For Tim,
Wishes

When Russia declared war on the Ottoman Empire in Ap
during the nineteenth century that hostilities had broken . . . .c two empires.
On this occasion the other Great Powers had done all they could to prevent it, although
public opinion in the West had been shocked by Turkey's brutal repression of the
Bulgarian uprising.

The war was to be fought in two distinct theatres. In Europe, as on previous
occasions, the Russian objective was to cross first the Danube and then the formidable
Balkan Mountains before striking for Constantinople. In Asia, over territory also
contested many times before, the Russians aimed to seize Kars and then Erzerum.

At first all went well for the invaders, the Turks making no serious attempt to
hold the line of the Danube, while a thrust south by General Gourko succeeded in
crossing the Balkans by a pass not previously considered practicable. At Plevna, however,
the Russian advance stalled in the face of the determined defence of the place by the
redoubtable Osman Pasha. In Asia, meanwhile, after initial success, the Russian advance
was halted by defeat at Zevin.

Poor strategic judgment on the part of the Turks led to their failure to take advantage
of the opportunity provided by Osman, even after the Russians had suffered three bloody
defeats at Plevna. Eventually, after the town was closely invested, it fell to the besiegers.
In Asia, the Turks suffered a major defeat in the battle of God's Mountain, and were
driven back to Erzerum, while Kars fell to a brilliant assault by the Russian forces. These
defeats marked the beginning of the end for the Turks. By January 1878 the Russians
were over the Balkans in force, and the last viable Turkish army was surrounded and
captured at Shenovo. Armistice negotiations led to a suspension of hostilities and to the
Treaty of San Stefano.

The other Great Powers had watched the conflict with mounting anxiety and were
determined to moderate the terms of San Stefano, which had imposed harsh conditions
on the Ottoman Empire. This, following tortuous diplomatic negotiations, they
succeeded in doing at the Congress of Berlin in July 1878.

This book, the first military history of the war in English for over a century, traces
the course of the campaigns, examining the many occasions on which the outcome of
a battle might have gone the other way, and the performance of the combatants, both
leaders and led. The book considers the extent to which the parties applied the lessons
of recent wars, as well as the conclusions that could be drawn from the experience of
combat with the latest weapons. It also explores the complicated motives of the Great
Powers in general, and Britain in particular, in bringing about a final settlement which
postponed the dissolution of the Ottoman Empire.

The author's detailed text is accompanied by an extensive number of black and white
illustrations, an impressive colour plate section containing reproductions of paintings by
artists such as Vereshchagin, plus black and white and colour battle maps. Extensive
orders of battle are also provided.

Quintin Barry is a solicitor and retired Employment Judge. He has also held a variety of offices in both the public and private sector, including the NHS and local radio. He is presently Secretary General of an international group of law firms. Throughout his professional career he has maintained his lifelong interest in military and naval history. He has made a special study of the period 1848-78, and has previously published three titles with Helion to wide acclaim – a two-volume study of the Franco-Prussian War 1870-71 and a single volume account of the Austro-Prussian War 1866. He is married and lives in Sussex.

WAR IN THE EAST

A MILITARY HISTORY OF THE RUSSO-TURKISH WAR 1877-78

Quintin Barry

Helion & Company Ltd

To my Father and Mother

Helion & Company Limited
26 Willow Road
Solihull
West Midlands B91 1UE
England
Tel. 0121 705 3393
Fax 0121 711 4075
Email: info@helion.co.uk
Website: www.helion.co.uk
Twitter: @helionbooks
Visit our blog http://blog.helion.co.uk/

Published by Helion & Company 2012. Reprinted in paperback 2016

Designed and typeset by Farr out Publications, Wokingham, Berkshire
Cover designed by Farr out Publications, Wokingham, Berkshire
Printed by Lightning Source, Milton Keynes, Buckinghamshire

Covers: The defence of the 'eagle's eyrie', Shipka Pass, August 23 1877. (Andrei Popov, 1893)

ISBN 978-1-911096-69-6

British Library Cataloguing-in-Publication Data.
A catalogue record for this book is available from the British Library.

For details of other military history titles published by Helion & Company Limited contact the above address, or visit our website: http://www.helion.co.uk.

We always welcome receiving book proposals from prospective authors.

Contents

List of Illustrations

Colour plates

Skobelev at Shenovo, January 8 1878. (Vasily Vereshchagin, 1878)
'Back from the front'. (Sami Yetik, 1920)

Images in colour maps section
Sketches by Irving Montagu, artist of *The Illustrated London News*.
Irving Montagu
A Russian Cossack
Erzerum
'Pending divorce'
'Incompatibility of temper'
'Saluting "The Illustrated News" in Asia Minor'
'Tween decks on a Turkish ironclad'
'Snowed up'

Key to Sources

Anon *Album della Guerra Russo-Turca del 1877-78* (Milan, 1878)
Anon *Histoire de la Guerre d'Orient 1877-1878* (Brussels, 1878)
Anon *Russes et Turcs. Guerre d'Orient* (Paris 1878, 2 volumes)
Budev *Grabados Españoles de la Guerra Ruso-Turco de 1877-1878* (Sofia, 1977)
Bullard *Famous War Correspondents* (Boston 1914)
Fauré *Histoire de la Guerre d'Orient (1877-1878)* (Paris, 1878, 2 vols)
The Graphic 1876-78
Hozier *The Russo-Turkish War. Including an Account of the Rise and Decline of the Ottoman Power, and the History of the Eastern Question* (London nd, 5 volumes)
Illustrated London News 1876-78
Ollier *Cassell's Illustrated History of the Russo-Turkish War* (London nd, 2 volumes)
Rogers – original photographs and other material from the collection of Duncan Rogers
Springer *Der Russisch-türkische Krieg 1877-1878 in Europa* (Vienna, 1891-93, 7 volumes)
Strantz *Illustrirte Kriegs-Chronik. Gedenkbuch an den Russisch-Türkischen Feldzug von 1876-1878* (Leipzig, 1878)
Wellesley *With the Russians in Peace and War: Recollections of a Military Attaché* (London 1905)
Zimmermann *Illustrirte Geschichte des Orientalischen Krieges von 1876-1878* (Vienna 1878)

List of Maps

The following appear in a colour section

All maps from Greene *Report on the Russian Army and its Campaigns in Turkey in 1877-1878* (New York, 1879, atlas volume)

Acknowledgements

I am glad to have this opportunity of expressing my gratitude to all those who have helped me in the preparation of this book, a number of whom, in no special order, deserve my particular thanks. Tim Readman read through the final draft and made a number of valuable suggestions.

Jean Hawkes once again overcame all the difficulties caused by my execrable handwriting (and on this occasion also the problems of very unfamiliar names of places and individuals) in patiently typing the book.

Colonel Ali Denizli of the Turkish Army (retd) gave valuable assistance on several aspects of the history of the Ottoman Army. In Plevna, Nicolay Petrov was a most helpful and courteous guide to the Panorama there, and subsequently assisted on a number of points relating to the Bulgarian Legion. In Bucharest, Alina Lefter helped me in explaining the use of some Roumanian military terms. Bob Williams provided invaluable help, particularly with the proper transliteration of Russian names, which I was able to include in the glossary.

As always I am greatly indebted to Duncan Rogers of Helion, who offered continual encouragement and support throughout the writing of the book. In particular he has been instrumental in the matter of illustrations and maps. On this occasion he has surpassed himself. Finally, my family have been patient and supportive throughout the project.

Preface

The Russian and Ottoman Empires clashed repeatedly during the 19th Century. It was a process that progressively weakened the Ottoman Empire and rolled back its frontier from the high tide mark of its expansion. Only when supported by powerful allies during the Crimean War of 1854–1856 did the Turks end on the winning side. The war of 1877–1878 was the latest in a series of conflicts caused principally by the relentless ambition of the Russian Empire. Russian concern for the subject Slav peoples of the Ottoman Empire was an ostensible, though subsidiary, motive for military action.

It was a brutal war, involving very substantial armies and enormous casualties on both sides, fought in conditions that were almost indescribably demanding. It was portrayed in chilling detail by a host of Western observers – diplomats, military *attachés*, artists and journalists; shocked both by the atrocities which they encountered and the gross incompetence of some of the generalship, they concluded that it was most decidedly not a European war fought between European nations.

In the years following the war it generated, understandably, a flood of books covering all its aspects; but by the dawn of the 20th Century there were other more evidently relevant wars to describe. The Russo-Turkish War ceased to be a subject for Western historians and military commentators, although it continued to receive attention in the countries of the participants. During the 20th Century the only English language narrative studies of the war were *The Siege of Plevna,* by Rupert Furneaux, published in 1958, which was not solely confined to the events of the siege; and the excellent *Caucasian Battlefields* by W E D Allen and Paul Muratoff, published in 1953, which devoted nine chapters to a penetrating and scholarly account of the campaign in the Caucasus.

I hope, therefore, that this book may go a little way to filling a historical gap, and to reviving interest both in the colossal struggle that took place in 1877–1878 and in its devastating consequences for the soldiers and civilian populations involved.

1

The Congress of Paris

Once Sebastopol had fallen on September 11 1855 there was no good reason why the Crimean War, the fourth war in the 19th century involving Russia and Turkey, should not be brought to an end. But it was not as simple as that. All the participants were inhibited in one way or another from embarking at once on direct negotiations. For Tsar Alexander II, the recognition of military defeat was a fearful blow to Russian prestige; but Russian public opinion was dead against the war and the nation's resources were severely overstrained, and it was obvious to his ministers that pride must take second place to reality. Napoleon III still had considerable ambitions to remake the map of Europe; but his ministers were determined on peace, and French public opinion was also against continuance of the war. Sooner rather than later Napoleon must bow to the inevitable. British public opinion, however, was still bellicose, and so was Lord Palmerston, not least because, unlike the French, the British army had no substantial victories to show for all its efforts. The Sardinian government had got all it needed from its participation, which ensured it could count on the favour of the Western powers. For Turkey, the Russian military threat in the Balkans had gone away, while there was nothing to be gained in the Caucasus, where things were not going well, and where the fortress of Kars finally succumbed on November 26.

The Crimean War, having begun as one of the most pointless wars of modern times, fought for obscure aims which had little to do with real national interests, now proved to be peculiarly difficult to terminate. It was only after immensely intricate diplomatic negotiations in November 1855 that the shape of a settlement began to emerge, which would culminate in the peace congress in Paris of the following year. Negotiations began in Vienna between the French ambassador there, Count François Bourqueney, and Count Karl Ferdinand Buol, the Austrian foreign minister. These discussions at first proceeded behind Napoleon's back, although subsequently his devious foreign minister Count Alexandre de Walewski persuaded him to authorise negotiations. Fundamentally the deal proposed followed the 'Four Points' put forward earlier in the course of the war, redefined and strengthened. Point 1, the abolition of the Russian protectorate over the Principalities of Moldavia and Wallachia, now also included a requirement that Russia transfer to Moldavia a strip of territory in Bessarabia that would deprive Russia of control over the mouths of the Danube. Point 2 provided for freedom of navigation on the Danube and its mouths, 'to be effectively assured through European institutions.' Point 3 required that the Black Sea be open to all nations, and that all military and naval facilities were to be abolished, no fleets being maintained there. The fourth point involved the abandonment of the Russian claim to a protectorate over the Christian subjects of Turkey, substituting for it assurances as to their security to be given by the Porte. To the Four Points Buol agreed to add a fifth, in the interest of securing French agreement; studiously vague, it stated that the belligerent powers reserved the right

Tsar Alexander II. (Hozier)

vested in them to bring forward in the European interest special conditions in addition to the Four Points.[1]

The British Cabinet, to Palmerston's dismay, voted to accept these terms as the basis for preliminary peace conditions, subject to modifications; however, Palmerston and Lord Clarendon, the Foreign Secretary, were left to define the modifications, which gave them to chance to ensure that negotiations with Russia broke down. In any case, Clarendon, together with a lot of other observers, thought the terms too tough for the Russians to accept. If they did not, the Austrians would break off diplomatic negotiations, and Russia would be still more isolated.

Predictably, the Russian reaction was at first to try to water down the terms, but Buol refused to make any concessions, although telling Count Esterhazy, his ambassador in St Petersburg, that he could reassure the Russians privately that the fifth point would present 'no serious obstacle to the conclusion of peace.' Thereafter, the matter was considered at the Russian Crown Council on January 15, when the consequences of rejecting the proposals were minutely examined; the outcome, announced next day, was to accept them unconditionally. The reality of Russia's situation, from the political, diplomatic, economic and military standpoints, could not be gainsaid. It has been suggested that perhaps the clinching argument in favour of acceptance was that the terms proposed would not hinder the development of the country's resources or impair its future prospects.[2]

Thus the hope cherished by Palmerston and Clarendon that the Russians would refuse the deal offered them proved illusory. They did what they could to scupper an armistice, turning first to Buol and, when he refused to play, to Napoleon. The latter was in a quandary; he wanted on the one hand to maintain the British alliance but on the other not to ignore French public opinion as to the financial consequences of continuing the war. Palmerston's position was that there could be no armistice unless Russia accepted the British special conditions, which required demilitarisation of the Aaland Islands in the Baltic, the admission of foreign consuls to Russian ports in the Black Sea and discussion of the future of the Russian provinces on the east coast of the Black Sea. The independence of Georgia and Circassia was a project that always formed part of Palmerston's war aims.

Walewski produced a fudge that enabled Britain to agree to the armistice; the special conditions would be notified to Russia by France, but only unofficially, while France would privately undertake to support Britain in getting them agreed. Professor Taylor has speculated 'whether Walewski meant ultimately to cheat the British or the Russians or both.' It was, he thought, another instance of 'a translation into diplomatic terms of the hope that something would turn up.'[3] Palmerston got his way on one thing; there would be an early meeting of the congress. Once the war had cooled down in the post armistice period, it would be progressively more difficult to bring it back to the boil, and he wanted to keep alive the threat of a renewal of hostilities.

Thus it was that on February 1 the peace preliminaries were finally signed, bringing to an end a war that had cost over half a million lives, two-thirds of them Russian.[4] The delegates to the peace congress began thereafter to arrive in Paris. The French delegates were Walewski and Bourqueney; the Austrian delegates were Buol and Hübner, his ambassador to Paris. Mehmed Emin Ali Pasha, the Grand Vizier and Mohammed Djemil Bey, his ambassador to Paris, represented the Sublime Porte, while Sardinia's delegates were Cavour, the Minister President, and Villamarina. Russia was represented by Counts Orlov and Brunnow, the latter being ambassador to London. Prussia, whose neutrality during the war meant exclusion from the congress until it discussed the Straits Convention of 1841, was represented by Otto von Manteuffel, the Minister President and Count von Hatzfeldt, the minister to Paris. Finally, the British delegation was led by Clarendon and Lord Cowley, the ambassador to Paris. Clarendon brought to the congress a profound personal distaste for the war, the original outbreak of which he had regarded as a 'horrible calamity' brought about as a result of 'two sets of barbarians quarrelling over a form of words.'[5]

Now, ironically, his mission was to ensure the continuance of the war if the most extreme terms could not be imposed on Russia. This objective was generally recognized, as he wrote to Palmerston:

> I understand that I am not considered by nature a wild beast, but that I am a slave of the English newspapers and the representative of your anti-Russian feelings; and that as peace would be fatal to your Government I am here for the purpose of making it impossible.[6]

It had been apparent to Clarendon before he arrived in Paris that the French would not go along with the British determination to prolong the war; he wrote dismissively that all of France was 'bent on peace at any price... The French people have gone mad, kissing each other upon the restoration of peace.'[7] When he got there, he was soon warning Palmerston that Britain would stand alone in going on with the war; there was

The Congress of Paris, 1856. (Rogers)

nobody in France, apart from the Emperor and Walewski 'who was not prepared to make any peace.'

The Congress opened on February 25, and it soon became evident that it was the Bessarabian issue that was going to prove the most difficult to resolve. Orlov's position was that no territory should be ceded, and that this should be to compensate Russia for returning Kars to Turkey. Neither issue was important to Napoleon, whose concern was to conciliate Russia. It had been a make or break question for Palmerston; he insisted that Clarendon should stand firm on the issue. Professor Taylor, slightly unfairly, put it this way: 'Clarendon, as usual, lost his nerve, particularly when he saw that Napoleon was bent on peace. Palmerston, as usual, believed that resolution would carry the day.'[8] In the end a compromise was reached; the Russians were allowed to keep about two-thirds of the Bessarabian territory in question, but ceded to Moldavia the key sector at the mouths of the Danube.

The other central terms were agreed with relative ease. The Russians acquiesced in the neutralisation of the Aaland Islands. Clarendon was obliged to abandon the move to give independence to the Caucasus provinces in the face of a general refusal by the other delegates to contemplate a resumption of the war to achieve this. As to the Danubian Principalities, the ticklish question of their union was deferred, and they were to remain under the nominal suzerainty of the Porte; the treaty provided that 'no exclusive Protection shall be exercised over them by any of the guaranteeing Powers.' Arrangements were put in place to oversee freedom of navigation over the whole length of the Danube.

The issue of the rights of Christians, which had been the ostensible cause of the war in the first place, might have proved a stumbling block, had not the Sultan issued a general decree on February 18 confirming the rights of all Christian and non-Muslim subjects of the Ottoman Empires, and setting out an extensive programme of political, administrative, legal and economic reforms. This was in part the work of Stratford Canning, the British Ambassador to Constantinople, and was intended to avoid any direct provision for reform in the final treaty; the question of the rights of Christians was confined to a reference to the Sultan's decree. To make the best of a bad job, Alexander announced to his people that the decree met the 'original and principal aims of the war.' The rights of Christians were assured: 'Russians! Your efforts and your sacrifices were not in vain. The great work is accomplished.'[9]

The future integrity of the Ottoman Empire was guaranteed by all the powers signing the treaty, and the Empire was formally admitted to the concert of Europe. The most important issue affecting Turkish sovereignty, however, was that which also most directly humiliated Russia. The clauses regulating the future of the Black Sea called for it to be neutralised and demilitarised; the waters of the Black Sea were to be open to all merchant vessels but barred to all warships, with the exception of light vessels, necessary for the policing of the coast lines determined by a separate Russo-Turkish convention. All military and naval bases were to be scrapped, and no shipbuilding was to be undertaken on the Black Sea (although Russia successfully resisted British demands that the demilitarisation should extend also to the Sea of Azov and the rivers flowing into the Black Sea). For Turkey, the loss of Sinope as a base was not of great consequence, and the development of a powerful navy on the Mediterranean was unaffected. For Russia, it was a bitter pill, particularly for Alexander, but it was swallowed readily enough, perhaps because it was without any long-term sanction.[10]

The Straits Convention, to be signed at the same time as the treaty, reaffirmed the 1841 convention closing the Straits to foreign warships in time of peace, save for light vessels in the service of diplomatic missions, with the Sultan's permission.

The Treaty of Paris was finally signed on March 30, to general relief, and was celebrated by a huge military review and artillery salutes in Paris. With the delegates still assembled, the Congress went on to talk about wider issues. To Napoleon's disappointment, these discussions led nowhere, although the Congress did adopt the Declaration of Paris, an international agreement on the rules of naval warfare to which within two years over forty nations subscribed; one significant refusal to do so came from the United States. Cavour suggested that 'perhaps the Congress of Paris will owe it to this act that it will not occupy an entirely obscure page in the annals of history.'[11]

The specific terms of the Treaty of Paris may have been less harsh than might have been the consequence of military defeat; but, as Hugh Seton-Watson has pointed out, 'Russia's position in Europe was changed for nearly a hundred years.'[12] And its terms were not forgotten or forgiven by Russia's leaders; the history of the next two decades would lead inexorably towards further conflict between the Russian and Ottoman Empires, and the outcome of such a conflict would depend on the extent to which in the meantime lessons were learned, both from the Crimean War and, more significantly, from the experiences of other nations during a period of huge military and industrial change.

2

Political and Social Reform in Russia

The accession to the throne of Russia of Alexander II had been melancholy and dramatic. Heartbroken by the events in the Crimea, and the fearful damage inflicted on the army that was so dear to him, Tsar Nicholas I seemed almost to be deliberately courting death in the freezing temperatures of St Petersburg in February 1855. Catching a cold, he ignored his doctors' advice and continued with his duties. His cold became worse; influenza was diagnosed. At first his doctors felt no real concern; but early in the morning of February 18 the true situation became clear. Nicholas faced his end with dignity, giving orders and dictating despatches, including a message to King William of Prussia begging him never to alter the alliance with Russia. He spoke his last words to his son:

> I wanted to take everything difficult, everything serious, upon my shoulders and to leave you a peaceful, well-ordered and happy realm. Providence decreed otherwise. Now I go to pray for Russia and for you all. After Russia I loved you [his family] more than anything else in the world. Serve Russia.[1]

With his death, the system created by Nicholas, which has been described as 'the epitome of an 18th Century Western European police state,' effectively collapsed. For Alexander and his advisers a wide programme of change in practically all aspects of the Russian state was absolutely necessary.

The Crimean War, and its disastrous outcome, demonstrated with pitiless clarity a number of aspects of Russian government and society that demanded reform. One was of course the extent to which the army needed root and branch overhaul. It was dependent on the loyalty of the peasant soldiers, who had shown their willingness to tolerate appalling privations during the war. But it was increasingly clear to intelligent observers that this loyalty could not be depended on indefinitely, and that the emancipation of the serfs must be high on the reform agenda.

Alexander II was thirty-seven when he became Tsar. He had had the benefit of a much more sympathetic upbringing than his father, the tutors assigned to him being humane and sensitive. His education was well fitted for a future ruler, addressing all aspects of the civil and military duties he would undertake, and gave him a humane and understanding view of the world.[2] In 1842 he married Princess Marie of Hesse-Darmstadt, (over his parents' objections) who became the Grand Duchess Maria Alexandrovna, and who bore him six sons and two daughters. One historian has described him, in somewhat highly coloured terms, as 'an unpredictable mixture of stubbornness and feebleness, boldness and timidity, enlightenment and obscurantism.'[3]

Nicholas I had been careful to give his son steadily increasing responsibilities: he stood in for his father when the Tsar left the capital for any lengthy period. In 1849 Alexander was given command of the Corps of Guards, and of all military colleges and schools. He was less of a soldier than his father but, on the other hand, had had much more experience of the problems of government by the time he came to the throne. He has been characterized as 'milder, less imperious than his father.' But at the same time he did not relinquish the decision-making process to anyone else.[4] He would usually back the advisers he appointed against all criticism.

Alexander wasted little time in tackling the question of the emancipation of the serfs. In a speech in Moscow on March 30 1856 he said: 'It is better to abolish serfdom from above than to wait until the serfs begin to liberate themselves from below.'[5] At the beginning of 1857 a secret committee began to address the key questions involved in carrying through a reform that was far reaching in its social and economic implications. During 1858 committees were set up in most provinces to study the issues; many could not reach unanimous agreement and sent in both a majority and minority view. Alexander was himself moving to a more generous view of what it was necessary to give the serfs in terms of the right to buy not only their own homes but also the surrounding land. One of his key advisers, General Rostovtsev, previously supposed to be a reactionary, was also moving to a more liberal position; his appointment to head the 'Editorial Commissions' that were set up to sort out the issues was a key factor in enabling the emancipation programme to move forward.

Rostovtsev died in February 1860, and Count Panin was appointed in his place. Although more reactionary than his predecessor, he accepted the liberal thrust of the proposals. To get the process completed it was necessary to overcome the bitter hostility that existed between the bureaucrats of the Ministry of the Interior and the landowners. The final proposals were discussed by the Council of State in January 1861 and the legislation was introduced in the following month. The serfs were emancipated from the possession of the landowners and were to receive land of their own. There were complex arrangements for the process which would gradually release them and enable them to acquire their land.

While noting that the settlement did not solve the peasant question, Hugh Seton Watson remarked on the fact that serfdom had been 'peacefully abolished in the same year in which failure to abolish slavery in another great country was a principal cause of one of the most bloody wars of the 19th century.' In seeking an explanation for the difference, he pointed out that Government authority was much stronger in Russia than in the United States, while the sanctity of private property was less.[6]

The Crimean War had demonstrated the complete inadequacy of the system of communications in Russia. In the year after the war ended there were just over a thousand kilometres of railway in the whole country; in the next twenty years this increased by a factor of nearly twenty. Largely developed by private companies, the encouragement given to them by the government was prompted by strategic considerations, but in such a huge country the economic benefits were enormous and immediate. Industries which had hitherto depended on serf labour naturally faced a downturn for a number of years after the emancipation, while those employing wage labour prospered. Gradually the industries that had fallen back recovered; in the 1860s there was an annual average of 798,000 workers employed in manufacturing, mining and metallurgy, a figure which rose in the next decade to 946,000. Output of pig iron more than doubled between 1862 and 1886, although the total still remained relatively small compared to other industrial nations.[7]

The progressive expansion of Russia from the principality of Moscow which Ivan III inherited in 1462 to the vast territorial empire to which Alexander II acceded nearly four hundred years later involved the absorption of many different peoples and ethnic and religious groups, and by no means all of these completely lost their cultural identity or their desire for autonomy and, in some cases, for independence. This meant that the Russian government, to preserve the integrity of the empire, must impose a rigid and autocratic rule over the provinces in which unrest might occur; and, of course, the imposition of such a system itself stimulated protest.

The vast areas covered by the Russian Empire would in any case make its government an especially difficult task. This problem was, however, exacerbated by the backwardness of its communications system, particularly when compared to that of other Great Powers. In spite of the accelerated building programme, Russia still possessed in 1870 only 10,700 kilometers of railroads compared with 17,900 in France and 18,700 in Germany. The network of paved roads was equally unsatisfactory. Troops could, therefore, not be moved quickly to prevent or put down insurrections or to meet external threats.[8]

By the time Alexander came to the throne, continuing Russian expansion was directed to the south, in the Caucasus; to the east and south-east in Turkestan and Turkmenistan; and to the Far East as far as the Pacific. Expansion into the Caucasus had encountered bitter opposition, particularly in Circassia in the west and Dagestan in the east. In Dagestan resistance was led by religious leaders, and in particular by Shamil, a brilliant guerilla fighter and a man of passionate conviction who inspired absolute loyalty in his followers. A campaign by the viceroy of the Caucasus, Count Michael Vorontsov, ultimately took Grozny, the capital of Chechnya, after an eighteen-month campaign which cost many thousands of Russian casualties. In spite of huge efforts, Chechnya, Dagestan and the mountainous regions of Circassia remained out of Russian control up to the Crimean War.[9]

In Kazakhstan, Russian influence had been steadily consolidated, in spite of a series of revolts in the 1830s and 1840s. Further east, beyond the Aral Sea, Turkestan was divided into three khanates of Khiva, Bokhara and Khokand. Between the Aral Sea and the Caspian Sea lay Turkmenistan. In 1858 Count Ignatiev led a Russian mission to Khiva and Bokhara which opened the way for the development of trade. Russian interest in the region grew in the 1860s, and in 1864 a series of military operations began, which steadily expanded the area of Russian control. The most successful of the Russian leaders was Cherniaev, who took the city of Tashkent in June 1865. In the following year some territory in Bokhara was occupied.

In 1867 a governor general of Turkestan was appointed, which was a confirmation of the forward policy being adopted by St Petersburg. By 1873, first Khiva and then Bokhara had each become a Russian protectorate. In 1875 a rebellion in Khokand spread to Russian territory; Kauffman, the governor general, pursued the rebels into Khokand and by January 1876 Major-General Michael Skobelev had taken Andizhan, following which the Russian government annexed the whole of Khokand.[10]

In the Far East the governor general of Siberia, N N Muraviev, pursued a vigorous policy, including the exploration of the Amur river, at the mouth of which a Russian settlement was established in 1850. This was not recognised by the Chinese government until 1858. In the following year, the site for a port further down the coast was selected. Then, in 1860, the Russians successfully negotiated the cession of all the territory claimed between the Ussari River and the Pacific, and the building of the port of Vladivostok began.

Meanwhile in the Caucasus the Russians, once the Crimean War had ended, embarked on a methodical military strategy to impose their control on the rebellious regions. Between 1857 and 1859 strong Russian forces penetrated further and further into the areas hitherto dominated by Shamil, and one by one the Chechens and the tribes of Dagestan surrendered. Shamil himself finally surrendered in August 1859. In 1862 a similar campaign began against the Circassians; by May 1864 the Russians were in complete control, although more than half the Circassian population chose to emigrate to Turkey rather than remain under Russian rule.[11] The two Christian nations of Transcaucasia, Georgia and Armenia, were perfectly content to remain under Russian rule, although as time went by there was some social discontent which made the region a fertile ground for revolutionary ideas.

Within Russia itself by far the most serious security problem faced by the government was the Polish rebellion of 1863. The population of Poland was somewhat less than five million, of whom three-quarters were Poles; there were 600,000 Jews and a quarter of a million each of Germans and Lithuanians. The Poles and Lithuanians, and some of the Germans, were Catholic. The question of the future of the peasants in Poland could not be avoided at a time when in Russia itself progress was being made towards the emancipation of the serfs; and the introduction of reforms in Russia made it expedient for the government to extend reform to Poland.

Unfortunately, the reform programme introduced by Alexander in 1861 had the effect of stimulating demand in Poland for still greater concessions. There was a difference of view in Poland between those leaders who believed that it was useless to struggle for independence and that what should be done was to make Russian rule more tolerable, and those who refused to compromise in this way. Street demonstrations in April 1861 led to Russian troops firing on the crowds; unofficially, the death toll was estimated at 200. Later that year there were further demonstrations, culminating in the declaration of a state of siege.

There was also a difference of view on the Russian side, between those who favoured further concessions and those who wished to take a hard line. In May 1862 Alexander approved a fresh reform programme and appointed his brother, the Grand Duke Constantine, as viceroy. He also appointed Poles to the positions of provincial governors, and conceded the adoption of Polish as the official language. In spite of reforms such as the reopening of Warsaw University, Polish extremists made attempts on the lives of the viceroy and Marquis Alexander Wielopolski, who headed the commission on education and religious affairs. The banishment of the Polish moderate leader Count Andrew Zamoyski, and the announcement of conscription for young Poles, added fuel to the fire, and the radicals began to set up provincial committees for armed rebellion, which broke out on January 22 1863.

Public opinion throughout Europe was in sympathy with the Poles. France, Britain and Austria united in protesting against repressive Russian measures against the rebels, and called for Polish autonomy. It was not unexpected that Napoleon III, always

Prince Bismarck. (*Russes et Turcs*)

supportive of the right to national self-determination, should take this line; but it marked an end to the cooperative relationship that had existed between France and Russia since the Tsar and Napoleon met at Stuttgart in 1857. But for Prussia, Russia would have been completely isolated. Bismarck, however, looked askance at the prospect of a successful Polish rebellion, which he considered would be a threat to Prussia; besides, for future purposes, he wanted Russia to be beholden to him. He sent General Konstantin von Alvensleben to conclude a convention whereby the rebels might be pursued across the border by either government. It was a step which caused the most bitter opposition within Prussia, where public opinion was entirely in support of the line taken by the other Great Powers.

Bismarck, however, was unmoved. By early 1864 the rebellion was crushed. The French attitude effectively prevented Napoleon from getting any support from Russia over the Schleswig Holstein question, and the ensuing action taken against Denmark by Prussia and Austria. Bismarck's policy assured him of Russian friendship in the future, and he was no more concerned by the hostility of the other Great Powers than he was by political sentiment at home. He was playing a much larger game.

The suppression of the Polish rebellion was in the end brutally efficient, particularly in Lithuania. This was in spite of the efforts of Grand Duke Constantine to secure leniency for the Polish people; by now Alexander was no longer prepared to resist those of his advisers who called for the strictest measures to be taken within Poland to maintain internal security. He was, however, prepared to introduce agrarian reform; by the settlement of March 1864 about 700,000 Polish peasant families obtained freeholds, while keeping their rights to the use of common pastures and forests. The Russian objective was in this way to separate the interests of the peasants from the Polish ruling class. However, it has been pointed out that although the Polish peasants did better out

War preparations in Russia – impressing wagons and horses
for army transport. (*Illustrated London News*)

of the deal than they would have done had there been no rebellion, their ownership of the land itself confirmed them in their conviction that Poland was their country.[12]

This ineradicable belief was maintained in spite of the application to Poland of the russification policy, which included the confiscation of all properties of the Catholic Church, and the maintenance of government control over the administration of the Church. In 1864 the Russian judicial system was substantially introduced into Poland; and in 1872 the Russian system of secondary education. The Russian government was also now extremely sensitive to any signs of nationalism arising in the Ukraine, and in particular to the effect of Austrian policy in the neighbouring province of Galicia, the population of which was made up of Poles and Ukrainians.

Russia also faced the incipient problems of nationalism in the Baltic States, and in Finland. In Estonia and Latvia there developed literary movements that carried with them a growing sense of national identity. In Finland, the Swedish minority dominated the landowning and business classes. The Russian government was inclined to favour the Finnish majority, introducing legislation to promote the use of the Finnish language in public business, and bringing into effect laws on education which had the result of hugely expanding the number of schools taught in that language.

The Tsar in Nevski Prospect, St Petersburg, April 1877. (*Illustrated London News*)

All of this meant that the internal government of Russia was an extremely complicated business. In the development of its foreign policy, it was obliged, notwithstanding the autocratic nature of its institutions, to have regard to the possible effect of that policy on the various interest groups that must be kept in mind. There was a strong body of public opinion which retained a belief in the common destiny of the Slav people.[13] The foundation in Moscow in 1858 of the Moscow Slavonic Benevolent Committee was the first of a number of organisations that came into being with the support of the government. Gradually the strident policies of the Pan-Slavs displaced the rather more diffident approach of the Slavophils. Russian Pan-Slavism was based on a belief that it was Russia's destiny to lead the smaller Slav nations, and that only those nations with an Orthodox rather than a Protestant or Catholic population could be trusted. The strength of Pan-Slav opinion would in due course exert a considerable influence over Russian policy, and its response to international events.

As the nation on its borders that was itself adjacent to the Ottoman Empire, Roumania was, of course, still notionally subject to Ottoman sovereignty, but its future was very much a matter of concern to Russia. Napoleon's idea that Austria might acquire it in exchange for Venetia was wholly unacceptable; Alexander said that the suggestion was 'inadmissible jusqu'à la guerre,' and Gorchakov was equally outspoken.[14] The idea

Prince Charles of Roumania. (Ollier)

had arisen when Prince Nicholas Couza, the Prince of Roumania, was compelled to abdicate in February 1866. When the Roumanian leaders sought a foreign prince, and their choice fell on Prince Charles of Hohenzollern-Sigmaringen, the Russians were far from pleased. Nor was Austria; but the other Great Powers supported his election (achieved with an overwhelmingly popular majority in the national plebiscite) and in October 1866 the Ottoman government accepted the position. Roumania's new ruler would have an important part to play in the years ahead.

3

The Ottoman Empire

In the period after the end of the Crimean War, the Turkish attitude to Western style reforms was crisply summed up by Stratford Canning, now Lord Stratford de Redcliffe:

> European systems of government, European ideas, European laws or customs – no honest Turk will ever pretend to admire any of these… If ever Easterns (sic.) get imbued with Liberal ideas of government their own doom is sealed.[1]

Nevertheless, under the leadership of Mehmed Emin Ali, the 'Tanzimat' reformers did make considerable progress in bringing the Ottoman Empire's institutions into the 19th century. The process was given a considerable boost by the Imperial Rescript of February 1856, with a pledge of a wide range of administrative reforms and racial equality. The more tolerant regime which this promised attracted refugees from Hungary and Poland, who brought with them new technical skills, imparting a new vitality and, it has been argued, the romantic nationalism of Central Europe.[2]

Among the practical problems faced by Ali and his reformist colleagues, however, was the extravagant spending of Sultan Abdul Mecid, who consumed a large part of the foreign capital which had been raised; in the end it led to Ali's resignation. The foreign investment did bring some lasting benefit; the development of a railway system began in 1856 with the construction of a line from Varna to the Danube, and another line running back from Smyrna. The improvement of the lamentable communications system was an obvious priority, and spending on improvements to the road system and on the electric telegraph reflected this. Sir Charles Eliot sardonically observed the advantages which such rapid communication could bring:

> It is no longer necessary to leave a province to the discretion of a governor, and trust that he will come home to be beheaded when that operation seems desirable. With the telegraph one can order him about, find out what he is doing, reprimand him, recall him, instruct his subordinates to report against him, and generally deprive him of all power.[3]

Although the Treaty of Paris preserved the Ottoman Empire from outside interference, in the decades that followed it effectively lost control over a significant part of its possessions. The nominal sovereignty over Serbia, Montenegro and the Danubian provinces was of less and less significance. It was, however, sufficient to embroil the Empire in a number of damaging disputes. So far as Serbia was concerned, there was a progressive retreat from the position of suzerainty. A settlement in 1862 resolved many of the issues that had arisen between the Serbs and the small Turkish minority; the civilian Turks were to sell their property and be removed from Belgrade; the Turkish military presence was confined to the occupation of their fortress at Belgrade and a number of river fortresses. In 1867 even these manifestations of Ottoman power were abandoned, and the garrisons were withdrawn.[4]

Relations between the Ottoman Empire and Montenegro had been equally stormy. In 1858 a Turkish attempt to invade Montenegro in yet another attempt to exercise some control over this tiny, mountainous and persistently rebellious principality ended in a crushing defeat at Grahovo. The Turks withdrew, and terms of settlement were negotiated by a conference of ambassadors at Constantinople. This settlement lasted only four years before Omar Pasha led another invasion of Montenegro, which was ultimately successful; the fighting ended with the Convention of Scutari.[5]

Egypt, which under the viceroyalty of Abbas Hilmi had behaved as a subject province of the Ottoman Empire at the start of the Crimean War, almost immediately reverted to practical independence after his death in 1864. His successor, Muhammad Said, still paid the annual tribute to Constantinople, but all important decisions, such as the approval of the Suez Canal project, were taken without reference to the Ottoman government.

The Danubian provinces, whose union the Congress of Paris had failed to achieve, were soon able to make significant progress towards this objective without the help of the Western Powers. Moldavia and Wallachia, holding separate elections, in 1859 each elected Alexander Couza as hospodar, an event for which the Congress of Paris had made no provision. The formal union of the provinces as the United Principalities of Roumania came about two years later; this was formally recognised by the signatories to the Treaty of Paris, who in fact had no choice. Although the Ottoman suzerainty was theoretically unaffected, the new state conducted its affairs without reference to Constantinople. In 1866, after the fall of Couza, Prince Charles of Hohenzollern-Sigmaringen was elected ruler. The country's independence was effectively acknowledged in 1877 at the time of the outbreak of the Russo Turkish War when the Turkish commanders sedulously avoided any operations that might amount to an invasion of Roumania.

Perhaps the most serious problem that the Sublime Porte had to deal with was to be found in the Levant. In May 1860 discord between the Roman Catholic Maronites of the Lebanon and the Muslim Druses began to lead to attacks by the latter. In July the situation deteriorated further with a violent assault by Muslims on the Christian quarter of Damascus, causing thousands of deaths. The Turkish authorities in Syria had done nothing to prevent it; if anything, they had encouraged the action. Even before the massacre began, Thouvenel, the French foreign minister, proposed that a European-Turkish commission be set up to investigate responsibility for the attacks which had previously occurred, to punish the guilty and take steps to prevent its repetition. Britain had dispatched a number of warships to the scene, and the French followed suit. With the worsening of the situation the Great Powers contemplated armed intervention, although there was enormous difficulty in getting agreement on this. Gorchakov, now the Russian foreign minister, was all for a very wide commitment that went well beyond what Britain, for instance, was prepared to accept.[6]

Ultimately an agreement on European intervention was cobbled together, and on August 22 four thousand French troops led by General Beaufort d'Hautpoul (who as a captain had been an adviser with Ibrahim's army at Nisib in 1839) landed at Beirut, with a mandate for an occupation of six months. In fact, this proved insufficient time in

Prince Gorchakov, Russian Foreign Minister. (Hozier)

which to restore stability, as a result of which there were further anguished negotiations to extend the occupation. In the end, terms acceptable to Napoleon having been negotiated, French troops departed in June, although the Anglo-French fleet remained to exert restraint upon the Turks.[7]

Napoleon's willingness to intervene in the Ottoman Empire was not wholly altruistic; apart from increasing French influence in the Levant, it also enhanced France's international prestige, which was extremely valuable to a ruler whose fertile brain was constantly devising schemes to rearrange the map of Europe. These not infrequently involved the Turkish provinces in Europe, which he was always prepared to use as a bargaining chip to resolve otherwise unrelated issues. One example had been the idea of allowing Austria to acquire the Danubian provinces in exchange for ceding Venetia to Italy; this idea was firmly crushed by the Russians. Another scheme involved a commercial approach; in 1861 he put it to Lord Cowley:

'What would be more natural than to arrange a transaction of this nature – let Italy purchase Venetia of Austria and let Austria purchase Bosnia or Herzegovina of the Porte. Austria wants territory and the Porte wants money. Let Austria keep the half of what she obtains for Venetia and give the other half to the Porte.'[8]

He added, regretfully, that Britain would probably not consent and that in any case he knew that Russia would not.

The Serbian inhabitants of Bosnia would not have been amused to know of Napoleon's ideas. The province was constantly on the point of coming to the boil, as it did in 1857, and as it would do so again in 1875. The idea that in due course Bosnia and Herzegovina would fall into Austrian hands did not go away; many of the schemes of

Newspapers being read aloud in a Constantinople café. (*The Graphic*)

rearrangement so energetically debated by diplomats during the two decades after the Congress of Paris reflected this.

Although the Turkish representatives at the lengthy negotiations to deal with the problem of the Levant succeeded in avoiding the discussion of any specifically Syrian issues, there had been agreement on an international settlement of the situation in the Lebanon, which provided a structure that reflected the interests of the contending sects, on a district by district basis. With the centre of power thus localised, the inhabitants were spared the effect of remote maladministration from Constantinople.[9]

At the end of June 1861 Abdul Mecid, only thirty-eight years old, died of tuberculosis, and was succeeded by his half-brother Abdul Aziz. A huge man, weighing over sixteen stone, he was of a particularly autocratic disposition. He shared his predecessor's extravagant tastes, and his general demeanour did not suggest a willingness to adopt Western liberal ideas. In spite of this, however, under the leadership of Emin Ali the Tanzimat reformers were able to introduce a number of measures that markedly improved the structure of provincial government; produced a reformed legal system; established a commercial code and, in due course a civil code. A lot of this reflected French culture and systems.[10]

The enormous British influence over Ottoman policy, as exerted by Stratford de Redcliffe, continued until he finally left Constantinople in 1858, when he was succeeded by Sir William Bulwer, a much less dominant personality. He shared with his predecessor a greater concern for the efficiency of the Ottoman government than for its adoption of liberal concepts. He was particularly concerned with reforms which provided opportunities for finance in an economic climate in which Western bankers, and their governments, actively supported investment in the Ottoman Empire. In his turn Bulwer was followed in 1865 by Sir Henry Elliot, whose views on the Ottoman Empire and what was permissible in its policies were in due course to be revealed to be entirely at odds with British public opinion.

Sir Henry Elliot, controversial British
Ambassador to Turkey. (Ollier)

Emperor Franz Joseph of Austria. (*Illustrirte
Geschichte des Orientalischen Krieges*)

The reform process that continued in spite of the accession of Abdul Aziz did face intellectual opposition from a number of dissident writers who adopted a Muslim fundamentalist position. It has, however, been pointed out that in spite of opportunist support which they received from the son of Ibrahim Pasha, these intellectuals were loyal to the concept of the Ottoman state, and that they expressed a form of Turkish nationalism.

Abdul Aziz was looked on by Western governments favourably, not so much for his own views as for the apparent movement towards westernized institutions; he was received by Napoleon III at the 'Great Universal Exhibition' in Paris in 1867, by Franz Joseph in Vienna and by Victoria at Windsor. This tour of European capitals greatly stimulated the Sultan's already considerable desire to possess more of the outward trappings of power and was, for instance, to lead to the rapid expansion of the Turkish fleet.

When Abdul Aziz came to the throne the influence of Emin Ali was the dominant force in Ottoman government. For eighteen years, during which he was Grand Vizier on five occasions, he had struggled, sometimes successfully and sometimes not, to maintain the reform process and to sustain the shaky finances of the Ottoman Empire. Much of the time his influence was sufficient to overcome the extravagant whims of both Abdul Aziz and his predecessor. When he died in 1871 it gave the Sultan the opportunity to choose Grand Viziers less ready to stand up to him; six took office in the first two and a half years after the death of Emin Ali, while the average length of term for a provincial governor was about four months.[11]

One of the strongest reformers was Midhat Pasha, who had been an extremely successful governor of the Danube *vilayet*; he became Grand Vizier in July 1872 but, unsurprisingly, lasted only three months, the Sultan taking exception to his proposals for a federal system of government, then to his establishment of an accounting department, and finally to his investigation of corruption within the Imperial Palace. Another Grand

Midhat Pasha, one-time Grand Vizier. (Ollier)

Vizier who was in due course to fall foul of the Sultan's autocratic resistance to any encroachment on his power was the former commander in chief of the army, Hüseyin Avni, who served from February 1874 until April 1875. He was dismissed because of his efforts to divert funds from the imperial palace to the army.

By now the Ottoman state was hopelessly insolvent. The series of loans from Western banks, the fruits of which had been squandered to a substantial extent on the whims of the Sultan, had left the Ottoman Empire with an enormous debt and consequently a huge liability for interest. In October 1875 the pro-Russian Grand Vizier Mahmud Nedim was forced to announce the government's inability to meet the interest payments on the debt. The disastrous mismanagement of the state's finances coincided with a series of internal events that were in due course to lead not only to the downfall of the Sultan but also, ultimately, to the fifth Russo-Turkish War of the century.

This progress towards disaster had small beginnings. The inhabitants of the little village of Nevesinje, some 25 miles from Mostar, in Herzegovina, protesting against the unreasonable tax assessments levied upon them, fled to Montenegro in February 1875. Prince Nicholas of Montenegro obtained leave for the refugees to return home, which they did, only to find that some of their homes had been burned. One thing led to another, the Turkish authorities displaying their accustomed brutality in dealing with the villagers' protests; and finally the local population rose in revolt in July 1875. The rising quickly spread; Montenegrin rebels crossed the frontier, and other tax-related protests led to insurrection in Bosnia as well. The Turkish garrison, already struggling to contain the rising in Herzegovina, was unable to cope; the rebels received considerable encouragement from sympathisers within Austria-Hungary as well as Serbia, including shipments of arms; and it was soon clear to the Great Powers that these were events which would necessitate their diplomatic intervention. Ever since the Crimean War the Balkans had been seen as likely to provoke a serious international crisis.

Discussing war with Serbia in a café in Constantinople. (*Illustrated London News*)

Before, however, considering the events on the international stage, it is necessary to follow the course of events within the Ottoman Empire. As the risings in Bosnia and Herzegovina continued, they were matched by a rebellion in the villages of the Rhodope Mountains, in Bulgaria. In due course the brutal repression of this insurrection would prove the decisive event in the course of the descent into war; but for the moment it was a riot in Salonika in May 1876 that occupied public attention in Constantinople. This had been caused by the treatment by Greeks of a Bulgarian girl wrongly believed to have been a forced convert to Islam. In the ensuing riot, fanatical Muslims murdered the French and German consuls (the latter a British subject). The Great Powers, outraged at the failure of the Ottoman government to prevent the incident, protested violently; on the other hand, nationalist discontent about outside pressure brought thousands of theological students on to the streets of Constantinople to demand the removal of Nedim. The crisis gave Hüseyin and Midhat the opportunity they needed to plan the Sultan's removal. In an attempt to preserve his position, Abdul Aziz appointed the former to his previous position of Commander in Chief. It was by no means enough; the situation in the capital continued to be so grave that the British government ordered the Mediterranean Fleet to Besika Bay. The moment for a coup had arrived; a *fatwa* of deposition was obtained from the Caliph, and Hüseyin ordered two battalions of infantry to surround the Dolmabahce palace.

There, on the night of May 29/30, Hüseyin presented the *fatwa* to Abdul Aziz who accepted his deposition. His nephew, the feeble and irresolute Prince Murad, was

Sultan Abdul Hamid II. (Hozier)

Turkish troops in a village in Bulgaria. (*Russes et Turcs*)

proclaimed as Sultan in his stead. He was, however, clearly not up to the task; a report in *The Times* of August 3 described him as sitting motionless on his sofa 'meditating on his abdication and only wondering on which of his brothers may devolve the burden which is too much for his shoulders.'[12]

His utter demoralisation had begun when Abdul Aziz was found dead on June 4, allegedly as a result of his suicide. It was accelerated by the assassination on June 14 of Hüseyin Avni and the Foreign Minister Rashid Pasha by the grieving brother of the former Sultan's favourite wife, who had died on June 12 apparently in childbirth.

By August 17 Elliot was reporting on a visit by an Austrian neurologist to Murad, who had diagnosed 'chronic alcoholism aggravated by the emotions he has gone though.' It was evident to Midhat that the new Sultan must go; another *fatwa* of deposition was obtained on the basis of his insanity, and Murad was immured in the Ciragan Palace on the Bosphorus where he remained until his death in 1904.[13]

His place was taken by his brother Abdul Hamid II, who was proclaimed Sultan on August 31. Notwithstanding the immensely difficult situation which he had inherited, Abdul Hamid came to the throne determined to exert its power. Unlike his brother, he was a strong willed man with a clear idea of what he wanted to achieve. His elevation had only come about after the assurances he had given to Midhat as to his support for continued reform, and he duly appointed Midhat as Grand Vizier. Elliot reported that the new Sultan was of a 'kindliness of disposition' with 'enlightened views,' but that it was doubtful whether he would accept the restrictions which the reformers might seek to place on him.[14]

4

The Eastern Question

The complexities of the Eastern Question, which so troubled the chancelleries of Europe, were greatly exacerbated by the insurrections that rocked the Ottoman Empire from 1875. All the Great Powers had kept a watchful eye on events within the Empire, and none more so than Russia. In St Petersburg, as in other capitals, the possibility of the final disintegration of the Ottoman Empire was kept under constant review. For Gorchakov, and for Tsar Alexander II, there was a particular concern, and that was the destruction of the Black Sea Clauses of the settlement of 1856. Russian diplomacy had always had this as one of its objectives, and the Franco Prussian War of 1870 provided a golden opportunity.

Accordingly, on October 31 1870 the Russian government formally denounced the neutralisation of the Black Sea. It was not so much a decision born of a perception of military need; it was more a step taken to remove the humiliation of the Treaty of Paris. It found the signatories to that treaty in too weak a position to do anything about it. France could in any case do nothing. Bismarck, of course, with a war to win and always concerned to maintain Russia's friendship, had no problem at all with the Russian objective, although he could have wished that the declaration had come later. His concern was that it might lead to a conflict between Russia and Britain, and it was for this reason that he proposed a conference. For Britain, the issue was the sanctity of treaties; Bismarck's concern was sharpened by a threat from Lord Odo Russell that Britain would go to war to uphold a treaty with or without allies.[1] Bismarck saw this as mere bravado, but it was an uncomfortable situation. On the other hand, an international conference, provided that it was excluded from consideration of the Franco Prussian war or its outcome, would defuse the situation. So it proved; with the tacit understanding that the Russian demand would be met if the declaration was withdrawn and the proposal put forward at a conference, the Great Powers agreed to meet in London. If this merely rubberstamped the inevitable outcome of the issue, it did nonetheless have the important consequence that the parties accepted the principle that the terms of an international treaty could not be arbitrarily changed by unilateral action.[2]

If the revision of the Black Sea clauses effectively reopened the Eastern Question, it was the events of 1875-6 in the Balkans which made it a question that must be answered. The problems facing the Christian Slavs of Bosnia and Herzegovina led to a tour in May 1875 by Franz Joseph of Dalmatia; it was, as was intended, seen as a gesture of support to the discontented Slavs within the Ottoman Empire. Meanwhile the Pan-Slavist party in Russia, with whose aims Ignatiev, the Russian ambassador in Constantinople, was certainly in sympathy, stepped up their support for the Slav populations of the Balkans. Throughout the Russian Empire charities were founded to provide funds for the relief of the mounting number of refugees that crossed Turkish borders into Austria-Hungary, Serbia and Montenegro.[3]

Count Ignatiev, Russian Ambassador to Turkey. (*Russes et Turcs*)

Misha Glenny has pointed out that the rise of Pan-Slavism, which united many strands of Russian society, had by the end of the 1860s become synonymous with the Orthodox Church. This, in turn, created dilemmas for the movement, not least when a dispute between the Greek and Bulgarian churches broke out. Ignatiev was the most prominent and most assertive of the Pan-Slavists; he was also the most ambitious, seeking for Russia the command of Constantinople and the Straits, and the unquestioned leadership of the Slavs. It was for Russia, not for the Slavs, that he wanted to see sweeping political change, as he explained:

> Sooner or later... Russia must fight Austria-Hungary for the first place in the Balkans and for the leadership of Slavdom: only for the attainment of this task should Russia make sacrifices for the Slavs under Austrian and Turkish rule and be solicitous for their freedom and growth in strength. To aim merely at emancipating the Slavs, to be satisfied with merely humanitarian success, would be foolish and reprehensible.[4]

Ignatiev did not himself make Russian policy, although he influenced it substantially at times; there were others who took a much more conservative view, including his opposite number in London, Count Peter Shuvalov. Gorchakov's position was somewhat between the two, and his direction of Russian policy was wholly pragmatic. Pragmatism also dictated the policy of Count Julius Andrassy, the onetime Hungarian rebel who became minister of foreign affairs in Vienna in 1871. The military leaders of the Dual Monarchy, whose influence over the Emperor was considerable, were unequivocal in their attitude to Bosnia and Herzegovina; for them, to annex the provinces was essential, for the protection of Dalmatia and to enable the constant unrest in the provinces on Austria-Hungary's borders to be brought under control. Andrassy, whose first concern

Count Shuvalov, Russian Ambassador to Britain. (*Russes et Turcs*)

was to see the Ottoman Empire kept in existence as long as possible, did not want an increase of the Slav population of the Dual Monarchy, telling Gorchakov that annexations 'would lead to the ruin of the empire and would therefore amount to suicide.'[5] He could see all too clearly that the absorption of these provinces would be a meal that would prove completely indigestible. Only if the Ottoman Empire completely disintegrated would it be necessary for Austria-Hungary, as a defensive measure, to annex Bosnia and Herzegovina in order to deny them to Serbia.

In Serbia, Prince Milan Obrenovic was of a much more conservative disposition than his predecessor Prince Michael; but although official Serbian policy was no longer irredentist, popular feeling certainly was, and by the time of the revolt in Herzegovina the national mood was militant in the extreme. As tension rose in the Balkans, therefore, Serbia could no longer be counted on not to intervene.

For Germany the Eastern Question had only a downside. Bismarck, who famously observed in December 1876 that there was nothing in the Balkans worth the healthy bones of a single Pomeranian musketeer, was concerned only to ensure that a balance was kept between Russian and Austria-Hungary, and was ready to agree to anything with which they both agreed. Britain, on the other hand, had a greater concern; in her case it was to preserve the existence of the Ottoman Empire, so that here at least there was a common interest with Austria-Hungary. From the British point of view it would be the tidiest solution for the Turks to suppress the insurrections on their own without involving the international community. Finally France, for her part, had no particular interest.

Andrassy, effectively taking the lead among the Great Powers, put forward a proposal on the part of the Three Emperors' League that they should send their consuls into the affected provinces to endeavour to mediate. France, which objected to being ignored, was on August 14 invited to join the mission, as was Italy; and, albeit reluctantly, the

British consul also took part. His view was that the trouble had been caused by Serbian agitation. The consuls heard much of the local grievances; but the rebel leaders wanted autonomy under a Christian prince or occupation by a foreign power until the grievances were resolved. This was unacceptable to Andrassy; and the Sublime Porte was not under any circumstances prepared to agree to this. Instead, a decree was published which promised alleviation of taxation, religious freedom and equality before the law, all of which had been promised before and never honoured.[6]

Next, Andrassy contemplated the imposition of a reform programme on the Ottoman government. Becoming aware of this, Abdul Aziz was determined to beat him to it by issuing his own programme for reform on December 12; he told Ignatiev that to allow foreign interference would be like committing suicide. However, this reform programme was merely a rehash of the former programmes, and Andrassy continued to work on his own plan, which he embodied in a note to the Great Powers on December 30. They all accepted it (although in Britain's case only because the Turks asked them to) and it was formally presented to the Porte on January 31 1876. However, although the Turks found it broadly acceptable, the insurgents did not, regarding the reforms as inadequate and worthless without international guarantees. It was an outcome which came as no surprise to Bismarck, for one, and he had already begun to consider alternative ways in which the increasingly pressing issues might be resolved.

His first approaches, to Britain and to Russia at the beginning of January 1876, fell upon stony ground. Although Russell thought Bismarck's desire for some understanding with Britain was sincere, he did not think that there was need for an immediate response; and Lord Derby, the Foreign Secretary, was content to let the matter rest. Gorchakov was also suspicious of Bismarck's motive in offering to mediate as well as his suggestion that Bosnia go to Austria and Bessarabia to Russia; he preferred to deal directly with Andrassy. A further approach in February through Lord Odo Russell was met with still greater suspicion by Lord Derby. It was still widely believed that Bismarck was a wolf in sheep's clothing, and that at this time dealing with him was extremely risky.[7] On this occasion at any rate Bismarck was being misjudged; he sincerely wanted to see a settlement of the Eastern Question since above all he wanted to avoid conflict between Russia and Austria; if the reform plans were not going to succeed, his suggestion of some limited territorial rearrangement might achieve his object.

On May 11 1876 Bismarck met with Andrassy and Gorchakov in Berlin to make another attempt to produce a generally acceptable solution. Bismarck had had a premeeting with Andrassy, and had tried and failed to convert him to the notion of some partition arrangements; when Gorchakov joined them he had brought with him the hope of creating autonomous states. Andrassy would not wear that either; and in the end the Berlin Memorandum that emerged was effectively a restatement of the original Andrassy Note. It called for the Ottoman government to provide means for the resettlement of refugees, for these means to be distributed by a mixed commission, for Turkish troops to be concentrated in a few specified locations, for Christians to be allowed to retain their arms for the time being and for the consuls to monitor the reforms.

As before, France and Italy agreed; but this time Britain did not. Affecting to be offended by the manner in which the Memorandum was communicated – Disraeli complained that 'England has been treated as though we were Montenegro or Bosnia' – the British government feared that the proposals were designed for the 'disintegration

Lord Derby, Britain's Foreign Secretary. (Fauré)

of Turkey.[8] Disraeli was pleased with himself, believing that in his rejection of the Memorandum he had driven a wedge between Austria and Russia.

While all this was going on the situation within the Ottoman Empire was steadily deteriorating. On May 29 Abdul Aziz had been deposed, while in April the revolt had spread to Bulgaria. Then, at the end of June 1876 Serbia and Montenegro declared war on Turkey.

Serbia took this step in the teeth of the official advice from the Russian government. Immediately before the declaration of war the Tsar sent a message to Prince Milan urging him to preserve peace at any price, and warning that he would be left to his fate if he did not do so. But Serbia's leaders were more impressed with the urging of Ignatiev that now was the time to take action.[9]

Command of the army was entrusted to the Russian General Mikhail Cherniaev, previously successful in Russian operations in Turkestan. Known as the 'Lion of Tashkent,' Cherniaev was an unfortunate choice. Although his capture of Tashkent in 1865 with less than two thousand men ensured that he was the hero of Russian imperialists, he was not a sound military commander. It was because of his championship of the Slav cause that he was selected, and his personality was unsuited to the demands which leadership of the Serbian army would make of him. One commentator observed:

Cherniaev was not a practical person – he lived in his imagination. He was always surrounded by a multitude of people who said yes to his fantasies and secured his trust. Like Don Quixote Cherniaev never recognised obstacles, he fought all his life against evil genii and giants … As a commander his qualities of will unquestionably predominated over his critical faculties, his heart over his reason.[10]

General Mikhail Cherniaev, the 'Lion of Tashkent'. (Strantz)

Emperor William I of Germany. (*Illustrirte Geschichte des Orientalischen Krieges*)

Cherniaev had arrived in Belgrade in May, and was followed by some 700 Russian officers as volunteers. In all it was estimated that some 4,000 Russian volunteers ultimately went to Serbia to take part in the war. As well as the provision of human resources in this way, the Russian organisations collecting funds in the Pan-Slavist interest were said to have transferred the equivalent of twenty million francs to Serbia. All this meant that the Russian government must prepare itself for the possibility of a great Slav victory, with all the uncertainties that this would create. Accordingly Gorchakov readily accepted the suggestion made by the Emperor William I that he should consult with Andrassy on a one to one basis to hammer out a joint programme of action in relation to the Serbo-Turkish conflict and its possible outcome.

Their meeting, at which they were accompanied by Tsar Alexander and the Emperor Franz Joseph, took place at Reichstadt on July 8. Their agreement was not reduced to writing, but essentially it amounted to an acceptance of the principle of non-intervention. If Turkey won, the status quo would be restored. Bosnia and Herzegovina were to be dealt with in accordance with the Andrassy Note and the Berlin Memorandum. If, on the other hand, Turkey was beaten, Serbia and Montenegro would gain some territory in Bosnia and Herzegovina, the rest of which would be annexed by Austria. Russia would recover Bessarabia and some territory in Armenia. If the Ottoman Empire collapsed altogether, Bulgaria and Rumelia would become autonomous, and also Albania (although this did not appear in the Russian note of the understanding). Greece would be allowed to make territorial gains. The deal pleased both sides; but it did not provide for direct Russian action in the Balkans, and this was in due course to appear a grave defect.

Serbian leaders hoped by their action in declaring war to promote a general insurrection across the Balkans; but neither Roumania or Greece responded, believing that it could not succeed without the active support of at least one of the Great Powers.

Bulgarian refugees. (Ollier)

This was not forthcoming, despite the conviction of Jovan Ristic, the Serbian Foreign Minister, that Russia could not remain passive. In this view he was sustained by a belief that the Pan-Slavs would define Russian policy.

The original intention was that the Serbian army, some 130,000 strong, should concentrate for an advance on Nish, where the principal Turkish forces were located. The plan was revised because of the risk of Turkish attacks upon both eastern and western flanks of the advance, and the Serbian army was organised in four corps with a view to advancing on all fronts. This was a dangerous dispersal of force; there was a frontier line of over 120 miles. The Serbian high command had, it has been pointed out, totally failed to pay attention to recent military history, which had conclusively shown that the power of modern infantry weapons enabled good defensive positions to withstand heavy assaults, and that only well trained, highly disciplined and well equipped troops could succeed in the assault.[11] The shrewd old Turkish leader Omar Pasha, who had watched Serbian manoeuvres for many years, thought that the peasant mass that constituted the army 'would take to its heels after the first bullet had been fired.'

At first all seemed to be going well. The Serbs crossed the frontier and made ground at all points. By the end of July, however, the Turks, commanded by Suleiman Pasha, were in a position to counter-attack. Suleiman Pasha, aged only thirty-eight, had acquired a high reputation. He had fought in Montenegro, Crete and the Yemen, and had risen to be Director of the Military Academy at Constantinople. There, he was very much at the centre of power, and he had taken an active part in the deposition of Abdul Aziz. Now,

Suleiman Pasha. (Hozier)

with a large army of well-equipped and well-trained troops he drove back the Serbs at the end of July, capturing Knjazevac and Zajecar.

Prince Milan lost his nerve completely, but was prevented by the government from seeking an armistice. Instead it was resolved to return to the original plan take to up a position in front of Nish, from where the Turks threatened Belgrade. For another month the Serbs, much better in defence than attack, held their positions. On September 1 however, at Alexinatz on the Morava river some seventeen miles north north-west of Nish, Cherniaev's army was decisively defeated, and the road to Belgrade lay open. Even the most fervent nationalists now lost heart, and a ten day ceasefire was negotiated upon stiff terms insisted on by the Turks.

While this was being negotiated, the situation in Serbia began to change. The increasing flow of Russian volunteers, and the upsurge in pro-Slav activity in Russia, brought above a complete change in the public mood, both there and in Serbia. It was not something that the Russian government could ignore, and the Tsar made a speech after the Russian army manoeuvres that autumn in which he said he had tried to preserve peace, but that if the country's honour was attacked he would know how to vindicate it.

All this immensely strengthened Cherniaev's position, and at his urging the armistice, which had been briefly renewed, was allowed to lapse on September 28. The resumption of hostilities, however, ultimately brought the Serbs no better fortune. Fierce fighting on the River Morava culminated in the Battle of Djunis on October 29, when a Turkish offensive smashed the Serbian army and advanced towards Belgrade. Cherniaev, enraged by his defeat, cried out to every Serbian officer he could find: 'Your Serbs all fled, and my Russians all perished!'[12] Confronted with the obvious and total defeat of the Serbs, Russia intervened to demand another armistice, to which the Turks at once agreed. The Great Powers now proposed a conference in Constantinople to settle the

Bulgarians destroying a Turkish mosque. (*Illustrirte Geschichte des Orientalischen Krieges von 1876-1878*)

terms of peace, which must necessarily include Montenegro, whose forces had succeeded in overrunning most of Herzegovina.

The war had been disastrous for Serbia. It is estimated that one sixth of her total population had been mobilised and that 10% of the male population was killed or wounded. The country's economy completely collapsed. These sacrifices on the part of Serbia had not only failed to achieve their object; they never could have done so:

> She was too weak and too unprepared to conduct the war with Turkey with any prospect of success. Even if she had overcome Turkey she could not have obtained Bosnia and Herzegovina, since they had already been allotted to Austria. But the significance of her entry into war lay not in its immediate result, but in the moral influence it had on the South Slavs, and in the further events it conditioned.[13]

In the immediate future, however, it was events that had already occurred in Bulgaria that were ultimately to determine the course of Balkan history.

5

The Approach to War

The news of the Bulgarian rebellion and the manner of its suppression brought about an astonishing reaction on the part of British public opinion. Soon after reports of atrocities committed by the Turks began to appear in the British press, an intense expression of popular outrage developed. W T Stead, the influential newspaper editor, wrote to Gladstone on September 6 to propose a national day of humiliation, a 'Bulgarian Sunday,' on which collections would be taken for the victims of the Turkish atrocities.[1]

And later that year another commentator observed that 'the mind and spirit of Englishmen were moved more than ever happened in my recollection.'

The progress of the Bulgarian agitation had coincided with the attempts of the Great Powers to bring about an end to the Serbo-Turkish War, and for the British government it soon began seriously to limit its options. When on August 24 Serbia began to seek Great Power support in arranging an armistice, Derby made plain to Elliot in Constantinople the extent to which British policy had been affected:

I think it right to mention, for your guidance, that the impression produced here by events in Bulgaria has completely destroyed sympathy with Turkey. The feeling is universal and so strong that even if Russia were to declare war against the Porte, Her Majesty's Government would find it practically impossible to interfere.[2]

Elliot replied in terms which demonstrated just how strongly pro-Turkish had been his interpretation of British policy, and how much he deplored the influence of public opinion on its development. He told the Foreign Secretary that he had 'over and over again' raised strong protests, and denied having been 'a blind partisan' of the Turks, arguing that he had been seeking to uphold the interests of Great Britain. He went on, however, to add:

We may and must feel indignant at the needless and monstrous severity with which the Bulgarian insurrection was put down, but the necessity which exists for England to prevent changes from occurring here which would be most detrimental to ourselves, is not affected by the question whether it was 10,000 or 20,000 persons which perished in the oppression. We have been upholding what we know to be a semi-civilised nation, liable under certain circumstances to be carried into fearful excesses: but the fact of this having just now been strikingly brought home to us all cannot be a sufficient reason for abandoning a policy which is the only one that can be followed with a due regard to our own interests.[3]

William Ewart Gladstone, a leading member of the Liberal Party, in
opposition in Britain, and vociferous opponent of Turkey.

The barely concealed suggestion of national hypocrisy did not go down well with
Derby, who responded that 'no political considerations would justify the toleration of
such acts.'

By the time William Ewart Gladstone published his pamphlet *Bulgarian Horrors
and the Question of the East* on September 6, the evidence of observers in Bulgaria had
established beyond doubt the extent to which the Turks, and especially the Bashi-
Bazouks, the irregular soldiers employed there, were guilty of atrocities. And yet that
evidence was in some respects both partial and unreliable. It is impossible to estimate
with any degree of accuracy the number of Bulgarians who died, whether in arms or
not, or the number of villages destroyed by the Turks, or the circumstances in which
these incidents occurred. Walter Baring, a second secretary in the British embassy at
Constantinople, was sent to investigate. He had been preceded by Dupuis, the vice
consul at Adrianople, whose first telegram to the Foreign Office on July 21 reported
that 'although great atrocities have been committed by Turkish irregulars against the
Bulgarians, they have been exaggerated.'[4] Baring's first reports from Bulgaria offered
dramatic evidence of those atrocities. After visiting the village of Batak he described
what he found:

> The village consisted of 800 houses, and about 8,000 inhabitants. Of these at least
> 6,000 have been massacred... The first thing I saw was some twenty or thirty dogs
> devouring human bodies, and in the place they had been feasting in I counted
> sixty-two skulls in about 20 yards. Here [inside and around the church] the corpses
> lay so thick that one could hardly avoid treading on them, and the stench was so
> fearful, that any examination was next to impossible.[5]

Safvet Pasha, Turkish Foreign Minister. (Ollier)

When Elliot, at a meting with the Turkish Foreign Minister, Safvet Pasha, put this report to him, the Turk's response was bitter. European newspapers, he complained, exaggerated every Turkish excess and suppressed all mention of those committed by the insurgents.

Baring's reports were substantiated by the American journalist Januarius MacGahan, sent by the *Daily News* to report on events in Bulgaria. His account of events in Batak was published on August 7. Its credibility was reinforced by the fact that MacGahan was accompanying Eugene Schuyler, sent by the United States Minister in Constantinople to investigate the reports of atrocities. Gladstone, in his pamphlet, violently attacked the British government for its failure to act:

> I entreat my countrymen, upon whom far more than perhaps any other people in Europe it depends, to require and insist that our Government which has been working in one direction, shall work in the other, and shall apply all its vigour to concur with the other States of Europe in obtaining the extinction of the Turkish executive power in Bulgaria. Let the Turks now carry away their abuses in the only possible manner, namely by carrying off themselves.[6]

Gladstone's position was readily distinguishable from that of Disraeli, rejecting the proposition that British interests should be the sole measure of what was right or wrong. What he had done was to politicise the issue, so that the question of Turkish atrocities became an issue between government and opposition and as such exerted a powerful influence on the development of foreign policy.[7]

It was not, however, only in London that public opinion as to events in Bulgaria affected the consideration of the Eastern Question. As Misha Glenny has pointed out,

Influential American war correspondents
J.A. MacGahan and F.D. Millet. (Bullard)

in almost every capital in Europe involved in the crisis public reaction to the newspaper reports swayed official policy.[8] The suspension of hostilities between Serbia and the Ottoman Empire had by no means brought the crisis to an end; and it was the Russians who made the next effective move.

This was prompted by Alexander, who had come to the conclusion that Russia must now take action following the defeat of Serbia and Montenegro. It has been suggested that his determination was crystallised by the fact that he was at Livadia in the Crimea, 'surrounded by Pan-Slav advisers and relatives and far away from the European atmosphere of St Petersburg.' There, Gorchakov had been hoping that Bismarck would lead the way in proposing a European congress or conference to deal with the situation but Bismarck had declined to take the bait. He had also been put out by an approach by Alexander to General Bernhard von Werder, the German military plenipotentiary, to enquire whether Germany would remain neutral in the event of a Russo-Austrian war.

This enquiry had its origin in a conversation between Field Marshal Edwin von Manteuffel, sent on a special mission to Russia, and the Tsar, who had expressed the hope to him that if there was conflict with Austria, Germany would act as Russia had done in 1870. He complained that Russia had so far made all the concessions to Austria, but quoted Gorchakov as having 'the conviction that if Germany supported the views of Russia in any positive form, Austria would join him completely.'[9] A platonic declaration of friendship from Germany was not enough.

Bismarck tried to avoid answering; Gorchakov pressed him further through his ambassador. Then the Tsar repeated the question, this time to Werder, who reported it to Bismarck on October 1. Considering the approach to be a trap, Bismarck still failed to answer, advising the Emperor William that he should not either. He was irritated also by the use of Werder as the medium of communication. The appointment of a more senior officer as military plenipotentiary was an arrangement exclusive to St Petersburg. His reports went in the first instance to the military cabinet, being then forwarded to the Foreign Office. Bismarck thought that the arrangement gave Gorchakov a decided advantage:

> We can never hold the Russians to their word or make them responsible for what they say to us through Werder, because the commissions which Prince Gorchakov gives General von Werder for us reach the latter solely through the medium of verbal confidential conversation between a monarch and his 'adjutant.'[10]

He also thought that it was a 'calamity' that an officer 'completely unversed in politics' should become in effect 'a Russian tool to help blackmail us for an embarrassing and untimely declaration,' which was being a bit hard on Werder, who could hardly help reporting what the Tsar might say to him. Bismarck, though, never forgave Werder for his part in all this.

He recorded in his memoirs the stance which he believed Germany should take up in this situation:

> We could indeed endure that our friends should lose or win battles against each other, but not that one of the two should be so severely wounded and injured that its position as an independent great power, taking its part in the councils of Europe, would be endangered.[11]

The Russians were not the only suitors for some indications of Bismarck's favour. First the Austrians, anxious about Russian intentions, and then Disraeli, made overtures to the German Chancellor. In *The Times* of October 16 a leading article suggested that 'one plain word from Bismarck would stop Russia even on the brink of the abyss into which a very little more pressure would make her plunge,' and went on to propose 'a cordial alliance between Germany and England' to bring about the necessary changes in Turkey.'[12] There was not much hope of this; Bismarck thought that partition was the best way of obtaining a lasting settlement of the Eastern Question.

With the Turks having acceded to the Russian demand at the end of October for an armistice in Serbia, Derby proposed that a conference be held in Constantinople, and this was agreed by the Great Powers. Although, for what it was worth, the Turks had won the war against the Serbs there was not much they could do to avoid it, and they reluctantly accepted the conference. Regrettably, none of the other participants had much faith that the conference would resolve the outstanding issues. For their part, the Russians were already determined on taking action – provided, that is, that they could do so without most of the rest of Europe lining up against them, as had occurred at the start of the Crimean War. The Tsar was at pains to tell the British Ambassador that he desired no conquest and that 'he had not the smallest wish or intention to be possessed of Constantinople.'[13] What he sought was the amelioration of the position of the Christians but that this should be properly guaranteed, and not rest solely on Turkish promises. He had no real need to offer this kind of assurance; the British government's position was plainly heavily circumscribed by the strength of popular sentiment that would for the

Benjamin Disraeli, Earl of Beaconsfield,
British Prime Minister. (Hozier)

moment preclude any military action in support of Turkey, although by the end of the
year the attitude of the press to Turkey had somewhat softened.

However, the respective public attitudes of the two governments were made clear
in two speeches made almost simultaneously. At the Guildhall on November 9 Disraeli
asserted the British position in a characteristically bombastic manner:

> Although the policy of England is peace, there is no country so well prepared for
> war as our own. If she enters into a conflict in a righteous cause – and I will not
> believe that England will go to war except for a righteous cause – if the contest is
> one which concerns her liberty, her independence, or her empire, her resources, I
> feel, are inexhaustible.

Next day, although unaware of Disraeli's remarks, Alexander spoke at Moscow, on
his way home to St Petersburg:

> My ardent wish is for a peaceful agreement. Should we not obtain from the Porte
> such guarantees for carrying out the reforms we have a right to demand, I am firmly
> determined to act independently; and I am convinced that the whole of Russia will
> support me, should the honour of Russia require it, and that Moscow will set the
> example.[14]

In the light of these bellicose utterances, it was no surprise that both the Russian
and British government should have been preparing for war. The Russians mobilised four
army corps; a commission from the British War Office was sent to Constantinople to

examine positions on both sides of the Straits and to assess how they might be defended. There was, however, a difference in the attitude of the respective governments. Well before the Constantinople conference the Russian government was determined upon military action against Turkey; all that remained to be done was to ensure that its diplomatic position was maximised. In the British Cabinet, however, there was no unanimity; the preparations for war which Disraeli ordered produced serious disagreements. Derby was utterly opposed to any order to the British fleet to pass the Dardanelles, and other prominent members of the Cabinet were deeply concerned.

Meanwhile Lord Salisbury, the British delegate to the conference, set off on November 20, travelling via Paris, Berlin, Vienna and Rome. In Berlin he found Bismarck to be extremely pessimistic; he told Salisbury 'that what we were trying to do in Turkey was hopeless' and was gloomy about the prospects of peace:

> He did not think it possible that Russia after doing so much should draw back...
> He encouraged us to take Egypt as our share; failing that he thought it would be very useful for European civilisation that we should occupy Constantinople.[15]

When he got to Vienna Salisbury found Andrassy of such a similar mind that he assumed that he and Bismarck were in 'active communication and tolerably close concert between them.' In the course of his travels, he reported from Rome, he had not succeeded in finding the friend of the Turk – he did not exist. When he got to Constantinople on December 5, however, he was extremely surprised to find that Ignatiev was displaying a conciliatory and moderate attitude, and soon established a good relationship with him.

The representatives of the Great Powers who gathered in the Ottoman capital agreed to have a series of meetings amongst themselves before confronting the Turks. Lord Salisbury and Ignatiev met on December 6 and 7, and it was soon apparent that the key issue on which the Great Powers must agree was the question of Bulgaria. Ignatiev proposed the creation of an autonomous Bulgaria (a 'big Bulgaria') both north and south of the Balkan mountains, with a seacoast on the Black Sea at Bourgas and on the Aegean at Dedeagatch. This was opposed by the Austrians and Salisbury as well, the latter believing that its size would make it 'fatal to the independence of the Porte.' He prevailed on Ignatiev to agree to dividing it into two provinces, one in the west and one in the east.

Another issue which generated a lot of correspondence between Lords Derby and Salisbury was the proposal to introduce a foreign military force to police the region. Britain could never agree to a Russian force, and Russia was likewise opposed to a British force, so Baron von Werther, the German delegate, suggested that the troops should come from outside the Great Powers. A Belgian force was proposed, and this Salisbury urged Derby to accept. The latter saw that it had 'obvious advantages', but could not absolutely promise that the cabinet would agree.[16]

Salisbury's good relationship with Ignatiev occasioned considerable surprise, not least on the part of Elliot, who put it down to Salisbury's ignorance of conditions in Turkey as a result of which he had fallen under Ignatiev's influence. As a pronounced Turcophil, this development was very disturbing to the envoy. A more favourable interpretation has, however, been put forward: Salisbury certainly did not share Elliot's distrust of the Russian ambassador, but he also felt the need for an accommodation with Russia; in

Lord Salisbury. (*Russes et Turcs*)

particular, he was keen to avoid a Russian occupation of Bulgaria. Derby noted in his diary on Christmas Day that Salisbury seemed more hopeful of success than he was:

> He expresses the opinion that Ignatieff wants peace, on personal grounds: diplomatic triumph is a gain to him, Ignatieff, whereas a war can bring credit only to the generals who make it. He also thinks that the Russian govt desires peace on military and financial grounds, being ill prepared and poor: and this is very possible true, but they are too deeply pledged to be able to back out however they may wish it. He … says that Elliott and the English generally at Constantinople think he has been too hard on the Turks, but makes no complaint of being unsupported.[17]

The period that began with the start of the Constantinople conference and continued until Derby's resignation in March 1878 was one of the oddest in the history of the development of British foreign policy. One of its curious features was the overt influence of the wives of some of the principal players. In Constantinople Salisbury was accompanied by his wife, who from the outset displayed extreme Turcophobia. In England, Lady Derby, who was Salisbury's stepmother, had formed a very close and thoroughly indiscreet relationship with Shuvalov; through her, the Russian ambassador was kept closely informed of the various shifts of opinion with in the British Cabinet. The Cabinet was seriously divided, with Disraeli and a few colleagues, who did not include Derby, pursuing an extremely belligerent policy towards Russia. The notion of going to war with Russia on behalf of the Turks, for which Disraeli made ostentatious

The conference in Constantinople. From left to right – Zichy (Austrian
ambassador), Chaudordy (France), Bourgoing (France), Corti (Italy), Midhat Pasha,
Werther (Germany), Safvet Pasha, Elliot (Britain), Ignatiev (Russia), Salisbury
(Britain). (*Illustrirte Geschichte des Orientalischen Krieges von 1876-1878*)

preparations, was practically speaking impossible while the Bulgarian agitation continued
in Britain.

Gladstone, of course, was one of those at the head of the anti-Turkish movement,
so much so that some felt he was rather too Russian. Hammond, the former Under
Secretary at the Foreign Office, wrote:

'Gladstone seems resolved still to find the Russians immaculate, and he has now
undertaken to white-wash them against the dirt thrown upon them by Schuyler in
the part of his late book, where he reveals the orders of Kauffman to massacre all
sexes and ages, and ravage all districts in certain parts of Central Asia.'[18]

A conference was convened in London on December 8 at St James's Hall and
attended by a number of extremely prominent members of all walks of British society,
and Gladstone made up his mind to speak. He did so in the teeth of opposition from
a number of leaders of his own party. The conference speakers were in general united
in their absolute refusal to entertain war for Turkey against Russia, and called on the
government to compel the Porte to introduce guaranteed reforms.

The Queen, who was as shocked as the agitators by Turkish behaviour in Bulgaria,
was nonetheless extremely put out by the conference and the message that it sent. She
greatly mistrusted the Russians and supported the line taken by Disraeli. The strength of
the agitation could not however be ignored; in the space of six weeks during the autumn

of 1876 it has been estimated that some five hundred meetings were held in Britain to protest about the Bulgarian atrocities.

The first formal meeting of the conference in Constantinople opened on Saturday December 23. Four days earlier Abdul Hamid had appointed Midhat Pasha as Grand Vizier. During the opening address by Safvet Pasha, the Turkish Foreign Minister, the startled delegates heard the booming of guns. Safvet told them that this was a salute to honour the proclamation of the new constitution which Midhat had drafted, and which guaranteed equal rights for all the peoples of the Ottoman Empire. The delegates were reduced to silence; this continued for several minutes, but they then resumed the business of the meeting, a display of rudeness that has been described as an example of the 'arrogant self-righteousness' with which Europe dealt with the Porte. At the end of the first day's meeting the Turkish delegates were handed a copy of the proposals agreed upon by the Great Powers during their preliminary meetings.

The Turkish position was that the granting of the new constitution rendered the proceedings of the conference irrelevant. Their intransigence was strengthened by the enthusiasm displayed in public demonstrations in Constantinople, and their response at the next meeting on December 28 was to reject the proposals as to Bulgaria. The counter proposals produced by the Turks on December 30 either ignored or refused most of what had been put forward, and the Great Powers met together next day to consider what should now be done. It was agreed at the formal meeting on January 1 to seek to clarify what the Turks were rejecting, and insist that a more satisfactory response must be produced without delay.

Admiralty Palace, Constantinople, where the conference was held. (Ollier)

Next day the delegates warned the Turks of the danger into which they had come, and Salisbury saw Midhat to impress this on him. The latter, however, was unyielding. On January 4 the Turks set out their reasons for objecting to the proposals; the Great Power representatives again met to concert their response. In expectation of a refusal, they produced revised proposals which contained considerable concessions; Derby entirely approved the changes but doubted whether the Turks would accept them. Further meetings by Salisbury, first with Midhat and then with the Sultan, produced no result. On January 15 the Turks were told that if the new proposals were not agreed by January 18 (later extended to January 20) the conference would end. On January 20 the Turks remained obdurate, and the Great Power representatives agreed to pack up and go home.

Long before the end Salisbury had had enough of the Turks, expressing himself graphically to Werther, the German representative, as the latter reported to Bülow on January 14:

> For the Turkish Ministers Lord Salisbury merely expressed utter contempt. He considers them incapable of conducting any serious negotiations whatever, and has gained the conviction from his conversations with Midhat Pasha that he is shifty and inspired by extreme ill will and that his one object is to slip, by means of base and petty tricks, out of any agreement which may make for a genuine improvement of the Turkish administration. He doubts whether, even if the intentions of the rulers of Turkey were more honest than they are, the universal corruption of

The closing scene of the Constantinople conference – Safvet
Pasha rejects the ultimatum. (Ollier)

the governing classes would permit the establishment of stable conditions in the Turkish provinces.[19]

On February 4 Gorchakov circulated the other European powers, arguing that the Porte's refusal of the proposals struck at the 'dignity and repose of Europe:'

The Emperor, desirous of acting as far as possible in common with Europe, wishes before taking a decision, to ascertain views of the other Great Powers as to meeting this refusal of the Porte, and ensuring execution of their wishes.[20]

There were divided views among observers as to whether this was a sign of weakness, or whether the Russians were preparing for war. To some extent, the latter was the case; secret negotiations with Austria had led to the signature of a military convention at Budapest on January 15 between the two powers in anticipation of the failure of the Constantinople Conference. It provided that if Russia went to war with Turkey, Austria would be a benevolent neutral, and would do her best to prevent intervention or mediation by other powers; in exchange Austria was to be allowed to occupy Bosnia and Herzegovina at a moment of her choosing. These negotiations had begun as early as November 1876. The military convention was to be binding when a political convention had been agreed; this eventually occurred on March 15. The two parties were each in a position whereby a deal of this kind was necessary; Austria, because she could not afford to leave in the air the situation that might result from a Russian victory, and Russia because she could not contemplate war with Turkey unless her flank was secure from Austrian intervention.

In Constantinople, Midhat's position as Grand Vizier was abruptly terminated on February 5. Abdul Hamid, who did not like him but had found him a useful figure with which to impress the Great Powers, now chose to blame him for the apparent affront to their representatives, replacing him by Edhem Pasha. He was not merely sacked; the Sultan ordered his arrest and banishment. At the same time foreign envoys were told that this did not mean the end of the new constitution. And indeed, in March the Sultan opened the proceedings of the new Chamber of Deputies in a showy ceremony attended by the diplomatic corps.

6

Recourse to Arms

The Balkan roads left much to be desired, and were for practical purposes impassable by an army during the winter. Even after the failure of the Constantinople conference, therefore, there still remained a window of opportunity for peace, although with each week that went by it was closing rapidly. The suggestion put forward by Count Shuvalov, accordingly, that Lord Derby should urge the Sublime Porte to adopt some of the reform proposals, was one which the Foreign Secretary had no difficulty in taking up. He got a temporising reply. Shuvalov's approach had been prompted by a conversation between Lady Derby and her stepson, on his return from Constantinople, as to the possibility that even now, with the Porte's willingness to consent to reform, the Russians might draw back from a conflict that otherwise seemed inevitable. Shuvalov was also anxious that Gorchakov's circular should receive a prompt reply.[1]

Bismarck was also anxious to know what the British response to the circular would be, and was concerned to hear of the close working relationship that had developed at Constantinople between Salisbury and Ignatiev. Always anxious about potentially hostile alliances, and in an effort to keep Britain apart from France and Russia, he put out feelers for an understanding between Britain and Germany, not just in relation to the present crisis, about which he was not much concerned, but on a more permanent basis. Lord Odo Russell reported on February 3 the Chancellor's remarks at a meeting:

Bismarck became grave and silent after a while and said that one of his foremost political dreams had been an active and intimate alliance with England... [for peace] but that dream could not be realized by good offices and moral support only which appeared to be all England had to offer him in return for the intimate alliance of Germany. It was a good deal and he was grateful for it, but it was not enough when other Powers were actively preparing for war.[2]

When the British Cabinet discussed the German approach, there was the usual knee jerk reaction of suspicion of what Bismarck was up to, a suspicion shared by Queen Victoria, who wrote in her diary:

That monstrous Bismarck is again at his tricks, wanting us to go with him and is getting up the same cry as before against France, accusing her of the intention of attacking Germany. It is just what he did 2 years ago.[3]

Meanwhile to the alarm of Disraeli and his colleagues, Ignatiev was sent ostensibly to visit an oculist but in reality on a tour of the Western capitals with the draft of a protocol, which Bismarck approved. That alone aroused suspicion about Russian motives; but Salisbury was enthusiastic about its moderation, and Derby thought its terms studiously inoffensive: 'nothing is said of the conference proposals; the Turkish

Queen Victoria.

Reforms are accepted instead; no date is fixed for their execution.[4] Ignatiev's arrival in England on March 16 where, his reputation so bad that his presence was unlikely to assist the negotiations, there was nonetheless an opportunity for a series of meetings which offered some hope that the 'golden bridge' which would enable Russia to retreat might be constructed.

Discussions continued between the Great Powers during the second half of March. One cause of delay was the continuing negotiation between Turkey and Montenegro, in the course of which Prince Nicholas of Montenegro was making territorial demands which the Turks were not disposed to accept. Derby suggested that the Protocol should not be signed until these negotiations were completed, but they continued to drag on and the Russian pressure for acceptance of the Protocol continued to increase. A more serious problem, however, was the insistence by the British Cabinet that the Protocol could not be finalised until the question of the demobilisation of the Russian army had been resolved. The Russian position as to this was that before they could demobilise, the Montenegrin peace talks must be completed, the Turkish reforms must be put in place and the Turks must themselves begin to disarm.

Just how sincere the Russians were in all this must be a matter of some doubt. Quite early in the approach to war the Russians had effectively painted themselves into a corner. Bismarck correctly understood that beneath the bellicose exterior of Russian policy there was a genuine reluctance on the part of Alexander and Gorchakov to go to war; however, they were, he observed, in the position of the diner who no longer wants the steak he ordered but feels compelled to eat it because he has to pay for it.[5] If there was to be a war Alexander certainly did not want to find repeated the situation his father had faced before the Crimean War, when he was opposed directly or indirectly by the rest of Europe. Getting the Great Powers to agree to a protocol that was extremely vague, while being reasonably confident that the Turks would either reject it, or fail in practice to comply with its requirements, he could proceed without fear of interference.

In London, while the members of the Cabinet anguished over the wisdom or otherwise of signing the Protocol, the House of Commons continued to debate various aspects of the question. One of these was the issue of whether Elliot, notionally on leave, should return as ambassador to Constantinople. Rightly perceived as an extreme Turcophil who had been allowed to bend British policy in favour of Turkey over a long period, there was a strong expression of opinion in the House in debates during March that he should not go back. Inside the Cabinet, Disraeli, who had privately determined that he should not, had had a long struggle with Derby, who obstinately resisted what he saw as interference with the Foreign Office's right to decide who should serve as ambassadors. But Elliot's extreme pronouncements, and the Cabinet's progressive retreat from a strongly pro-Turkish position, meant that in the end there could be no question of his return. Indeed, his maintenance in his position in the latter part of 1876 probably owed as much as anything to the requests of Shuvalov that he be removed; such a demand from a foreign ambassador could never be complied with.

The best abused men in Europe
on the road to Glory —

Bashi-Bazouks as sketched by an artist with *The Graphic* illustrated newspaper. Note his legend – "The best abused men in Europe on the road to Glory". (*The Graphic*)

On March 28 Loftus, from St Petersburg, telegraphed Derby that the chances of peace were seriously put at risk by British insistence on Russian demobilisation:

> It is my duty to inform your Lordship that the present crisis here is one of serious gravity. I am privately informed that if the condition for demobilisation is maintained... war is certain. Emperor of Russia regards it as one of humiliation, and will prefer war to its acceptance. Unless difficulty as regards the demobilisation can be solved and the protocol signed it is my conviction that the Russian army will cross the Pruth in about three weeks.[6]

Later that day the Cabinet met again and in the face of such a threat had no option but to authorize the signature of the Protocol without further delay. The Foreign Secretary feared a trap, and told Shuvalov that if armament and war were not avoided, the Protocol would be regarded as invalid.

In last minute negotiations to ensure the signature of the Protocol, Shuvalov obtained his government's agreement to a Turkish envoy going to St Petersburg to discuss disarmament; and following this, on March 31 the London Protocol was duly signed by Derby, Shuvalov, the Marquis d'Harcourt for France, Münster for Germany, von Beust for Austria and Menabrea for Italy. The terms of the document were as follows:

> The protocol reaffirmed the interest of the powers in the amelioration of the condition of the Christian populations and in the reforms to be introduced in Bosnia, Herzegovina, and Bulgaria. It took cognisance of the peace concluded by the Porte with Serbia on March 1. The Turkish government was invited to consolidate the peace by putting its armies on a peace footing and by taking in hand the reforms which had been promised. The powers proposed to watch carefully, by means of their representatives, the manner in which the promises of the Porte were carried into effect. If their hopes should again be disappointed, they declared, such a state of affairs would be incompatible with their interests and those of Europe generally. In that case they reserved to themselves further consideration as to the means best fitted to secure the welfare of the Christian populations and the interests of general peace.

Derby added a declaration that if there was no reciprocal demobilisation the Protocol should be treated as null and void. He recorded in his diary his suspicion and dislike of the whole business of the Protocol:

> We are signing a paper which is a sham, on the assurance that Russia wants it as an excuse for disarming. The best that can be said is that guarded as we propose, it can do no harm: and that if we had refused, as possibly it is wished that we should – the whole blame of war breaking out would be thrown on us.[7]

Although, as the Foreign Secretary had observed, the Protocol was 'studiously inoffensive,' it was entirely possible that it would be rejected by the Turks. This in fact occurred on April 9, when the Turkish government protested against the imposition of the surveillance of its conduct which the Protocol contained, and appealed to the

Henry Layard, British Ambassador to Turkey following the transfer of Sir Henry Elliot. (Ollier)

provisions of the Treaty of Paris. Musurus Pasha, the Turkish ambassador, saw Derby two days later, prior to the formal publication of the Turkish circular. He suggested that 'it would be better for the Sultan to lose one or two provinces than his prestige and independence;' in reply the Foreign Secretary said that it was no longer just a matter of one or two provinces but of the future of the Ottoman Empire.

A number of factors contributed to the decision of the Turks to reject the London Protocol. First, there had of course been a recent change of government in Constantinople. The fall from power of Midhat after only a brief spell as Grand Vizier spelt the effective end of his constitution; its first function was to undermine the proceedings of the Constantinople Conference and its last was to secure 'parliamentary' rejection of the Protocol.[8] Secondly, there were strong objections to the suggestion in the Protocol of a rectification of the frontier in favour of Montenegro. Next, the announcement on March 31 of Henry Layard as British Ambassador (to start with, only as a temporary appointee) seemed to mark a return to the pro-Turkish policy espoused by his predecessor; there existed a feeling that, once the chips were down, the British government would perceive it to be in its interests to stand by Turkey. Finally, and perhaps crucially, the Turks believed that they would be calling Russia's bluff, and that St Petersburg would draw back from war. Russia's financial problems were well known, while the reorganisation of the Russian army pursuant to Miliutin's reforms still had some way to go.

But the attempt to call Russia's bluff was a fearful miscalculation; it was in any case unwise to do so when the hand of cards which the Turks held was itself so weak. Nationalist opinion in Russia in support of the Slavs might somewhat have abated; but those around the Tsar exerted sufficient influence to ensure that his courage

Edhem Pasha, Grand Vizier. (Hozier)

remained screwed to the sticking-place. Turkish rejection of the Protocol, even if not a surprise, inevitably resulted in a hardening of the Russian position. No step was taken to reopen discussions with the other Great Powers, although this had been contemplated in the event that the Turks did indeed reject the Protocol. Instead, the process of full mobilisation of the army was at once ordered. The Russians had, by their diplomacy, obtained the conditions which would enable them to make war on the Ottoman Empire without the fear of foreign interference. And, above all, the coming of spring would make the Balkan roads passable; the campaigning season had begun.

Layard arrived in Constantinople on April 20 and at once went to see Edhem Pasha, the Grand Vizier, who told him that it was too late to prevent the war. Layard made clear that if war broke out, Britain would not help; this kind of protestation had of course been made before, even by Elliot, and the Turks were inclined still not to believe it. Next day, with Safvet Pasha, the Foreign Minister, Layard discussed the possibility of mediation, and found him inclined to pursue the idea. Finally, on April 24, Layard had an audience with Abdul Hamid, who emphasised, with tears in his eyes, that he desired peace. Layard was impressed with the Sultan, and thought him sincere and 'a man out of whom much might be made.' However, in the course of their meeting the Sultan received a telegram from his ambassador in St Petersburg to the effect that he had received a note from Gorchakov containing the Russian declaration of war.

The Tsar's manifesto announcing this was issued from Kishinev, and was a lengthy one. It did not however, set out with any precision the Russian war aims. After referring to his strong interest in the oppressed Christian peoples of Turkey, Alexander referred to his constant solicitude for peace, and to the incessant efforts of the Great Powers to induce the Porte to effect the necessary reforms. He went on to explain the

The departure of the Tsar from Kishinev. (*Illustrirte Geschichte des Orientalischen Krieges von 1876-1878*)

London Protocol, which contained the most essential conditions of the Constantinople Conference, and the failure of the Turks to adhere to it:

> Having exhausted our pacific efforts, we are compelled by the haughty obstinacy of the Porte to proceed to more decisive acts. A feeling of equity and of our own dignity enjoins it. By her refusal Turkey places us under the necessity of having recourse to arms… We expressed the intention to act independently when we deemed it necessary, and when Russia's honour should demand it. In now invoking the blessing of God upon our valiant armies, we give the order to cross the Turkish frontier.[9]

On the same day Gorchakov issued a Circular Note to the other Great Powers informing them of Russia's declaration of war, a step which, he wrote, was fulfilling a duty which was imposed on him by the interests of Russia, whose peaceable development was impeded by the constant troubles in the East. In doing so, he expressed the belief of the Tsar that he was at the same time responding to the views of Europe.

Thus ended in futility two years of the most intricate diplomacy intended to avert the outbreak of hostilities, conducted by the participants in a manner that was at various times sincere, cynical, constructive, selfish and half-hearted. The prospect of the ceaseless negotiations ending in success was impaired by the fact that in St Petersburg and Constantinople there were differing opinions as to the policy to be pursued. Still more was this the case in London, where the British Cabinet was deeply divided; while popular opinion remained profoundly affected by the Bulgarian atrocities, Disraeli was just about able to hold together his Cabinet. He and Derby were however beginning to drift further apart; he was discontented with the Foreign Secretary's negative approach, while the latter constantly reiterated his belief that the middle class was 'strong against war.'[10]

Derby's attitude particularly annoyed the Queen, who told Disraeli that 'Lord Derby must be made to move; the Queen feels horribly anxious about this.' Her Russophobia was becoming more pronounced; in March she had complained to her Prime Minister of 'this mawkish sentimentality for people who hardly deserve the name of Christian … and forgetting the great interests of this great country.' Under no circumstance, she said, could Russia ever be permitted to occupy Constantinople.[11]

British suspicion of Russian motives may well have been unjustified. Of course there were many points of view within Russia as to the real war aims which might be achievable, and certainly the military men had some extremely ambitious ideas on the subject; but a memorandum written by Gorchakov at the beginning of June for the benefit of Shuvalov and the latter's anxiety to reassure Britain shows that in the Chancellor's mind at any rate British fears were without foundation. Addressing the key areas of concern, he wrote:

> As to Suez and Egypt, we shall not touch these two points: we have neither the interest, the desire, nor the means, to do so … Once the British Ministers are fully assured that we shall in no case remain at Constantinople, it depends on them to save us from the need of going near to it.

Britain could achieve this, he wrote, by exerting due pressure on Turkey. He went on to deal with fears of Russian action on the Euphrates and the Persian Gulf or at Erzerum, and its effects on the route to India:

> Our position is simple and clear. We have no interest to injure England in this direction, but we may be forced to seek measures of defence against her hostility. Our attitude depends entirely upon hers … We are quite disposed to come to terms frankly and loyally on all these questions with the London Cabinet: we believe such an *entente* to be possible and more advantageous than mutual distrust and suspicion. In general, we have no interest in troubling England in her Indian possessions or in her communications. The present war does not demand this, for its aim is clearly defined and it would only be complicated by so vast an extension of the struggle.

He offered an explanation of British misunderstanding of Russian motives:

The English find it hard to understand a war of religious and national sentiment, and being incapable of one themselves, they constantly look for *arrières pensées*. But they should at least be accessible to the material side of the question.

This was that Russia could no longer tolerate a situation which might affect her peaceful development and precipitate her into disastrous crises and wars. It was necessary to put an end to this by asserting Russia's military superiority in such a way that the Turks should not in future defy her lightly, while guaranteeing the situation of the Christians, especially of Bulgaria. Britain on the other hand desired the maintenance of the Ottoman Empire and the inviolability of Constantinople and the Straits. These views, he wrote, were 'not irreconcilable.'[12] Since this memorandum was intended for Shuvalov alone, it may reasonably be taken as a sincere account of Russian intentions.

In this memorandum Gorchakov also set out the specific terms on which Russia would make peace if Turkey put out feelers for negotiation before the Russian army crossed the Balkans. These comprised the following: Bulgaria as a vassal state under European guarantee, administrative guarantees for Bulgaria south of the Balkans and the other Christian provinces, additional territory for Serbia and Montenegro, autonomy for Bosnia-Herzegovina, and regulation by Europe of the relations between the Balkan states and Turkey. In addition Russia would require the cession of Bessarabia, for which Roumania would receive compensation in the Dobrudja; and Russia should also receive Batum. These might be seen as the minimum practical war aims of Russia at the commencement of hostilities.[13] Shuvalov communicated these terms to Derby on June 8. When these were reported to the Cabinet, a lengthy debate ensued. The lack of any assurance that the Russians would not, in the course of military operations, occupy

Russian aristocratic women help prepare medical supplies for the front. (Budev)

Constantinople or the Straits, caused concern. Although Derby thought them reasonable and the best that Turkey could hope for, Disraeli was not so happy, and nor was the Queen, who wrote to the Foreign Secretary to call on him to be firm and energetic. When asked, Layard replied that the Porte would in any case refuse to consider such terms.[14]

Meanwhile, as soon as it was clear that war was inevitable, Disraeli had been pondering British options. He was keen on a plan whereby British troops should be sent to occupy Gallipoli as a means of securing the Dardanelles. He talked to the two most prominent of his Cabinet colleagues who might, from very different points of view, be expected to dissent, as he reported to the Queen on April 17:

> This morning, a torturing hour with Ld. Derby, who was for doing nothing, and this afternoon, with Lord Salisbury, who evidently is thinking more of raising the Cross on the cupola of St Sophia, than the power of England.[15]

The Cabinet, when they discussed it, were reluctant to accept the plan, although a report from the Secretary of State for War, Gathorne Hardy, that the Russians intended to occupy the Dardanelles before advancing on Constantinople, shocked them into agreeing that something must be done, even if that was for the moment unresolved.

The British Cabinet continued to meet frequently; on May 1, its fifth meeting in eleven days, it agreed on the text of the formal reply to Gorchakov's Circular Note, rejecting the arguments put forward for the Russian decision to go to war. In particular, the reply complained that by its action the Russian government had departed from the position it had correctly adopted in 1871 'that no power can liberate itself from the engagements of a treaty' without the consent of the other parties, in relation to the Treaty of Paris.

Stocking public buildings at Nish with biscuits. (*The Graphic*)

Britain would, however, remain neutral. However, having failed to get the Cabinet to approve his Gallipoli scheme, Disraeli insisted that the British position be made clear to Russia. On May 6 Lord Derby's Note set out the conditions upon which that neutrality would be maintained. There were a number of key British interests which Her Majesty's Government would be determined to defend, and he wished to make clear what these were. First was the necessity of keeping open the Suez Canal; any attempt to blockade or otherwise interfere with it would be regarded as a menace to India. Next, Britain could not 'witness with indifference the fate of Constantinople or the passing into other hands than those of its present possessors, of a capital holding so peculiar and commanding a position.' Third, there might be other interests, such as those on the Persian Gulf, which Britain might have a duty to protect.[16]

As the war went on, the diplomats of the Great Powers continued ceaselessly to negotiate possible ways in which the conflict might be ended. Thus far, the chief ministers had not achieved a great deal; Andrassy had been defensive, and had fallen back on seeking territorial compensation; Disraeli had been inconsistent, beset by cabinet dissensions; only Bismarck had a clear grasp of the situation. He saw no German interest in the future of the Ottoman Empire, save only to avoid a European war in which his nation might become involved.[17]

7

The Russian Army

The disastrous outcome of the Crimean War left the Russian army in a parlous state. It had begun that war with a reputation (based in part on its size) that, as events soon showed, was undeserved. It was, of course, an enormous army; it had emerged with credit from the Napoleonic Wars and had been ultimately successful in the Russo-Turkish

War of 1828-1829. But its very size, its clumsiness and inflexibility, and the social structure which it reflected, had brought it to a humiliating failure.

Even before the Crimean War it was apparent to some observers, although not to the high command and certainly not to Nicholas I, that reforms were necessary. One General Staff officer, A I Astafeev, argued that the army should look to the principles of Suvorov rather than those of Napoleon; while F I Goremykin, a military writer at the Nicholas Military Academy, complained of the pedantry that affected the whole army: 'It is time to leave behind the oppressing and strange forms in which military learning is sometimes wrapped.'[1]

An even clearer voice was that of Dmitri Alexeievich Miliutin, who unlike most theoreticians was to be able in due course to put his ideas into practice. He was born in 1816 into an impoverished noble family. His mother, however, was a sister of the influential Count Paul Kiselev who was able to be of assistance both directly and indirectly to his nephew's early career.[2] After obtaining a commission in the Life Guards, Miliutin graduated in 1837 from the Nicholas Military Academy with a silver medal, and was appointed to the Guards General Staff. After two terms of service in the Caucasus, in the first of which in 1839 he was severely wounded, he joined the faculty of the Nicholas Military Academy as a lieutenant colonel in 1845. For the next decade he led the life of an academic as Professor of Military Geography, studying in detail a wide range of military issues. At the request of Prince Chernyshev, the War Minister, he completed a history of the Russian army in Suvorov's campaigns against France in 1799. By the outbreak of the Crimean War Miliutin had risen to the rank of major general. During the war he was employed as an adviser to the War Minister, Prince Dolgorukov, and served on a number of key committees. He was now close to the centre of military power in Russia, a position in which his writings, calling energetically for military reform, began to be increasingly noticed.

Alexander II was far more ready than his predecessor to accept the need for military reform. However, his appointment in 1856 of the conservative General Sukhozanet to succeed Dolgorukov as War Minister did not at first signal a recognition of the need for change, and later that year Miliutin accepted a posting as Chief of Staff to Prince Bariatinsky, the Commander in Chief in the Caucasus. During this assignment he enjoyed an excellent relationship with his chief. It was not until the summer of 1860 that he returned to St Petersburg, after the Russian forces in the Caucasus had in 1859 defeated and captured the famous rebel Shamil. As Chief of Staff Miliutin had been

General Dmitri Alexeievich Miliutin. (Ollier)

largely responsible for the innovative reforms in the military administration in the Caucasus and earned much of the credit for their success.[4] He had been called back to take up an appointment as deputy to Sukhozanet, a decision made by Alexander on the recommendation of Bariatinsky. In November 1861 Sukhozanet was given the post of Viceroy of Poland, and Miliutin was appointed as War Minister in his place.

With his hands at last on the levers of power, Miliutin wasted no time in putting before the Tsar a comprehensive reform programme. His objective was to devise a way in which the colossal army budget might be reduced while at the same time giving Russia an army worthy of her. This meant adopting the kind of system in place elsewhere in Europe, which enabled a rapid expansion of the army in time of war. Drawing attention to the extent which other Great Powers could do this, he wrote:

> Under present conditions of the European powers' situation, when each of them has a significant standing army and the assured means of expanding its military forces in case of war, the relative political significance of Russia can be supported in no other way than by corresponding armed forces with the same foundation for proper expansion in wartime.[5]

The emancipation of the serfs made a policy of national conscription a target at which to aim, although political resistance and the scale of the changes necessary delayed its introduction until January 1874. In the meantime in 1862 Miliutin set about the reorganisation of the Field Army, basing it at first on four military districts; six more were added in 1864 and four more in the following year. He also embarked on a reorganisation of the War Ministry, slashing its total workforce by 1,000. By 1869 it was

General Nepokoitschitsky, Chief of Staff of the Russian Army in Europe. (*Russes et Turcs*)

divided into five principal departments, the Imperial Headquarters, Military Council, High Military Court, War Ministry Chancellery and Main Staff. Supporting these were the specialist administrations, inspectorates and main committees.[6]

Miliutin's reforms encountered opposition, not least from his former chief, Prince Bariatinsky, who favoured an organisation on the Prussian model. The outstanding success of the Prussian army in 1866, to be followed again in 1870-1871, made this an attractive option. But in spite of the very considerable weight of Bariatinsky's influence, the Tsar backed his War Minister. This left the emerging Main Staff, headed by the chief of the General Staff, as having very wide administrative powers; it has been suggested that these were in fact too wide to allow proper attention to complex information-gathering and planning processes.[7]

The administrative improvements had greatly enhanced Russia's ability to mobilise. By 1863, the entire army could be put on a full wartime footing within ten weeks; by 1867 the mobilisation period had come down to twenty-five days in the Kiev Military District although still one hundred and eleven days in the Caucasus. Five years later the corresponding periods were nine days and thirty-nine days. Unfortunately it was evident that the mobilisation periods for potential enemies such as Germany and Austria-Hungary were still much less.

Quite apart from the process of mobilisation, the Russian army's need of men had always been enormous. The existence of a standing army of over 800,000 throughout the period that followed the ending of the Napoleonic Wars had put a colossal burden on the national exchequer, and it was this problem that Miliutin was resolved to address. However, even the maintenance of such a large standing army did not provide sufficient

Russian infantry in camp. (Budev)

forces for the many conflicts with which the army was involved, since the country's foreign policy always required that a large part of the available force remained in position along the Western frontiers. This policy had ensured that in most of its campaigns the Russian army fought with inadequate numbers for the tasks which confronted it. The most startling illustration of this had been during the Crimean War, during which it has been estimated that, inclusive of irregulars and militia, the Russian army reached a size of over two and a half million men. The total of the allied forces actually engaged with them in the Balkans, the Crimea and the Caucasus was not a great deal more than 300,000.[8] Another instance of this had been seen in 1828, when the Russians crossed the Pruth with 100,000 men, an entirely inadequate number for the campaign that was to follow.

Miliutin's reforms had by 1872 produced a cadre and reserve system that would provide, on full mobilisation, a total of 1,358,000 men, a figure well short of what he believed was needed. In the autumn of 1870, therefore, he began a campaign for the introduction of universal conscription; two commissions were set up to investigate the issue, and these reported by mid 1872. Miliutin now pressed the Tsar to initiate a comprehensive review of exactly what was required, and in February 1873 a month long special conference was secretly convened to study the matter.

Grand Duke Nicholas of Russia, commander of the Army of the South. (Hozier)

Grand Duke Michael of Russia. (Ollier)

As it turned out, the conference very nearly did for Miliutin's reforms. It brought together a number of key ministers and others intimately concerned with the issues of Russia's military future, and among them were a number of serious critics of Miliutin's programme. These included, of course, Bariatinsky, but also the Tsarevich, the Grand Dukes Michael and Nicholas, and Count Paul Shuvalov, the head of Imperial Security. As soon as the conference began to look at army organisation, Miliutin found himself assailed by a number of his critics. A sub-committee appointed by Alexander to look at ways of cutting costs was, to Miliutin's fury, to be chaired by Bariatinsky. However, the sub-committee's report was delayed, and the Tsar supported his War Minister and his call for conscription, and in due course the decree introducing it came into effect on January 1 1874.[9]

All men were required to give military service of six years in the active army and nine in the reserve. Exemptions relieved some 48 per cent from peacetime service and 24 per cent in wartime; the annual intake now gave Russia an adequate standing army and wartime reserve. The Active Army was organised into field troops and local troops, the latter consisting of garrison troops in European Russia, regular troops in Asia and stationary troops, gendarmes and other local units. The Reserve would, upon mobilization, provide the troops necessary to bring the Active Army to its war establishment, together with an ersatz reserve to make good wartime losses and, separately, reserve regiments available wherever required. The field troops were organised into 48 Infantry Divisions, of which three were Guard Divisions, four Grenadier Divisions and the rest Line Divisions. There were 8 Rifle Brigades, 48 Field Artillery Brigades, 19 Cavalry Divisions, 35 Horse

Artillery Batteries and 19 Engineer Battalions, together with supporting units. Divisions were organised into army corps, of two or three divisions, with corresponding field artillery, a cavalry division and two horse artillery batteries.[10] Apart from headquarters and support services, the establishment of an army corps of two divisions would be 20,160 infantry, 2,048 cavalry, 96 field guns and 12 horse artillery guns.

In addition to the regular and reserve troops described above there was also a militia, called the *opolchenie*, which comprised men with exemption from conscription and those under the age of forty who had completed their service terms. The *opolchenie* could only be called upon by a special Imperial decree.

The organisation of artillery and cavalry units was overhauled. Reserve artillery formations were created, capable of expansion on mobilisation, which could produce 144 reserve artillery batteries, of which two-thirds were available to support reserve divisions and the remaining third to provide replacements. Although the introduction of rifled guns had been completed, the four and nine pounder guns were already obsolescent, and the training of the artillery was seriously deficient, as was the understanding of senior commanders as to their proper employment. The cavalry, organised into two Guard divisions, two Cossack divisions, one Caucasian division and fourteen regular cavalry divisions, had been somewhat expanded in the light of the experience of other European armies in the wars fought since the Crimean War. This expansion had especially affected the Cossack units, which were integrated into the regular army and mobilisation structure.

In planning for a Russian army that was so much larger, Miliutin was taking account of the ever-present fear that war with a European adversary would at once stimulate a further uprising in Poland. This meant that a large garrison must be maintained there

A Russian column on the march. (*Illustrated London News*)

at all times. Similarly there were pressing requirements that the army must fulfil in other borderlands of the Russian Empire, each of which further reduced the number of troops available for other theatres, such as the Caucasus region and in Central Asia.[11] The complete change in the balance of power in Europe following the Franco-Prussian War of 1870-1871 obliged Russian strategists to review the nation's capability to deal, for instance, with the possibility of a war against an Austro-Prussian alliance, which would particularly threaten Poland, where the slower Russian mobilisation would enable the enemy to overrun large areas of the country. The conference of February-March 1873 paid particular attention to this.

Although by 1877 Miliutin's reforms had not yet produced a peacetime army or an army on mobilisation of the size that he judged would be required in the event of war with Germany and Austria-Hungary, it was nonetheless a huge improvement on the situation following the Crimean War. In 1874 the active army stood at a total of 754,265; on January 1 1878 the total strength available had grown to just over one and a half million.[12]

The War Ministry also embarked on the reequipping of the army, a task rendered urgently necessary by the evident requirement for breechloading rifles. Various efforts were made to find a system suitable for converting muzzle-loaders to breechloaders, and in 1869 the Krenk conversion was adopted, when 800,000 of these weapons were purchased. However, an alternative had also been identified in the rifle manufactured in the United States by Hiram Berdan, which was considerably more robust than the Krenk. By the spring of 1877 the Guard Grenadiers and nine Line divisions had been equipped with the Berdan, as had the Rifle brigades; the remaining Line divisions had the Krenk. The Berdan was sighted to 1,500 yards, while the Krenk was limited to 600 yards.

The Russian army had not, however, properly grasped the lessons that were to be learned from the effect of breechloaders in the Wars of German Unification, and there was still a strong disposition to regard the bayonet as the crucial weapon for the infantry:

> They were trained to advance to the attack in column of companies, and to move to the assault while still at a distance from the position to be captured. The bayonet assault was looked upon as the one decisive feature in an infantry attack; no attempt was made to obtain superiority of fire over the enemy. In short the possibilities of the breechloading rifle were not understood. There was no provision for a mobile battalion ammunition reserve which could follow the infantry in the attack.[13]

In addition, unlike their Turkish adversaries, the Russian infantry were inadequately provided with entrenching equipment.

The Imperial family provided the commanders in chief for each of the European and Caucasus theatres. In all, twelve members of the family came to the war, occupying positions at all levels down to the rank of captain. The Tsar's brother, the Grand Duke Nicholas, was assigned to command the army assembling to invade the Principalities. Born in 1831, he was from the outset destined for a military career, and became commander of the Imperial Guard in 1864. A notorious womaniser, he was of limited intelligence. Francis Greene thought him a man of 'remarkably frank and genial nature,' and considered that if he had not been a grand duke 'would probably have made a dashing

Russian Cossack officers, summer 1877. (Rogers)

leader of a cavalry division.' If his military talents alone would not have made him a commander in chief, Greene thought it doubtful if any general could have been selected who would have been more acceptable to the army.[14] As it was much of the responsibility for directing his army would fall upon his Chief of Staff, General Nepokoitschitsky. The latter appears to have had a high reputation in Russia, where he was known as 'our Moltke,' since he had made a careful study of Moltke's methods. He was interviewed at the start of the campaign by a correspondent of the *Daily News*, who provided this description for his readers:

> The General is a short, square-set, but active-looking man, hale and hearty, in spite of his seventy years; he looks as fit to make a campaign as if he were twenty years younger … General Nepokoitschitsky's hair, whiskers and moustache are snow-white, but there is a flush of hale colour on his cheek; his eye is not dim, neither is his natural force abated.[15]

The *Daily News* correspondent, noting the Chief of Staff's placidity of temperament, was struck by the fact that his personality was complemented by the excitable Assistant Chief of Staff, General Levitsky. Francis Greene, on the other hand, had a particularly low opinion of the Chief of Staff and his Assistant Chief, regarding them as 'men of very mediocre abilities,' commenting:

Lieutenant-General Baron Krüdener,
commander of the Russian IX
Corps. (*Russes et Turcs*)

Lieutenant-General Zotov, commander of
the Russian IV Corps. (*Russes et Turcs*)

The first was never more than a chief clerk, and the second was reduced to being one after having committed two or three crass blunders early in the campaign. Yet these two men, whose incompetency nobody disputed, were, for reasons never fully understood, retained in their places to the end of the campaign.[16]

In the first instance the Army of the South, commanded by Grand Duke Nicholas, comprised four army corps, the VIII (Lieutenant-General Radetzky), IX (Lieutenant-General Baron Krüdener) XI (Lieutenant-General Prince Shakofskoi and XII (Lieutenant-General Vannovsky). There were in addition two rifle brigades (Major-Generals Dobrovolski and Zviazinsky) and a Cossack division commanded by Lieutenant-General Skobelev I, father of the rather more famous Major-General Michael Skobelev II. Two other corps, the VII and X Corps, were also mobilised and deployed for the protection of the coast, based on Odessa and Nicolaiev respectively. These six corps represented the first wave of the Russian mobilisation, and had been mobilised as long ago as October 17 1876. It was soon evident that the four corps initially constituting the Army of the South would be insufficient; three more corps were added on May 6 1877 – XIV Corps (Lieutenant-General Zimmerman), IV Corps (Lieutenant-General Zotov), and XIII Corps (Lieutenant-General Prince Korsakov).

Michael Skobelev was already the most famous soldier in the Russian army. His exploits had provided journalists with an immense amount of material, and the war correspondents who accompanied Russian headquarters naturally fastened on him as a source of copy. On May 20, Januarius MacGahan encountered him as a familiar figure:

Lieutenant-General Radetzky, commander
of the Russian VIII Corps. (Rogers)

Lieutenant-General Shakofskoi, commander
of the Russian XI Corps. (*Illustrirte Geschichte
des Orientalischen Krieges von 1876-1878*)

Among the many officers on the Grand Duke's staff, there is one who would attract
attention anywhere, and whose career has been curious and brilliant. He is a tall
handsome man, with a lithe, slender, active figure, a clear blue eye, and a large,
prominent, but straight, well-shaped nose, the kind of nose it is said Napoleon
used to look for among his officers when he wished to find a general, and a face
young enough for a second lieutenant although he is a general – the youngest in
the Russian army. It is the famous General Skobelev, the conqueror of Ferghana, or
Khokand. The last time I saw him we were both standing on the banks of the Oxus,
in the Khanate of Khiva.[17]

Another correspondent met Skobelev a few days later, and was also struck by his
apparent youth, finding him a 'tall, stalwart, fresh-coloured young man, looking so like
an English squire.' His unprecedently swift promotion was, he noted, nothing to do with
his having an influential mentor:

He owes, indeed, something to luck – that good fortune which has placed him so
often where opportunity offered to distinguish himself; nor has he omitted to make
the most of every opportunity. It is something for a man while yet in his young
prime to have added to his country a territory larger than the whole of Great Britain
– the Khanate of Khokand.[18]

In one respect, however, Skobelev had not been lucky. His successes in the East,
and his rapid promotion, had earned him the jealousy of rivals and the hatred of the

Major-General Michael Skobelev, legendary commander. Due to the presence
of his father in the army, Lieutenant-General Skobelev, commander of a
Cossack division, he was sometimes referred to as Skobelev II. (Ollier)

Russian infantry on campaign in Bulgaria, summer 1877. An
excellent on-the-spot sketch by José Luis Pellicer. (Budev)

Lieutenant-General Loris-Melikov was an Armenian by birth, and
played an important part in the Caucasian campaign. (Hozier)

contractors whose fraudulent practices he had exposed. The latter promoted stories of
atrocities perpetrated by the troops under Skobelev's command and of his embezzlement
of millions of roubles. He returned from Khokand to clear his name, and was obliged to
remain in St Petersburg until the Government's auditors had assured themselves of his
honesty. Only then could he seek to repair his reputation in the eyes of the Tsar, who had
however already left for the front. When Skobelev arrived there, he found that the Tsar's
mind had been effectively poisoned against him, and he was denied a command, being
assigned instead to act as his father's chief of staff. It was to be some time before the Tsar
remedied this gross injustice.[19]

In the Caucasus, the nominal Commander in Chief was the amiable Grand Duke
Michael, the eldest brother of the Tsar, who held the office of Viceroy. His deputy
was Prince Dmitri Sviatopolk-Mirsky, described variously as lacking both energy and
military talent, and as irresponsible.[20] He had under his command, organised in four
detachments based respectively on Rion, Akhaltsik, Alexandropol and Erivan, a total
of five infantry divisions, a Cossack rifle brigade, two Cossack cavalry divisions and ten
Cossack regiments. The most senior of the subordinate commanders was the Armenian
Lieutenant-General Loris-Melikov, who had served in the Caucasus for very many years;
a competent if cautious leader, he lacked any clear strategic vision.

8

The Ottoman Army

The need for extensive reform of the Turkish army and its institutions had by the early 19th century been obvious for a considerable time. The process of reform began under Sultan Mahmud II. This only became possible after the bloody suppression of the Janissaries in June 1826. The process was far from complete by the outbreak of the Russo-Turkish War of 1828-1829, but a new system of organisation, based upon that of France, had been introduced, together with a westernised form of dress. Helmuth von Moltke, in his history of that war, noted the essential change that had been brought about:

> The splendid appearance, the beautiful arms, the reckless bravery of the former Muslim horde, had disappeared; but yet this new army had one quality which placed it above the numerous host which in former times the Porte could summon to the field – it obeyed.[1]

During this war the Ottoman army performed somewhat better than expected, and at times put up a strong resistance against the invading Russian army; the campaign proved to be far from the cakewalk to which the Russians had looked forward. Ultimately, however, the outbreak of war seriously set back the military reforms, as Moltke observed:

> If Turkey had enjoyed ten years of peace after the destruction of the Janissaries, Sultan Mahmud's military creation might in that time have gained some strength; and, supported by an army on which he could depend, the Sultan might … have made himself formidable to his neighbours. All this was prevented by Russia, which nipped the Sultan's military reforms in the bud.[2]

The army's weakness was dramatically demonstrated in the campaigns it fought against the forces of Muhammed Ali, the rebellious Viceroy of Egypt. In December 1832 the Egyptian forces under Muhammed's son Ibrahim routed a Turkish army at Konya, and threatened to strike deep into Anatolia. Further humiliation was averted when a peace deal was patched up with French mediation; but the Sultan accepted the arrangement with reluctance, and for the rest of the decade hankered after a renewal of the war. He finally resumed hostilities in 1839, when Moltke had a first hand opportunity of seeing for himself the quality of the Turkish army, when serving on the staff of Hafiz Pasha, the commander of an army with the task of advancing south on Aleppo. Moltke's sound advice was rejected by his commander, who preferred the opinion of the mullahs who accompanied the army. When confronting Ibrahim's forces near Nisib on June 24 1839 Hafiz was comprehensively defeated, as Moltke had predicted. Moltke himself was lucky in the resultant chaos to escape with his life. He described the disaster in a letter written a fortnight later:

The army of Hafiz Pasha has ceased to exist. The Turks threw down their arms and abandoned their artillery, flying in every direction.[3]

Mahmud II died before the full reports of Nisib were received, and was succeeded by his son, the sixteen year old Abdul Mecid. The intervention of the Great Powers resulted in the curtailment of Muhammed's ambitions; and the removal of this military threat ushered in the 'Tanzimat' era of reform. The political and social changes that were contemplated by the Imperial Rescript of the Rose Chamber, announced in November 1839, involved an extensive programme of westernisation. In the year that followed the reform programme extended to the armed forces of the Ottoman Empire, and the benefit of this was seen in the performance of the Turkish forces in the Crimean War. Under Omar Pasha they gave at least as good as they got in the fighting along the Danube in 1853-1854, until, under Austrian pressure, the Russians evacuated the Principalities in July 1854. When it was decided to make Sebastopol the war's principal objective, 6,000 Turkish troops formed part of the Allied invasion force that landed at Eupatoria in the Crimea.

During the ensuing campaign the French and British had mixed views of the Turkish infantry. 13,000 Turkish troops fought well in defending Eupatoria against an energetic assault by 20,000 Russian troops in February 1855, throwing back the attackers with heavy loss. They were also effective in the part they played during the Battle of the

Recruits from Salonika arriving in Constantinople to be clothed and armed. (*Illustrated London News*)

Turkish infantry on the march. (*Russes et Turcs*)

Tchernaya in repulsing a Russian sortie in August of that year, as they had been in the Franco-Turkish expedition to seize the town of Kerch on the eastern coast of the Crimea.

In the Caucasus, the Turkish forces did not do so well at first, and were defeated a number of times in the winter of 1854 and again during the following year. In the siege of Kars, however, under a British commander in General Fenwick Williams, they fought bravely against heavy odds, and although the fortress ultimately fell on November 25, its Turkish defenders could feel pride in their lengthy defence of the place.

All in all, therefore, the Turkish army had come out well from the Crimean War, with its reputation to some extent enhanced.

In 1877 the Turkish army was still recruited only from the Muslim population, Christians not being allowed to bear arms but instead obliged to pay a poll tax in lieu of military service. The army was divided into four categories. The standing army, or *Nizam*, consisted of infantry who served for four years and cavalry and artillery who served for five. After completing their terms of service all soldiers passed into the *Ithiat*, or first reserve, where they served a further term to make up a total of six years. Next came the *Redif*, or second reserve. This consisted of men who had served in the *Nizam* and the *Ithiat*, together with those who had avoided conscription. Service in the *Redif* was divided into four classes. The first class consisted of soldiers that had served in the *Nizam*; after four years in this class they passed into the second class. Men who had escaped conscription received a certain amount of military training during a term of four years in the third class, at the end of which they passed into the fourth class. The whole of the *Redif* was organised in battalions by classes, and these battalions were formed and called out for service as complete units. Finally there was the *Mustafiz*, which consisted of all men who had completed their time in the *Redif*, in which they served for a further term of six years.[4]

During the reign of Abdul Aziz, progress was made in improving the standard of military education, with the opening of new military high schools to support the Military Academy and the Military Engineering School. By 1877, however, the process had produced for too few academy trained officers, or *Mekteblis*; out of a total of 20,000 regular officers, only 1,600 were from the academy. Even more seriously, there were only 132 academy trained general staff officers for all the armies which the Ottoman Empire put into the field, with potentially disastrous consequences for their manoeuvrability. On the other hand, the artillery was more fortunate, some 20% of its officers being *Mekteblis*.[5]

The basic unit of the Turkish army was the battalion, which notionally consisted of 800 men, divided into eight companies. All larger units were assembled on an *ad hoc* basis, although for administrative purposes in peacetime the standing army was organized in seven army corps, two of which were based in European Turkey and the remainder in Asia Minor.

Considerable confusion resulted from the way in which the army was organised, as was noted by one British observer serving with the Turks:

The administrative and tactical unit was the battalion, not the regiment. For administrative purposes three battalions are formed into a regiment; but the tactical formation of a regiment was arbitrary, differed nearly always from the administrative one, and was often changed from one *ordre de bataille* to another.

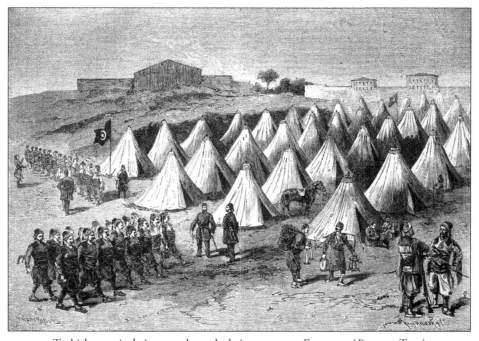

Turkish recruits being put through their paces near Erzerum. (*Russes et Turcs*)

Turkish troops transported by railway. (*Russes et Turcs*)

Thus the colonelcy had no real tactical value. The major was the fountain-head, the source, the authority.[6]

One consequence of this is that historians have found it to be extremely difficult to calculate accurately the distribution of the Turkish units during the war and the numbers of troops engaged.

Although the nominal strength of a battalion was 800 men, practically all Turkish units were well below their establishment, due to the losses sustained in the recent campaigns against insurgents, which had not been made good from the *Ithiat*. However, the army was better prepared for war in 1877 than had been the case for many years. The *Ithiat* and the first class of the *Redif* had been called up to reinforce the *Nizam* on the outbreak of fighting in Herzegovina in 1875. Early in 1876 a large part of the second class of the *Redif* was called up when war broke out with Serbia and Montenegro. Finally, the third class of the *Redif* had been called up in November 1876 when the Russian army began to concentrate in Bessarabia.

The Turkish army was also very much better equipped than ever before, a large part of the national budget, as well as the proceeds of international loans raised in Europe, having been lavished upon it. Three-quarters of the infantry were now armed with the Peabody-Martini rifle, sighted to 1,800 yards, which has been described as being as good a weapon of its kind as any in the world. The rest of the Turkish infantry were equipped with Snider rifles, with a shorter range; and the contingent of twelve battalions that arrived from Egypt had Remingtons. Major Maurice, in his history of the war, described the qualities of the Turkish infantry:

Types seen accompanying a Turkish baggage train. (*Histoire de la Guerre d'Orient 1877-1878*)

The Turkish foot soldier only requires leading and training to make him one of the finest fighting men in the world; he is sober, capable of enduring great privation, and a good marcher; a fatalist by religion, he is without fear of death. While insufficiently trained to be able to manoeuvre under fire and to attack, the Turkish infantry were by their natural qualities admirably suited for defensive tactics.[7]

The supporting services of the Turkish army were decidedly mixed. There was a plentiful supply of ammunition, although the Turkish infantry were generally extremely wasteful in its use. They were also very well equipped with entrenching tools, and were trained to dig in at once on occupying a position. On the other hand, the commissariat was dreadful; a regular supply of adequate rations could never be depended on, and Turkish troops were obliged to forage for themselves, which led to much straggling on the march. Transport, too, was unreliable and often non-existent.

The cavalry units were poorly trained and badly mounted. A cavalry regiment consisted of six squadrons, each nominally of 150 men. Dragoons were armed with Winchester repeating rifles, as were the two flank squadrons of a Lancer regiment, the remaining four squadrons being equipped with lances instead of rifles. The artillery was well equipped with modern four and six pounder breechloaders from Krupp. Like the cavalry, they were badly horsed, and were insufficiently trained. Finally, there were the Bashi-Bazouks, the irregular cavalry, which were untrained and almost completely lacking in discipline. Frederick William von Herbert succinctly described his own experience of Turkish troops in the field:

A Turkish battery near Rustchuk. (Strantz)

Abdul Kerim Pasha. (Hozier)

The artillery was splendid (despite the bad supply of horses), the infantry very good, the regular cavalry mediocre (apart from the fact that it was insufficient in numbers), the irregular, on the whole, useless. Train, commissariat, sanitary service, engineers etc were either absent altogether or bad.[8]

The higher leading of the Ottoman army left in general a lot to be desired. The first commander appointed to lead the Turkish army to face the Russians was Abdul Kerim Pasha. Aged seventy-one in 1877, he had studied for five years in Vienna, which gave him the reputation of being something of a military intellectual. During the Crimean War he served on the Caucasus front, where forces under his command won the Battle of Bayandir. He acted as commandant for some time of the fortress of Kars, a position from which he was removed after a defeat in January 1854. He commanded the army in the war against Serbia, but his success in that campaign was due more to the efforts of his subordinates and the troops under their command than to his own leadership; he is said to have conducted most of the campaign at a distance, remaining in Sofia. He was vividly described by a correspondent of the *Daily News*:

The Commander in Chief is a Turk of the good old time, about sixty-seven years old, with white hair and beard, lively round brown eyes, and dark complexion. His jovial face and corpulent body do not at all indicate a soldier of nervous disposition, consumed by arduous activity and ambition, but one of passive energy, capable of stubborn resistance.[9]

Osman Pasha, defender of Plevna. (Hozier)

Ahmed Eyoub Pasha. (*Russes et Turcs*)

Mehemet Ali Pasha. (Hozier)

Mukhtar Pasha. (Hozier)

Faizi Pasha, the Chief of Staff of the Turkish forces in the
Caucasus. (*Album della Guerra Russo-Turca del 1877-78*)

The most influential of Abdul Kerim's immediate subordinates was Ahmed Eyoub
Pasha, commander of the corps based at Shumla, the largest individual concentration of
Turkish forces. To the west, however, on the extreme left of the Turkish line along the
Danube, was the force commanded by Osman Nuri Pasha, based at Widdin. Osman
was to prove the outstanding military hero on the Turkish side. He was born in 1837. He
served under Omar Pasha in the Principalities in 1853-1855, and fought at Eupatoria in
the Turkish victory there. He distinguished himself in a number of minor campaigns in
the Lebanon, Crete and the Yemen before in 1876 he was appointed to the command of
an army corps in the war against Serbia. He defeated Cherniaev, the Russian commander
of the Serbian forces, at the battles of Saitschev and Yavor, and advanced to the invasion
of Serbia, where he captured Alexinatz and Deligrad. His Chief of Staff was the able
Tahir Pasha.

Herbert, who admired him greatly, described Osman thus:

> Osman, though not tall, was of dignified presence. He was taciturn and grave,
> abrupt of speech and manner, rather disdainful in looks and words, and had naught
> about him of the petty forms of politeness. A peculiarity of his was a violent dislike
> of foreigners – English, French, Germans, Russians, all alike.[10]

The Turkish commander in the Caucasus was Ahmed Mukhtar Pasha. Born in
1832, he served as an adjutant during the Crimean War, and later took part in the
Montenegrin campaign of 1862 and the Yemen campaign of 1870-1871. In 1873, he
was given command of an army corps, and in 1875 led the Turkish forces in Bosnia and
Herzegovina. He knew the Asian theatre well, having been Governor of Erzerum for

a number of years before the war. He had the benefit of a particularly reliable Chief of Staff in Faizi Pasha. Born in Hungary, the latter had served as Chief of Staff to General Williams during the siege of Kars in the Crimean War.

At the start of the war the Ottoman Empire had some 378,000 men under arms. Of these, 168,000 were under the command of Abdul Kerim. Elsewhere in Europe another 140,000 men were deployed to deal with a large number of threats to Ottoman security. The single largest force, under Suleiman Pasha, was in Montenegro and Herzegovina, with 15,000 more under Veli Pasha in Bosnia. 20,000 men were concentrated in Albania under Ali Saib Pasha, with 10,000 more at Novi-Bazar under Mehemet Ali Pasha. In addition to these there were some 45,000 men scattered in small garrisons throughout European Turkey and Crete. On the Caucasus front there were a total of 70,000 men, of which Ahmed Mukhtar directly commanded 50,000, with another 20,000 at Batum.[11]

9

Command of the Sea

One potential advantage possessed by the Ottoman Empire was the command of the Black Sea, and the not inconsiderable fleet that was available to exercise it. The Turks had acquired a number of vessels that would have been the envy of any navy. The most powerful of the ironclads was the *Messudieh*, built by Thames Iron Works and commissioned in December 1875. Of just under 9,000 tons, she was armed with twelve ten-inch muzzle-loading rifled guns and three seven-inch muzzle-loaders. On her trials she achieved a speed of just under 14 knots. She was originally to have been joined by a sister ship, launched as the *Mahmoudieh* but subsequently renamed *Hamidieh*; this vessel was, however, compulsorily purchased by the British government and entered the Royal Navy as HMS *Superb*. Described as 'one of the most formidable vessels of her class afloat,' the *Messudieh* had a belt of 14 inch armour plate.[1]

In addition there were the four ironclads of the *Osmanieh* class, three of which were built by R Napier and Son and one by Thames Iron Works. These were of 6,400 tons, and were armed with one nine-inch muzzle-loader and 14 eight inch muzzle-loaders. Named *Osmanieh*, *Azizieh*, *Orkhanie* and *Mahmoudieh*, they were protected by a belt of 4.5 inch armour, and had a speed of 13.5 knots.[2] There were also ten other ironclads, five wooden steam frigates, eleven wooden corvettes, two wooden gun vessels and eleven gunboats. Seven of the gunboats were armoured, and these constituted the flotilla based on the Danube.

In terms of numbers, a *Daily News* correspondent reckoned that Turkey had 'one of the finest fleets in the world,' sufficient for a comprehensive blockade of the Russian coast:

> Properly watched, not a vessel ought to be allowed to escape out of a Russian port; and although there is a fine fleet of merchant steamers at its disposal, the Turks ought to be able to prevent the Russian Government from sending any supplies to its various corps d'armée except overland.[3]

The commander of the Turkish navy was a flamboyant Englishman. Hobart Pasha, as he was known, was the son of the Earl of Buckingham. He was born in 1822, and served in the Royal Navy for over thirty years. He saw service against Russia in the Baltic during the Crimean War but later, having reached the rank of post captain, he was according to the procedure at that time obliged to remain on shore for four years to await assignment to an appropriate command. Bored with this, during the American Civil War he became an extremely successful blockade-runner, operating under the pseudonym of 'Captain Roberts.' After the war ended, he went on a tour of Europe, and found himself in Constantinople, where he greatly impressed the Grand Vizier, Fuad Pasha, and was as a result offered the post of Naval Adviser to the Turkish government, a post that had just become vacant on the retirement of Admiral Sir Adolphus Slade. Hobart's acceptance of

Hobart Pasha.

The Turkish fleet at Buyukdere. (Ollier)

the post seriously annoyed the Admiralty, where the assignment of an officer to the post was regarded as being in the gift of the British government.[4]

Hobart was a man of enquiring mind, and was particularly struck by the potential of the torpedo as a naval weapon. Not long before the outbreak of the Russo-Turkish War, while on a visit to his home in England he had conducted experiments with torpedoes on the village pond. Hobart was a man of strong opinions, which he usually expressed with more force than tact. In command of the Turkish fleet he achieved some success off Crete during the insurgency there; but he has been described as 'a reluctant and intolerant administrator.'[5]

The fact that the Turkish fleet possessed so many large units owed a good deal to the personality of Sultan Abdul Aziz. Always a man of extravagant tastes, he had been hugely impressed by the British fleet which he saw in the course of a visit to England in 1867. After receiving him at Windsor, Queen Victoria took him on a fast train to Portsmouth, where she appointed him a Knight of the Garter, and where he watched the ships of her fleet pass before him. The Queen was greatly impressed by the Sultan, and wrote to her daughter, the Crown Princess of Prussia, to describe the Portsmouth visit:

Our Naval Review was a very fine sight in spite of the most awful weather – and really it was an act of great *dévouement* to my Oriental Brother to go out in it and to have to go in and out in of boats in a horrid swell which always frightens me so... The poor Sultan was not comfortable and had to lie down a good deal below.[6]

In spite of the discomfort he had endured, the Sultan returned home with the conviction that he must have a fleet to be proud of. He had always been interested in naval affairs, and was convinced of the value of a strong navy. His succession to the sultanate had given him the opportunity to indulge his interests:

On tasting power he rapidly fell into extravagant ways, including spending large sums on the armed forces. Unfortunately, although he was intrigued by new technology, he was not sufficiently educated to discriminate between a practical invention and a visionary scheme, and so was prey to every projector and salesman. This weakness extended to warship procurement, and the Sultan's whims burdened the navy with warships it did not need and could not effectively use.[7]

Nonetheless, it did mean that in 1877 the Turks had a formidable weapon in their hands which could and should have had the effect pointed out by the correspondent of the *Daily News*.

Its overall size may be judged from the fact that its Navy List for 1876 recorded it as possessing a total of 132 vessels and 18,292 officers, seamen and marines. In building up such a force, the Turkish government had called upon the services of a number of overseas officers, whose contribution was, however, not as effective as might have been hoped, as has been pointed out by the historians of the Ottoman Navy:

The Sultan was also unfortunate in his technical advisers, most of whom were recruited in Britain. With the exception of the long serving Slade, who was mainly employed on naval staff work, and Henry S Wood, who took over command of the

Turkish sailors. (*Illustrated London News*)

Russian batteries shelling a Turkish monitor. (Fauré)

The Turkish gunboat *Lufti Djelil*, sunk by the Russian
batteries near Braila. (*Illustrated London News*)

naval school at Heybeliarda, they were generally adventurers who were ill-equipped,
or ill-disposed, to deal with the obstructionism of the navy ministry.[8]

This was perhaps not a problem confined to the Turkish navy; the chaotic and corrupt
administration and low morale of its officers and men was a more general reflection of
the style and behaviour of the Turkish government.[9]

So far as major naval units were concerned, the Russian navy could not compare
with its adversary. In 1877 it possessed only seven seagoing ironclads, and six of these
were in the Baltic. One, the elderly *Petropavlovsk*, was at Spezia in southern Italy, where
she remained, taking no part in the war. In the Black Sea the Russians had not taken
advantage of the removal of the Black Sea clauses to build up their naval resources to an
effective level. There, they had the extraordinary and quite useless circular ironclads, the
Admiral Popov and *Novgorod*, which if they had served any purpose at all would have
been as floating forts. For the rest, Fred T Jane summarised the Russian situation:

In the Black Sea there was nothing; or rather, there was worse than nothing,
a number of old tubs of no fighting value whatsoever. About twenty merchant
steamers were purchased and armed, and a number of torpedo boats (launches we
should call them nowadays) were sent across country by rail from St Petersburg, but
practically at the outbreak, and in the early stages of the war, Russia was worse off
than she would have been without a fleet at all. For the consequent forced inactivity,
as in the case of the *Petropavlovsk* at Spezia, might be assumed to have a fatal effect
on the morale of the men. Inaction soon neutralises the finest fleet, and its effects
are likely enough to spread to the military in a long campaign.[10]

The Turkish Egyptian squadron leaving Alexandria for
Constantinople with Egyptian troops. (*The Graphic*)

Ironically, considering Hobart's interest in torpedoes, it was to be the Russians who
made most use of these weapons. Even before the war, their development of the torpedo
was generally regarded as noteworthy:

> In those days the torpedo was a new weapon, and though possessed by all Powers,
> was more associated with the name of Russia than any other. These torpedoes the
> Turks were supposed to be particularly afraid of, and this has been put forward as
> a reason for their extraordinary inactivity; actually, however, circumstances, lack of
> ammunition, or defects in machinery, may be considered more probable causes.[11]

The weakness of the Russian navy in the Black Sea was principally due to the
government's reluctance to spend very much on building up an ironclad fleet there. In
addition, the redevelopment of Sebastopol's shipbuilding capacity was not, by 1877, very
far advanced. The only vessels built for operation in the Black Sea after the removal of
the restraints of the Treaty of Paris in 1871 had been the absurd circular ships designed
by Admiral Popov. No attempt was in fact made to employ them in 1877 since they
were, as Fred T Jane put it, 'unique curios of naval architecture – nothing more.' He
described what happened on their trials:

> Such mobility as they had was soon heavily discounted. On a trial cruise they went
> up the Dnieper very nicely for some distance, till they turned to retire. Then the
> current caught them, and they were carried out to sea, whirled helplessly round and
> round, every soul on board hopelessly incapacitated by vertigo.[12]

It might have been expected that with such a pronounced advantage at sea, the Turks would, in the period leading up to what was seen as a virtually inevitable war, do all they could to prepare their navy for the coming struggle. Clearly the Russian strategy would be based on an invasion of Bulgaria, and the Turkish fleet would, or could, have a big part to play in resisting it. Hobart was sent to the Danube delta to advise on the situation, and when he got there was at first optimistic:

It was soon made clear to me that much could be done, in the way of defending that great estuary, had nautical experience and the splendid material of which the Turkish sailor is made of been properly utilised. But alas! I found that, contrary to the views of His Majesty the Sultan a line of action was followed showing that pigheaded obstinacy and the grossest ignorance prevailed in the councils of those who had supreme command in that great river. I found that my advice and that of competent Turkish officers, in comparatively subordinate positions like myself, was entirely ignored.[13]

10

Plans of Campaign

A number of geopolitical considerations dictated the nature of the Russian plans for war against Turkey. As in the past, there must be two separate campaigns on land, in the Balkans in order to threaten Constantinople, and in the Caucasus with Erzerum as the objective. Turkish control of the sea would be a key factor; the advancing Russian armies would be obliged to keep away from the coast. And external considerations required a quick victory; otherwise the Great Powers might be tempted to intervene.

Among the leading military planners was General Nicholas Obruchev, a protégé of Miliutin who had come under a cloud in the 1860's when becoming involved with a revolutionary organization called 'Land and Liberty', a connection which tainted his subsequent career, but which, surprisingly, did not end it completely. Instead, within a decade, Obruchev became one of Miliutin's most valued collaborators, and was at the centre of the process of recasting Russian strategy which began in 1873 with his publication of a memorandum entitled 'Considerations on the Defence of Russia.' Looking at the military threats which faced the Russian Empire in Europe, he concluded that 'the armed forces of Russia in their present condition [were] insufficient for the defence of her security.'[1] In 1876 he prepared a series of lectures outlining plans for a war against Turkey. He aimed for a swift decision by an advance over the Danube southwards to force the passes over the Balkans, and thence towards Constantinople. This avoided an advance along the coast through the Dobrudja into the Quadrilateral of powerful fortresses of Rustchuk, Shumla, Varna and Silistria.

Obruchev, who had reached such a pessimistic conclusion about war in Europe that he believed that only a long war would give Russia a chance of winning, had been obliged by the particular circumstances of a war with Turkey, and the external political factors, to go for a short blitzkrieg. He was clear about the need for this:

> We have no choice. We are not free to pose the question: is it possible or impossible to end the war in one campaign? It must be ended in one campaign, as we do not have the resources for a second, and moreover, because we would then have to fight not only Turkey but with all of those who are only waiting for our exhaustion. It is necessary quickly to put an end to the matter and suppress the Turks, while we still preserve the entire extent of our strength and have not revealed our weakness.[2]

Obruchev proposed that the force invading Bulgaria should be divided into two armies. The first of these, up to about 120,000 strong, should once over the Danube advance southwards in a lunge towards and then through the Balkans, and thence to Constantinople, a target to be reached if possible in four to five weeks. The second army, which would comprise eight infantry divisions, four cavalry divisions and ten to twelve Cossack regiments, would have the task of protecting the lines of communication and the

General Obruchev. (*Russes et Turcs*)

rear of the first army. This would mean the taking of the powerful fortress of Rustchuk at least, and perhaps Shumla as well. Contemplating this plan, the Grand Duke Nicholas and his advisers, who would conduct the operation, felt rather less bullish, and as the campaign proceeded were to water down Obruchev's bold concept.[3]

Whatever deployment was decided upon, it would first be necessary to obtain the consent of Roumania for the passage through Moldavia and Wallachia. Notionally subject to Turkish suzerainty, the Roumanian government was placed in a quandary. There was no point in declaring Roumania neutral in the coming war, since the Great Powers would not guarantee her position; nonetheless, this would have been the preferred option of some members of the government. In the alternative, an alliance could be made with Russia whereby Roumania would take no part in the war itself; or there might be a full-blown alliance with Roumania taking an active part in hostilities. Prince Charles and his leading ministers preferred this course, but initially this was rejected by Gorchakov and the Tsar. In due course, however this came about, although ultimately Russia was to prove an ungrateful ally. In the face of the large Russian army that was assembling in Bessarabia, the Roumanians had little choice but to accede to Russian requests for a free passage of the army; in addition Roumania also agreed to provide camping grounds, the use of the railway system and supplies (upon payment). Expecting that such an agreement might lead to Turkish troops crossing the border, the Roumanian government took the step of mobilising its own army on April 18 organised in two corps, each of two divisions. It reached a strength of 32,000 infantry, 4,500 cavalry and 84 guns by the end of May. Ultimately the Roumanians mobilised a total of 1,602 officers and 100,000 men and put into the field 58,700 men with 12,300 horses and 190 guns. These forces comprised both regular and territorial units; neither their

Varna. (Fauré)

Shumla. (Fauré)

high command nor the regimental officers had any practical experience of war. There was a shortage of junior officers. The infantry were equipped with a variety of weapons; the artillery had two models of Krupp field guns. One piece of equipment was to come in particularly useful in the trenches before Plevna; this was the Linneman portable spade.[4]

In determining how to cross Wallachia in order to reach the Danube, it was evident that the delta of the Danube itself must be avoided. The marshes and lakes of this region were, in the spring, prone to sudden flooding, and were unsuitable for the passage of a large army. Accordingly, in order to deploy into the basin of the Danube, the Russian army must cross the Pruth, moving westwards, before executing a left wheel to head south towards the Danube. Six roads were available for this, two via Fokchany leading to Bucharest, and four converging at Galatz. There was also a railway that ran south from Odessa to Kishinev, crossing the Roumanian border at Umgeni; there, however, the gauge changed, and the single line through Jassy to Bucharest was poorly laid, and could take only limited traffic.

Upon reaching the Danube the Russian army faced a very serious obstacle. From the Iron Gates the river runs east for some three hundred miles before, at Rassova, turning north to Galatz for eighty miles before resuming its eastward course to flow into the Black Sea. At Widdin, close to the Serbian border and forty miles south-east of the Iron Gates, the Danube was in the dry season some 800 yards wide and at Galatz a mile wide. When in flood the river could, at its eastern end, attain a breadth of four miles. Except at one or two points, the southern bank commands the northern which in many places is marshy and often flooded. Many of the towns at crossing points were fortified, although only Widdin, Rustchuk and Silistria could be said to be in good repair.

Westwards of Nicopolis, the roads southward through Bulgaria converged on Sofia, a direction taking an invading army too far to the west for an advance on

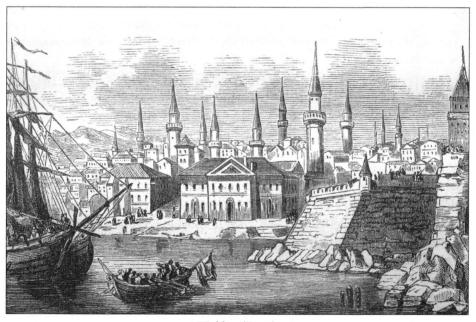

Widdin. (Fauré)

Turkish fortifications outside Rustchuk, giving a good impression of the type of field fortification also seen at Plevna. (*Album della Guerra Russo-Turca del 1877-78*)

Constantinople. The more direct route would involve crossing the Danube between Nicopolis and Rustchuk, good roads leading from there through Lovtcha and Tirnova and thence southwards to the Balkan passes. Accordingly, the plan adopted was to cross the Danube there, pushing strong forces to right and left to mask the Turkish armies based on Widddin and the Quadrilateral respectively, and to thrust south as swiftly as possible through Tirnova to seize the Balkan passes. It was a plan that attracted severe criticism:

> Nepokoitschitski's studies of the 1870 campaign and of von Moltke's strategy had led him to a false conclusion. Had he been content to carry his plan of campaign up to the passage of the Danube, and arranged his strategic deployment so that on crossing that river he would have been in superior force to either of the detachments, into which the Turks had weakly divided their forces; had he set himself the task of crushing the enemy's armies, before proceeding to threaten their capital, he might have passed as an apt disciple of the great Prussian. Moltke did not carry his original plan of campaign beyond the first collision with the French. His strategic deployment was so arranged that his armies should meet the enemy in superior force.[5]

Although an enemy's capital might properly be the ultimate objective, the key task was the defeat of the opposing armies.

The Russian plan depended for its success on the effect of their rapid advance southward. It was based on what was unquestionably a serious underestimate of Turkish capabilities. This, in a sense was perfectly understandable; in the past Ottoman leaders had usually been strikingly unambitious, and the Russians might well consider that speed of action would be all that would be required. And in fact what was known of the early Turkish dispositions must have confirmed the Russians in this belief.

The Russian deployment involved a striking force of some 200,000 men, an army judged to be sufficient to carry out the plan. It could have been stronger; there were substantial additional forces available that had not yet been mobilised, and in addition there were some 60,000 troops assigned to operations in the Caucasus. This deployment was found by Maurice to be strategically unsound. He commented on the plan to invade Asia Minor, with an advance on Scutari:

This operation was planned in the same optimistic spirit which devised the dash through the Balkans and Constantinople. Their desire to be strong in both theatres of war led the Russians to be strong in neither. 20,000 men would with the assistance of local levies have sufficed to defend the passes of the Caucasus against Turkish aggression.[6]

His conclusion was that Nepokoitschitski had failed to learn from Moltke that it is impossible to be too strong at the decisive point. The containment of two armies,

Turkish battery at Rustchuk. (*Illustrirte Geschichte des Orientalischen Krieges von 1876-1878*)

together not much less than his own, would leave only a small force available to plunge southwards, while he overlooked the mobility which command of the sea, and a more or less adequate rail system, had given to his opponent. And, quite apart from seriously misjudging the military effectiveness of the enemy, the logistical difficulties, and the effect of the weather, had been insufficiently taken into account. A very wet spring would badly affect the Roumanian road system, and would keep rivers and streams unusually high, while the rail transport system proved even less effective than had been hoped. It has been pointed out that distance, and the inability to use seaborne communications, intensified these difficulties, a march from Kishinev via the Shipka Pass to San Stefano amounting to over 650 miles.[7]

As has been already noted, the initial Turkish dispositions were widely scattered as a result of pre-existing commitments. In March 1877 Turkish forces stood in Bosnia, Herzegovina, around Novibazar, at Widdin, in Albania, around Sofia and in the Dobrudja and the Quadrilateral. Abdul Kerim could see that this dispersal of force must urgently be corrected if he was to have any chance of resisting a Russian advance. He faced however the difficulty that local governors of towns and provinces, who were reluctant to lose the protection of their garrisons, appealed to Constantinople to allow these to remain. As a result, there was a good deal of confusion, and Abdul Kerim's intention to concentrate in the Quadrilateral was seriously impaired.

His purpose was to offer a strictly passive defence. While this might play to the strengths of the troops under his command, it conceded completely the initiative to the Russians. He appears to have believed that he could not successfully defend the line of the Danube, and that his best chance lay in attacking the Russians while they were

Shipping horses at Constantinople for the seat of war in Asia Minor. (*Illustrated London News*)

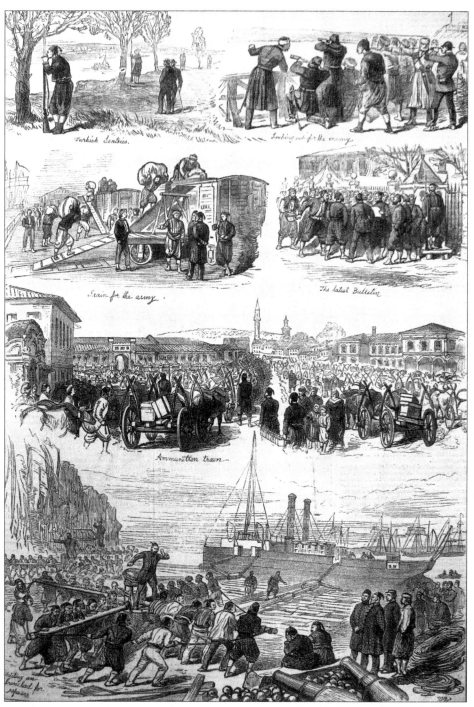

Sketches of Turkish war activity at Rustchuk. (*Illustrated London News*)

Progress Map No 1 – First period of the Campaign. From the declaration of war to the crossing of the Danube. April 24 to June 27 1877

Locals called out to work at the fortifications at Varna. (*Illustrated London News*)

engaging in masking or besieging the four fortresses. Maurice was even more severe about this strategy than that of the Russians:

> Such a plan of campaign is more than puerile. Even the youngest spider does not expect to catch flies without spinning a web. Abdul Kerim might have foreseen that the reasons which led him to wish that the Russians should enter the Quadrilateral, would keep them out of it.[8]

An alternative strategy would, however, have had its own risks. The ability of subordinate commanders to execute offensive movements in a timely manner was far from reliable; the larger Turkish formations, hurriedly assembled from the basic battalion units, had only limited experience of working as a whole, and at all levels were diffident about abandoning prepared positions to take the offensive. On the other hand, there was much to be hoped from a delay to the Russian advance, which could only be checked by an active defence, unless, of course, the Russians obliged Abdul Kerim by attacking the Quadrilateral. International intervention might well occur if the campaign were protracted in this way.

Looking at the alternatives open to the Turkish strategists, Francis Greene concluded that if 'the Turks meant to oppose an energetic resistance to the Russian advance, it was very plain that their most advantageous position from which to do so was the Dobrudja.' From here, an army of 100,000 men could be poised either to oppose a crossing of

Colonel Frederick Wellesley, British military *attaché* to Russia. (Wellesley)

the lower Danube or, if the Russians attempted to march past, could attack them in the flank. Immediately war was declared, a powerful Turkish force could seize the key towns on the northern bank of the Danube, and fortify them, and seize the key bridges. However, instead of preparing for this, the Turks remained static:

> The Turks passed the winter preceding the declaration of war with an army of 50,000 to 60,000 men in the Quadrilateral, another of the same size 200 miles away at Widdin, and a few weak garrisons along the Danube. Whether it was Oriental procrastination, or because, as has been pretended, they had a deep plan of luring the Russians across the Danube and then overwhelming them, or, as is more likely, because they had no very definite plan of campaign beyond simply waiting, according to their traditional mode of warfare, behind fortifications to be attacked, it is hardly possible to state.[9]

It is also remarkable that Abdul Kerim should have paid no regard to the use which might have been made of the powerful Turkish navy. This had already had its effect in pinning down two Russian corps for coastal defence. But a great deal more might have been achieved by using the command of the sea to concentrate Turkish forces more speedily at critical points. In particular, the existence of a large fleet of armoured and unarmoured vessels on the Danube, together with a fleet of twenty more armoured vessels off the Sulina mouth of the river, could have enabled Abdul Kerim to hold the river line at Braila, Galatz and Reni, and in this way seriously damage the Russian advance. It was probably not putting it too high to observe, as Maurice did, that 'in all her many struggles against Russia, Turkey had never had such opportunities as she possessed in the spring of 1877 for delaying the Russian advance across the Danube.'[10]

Hobart had been, not surprisingly, particularly put out by the cavalier treatment he and his navy received at the hands of the Ottoman commanders, as he recorded:

> On the day that war was declared I was at Rustchuk, the headquarters of the Turkish army. On that occasion I made a final effort, by making propositions which events have proved would have arrested the advance of the enemy. I was simply told to mind my own business, and ordered to immediately rejoin my ships, which were at the moment lying at the Sulina mouth of the Danube.[11]

He subsequently pointed out that this was not going to be easy, since the Russians had by then reached the river, and placed batteries commanding it. Hobart was told that if necessary he could rejoin his fleet overland via Varna. Still further enraged by this, he decided to run the gauntlet of the Russian guns in order, as he put it, to show his contempt for them all. After an adventurous run down the river, he reached Toltcha at the mouth of the Danube, where he received further orders to leave the area:

> I cannot express my annoyance, as even at that moment I could have brought a couple of small iron-clads that were lying at Sulina into the river and played 'old Harry' with the Russian army, then advancing into Roumania, via Galatz. The bridge near Galatz could certainly have been destroyed. It was hard on the gallant Turks, hard on the Sultan and his government, and hard on me, to see such magnificent chances thrown away.[12]

As was usual the Russian army would be accompanied by military *attachés* from other Great Powers, both at headquarters and in the field. In the case of the British military *attaché*, however, this led to a serious diplomatic incident. Colonel Frederick Wellesley, the son of the former British ambassador to Paris, Lord Cowley (himself a nephew of the Duke of Wellington) had been in post at St Petersburg for a number of years. When the Russians mobilised, in January 1877, he reported to London on a number of grave defects in the process, including the fact that rather than the 400,000 men claimed, only 118,000 had been assembled after great confusion, with an inefficient and inadequate commissariat and chaotic disorganisation on the railways. As he wrote in his memoirs, it was naturally his duty to report 'the lamentable shortcomings of the Russian army respecting this most important portion of its military organisation.'[13]

His report was of course sent secretly; but a British Cabinet minister leaked the contents to the French ambassador, who reported it to Paris. Since his own military *attaché* had described the mobilisation in different terms, the French Foreign Minister enquired of his ambassador in Moscow, General Le Flô, as to which report was correct. The latter mentioned the matter to Jomini, in the Russian Foreign Office, and the fat was in the fire. The upper echelons of the Russian military, and especially the Tsar and Grand Duke Nicholas, were outraged at this affront to the national honour. The first manifestation of this came when the Tsar ignored Wellesley at the Sunday guard mounting parade, and this was followed by a failure to invite him, unlike his German and Austrian colleagues, to accompany the Tsar to join the army on the completion of the mobilisation. It took an intervention by Lord Derby to secure the invitation.

On arriving at the Imperial headquarters he was told he was to be attached to the headquarters of the Grand Duke. When arriving there, however, he was treated with the grossest incivility by the commander in chief, to such an extent that Wellesley deemed it best to say nothing but to report the matter to Derby and seek further instructions.[14] The Foreign Secretary on this occasion at any rate acted swiftly, taking the matter up with Count Shuvalov, who was informed that the Queen and her government were 'deeply grieved' at the treatment of the military *attaché*. This did the trick; within a few days Prince Gorchakov himself arrived, to congratulate Wellesley on his restraint which he thought had probably averted a war, and to invite him to join the Imperial headquarters.

Wellesley arrived there on July 2; except for Ignatiev, who was charming, he was shunned by the Russian staff. Nicholas, however, who said that it was a 'nice scrape' that Wellesley had got him into, came as near to an apology as a Grand Duke could, and they shook hands. Likewise Alexander, who sent for Wellesley, and made peace with him, and thereafter the relationship with the Imperial family and the Russian high command was restored.[15] It had been a difficult incident, which illuminated the sensitivity of the Russians to any perception of their military weakness.

Wellesley was an interesting character, being something of a chancer; indeed, Professor John Vincent, the editor of Lord Derby's diaries, called him 'a classic Victorian scoundrel.' He was sceptical about Wellesley's reliability in the contents of his diplomatic reports. However, although he may have been 'not just a rogue, but a young rogue, a Disraelian young man,' as Professor Vincent puts it, Wellesley was present on a number of significant occasions during the war, and his descriptions of them are important, even if his general character should be taken into account when considering them.[16] Significantly, in July 1877, Salisbury suggested in Cabinet that Wellesley should be replaced not only as being unpopular with the Russians but as 'lying under strong suspicions of corruption.'[17]

11

The Barboshi Bridge

To protect the left flank of their advance it was necessary that the Russians should swiftly seize Reni, Braila and Galatz, the only firm crossing places in the area in which the Danube swings eastwards towards the Black Sea. Just south of Galatz the River Sereth flows into the Danube, at which point it is one hundred and eighty yards wide and is deep and swift flowing. Across it there were three bridges; there was one bridge at Roman, one narrow bridge in bad repair between Tekutch and Fokchany and a modern iron rail and road bridge at Barboshi, near Galatz, which crossed the Sereth just before it joined the Danube. The latter was 300 yards long and its possession, undamaged, was essential; the heavy April rains had flooded the marshes near Barboshi, and the construction of a temporary bridge was impossible.

The agreement with the Roumanian Government permitting the Russian forces to cross the country was not to come before parliament until April 29, and the Russians believed that the Turks would not expect hostilities to begin until it had been ratified. Accordingly, they moved their advanced forces up to the frontier, and then made a formal declaration of war on April 24. During the previous night a column commanded by Colonel Biskoupski, the Chief of Staff of the XI Corps, assembled on the frontier between Kubei and Bolgrad, crossing at 3.00 am. Its task was to race for the Barboshi bridge and prevent its destruction by the Turks. It consisted of three Don Cossack regiments, two battalions of the 41st Regiment and two field and two Cossack batteries. From Kubei to Galatz it is about fifty miles; the cavalry, leading the column, quickly reached the flooded River Pruth, but were here delayed for some five hours while crossing in boats. The Barboshi bridge was reached at 7.00 pm. Meanwhile the rest of the column, which reached Reni between 5.00 pm and 6.00 pm, was held up by the discovery of two Turkish gunboats at the mouth of the Pruth, where the ferry had been damaged. However, by 10.00 pm the column began to cross and by 9.00 am on the following day Biskoupski had one battalion and the two Cossack batteries over the river, with which he marched at once on Galatz, reaching the Barboshi bridge at noon. In spite of the delay the infantry had marched the fifty miles in thirty-four hours, and were rewarded when the bridge was seized undamaged. The artillery quickly took up position to cover the bridge; this was just in time, because Turkish monitors arrived at the mouth of the Sereth but were driven off by the Russian guns.

Hozier, in his history of the war, noted that the Russians knew, and the Turks should have known, that the Barboshi bridge was critical to their main line of communications:

> Immediately on the threat of active hostilities that bridge should undoubtedly have been destroyed by the Turks. With a fatal apathy, however, this precaution was neglected until too late ... Being situated but a few hours march from the Turkish frontier, the bridge might easily have been seized and blown up by Ottoman troops. While the Russian flying column performed considerably over 100 miles to seize it,

Cossacks on the road from Galatz to Barboshi. (*Illustrated London News*)

the Turks from Matchin, or some other point on the Danube, might have reached Barboshi in eight hours. The *coup de main* which, in a few hours after the beginning of the campaign, made the Russian masters of this bridge, was a stroke worthy of the conception and genius of Moltke.[1]

The bridge was commanded by ancient Roman fortifications on the plateau overlooking it, which proved surprisingly suitable for modern artillery; thus, when on April 25 the Turkish monitors arrived, they were easily driven off.

Meanwhile other detachments of the XI Corps had seized Ismail and Kilin, securing the Russian left flank. By the end of April 27 the 11th Division, with the 2nd Brigade of the 32nd Division, had occupied Galatz, and within two days the rest of the XI Corps had arrived, supported by the Naval Brigade. This *coup de main* gave the Russians the chance to make up for delays caused by the almost ceaseless rains, as McGahan reported:

> The roads, therefore, remain in a fearful condition, and the progress of that part of the army which is moving forward on foot is but slow. Nevertheless, the Russians have, by their energy and rapid marching, won the first move in the game just opened, or rather the two first moves – first, in preventing the destruction of the railway bridge near Galatz by a wonderful march; and secondly, in throwing forward a sufficient number of troops to prevent the occupation of Roumania by the Turks. It was evidently so clearly the proper move of the Turks to cross the Danube, destroy the railways and bridges of all kinds, skirmish with the advance guard, and retard and harass the march of the army, that the Russians were quite convinced that they would do this.[2]

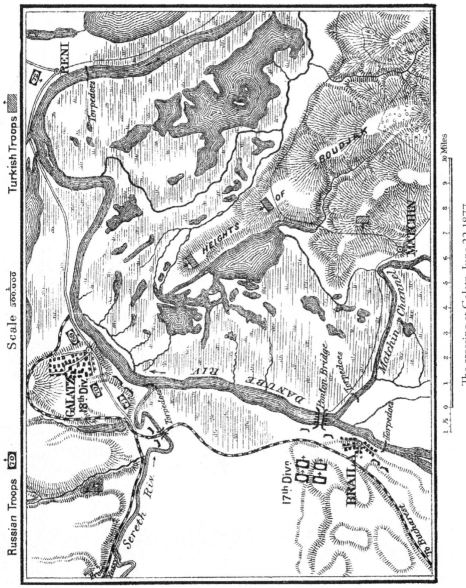

The crossing at Galatz, June 22 1877

Russian council of war at Barboshi railway station. (*Illustrated London News*)

Russian torpedo launches attacking a Turkish monitor at Matghin. (Ollier)

Russian infantry at the railway station, Jassy. (*Illustrated London News*)

Further steps were at once taken to secure the Barboshi bridge and the other crossings against any attack by the Turkish navy. The mouth of the Sereth was mined, and by April 30 a line of mines was laid across the Danube at Braila and Reni. This had the effect of cutting off the Danube flotilla, consisting of seven armoured gunboats and eighteen wooden vessels, from the Turkish fleet off the Sulina mouth of the river. To the fury of the neutral merchantmen awaiting cargoes at Galatz, all ships were ordered to clear the port by 6.00 pm on April 27. Protests by the consuls of the various nationalities were of no avail; Prince Shakofskoi, the commander of the XI Corps, insisted that his orders from the headquarters of the Army of the South were inflexible.[3]

Having achieved nothing to prevent or delay the Russian move southward, ships from the upriver flotilla, consisting of five armoured gunboats and two wooden ships, came down on May 6 to Braila and opened fire on the Russian batteries and the town. They had previously taken refuge in an arm of the river at Matchin, and this was apparently an effort to break out to join the principal naval forces at the mouth of the Danube. The Turkish vessels exchanged fire with the Russian batteries over several days; finally, on May 10 a shell from a Russian mortar penetrated the armoured deck of the flagship *Luft-i-Djelil*, which blew up and sank with the loss of 217 crew. This was a twin-screw seagoing monitor, carrying four 150 pounder Armstrong guns.[4]

On May 25 the Russians went over to the offensive, when Lieutenant Dubassov, with four steam launches armed with spar torpedoes, went up river to the Matchin channel where, on a dark and rainy night he found two Turkish ironclads, and a wooden vessel, at anchor. When the alarm was given he put on full steam, exploding his torpedo under the port quarter of the largest monitor, the *Havzi Rahman*. Dubassov's launch had

Nicopolis. (Fauré)

been filled with water by the explosion; he called out to Lieutenant Shestakov in the next launch to come on; he did so, and exploded his torpedo amidships, and the ship sank within a few minutes, only her masts showing above the water.[5] MacGahan saw in this feat a grim warning for the future:

> This is the first instance, I believe, in which a vessel has been destroyed in time of war by an enemy's torpedoes, and the ease with which this was accomplished makes it a most important event in naval warfare. What gives it more significance is that the Turks apparently were not taken by surprise. They had as much warning as they could expect under the circumstances, and they found it utterly impossible to arrest or injure the swift and terrible instruments of destruction that were flitting about them in the darkness. The Turks are notoriously bad sailors, but it does not appear that even good sailors under such circumstances could have done any better.[6]

Meanwhile the Army of the South was engaged in its deployment in Roumania, a process that was undisturbed by the enemy. The bulk of the army had begun to cross the frontier on April 24, preceded and screened by the cavalry, in three principal columns. On the right, one column moved from Umgeni through Jassy and Roman to Fokchany. The centre column, also with Fokchany as its first objective, moved by Berlat. The left column, which crossed the Pruth at Leova, had a particular mission. Led by Skobelev I, it headed for Galatz and Braila. It consisted of the Caucasian Cossack Cavalry Division, the 23rd Don Cossack Regiment, the 4th Rifle Brigade and the 5th Engineer Battalion. Skobelev's task was to occupy all the possible river crossings on the Danube above Braila, and thereby to screen the movement of the rest of the Army of the South. It was followed

Russian troops making rafts on the banks of the Danube. (Ollier)

in its march by the 11th Cavalry Division and the infantry and artillery of the VIII Corps.

By May 8 the VIII, XI and part of the VII Corps was concentrated around Reni, Galatz and Braila. The XII Corps was at Tekutch. Skobelev had carried out his mission to occupy the left bank of the Danube as far as Gora-Yalumitza; westward of here the Roumanian army watched the line of the river, handing over their positions to Russian troops as they moved west. Turkish activity during the month of May was confined to the occasional bombardment of Roumanian towns on the northern shore of the Danube, a process which strengthened the hand of the more belligerent faction in the Roumanian government and army, and inclined public opinion to their support. Prince Charles of Roumania, the country's Hohenzollern prince, who was concerned to identify himself with his people, also assumed a warlike attitude.

On May 11 Roumanian relations with the Ottoman Empire were finally broken off, and the formal independence of the country was declared four days later. Following this another agreement was reached with Russia, by which the independence of Roumania was recognised, and a promise made to require Turkey to cede to her the northern part of the Dobrudja. In exchange for this Roumania was to transfer part of Roumanian Bessarabia to Russia, from Reni to the Black Sea. It was a term of the agreement that Roumania should enter the war with an army of 70,000 men, and should receive 200,000 rifles. The actual basis of Roumanian participation was not agreed, and this was for the moment postponed. The Russian high command was largely indifferent to this, regarding the possibility of active Roumanian involvement as unnecessary and probably undesirable. It was an attitude of which they would in due course repent.[7]

This attitude of indifference was maintained notwithstanding the fact that it had already become clear that there were insufficient Russian troops on the ground; it was as a result of this that the three further corps had been added to the Army of the South on May 6. It would necessarily be some time before these could come into line. The XIV Corps would be the first to arrive, being directed on Galatz on June 13, where it was to relieve the XI Corps which would move west to a position opposite Turtukai. The XIII Corps was to go to Alexandria, sixty miles south-west of Bucharest, arriving on June 27; and the IV Corps was for the moment to go to Bucharest, where it was held in reserve.

By May 24 the Army of the South had completed its initial deployment. Headquarters was now at Ploesti. Two and a half corps were at Bucharest, with a half corps at Slatina.

The cavalry continued to cover the line of the Danube from Nicopolis to Silistria, at which point began the marshy section of the river unsuitable for a crossing. The army was thus in the position required for the crossing of the Danube at the selected point, but it was soon clear that the wet spring meant that the operation must be delayed. The level of the river at Galatz was on June 1 some fifteen feet higher than usual at that time; several railroad bridges had been swept away by floods and many roads had become impassable. The limited capacity of the railroad had been largely taken up with the transport of heavy artillery, ammunition and siege materials, pontoon trains and the steam torpedo boats and their equipment that were performing so creditably.[8]

The target date of June 6 for the crossing of the Danube was accordingly put back, and the Army of the South remained immobile in the positions it had taken up. The deployment had certainly been remarkable successful, having regard to the practical difficulties it had faced. The efficient use of cavalry to screen the movement into Roumania gave the Ottoman commanders little indication of the real line of advance to be taken. Such information as could be gleaned from the concentration around Braila and Galatz appeared to point to a Russian advance through the Dobrudja.

Meanwhile the Russian navy continued its efforts to neutralize the Turkish fleet. On June 10 the steamer *Constantine* with six torpedo launches in tow, sailed from Odessa on course for Sulina. Arriving that night, the launches were sent in to attack the Turkish ironclads. Three were at anchor; another had steam up in the roadstead, and this was made the target. The spar torpedo of the leading launch exploded short of its object, probably due to protective wire netting. This caused the alarm to be raised, and the launches made their retreat to the *Constantine*, although one was disabled and captured.[9]

On June 20 ten steam launches succeeded, in spite of the intervention of a Turkish monitor from Rustchuk, in placing a barricade of torpedoes across the Danube above that place. Three days later, Commander Novikov, who had led that operation, used rowing boats to do the same above Nicopolis. A Turkish monitor came down river, and was attacked unsuccessfully by two launches; in the face of heavy gunfire from Russian artillery on the northern bank it speedily withdrew.

This marked the end of active operations by Turkish gunboats on the Danube. The considerable threat which they might have posed to the Russian advance never materialised. Two of the ironclads had been sunk; two would in due course be captured at Nicopolis when that place was taken, while the other three remained at Rustchuk until the end of the war.

The Crossing of the Danube

Since the early 1860s Mikhail Ivanovich Dragomirov had been the most influential military thinker on the tactics that should be adopted by the Russian army. He was born in 1830, the son of a distinguished soldier of the Napoleonic wars. After graduating from the Nicholas Military Academy he travelled to Western Europe, studying training methods in France and Britain. From the outset he believed that attack with the bayonet was the decisive act in battle. It was a conviction from which he never retreated, in spite of the evidence from the Wars of German Unification that the advent of the breechloading rifle had entirely changed the battlefield environment.[1]

Dragomirov became Adjunct Professor of Tactics at the Military Academy in 1860, and from 1862 served as a member of a committee on structure and training. As a protegé of the War Minister, he was able to influence the emerging Russian tactical doctrine. He did not accept the conclusion of Astafeev that the new firepower required the adoption of dispersed formations and skirmish lines, and that if a bayonet attack was necessary the units concerned would concentrate only temporarily for the purpose. Cold steel, argued Dragomirov, required closed formations, and these would remain the primary mode of attack. His emphasis on this did not entirely blind him to the power of the breechloader; but he feared that to encourage the infantry to individual marksmanship rather than volley firing would increase their concern for self preservation and hence their enthusiasm for the bayonet assault.[2]

The infantry regulations introduced in 1866 reflected Dragomirov's strongly held beliefs. The formation to be adopted was, as Bruce Menning has pointed out, to place the emphasis as to four fifths on cold steel and one fifth on firepower. There was a noteworthy regard to the importance of conserving ammunition, a requirement that was in striking contrast to their Turkish opponents in 1877-1878. Volley firing was still seen as the principal utilisation of the breechloading rifle. In the aftermath of the Franco-Prussian war there was a vigorous debate about the appropriateness of Dragomirov's doctrine; Baron Zeddeler, a Russian observer, noted that 'fire was always preferred to the bayonet,' because 'firearms had attained a power so unprecedented that it superseded the bayonet attack, at least in this last war.'[3] Such heresy, however, cut little ice with those in authority, and Dragomirov's beliefs continued to prevail.

In 1877 Dragomirov, now a Lieutenant-General, was in command of the 14th Division, forming part of Radetzky's VIII Corps, and it was to him that was assigned the task of forcing the passage of the Danube. During the enforced delay the Russian engineers had been carefully reconnoitering the country on either bank of the river. It was clearly essential that the crossing point should be kept secret from the Turks until the last possible moment and elaborate steps were taken to ensure this. A suitable location for the assembly of the bridging material was found in the River Aluta, which joins the Danube just above Nicopolis; the point selected for the crossing must therefore be reasonably adjacent to that river. The point chosen was originally at Simnitza; but it soon

Lieutenant-General Dragomirov, commander of the Russian 14th
Division, part of Radetzky's VIII Corps. (*Russes et Turcs*)

appeared that the level of the Danube there was so high that it would be impossible.[4]
Instead, therefore, it was determined to cross near Nicopolis, and the date provisionally
chosen for the operation was June 24. However, in personally reconnoitering this stretch
of the river on June 20, Nicholas and Nepokoitschitski became convinced that the
strong Turkish works there would be difficult to force; at the same time the river level at
Simnitza had fallen, and it was decided to revert to the original location.

Meanwhile in order to focus Turkish attention on the left flank of the Russians,
and to confirm the impression that the main line of advance would be through the
Dobrudja, it was decided that before Dragomirov attempted his crossing Lieutenant-
General Zimmerman's XIV Corps should cross the Danube between Galatz and Braila.
In addition to his own corps Zimmerman also had one division of the IV Corps under
his command. On June 12 construction began of a pontoon bridge half a mile north of
Braila opposite Getchet; however, the Danube was still fifteen feet above its normal level
and at this point the waters were 2,500 yards wide. Zimmerman reported that a crossing
was for the moment impossible. This was certainly not good enough, and he was sharply
directed that he must be over the river by June 22.[5]

Since the bridge could not be completed in time, he resolved to cross in rowing
boats, rafts and steam tugs from Galatz, his first objective being the Budschak Hills,
which overlooked the marshes where it was intended to land. On June 22 at 3.00 am
two groups each of five companies of infantry began the crossing; at first the landing was
hotly disputed by the Turkish troops on the Budschak Hills, but as more Russian troops
came across the Turks fell back first to Matchin and then further to the south.

Russian casualties in the seizure of the Budschak Hills amounted to a total of 142 officers and men. When MacGahan was able to cross, he found that the operation was well under way. Looking towards Matchin, he could see the advance into the hills:

> Long lines of white smoke rose up from the mountain side, and were borne away on the air in thin fleecy clouds. The dull, booming heavy sound of cannon, a distant roar of artillery, and the continued and rattling crash of small arms were borne to us in a softened kind of roll on the still sunny air … Slowly the two lines of smoke advanced along the range of hills towards Matchin, one pursuing the other, and marking the progress of the battle. Slowly the Russians drove back the Turks, following them from rock to rock, from point to point, from summit to summit, from hill to valley, and from valley to hill, over the irregular and uneven ground.[6]

The hills once taken, Zimmerman completed his crossing without further interruption, and slowly followed the retreating Turks, occupying Iskatchi, Toltcha and Hirsova unopposed. By the end of June the Turks, under Ali Pasha, who were about 15,000 strong, had retreated down the Dobrudja to Trajan's Wall. Zimmerman arrived at this position by July 19, where he settled down to observe the enemy but took no action to disturb them.[7]

By now Tsar Alexander had arrived to join his army. As part of the efforts to deceive the enemy as to the chosen crossing point, it was announced that he planned to witness his troops enter Bulgaria, and he established his headquarters at Turnu Magurelle, close to Flamunda. The latter was one of the alternative sites near Nicopolis considered when Simnitza appeared impossible.

Russian troops crossing the Danube at Braila. (*Russes et Turcs*)

The legendary Archibald Forbes, war correspondent. (Bullard)

By June 24, the date originally selected for the attempt, the Russian forces had not yet reached their jumping off point, and it was delayed until the night of June 26-27. Even the Tsar was not told of the chosen site for the crossing until 8.00 pm on June 26, so stringent were the security precautions.[8]

Dragomirov had his own 14th Division, which comprised four regiments (53rd, 54th, 55th, and 56th), the 4th Rifle Brigade, and supporting troops, a force that in all comprised 17 battalions, 6 Cossack squadrons and 64 guns. The XIII Corps was ordered to advance from Alexandria to Piatra, and the IX Corps to make a feint of crossing at Flamunda, as part of the deception plan. Siege batteries were established opposite to the fortresses of Nicopolis and Rustchuk. Dragomirov split the forces available to him into six groups each of about 2,500 men, comprising twelve companies of infantry, with 60 Cossacks. To the two detachments intended to form the first wave of the attackers he attached eight mountain guns, with four field guns to support each of the other four. Strict orders were issued that not a shot was to be fired until the opposite bank was reached.

Supporting Dragomirov's division was Prince Mirsky's 13th Division; stationed at Lissa, it was under orders to move up to Simnitza at 7.00 am on the morning of June 27. For Archibald Forbes, who had attached himself to Dragomirov's division, the move of the 13th Division was evidence that the Russians intended to succeed in the crossing whatever the cost; in the event that Dragomirov was checked, Mirsky's division was then to be committed:

In the event of failure it was to take up the fighting, and force a passage at all sacrifices; for the Archduke Nicholas had announced that he would take no denial. The river had to be crossed at Simnitza, cost what it might. Other divisions stood within call if need were. The waters might be reddened, but they must be crossed.[9]

On June 24 the Russian artillery concentrated opposite Rustchuk began a heavy bombardment of the city; and on the evening of the following day the artillery began a bombardment of Nicopolis and the Turkish batteries on either side of that fortress, and covering the mouth of the Aluta river. The shelling continued throughout June 26 and 27, the Turkish artillery being entirely silenced, and two of the batteries destroyed. This, with the other steps taken to ensure complete security, fixed firmly in the minds of the Turkish commanders that Nicopolis would be the crossing site.

Although Moltke was reputed to have said that the line of the Danube could not be defended, a contested river crossing was bound to be a difficult operation, particularly given the breadth of the Danube. Simnitza lay almost opposite the town of Sistova on the southern bank. Below Sistova, the Turkish bank was steep, at some points precipitous. About two miles down river the Tekir brook formed a small cove, to the right of which there was a small camp occupied by a company of *Mustafiz*, while on the hills behind there was a battery of heavy guns. The total Turkish force in and around Sistova amounted to about 4,000 men, consisting of the brigade of Ismid Pasha and supporting artillery. The overall commander at this point was Ahmed Namdy Pasha.

In a number of respects the chosen crossing place presented difficulties. Although around Simnitza the Roumanian bank was high, it was separated from the Danube proper by a low lying stretch of land partly of meadow, partly of sand and partly of mud, which at this time was just emerging from inundation. These flats were cut off from Simnitza by a narrow arm of the Danube, so that it was effectively an island. It was not the most advantageous jumping off point. The recent floods had wrecked the bridge, so the Russians erected a short pontoon bridge to reach the flats. They were intersected by many streams; marshy land was punctuated by standing water left by the floods. The flats were bare, apart from a wood of willows and alders facing, across the Danube, the cove formed by the Tekir brook, and this did offer some cover.[10]

In the late afternoon of June 26 Dragomirov's troops had been discreetly concentrated on the shore near Simnitza, with their pontoons. As night fell they began to move out to cross the bridges to the flats. The bridges creaked so loudly and the wheels of the guns and vehicles rattled so much that it was feared that the Turks would discover the movement. Hay was taken from the horses and laid over the bridges, which to some extent muted the passage of the troops who next took up a position in the willow wood. The troops carried food for three days; they had discarded their white uniforms, and were wearing their heavy duty blue uniforms, the reasons for this being given as the greater warmth that would be afforded to wounded lying exposed to the cool of the night, and that the white uniforms rendered them too conspicuous. Forbes was derisive:

The latter reason is rubbish. Blue on the light ground of the Danube sand is more conspicuous than white. Everywhere British Scarlet is more conspicuous than any other. The true fighting colour is the dingy kharki (sic) of our Indian irregulars.[11]

Bridge of boats over the Danube between Simnitza and Sistova. (Ollier)

Russian infantry on the march. (*The Graphic*)

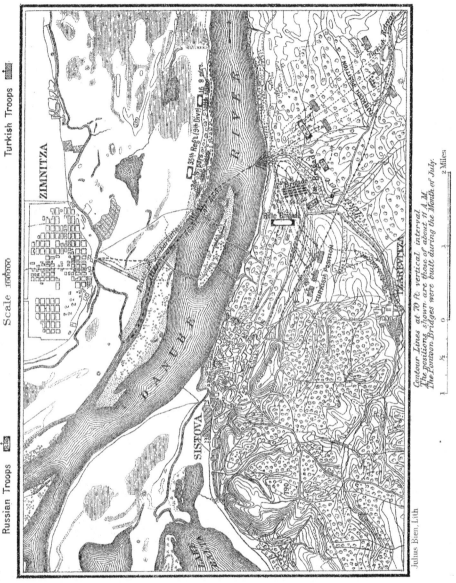

The crossing at Simnitza-Sistova, June 27 1877

Turkish Troops

Russian Troops

Scale 100000

Julius Bien, Lith

Russian troops landing at Sistova. (Strantz)

The troops began embarking around midnight, but it was not until between 1.00 and 2.00 that the first wave began the crossing. This was Yolchine's brigade, comprising the 53rd and 54th Infantry Regiments. The boats set out in a line, but soon the current, and the different speeds attained by the rowers, resulted in their separation. They were soon spotted by the Turkish lookouts, and before they were half way across first the Turkish infantry and then the artillery opened fire. One boat, with forty officers and men, was hit and sank; two others, lashed together either side of a stage carrying two of the mountain guns, were hit repeatedly and sank abruptly, with all their passengers. Apart from these, the losses during the crossing itself were not great. As dawn came up some 208 boats had made the crossing.

The first wave landed, and the troops were led ashore by Yolchine, who ordered them to lie down in the mud of the cove to await the following reinforcements. They then ran forward with fixed bayonets to seize the cliffs, driving back the Turkish skirmishers.[12] By 2.00 am the leading Russian troops were already advancing some three-quarters of a mile from the shore to the east of the Tekir brook. As dawn broke Ahmed Namdy had sent forward two battalions; these were, however, quite unable to hold their position as more and more Russian troops came ashore. Before the crossing began, one of Ahmed Namdy's battalions had been stationed in Sistova itself, while the other three were in camp some two miles to the east of the town, about a mile and a half back from the river, and hence well placed to move forward to confront the first wave of the attackers. But the Russian obsession with security had paid off, and the surprise of their enemy was complete. However, even after Ahmed Namdy had become aware of the strength of the landing, he missed his chance of inflicting a serious check on the Russian advance:

Russian troops are welcomed on their entry into Sistova. (Ollier)

The moment that it became clear that the Russians were making a serious attempt to force the passage of the river, it was Ahmed Namdy Pasha's duty to throw in every man he had available, to oppose the Russians on the river bank, and to delay them by every means in his power, pending the arrival of reinforcements from Rustchuk, distant only thirty-five miles. By sending up his reinforcements piecemeal, he allowed the Russians to obtain a foothold on the right bank, and the success of the crossing was thereby assured.[13]

At about 5.00 am Dragomirov arrived on the southern bank and assumed command. He was accompanied by Michael Skobelev as a volunteer, who evidently found acting as his father's Chief of Staff to be insufficiently stimulating. Dragomirov sent fifteen companies to attack the Turkish troops in camp to the left of the Tekir brook, and proceeded to push the rest of his force as it arrived down the valley and on the heights on either side to form a defensive perimeter. Reinforcements began to arrive more rapidly, a steamer having run past the Turkish batteries at Nicopolis to help get more troops across. The troops crossing did not escape unscathed; in all some five boats were sunk, with the loss of about 100 men killed and wounded.[14]

Skobelev was everywhere in the thick of things. He was encountered by Forbes on the morning of the crossing:

> I shook hands with him on the edge of the bank of the Danube after the bayonet charge in which he had taken part. His face was black with powder, and he, general as he is, carried a soldier's rifle, with the bayonet fixed.[15]

Russian Cossack scouts. (Rogers)

By 11.00 am Dragomirov had sufficient men on the ground to think of making a significant advance. He had most of the 14th Division in hand, with part of the 4th Rifle Brigade, and he now ordered an advance on the Sistova Heights. By 3.00 pm these were in his hands and his troops had entered Sistova itself. Turkish opposition now crumbled away; the bulk of Ahmed Namdy's troops retreated in the direction of Tirnova, with those on the western side of their position retreating to Nicopolis. At 3.00 pm Radetzky, the VIII Corps commander, crossed to the southern bank; by 9.00 pm the whole of the corps had made the crossing. It had been a brilliantly successful operation. The total of Russian killed and wounded was 821.[16] Turkish losses were said to be about 700. The Russian plan had been a bold one; it could have gone very wrong, but unfortunately the fact of its success confirmed the Russian disposition to underestimate the enemy.

Dragomirov, in his report, drew a number of conclusions, observing that the Russian troops, once over the river, did not fight in their regular formations:

> The characteristic feature of the combat of June 27 was that the first troops engaged did not form whole battalions, nor companies, nor even platoons; on landing the troops formed themselves into improvised groups; ... each group observed attentively what its neighbours were doing, each regulating its movements by those of the others, and lending each other a mutual support. It was not possible to think of forming a general reserve, until after the passage of the last detachments of the 14th Division, i.e. about 9.30 am, nearly eight hours after the beginning of the action.[17]

Greene thought that the Russian success and the relatively small number of casualties might be due to this individuality of the Russian soldiers.

Next day the Russian engineers now made strenuous efforts with the bridging material collected in the River Aluta to complete the first of two pontoon bridges over the Danube, not without difficulty; on June 29 a Turkish monitor appeared, but for reasons unexplained sailed away again without opening fire. Next day a storm delayed the work. On June 28 the Tsar had crossed the Danube to visit the troops that had forced the passage of the river; the bridge was completed on July 2, and large bodies of troops were now able to move into Bulgaria.

The Tsar's arrival at the battle front had an immediate effect on the planning of the next stage of the war. Although not formally taking any part in the deliberations of the high command, the Tsar was soon exhibiting decided uneasiness about the best way forward, to the understandable annoyance of the Grand Duke Nicholas. The problems which the latter now faced were complex; the Ottoman commanders in the field whose resistance must be overcome possessed large numbers of troops, and further reinforcements, brought in from Montenegro and Albania, might add something of the order of 50,000 men. Apart from the garrisons of the principal Turkish fortresses at Widdin, Nicopolis, Rustchuk, Turtukai, Silistria and Varna, which probably amounted in all to about 50,000 men, there were three principal field armies with which the Russians would have to deal. Ali Pasha had about 15,000 men and 40 guns in the southern part of the Dobrudja, while Osman Pasha was said to have 40,000 men and 100 guns in the Widdin area. Finally, there was Abdul Kerim's principal army, currently located around Shumla, of about 60,000 men and 230 guns.[18]

Although everything had so far gone according to plan for the Russians, the units composing the Army of the South were by now well below establishment. The long sojourn in Roumania during a lengthy period of wet weather, and the marshes of the Danube, had put large numbers of men on the sick list, and it had been necessary to make a number of detachments for the protection of the long line of communication, while the threat from the Turkish navy, although not having amounted to much so far, had still to be taken into account. It remained to be seen how far the original bold concept of a rapid strike south to the Balkans could still remain the basis of Russian strategy. So far, everything had gone well; the difficult part was about to begin.

13

Gourko

The long wait to cross the Danube occasioned considerable frustration among the war correspondents eager to report spectacular action, but it was caused not only by the need to allow the waters to fall, but also to the most careful and deliberate preparations to ensure the operation's success. In the next phase of the campaign, however, the Russians stuck to their original plan and went from one extreme to the other, showing themselves willing to throw caution to the winds. Certainly the sluggish and ineffectual Turkish response so far encountered might be thought enough to justify the bold stroke southward which had always been the intention.

But before that bold stroke could be undertaken there was some further delay which brought forth serious criticism of the Russian army by at least one observer. Archibald Forbes was sceptical that the reason was solely due to the need to bring up supplies, writing on July 9:

> My own belief is that a great part of the reason is to be assigned to the pottering rearrangements of the commands in order that young gentlemen of the blood imperial may gain military fame and St George's Crosses. But this is not all. There is a lack of go, of energy, of system, of purpose, about the direction of the army. The machine is a very fine one, the material is admirable, the workmanship is good, the finishing is fair – but there is not motive power sufficient to bring out its excellences and to do it justice.[1]

Nonetheless, there was a lot to be done before embarking on the next phase. First it would be necessary to complete the pontoon bridge over the Danube. Construction of this had begun during June 28 and was finished on July 2. While this was going on, orders were drawn up for the formation of a special detachment to lead the strike to the south, and for the operations of the main army once its move across the Danube had been completed. Basically, the plan to be adopted was that drawn up before the outbreak of war. The advance guard was to be led by Lieutenant-General Joseph Vladimirovich Gourko, the commander of a division of Guard cavalry at St Petersburg. Gourko was born in 1828, fought in the Crimea and in the Polish insurrection, became a regimental commander in 1866 and was promoted to Major-General in the following year. Since then he had held various commands in the Guard cavalry and hence was close to the imperial court. Since his division had not been mobilised at the start of the war, he came to the front as a volunteer, and was personally selected by Grand Duke Nicholas to lead the advance guard.[2]

Gourko's detachment consisted of 10½ battalions (8,000 men), 31½ squadrons (4,000 men), with 18 horse artillery and 14 mountain guns. It comprised the 4th Rifle Brigade, (Drietsinsky), two companies of Cossack infantry, the six battalions of the Bulgarian Legion (Stoletov), a Dragoon Brigade (Prince Eugene Maximilianovich) a

Lieutenant-General Joseph Vladimirovich Gourko. (Hozier)

composite brigade of Hussars and Cossacks (Prince Nicolai Maximilianovich), a Don Cossack Brigade (Chernozubov) and a Caucasus Cossack Brigade (Tutolmin). The force crossed the Danube over the newly completed bridge on July 3 and at once moved south in the direction of Tirnova. Behind the advance guard in support came the VIII Corps (Radetzky). On the left the XII Corps (Vannovsky) and XIII Corps (Hahn) made up the Army of Rustchuk, which was placed under the command of the Tsarevich. Its mission was to advance on Biela, to occupy the line of the River Jantra, to contain the Turkish forces in the Quadrilateral and if possible to take Rustchuk. To the right, Krüdener's IX Corps, with a brigade of Caucasus Cossacks was designated as the Western Army, with orders to seize Nicopolis and occupy the line of the Vid, thus covering the right flank. The reserve consisted of the XI Corps (Shakofskoi) and IV Corps (Zotov) and was concentrated around Simnitza. Finally, Zimmerman's XIV Corps was to watch the northern part of the Quadrilateral.[3]

Gourko's objective was to be the crossing of the Balkan Mountains – in other words the penetration of what Moltke regarded as the true line of defence upon which the Turks should concentrate to resist an invasion from the north. In his history of the war of 1828-29, he reviewed the effectiveness of the Balkans as a barrier. The suggestion that it was insurmountable was not, he thought, warranted by the height or formation of the mountains, but

> partly upon tradition, partly upon the number of small difficulties which are accumulated within five or six marches, and which have to be encountered by all the troops in succession, and lastly upon the paucity and badness of the roads across the mountains.[4]

Tsarevich Alexander, commander of
the Army of Rustchuk. (Hozier)

General Stoletov. (Rogers)

He went on to list the routes across the Balkans that were, he considered, practicable for troops; there were, he thought, six of these, and much the best was that from Tirnova via the Shipka Pass to Kazanlik. Eastward of this he next identified the Iron Gate, through which passed the road from Tirnova to Slivno. In Moltke's view, these passes would best be defended not so much by the erection of forts but by assigning bodies of troops to occupy them and, with barricades and abattis, to 'oppose a very formidable resistance to any force attempting to cross the mountains.' There were, of course, other passes to the west of those described, but these did not lead towards Adrianople and Constantinople.

The very substantial forces set aside to cover the flanks of the advance and of the lines of communication meant that the thrust southward was being undertaken by only a small part of the Russian forces that had crossed the Danube. Thus far the Turkish response to the invasion had been notably passive, but it by no means followed that this would continue to be the case. Gourko's advance carried with it the responsibility for the success of the whole of the Russian operations in Bulgaria. As Maurice pointed out, four fifths of the Russian army had thus been dissipated in what could reasonably be termed minor operations.

By the night of July 4 Gourko's cavalry had reached a point some twenty miles south of their start line, and had so far encountered no opposition. His first objective was Tirnova, and the information which he gathered as he moved south was that this was held by the Turks with five battalions of infantry together with cavalry and artillery. July 5 was a rest day, made necessary by the slow process of getting the Russian army over to

Tirnova. (Fauré)

the south bank of the Danube at Sistova. Gourko's cavalry maintained contact with the leading cavalry units of both the Western Army and the Army of Rustchuk.

Approaching Tirnova from the north, the traveller entered a countryside still more fertile, the meadows greener and the scenery more striking. Moltke, in his *Letters sur l'Orient*, remarked on the beauty of the region:

> What a marvellous country this Bulgaria is! Everything is green. The sides of the deep valleys are planted with lime and wild pear trees, wide meadows form framework for the rivers, rich cornfields cover the plains, and even the vast uncultivated tracts are covered with luxuriant herbage. The numerous trees, planted singly, cast their black shadows upon the plains of brilliant green.[6]

Tirnova was the ancient capital of the former rulers of Bulgaria before it was occupied in 1393 by the Ottomans. Many of the finest buildings were then destroyed during and after a three months siege. In 1877 the town had between 40,000 and 50,000 inhabitants. It stands on a hill about 1,000 feet high on the banks of the River Jantra. It was and still is dominated by a citadel and is surrounded by higher hills on which strong redoubts and earthworks could have been constructed, and was accordingly extremely well suited for a strong defence. It was a crucially important road junction, giving access to the best passes through the Balkans as well as being the junction of roads east and west to Osman Bazar and Selvi respectively. The roads entered the town from four directions through narrow defiles between high limestone cliffs.[7]

It was, therefore, not only the first principal objective of Gourko's force but also one which must be approached carefully. In fact, however, the Turks had not taken the opportunity to create a strong defensive position in and around the town. Its defenders consisted of five battalions of infantry (about 3,000 *Nizams*), a body of *Redifs* and one battery. On July 7 Gourko reconnoitred the place, advancing with the brigade of dragoons from the west. It soon became apparent that the Turks were not in great force, and on getting a message from the Christian inhabitants that their lives might be in danger he resolved to move forward at once with the whole brigade, supported by a horse artillery battery of six guns. Four *sotnias* of Don Cossacks had arrived, and these he sent forward on his left, to turn the Turkish flank and rear, while he advanced directly on the town. The Turks put up little resistance, retreating hastily down the slope of the hill on which they stood, and taking the road to Osman Bazar:

> Round the point of the spur they ran, flinging away their cartridge boxes and their arms, leaving huge heaps of ammunition boxes. Everything that could be was thrown away, and the place was literally strewed with the débris of their flight. Once, indeed, they formed line to the left as they passed across the field; but a shell or two falling amongst them put them to flight again.[8]

The precipitate flight of the town's defenders was later explained by the delay in the arrival of reinforcements for which Said Pasha had asked. These were to come from Shumla under the command of Safvet Pasha; they had advanced as far as Osman Bazar and halted there. Meanwhile, because there existed no telegraph between that point and Tirnova, Said Pasha's messages had to go through Adrianople, Constantinople and Shumla before they were received, and in the event Safvet could not reach Tirnova in time to take part in the town's defence. It is a moot point as to whether it had made much difference, and when Said's retreating forces met those of Safvet, nothing was done by way of any attempt to retake Tirnova.[9] Said's orders from Abdul Kerim had been to hold out to the last pending the arrival at the town of Safvet's force.

It was an almost bloodless victory; Gourko lost two men and eight horses wounded. The possession of Tirnova meant that he was now well placed for his advance on the Balkan passes. The remainder of Gourko's force now came up to Tirnova, not without difficulty, as Colonel Epauchin, in his history of the advance guard's operations, described:

> The heat was terrible. The men got dreadfully tired, and so faint from thirst that they could not be kept from drinking from every pond they passed. They dipped it up in their caps, poured it over their necks, wetted their heads, and sluiced each other with it.[10]

Gourko spent the next four days in the town, gathering intelligence about the Turkish forces and the state of the passes over the mountains, organising a pack train and preparing for his advance. His information was that the Turkish authorities and most of the population had left Tirnova for Shumla. So far none of the passes appeared to be defended except the Shipka Pass where there were apparently some 3,000 infantry, some mountain guns and some Bashi-Bazouks. Pondering the best way to cross the Balkans, Gourko concluded that he should not attack the Shipka Pass directly. Instead he proposed to cross by one of the most difficult and least known passes, that at Hainkioi, ignoring the local proverb that 'ill luck awaits him who crosses the Hainkioi Pass,' on the basis that he would meet with the least resistance there. It was by no means certain, however, that this pass would be viable for any substantial force. Moltke, indeed, in his history of the war of 1828-29, did not consider it one of those practicable for an army.[11] Gourko's intention was that, having crossed the mountains and descended into the Tundja valley, he should turn westward, and having occupied Kazanlik take the Turks holding the Shipka Pass in their rear. He planned to take his whole force through the Hainkioi pass, leaving behind only the 30th Don Cossack Regiment with two guns. For the moment four squadrons of this regiment would remain at Tirnova, while two squadrons and the guns would watch the Shipka Pass. A small detachment would reconnoitre the Elena passes, to check that there were no Turkish forces there.[12] Gourko's plan was approved by the Grand Duke, who himself reached Tirnova on July 12, the day in which the advance guard set off on its hazardous mission. In conveying the approval of headquarters, Levitsky wrote in somewhat restrictive terms:

> The Grand Duke ... desires you to understand that you must without fail confine yourself to merely seizing the passes and their outlets, and move no further without orders. In support of your movement against the Shipka Pass HIH will send from Tirnova to Gabrova on the 14 July a regiment of infantry and a battery from the

Some of Gourko's men burning a railway station. (*Illustrated London News*)

2nd Brigade of the 9th Division, which is to arrive at Tirnova tomorrow, the 12 July.[13]

Levitsky went on to refer to the retention at Tirnova of two of the Bulgarian battalions and a Hussar regiment, a suggestion that caused Gourko some anxiety; however, following two letters to the Grand Duke pointing out that his force was weak enough already, headquarters relented, and Gourko was allowed to proceed with the whole of his force.

When the Grand Duke himself arrived at Tirnova on July 12, he was accompanied by the leading units of the VIII Corps. A detachment of these was moved to Gabrova, under the command of Major-General Darozhinsky, consisting of the 36th (Orel) Regiment, the remainder of the 30th Don Cossacks (two *sotnias* were already at Gabrova) and 10 guns. The intention was that this force should advance to attack the Shipka Pass from the north on July 17. Subsequently on July 16 Prince Nicholas Sviatopolk-Mirsky, the younger brother of Grand Duke Michael's deputy in the Caucasus, who was the commander of the 9th Division, arrived and took over the conduct of the operation.

Central to the success of Gourko's enterprise would be the work of the pioneers in ensuring that the route to be taken would be passable by the whole of the advance guard, including the artillery. The trail to be followed was essentially not much more than a footpath. The mounted pioneers, taking with them carts carrying dynamite and tools, under Major-General Rauch of the Engineers, in two days made a road over which it was possible by one means or another to transport the guns.[14] The ascent began at Parovtchi, at an elevation of 1,800 feet, and in the following eight miles rose a further 1,900 feet at which point the summit was reached. On the far side the pass descended 2,300 feet to Hainkioi. For part of the journey it was necessary for the guns to be dragged by the infantry. Hozier described the ordeal of the gunners:

> At one place two of the mountain guns rolled down from the path to the bottom of the valley, but without injuring horse or man. The guns which passed first cut up the road a great deal, and for the last battery the day's work was terrible; nearly all the drivers pressing their horses and laying on their whips – the gunners assisting by pushing or pulling. Never did horses work harder, yet the guns hung behind; but it is doubtful whether artillery was ever taken along such roads before even at such a pace.[15]

MacGahan, who was intent on accompanying Gourko in his march over the mountains, left Tirnova on the day after the advance guard, confident at first that he should easily catch it up. Taking first the Elena road, he soon learned that Gourko had not followed this route; he concluded that, instead, he must have gone through Gabrova in order to cross the Shipka Pass and rode off in that direction. Here again he was disappointed, and reasoned that the advance guard must have taken a route between those he had tried; eventually, he learned from the inhabitants that this was indeed the case, and that a pass began near the village of Parovtchi which was, however, not marked on the Russian staff map. He duly followed this road, which led him to a sight which he described lyrically in a dispatch of July 15:

We emerged from the forest upon a high narrow ridge that seemed to be a watershed, where we had the most splendid view of the Balkans I have ever seen. There was first a low uneven hilly country, full of green little valleys and hollows, rich and luxuriant with orchards, trees and growing grain that almost hid the villages of fifteen or twenty houses which they surrounded. Then, beyond, the range of the great Balkans, their huge round forms rising up against the sky, in glorious robes of misty purple, and extending far away to the west until they mingled imperceptibly high up in the sky with the golden-edged, many-tinted clouds.[16]

Ahead of him Gourko's detachment was led by a force of 200 Cossacks. Serving with them as a volunteer was the young diplomat Prince Tsertelev, who had been on Ignatiev's staff at Constantinople. They were also accompanied by McGahan, despite his suffering from a broken ankle. It was Tsertelev who had, on reaching Tirnova, heard of the Hainkioi Pass and recommended Gourko to take that route. Now, on July 13, as the Cossacks neared the exit of the pass, he had gone ahead in the dress of a peasant and found that Turkish troops had been posted there, although no entrenchments had been formed. When this report reached Gourko, he pushed on with the advance, not stopping until midnight. At 6.00 am on the following day the advance was resumed. At 10.00 am the Cossacks reached the mouth of the defile which opened to the width of half a mile, and there before them lay the beautiful valley of the Tundja, known as the 'Valley of the Roses.' The Turkish troops posted to watch the exit to the pass were taken entirely by surprise, and retreated rapidly toward Slivno. On reaching Tvarditsa, about five miles south of Hainkioi, they were joined by the garrison of that place, making a total force of about 2,000 men in four battalions.[17]

The retreating Turks were followed up by two battalions of the 4th Rifle Brigade. During the late afternoon the Turks launched a brief counter-attack, advancing to Tvarditsa. After only a brief engagement, in the course of which the riflemen were reinforced by a third battalion, the Turks broke off the action and fell back to Slivno. The Russians occupied the abandoned Turkish camps. With the passage of the Balkans completed successfully, Gourko ordered a rest day for July 15, assembling his complete force for the next stage of his operations.

He did, however, send out a number of reconnaissances. Two squadrons of Cossacks moved out towards Slivno under Baron Korf. Near Orezary they ran into a large group of Bashi-Bazouks and Circassians, supported by three battalions of infantry with two guns. The Cossacks fell back on Zapanli, where they were reinforced by two further squadrons. At 6.00 pm further reinforcements reached them in the shape of the Kazan Dragoons, a Bulgarian brigade and four guns, and the Turks soon retreated in disorder. An attempt was made to stand at Tvarditsa, but the Turks soon broke again and were pursued by the Cossacks for seven miles. Total Russian losses were one killed and three wounded.

Two squadrons under Captain Martinov probed towards Yeni Zagra, where they destroyed an eighty wagon transport train. However, they then encountered strong Turkish forces, and were threatened in flank by two Circassian squadrons; they fell back to Kavlikoi and thence to their camp at Esekeye, having ascertained the total strength of the Turkish forces as three battalions, with a battery and the Circassians. Their losses amounted to three horses. These actions led the Turks to suppose that Gourko's next

Gourko and his staff near the Shipka Pass. (*Album della Guerra Russo-Turca del 1877-78*)

move would be on Yeni Zagra, which they decided to await, leaving Gourko free to make his move on Kazanlik. A third reconnaissance had a minor encounter on the Kazanlik road.

On July 16 Gourko began his advance toward Kazanlik. He had twenty miles to cover to reach that town, and hoped after taking the place to be in position to attack the Shipka Pass on the following morning. He took with him a force of six and a half battalions (5,000 men), nineteen and a half squadrons (3,000 men) and 16 guns. He left behind four battalions (3,000 men), six squadrons of 500 men and 14 guns at Hainkioi under Major-General Stoletev.[19]

The advancing Russian troops encountered at about 10.00 am a Turkish force about 3,000 strong in position behind a stream at the village of Uflani. MacGahan described the outcome:

This force retreating before us proved to be a most unfortunate circumstance for four or five Turkish villages on the way to Kazanlik. They took refuge in these villages, and either they or the inhabitants fired on us from the houses. The result was that we set fire to every house from which we had been fired at, and, the fire spreading, these villages were for the most part destroyed. The Turks seem to have the faculty of always doing the wrong thing and never the right one. Had they fired at us from behind the rocks and trees in the defiles of the Balkans it would have annoyed us very considerably, delayed our progress, and have done the Turkish population no harm. Instead of that, they fire at us from villages in the plain in the most senseless and useless manner, where this kind of resistance could not delay our march an hour, with the natural result of getting these villages burned. They leave no mistake uncommitted that perversity, ignorance, and stupidity can commit.[20]

The engagement at Uflani did however seriously delay Gourko's march, with the result that by the time the Turks were finally driven back to a position near Kazanlik, Gourko's timetable had been disrupted, and he bivouacked for the night with his force at Magilish. Russian losses in the engagement were relatively light, amounting to sixty-two killed and wounded. Turkish casualties were far greater, over four hundred being killed, in addition to a large number of wounded and a considerable number of prisoners.[21] Seeing how heavily the Turks had suffered, when he rode across the battlefield that evening, Gourko reckoned the moral effect of the defeat meant that they were unlikely to venture on an advance against his rear from the direction of Yeni Zagra. Accordingly he gave orders for the four Bulgarian battalions left with Stoletev at Hainkioi to march to rejoin his main body at Magilish.[22]

Next morning Gourko resumed his advance, moving on Kazanlik in three columns; on his right one and a half battalions moved into the mountains to come down on the town from the north-east, while in the centre five battalions with ten guns advanced directly from the east. On the left the cavalry, with six guns, was to follow the Tundja valley and turn the Turkish right. The Turks were found to have taken up a position along the Kara Dere, about five miles in front of Kazanlik, with three battalions and three guns, with another column on the left coming down from Shipka. The engagement began at 7.00 am and lasted about three hours before the Russian cavalry, having turned the Turkish right, drove the whole force back in disorder; it retreated to Kazanlik, where it briefly made a stand before falling back to Shipka, having lost heavily, including four hundred prisoners and the three guns. The Russian loss was fourteen men.[23] Gourko was in Kazanlik by noon, where he was enthusiastically welcomed by the population. However, his hope of mounting an attack on the Shipka Pass that day was over optimistic; in the intense heat his men were exhausted. He rode on with the cavalry to reconnoitre the enemy position, and was joined by the infantry in front of Shipka as the sun was setting. The Turks had abandoned the village of Shipka, and their camp, falling back to the pass, where it was said some 5,000 men were in position. Gourko's inability to assault the pass that day meant that he was going to be one day late for the joint attack from north and south which had been planned for July 17. At Shipka, firing could be heard from the other side of the pass, indicating that the attack there was under way.

On the south side of the Balkans there are scarcely any foothills, the mountains falling abruptly to the plain, as MacGahan described:

As you ride along the valley of the Tundja you see these monster masses of earth and rock and forest rising abruptly out of the plain without any intermediate hills or irregularities, like a row of sugar loaves placed along a floor and rounded off at

A Russian Cossack encampment. (Rogers)

the top. The pass is therefore only a couple of miles from the foot of the mountain on this side and the road up to it is very steep and difficult.[24]

Gourko's intention was now to launch an attack early on the morning of July 18, and he sent off a message over the mountains to Prince Mirsky asking him to support the attack from the north. The message did not get through, however, until noon, too late for anything to be done. Mirsky had, as arranged, at 7.00 am on July 17 launched his attack from the north from Gabrova, moving in four columns on what was clearly a strong Turkish position in several lines of trenches across the road leading to the Shipka Pass. East and west of this position there rose a number of commanding heights, of which the highest was Bald Mountain, some 4,875 feet high, which dominated the whole area. The Turks were commanded by Khulussi Pasha, whose force was about six and a half battalions strong, between 4,000 and 5,000 men, with a number of Bashi-Bazouks and twelve guns. Mirsky had only the 35th (Briansk) Infantry Regiment, about 2,400 strong, with six guns. To drive the Turks out of a very strong position with such a small force was a tall order.

The column on the right, of four companies, led by Lieutenant Colonel Khomenko, was directed on Bald Mountain, which it did not reach until 7.00 pm, without having encountered any resistance. The centre column, also composed of four companies, was pinned down in front of the most advanced Turkish trenches, a position too strong to assault. On the left, two companies advanced through the woods towards the St Nicholas hill which was in fact the strongest part of the defences; this column soon ran into trouble, but held its ground until about 4.00 pm, when it fell back, pursued by the enemy, suffering losses of 115 out of the total of 320 men. Finally, the column on the extreme left, also of two companies, advanced through the woods on Mount Berdek, three miles from St Nicholas. This column, commanded by Major Rodzevich, which moved off much earlier than the others, enjoyed the only success of the day, storming the Turkish position and driving the enemy back to St Nicholas. But it was not sufficient to redeem the failure of the other columns, and during the night all the Russian troops fell back to Gabrova, with total casualties of 205.[25]

Gourko's attack on the southern end of the pass on July 18 was similarly unsuccessful. Pushing through the woods on either side of the main road they arrived at the strong position on St Nicholas. Soon after the Russians opened fire, the Turks displayed white flags and the Russians ceased fire and sent forward a flag of truce. MacGahan recorded what followed on the part of the Turks:

> They seized the bearer of the flag, murdered him, and opened fire upon the Russians without warning. The whole business is so barbarous and so savage that the story would probably not be believed if it rested on Russian authority alone. Fortunately it does not. There was a Prussian officer present, Major Liegnitz, on whose authority, as well as on that of many Russian officers, the truth of the story rests.

When the Turks displayed the white flags they ceased firing, as did the Russians, who imprudently emerged from cover. When the Russian flag of truce went forward, there was a general relaxation and Liegnitz went close enough to the Turkish position to speak to a Turkish soldier. Once the flag bearer entered the fort, fire was opened without warning, not accidentally but, as MacGahan reported, in response to a trumpet call. Next day when the Russians entered the fort the mutilated and decapitated body of the flag bearer was found.[26]

With the ending of the apparent truce Gourko's men launched a charge against the Turkish position, capturing some of the first line of trenches, but were not strong enough to make any further progress into the main works on St Nicholas. They fell back on Shipka, having suffered casualties of over 150.

These uncoordinated attacks on the Turkish position in the Shipka Pass having failed, it was resolved to launch further attacks from both north and south on July 19. Khulussi, however, despaired of being able to hold the position, and during the night of July 18/19 and the following morning, the Turks evacuated St Nicholas in small parties which made their way through the mountains. To buy time for this manoeuvre a letter was brought to Gourko's headquarters at 7.00 am with an offer to surrender; the Turkish officer took back a proposal that the capitulation take place at noon, promising to return within two hours. Gourko sent forward some hospital attendants to care for the wounded. The Turkish officer did not return; when noon passed without further contact, Gourko sent forward a reconnoitring party and was preparing to advance with two battalions when some of the hospital attendants returned to say that Skobelev was on St Nicholas. This was soon confirmed by a note from the latter to say that the Turks had abandoned the position, leaving behind eight guns and a large quantity of ammunition and supplies. What had happened was that Skobelev, always thirsting for action, had taken nine companies of the 36th Regiment with four guns to attack St Nicholas; but as he advanced through the defences found that the enemy had gone, leaving behind the mutilated bodies of many dead Russian soldiers.[27]

With this, Gourko's objective had been accomplished. It had been a remarkable success. At the cost of less than 500 casualties he had occupied Tirnova, seized three passes through the Balkans, opened the road into Rumelia, dispersed Turkish detachments totaling over 10,000 men, and disarmed the Turkish population in a large part of the Tundja valley. He had taken two flags, thirteen guns and 800 prisoners, and had vindicated the boldness of the Russian plan.

14

Krüdener

The first objective given to the IX Corps, in its capacity as the Western flank guard of the Russian advance, was the taking of Nicopolis. Some fifteen miles west of the crossing point at Simnitza, Nicopolis was a town of between 8,000 and 10,000 inhabitants. It was by no means heavily fortified. An old citadel on a bluff overhanging the Danube was in substantial disrepair; it was commanded by the hills to the south. Most of the town lay outside the walls of this fortress. The River Osma joins the Danube two miles to the west of the town; on the east it was covered by the Danube marshes. Immediately south of the town a plateau, about 700 feet above the level of the river, runs from the Osma to the marshes. Three miles further to the west, the River Vid runs north-east into the Danube, passing about seven miles west of the town of Plevna, which is about twenty three miles from Nicopolis.

During the period before the crossing of the Danube, the Russians had been active on the northern bank of the Danube opposite Nicopolis and the Turks had established a number of batteries to fire over the river, together with rifle pits on the bluffs of the Osma and the Ermenli Ravine to the east. Once the Russians were over the river, hasty efforts were made to construct earthworks on the south side of the town. The garrison of Nicopolis, about 12,000 strong, was under Hassan Pasha. He positioned the bulk of his troops in the new earthworks, in which there were about ten guns; between 3,000 and 4,000 men were in the hills between the Osma and the Vid.[1]

The IX Corps had been obliged to surrender two cavalry regiments to Gourko's advance guard; in their place, Krüdener had a brigade of Caucasian Cossacks of twelve squadrons. He left one infantry regiment at Sistova, while another was pushed south-westwards from that place to Bulgareni, on the main road from Plevna to Biela and Rustchuk. With the remainder of his force he marched westwards to Nicopolis, arriving in front of the Turkish positions on July 13. During the following day he reconnoitred and made his plans for an assault on July 15.

Since Krüdener's orders were to take Nicopolis he concentrated all his attention on carrying out this task which, as the Russians soon found out, was a serious mistake, and an unnecessary one. The Caucasian Cossack Brigade had come under the command of the IX Corps on July 9; but two days prior to this its commander, Colonel Tutolmin, had reported intelligence from the local population to the effect that a company of Turkish troops had occupied Plevna and confirmed the presence of a few Turkish troops which had withdrawn to Rahova. Tutolmin requested an infantry battalion to enable him to take the town, but Krüdener refused, saying that Nicopolis must first be captured. Those units of the IX Corps already over the river halted, awaiting the rest of the corps. On July 10 Krüdener had been told that a mixed force of enemy troops had entered Plevna, apparently from Nicopolis: next day the Cossacks reported that there were now at least four battalions with six guns there.

Turkish reinforcements for Nicopolis. (Strantz)

These troops, under Atouf Pasha, had been sent by Hassan to keep open his communications particularly with Osman Pasha in Widdin, and had arrived there on July 9, a few hours before Tutolmin's leading patrols reached the town. While Krüdener was preparing his assault on Nicopolis, Atouf's force was all that there was in Plevna. Krüdener, however, denied himself the chance of gathering further intelligence by employing Tutolmin's brigade in support of his action against Nicopolis, and Atouf's troops were left undisturbed. Maurice was sharply critical:

> Had this cavalry been employed in work round Plevna and in learning what was going on in the direction of Widdin, it is probable that Krüdener would have discovered that the occupation of the line of the Lower Vid and of Plevna as its key were of greater importance to the Russian plan of campaign than the immediate capture of Nicopolis. To withdraw cavalry which has once gained contact can rarely be justified.[2]

As it was, there was no means of telling what Osman might be getting up to in Widdin. It was certainly known that there stood much the largest and most dangerous Turkish force in the western part of the country, and information as to its movements was crucial. In fact Osman had been champing at the bit to move eastwards, and it was only after he had submitted five proposals to Abdul Kerim that he finally received authority to move. On July 12 Osman's preparations were complete; on the following

Constructing a Russian battery. (*Illustrated London News*)

morning at 4.00 am he marched out from Widdin with a force comprising 19 battalions, 6 squadrons, and 9 batteries, a total of 12,000 men with 54 guns.[3] His intention was, if possible, to join forces with Hassan, if he did not arrive too late.

For his assault on Nicopolis Krüdener divided his forces in two; one part, under Lieutenant-General Schilder-Schuldner, the commander of the 5th Division, was to advance down the left bank of the Osma, seizing the hills and cutting off any escape route to Plevna. With the remainder of his force Krüdener intended to assault the Turkish positions to the south of Nicopolis. Schilder-Schuldner had the 17th (Archangel) and 18th (Vologda) Infantry Regiments, a regiment of lancers and the Cossack Brigade. The latter was to cover the left and rear against any Turkish reinforcements. His force was linked to the main body by the 123rd (Koslov) Infantry Regiment. For his assault, Krüdener had the 121st (Penza) and 20th (Galicia)Infantry Regiments with five batteries, with the 122nd (Tambov) Regiment in reserve, together with three more batteries and two *sotnias*. Three *sotnias* observed the eastern flank of the Turkish position. The intention was to drive Hassan's forces into Nicopolis and to compel their surrender.[4]

The Russian artillery opened fire at 4.00 am on July 15, and Schilder-Schuldner's infantry began to move forward, arriving in front of the Turkish heights at 7.00 am. An assault on the enemy positions soon followed and after a struggle the hills were occupied and their defenders driven over the Osma towards Nicopolis. The 123rd Regiment now moved up to harass the retreating Turks. Two battalions of the 18th Regiment crossed to the right bank of the Osma and joined the 123rd Regiment in climbing the heights above Djournevo, a village on the river about four miles from Nicopolis. It was now about 2.00 pm, and seeing the success on his left Krüdener launched the 20th Regiment

Lieutenant-General Schilder-Schuldner, commander of the Russian 5th
Division. (*Illustrirte Geschichte des Orientalischen Krieges von 1876-1878*)

towards the Turkish position in the centre. After three assaults the key Turkish redoubt
was captured, and the Russian infantry moved up to the walls of the fortress.

Meanwhile, on the left, Schilder-Schuldner's advance along the road parallel to
the Danube continued, and he launched an attack on a large redoubt to the west of
Nicopolis; darkness, however, intervened before it could be taken. During the night
part of the Turkish garrison attempted to break out in the direction of Plevna, but were
repulsed by the Caucasian Cossack Brigade.

Krüdener had therefore been able to complete his investment of Nicopolis and had
seized two out of the three most important positions held by the Turks for its defence. For
the following day he planned an all out assault, supported by the Russian siege batteries
on the northern bank of the Danube, and at 4.00 am on July 16 the storming columns
moved forward. Almost at once, however, the Turks hoisted a white flag, and negotiations
were soon concluded for the capitulation of the town. The Turks surrendered 7,000 men,
including 300 wounded, together with 110 guns and a large quantity of small arms and
ammunition. Their casualties during the fighting were not known. The Russians lost 276
killed, 949 wounded and 84 missing.[5] Hassan's surrender was undoubtedly premature;
had he resisted for several days before laying down his arms Osman would have been able
to fall on Krüdener's rear and compel him to lift the investment of Nicopolis. Although
possession of that town was crucial to neither side, Krüdener's retreat to Simnitza would
have put Osman in a position to threaten the whole Russian operation in Bulgaria.

It is surprising, therefore, that the Russians should have made so much of Hassan;
Forbes described him as 'the valiant Turkish defender of Nicopolis, of whose fighting

prowess the Russian speak with generous appreciation.' Hassan was reported as saying that he had capitulated because his ammunition was all gone, 'and he had been obliged to kill with his own hand three or four soldiers who left their duty.' He added that it was a stupid war into which the Turks had been led by the attitude of England.[6]

While the Russians were engaged in the reduction of Nicopolis, Osman's march eastward had proceeded under cloudless skies in extreme heat. The news received on July 14 that Gourko was over the Balkans came as a shock, as a result of which Osman's troops were ordered to march all through the night, pausing only at noon on the following day. Late on the evening of July 15 came news of the commencement of the Russian attack on Nicopolis, with orders from Abdul Kerim to move with the utmost speed to save not only Nicopolis but also Plevna and Lovtcha. Osman sent on three battalions in advance of the main body to join Atouf in Plevna; the rest set off at 4.00 am, with a twenty-four mile stage ahead of them. They finally reached their objective, the River Skit, at midnight, and bivouacked in a state of extreme exhaustion. It was 4.00 pm on July 17 before they set off again.

The march continued in the intense heat. At noon on July 18 the main body reached the River Isker, where a makeshift bridge of submerged carts and boards had been constructed. News of the fall of Nicopolis which reached Osman at this point did not unduly disturb him, apart from the loss of its garrison; he was more worried about the Russian occupation of Lovtcha, which he regarded as a key point. On July 19 the main body set off at 5.00 am, and marched so quickly as to leave far behind the tail of the

The Turkish garrison of Nicopolis surrenders. (*Illustrirte Geschichte des Orientalischen Krieges von 1876-1878*)

column with its ponderous train. William Herbert's battalion marched at the rear; he described their arrival at Plevna:

> Despite all our haste the tired, overburdened horses detained us; it was past 2.00
> pm before we arrived at the stone bridge by means of which the Orkhanie – Plevna
> road closes the Vid. Behind a bend of this road – on the right of which is a hill
> covered with vineyard and orchards – we came in sight of Plevna, which, lying in
> a deep, fertile valley, presented a strikingly beautiful picture with its minarets and
> domes, its white houses, its patches of foliage, its background of hills. At 4.00 pm
> we marched, or rather dragged ourselves, into the town without having seen an
> enemy.[7]

The main body had arrived at Plevna during the course of the morning, and Osman immediately moved them out of the town into positions identified by Atouf. Anticipating Osman's arrival, Atouf had collected large quantities of food and other stores, and hot meals were prepared for the tired and hungry troops. The march from Widdin had covered 115 miles in seven days, an average of over sixteen miles a day.

In 1877 Plevna was a town of 17,000 inhabitants, of which 10,000 were Christian. 4,000 of the latter had fled, but since the Russians had crossed the Danube some 2,000 Turkish refugees had arrived in the town. Through the middle of the town ran the Tultchenitza, while the Grivitza ran round the northern edge; the two streams join two miles to the north-west and run into the Vid a mile further on. Herbert's first impressions of the town were favourable:

> Plevna was better built than any other Turkish town I had seen; yet here, too, there
> were the ruined and deserted houses, the waste spaces full of rubbish, which are a
> feature of the country. The filthy streets, badly paved or unpaved, and in wet weather
> impassable, the absence of sanitary arrangements, the thousand-and-one stenches
> characteristic of urban Turkey, were worthily represented. The Tultchenitza served
> as a natural (and only) main drain. The town is built without any obvious plan;
> but the streets were wider and straighter, the houses better, than, say, in Widdin.[8]

When Osman arrived the town was, as Herbert recorded, entirely unfortified. It was surrounded by hills; Herbert noted in particular the Janik Bair, north-east of Plevna, nearly four miles long, 1,300 feet high and running from west to east 350 feet above the Plevna valley. The hills to the north and east were bare; those to the south and west were covered with vineyards, gardens and orchards. To the west Plevna was protected by the Namasgula Bair and the River Vid.

Plevna was a point of great strategic importance for a number of reasons. First, it lay on the flank of the Russians' march into Bulgaria and threatened any operations which might be intended, particularly the advance to and over the Balkans. Secondly, it was a road junction through which six routes ran, to Widdin, Sofia, Lovtcha, Pelisat, Rustchuk and Nicopolis. These roads gave ready access to the circle of hills surrounding Plevna, and meant that reinforcements could rapidly be sent to any part of the lines of defence that might be threatened. Furthermore, the roads ran mainly through the valleys of the streams joining the Vid, thus providing a system of covered communications.[9]

At the Russian headquarters there had been no reports of Osman's march before July 17, when pickets of the Caucasian Cossack Brigade reported that a strong enemy force was moving on Plevna from a westerly direction. No great significance seems to have been attached to this report; Krüdener was, however ordered by the Grand Duke to 'occupy Plevna as promptly as possible.' Krüdener, preoccupied first with the capture of Nicopolis, and then the administrative arrangements for the town, and for its captive garrison, was already aware from prisoners before the town was taken that reinforcements were expected from the west, but he paid no heed to the warning.[10] It was not until July 18 that the Caucasian Cossack Brigade was directed to leave its position on the Vid, when it was sent off to the east to Bulgareni on the Osma.

Receiving on that day the instruction to occupy Plevna, Krüdener ordered Schilder-Schuldner to carry out the task. He was to take the 1st Brigade of the 5th Division (17th and 18th Regiments), four batteries and the 9th Don Cossack Regiment, and, marching through Bryslan, to proceed to Plevna. Krüdener also put under Schilder-Schuldner's orders the 19th (Kostroma) Regiment, which was already on the Rustchuk-Plevna road at Bulgareni and Poradim, and the Caucasian Cossack Brigade. Schilder-Schuldner set out at once, and by nightfall had marched ten miles from Nicopolis. Intending to approach Plevna on a wide arc, he ordered the 19th Regiment to Sgalevitza, about eight miles east of the town, while the Cossack Brigade was to reach the village of Tultchenitza, about six miles south-east of Plevna. Next day he continued his own march south-westwards, reaching the heights south of Verbitza at about 2.00 pm, where he was, to his surprise, held up by Turkish artillery posted on the heights of Grivitza, south-east of the Janik Bair. With no cavalry at all with his main body – he had sent the 9th Don Cossacks to the west – he had no information of the location of any of the Turkish forces in the area.[11] When they heard the gunfire, the Don Cossacks, who had been peaceably cooking soup, mounted and rode forward towards Plevna, encountering a party of Turkish infantry with whom they skirmished until nightfall. Meanwhile the rest of Schilder-Schuldner's forces had reached the objectives assigned to them, and bivouacked for the night, as did the main body.

Atouf had, since his arrival at Plevna, taken some steps to prepare defensive positions around the town, and Osman continued this work. By July 20, however, he had only completed a few field works commanding the Biela road and the Grivitza area. North of Plevna some trenches near Opanetz had been dug, and some of the buildings in the village of Bukova had been loopholed for defence. In the course of a reconnaissance of the Russian forces around Plevna on the afternoon of July 19 he had concluded that the principal attack would come from the units north of the town, and that those approaching Grivitza from the east would merely make a feint. Osman's total force now amounted to 25 battalions, 10 batteries and 6 squadrons. Of these, he concentrated his small force of cavalry at Opanetz, with two battalions. He assigned eight battalions, with three and a half batteries, to the defence of the Janik Bair, and three battalions and one battery to the hill just west of Grivitza, with four battalions forming a connecting link between these two forces. One battalion and half a battery occupied the hill south of Plevna which commanded the Tultchenitza valley. Two battalions stood between the Tultchenitza and Grivitza brooks, and Osman kept five battalions and three batteries in reserve.[12]

The heights north of Bukova, seen from the saddle south of the village. This is the ground over which Schilder-Schuldner's men attacked. (Springer)

Schilder-Schuldner advanced, on the morning of July 20 at 4.00 am, in two columns widely separated from each other. The northern column, of six battalions consisting of the Archangel and Vologda Regiments with four batteries, advanced to the attack on the ridge south-west of Verbitza. At 4.30 am the Russian guns opened fire, and at 5.30 am, after a scarcely adequate artillery preparation, the infantry moved out to the attack. Quickening their pace, they charged down the slope of a ravine and up the other side, driving back the Turks. The Vologda Regiment, with several companies of the Archangel Regiment, set off in pursuit; the enemy retreated constantly until the Russians found themselves entering the town of Plevna itself. At this point, quite unsuspected by the attackers, large masses of Turks who had positioned themselves in the houses at the edge of town opened a heavy fire, before charging upon the outnumbered Russian infantry. Hozier described what followed:

> In an instant the Russians suffered enormous losses; they fell by hundreds; and having lost Major-General Knorring, commander of the brigade, wounded, and Colonel Rosenbaum, commander of the Archangel Regiment, who was killed at the head of his men, they began slowly to retreat – still facing an enemy vastly superior in numbers. Many of the wounded were unfortunately obliged to be abandoned, and their comrades saw them massacred and mutilated under their very eyes in a most inhuman manner.[13]

The other column had reached Grivitza by 5.00 am, and the battery that accompanied it was soon in action against the trenches south of the main road. After only a short artillery preparation the 19th Regiment moved to the attack in columns of companies; it took the first two lines of trenches without difficulty, and then after a hard struggle the third line, and followed the retreating Turks to the edge of town, where the regiment was halted by heavy fire from the gardens and buildings. Colonel Kleinhaus, leading the attack, was first wounded and then as his wound was being dressed killed by a shell burst, shortly before the third line of trenches was taken. It was soon apparent that the foothold on the edge of Plevna could not be maintained, and the regiment fell back, having sustained heavy losses. The Turks followed them to the first line of trenches. The Caucasian Brigade, on the extreme left of the Russian force, had ineffectually fired its mountain guns, having been unable to mount a charge due to the nature of the ground; it moved to cover the retreat of the 19th Regiment as it fell back down the road to Bulgareni. Meanwhile the main body had fallen back to Bryslan, the right flank being covered by the Don Cossacks.

The Russians had sustained very heavy casualties, losing two-thirds of their officers and a third of their men; total losses amounted to 2,823 killed and wounded. William Herbert, whose battalion had been fighting on the Janik Bair, before falling back to Bukova, had taken part in the counter-attack which drove back the extreme right of the Russian assault. He put the total Turkish casualties at 2,000. He described the Russian retreat:

> The Russian books state that the troops retired in good order. I can testify to the fact that they were in a desperate hurry, to say the least of it. Closed ranks of our infantry, under perfect control, were at their heels. We joined these, and found ourselves next to a company of our own battalion, with whom we advanced through the fields eastward. Thus we pursued the enemy across fields and meadows, over hedges and

A Red Crescent ambulance and doctor. (Ollier)

ditches, up hill and down dale. The men's spirits had revived wonderfully, for the joy of victory is as contagious as the despondency of defeat.[14]

Francis Greene was particularly critical of Schilder-Schuldner, holding him responsible for the defeat:

> The almost criminal faults of this battle on the part of the Russian commander are so apparent that they hardly need to be pointed out. Without having learned anything about the strength or position of the enemy, and without any reserves whatever of his own, his troops were led blindly to the assault in company columns, along two lines which had no communication with each other, and against an enemy which, as the official report says, was subsequently discovered to be more than four times their own strength![15]

Osman, having only a very small cavalry force, did not attempt to pursue the enemy, and turned his attention to strengthening the defences of Plevna against the next assault, which he expected would come very soon. And, indeed, from Russian headquarters, where the euphoria engendered by the crossing of the Balkans ensured that confidence there was undiminished by the setback, orders went to Krüdener to drive Osman back at once. In preparing for this, Osman concentrated particular attention on the defences of the Grivitza redoubt, and the lines between it and Bukova. He also embarked on the construction of a series of redoubts just east of the town. Although he had won a complete victory on July 20, Osman had been sufficiently impressed by the Russian assaults to call for reinforcements. Mehemet Ali, who had only just taken over as commander in chief, put under Osman's command all the Turkish troops in Western Bulgaria, at Sofia and Novi Bazar. He did not, however, favour Osman's other request, which was for authority to link up with Raouf Pasha, commanding the Turkish troops in the Balkans. Instead, he ordered Osman to hold Plevna and continue to entrench himself there.[16]

15

Osman

I n strengthening the position which he held at Plevna, Osman could count on the traditional ability of the Turkish infantry to construct effective field fortifications. One historian of the siege of Plevna described it thus:

> Simple Anatolian peasants as many of them were, the Turkish linesmen were as at home with their few, rough tools as they had made themselves familiar with their excellent Martini-Peabody rifles. It was, indeed , the Osmanli's ability to 'dig himself in and, from his entrenched position, direct a steady stream of rapid fire against opponents advancing in outmoded column formation, that gave him an advantage over the Russian soldier which only factors beyond the power of the man in the Osmanli ranks to control eventually served to redress.[1]

The defensive works along the Janik Bair formed at this stage the key to the Turkish position. Four redoubts were constructed, two north-west of Grivitza and two more further along the ridge to the west. Herbert's battalion was engaged in the construction of Redoubt No 2, of which it formed part of the garrison. All four of these redoubts were square shaped. Herbert described No 2:

> The northern slope of the redoubt, facing the enemy, bordered upon the ravine which played such a conspicuous part in the first battle. It had one ditch or trench for the protection of skirmishers on the southern side of the ravine, and two, one above the other, on the crest of the opposite bank. There were on each flank trenches running at obtuse angles to the redoubt, whence an attacking enemy could be taken by flank fire.[2]

A covered way led southwards to Redoubt No 1. Each of these redoubts was occupied by two battalions, with half a battery, while the two smaller redoubts each contained one battalion and one or two guns. With these hastily constructed fortifications the Turks had created a formidable stronghold shaped by the Janik Bair; from east to west it was three and a half miles long.

The design of these works was fairly basic, and reflected the defensive problem that Osman and his staff must solve. It was necessary to hold a very long line of defence, so the decision was taken to create a series of closed redoubts at key points, with light trenches on the front and flanks. Since the principal weapon to be employed was the rifle, the design must allow for clear fields of fire; it was evident that the Russians would always enjoy a heavy superiority in artillery. The redoubts provided good cover for their garrisons and were mainly located where the ground fell away to their rear, so that the reserves could take up a sheltered position there. As Sir George Clarke pointed out, and as the Russians were to discover to their cost, well sited redoubts that were fully garrisoned could wreak terrible havoc upon attacking infantry; 'with an excellent breechloader and plenty of ammunition, the distance required to repulse an assault is comparatively short.'[3]

The troops worked in relays, by day and night. In the relatively short time available before the coming Russian assault they had created formidable field works. Redoubt No 1 was the largest of the four redoubts, covering Grivitza itself and the Bulgareni road. The parapet was nearly fourteen feet thick, and nine feet high; it was surrounded by deep and broad ditches. In addition to the shelter trenches described by Herbert, a series of rifle pits was dug in front of them, effectively providing three tiers of rifle fire.[4]

In taking up his position at Plevna, Osman was very much aware of the importance of Lovtcha, some twenty miles to the south. It had been occupied by a Cossack unit on July 16, but had not been reinforced. On July 25 Osman dispatched a force of six battalions, under Rifaat Pasha, with one battery and some Circassian cavalry to retake the place. Lovtcha had a population of about 14,000; according to Herbert it 'was considered one of the richest, prettiest, best built, and most advanced towns of Bulgaria.'[5] Rifaat had no difficulty in reoccupying Lovtcha, driving back the Cossacks who had been vigorously supported by many of the Bulgarian inhabitants. Osman may have hoped that reinforcements might have been sent from south of the Balkans to garrison Lovtcha; as it was, Rifaat was left to put it in a state of defence.

Osman, having been given command over the forces in western Bulgaria at Sofia and Novi Bazar, had brought up reinforcements to Plevna in the shape of a brigade from Widdin and eight battalions from Sofia. This gave him a total of thirty-nine battalions, six of which were at Lovtcha with Rifaat. The remainder he reorganised into two divisions each of twelve battalions, two squadrons and twelve guns, with a general reserve of nine battalions, one squadron and thirty-four guns. The 1st Division, commanded by Adil Pasha, was responsible for the northern section, while the 2nd Division (Hassan Pasha) held the eastern and southern sections of the defence works. These included four small redoubts that were more or less completed, but apart from those consisted principally of shelter trenches. The stiff clay soil around Plevna lent itself well to the construction of earthworks and trenches; the latter were deep and narrow, with perpendicular sides. As in the northern sectors, rifle pits had been dug for sharpshooters in advance of the main line of trenches.[6]

It was decided at Russian headquarters that, in order to ensure the success of the next assault on Plevna, additional forces should be made available. Krüdener had in hand Schilder-Schuldner's force, plus three regiments of the 31st Division, the 9th Regiment of Lancers and eight batteries. The 19th Regiment was moved to Nicopolis, to recover from its mauling on July 20. The 124th Regiment was still covering the bridgeheads at Sistova, and two cavalry regiments were with Gourko. He was reinforced on July 29 by the arrival of the 30th Division from the IV Corps, the 1st Brigade of the 32nd Division (from the XI Corps) and the 1st Brigade of the 11th Cavalry Division. This force was under the command of Lieutenant-General Prince Shakofskoi.

Krüdener had, on July 28, telegraphed Russian headquarters for instructions after having carried out a thorough personal reconnaissance of the Turkish positions. He did not at all like what he saw. He received a peremptory reply from the Grand Duke, who could not understand Krüdener's hesitation in carrying out the orders previously given to him. In the face of this, Krüdener had no option but to order an assault, to take place

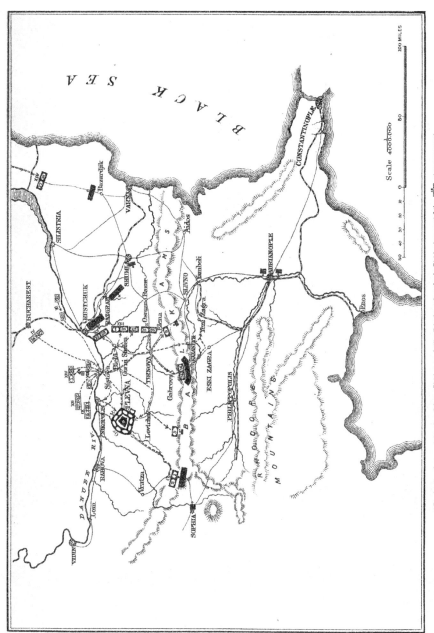

Progress Map No.2 – Second period of the Campaign. From the crossing of the
Danube to the fall of Plevna, June 27 to December 10 1877

Russian infantry assault the Turkish entrenchments at Plevna. (Ollier)

on July 30. Although, being slightly senior, he was in command, he shared responsibility for the attack with Prince Shakofskoi. It was a partnership that might well not work well, as Maurice observed:

> The two men were of very different character. Krüdener had the reputation of being a good soldier, but a man who was inclined to take life easily. Shakofskoi was a man who believed that nobody but an aristocrat could be a good general; he was very quick tempered and impetuous, and was in no sense a scientific soldier.[7]

One particularly valuable part of the reinforcement was however Michael Skobelev, newly returned from the Shipka Pass, who joined Shakofskoi on the latter's march from Tirnova. On July 28 Shakofskoi ordered Skobelev to take the Caucasian Cossack Brigade and advance on Lovtcha, and occupy the place. When he reached his objective Skobelev found that Rifaat had forestalled him, and reported back that the Turks were engaged in strengthening the good defensive position which they had taken up, and that it would require at least an infantry division to support the cavalry if an attempt was to be made to take it. This was much more than could be spared, so Skobelev was directed for the moment merely to watch Lovtcha while the rest of the army concentrated for the assault on Plevna.

When he arrived Shakofskoi reconnoitred the Turkish positions before conferring with Krüdener as to the plan to be adopted. Shakofskoi, who had a great contempt for the Turks, had no doubt that the defeat on July 20 was the fault of Schilder-Schuldner and his lack of determination. He was equally certain that he could do much better, and

Russian infantry contest the outskirts of Plevna. (Budev)

pressured Krüdener into agreeing to dispositions which would give him as free a hand as possible. The intention was to attack in two columns, one advancing from the north-east under Lieutenant-General Veliaminov with the 31st Division, with Schilder-Schuldner's 5th Division in support, and one from the south-east under Shakofskoi with the 1st Brigade of the 30th Division and the 1st Brigade of the 32nd Division. In the rear, near Poradim and between the two columns, stood the general reserve under Krüdener's direct orders, consisting of the 2nd Brigade of the 30th Division and four squadrons of cavalry. Four more squadrons were to act as a link between the two columns. On the extreme right, a cavalry brigade under Major-General Lockarev was to be ready to cross the Vid in order to cut off a Turkish retreat to Sofia, while on the left Skobelev, reinforced with a battalion and four guns, was in addition to watching Lovtcha, to cover Shakofskoi's left and rear. It was Shakofskoi's conviction that the heights above Radischevo would prove to be the critical point of attack.[8] Krüdener's headquarters were on the left of the line of Veliaminov's advance, on the heights about a mile and a half to the east of Grivitza.

The advance began at 7.00 am in thick fog. By 8.00 am the leading troops of the right wing came within range of the Turks who opened fire. The Russian artillery, which had deployed about two miles east of the Grivitza Redoubt (No 1), opened fire at about 8.30 am. For the next four hours there was a vigorous artillery duel, in which the Russians, with eighty guns in action, had the advantage in numbers. It was not until 2.30 pm that Krüdener gave the order for the advance of the infantry This was to be in two columns, one from the north and one from the east. The first column consisted of the 121st Regiment and two battalions of the 123rd Regiment, followed by the 17th and 18th Regiments in reserve. The other column comprised the 1st Battalion of the 123rd Regiment and the 122nd Regiment, with the 20th Regiment in reserve. The leading battalion of the 121st Regiment carried the first line of trenches, but was held up by the second. Soon, however, the following battalion came up and they drove the Turks across the ravine and dashed for the redoubt, where many of them were cut down by the fierce rifle fire. The 121st Regiment fell back across the ravine having lost more than a third of its men and half its officers.[9] The arrival of the 17th and 18th Regiments failed to restore the position; their assaults on the redoubt were also thrown back. The column advancing from the east was equally unsuccessful; the 122nd Regiment was held up on a little mound four hundred yards short of the redoubt and the 20th Regiment's advance was also stalled.

Krüdener had released one of his regiments (the 119th) from his reserve to Shakofskoi; he now at 6.00 pm sent forward one battalion of the 120th Regiment with a squadron of dragoons and two horse guns to the help of the 17th and 18th Regiments who were hard pressed; with this reinforcement they managed to hold their position. As the sun went down, Krüdener ordered another general assault. It went in with desperate courage but broke down in the face of the heavy fire. Obliged to recognise the complete defeat of the right wing of the Russian assault, Krüdener ordered a retreat, covered by the two remaining battalions of the 120th Regiment, and by the 124th Regiment, which had just arrived from Sistova. Exchanges of fire continued all night, and it was daylight on July 31 before the last of the Russian infantry retired to an assembly position at Tristenik and Karagatch.

Russian infantry at Plevna. (Ollier)

Meanwhile Shakofskoi's attack with the left wing had begun with the descent of the Radischevo ridge by the 125th (Kursk) and 126th (Rylsk) Regiments. However, as they began to climb the opposite slope, the troops were met by murderous rifle fire, and suffered fearful losses. Nonetheless, by 5.00 pm they had carried the two small redoubts in their immediate front, from which the Turks withdrew, saving all their guns bar two. On Shakofskoi's left, parties of his troops had managed to advance through a ravine to the edge of Plevna itself. He had committed his 118th Regiment, so now had only one regiment in reserve; of his artillery, four guns were with Skobelev and three had been knocked out, so he had 21 in reserve. His position was precarious; although he had captured two redoubts, the Turks were clearly massing for a counter-attack. There was no hope of support from the right wing; even if it had not taken the fearful pounding which it had endured, it was over five miles march from Shakofskoi's column. The 119th Regiment, which had been sent to reinforce him, had been diverted to face a Turkish column advancing into the gap. Shakofskoi now committed his final reserve, so that by 6.00 pm all his troops were engaged. It was soon clear that no further progress was possible, with the Turks threatening the Russian troops on three sides, and as soon as it was dark the order was given to fall back to the Radischevo ridge. Next morning the whole force retreated to Poradim.[10]

Although he had been heavily defeated, Shakofskoi had Skobelev to thank for not having faced an even more serious disaster. Under cover of the thick fog, Skobelev moved his force out of Bogot at 5.00 am, and succeeded in reaching the village of Krishin, having taken the Turks entirely by surprise. He occupied the heights above the village and then with two squadrons and four guns worked his way through the vineyards to within 300 yards of Plevna. From the heights he looked down on the whole Turkish position, seeing the large Turkish reserve, which he estimated at 20,000 men. When Shakofskoi opened fire at about 10.00 am, Skobelev's four guns joined in, whereupon a force of some 4,000 of the enemy advanced against him. He fell back to Krishin; but he had spotted that if the Turks moved some two miles down the road from Plevna to Lovtcha they could take a hill from which they could enfilade the whole of Shakofskoi's line. He scattered the bulk of his cavalry to cover the flank in accordance with his orders and then, with the remaining four *sotnias*, the infantry battalion and four guns moved to the attack of the Turkish infantry that had assailed him.

Keeping three companies and two *sotnias* in reserve until 4.00 pm he maintained the fight all day and until after dark, when he withdrew, taking with him his wounded, reassembling what was left of his scattered force at Krishin before retreating first to Bogot and then to Pelisat. Greene wrote of Skobelev's force that 'it was hotly engaged during the whole day, and, although small in numbers, was handled with such skill as to establish beyond doubt the military genius of this brilliant young general.'[11]

The Russian defeat was complete. Out of 30,000 men engaged, they had lost 169 officers and 7,136 men; 2,400 had been killed. The regiments which had suffered the most were the 121st and 126th Regiments; the latter lost 725 killed and 1,200 wounded, or 75% of its whole strength. Turkish casualties are unclear; they admitted to 1,200 killed and wounded, but the total was almost certainly much greater than this.[12] News of the defeat was carried back to Sistova by evacuated wounded, and in a highly exaggerated form, causing a grand stampede among both inhabitants and camp followers on both sides of the bridge.

The assault on Plevna as sketched by the *Illustrated London News* artist. (*Illustrated London News*)

As had been the case after his victory on July 20, Osman made no move to follow up his beaten enemy. Greene weighed the wisdom of this:

It would appear at first sight as if Osman made a great mistake in not pursuing the force which he had so signally defeated, especially as he probably had a considerable force of fresh troops which had not been engaged at all, and as the Russians had retreated in two columns on divergent country roads totally independent of each other, leaving the great high-road midway between them perfectly open. Yet it is a fact that every offensive movement of the Turks throughout the war came to naught, and it is more than probable that Osman did exactly the wisest thing; he felt sure that the Russians would come to him again as soon as they got a few more men together, and he therefore kept his troops on their own ground, and set them to work as hard as they could with their spades.[13]

Maurice was of much the same view, observing that 'Osman had little cavalry, few trained staff officers, and neither the character nor organisation of his force were suited to sudden and unforeseen efforts.'[14]

In fact, there was a brief encounter on the following morning, which Herbert described, when a Russian regiment and some batteries came back within range and opened fire. Osman sent all his available cavalry, a light battery and an infantry battalion; but the Russian movement had no doubt been made only to cover the retreat, and they soon fell back. Herbert remarked that 'no pursuit took place; for, truly, the Turks were not in a condition to pursue.'[15]

Not surprisingly, commentators have been extremely critical of the Russian leadership. Krüdener's abandonment to Shakofskoi of all responsibility for the left wing has been particularly censured, as has the weakness of the general reserve. The reconnaissances made had failed to reveal much information about the Turkish positions. The infantry assaults had not been preceded by the action of skirmishers, a fact which Herbert noticed and which surprised him. And, in particular, there was little cooperation between the three arms in the course of the battle – with the striking exception of Skobelev's little force, whose exploits were the one redeeming feature of Russian operations.[16]

Regrettably the Russian leaders were swift to blame each other. Shakofskoi complained that Krüdener had not supported him; on the other hand Krüdener asserted that Shakofskoi had not obeyed his orders, and that he should not have moved to the assault without further orders. Nor was Grand Duke Nicholas free from blame; he gave the orders for an assault against a position about which he knew little or nothing, and in the teeth of the reservations of the man on the spot.

Archibald Forbes, who had been present at Shakofskoi's headquarters throughout the battle, took his report personally first to Bucharest and then, fearing that the Russians might censor his news of their defeat, decided to ride the eighty miles across the Carpathians and over the Hungarian border to Kronstadt. Reflecting on the outcome of the battle a day or two later from Bucharest, he contemplated the possibility that the Turks might advance to cut the Russian line of communications, sweeping aside the broken forces of Krüdener and Shakofskoi:

Beaten, disorganised, and weakened, there can be no certainty that this force is able to withstand the Turks advancing in force against it, and the result of another battle that should go against the Russians would be the clearance for the Turks of the road to Sistova, and the absolute severance of the whole Russian force in Bulgaria from its base in Roumania.[17]

Alternatively, he thought, Osman might march on Tirnova and join hands there with Mehemet Ali, in which case, he wondered, what would be the plight of Gourko and Radetzky's VIII Corps, 'jammed in the Balkans or dispersed in reckless raids on the further side'?

It was now evident not only to the Russian high command, but also to Gorchakov, that Roumanian assistance was essential. There had already been some cooperation, with Roumanian troops covering the Russian deployment and supporting with their artillery the Danube crossing and the attack on Nicopolis. Receiving a pressing demand for further support, Prince Charles and his ministers agreed to provide it, but only on the basis of settled terms. Agreeing these was not entirely straightforward, since the Russians attempted to impose unreasonable conditions, such as the incorporation of Roumanian troops in Russian units.[18] For its part, the Roumanian government insisted on a separate line of operations along the River Isker. Finally, after protracted negotiations, it was agreed that, retaining their separate identity and leadership, the Roumanian divisions should form the right wing of the Russian army. From the Roumanian point of view it was necessary that the independence of the country proclaimed by its parliament should be underlined by military success, and that it should be seen that Roumania had come to Russia's aid.

There was one ticklish question to be resolved. At a meeting on August 28 with Grand Duke Nicholas and the Tsar, Prince Charles made it clear that he intended to command his own troops in person. In his memoirs he recorded the reaction:

> The Grand Duke objects then that this decision will cause difficulties, as naturally it is not possible that the Prince should be placed under the orders of a Russian general. The Prince answered rather vivaciously; certainly he can't accept that, it is an impossibility; but on the contrary one could put ten Russian generals under his orders. The Emperor listened in silence to this exchange of words ... But before the Prince had finished dressing Grand Duke Nicholas comes to him, and offers him, by order of the Emperor, the supreme command over all Russian troops around Plevna.[19]

Lieutenant-General Zotov, the commander of the IV Corps, was to serve as his Chief of Staff, and second in command, thus ensuring effective Russian control of the operations, and over the Roumanian troops taking part.

It would, however, take some time before the Roumanian divisions could be brought over the Danube and fully deployed. Now was the time for the Turks to take advantage of their situation and strike an effective blow. It would be for Mehemet Pasha to lead it; he had arrived at Shumla on July 22 to take over the supreme command from Abdul Kerim.

16

Mukhtar

Far away to the east, in the remote mountains of the Caucasus a different, and entirely separate war was being fought. Like the war in Europe, however, it was being fought over terrain that had frequently been traversed by these combatants. And both the terrain and the climate presented severe difficulties for the armies that must operate there. The climate was marked by extremes of heat and cold:

> In the summer in the highlands and mountain passes the sun burns like fire; but the air is sharp, exciting and keen, and the skin of the face and hands, unsoftened by the least moisture, becomes cracked and dried, and peels off, leaving a scar resembling the marks produced by a burn, while at the same time the body is so cold that winter clothing is necessary. In the winter, when the sun is hidden by heavy clouds, vast quantities of snow cover the country to a depth of several feet, the tracks become obliterated, all communication between the villages is stopped, and the wretched inhabitants are obliged, like people on board ship, to make such provision for themselves and their animals as may sustain them for days altogether.[1]

Bayazid. (*Illustrirte Geschichte des Orientalischen Krieges von 1876-1878*)

170

Erzerum. (Fauré)

The principal area of operations was the Armenian plateau, of which Erzerum was the centre and much the most important city. It had figured prominently in all the previous wars between Russia and Turkey. The plateau rises some 6,000 feet above sea level. The population of Erzerum in 1877 was about 60,000; it was the capital of the *vilayet* or province to which it gave its name. Its importance was such that it must necessarily be the principal objective of any Russian advance into Armenia. Erzerum lies 115 miles from Trebizond and the same distance from Batum, both important ports on the Black Sea. Kars, the fortress so ably defended by Sir Fenwick Williams during the Crimean War, is about 110 miles north-east of Erzerum. This was one of the key defensive points inside the Turkish frontier, the others being the fortresses of Ardahan and Bayazid, in addition to Batum. Bayazid, which lies in a valley south of Mount Ararat, was in a poor state of defence, but the other three had, in the twenty years since the Crimean War, been strengthened and extended. Each consisted of a stone citadel, with from eight to twelve detached forts, partly in masonry and partly composed of earthworks. Kars was much the best equipped, with 300 guns. The work of improving the defences of those fortresses had been superintended by Faizi Pasha, who would serve as Mukhtar's chief of staff in the coming campaign.[2]

On the Russian side of the boarder the principal towns were Tiflis, Erivan, Alexandropol and Poti. The latter was Russia's southernmost port on the Black Sea, at the mouth of the River Rion, but it was much inferior to Batum, whose excellent port the Russians had long coveted. Tiflis, the capital of Georgia, was much the largest city in Russian Trans Caucasus, having in 1877 some 100,000 inhabitants. It was connected by rail to Poti. Erivan, about 110 miles to the south of Tiflis, was a walled city with a population of 12,000. Fifty-five miles north-west of Erivan lies Alexandropol, of about

Trebizond. (Fauré)

Tiflis. (Fauré)

17,000 inhabitants. Heavily fortified by Russia since its acquisition, Alexandropol did not present an attractive appearance:

> Its surroundings are desolate and gloomy in the extreme. It would be difficult to conceive any country more bare and sterile than the plateau on which it is built. In the town itself there are a few trees, but there are none to be seen in the surrounding country. The destruction of wood on the slopes of the Ararat chain has ruined the agriculture of the district. The rivers, which were formerly well filled, now only consist of small streams deep down between high and sterile banks.[3]

In this unappetising place the Russians had concentrated some 60,000 men during the winter of 1876-1877, camped mainly to the north and south of the town. For the unfortunate troops it cannot have been a comfortable time. As the winter passed, the Russian army was distributed to the centres from which, in the spring, it was intended to advance. There were four of such bases, and they had been chosen for their proximity to the principal Turkish fortresses that would be the first objectives of the invasion.

On the right, based on Kutais, was the Rion detachment under Lieutenant-General Oklobju, consisting of sixteen battalions, six field batteries of 48 guns and two regiments of Cossack cavalry with 12 horse artillery guns. Its orders were to cover the Black Sea coast and to operate against Batum. It was connected with the remaining main columns, operating separately. Next in line came the Akhaltsik detachment consisting of the 39th Division, with ten Cossack squadrons, 28 guns and 6 of horse artillery, commanded by Lieutenant-General Devel, with Ardahan as its objective. The Alexandropol detachment, aimed at Kars, led by Lieutenant-General Heimann, was accompanied by General Loris-Melikov, himself an Armenian, and was the largest group. It consisted of the 4th Grenadier Division of the Caucasus, the 19th Division, 16 squadrons of Caucasian Dragoons, 22 of Caucasian Cossacks, 6 of Daghestan Cossacks and 8 of Volga Cossacks, together organised in two cavalry divisions. This detachment had 92 field guns and 30 of horse artillery. Finally, on the left, came the Erivan detachment, under Lieutenant-General Tergukassov. This consisted of the 38th Division (with 32 guns) a Dragoon regiment, and four regiments of Kuban Cossacks, 18 squadrons in all, with 6 horse artillery guns. This force had Bayazid as its target.[4]

On paper this was a considerable force. There was, however, a considerable disparity between the nominal and actual strength of the Russian forces available. Captain Norman, *The Times* correspondent, gave a lecture after the war to the United Services Institute in which he asserted that 'he was assured on the most excellent authority that the Russian forces in Armenia were only half their nominal strength.'[5]

The original Russian plan for hostilities in Asia had called for a rapid incursion into Turkish territory with a view to seizing Erzerum within six weeks of opening the campaign. For Grand Duke Michael, anxious about the possibility of insurgent activity, this was altogether too bold. Two divisions were required for internal security duties, while another was required for coastal defence. Shortly before the outbreak of war another division was held back in case of trouble in Chechnya and Dagestan. The revised plan now contemplated reconnaissances in force in the western sector against Ardahan and Batum, while in the centre and to the east Kars was to be kept under observation and a demonstration made against Bayazid.[6]

General Heimann, commander of the Russian Alexandropol Detachment. (*Russes et Turcs*)

General Tergukassov, commander of the Russian Erivan Detachment. (*Russes et Turcs*)

Mukhtar Pasha arrived in Erzerum to take up his command on March 30. Hozier rated him highly:

> Young, active, and intelligent, of a genial disposition, cheerful manners, hard working, and able to enter into the details of everything connected with his command, he soon gained the confidence and respect of both officers and men ... His appearance was soldier like, his tones decisive, and his arms and accoutrements always clean and well put on ... At all times energetic and diligent, he likewise possessed great personal courage and coolness.[7]

In addition to those qualities Mukhtar, who spoke French well, was also invariably helpful and considerate to the European journalists who accompanied his headquarters.

The size of Mukhtar's army at the outbreak of war is uncertain. Greene, relying on the information obtained in April by Charles Williams of *The Standard* from the British military commissioner General Sir Arnold Kemball, put the total at 67 battalions including regulars and first, second and third reserves, with about 1,000 cavalry. Taking the battalions as having an average strength of 750 men, he arrived at a total of 70,250, although he noted that Williams thought the number much less, putting it at 47,500. The *Daily News* correspondent reported that Mukhtar had told him that, exclusive of the garrison of Batum, he had a total of 52,000 men. Hozier arrived at a different figure again, concluding that the grand total comprised 63,000 infantry, 5,000 cavalry and 180 guns.[8]

These figures all excluded the garrison artillery, which had been assigned to the four fortresses. The Turkish artillery was considered to be the best arm of the service. Its field guns were principally Krupp six pounder steel breechloaders; the horse artillery had four

General Oklobju, commander of the Russian Rion Detachment. (*Russes et Turcs*)

pounders, and the mountain guns were Krupp bronze 2¼ inch rifled pieces. The draught horses, some of which had been imported from Hungary, were strong and useful animals capable of great endurance. On the other hand, Mukhtar was severely handicapped by his shortage of cavalry, and the fact that what he had was no good:

> Badly mounted, indifferently armed, without discipline, and perfectly ignorant of even the rudiments of drill, the Turkish commander was unable to avail himself of the services of the cavalry in his army for the performance of those legitimate duties on which the safety of a corps mainly depends.[9]

The inevitable consequence was that Mukhtar was often completely unable to monitor the movements of the Russian forces opposed to him.

The infantry, on the other hand, although badly dressed and ill equipped in other respects, had at least for the most part the excellent Peabody-Martini rifle. In Asia, as in Europe, it was found to be strong and durable, standing up well to a lot of rough usage. Each soldier was supposed to carry 150 rounds of ammunition, with reserves carried on 32 ponies attached to each battalion. In practice, however, they frequently went into action with a much smaller supply.

The Russian advance began immediately upon the declaration of war on April 24. The Grand Duke Michael urged his troops on with a grandiloquent order of the day calling on them to defend the honour and dignity of their country: 'You have behind you the glorious past of the Army of the Caucasus, before you the plains and mountains red with the blood of your fathers and your brothers!' Kars being obviously the toughest nut to crack, it was natural that Loris-Melikov, the de facto leader of the army, should take effective command of the Alexandropol group aimed at that fortress. He had served for many years in the Caucasus, and had particularly distinguished himself in the siege of Kars in the Crimean War. Now aged fifty-three, he was fluent in French, Armenian, Turkish, Tartar and Persian, and was particularly well fitted to lead the campaign, although instinctively cautious, and protective of the lives of his men.

After his cavalry had crossed the River Arpa at various points, Loris-Melikov's engineers immediately began the construction of two pontoon bridges over the river. One, below Alexandropol, took seven hours to complete while the other, at Baiadour, took only two and a half hours. As soon as that was complete, the two brigades of the 4th Grenadier Division crossed and set off on the road to Kars. The weather was foul, with heavy rain and a violent cold wind, and the roads were deep in mud. Progress during the first few days was slow, although no Turkish resistance was encountered; such troops as there were between the frontier and Kars at once fell back on the fortress.[10]

By April 28 Loris-Melikov had reached Zaim, on the River Kars, some fifteen miles north-west of the fortress, on the road to Ardahan, thus cutting off communication between the two places. It seemed clear to Mukhtar that his forces would be heavily outnumbered, so leaving some 15,000 men as a garrison in Kars, he retreated with 5,000 men to the Saghanli Dagh, a mountain range about 35 miles south-west. Kars was for the moment the least of his problems; it was well armed and provisioned, and the garrison was strong enough to ensure a prolonged defence. The rest of Mukhtar's command was in by no means such a satisfactory state, being completely disorganised and unprepared to resist a Russian invasion. Since war had been threatening for so very long, and the strength of the Russian forces well known, this was inexcusable. It meant that Mukhtar must for the moment avoid a major encounter in the open field, and hope that the fortresses would be able to hold up the Russian advance for long enough for him to get his army into a proper shape to resist it.

Kars. (*Illustrirte Geschichte des Orientalischen Krieges von 1876-1878*)

In fact the Turks believed the Russians to be in much greater strength than was actually the case, and Mukhtar took his force still further back, taking up a position on June 2 at Zevin, about 55 miles north-east of Erzerum. Meanwhile Loris-Melikov began probing the defences of Kars, while sending a force of cavalry southwards to Khagisman on the Passin-Su. On May 8 his patrols picked up a Turkish courier; the dispatches which he carried included a letter from the commandant of Ardahan, Hussein Sabri Pasha, setting out the concerns which he had with regard to his troops and detailing the weak points of the fortifications.[11] Loris-Melikov decided to strike while the iron was hot. He detached a substantial force under Lieutenant-General Heimann to reinforce Devel's detachment from Akhaltsik, which had arrived in front of Ardahan on April 28.

Heimann took with him the 13th (Erivan) and 15th (Tiflis) Grenadier Regiments, 24 guns, a Dragoon regiment and eight *sotnias* of Cossacks, a force of some 8,000 in all. He reached Ardahan on May 13, as did Loris-Melikov himself, who had decided to take personal command of the assault on the fortress. The latter reconnoitred the place next day, finding that there were six particularly strong forts armed with heavy guns, but which were commanded by hills some two miles off. On two of these hills, Gheliaverde on the east and Ramazan on the west there had been constructed further strong fortifications. The Emir-Oglu Tabia, on Gheliaverde, was unfinished.

Hussein Sabri was a man of little ability. He commanded a garrison of some 10,000 troops, and his concerns about their quality were well founded. They largely consisted of Kurdish recruits, and were mingled with the few regular troops at his disposal. His commanders were not much use, either; the only one of any energy was a European, Colonel Kaftar Bey. In planning for an attack on Ardahan, Devel had thought it necessary to begin by assaulting Ramazan; Loris-Melikov disagreed, believing that this would take too long, and would involve heavy casualties. Having read Hussein Sabri's letter, he favoured an attack on Gheliaverde on its southern side, where the defences were in a poor condition.[12]

On May 15 the Russian siege artillery arrived, and during the night batteries were constructed, enabling a heavy bombardment of Gheliaverde to begin on the following morning. This inflicted great damage on the fortifications and heavy casualties among the defenders. Meanwhile Devel pushed forward two regiments, the 153rd (Baku) and 156th (Elisavetpol), up the hill on its eastern side, reaching the summit at 1.00 am, from where they drove the Turkish infantry back 600 yards to the fort of Emir-Oglu Tabia. After a brief rest, Devel advanced against this work, capturing it at 1.00 pm. That night and next day the Russians brought up their artillery in preparation for a bombardment of the remaining Turkish positions, which began at 3.00 pm. On May 17 Loris-Melikov sent in an emissary to Hussein Sabri with a summons to surrender, which was ignored. He had intended to defer any assault until May 19, to ensure that the bombardment had the maximum effect; but late on May 17 it was clear that it had taken a tremendous toll on both the Turkish fortifications and their defenders, some of whom appeared to be withdrawing. In reponse to Heimann's entreaties, Loris-Melikov decided to put in an immediate attack; at 6.00 pm the 13th and 16th Grenadier Regiment and the 153rd Regiments were launched against the south-east of Ardahan.

Once the Russians broke into the town there was a period of intensive house-to-house fighting. Hussein Sabri defended himself for some time in a solidly built house, during which his Chief of Staff, Colonel Ahmed Aga, was killed at his side. But the

Turkish resistance gradually slackened, as the Kurdish recruits and irregular troops began to panic and, falling back, took with them the regular troops that had been putting up a stout defence. The Turkish retreat gathered pace, and they disappeared into the mountains to the west; no attempt was made to defend Ramazan at all.

An English correspondent described the retreat of what was left of Hussein Sabri's force:

> The remains of the unfortunate garrison of Ardahan straggle along the road in the direction of Erzerum; and as these men carry arms and are generally without food, and always without money, they plunder, and often with extreme violence, the wayfarers or villagers of the surrounding country. The condition of these runaway soldiers is very pitiable; and as in civilised places hunger often drives men towards crime, it is not surprising that such famished wretches are careless about the injuries they inflict upon others in order to provide themselves with food.[13]

By 9.00 pm the whole of Ardahan was in Russian hands. Total Russian losses during the operation were 539. They had captured 1,000 prisoners, 92 guns and a large quantity of ammunition and stores. The bodies of some 1,750 Turkish troops were buried after the battle, and it was estimated that total Turkish casualties, in addition to those taken prisoner, were over 3,000.[14] The defeat caused dismay and discouragement on the Turkish side; but it has been pointed out that one side effect was to confirm old Caucasus hands like Heimann in their disregard of the power of modern weapons, and their belief in the effectiveness of the bayonet.[15]

Lieutenant-General Heimann's troops storm Ardahan. (*Russes et Turcs*)

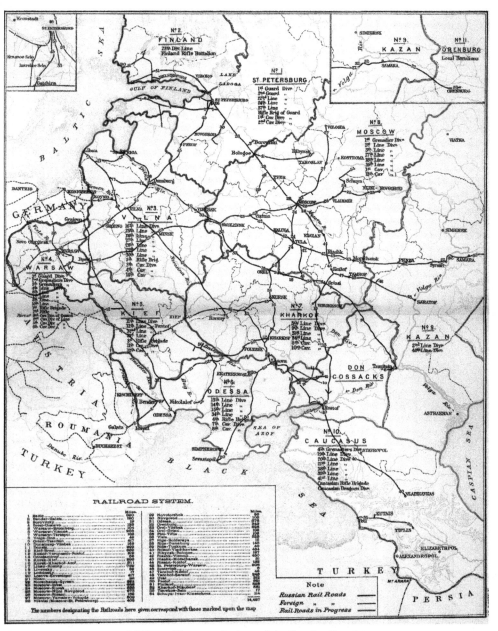

Military Circumscriptions of the Russian Empire

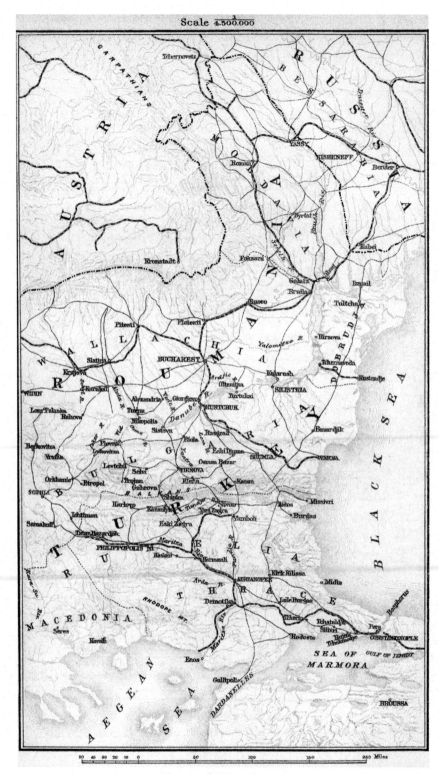

Theatre of War in Europe

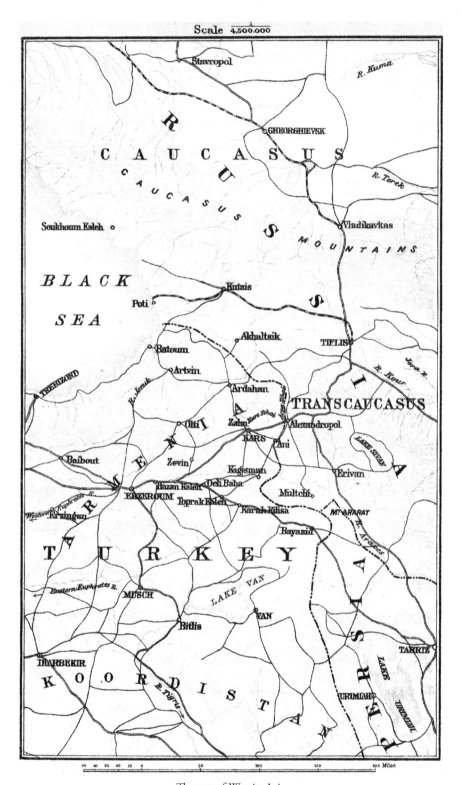

Scale 1/4,500,000

Theatre of War in Asia

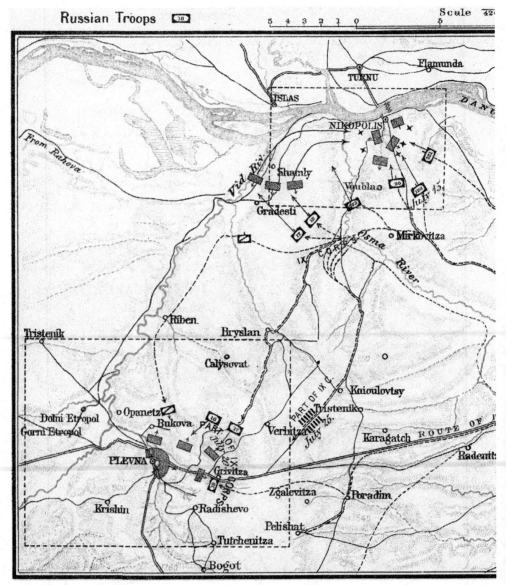

Map of the vicinity of Sistova, Nicopolis and Plevna to illustrate the movements of the Russians immediately after the passage of the Danube. The rectangles shown are reduced versions of three

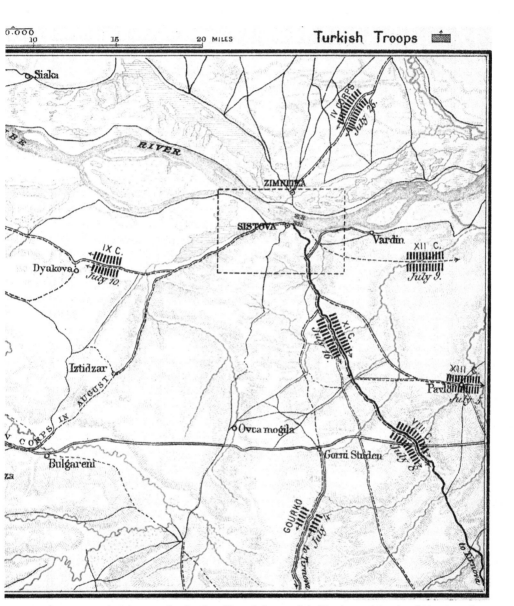

0.000
10   15   20   MILES

Siaka

DE

RIVER

IV CORPS
July 25.

ZIMNITZA

SISTOVA

Vardin

IX C.
Dyakova
July 10.

XII C.
July 9.

Iztidzar

X C.
July 6.

V   CORPS   IN   AUGUST

XIII C.
Pavlo
July 5.

Bulgareni

za

Ovca mogila

Gorni Studen

VIII C.
July 8.

GOURKO
July 4.

to Ternova

to Tirnova

maps that appear elsewhere in this book – (from left to right): The Second Battle of Plevna, July 30 1877; Plan of the positions near Nicopolis; The crossing at Simnitza-Sistova, June 27 1877

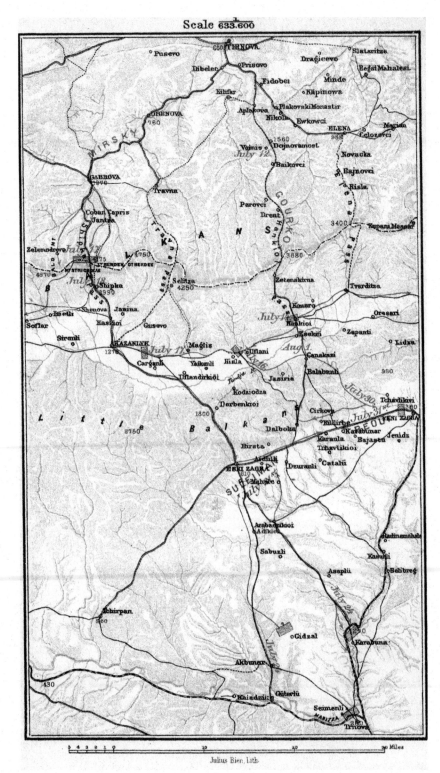

Julius Bien, Lith.

Map of the Balkans near the Shipka Pass to illustrate Gourko's operations in July

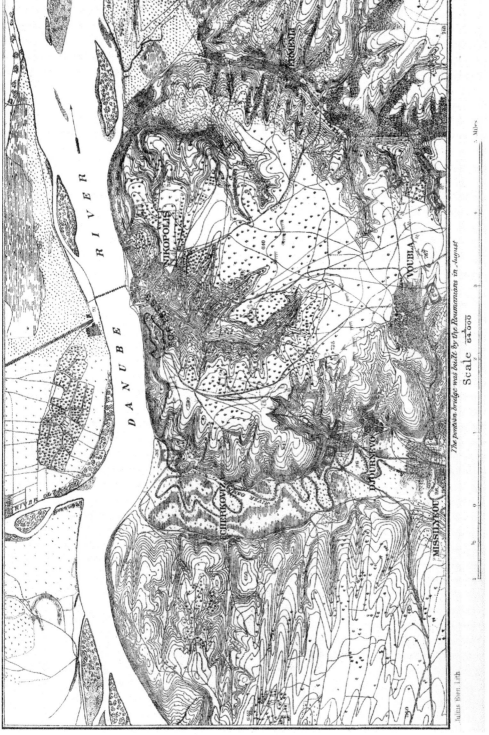

The pontoon bridge was built by the Roumanians in August

Scale 1/64,000

Julius Bien, Lith.

Plan of the positions near Nicopolis

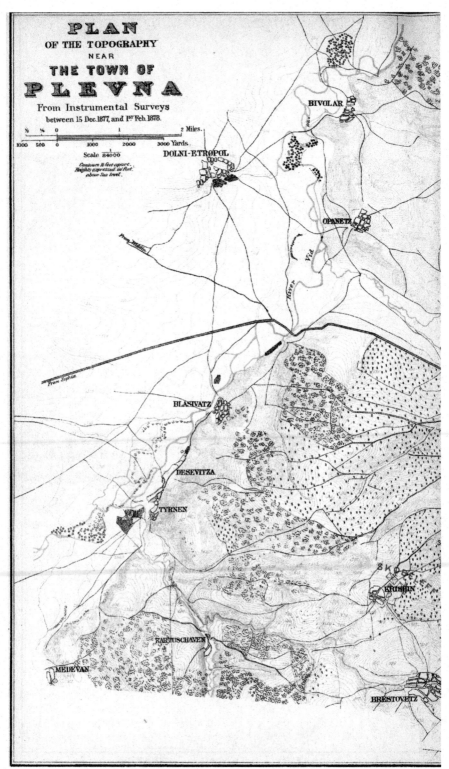

The Second Battle of Plevna, July 30 1877

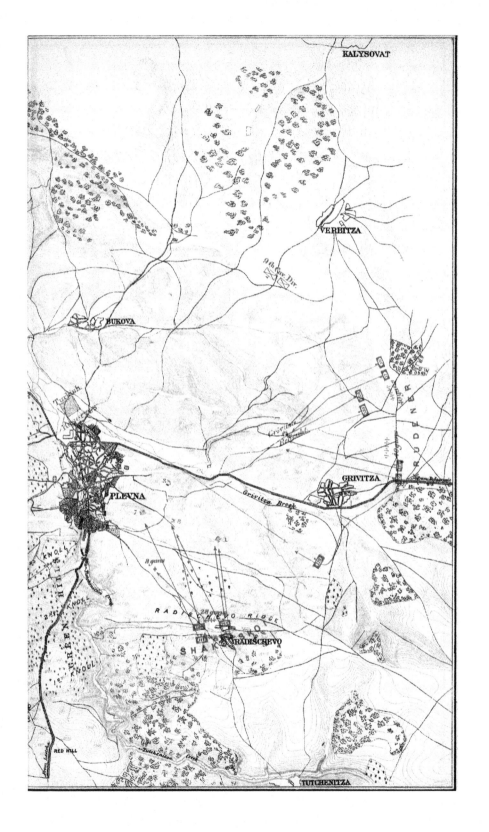

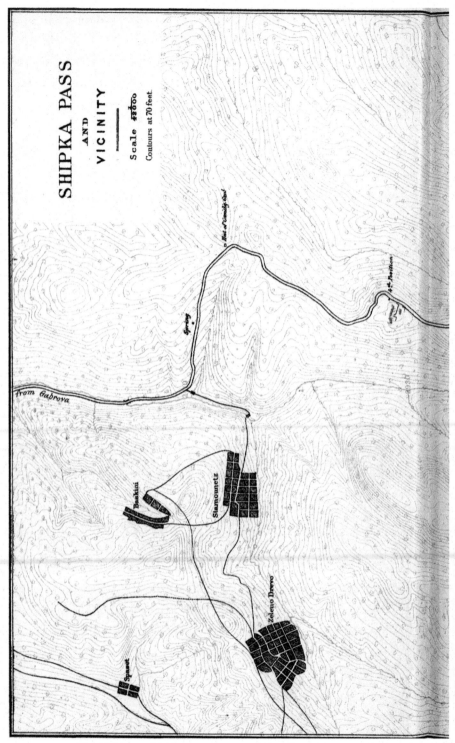

Shipka Pass and vicinity, with troop dispositions, August 1877

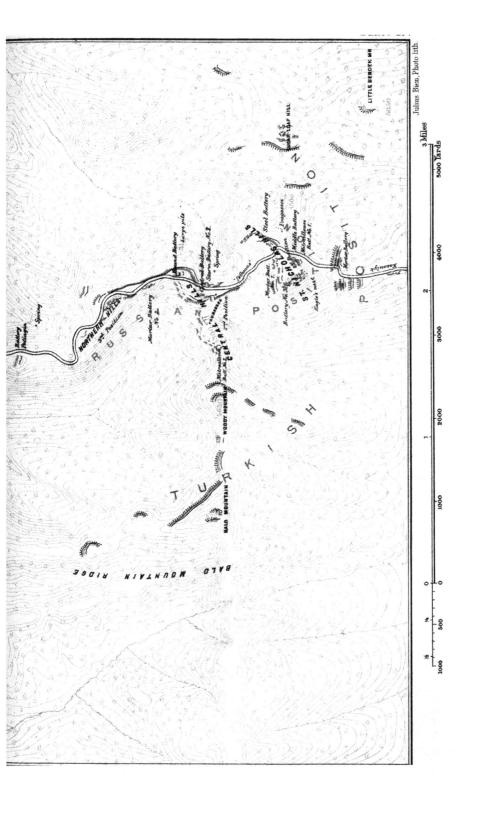

Julius Bien, Photo lith.

BALD MOUNTAIN RIDGE

BALD MOUNTAIN

T U R K I S H

WOODY MOUNTAIN

CENTRAL — Position

Mitrailleuse Batt.

Battery Position

Spring

NORTHERN HILLS

3rd Position

R U S S A N

Mortar Battery No. 2

Battery

Goor. Battery No. 2

Spring

Abattis

Platform

Sprye pits

Battery Position

P O S I

Mortar Feint

Batteryi

Battery No. 1

Eagle's nest

Middle Battery

S N I C H O L A S

Steel Battery

Magazines

Kamuuijk

Mortar Battery

Prism

P O S I T I O N

SUGAR LOAF HILL

LITTLE BERDEK MR

5650

5600

5500

3 Miles

5000 Yards

4000

3000

2000

1000

500

1000

0

¾

½

0

1

2

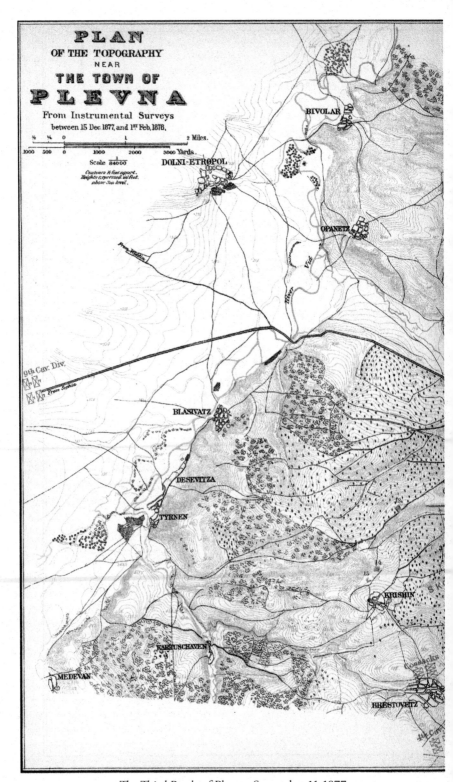

The Third Battle of Plevna, September 11 1877

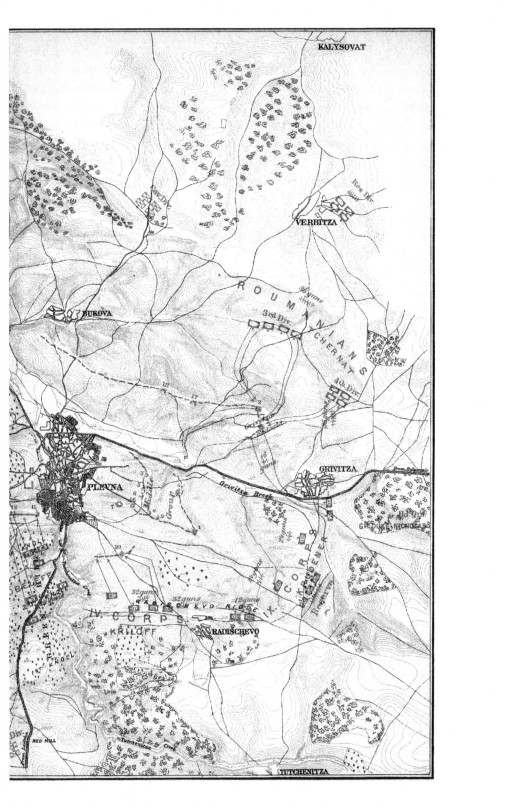

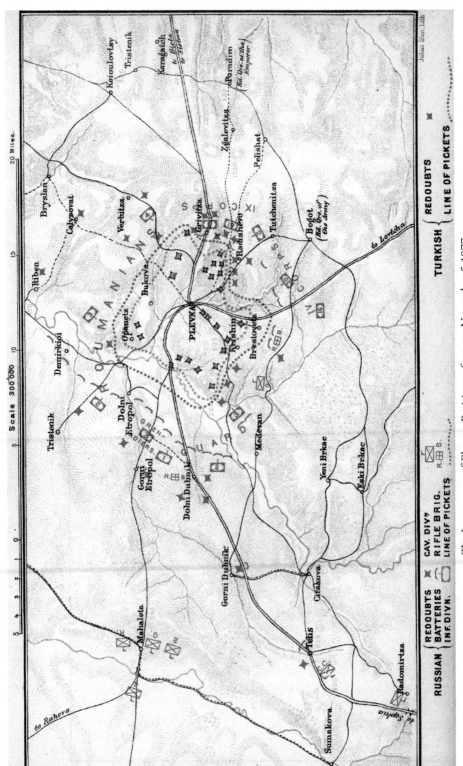

The Investment of Plevna. Positions of troops November 5 1877

RUSSIAN { REDOUBTS ▦
BATTERIES ⊠
INF. DIVN. ▭

CAV. DIV⁵ ★
RIFLE BRIG. ▭
LINE OF PICKETS ········

⊠ R.▦ B.

TURKISH { REDOUBTS ▨
LINE OF PICKETS ········

Julius Bien, Lith.

Scale 300'000

20 Miles.

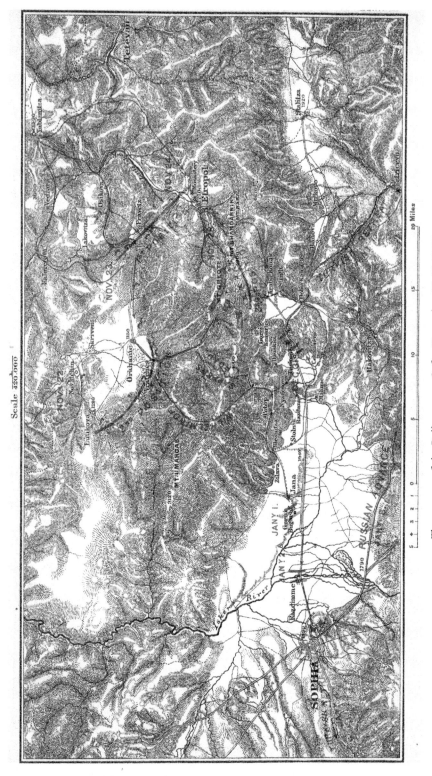

The passage of the Balkans near Sofia, December 25-31 1877

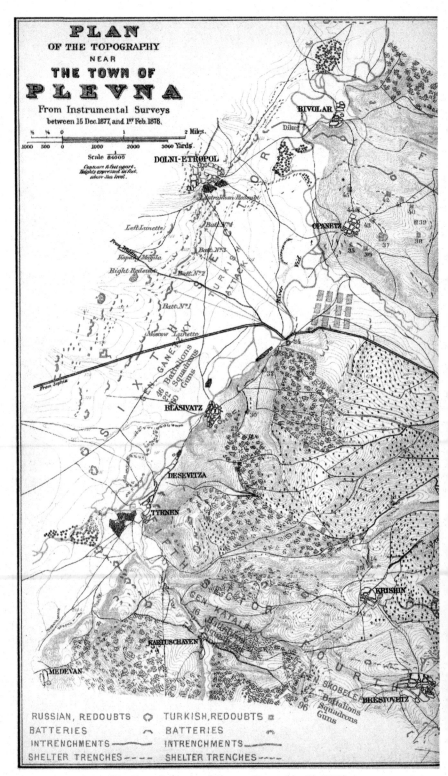

The Fourth Battle of Plevna, December 10 1877

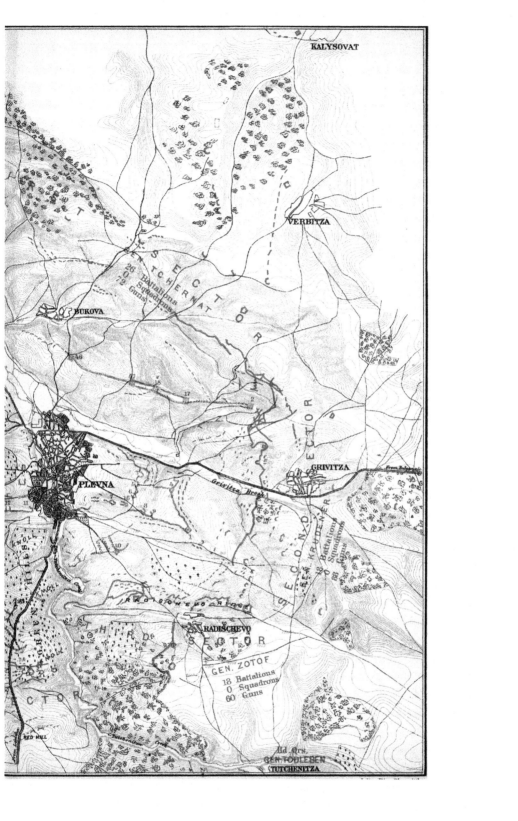

KALYSOVAT

VERBITZA

TCHERNAT SECTOR
26 Battalions
99 Squadrons
72 Guns

BUKOVA

GRIVITZA

PLEVNA

Grivitza Brook

SECOND SECTOR
GEN KRÜDENER
Battalions
Squadrons
Guns

KNOLL

RADISCHEVO RIDGE

RADISCHEVO

HIRD SECTOR
GEN. ZOTOF
18 Battalions
0 Squadrons
60 Guns

RED HILL

Hd Qrs.
GEN TODLEBEN
TUTCHENITZA

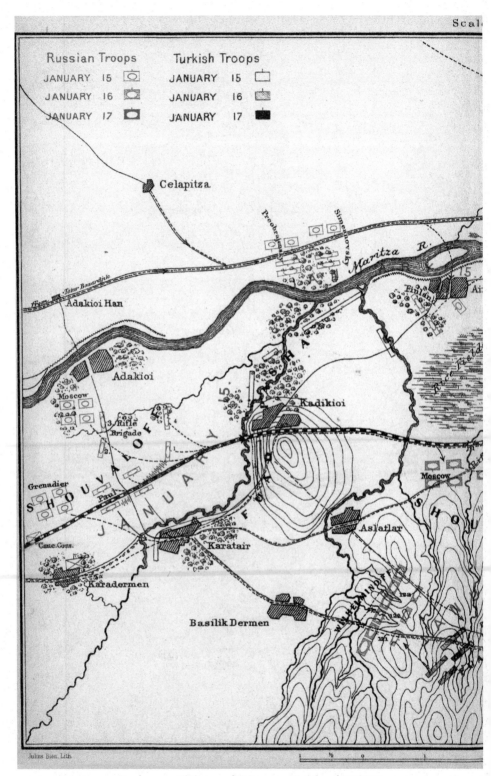

Battles near Philippopolis, January 15, 16 and 17 1878

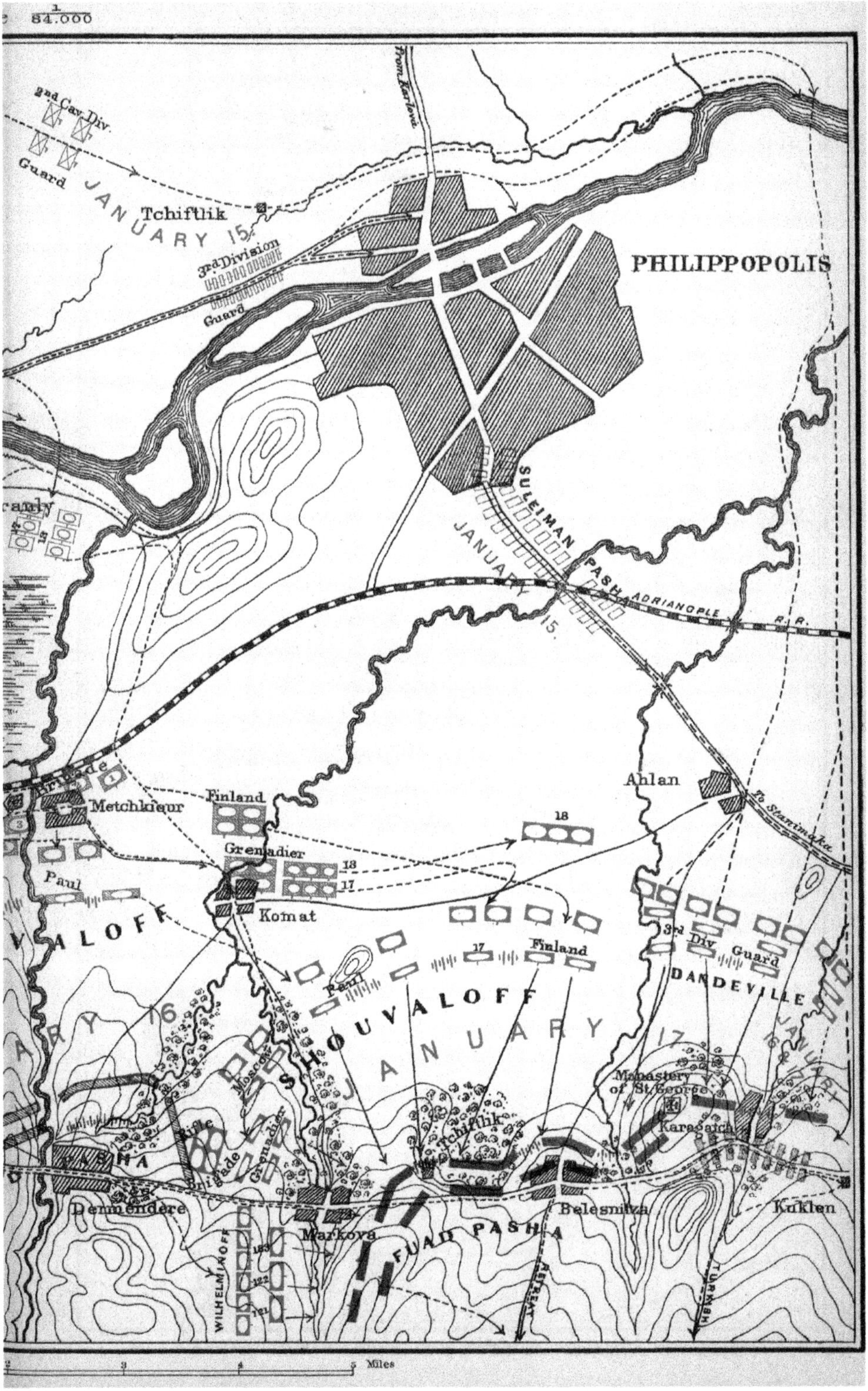

2nd Cav Div.

Guard

Tchiftlik

3rd Division
Guard

JANUARY 15.

PHILIPPOPOLIS

SULEIMAN PASHA

JANUARY 15.

ADRIANOPLE

R.R.

To Starimakra

Ahlan

18

Metchkieur

Finland

Grenadier

18
11

Komat

Paul

VALOFF

Paul

17

Finland

3rd Div Guard

DANDEVILLE

SHOUVALOFF

JANUARY 16

JANUARY 17

JANUARY

Monastery
of St George

Karagatch

Tchiftlik

PASHA

Dennendere

WILHELMINOFF

Markova

FUAD PASHA

Beslesnitza

Kuklen

Miles

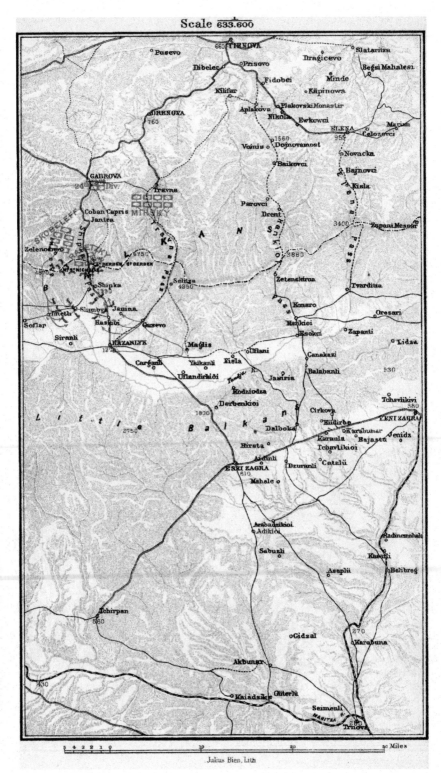

Map of the Balkans near the Shipka Pass to illustrate the capture of the Turkish Army at Shipka

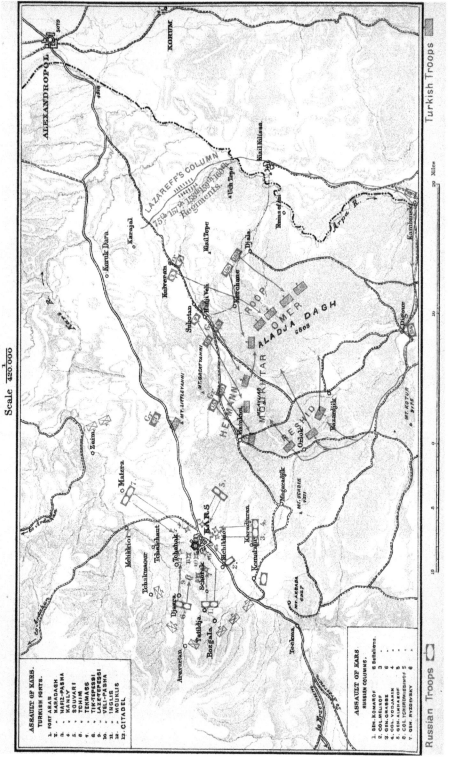

Scale $\frac{1}{420:000}$

Battle of Aladja Dagh, October 15 1877 and the Assault on Kars November 17 1877

Turkish Troops

Russian Troops

ASSAULT OF KARS.
TURKISH FORTS.

1. FORT ARAB
2. " KARADAGH
3. " HAFIZ-PASHA
4. " KANLY
5. " SOUVARI
6. " TCHIM
7. " TEKMASS
8. " TIKTEPESSI
9. " LAZ-TEPESSI
10. " VELI-PASHA
11. " INGLIS
12. " MOUKLIS
13. CITADEL

ASSAULT OF KARS.
RUSSIAN COLUMNS.

1. GEN. KOMAROF .... 8 Battalions.
2. " MELIKOF ..... 3 "
3. " GRABBE ...... 4 "
4. COL. VODJAKIN ... 4 "
5. GEN. ALKHAZOF ... 5 "
6. COL. TCHEREMISSINOF 5 "
7. GEN. RYZDVSKY .. 8 "

LAZAREFF'S COLUMN
7.5th 17.5th & 155th. 156th
Regiments.

Sketches by Irving Montagu, artist of *The Illustrated London News.*

Irving Montagu

A Russian Cossack

Erzerum

'Pending divorce'

'Incompatibility of temper'

'Saluting "The Illustrated News" in Asia Minor'

'Tween decks on a Turkish ironclad'

'Snowed up'

Sketches taken from Irving Montagu, *Camp and Studio* (London 1892).

Russian troops storming Ardahan, May 17 1877. (Strantz)

The fall of Ardahan opened the road to Olti, to which Colonel Komarov, left in command at Ardahan, sent a small detachment, which occupied the place on June 1, the Turkish garrison retreating to Erzerum. Meanwhile Loris-Melikov, with Heimann's detachment, returned to Kars, where he began to establish siege batteries to the north, west and east of the place. At the same time he sent out extensive cavalry patrols to ascertain Mukhtar's position at Zevin, and to maintain contact with the easternmost of the Russian columns under Tergukassov, which had been advancing from Igdir, sixteen miles from the frontier.

Its advance began on April 27. The Turks supposed that the only practicable route to Bayazid, other than through Persian territory, lay between Mount Ararat and Little Ararat, a narrow rocky pass with scarcely any room for two men to march abreast, and utterly impassable by artillery. As a result only a small garrison had been left in Bayazid. However, there existed another route to the west, which the Russians had secretly prepared for the passage of artillery, and it was by this way that Tergukassov's detachment marched. In spite of the preparations made, the route was still appallingly bad, and progress was limited to ten miles per day.[16] By 3.00 am on April 30 Colonel Philippov, Tergukassov's chief of staff, was with the advance guard about ten miles from Bayazid. Moving forward, he occupied the village of Zanghezour; the Turks he found there fell back quickly beyond the heights surrounding Bayazid. Philippov soon saw a column of some 2,000 Turks withdrawing in a south-westerly direction from the fortress by way of a mountain path; it was the entire garrison of Bayazid, and Tergukassov at once moved to occupy the place.

On May 8 Tergukassov resumed his march, occupying Dyndin, north of the Ala Dagh without resistance, and continuing westward along the valley of the Murad-Su. On May 20 his patrols located three separate bodies of Turkish troops at Karakilissa, Alashkert and Az-Khan, which together contained about 10,000 infantry and some Kurdish cavalry. This was the right wing of Mukhtar's army, under Faik Pasha, which he had assembled to cover the road from Bayazid to Erzerum. It put up no resistance, however, and on June 4 the leading Russian troops occupied Karakilissa. North of the town ran the Shahjehol or 'King's Road' to Khagisman, which had been occupied by the Alexandropol detachment, so the objective of establishing contact with Loris- Melikov's main force had been achieved.

Meanwhile Mukhtar, while waiting for reinforcements, had set about fortifying the position which he had taken up at Zevin. 6,000 feet above sea level, it had been carefully planned by Faizi, and was formed in two lines, the front along a ridge about a mile and a quarter long with a deep ravine before it. In the centre was a knoll, about 300 feet higher, on which was positioned on earthwork with four guns, with another on the extreme right, also covered by a battery. Behind the first line on the reverse slope five battalions were encamped. Beyond them came a deep ravine, with a gentle slope on the opposite side to the second position, in which were earthworks housing six field guns and eight mountain guns, behind which a further eleven battalions were posted. Two other hills were also fortified and each garrisoned by one battalion.[17] Gradually reinforcements began to arrive; but in the face of what he still believed to be the overwhelming Russian superiority in numbers, Mukhtar intended to make no forward move for the present.

About 18 miles south south-west of Zevin, at Delibaba, Mukhtar had posted Mahomed Pasha, with a force of eight battalions and two batteries, blocking the road from Bayazid to Erzerum at the pass through the Kosegh Dagh, in an entrenched position. His left flank was somewhat exposed; the troops originally at Pennek, Olti and Bardez had hurriedly retreated either to Erzerum or to the main body at Zevin. It was not long, however, before the belief that the Russian had pushed forward a large force to Olti gave way to a realisation that in fact that it was only lightly held. Mukhtar accordingly pushed forward his left wing towards Bardez, and the Russian troops in Olti precipitately evacuated the place on June 8 on the orders of Loris-Melikov and fell back on the main body investing Kars.

Loris-Melikov had brought the bulk of the forces under Devel to join his principal forces at Kars, which he now proceeded to invest completely. The line of investment had a circumference of about thirty miles; the Russian forces occupying that line were organised in three groups, under Heimann, Devel and Loris-Melikov himself. The plateau on which Kars stands dominates the country on all sides. After 1856 a great deal of effort had gone into strengthening the fortress, with new works covering the whole plateau; the design took account of the lessons learned in the long siege of the place. It was well provided with artillery; there were a hundred rifled 24-pounders, most however being muzzle-loaders, and forty-four smoothbore 24-pounders. In addition there were sixty-six field guns. The garrison consisted of about 33,000 men, which included eighteen battalions of regular infantry.

One of the difficulties faced by the Russians was that in constructing siege batteries opposite the key fortifications, they must do so at a height some 300 feet lower than the forts. The most powerful of these was Fort Karadagh, on the north-east front of the

Mukhtar Pasha reconnoitring Kars. (*Illustrated London News*)

fortress, which dominated the town. It did however give to the attackers one advantage; the rocky ground prevented a ditch being dug, while the lack of earth made it difficult to repair damage caused by enemy bombardment. The Russian attack was concentrated at this point, and also at Fort Tekmass, on the west side. It was this latter point at which the Russian bombardment was first directed, continuing throughout the first two weeks of June. On June 17 eight batteries commenced a heavy bombardment of Forts Karadagh and Arab. The bombardment paused every afternoon, when both sides took the opportunity for a midday meal, and also during the night. The Turkish counter-battery fire was very effective, although it did not prevent the Russian batteries from creeping nearer to the fortress.

While the main body attempted to reduce Kars, Tergukassov, with 8,000 men, continued his movement towards Erzerum from Karakilissa. He was now over 100 miles from his base. This further advance had been ordered by Loris-Melikov, in the belief that a threat to the Passin-Su valley would prevent ay interference by Mukhtar with the operations round Kars. It was a rash move, which could seriously endanger Tergukasssov.[18] He had left behind 1,600 men in the fortress of Bayazid, the condition of which made defence difficult. And, unknown to him, there was a substantial force in his front while another was forming on his left flank. By June 9 Tergukassov had reached Zaidikan, by which time it had become clear that he was not in great strength. Mukhtar accordingly directed the local commander, Mahomed Pasha, to block his progress, reinforcing him with two infantry battalions, a battery, and 1,000 irregular cavalry. This brought the total force available to seventeen battalions, with three batteries and 2,000 cavalry – or would have done, if they had all come up in time. As it was, Mahomed was obliged to fight with only part of his force.

Turks and British observers watching the bombardment of Kars
from the Tchakmak Tabia. (*Illustrated London News*)

Tergukassov's patrols encountered the Turkish forces on June 14, finding that Mahomed had taken up a naturally strong position some three miles long covering the village of Taghir, with its right flank covered by two long ridges and its left by a chain of hills. In front of the position lay a deep steep-sided ravine, beyond which the ground was devoid of cover. The Turks had dug a series of shelter trenches to strengthen the position, which was held by ten battalions and two batteries. Two battalions and a battery were posted to cover the line of retreat.[19] On June 15 the Russians occupied a long ridge in front of the Turkish position, and brought up sixteen guns which they protected by shelter trenches.

At about 4.00 am the Russian infantry began to move forward. Charles Williams, who with General Kemball and Captain Norman accompanied Mahomed's force, noted that from no point was it possible to see the whole of the terrain over which the action was fought; he was struck in particular by the profligate use of ammunition:

The rattle of Berdan rifles was incessant, but no more prevalent than the replies of the Sniders and Martini-Peabodys from our side. On both sides there was an enormous waste of cartridges, aim being taken, where it was taken at all, at impracticable distances; but more frequently the great object of the men was to engage in a rapid firing competition, and get rid of as many shots as possible in a given space of time.[20]

General Sir Arnold Kemball, British military commissioner
with the Turkish army in Asia. (*Vanity Fair*)

The Russian artillery soon gained the upper hand, and the Turks, in order to turn their flank and seize some heights from which to enfilade the Russian guns, attempted an advance on their left, but were driven back by the rifle fire of the Russian infantry. In the centre, three Russian battalions, supported by four guns, moved forward, and began to inflict heavy casualties on the Turks in their front. Mahomed committed two battalions from his reserve, but in turn Tergukassov fed in two more battalions to reinforce his front line. Shortly before 9.00 am parties of Russian skirmishers began to move around Mahomed's right flank; efforts to stop them by fire from the two battalions posted on a knoll on that flank broke down under heavy Russian artillery fire, and the skirmishers began to advance, supported by four cavalry regiments. At this crucial moment, at 11.35 am, Mahomed was killed; with their ammunition running out, the Turks fell back, their retreat soon becoming general.

As the Russian cavalry advanced they spotted Kemball and Norman; convinced that they had taken part in the battle on the Turkish side, a party of Cossacks was detached to seize them. The two Englishmen mounted, and managed to get a start of the Cossacks, riding over the Taghir stream towards Delibaba. They were, however, not yet out of danger:

The Cossacks, pursuing by another route, reached the village of Delibaba before the fugitives, and had the latter not received timely warning from a friendly Turk, they would most probably have been taken prisoners. As it was, they had to urge their horses to the utmost to escape, the pursuit being pressed with the greatest determination.[21]

Writing at the turn of the century, a distinguished Russian international lawyer commented on Kemball's activities in terms which suggested that the latter had been well advised to do all he could to avoid being taken:

If the commander-in-chief of the Russian army in Transcaucasia had possessed irrefutable proof as regards the participation of Sir Arnold in the operation of the Turkish armies, the latter, in case he should have been captured, would necessarily have been treated as a Turkish prisoner of war, and not as a British general or as the military *attaché* of the British Government. Sir Arnold Kemball seems to have realised this himself for in consequence of setbacks suffered by the Turkish army and when it turned tail *en masse*, he took care not to be with the rearguard.[22]

The Turks retreated some eight miles, and took up a position which was immediately entrenched. Casualties during this encounter were not high on either side; Williams put the Turkish losses as not more than 300, and thought that the Russian losses must be about the same. In fact the Turkish loss was much greater, some 1,000 casualties being

General Sir Arnold Kemball (left) and Lieutenant McDougall with the Turkish forces in the Caucasus. (*Illustrated London News*)

left on the field, and 1,000 prisoners being taken, with ten guns.[23] It was a Russian victory; but the performance of the Turkish troops gave warning that they were capable of stout resistance.

On the day before the Battle of Taghir a sortie had been attempted from the fortress of Kars on the north-west; it was repulsed by a Grenadier regiment from Heimann's command, and retreated having sustained about 200 casualties. The Russians lost about 150 men in the course of the engagement.[24]

Following his victory on June 16, Tergukassov was very much aware that his situation was precarious. His force was not large, and was heavily outnumbered by the Turks in his immediate front, while he had now learned that his rear was threatened by the force of Faik Pasha, who was marching on Bayazid. He reported his concerns to Loris-Melikov, who at once decided to relieve the pressure on Tergukassov by marching directly against Mukhtar's main force at Zevin. Tergukassov resolved to await the outcome of this movement, and halted at Eshki-Kaliass, where he fortified his camp on the Mourad River.

Mukhtar had also become aware of the true position, and although he was informed of Loris-Melikov's advance he reckoned that he had time to defeat Tergukassov and get back to his main body at Zevin. Leaving Ismail Pasha and Faizi Pasha in charge there, he made his way to Delibaba and took personal command of the Turkish forces around the place, arriving on June 19. On June 21 he advanced in three columns against the Russian position at Eshki-Kaliass, which was three miles in length and thinly held. The rugged nature of the country, however, considerably favoured the defence. On the left, where the steepness of the slopes made it impossible for the Turks to bring up any artillery, there was soon a stalemate, the fighting being confined to a long-range exchange of rifle fire.

In the centre the Turks succeeded in getting up three Krupp guns, which opened fire against the Russian position. In their turn, the Russian deployed three batteries, which fired with greater effect on the Top Dagh, the mountain on which Mukhtar had located his headquarters. On the Russian left, Tergukassov sent forward two Cossack regiments to cross the Mourad and take the Turks in flank. Mukhtar committed his cavalry to stop them, but they were met with a murderous fire and obliged to retreat with heavy loss. The Cossacks rode forward in pursuit, but were stopped and then obliged to retire by some *Redif* battalions, who took up a position from which neither the Russian artillery nor an infantry assault were able to dislodge them.

Thwarted here, Tergukassov made an attempt to turn the Turkish left. Fierce fighting ensued, in which Mukhtar was obliged to commit his last reserves; in the end the Turks fell back to their start line. As night fell, the two forces remained in their positions, each, unknown to the other, in serious want of artillery ammunition. Mukhtar was in two minds as to whether to resume this attack on the following day; but when the fog lifted the following morning a Turkish reconnaissance found to its surprise that the Russians had pulled out of their position, and could be seen disappearing into the mountains. During the battle the Turks had suffered a total of about 2,000 casualties, although Williams initially put the figure at much less; the Russian loss was about 700.[25]

The retreat of the Russians certainly entitled Mukhtar to claim the battle as a victory, and it greatly heartened his troops who had hitherto been very demoralised by the succession of retreats. Mukhtar himself was anxious to hurry back to his main body at Zevin. He was in no doubt that a potentially decisive battle there might be imminent,

Turkish infantry throwing up shelter trenches just before the
battle at Eshki-Kaliass, June 21. (*The Graphic*)

and on June 22, certain now that there was no more to fear from Tergukassov, he set out
to rejoin his troops at Zevin.

17

Batum

Apart from the fortresses of Kars and Erzerum, the acquisition of Batum was for Russia much the most attractive territorial war aim in Asia. It was an excellent harbour, and its possession would greatly strengthen Russia's grip on its turbulent provinces in the region. Hobart thought Batum to be 'the key to Asia Minor.'[1] It will be recalled that the Rion detachment based on Kutais had Batum as its objective, together with the protection of the Black Sea coast. Its proceedings were largely unaffected by, and did not affect, the operations of the other three columns invading Turkish territory.

It was recognised from the outset that Oklobju, in command of the Rion detachment, had a peculiarly difficult task. The terrain it must cross to get at Batum was especially forbidding, while the Turks could derive considerable assistance from their command of the sea. They were able to bring in reinforcements unhindered, while the guns of their ironclads could help with the defence of some of the approaches to the town. Added to this, the Turkish garrison was commanded by the able and energetic Hassein Tashmi Pasha, who had available between 10,000 and 12,000 regular troops, plus between 7,000 and 8,000 irregulars recruited locally, who were particularly well versed in mountain warfare. His nominal strength was thirty-four battalions with thirty guns.

The particular geographic problems faced by Oklobju were considerable:

> The distance in a direct line between the Russian frontier and Batum is only about fifteen miles; but it presents the greatest difficulties to the advance of an army. It consists of a strip of land enclosed between a range of nearly inaccessible mountains and the sea, and crossed by seven mountain torrents, together with numerous tributaries of the Tcholouk. The ravines at the bottom of which they flow are separated by steep wooded heights, affording great facilities for defence. Nor had the Russian general much choice as to his mode of approach. From his starting point it was possible to enter the Turkish territory by three roads, which after a short distance reunite near Muchaster, from whence there is only one available road, passing down to the sea at Tsikhe Dsiri and proceeding along the coast to Batum.[2]

As usual, the Turks had been assiduous in fortifying the heights around the town, and it was evident that Oklobju's force would be obliged to attack these positions directly. The surrounding terrain would render any ambitious turning movements impossible. Oklobju had been provided with only a small force of cavalry, consisting of two Cossack regiments with twelve guns, since the nature of the country was unsuitable for cavalry operations on any large scale, and it was not to be expected that he would be making long marches. Oklobju had about 12,000 men and 48 guns available together with 7,000 more in reserve at Kutais and Ozurgeti. Bearing in mind the advantage afforded the defence by the nature of the country, it was scarcely enough.[3]

A Turkish supply column. (*Illustrirte Geschichte des Orientalischen Krieges von 1876-1878*)

Oklobju began his advance on April 24, immediately following the declaration of war, moving in three columns. Those on the right and the centre were to reunite under the command of General Shelemetiev; that on the left was a commanded by General Denibekov. To their surprise the Russians almost immediately encountered Turkish skirmishers on the heights in their immediate front, and it was necessary for these to be driven off before the advance could continue. When Shelemetiev was able to push forward he found that the Turks had established a strong defensive position around Muchaster, held by five battalions of irregular infantry and three squadrons of cavalry under the command of Ali Pasha. These resisted Shelemetiev's advance throughout April 25, inflicting heavy casualties. On the following day, however, the Russian troops succeeded in taking Muchaster, while on the left Denibekov occupied the village of Alamberi. The advance had got no more than five miles beyond the frontier; but for the next two weeks Oklobju contented himself with strengthening his position at Muchaster before making his next forward move.[4]

During this period Hassein was fortifying the line of the River Kintrish, and occupying the Khontsoubani heights. Oklobju was aware of considerable and increasing restlessness among the local population and it was as much to push back the Turks and thus discourage any rising, as to move on Batum, that he prepared to advance against Hassein's positions on May 11. Denibekov, with the 164th (Zakatala) Regiment, two battalions of Caucasian Rifles, a Kuban *plastun* battalion (Cossack infantry unit), the Gurian militia and two batteries, was to advance against the village of Khontsoubani, while Shelemetiev, with the 163rd (Lenkoran) Regiment, the Imeretian militia and four batteries, was to move out of the Muchaster position towards the mouth of the Kintrish. The road to be taken by Denibekov led to the River Acho, but to get there he had to cross a range of natural terraces, which had been heavily fortified, while the road itself had been barricaded at several points. Denibekov marched in two columns, the larger on the right of the road consisting of fifteen companies of infantry and four guns, while that on the left took the road with six companies and two guns. The advance was supported by a battery of 24 nine pounders in front of Muchaster.

Hassein had posted some 5,000 men on the line of the Acho, and Denibekov was made to fight every yard of the way. For five hours he was pinned down in front of the Turkish entrenchments, and Oklobju was obliged to bring up reinforcements. The heavy artillery fire from Muchaster was effective in smashing the buildings dotted among the trees, but it was only when Denibekov personally led a bayonet charge on the position that the Turks finally gave way and retreated.

Meanwhile Shelemetiev's advance had run into similar difficulties after crossing the Acho; an attempt to storm the heights in front broke down, and the attackers were forced to retire. Shelemetiev contented himself with an artillery bombardment of the Turkish positions. While this was going on Hassein advanced with about 2,000 infantry and attacked the column's right flank, and almost overwhelmed it, before being driven back by reinforcements hurriedly brought up. At this point an ironclad gunboat came up river, and began shelling the Russian troops on the north bank of the Acho. The artillery duel continued for about four hours before Shelemetiev judged it right to resume his advance, pushing forward a company of sharpshooters which turned the enemy left, whereupon the Turks fell back rapidly.

The fighting had been severe, but no official return of casualties was published on the Turkish side. Some 200 were found dead on the field of battle; other losses are unknown. The Russians admitted only eighteen killed and 150 wounded, but Hozier reckoned that their casualties must have been greater than the Turks. The latter made the preposterous claim to have killed 4,000.[5]

Russian steam engines at work helping to load and unload war matériel. (Budev)

After a further pause of two weeks Oklobju again moved forward with a view to occupying the line of the Kintrish, which had been more strongly fortified than the Acho position. However, an advance in two columns quickly succeeded in crossing the river, whereupon the Turks fell back quickly towards their principal position at Batum. If the outlying works had been strong, those surrounding the town were even more formidable.

Oklobju, who had now only got halfway from the frontier towards Batum and was not yet even in sight of the town, resolved to wait for the time being in the positions he had taken. The Turks continued to resupply Batum by sea, while their ironclads effectively interdicted the coast road to the town, which would otherwise have provided the most straightforward route for an advance.

While this deadlock continued, the Turks determined to take advantage of their command of the sea by launching an attack on the coast of the Russian Trans Caucasian provinces. They had already, soon after the outbreak of war, bombarded Poti, where they employed courageous divers to cut the cables of the torpedoes, or mines as we should call them, which had been laid extensively around the port in an attempt to keep any assailant out of range. Once floated, the mines were towed away to be destroyed. These mine clearing operations were extremely successful, and the Turkish ironclads were able to steam close inshore and do considerable damage to the buildings of Poti.

Hobart had taken personal command of the Turkish fleet off Batum, which consisted of eight ironclads together with a large number of transports bringing in supplies. Warned by spies in Sebastopol that torpedoes would be used against the fleet, he put a barrier of booms ahead of the ships, in the port, with guard boats to cover the harbour entrance. His precautions were wise; attempts were made on a number of occasions by two fast Russian steamers, carrying torpedo boats, to launch attacks against the Turkish ironclads.[6]

The operations against the Russian forces threatening Batum, and against Poti and other places on the coast, were suspended for a more ambitious operation. The Turkish plan was to stimulate a rising against the Russians in Abkhazia, where the population had been unremittingly hostile to the Russian occupation; most recently there had been an insurrection in 1866, put down by Russian troops. The Abkhazians, however, did not

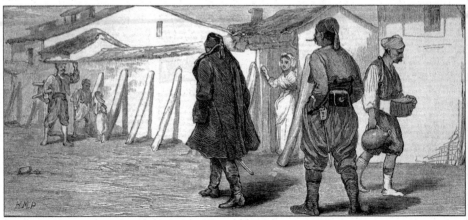

A Turkish officer with his orderly. (*The Graphic*)

make the most dependable of allies; a British traveller compared them to some of the tribes on the North-west frontier of India:

> Of all the rascally robber tribes of the Caucasus, whose regular occupation up to the period of Russian ascendancy was vendetta, kidnapping, and horse stealing, the Abkhazians are by many degrees the worst, worse even than the Tcherkess, which is saying a great deal. Their character very much resembles that of the Afridis, Bajouris and Bonairs of our North-west frontier in India, being a compound of avarice, treachery, caprice, and ferocity, joined to considerable courage, and great aptitude for guerrilla warfare.[7]

Turkish agents had been secretly sent to stir up the population in advance of a landing on the Russian coast. This was to take place at Soukhoum Kaleh, some twenty miles north of Poti. The town was largely populated by Greeks and Armenians, and by the Russian officials; the native Abkhazians came into town to trade on market days. Hozier described Soukhoum Kaleh as 'a place of very great beauty, enclosed by an amphitheatre of hills, with a gorge and snow–clad mountains behind.' The Russians had not done much to fortify it; there was a bastioned square, a work called the New Battery and a large fortified barracks.

Hobart detached four ironclads for the expedition, commanded by one of his best officers. Admiral Hassan Pasha had served in the British navy, and was extremely competent. On May 12, after a series of feigned attacks on the village of Gudati, east of Pitsunda Point and about ten miles north-west of Soukhoum Kaleh, the commander of the garrison, General Kravchenko, panicked and sent part of his force in that direction. The Turkish squadron accordingly steamed off to Soukhoum Kaleh, and began a heavy bombardment of the town. Kravchenko retreated with the rest of his force into the hills behind the town on May 15; the main force intended for the landing was not yet at sea, but he fell back further into the interior. Large numbers of Abkhazians assembled to take up the arms distributed by the Turks. Kravchenko took with him a large part of the population who suffered severely on the journey through the mountains; many of those who fell behind were massacred by the Abkhazians.[9]

On May 23 a force of 3,000 Circassian troops was landed at Adler, thirty miles further north, causing a further Russian retreat; about 100 miles of coast had been abandoned to the Turks. 10,000 further Turkish troops were sent to Soukhoum Kaleh to follow up the initial successes, but to no purpose; hemmed in by the mountains, and by the Russian forces assembled to resist them, they were completely ineffective. It was soon realised that there was no choice but to evacuate them, a task which fell to Hobart.

He was obliged first to take off the force at Adler, an operation which he described with considerable self satisfaction:

> The corvettes and the paddle transports were moored in as close to the shore as possible, my intention being to cram them with men and stores first, leaving my flagship free to the last to manoeuvre off the Russian camp and shell it, should the slightest opposition be offered to the embarkation. The work commenced at daylight, and was actively carried on throughout the day and following night, the last batch of men coming off at dawn. The men were taken off under the very teeth,

Dervish Pasha. (Russes et Turcs)

as it were, of the Russians. The ships in shore were well within rifle range, and the boats passing to and fro were exposed the whole time to a fire from hidden foes.[10]

The troops were taken in the first instance to Soukhoum Kaleh; but it was evident that this place must also be abandoned, and Hobart was ordered to evacuate not only the troops, but also all those of the indigenous population who preferred to leave rather than face Russian vengeance. In the end, within about a fortnight, Hobart was able to take off some 50,000 people, landing them at the nearby Turkish ports, completing the operation by 31 August. During the evacuation a bold torpedo attack was made on the Turkish ships by converted launches from the Russian sloop *Constantine*, on 23/24 August during an eclipse of the moon. Although it failed, the confidence of the Turks was badly shaken.[11] In military terms the operation had been a failure; but it did illustrate what might have been done if a more ambitious use had been made of the Turkish command of the sea.

Meanwhile in the fourth week of June Oklobju had prepared for a further offensive. After ten days of preparation, not only in bringing up artillery and supplies, but also in constructing some eighty miles of roads and thirty bridges, the Russians were ready to advance. By now they faced a new opponent, command of the Turkish forces in the Batum area having passed to the extremely able Dervish Pasha. He was able to deploy additional troops, reinforcements having come in by sea from Trebizond; he had some 20,000 troops at his disposal, half of whom were regulars, with 35 guns, some of which were heavy calibre pieces with a considerable range.[12]

Oklobju organised his force in five groups. On the right, Shelemetiev, with the 2nd Caucasian Rifles, two battalions of the 163rd Regiment, and Imeretian militia, with three battalions of the 101st (Piatigorsk) Regiment, was to push forward in support of the attack on the Kvirike ridge. This was to be made by Colonel Gurchin, with the 1st and 4th Caucasian Rifles and Gurian and Imeretian militia, with two battalions of the 76th (Kuban) Regiment in reserve. A general reserve consisting of the 151st Regiment and two battalions of the 75th Regiment stood on the Khontsoubani heights; three battalions were held to the left rear of the assault, and the 164th Regiment watched the lower Kintrish. Oklobju was keeping his options open; he planned a reconnaissance in force, but if the attack was successful he would throw in his reserves to exploit it.[13]

Dervish was ready to meet the attack. He had ten battalions on the Kvirike ridge; his right flank in the dense forest of the Kintrish ravine was covered by 3,000 irregulars. The Kvirike ridge was his second line; behind it, the Deva heights had been prepared for defence and four batteries installed, while at sea the guns of a 9 inch monitor had the Khontsoubani heights within range.

On June 23 the Russian artillery opened fire on the Kvirike ridge, quickly silencing the Turkish guns. Gurchin's infantry advance, however, made slow progress, while the Turkish artillery on the Deva heights came into action to prevent the Russian gunners from coming forward. By nightfall Oklobju had taken about 1,000 casualties, and had had enough, ordering a withdrawal to the Sameba Heights and Table Hill. Next day Dervish counter-attacked, his men advancing boldly to a point at which the Russian guns were in danger of capture; in the end, however, they were driven back by bayonet charges, and Dervish called off the attack. Oklobju, reckoning that his exposed position was extremely vulnerable, fell back on June 30 to the Muchaster position that he had occupied two months before. He had suffered some 2,000 casualties during the fighting, plus a similar number sick from the prevalent coastal fever.[14] At Muchaster he constructed powerful fortifications, and there he remained to the end of the war. This front saw no further action until January 30 of the following year, when an unsuccessful attack was launched under the command of Komarov; it cost the Russians some 1,200 men in killed and wounded. Among the dead was Shelemetiev, killed under long-range fire from Turkish ironclads as he was establishing his batteries. The Russians fell back to their start line, and the Turks remained in possession of Batum until the Congress of Berlin, where the successful defence of their position which they had maintained in the face of constant attacks, certainly strengthened their hand in the peace negotiations.[15]

18

Zevin

Loris-Melikov had received news from Tergukassov of the Battle of Taghir on June 18; the latter's despatch had explained the difficulties in which he was placed, and after a Council of War was held it was resolved to advance from the vicinity of Kars to provide some relief. On June 20 Loris-Melikov, leaving Devel to manage the siege of Kars with part of the army, marched off with some 17,000 men. Unlike a number of subordinates, (in particular Heimann), he did not suppose that the operation against Mukhtar's well-entrenched army would be a walkover. He was well aware of the stream of reinforcements that the Turks had been sending forward, and although he had been in favour of pushing on to Erzerum three weeks earlier, he now realised that the chance of doing so successfully might have gone.

By nightfall on June 22 the army had reached Sarakamish, at the entrance to the mountains. There were two routes that might be followed; to the north, via Bardez, and to the south by Meliduz and Mejingerd. Loris-Melikov opted for the southern route, in order to give the impression that he was aiming for the entrenched camp at Khorassan before swinging to his right to attack Zevin. If in the meanwhile Mukhtar had moved to support the Khorassan position, Loris-Melikov could fall on his flank after taking Zevin. As a plan, this was well enough; but it remained to be seen if the Russian army was strong enough to take Zevin.[1]

On June 23 the Russians began their painful climb up the mountain. Sappers had been sent forward to prepare the way, but for the artillery it called for a colossal effort:

> By yoking eight horses to one piece, and making the soldiers push at the wheels, the passage of the guns was accomplished, but not without much trouble and great fatigue to the men and horses. At last they reached the plateau of Meliduz, which is about half the height of Mont Blanc, and where the cold was very severe. A magnificent panorama was enjoyed from this point, and as far as the eye could reach shone the snow-clad peaks of the range of mountains.[2]

On June 24 Loris-Melikov decreed a rest day, while he sent forward patrols to examine the Turkish positions. They were quite as strong as he had feared. The natural strength of the terrain, described in Chapter 16, had been utilised with great skill by Mukhtar's engineers to render it almost impregnable.

The Turkish position effectively barred the main road to the west of the heights from Kars to Erzerum, and lying as it did on the flank of the road to Khorassan it threatened any Russian advance on that line. It extended along the western side of the River Zevin ravine for some five miles south of Zevin itself. The one defect of the position was its length; the inadequate Turkish force available for its defence must necessarily be spread very thinly.[3]

A Turkish mountain gun battery. (*Album della Guerra Russo-Turca del 1877-78*)

Although the command was nominally in the hands of Ismail Hakki Pasha, the Governor of Erzerum, it was Faizi Pasha, in the absence of Mukhtar, who was effectively in control of the Turkish army at Zevin, where his task was relatively simple. All he had to do was to sit tight, and allow the Russians to break their heads in vain assaults on his position. It is not entirely clear how many troops he had available, but his strength was put by Williams at 16,000.[4] Other estimates put the total at much lower, probably correctly.

On June 25, at 7.00 am, the Russian troops began their advance, pushing forward through extremely difficult and broken country, climbing and descending steep slopes. The baggage and ammunition train was left on the Meliduz plateau, guarded by a battalion with one battery. The assaulting force consisted of fifteen battalions with twenty-four guns. Loris-Melikov detached his cavalry, consisting of six regiments with two batteries, under Prince Tchavtchavadze for a thrust towards Khorassan, in the hope of weakening the Turkish army in the Zevin position or at least diverting all or part of the force with which Mukhtar had beaten Tergukassov. However, he postponed this manoeuvre until the day of the assault on Zevin, which gave the Turks no time to take the bait in any case. As it turned out, the two batteries were unable to traverse the road to Khorassan, so their detachment was wasted, while the Turkish cavalry guarding the place simply withdrew to Kaprikoi. Nothing therefore had been gained by the reduction in strength of the force before Zevin.

At 8.00 am there was a dramatic development, when Loris-Melikov at last received news from Tergukassov, for which he had been waiting for the last two days. It read: 'Attacked at Taghir by superior forces. I have fought for ten consecutive hours, and maintained my position. Manoeuvre so as to extricate me.' Loris-Melikov halted the advance while he pondered the situation. Another Council of War was convened. As usual Heimann and the other veterans of wars in the Caucasus were all for launching an immediate assault. Others were not so sure, preferring to put off the attack until the following day. In the face of Tergukassov's appeal, and in the knowledge that Mukhtar was on his way back to strengthen the garrison, Loris-Melikov reluctantly decided that the assault must go in that day.[5]

The attackers had arrived in front of the Zevin position at about 11.00 am. The enormity of their task was immediately apparent. The Russian batteries could not get nearer than 5,000 yards to their targets, while the strength of the three tiers of Turkish field works was all too clear. The principal assault was to be undertaken by the centre column, under Major-General Komarov, who led forward the 15th (Tiflis) Regiment, with three battalions of the 14th (Georgian) Regiment and one battery. His task was to cross the steep-sided valley of the River Khani and attack the principal feature of the Turkish position, known as the 'Yellow Mamelon.' On Komarov's right, with orders to support this operation, was the 13th (Erivan) Regiment and three batteries under Major-General Avinov. On the left, the 16th (Mingrelian) Regiment, with one battery, was to cross the River Zevin and assault the left of the Turkish position, which was separated from the centre by a deep ravine.

At 1.00 pm the Russian artillery began its bombardment of the entrenchments, but firing at a great range, and at targets that stood some 1,500 feet higher than the guns, the shells fell at a high angle and did relatively little damage, although a high rate of fire was maintained. On the left the Mingrelian Regiment crossed the ravine of the Zevin and clambered up to the heights to the first line of the Turkish trenches. To Loris-Melikov's delight, as he watched through his binoculars, they first disappeared into the smoke and then beyond it, having taken the trenches.

Russian wounded being transported in the Caucasus. (Strantz)

In the centre, Komarov's troops crossed the Khani, forming up on the road at the foot of the heights at the village of Zevin. The first line of Turkish infantry was behind a crest at a bend in the road as the Russians came up:

> A magnificent display of discipline was then exhibited. The Russian soldiers advanced in perfect order, without firing a shot, under a tremendous fusillade which had suddenly burst out along the whole Turkish line, to the right, left and in front of them. Arrived within about 200 yards of the trenches the Russians opened fire, and then almost immediately rushed on the enemy with the bayonet. The attack was of brief duration; the Turks hastily fell back, and thus another entrenchment was taken.[6]

This success, however, represented the high watermark of the Russian assault. The Yellow Mamelon still confronted the Russian troops, and from its first line sharpshooters poured a heavy fire on the attackers, while from either side the Turkish infantry in the trenches opened fire. Nevertheless, the Russian troops did all they could, sometimes using their bayonets as alpenstocks to help them up the steep slopes. So threatening was their advance that at one point a body of Turkish soldiers retreated *en masse* to a higher trench line. Faizi, however, who was on the spot, ran to them and led them back. For a while the attack hung in the balance. The Russians made no less than ten attempts to gain the crest of the mamelon, but each time they were driven back by the hail of fire from the trenches. The fight went on till after dark and it was only by the light of the moon that Loris-Melikov finally pulled back the exhausted attackers.

Faizi, anxiously watching from the centre, did not at first realise what had happened. It was Baron Schluga, of the *Neue Freie Presse*, who first spotted the Russian move, and he galloped up to Faizi, shouting 'The Russians are retreating!' Faizi, although lacking cavalry that might have been able to pursue the enemy, made the most of his advantage, inflicting heavy loss on the retiring enemy as they fell back down the slopes.

Meanwhile on the right flank the Erivan Regiment had got itself into a dreadful mess. Avinov got a message to send two battalions to the assistance of Komarov, with which he complied; he then received the same message again, and not realising that it was a duplicate sent off two more battalions. This mistake was compounded by further confusion in the commands that reached him, and he crossed and recrossed the river four or five times, uncertain as to his instructions.

During the afternoon there had been no news from Prince Tchavtchavadze as to his movement towards Khorassan. The Mingrelian battalions remained in the positions which they had occupied while awaiting the arrival of the cavalry. It was not until 7.30 pm that Tchavtchavadze was able to push forward parties of dismounted cavalrymen, and these joined the Mingrelian battalion on the hill at the southern end of the Turkish position. Without artillery, however, no further forward movement was possible, and these troops joined the general withdrawal ordered by Loris-Melikov.[7] The Russian official casualty reports indicated that 880 officers and men had been killed or wounded. Hozier noted that the Turkish losses having been acknowledged as 138 killed and 1,328 wounded, it was probable that the Russian loss as given was an understatement[8]. The manner of their advance, and the ferocity of the storm of rifle and artillery fire which they faced, suggests that the Russians did indeed suffer heavily.

Charles Williams, writing on the day after the battle, commented on the improved performance of the Turkish infantry:

> Behind breastworks, or in rifle pits, at any rate, the Turks are quite a match for the invader; and after a few weeks of this sort of thing, they will not be far behind them in the open field, though it will be long before they learn to come into action, like the Russians, with such beautiful regularity that, from a parade point of view, old soldiers are struck with admiration. There is just a question, however, whether this machine-like style does not cost a good many lives that a more scrambling system would save. There is no doubt it gives immense confidence to the men, both in themselves and in their officers.[9]

During the night Mukhtar arrived in the Zevin position with twenty-two battalions, more than doubling the size of the Turkish army there. It was certainly possible for him to launch a counter-attack upon his beaten enemy, but he resolved to continue with his defensive tactics, and did no more than to prepare for a second Russian assault. Heimann urged strongly on Loris-Melikov that he should order this, but the latter, saying that enough brave men had already died in a rash venture, ordered a retreat to rejoin the army around Kars. Remaining in its overnight position throughout June 26, his force fell back first to the Meliduz plateau on the following day and then crossed the Saghanli Dagh. By July 3 it was reunited with the rest of the army.

Camels conveying ammunition to the front. (Ollier)

Mukhtar made no attempt at a close pursuit. On June 30 he advanced from Zevin with twelve battalions, twelve guns and a large part of the cavalry, being followed by Faizi next day with twelve more battalions and twelve guns. He ordered Ismail to take the remainder of the army, comprising twenty-three battalions, 1,500 cavalry and two field and two mountain batteries, and operate on the right wing, keeping in touch with the centre and putting pressure on Tergukassov's force. Mukhtar resolved now to march to the relief of Kars, reached the Meliduz plateau on July 1, and next day moved through the Meliduz pass, taking advantage of the greatly improved roads which the Russians had left behind. On July 4 he halted at Kirk Bunar, some twenty miles south-east of Kars, to await reinforcements, which arrived two days later. His force now consisted of thirty battalions, and on July 7 he advanced to within seven miles of Kars.

All this time the Russian besiegers of Kars had kept up a heavy bombardment. As Mukhtar approached, the Cossack cavalry screening the siege operations fell back, and on July 8, accompanied by his staff and Sir Arnold Kemball, the Turkish commander in chief was able to ride in to the city. During the day the Russian gunfire began to slacken, and the Turkish outposts suspected that the Russians might be retiring. That night there were large fires in the Russian siege works, and next morning all was quiet. Loris-Melikov had retreated, taking all his stores and equipment, to a position that had previously been prepared at Kuruk-Dere Pass, only a few miles from the frontier, covering the two roads to Alexandropol. Mukhtar, having ordered Kars to be resupplied sufficiently to stand a twelve months' siege, moved forward to take up a position along the edge of a high plateau, from Visinkoi to Ani, on the River Arpa. This position, like that of his adversary, was soon strongly fortified.[10]

The Russian retirement had come as a considerable surprise to Mukhtar. The force with which he had advanced from Zevin was no stronger than the Russian force which had been beaten there; the latter, combined with the troops with which Devel had been investing Kars, substantially outnumbered Mukhtar's army. The retreat had been ordered following instructions from the imperial headquarters on the Danube, where the current success of the operations there made it seem that an adventurous policy in the Caucasus was unnecessary as well as risky.[11]

There matters remained for some considerable time, the only activity amounting to an occasional cavalry skirmish. On his side Mukhtar was bound by the strictest orders from Constantinople to remain on the defensive. For his part, Loris-Melikov had already realised that his army had bitten off more than it could chew, and in view of the orders received was obliged to await reinforcements before he undertook a further offensive. For the moment he enjoyed the benefit of a much shorter line of communication with his base, at Alexandropol; Mukhtar, on the other hand, had to bring up all his supplies from Erzerum. Nonetheless, in the euphoria which gripped the Turkish headquarters following the Battle of Zevin and the relief of Kars, it seemed to Charles Williams that the victorious progress of the Turks might continue to a remarkable extent:

> Turkey can hope for no conquests in Europe – it is even possible that she may lose all control over the provinces north and west of the Balkans; but what if she were able, unaided, to repossess herself of Georgia, and to win Circassia even, across the vast chain of the Caucasus, part of which is before my eyes as I write, which is

An encounter between an artist from the *Illustrated London News*
and some Cossacks. (*Illustrated London News*)

the nursing mother of all the nations of the West, and which has been described
somewhere or other as the natural northern frontier of Islam?[12]

Meanwhile the events at Zevin gave Tergukassov no alternative but to retreat as
quickly as he could. Threatened in front by the large force under the command of Ismail,
he was already aware that his line of retreat was under threat. A Turkish force of six
battalions of regular infantry, with three batteries and some 8,000 Kurdish irregulars,
commanded by Faik Pasha, had marched on Bayazid, besieging the small garrison of
about 1,600 in the citadel of that place. Unknown to Tergukassov at the time, Bayazid
had been the scene of an appalling atrocity. Marching on the town on June 17, Faik's
leading troops encountered an enemy patrol, which fell back on the garrison. That night
a small Russian force advanced from Bayazid in the direction from which the Turkish
forces had come, only to encounter a very much larger force some ten miles from the
city. The Russians retreated, pursued by Kurdish cavalry, leaving behind their wounded.
Hozier described what followed:

All these wounded, together with a few prisoners cut off by the Kurds, were
remorselessly butchered. With the aid of two field guns the commandants managed
for a time to keep the Turks at bay; but Faik sending Munib Pasha, with two
battalions and three mountain guns, to occupy a hill about 1,200 yards east of
the castle, the Turks were enabled to command the Russian position, and finally

rendered it untenable, driving the whole of the garrison within the citadel, and what was of more importance to them, cutting off their supply of water.[13]

Worse was to follow. The Russian commander, Colonel Kovalevsky, reckoning that the situation was hopeless, sought to negotiate terms of surrender. Agreement was reached, and at 4.00 pm on June 19, the gates were opened and the unarmed garrison began to file out of the citadel between lines of Turkish regular troops. About 200 had left when a large body of Kurdish irregulars rushed on the defenceless men and began a massacre. Neither the Russian officers nor the Turkish regulars could prevent them all being slaughtered; only the hurried shutting of the gates and a brisk fire from the citadel prevented the Kurds from breaking in. Thwarted in this endeavour, the Kurds turned their attention to the unfortunate inhabitants of Bayazid, murdering nearly the whole population of 1,400. Kovalevsky had been killed; his wife, who was still in the citadel, urged the rest of the garrison to resist, taking a rifle to fight alongside the soldiers. The command was taken by Colonel Stokvitch, who proved a reliable and enterprising leader. On June 21 he was able to send messengers to Tergukassov to report what had occurred.

Tergukassov remained in his position on the Koseh Dagh, near Delibaba until June 27, confident that the extensive earthworks which he had constructed there left him safe against attack while he made his preparations to retreat. The Turks soon pursued him, as he fell back through Karakilissa and Dyadin and all the way to Igdir, the other side of the frontier. His progress had been severely hampered by the large number of Armenian families, to whom had been promised the Tsar's protection, who followed his retreating columns. In the face of the pleas of these unfortunates that they should not be abandoned to the untender mercies of Turkish irregulars, Tergukassov felt obliged to cover their march to Russian territory, and safety, by the vigorous operations of his rearguard. The whole column finally reached Igdir on July 5, having suffered casualties during a difficult and dangerous retreat of only 31 men.[14] Preparations were made to turn the force around for a relief march to Bayazid as soon as possible, for which some reinforcement had been sent to Tergukassov.

He set out on July 8, appearing to the north-east of Bayazid at dawn on July 10. The Turkish forces at Faik's disposal were some three times as strong as those with which Tergukassov advanced, having been reinforced by a brigade under Nakif Bey sent forward by Ismail. Although the Russian cavalry succeeded in cutting off Munib's retreat from the position he had taken up to rejoin Faik, they could not prevent him from uniting with the approaching brigade of Nakif. Nonetheless a prompt Russian attack soon drove the Turks back with heavy losses; Faik did nothing to assist, and himself rapidly retreated from Bayazid.

Since the beginning of the siege, the garrison had lost 116 men killed and 366 wounded; the survivors were practically all ill, and were swiftly taken back to Russian territory for rehabilitation. Having raised the siege, Tergukassov at once returned with all his sick and wounded, and those of the civilian population who had survived the Kurdish massacre, to Igdir, without further contact with the enemy.[15]

19

Eski Zagra

Having seized the Shipka Pass, Gourko at once set about strengthening its defences. The existing works were occupied by a newly arrived brigade of the 9th Division, and were armed by a battery consisting of the three mountain guns and five Krupp guns captured during the fighting. Once the reinforcements had arrived Gourko was able to move his whole force, save for the 30th Don Cossack Regiment which was still north of the Balkans, to Kazanlik. There it was able to rest for a while.

But not for long. Gourko was quite convinced that only by pressing on could the moral effect of his success be maintained. He set out his intentions clearly:

> If we stay where we are we shall accomplish nothing, nay, we shall risk losing everything. The Turks will recover from their panic, collect their scattered forces, receive reinforcements by train, realise how weak we are, and, reassuming the offensive with greatly increased numbers, drive us from the valley of the Tundja.[1]

On the other hand, if the offensive was continued, further hard blows might be struck at the enemy; at worst, the force could retreat into the Shipka Pass.

Accordingly, Gourko wrote on July 20 a personal letter to Nicholas to seek approval to advance towards Adrianople, for which he asked for an additional infantry brigade and the return of the 30th Don Cossacks, together with an additional nine pounder battery. If he lost a day in his present position, he wrote, he might lose all the advantages he had gained. The letter crossed with one from Nicholas, which Gourko received on July 21, congratulating him on his successes but asking him not to move his infantry beyond the Tundja, while sending his cavalry forward on a wide front. It was followed by an order from Nepokoitshitsky on the following day, which reported on the setback at Plevna, and also required him to hold his infantry at Kazanlik. Information was also given on the movement of Suleiman Pasha's army from Montenegro, news of which had already begun to reach Gourko from local sources.[2]

Gourko was disappointed; standing still in this way was to court disaster, but he had no choice but to obey. In the meantime he sent his cavalry forward as requested. On July 22 the 9th Dragoons and a section of horse artillery went to Eski Zagra at the request of the Christian inhabitants. Next day came news of Turkish reinforcement arriving at Adrianople, and Gourko resolved to break up the railways from there to Philippopolis and Yeni Zagra. Two cavalry regiments and a section of horse artillery were sent to wreck the railway station at Karabunar and a similar force went to Kajadzik on the same errand. Gourko himself accompanied the 9th Hussars and two Bulgarian regiments which were moved to Eski Zagra.[3]

The cavalry reconnaissances each succeeded in breaking the railway, but in each case found the stations strongly defended. They returned with the news that the Turks were concentrating at the railway junction at Semenli.

Cossacks cutting telegraph lines. (*The Graphic*)

On July 28 a further reconnaissance showed that the Turkish strength there was about two brigades in strength; another brigade was at Yeni Zagra, and the force opposed to him was growing daily in strength. That this was possible was due solely to the Turkish command of the sea, as Maurice pointed out:

> This movement of Suleiman's army from Montenegro to Rumelia is one of the most striking examples in military history of the value of sea power to operations on land. The distance in a straight line from Antivari to Hermanli is 300 miles, the actual distance by sea and rail is 1,200. Thirty thousand men had been conveyed between these points without fatigue and without risk of interruption by the enemy … This operation was made possible by the preponderance of the Turkish fleet; a single Russian cruiser unaccounted for in the Mediterranean would have confined Suleiman to Montenegro.[4]

Gourko's intelligence as to the enemy strength was incomplete; unknown to him the Turks had some 48,000 men between Slivno and Semenli. Always in favour of the aggressive approach, Gourko decided to bring forward not only his 4th Rifle Brigade from Kazanlik but also the 1st Brigade of the 9th Division which was holding the Hainkioi Pass. His aim was to smash the Turkish force at Yeni Zagra before the main body at Semenli could intervene. His information was that it was extremely demoralised.

A Cossack reconnaissance party near Yeni Zagra. (Budev)

Gourko was not, however, indifferent to the risk he was running, already reporting to headquarters on July 25 that Suleiman's army would be dangerously close to him within five or six days.

On July 27 he wrote from Kazanlik to Nicholas to break the news of his intention to disobey orders by concentrating at Eski Zagra. Explaining the disadvantages of the position at Kazanlik, he pointed out the danger in which he would be placed by a Turkish offensive. He went on to explain in extravagant language why the move was essential:

> To shift my headquarters to Eski Zagra is to me a matter of life and death. Here my base is the narrow strip of the valley of the Tundja, and I cannot use my cavalry to reconnoitre in front, while at my back is the precipitous chain of the Balkans, which, in case the enemy should advance in overwhelming numbers, leaves my force no alternative but to seek a glorious death.[5]

At Eski Zagra, on the other hand, reconnaissance would be straightforward, and if he concentrated his force he would have 'every chance of getting the better of the enemy.' There was another compelling reason to hold on to Eski Zagra; if he left, the Bulgarians would kill and plunder the unarmed Turkish civilians there and the Bashi-Bazouks and Circassians would massacre both.

On the same day as Gourko was trying to persuade Nicholas of the wisdom of his scheme, Suleiman had a meeting with Raouf Pasha, now commanding the forces at Yeni Zagra. Until July 22 the latter had been Minister of Marine; but the simultaneous dismissal of Abdul Kerim and his replacement by Mehemet Ali, and the dismissal of Redif Pasha, the War Minister, had led to a complete cabinet reshuffle. Raouf found it necessary to turn up for the meeting with an escort of no less than six battalions. At their meeting the two generals agreed on an advance on Eski Zagra in three columns,

Raouf from Yeni Zagra, Suleiman from Semenli and Khulussi from Philippopolis. The movement was to begin on July 29, the same day on which Gourko planned to launch his advance to Yeni Zagra.

Suleiman, who was to play a pivotal role for the remainder of the war, was highly regarded in Constantinople. His distinguishing characteristics were said to be energy and obstinacy; he was certainly to demonstrate the latter quality in the months ahead.

Gourko was also planning a move in three columns. The left, from Hainkioi, consisted of five battalions of the 9th Division, with a battery and four *sotnias*, under Major-General Boreisha. The centre column, under Major-General Tsvietsinsky, which Gourko accompanied, marched from Kazanlik through Magilish, Kisla and Balabanli, where it was to cross the Lesser Balkans; it comprised the 4th Rifle Brigade, with six *sotnias* and sixteen guns. The right column consisted of the troops already at Eski Zagra, under the command of Prince Nicholas Maximilianovich; these were four Bulgarian battalions, three cavalry regiments and two batteries, which were to take the main road to Yeni Zagra.

The right and centre columns united at Kavlikioi early on the morning of July 30, at which time nothing had been heard of the left column. Gourko decided not to wait, and advanced to the attack of Yeni Zagra.

The Turkish troops in Yeni Zagra amounted to five battalions with six guns. Gourko's attack soon drove them back, and by midday he had captured the station. At this point, however, Gourko received a message outlining the situation of the left column, which had been stopped in its movement east from Eski Zagra by superior forces. In fact the

The capture of Yeni Zagra. (Ollier)

The Times correspondent at Yeni Zagra. (Ollier)

troops which he had driven out of Yeni Zagra were part of Raouf's force, the bulk of which was in motion towards Eski Zagra to link with Suleiman.

As night fell on July 30 Prince Nicholas, with the Eski Zagra detachments, held the high road eastwards from that place for about six miles. The Bulgarian battalions and some Cossacks made up his right flank in the town itself while his cavalry was at Aidinli and Hirsta, about half way between Eski Zagra and Dzuranli. Gourko, now joined by Boreisha, had collected his troops ready to come to their aid on the following morning and he had ten battalions just to the west of Yeni Zagra. At Karubunar, Suleiman, with some 40,000 men in hand, was disposed on an arc about five miles from Eski Zagra from the Chirpan road on his left to the village of Dzuranli on his right; the troops here were the remainder of Raouf's contingent.[6]

Prince Nicholas had fought all day against these extremely heavy odds; it was obvious to him that it would be crucial to hold Eski Zagra if he could, since it covered the Russian retreat to Kazanlik. During the day the Russian cavalry, about 1,800 strong, had withstood the attacks of 4,000 infantry and several hundred irregular cavalry, fighting with great courage and skill. By now, however, as they prepared to face another day, they were close to the end of their tether.

On the morning of July 31 Gourko began his move along the high road towards Eski Zagra. When the Cossacks leading his force reached the vicinity of Dzuranli at about 7.00 am, they came under heavy fire from the Turks posted there. Seeing this, Prince Nicholas sent the 9th Hussars with four guns against the left flank of the Turks at Dzuranli to relieve the pressure on Gourko's leading troops. He then dispatched the 8th Dragoons against the right flank of the rest of Suleiman's army. The actions of these two cavalry regiments effectively kept the two parts of the Turkish army apart for several hours.

Further west Suleiman had begun a rather ponderous assault on the Bulgarian battalions holding Eski Zagra, moving forward at about 8.00 am along the roads reaching the town from the south and south-west. By 11.00 am the Bulgarians had been pushed back into the town; the 9th Dragoons were sent to their aid at the same time Gourko's main body came into action against Dzuranli, driving back the Turks, but at the same time losing touch with the Eski Zagra detachment when he pulled back all the rest of the cavalry to his right wing.[7]

The fighting in front of Dzuranli was prolonged and bitter; from the shelter of the dense woods in front of the village the Turks poured a fire so heavy on the attackers that Major Liegnitz, the German military *attaché*, described it as 'the most terrible musketry fire he had ever seen or heard.'[8] However, with the support of a well-timed cavalry charge, Boreisha's infantry pressed forward and drove the Turks back through the wood.

In Eski Zagra the fighting continued throughout the afternoon. By now Major-General Rauch, having reached the town after a circuitous ride around the Lesser Balkan Mountains, had taken command. It was evident that there was a serious risk of the town's defenders being cut off, and he ordered a retreat to a position on the heights some five miles north of the town.

Hozier, describing the Bulgarian resistance to the very strong forces sent against them, observed that they had defended themselves with great bravery; it was not surprising that, when the risk of being surrounded became apparent, they preferred to fall back rather than be taken and face massacre by the Turks. He added:

> In this struggle the Russians seemed to hold the lives of their Bulgarian allies somewhat cheap; at all events, the regiment of dragoons which remained occupied itself much more in extricating itself than in protecting the retreat of the Bulgarians.[9]

Gourko, in spite of his success at Dzuranli, could see that any attempt to reach the troops in and above Eski Zagra was doomed to failure, and with a heavy heart he ordered his contingent to fall back along a sheep track which ran through the mountains to Dalboka, and then rose up from that place through the pass to the Tundja valley. That night his troops bivouacked briefly at Dalboka. Early on the morning of August 1 they resumed their retreat through the pass, covered by the cavalry. Hozier, commenting on Gourko's operations, remarked on the courage displayed and the difficulties overcome during the advance, and added that 'the retreat was perhaps even more noticeable, both for its daring, being undertaken in the face of an enormously superior force, and for having to overcome the greatest natural obstacles.'[10] Trudging onwards, the force attained the relative safety of Hainkioi on August 3, and from there sent back patrols to see what Suleiman was doing.

These reported that the Turks were moving in considerable force from Eski Zagra to Yeni Zagra. One patrol rode through the burnt and ruined town of Eski Zagra, finding that only some Bashi Bazouks remained. The unfortunate inhabitants had suffered terribly at the hands of the Turks, although no reliable estimate of the civilian casualties could be made. It seems clear that Suleiman had authorised the destruction of the town as a reprisal for what was regarded by the Turks as the 'treason' of the inhabitants.[11] Quite what was the reason for Suleiman's move to Yeni Zagra is unclear, but it meant that the Russian retreat on Kazanlik and Hainkioi was largely undisturbed.

No separate account of the casualties suffered by Gourko's force during the fighting between July 22 and July 31 appears to have been published. Greene recorded the total casualties from the departure from Tirnova until August 6 as having been 981, of which he estimates that about 500 were lost during the Eski Zagra battles. These figures manifestly understate the true figures. Forbes reported on August 8 that 'of the severity of the fighting a judgment may be formed from the fact that of the Bulgarian Legion, which began sixteen hundred strong, only between four and five hundred reached Shipka.'

He went on to give a figure of three thousand casualties for Gourko's force during the fighting on July 30 and 31.[12] These figures, which were estimates made at the time with no official figures against which to check them, probably exaggerated the true position.

Epauchin, in his account of the operations of Gourko's advance guard, gives the total Russian casualties between the start of the advance from Tirnova to the return to the Balkan range as being 527 killed, 916 wounded and 85 missing, a total of 1,528, or more than ten percent of the whole force.[13] This, too, may be inaccurate, and may understate the loss. Epauchin was, naturally, at pains to depict the operation as an overall success, noting that the Russian advance through the Balkans had caused total panic in the Turkish government, one despatch referring to the Ottoman Empire as being 'placed between life and death.' In particular the threat to Adrianople caused great concern, and prompted the recall of Suleiman's army as well as the changes in the high command. Epauchin listed the trophies gained by the advance guard:

They were indeed great. Firstly, the Balkan chain for a considerable distance, (2) the two convenient passes of Hainkioi and Shipka, (3) the town of Tirnova, so important both in a military and political sense, (4) a wide belt of territory which passed into our hands, (5) numerous stores of all kinds, (6) some 1,500 prisoners, and three standards, fifteen guns, and lastly, twenty three battalions routed and dispersed.[14]

Turkish infantry advance to the attack. This image conveys an excellent impression of how infantry manoeuvred about the battlefields during the war, and how men were sent forward to feed a skirmish line. (*Illustrirte Geschichte des Orientalischen Krieges von 1876-1878*)

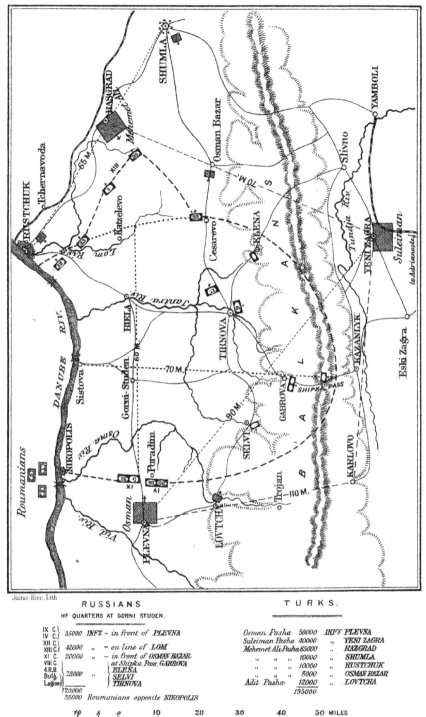

Relative positions of the Russian and Turkish armies August 5 1877

Julius Bien, Lith.

RUSSIANS		TURKS.

Hⁿ QUARTERS AT GORNI STUDEN.

IX C. IV C.	35000	INFᵞ – in front of *PLEVNA*	Osman Pasha	50000	INFᵞ	*PLEVNA*
XII C. XIII C.	42000	„ – on line of *LOM*	Suleiman Pasha	40000	„	*YENI ZAGRA*
XI C.	20000	„ – in front of *OSMAN BAZAR*	Mehemet Ali Pasha	65000	„	*RAZGRAD*
VIII C.		at Shipka Pass, GABROVA	„ „ „	10000	„	*SHUMLA*
4.R.B. Bulg. Legion	23000	*ELENA* *SELVI* *TIRNOVA*	„ „ „	10000	„	*RUSTCHUK*
			„ „ „	8000	„	*OSMAN BAZAR*
	120000		Adit Pasha	12000	„	*LOVTCHA*
	35000	Roumanians opposite *NIKOPOLIS*		195000		

Scale $\frac{1}{1350.000}$

10   5   0   10   20   30   40   50   MILES

Whatever Gourko's original ambitions for his operation may have been, he was soon convinced by the feebleness of the opposition that he encountered that he was in the presence of a beaten enemy, and that a bold push southwards would keep the Turks on the run. However, the objectives of the high command in planning the operation were more limited. Gourko was to seize one or more of the Balkan passes, stimulate a rising of the Christian population south of the Balkans, and disperse whatever Turkish forces he might encounter in the Tundja valley. In the period before the first two battles of Plevna he enjoyed a spectacular success, and but for Osman's intervention might have received the reinforcements necessary to exploit it. But after Krüdener's defeat on July 31 the Russian leaders lost their nerve. Colonel Brackenbury, who had accompanied the advance guard, wrote some months later:

> Unfortunately for Russia, perhaps for Europe, timid counsels were allowed to prevail, and instead of detaining the Turkish armies while the reinforcements were coming up, instead of pushing forward the VII Corps over the Shipka Pass so as to overawe the already panic-stricken forces in Roumelia, and claim a success ending in an honourable peace, the Russian chiefs threw away the reputation of their arms and the precious lives of their best soldiers by hurling them against the breastworks and batteries of Plevna. A very well informed officer of the Turkish army in Roumelia has assured me that the dash forward of the VIII Corps must have been crowned with success, for there were but few troops to oppose it, and these were both raw and demoralised.[15]

While this assessment, looked at with the benefit of hindsight, is almost certainly true, it pays no regard to the enormity of the threat that Osman, in Plevna, posed to the fragile line of communications or, indeed, to the menace of the entirely fresh troops to the east of the Lom, which had not yet made their presence felt. It would have taken leadership far abler than was to be found at the Russian headquarters to press on in the manner suggested.

What was clear to Nicholas and his staff at the beginning of August was that for the moment no further operations south of the Balkans would be possible. On August 5 Gourko was ordered to post the 9th Division, 4th Rifle Brigade and the Bulgarian battalions to hold the passes, while he was to take the cavalry back to Tirnova. From there, he was himself to return to St Petersburg to resume his command of the 2nd Cavalry Division of the Guard, which had now been mobilised and was preparing to leave for the front. This was part of a major reinforcement of the Army of the South which was seen as urgently necessary after the second battle of Plevna. On August 3 the Tsar signed an order for the mobilisation of the Guard, the Grenadiers, and two further infantry divisions (the 24th and 26th). This was in addition to the mobilisation of the 2nd and 3rd Infantry Divisions, which had been ordered soon after the outbreak of war. The additional forces made available by these steps comprised 125 battalions, 42 squadrons, 436 field guns and 24 horse artillery. Three reserve divisions, in addition to one already *en route*, were to be mobilised. The Tsar had also ordered the calling out of the first *ban* of the militia to replace the losses already suffered or which might be thereafter sustained.[16] There could hardly have been a clearer acknowledgment of the extent to which the Russians had underestimated their adversaries. The total effect of the measures taken was to provide 120,000 men for service at the front, with a further 220,000 to replace losses, and to provide garrisons and line of communications troops. Of course, it would be some time before these reinforcements arrived, which meant that the additional support of the Roumanian army was of crucial importance, while offensive operations must for the moment be avoided.

20

Suleiman at Shipka

Suleiman's arrival from Montenegro had made him, the *Daily News* correspondent in Constantinople thought, 'the hero of the hour.' Seeking an interview with the general, he was pleased to find that no restrictions were imposed on him, and he met him at his headquarters in the outskirts of Adrianople:

> The General is hardly forty years old, a man of middle height, and for a wonder not inclined to corpulency, as appears to be the almost invariable effect of high command in Turkey. To look at his fair complexion, sandy beard and whiskers, and his grey eyes, one would almost imagine oneself in the presence of a migratory Scotchman.[1]

This interview took place before the Battle of Eski Zagra, and Suleiman assured his interlocutor that as far as atrocities were concerned 'the strongest orders of which language was capable was ... had been issued to prevent the slightest excesses of the men.'

A few days later, just before the battle had began, this same correspondent was obliged to report that Suleiman's assurances had proved worthless. Writing from Karabunar, he observed:

> The villages between this little station on the Jamboli line and Eski Zagra appear likely to become as infamous in history as those in which the Turkish name will be branded to the end of time. The passion of revenge once let loose amongst a barbarous people is not to be stayed by military mandates, no matter how severe the language in which they may be couched. It is to be hoped that the Russian Commander in Chief is in earnest in his desire to carry on the war in a civilised manner; and it certainly appears almost incredible to find the Turkish side professing to be horror-stricken at outrages which they have so lately been doing their utmost to palliate.[2]

After his victory at Eski Zagra, Suleiman had, as has been seen, not made any effort to follow up Gourko's retreat, but encamped at Yeni Zagra, bringing up supplies and ammunition before preparing to take the offensive. The key question now was the direction in which to move. Mehemet Ali, the nominal Commander in Chief in the European theatre, was of equal rank to Osman and Suleiman, whose armies were operating independently of him; in practice their movement was coordinated, or was meant to have been, by telegraph from Constantinople by the so called War Council which had been established. As Greene pointed out, this was the worst possible system that could have been conceived.

The headquarters of Suleiman Pasha in the Tundja valley. (Ollier)

Essentially there were three options open to Suleiman. He might move to his right and cross the Balkans to join his army with that of Mehemet Ali at Shumla. Alternatively, operating on his opposite flank, he could march to link hands with Osman. In either case he must undertake a ten days' march; but thereafter a really powerful force would have been assembled to strike at the Russian line of communications at Sistova. The third option was more direct; it involved a frontal attack on one or more of the Balkan passes held by the Russians.

Of those options, the move westwards to join with Osman must have seemed the least promising. It would involve crossing the Trojan Pass, and the route would take Suleiman dangerously close to the Russian forces based on Selvi, while once reaching Plevna the fortress of Nicopolis must be retaken before attacking Sistova. On the other hand, the eastward advance would cross the Balkans by the Slivno-Shumla pass, one of the best routes through the mountains, and would stay well clear of any of the Russian positions. Allied to Mehemet Ali's army, the Turks would have 125,000 men concentrated to attack the Russian left, and would certainly oblige the enemy to abandon his position at the Shipka Pass. A Russian defeat would open the road to Sistova; on the other hand, if the attack failed, the Turks could fall back on the fortresses of the Quadrilateral.[3] This option was much preferred by Mehemet Ali, who saw the opportunity of a joint advance through Tirnova to join hands with Osman by way of Lovtcha. Neither of these two options appealed to his colleague:

Suleiman, however, was apparently more occupied in maintaining and increasing his influence with the Government than in endeavouring to assure the decisive

Guard for the colours of the Bulgarian Legion. (*The Graphic*)

success of a campaign, the honour of which would have accrued to his rival. He knew that if he could succeed in retaking the Shipka Pass he should flatter the national pride, which had been profoundly humiliated by the loss of this position. The extreme fear which the Russians inspired, combined with the ignorance of military matters, produced the idea at Constantinople that the evacuation of Shipka by the Russians was an indispensable condition of the security of the capital.[4]

Suleiman's nominal superior had a more objective grasp of what was required. Mehemet Ali's family had come originally from France, but settled in Germany. He was born Jules Detroit, and was brought up in Magdeburg, joining the merchant navy as a boy of fifteen. Visiting Constantinople, and anxious to escape the brutal regime he endured on board ship, he encountered a relative serving in the Turkish army, and through him joined the household of Ali Pasha, becoming a Muslim. Sent to the military school, he did well, and rose rapidly in the army. He served on the staff of Omar Pasha during the Crimean War. Later he served in Montenegro, Arabia, Bosnia and Crete, before being appointed to suppress the banditti in Thessaly. This task he performed very successfully, quickly restoring order. He was given the command of a division during the Serbian War of 1876. He had earned the personal confidence of the Sultan, in spite of his being a foreigner. While *Redif* was Minister for War, this latter circumstance would have made it unlikely that Mehemet Ali could be appointed as commander in chief; but *Redif*'s fall cleared the way. To his great surprise, Mehemet Ali was sent for by the Sultan, and told that he was to replace Abdul Kerim with immediate effect.

His origins, however, remained a serious handicap, and he soon found that a number of the pashas of the old school were determined to thwart him in any way they could.

Among those opposed to him was Suleiman, who was able to win support among the members of the War Council for his preference for a direct attack on the Shipka Pass. In the end this view prevailed, apparently on the basis that Suleiman's army had insufficient pack transport. Orders were issued accordingly. It was, however, not until August 13 that Suleiman began to put his forces into motion.

Suleiman had about 40,000 men available to him for his operation against the Shipka Pass, of which some 15,000 were first line regular troops; the remainder were reserves, together with some irregular cavalry. The latter were completely undisciplined, ignoring Suleiman's orders forbidding the burning of Bulgarian villages in the path of the advance; the destruction which they wrought was entirely self-defeating, since the houses burned down would have provided quarters in the event of a winter campaign.

Responsible for the defences of the Balkan passes was Radetzky, the commander of the VIII Corps. His troops were disposed to cover the three passes of Shipka, Hainkioi and Elena. At Shipka he posted the 36th Regiment (from the 9th Division) and five battalions of Bulgarian troops. Major-General Boreisha, with the 34th Regiment and the 13th Dragoons, was covering the easternmost of the passes held by the Russians, the Elena Pass, while the 33rd Regiment held the Hainkioi Pass. In reserve at Selvi were the 35th Regiment, and the 55th and 56th Regiments from the 14th Division. The rest of the 14th Division was at Tirnova, with the 4th Rifle Brigade, while one Bulgarian battalion held the pass at Triavna.[5]

Suleiman finally made his move on August 16, beginning with a feint against the Russian left, to give the impression that he intended to adopt the scheme advocated by Mehemet Ali. Six battalions together with a large body of Circassians attacked the 33rd Regiment at the entrance to the Hainkioi Pass; after several hours' exchange of rifle fire the Turkish force withdrew. Further east, a more substantial movement was made through the Demir Kapu Pass, the pass of the Iron Gate, driving back Boreisha's troops to Bebrova on August 16 and then on the following day attacking again and taking

The road through the Shipka Pass seen from the north, a near-contemporary view. (Springer)

The Shipka Pass viewed from the south, a near-contemporary view. (Springer)

the town. Boreisha fell back to Elena, while Bebrova was partly destroyed by the Bashi Bazouks. Radetzky took the bait; the advance through the Iron Gate was, he considered, a serious threat to his left flank, and he sent the 2nd Brigade of the 14th Division to Slatariska to block the road that ran through that place to Tirnova. He went himself with the 4th Rifle Brigade to Elena, through which ran the other road that the Turks might take to outflank him. There, he realised that the movement was no more than a reconnaissance in force. This enabled him to pull back the brigade at Slatariska to Tirnova, where it would be available to meet the real thrust when it came.

This was, of course, to be directed at Shipka. On August 18, at about 10.00 am, the garrison there observed considerable Turkish activity in and around Kazanlik. Six battalions were seen on the heights above the town, while the villages of Shenovo and Yabiba were occupied by cavalry. Stoletov, in command at Shipka, reported these movements to Radetzky, who set the 35th Regiment in motion to reinforce him. This was just as well; on the morning of August 19 it was clear that practically the whole of Suleiman's army was deploying for an attack on the Shipka Pass. However, Major-General Darozhinsky arrived on August 20, bringing the total garrison to eleven battalions, with 32 guns, including the seven steel Krupp guns captured by Gourko from the Turks.

The Shipka position which the Russians must defend had two serious disadvantages. The first of these was that at this point in the main Balkan range three spurs run both to the north and to the south. The central spur is the Shipka ridge, up which the road climbs. Before the summit is reached, however, there are three sets of small hills or ridges about 200 feet high running across the main ridge. Of these the highest and most southerly is St Nicholas, the key to the position. Behind it came the Central Hills, about a mile back, and finally the Northern Hills, a further mile back. The problem for the defenders was the fact that to the west and east the other spurs, the high points of which are Mount Aikiridjebel or 'Bald Mountain,' and Mount Berdek respectively, both dominate the Shipka position. Each is separated from the Shipka ridge by a deep ravine. Since the Russians had insufficient troops to enable them to hold these heights there was nothing to prevent the Turks from occupying them, and bringing up guns which could take advantage of the position to overcome the Russian artillery.

The second drawback was the nature of the broken ground in front of the position, which paradoxically might have appeared to be an advantage:

> The strength of a position does not, however, depend entirely upon its difficulty of access to a direct attack, but upon the extent of ground which can be swept by its guns, and upon its means of concentrating fire upon points of critical importance; and Shipka is not able to dominate with its fire the network of lateral valleys and heights which surround it. A brigade of infantry could be massed in a ravine at less than a hundred yards distant from the first Russian position out of reach of its artillery.[6]

The Russian positions were on the three sets of small hills described above. On St Nicholas, part of the southern side of which is a perpendicular rock, there were three

The Shipka Pass - the view south, looking from the Russian position towards the direction in which the Turks attacked, and the epicentre of the battle. (Dave Watson)

The peak from which desperate Russians threw any missile
they could find on August 23. (Dave Watson)

batteries with 25 guns, while to the north-east at the end of a spur some 250 yards long there were the seven steel Krupp guns. Trenches connected the two positions.

During August 20 Suleiman sent forward a substantial force composed of seven infantry battalions against the village of Shipka, which was held by several companies of Bulgarian troops. After several hours fighting the latter fell back toward the pass. The Turks advanced up the road under heavy fire; four battalions swung off down a ravine and into a copse, where they encountered Russian infantry. For a while, the Turks held their position, before falling back though the ruins of the village, which had been set on fire. It was obvious that a further, more substantial attack was to be expected next day; during the night the Bulgarian battalion that alone had remained in front of the Russian position was compelled to retreat to the pass. Stoletov had posted one battalion between the St Nicholas and Steel batteries; another battalion was in trenches on the right, with two companies in a forward position in front of it. Three Bulgarian battalions held the trenches on the left. Two more Bulgarian battalions, with a battalion and a half of Russian infantry, were in reserve between St Nicholas and the Central Hill.[7]

Soon after 7.00 am on August 21 Turkish infantry could be seen on Mount Berdek. The sun came up on what for the moment was a peaceful scene:

The day promised to be very warm; the sky was magnificently clear, balsamic odours ascended from the surrounding woods; while from the bottom of the gorges came the murmur of water under the leaves, and the songs of the birds that the noise of battle had not yet frightened away.[8]

The scale of the imminent assault was entirely clear to Stoletov and his men; the question in all their minds was whether the expected reinforcements would arrive in time.

Predictably the Turks were soon at work constructing a battery on Mount Berdek opposite the Steel battery at a range of about 2000 yards. Rifle fire failed to prevent the establishment by 10.00 am of four guns in the position. Meanwhile the Turkish infantry had begun to move up the road from Shipka village. The road had been mined with fougasses; as the Turks came up they were met with heavy artillery fire from the Steel battery and then the fougasses were exploded electrically, causing heavy casualties. The explosions also heavily damaged the road itself. Now the Turkish artillery on Mount Berdek opened fire, and the Turkish infantry deployed and maintained a heavy rifle fire on the Russian position. On the south-east side three Turkish assaults were made, all of which broke down in the face of the rifle fire of the defenders; the attackers fell back with heavy losses.

Suleiman, who appeared unconcerned about the casualties which his army might incur in the process, was resolved to launch a series of powerful probing attacks against different sectors of the Russian position, in the hope of finding the weakest point. Having failed on the south-east side of St Nicholas, he next launched strong columns against its western slopes. For a while, in spite of terrible losses from the artillery firing point blank into them, the Turks courageously held their ground; but the casualties they took were so great that they were obliged to fall back. It was now about 11.30 am; to the vast relief of the defenders the 35th Regiment now arrived, having marched without a break for 27 miles to reach the front.

Suleiman next varied his tactics, employing dense masses of sharpshooters to lay down a constant blanket of rifle fire, which fell not only on the troops in the trenches but also on the reserves in the valley behind. He then at about noon launched an attacking column towards the Steel battery, which advanced in three lines at a run to scramble up the mountain side with drums beating and to shouts of 'Allah! Allah!' Despite their bravery, they were cut down by murderous rifle fire; ten times they charged the Russian position, as Suleiman fed in reinforcements, but every time the attackers were forced to retreat. The final assault went in by moonlight at about 9.00 pm. Casualties during the day had been fearful; Hozier puts the total Turkish loss at 3,000 men. The Russian official figure of their loss was about 200 in total.[9]

During the night the Turks were busy constructing new batteries, and digging trenches as close as one hundred yards from the Russian positions; there was little that Stoletov could do to prevent this, since he had too few troops to undertake a sortie. As August 22 dawned the Turks now had ten guns in position on Mount Berdek, and six guns on Bald Mountain. Two more were on the height known as Woody Mountain to the north of Bald Mountain.

Throughout August 22 the Turkish artillery kept up a heavy fire, but no serious assault was made. During the day, however, ammunition for the Russian artillery began to run dangerously short. All day both sides worked hard at repairing their batteries; the Turks dug a series of shelter trenches to cover their forward positions. During the day

Bringing down the Turkish wounded. (Ollier)

also, Suleiman began to withdraw part of his reserve behind Mount Berdek, and moved them round to his extreme left, to Woody Mountain. His aim was to break the frail umbilical cord which linked the defenders of Shipka to the rest of the Russian forces north of the mountains. By the morning of August 23 the Russians were threatened on all sides; the narrow ridge, along which ran the high road, and which connected the hills which made up the Russian position, was entirely exposed to the cross fire of the Turks at a range of between 1,500 and 2,000 yards.[10]

Suleiman had by now realised the folly of making piecemeal attacks on what was unquestionably a strong position which was being resolutely defended. His intention for August 23 was to make a simultaneous assault taking advantage of the situation which his troops had occupied on practically all sides of the Russian position. In preparation for the assault the Turkish artillery kept up its bombardment throughout the night.

Early on the morning of August 23 he pushed forward two columns on either side of the Shipka ridge, up the valleys which were out of reach of the Russian artillery. That on the Russian right was directed at the western flank of the Central Hills, while that on the Russian left assaulted the eastern flank of the same position. At the same time two large columns advanced to the assault of the rocky slopes of St Nicholas.

On the left of this position, held by three Bulgarian battalions, Turkish troops attacked from two ravines on the east. As many as six battalions repeatedly attacked the Bulgarian trenches, but in spite of inflicting heavy losses were unable to gain a foothold. Meanwhile in the front of St Nicholas, on its southern face, the Turks made no less than four attempts on the Steel battery; all were driven back with heavy loss, but here again the defenders had also suffered terribly and were obliged hurriedly to dig additional rows of shelter trenches to provide cover.

Stoletov had sent two and a half companies under Lieutenant Colonel Schwabe to take up a position on the slopes of Mount Berdek, and thereby hamper any Turkish assault from this direction. Naturally the Turks made Schwabe's men the first object of their assault; at 5.00 am they moved forward in four columns, and Schwabe sent for reinforcements, receiving one and a half companies. The Turkish attack came in at 6.00 am. Heavily overpressed, Schwabe again appealed for help, and two more companies were sent to him. The Turks also received reinforcement and at 7.30 am launched a fresh attack, inflicting heavy casualties on the defenders. One of the latter said afterwards: 'The Turks fired at random, and only stray bullets reached us; but there was such a hail of shot, so many stray bullets, that the ranks thinned with frightful rapidity.'[11] The pressure on Schwabe was intense; in reply to a further appeal from him Stoletov sent yet more reinforcements.

The situation on this flank remained extremely serious, but there now came a development that could have been fatal to the Russians. A fresh Turkish column debouched from the forest on Woody Mountain, to assault the Northern Hills.

They advanced rapidly towards the high road, and at a range of a hundred yards the Turks opened fire on the one and a half companies of the 35th Regiment which confronted them. The Russian infantry charged forward with the bayonet without firing a shot, and drove back the attackers. Meanwhile on Mount Berdek Schwabe was grimly hanging on to his position. The last company which Stoletov still had in reserve was sent to him at about 10.00 am, and with this his small force, which had sustained heavy casualties, was able to hold on until 2.30 pm. At this time he sent a message to Stoletov that he could do so no longer without further reinforcement; but none was available, and he was told to hold the position at any cost for as long as he could, and only if absolutely necessary to fall back. Fortunately, at about this time the Turkish attack on the southern face of St Nicholas slackened, and Stoletov was able to withdraw troops from there to help Schwabe. By 5.00 pm, however, there was no more that the latter could do, and his troops began to retreat.

The lack of ammunition was by now having a marked effect; sensing that the Russians were coming to the end of their tether Suleiman renewed his assaults, which were met not only by bayonet charges but by a hail of stones, tree trunks and other missiles of all kinds. Archibald Forbes described the dramatic moment as Stoletov and Darozhinsky, having sent what they believed might be their final message reporting the situation, prepared to defend the position to the last:

It was six o'clock; there was a lull in the fighting, of which the Russians could take no advantage, since the reserves were all engaged. The grimed, sun-blistered men were beaten out with heat, fatigue, hunger and thirst. There had been no cooking for three days, and there was no water within the Russian lines. The poor fellows

The Russians defended themselves desperately when, on August 23, ammunition ran so low they used rocks, tree trunks and other missiles to repel the Turkish assaults. (*Russes et Turcs*)

lay panting on the bare ridge, reckless that it was swept by Turkish rifle fire. Others doggedly fought on down among the rocks, forced to give ground, but doing so grimly and sourly. The cliffs and valleys sent back the triumphant Turkish shouts of 'Allah il Allah!'[12]

Suddenly, as they watched, Stoletov caught sight of a long dark column moving down the high road. To their amazement the two generals saw that these were mounted men. They were not, however, cavalry; the column consisted of somewhat less than 300 men of the 4th Rifle Brigade. Radetzky had accompanied the brigade on its march to Gabrova on its way to reinforce the Shipka front. By the afternoon of August 23 they had, after marching thirty-three miles, reached the entrance to the Shipka Pass. There Radetzky was met by an orderly officer sent by Stoletov who, seeing the general, called out: 'Quick, General, we can hold out no longer, the Turks are on the point of cutting the road.' Seeing the horse lines of several *sotnias* of Cossacks who had camped at this point, and whose riders had made their way on foot into the pass, Radetzky ordered the riflemen to take off their knapsacks and to mount the Cossack ponies and ride hell for leather through the pass. As they galloped up the road they met more and more parties of walking wounded heading for Gabrova, but soon they were able to take their place

Radetzky's riflemen arrive in the nick of time at Shipka on August 23. (Budev)

alongside Stoletov's exhausted men, and their arrival, which the Turks took to be a much larger reinforcement than was in fact the case, caused the enemy to become demoralised. However, the rest of the 4th Rifle Brigade was following, albeit on foot. The battle was not, though, by any means over yet. The Turkish troops on Woody Mountain continued to pose a serious threat to the Russian rear. Radetzky, who with his staff had accompanied the mounted riflemen, took in the situation at a glance. The 16th Battalion of the 4th Rifle Brigade was just now beginning to arrive; pausing for half an hour for these troops to be collected. Radetzky launched them in a charge towards Woody Mountain. So successful was their attack that they drove the Turks back beyond their first line of trenches, which the riflemen occupied. By 8.00 pm silence at last descended on the battlefield.[13]

It had been a disastrous day for the Ottoman Empire. Estimates of the Turkish casualties during the three days fighting vary; Hozier puts the total figure as being at least 8,000 men, and Russian losses during the same period as more than 2,000. Until Radetzky brought up the reinforcements, Russian casualties were of the order of 50% of their total force engaged. The defence of the Russian position on Mount Berdek, which had absorbed so many of Stoletov's reserves, had been particularly expensive. Of the troops engaged there, only about 150 remained unwounded.[14]

For the Turks, however the consequences of the fighting on August 23 were immense. The symbolic significance of Shipka, which had enabled Suleiman to convince himself, and the government, that this was the correct military objective, had been profoundly enhanced by the sacrifice of so many lives. Thereafter Suleiman's military judgment was perverted by a desire to take the Shipka Pass, at whatever cost, with the result that the overall Turkish strategy lost whatever coherence it might have had.

The immediate battle was however, by no means over. At 5.00 am Dragomirov arrived with the 56th Regiment, the leading unit of his 14th Division, which had marched thirty-eight miles the previous day. It was followed closely by the 55th Regiment. Radetzky wasted no time in committing these fresh troops, sending the 1st Battalion of the 56th Regiment across the ravine to attack the Bald Mountain in flank, while the two remaining battalions were posted on the road in reserve. Radetzky was standing on the slope of the Northern hills, watching the progress of the attack, when Dragomirov joined him after posting his troops. The 1st Battalion of the 56th Regiment was pinned down by the Turkish rifle fire, and the 2nd Battalion was moved forward in support. As the two generals discussed the position Dragomirov, who had dismounted, was severely wounded in the knee. Forbes watched as Dragomirov's horrified staff turned to help:

> One of the best generals in the Russian Army is *hors de combat*. He is as brave as he is skilful. He never so much as takes his spectacles off, but when we have borne him into comparative shelter quietly sits down, and, ripping up his trouser leg, binds a handkerchief round the wound. Surgeons gather round him; but, like the true soldier he is, he says he will take his turn when it comes. He is carried further out of the line of fire, his boot removed, and the limb bandaged.[15]

As he was placed in a litter, the 2nd Battalion defiled past to take up its position. 'Go on, my brave fellows,' called out Dragomirov: 'Don't flinch before the fire. Everyone has his fate, and if one is killed, *ma foi*, it is no great matter.'[16]

Turkish dead at the Shipka Pass. (*Illustrated London News*)

For about two hours the battle at this point raged with first one side and then the other seeming to gain the upper hand; but at about noon the Turkish artillery were seen to withdraw, and Radetzky personally led forward all the troops that he could collect in an assault on the Turkish infantry. The attack met with limited success; the first line of Turkish trenches was taken, but the other positions on Bald Mountain were obstinately defended, and as night fell they remained in Turkish hands.

Meanwhile Suleiman, aware that the arrival of the Russian reinforcements meant that his opportunity was beginning to slip away, had launched a further assault on St Nicholas. The point of attack was once again the Steel battery, and on this occasion the leading Turkish troops succeeded in getting into the Russian trenches, where a fierce hand-to-hand struggle with the bayonet ensued. In the course of this fight, which ended with the attackers falling back to their start line, the leading Turkish battalion of about 500 men was virtually annihilated.[17]

During August 24 the rest of Dragomirov's division had continued to arrive, and by nightfall Radetzky had nearly 20,000 men at his disposal. This figure did not include the battered remnants of the Bulgarian battalions who were sent back through the pass to Gabrova for a well-earned rest. Radetzky's immediate concern was the continued Turkish possession of Woody Mountain, which commanded his right and posed a serious threat to the road, and for August 25 he planned a further assault in this sector. For this he proposed to employ the 1st Battalion of the 56th Regiment, together with three battalions stationed under Colonel Lipinsky on the right of the Central Hills. The 1st Battalion was soon in trouble, and it was not until noon that it succeeded in getting across the ravine and up the Bald Mountain spur. Once it was engaged with the Turkish troops there, the gunfire served as a signal to Radetzky to launch the other three battalions towards the Woody Mountain, During the morning Darozhinsky had fallen, shot through the heart; practically the whole of the Russian position was exposed to the dropping fire of the Turkish skirmishers, and casualties continued to mount in this way.

Lipinsky, moving up the high road and preceded by a dense cloud of skirmishers, reached the foot of Woody Mountain during the afternoon. His central column rushed up the slope and seized the first line of Turkish trenches, whose defenders fell quickly back, abandoning their second line as well. The Russians charged on, arriving in disorder at the principal line of Turkish trenches, where they were first halted, and then driven back. Two battalions of the 53rd Regiment were sent forward to reinforce them, and the battle continued through the evening and into the night. Colonel Count Adlerberg, commanding the troops occupying the first line of Turkish trenches, to which the Russians had retreated, was hard pressed and called for reinforcement; but Radetzky, with only one regiment left in reserve, felt unable to provide any further troops for this sector, and ordered Adlerberg to retreat on the morning of August 26.

The battle had continued throughout the night. An observer described the spectacle:

> It was a rare sight, this great battle in those dark woods at night. The flashes of fire passed along the line like an electric spark, and a strange effect was produced by the red light reflected on the columns of smoke that hung suspended over the combatants in the still night air. The whole of the top of the mountain seemed ablaze for hours with musketry and cannon discharges, and at certain moments the whole summit appeared to be on fire.[18]

During August 26 there was a brief and unofficial truce to allow the dead to be buried; when it ended, the firing was desultory, and the only attack was mounted during the evening by the Russians, but not in great force. Suleiman, whose artillery kept up an exchange with the Russian guns during the following two days, pulled back the bulk of his exhausted troops to Kazanlik, leaving small detachments to hold the positions that he had gained. On their side, the Russian troops in the Shipka Pass were also utterly worn out; during this period further troops were brought up to relieve them, and the total force in and around the pass was increased to thirty-nine battalions, ensuring that there was no danger of its capture. Nepokoitschitsky, arriving on August 29, concluded that no further reinforcement was necessary, and sent back the further units that were *en route*.

Assessing the final casualty list is difficult. The Russians reported that the total of wounded was 2,731 with about 1,000 men killed. Casualties had been particularly high among the officers, whose white uniforms made them an easy target for Turkish sharpshooters. On the Turkish side, estimates were made on the basis of the number of wounded counted by foreign observers as passing through Kazanlik, Philippopolis and Adrianople. A total of 8,350 was arrived at, while the number of killed was reckoned to be at least 4,000. If Suleiman had 40,000 troops at the start of the battle, this meant that he had suffered casualties of 30%. Later estimates put the total even higher.[19] Suleiman at once applied for reinforcements of 20.000 men, and by a remarkable effort the bulk of these were supplied, including units from the garrison of Constantinople and the police. For the moment, however, the sector remained quiet.

21

Karahassankoi

Abdul Kerim was undeniably physically torpid, and it had gradually became apparent to the government in Constantinople that this characteristic extended to his intellectual approach to the campaign in Bulgaria. Certainly it is true that, to his credit, he had authorised Osman's movement eastwards from Widdin; but that, in terms of his strategic contribution, was about all. Whether the Russian staff prepared the same kind of penetrating analysis of their prospective individual opponents as was the practice of the Prussian General Staff is not recorded. If they did, they should perhaps have paid more attention to the possibility of interference by Osman's large army at Widdin; on the other hand, they might have been more relaxed about the threat from the forces in the Quadrilateral under the direct command of Abdul Kerim.

As it was, the size of the Turkish forces based on Rustchuk and Shumla was such that two corps were considered necessary to deal with them. Designated as the Army of Rustchuk, and under the command of the Tsarevich, their initial objective was to occupy Biela and the line of the Jantra, to contain the Turkish forces in the Quadrilateral and, all being well, to take the fortress of Rustchuk itself. Energetically handled, the army under Abdul Kerim might have proved a formidable opponent. At the beginning of July he had a total of 136 battalions, 46 squadrons and 25 batteries under his command. Of these, 48 battalions constituted the garrisons of the four fortresses of the Quadrilateral; there were twelve battalions in each of Rustchuk, Shumla, Silistria and Varna. 20 battalions, with four squadrons and six batteries were with Ali Pasha in the Dobrudja. This still left a field army of 68 battalions, 42 squadrons and 19 batteries with which to oppose the Russian crossing of the Danube.[1]

At the time that the Russians crossed at Simnitza, the Turkish corps at Shumla was under the command of Ahmed Eyoub Pasha. It consisted of the 1st Division (Nedjib Pasha) of 8 battalions and 3 batteries; the 2nd Division (Assaf Pasha), of 16 battalions and 3 batteries; and a cavalry division under Fuad Pasha composed of 18 squadrons of regular cavalry, 6 squadrons of irregular cavalry and 3 horse artillery batteries. The corps at Eski Djuma was commanded by Salih Pasha, and was still in the process of being organised. It consisted of 22 battalions, 9 squadrons and 6 batteries; 5 batteries and 3 squadrons had been detached to Tirnova, while 9 battalions, 4 squadrons and 2 batteries held Osman Bazar. In addition a mobile brigade consisting of 8 battalions, 5 squadrons and 2 batteries had been assembled from the original garrison of Rustchuk, and was under Mustafa Zefi Pasha there.[2]

In addition to these a division made up from the contingent arriving from Egypt was at Varna, but was not yet ready for action. The total of mobile troops at the disposal of Abdul Kerim amounted to about 30,000 men, with another 45,000 garrisoning the fortresses of the Quadrilateral.

It had been expected that the Danube would prove a serious obstacle to the Russian invasion of Bulgaria, and the news that the Russians had succeeded in crossing with very little difficulty came as a nasty shock to the government in Constantinople. Abdul Kerim was called upon to explain what he was doing; his response was that permitting the Russians to get across the Danube was all part of his plan. Not surprisingly, he was then invited to explain what his plan consisted of; he refused, saying that if the government did not have confidence in him he should be relieved, but that the contents of his plan must remain a military secret.[3]

This was plainly not good enough, and he was peremptorily ordered on July 3 to advance and halt the progress of the invasion. In response to this, Abdul Kerim moved Fuad and Assaf to Rustchuk via Rasgrad. These were to be joined at Rustchuk by Mustafa Zefi's brigade, and the whole force was then to advance on the Jantra. Meanwhile Nedjib remained at Shumla and the Egyptian troops at Varna, while Salik was also not required to move for the time being.

The fortresses of the Quadrilateral, like their famous namesakes in Northern Italy, enjoyed a considerable reputation for defensive strength. They invariably figured largely in wars between Russia and Turkey, and in 1828-1829 held up the invasion for nearly a year. Notionally, the most powerful was Rustchuk, located where the River Lom joins the Danube. The city is on a plateau, which rises above the river to a height of about one hundred feet. In 1877 its population was about 30,000. Hozier described the city and its fortifications:

> The houses are mostly low wooden buildings scarcely better than huts, and the streets are dirty and ill paved. The defences included the old fortified girdle, and a series of independent outworks. The *enceinte* consisted of eleven bastioned fronts with proportionally short curtains. The ditch was about forty-feet wide and ten deep. The scarp and counterscarp were of masonry. The bastions were each armed with from four to six guns, some of them being of heavy Krupp calibre.[4]

Outworks, mostly of a very modern date, surrounded the town and citadel by a kind of double girdle beginning and ending with the Danube. Plans to turn the area around the city into an entrenched camp had not been carried out, due to a lack of money; but one entrenchment had been completed, on the Sari Bair, known as the Levant Tabia.

Shumla, where Abdul Kerim's headquarters were located, was an entrenched camp protected by a double line of forts erected on the highest points of its easily defensible position. It was a much more imposing city than Rustchuk, with a population of 40,000. In the reign of Mahmud II Moltke had drawn up plans for the first line of defence, and these had been the basis for the construction of the forts and the earthworks that linked them. Outside this line a second line of forts had been constructed, to take account of the greatly increased range of modern artillery. The two latest forts, constructed in accordance with the most modern designs, were built by two former Prussian officers, Reschid Pasha and Blum Pasha. The main works were armed with 200 guns, 50 of which were heavy Krupp guns. The entrenched camp provided shelter for an army of up to 150,000 men. Moltke noted the strength of the place in the war of 1828-1829:

> Shumla, with regard to its supply of provisions, was like a fortress on the seaboard, which, although besieged on one side, can only be blockaded from a distance on the other. The circumference of the high plateau, at the foot of which lies Shumla,

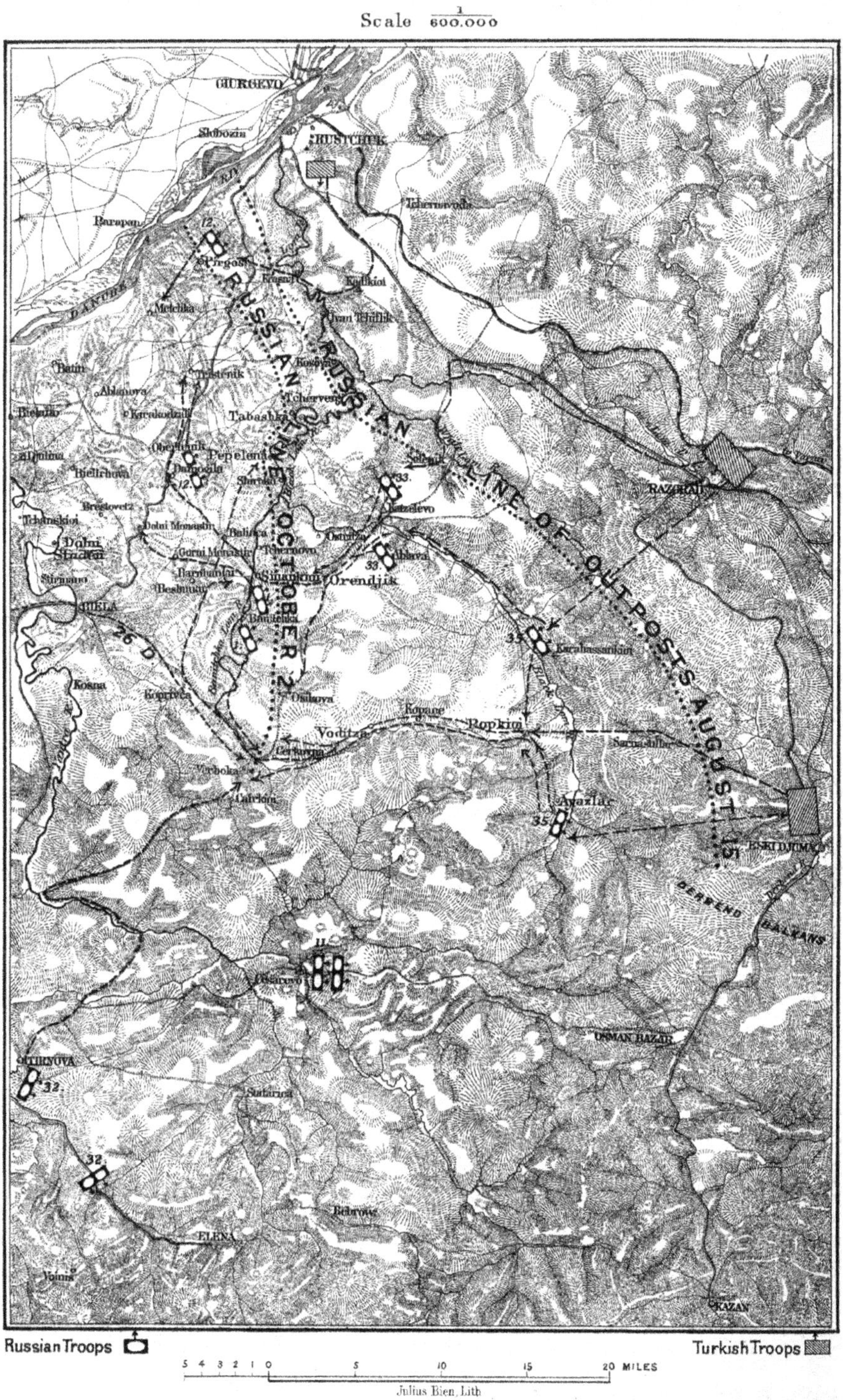

Scale $\frac{1}{600.000}$

Russian Troops

Turkish Troops

5 4 3 2 1 0   5   10   15   20 MILES

Julius Bien, Lith.

Country between the Lom and Yantra rivers

amounts to 18 or 20 miles. But unless troops can be placed close under the heights, they must extend their observation of the principal thoroughfares to a much greater distance round the town. To make the investment complete, it would be necessary to detach to distant points numerous divisions, which ought not to be weak, as in the woody and broken ground the enemy could steal upon them unawares, in considerable force, without running any risk of uncovering their own front.[5]

Silistria, always seen as crucially important from a strategical point of view, was unfavourably placed for the purposes of fortification. The town was smaller than either Widdin or Rustchuk. Its importance lay in the fact that it commanded one of the most practicable passages of the Danube, and posed a serious threat to the line of communication of an army advancing on either Shumla or Varna. The town was surrounded by a bastioned *enceinte* strong enough to protect it from being captured by storm. Since 1828-1829 it had been strengthened by the construction of two lines of outworks, 1,600 yards and 2,000 yards from the old walls, which were supported by modern bombproof redoubts.

Finally there was Varna, located on the Black Sea at the mouth of the River Devna. The town and fortress stood between two ranges of hills which run out to the sea and form the harbour. The inner fortifications had been modernised and rearmed with guns of a heavy calibre. Fourteen forts and redoubts had been constructed on the heights. In total the defences mounted some 300 guns. The resources lavished on this fortress were eminently justified by its crucial importance to the Turkish army in Bulgaria. Through it passed all the supplies and men destined for the defence of the country against invasion. If a Russian force got as far as Varna, it would be well placed to attack any Turkish field army operating north of the Balkans in its rear.

It was the strength of these fortresses which had persuaded Abdul Kerim that he was better off operating within the Quadrilateral. Whether he had any more of a plan than to sit and wait for the Russians to come and attack him is unclear, and the movements which he ordered following the directions from Constantinople do not disclose his intention. Certainly the defence of the line of the Jantra was his best bet for the moment, and for this he must hold Biela. To do that he must bring strong forces forward as quickly as possible. Fuad's cavalry was obviously the fastest moving unit, and could have quickly reached Biela from Shumla, a distance of fifty miles.[6]

It cannot be said, however, that on the other side the Russian movements displayed much sense of urgency. Of the two corps comprising the Army of Rustchuk, it was the XII Corps (Vannovsky) that was to invest that city and besiege it with the assistance of the heavy artillery installed on the north bank of the Danube at Giurgevo. The XIII Corps (Hahn) was to cover this operation and watch the Turkish forces around Shumla. The Russian cavalry entered Biela on July 4, but it was not until July 11 that the first infantry reached the town in the shape of the 33rd Division (from the XII Corps) (Timoslav). The other division of this corps (the 12th Division) (Firks) was at Pavlo, about six miles to the west of Biela. The two divisions of the XIII Corps, the 1st Division (Prosharov) & 35th Division (Baranov) were also by now closing up to the Jantra, and were within a few hours' march of Biela. The cavalry division of the XII Corps (Driesen) had advanced up the road toward Rustchuk, and was now some eight miles from Biela.

Ahmed Eyoub had, in accordance with his orders, effected his junction with Mustafa Zefki, south of Rustchuk, on July 9; his cavalry moved south on the Rustchuk-Biela road. They soon bumped into Driesen's cavalry coming up in the opposite direction, and there was a brief engagement before Abdul Kerim ordered Ahmed Eyoub to retreat. Mustafa Zefi went back to Rustchuk, while Ahmed Eyoub also went back the way he had come, taking up a position behind the Kara Lom. Four rivers bore the name Lom; the most westerly was the Banicka Lom which joined the Kara Lom; together they flowed into the Solenik Lom some fifteen miles south of Rustchuk. Finally the Beli Lom joined the Solenik Lom about eight miles south-east of that point. Abdul Kerim's abrupt reversal of his orders to move out of the comfort zone of the Quadrilateral was prompted in particular by the news of Gourko's occupation of Tirnova.

This latest demonstration of Abdul Kerim's ineptitude made up the Sultan's mind. Redif Pasha, the War Minister, and an elderly retired general, Namyk Pasha, were sent to Abdul Kerim's headquarters to find out just what was going on. Unknown to *Redif,* Namyk had orders to report not only on Abdul Kerim but upon *Redif* as well. When he got there, Namyk speedily made up his mind what must be done; producing his secret instructions, he ordered both *Redif* and Abdul Kerim to leave Shumla at once. Mehemet Ali arrived to take over command at Shumla on July 19.[7]

His arrival immediately energised the Turkish headquarters. On the day following, after the *firman* appointing him had been read to the troops, he made a personal address, saying that he was empowered to promote a deserving soldier to the rank of general, or to degrade the undeserving, or shoot a traitor. Following this, Mehemet Ali became a whirlwind of activity:

> Marchings and counter-marchings, reviews and inspections, were now the order of the day, till the so lately languid, dispirited legions of Shumla were stirred with all the fire of martial life, and heard of the deeds of their brothers-in-arms at Plevna with mixed feelings of admiration and envy. As the spirits of the soldiers revived, their health improved; and complete confidence being established in their new chief, the men were soon burning for an opportunity to distinguish themselves under his orders.[8]

Mehemet Ali's immediate concern was to ensure that his movements would be concealed from the Russian cavalry, and he sent out patrols in all directions. In the irregular Circassian cavalry he had a body of troops that could be as much of a nuisance to his own army as they were to the enemy; but they were well suited to match the Cossack cavalry, who were very effective in covering the movement of the main body of the Russians. By the time he took over there was not much contact between the opposing forces, although a body of Turkish cavalry under Eshreff Pasha was well forward in a position at Torlak, only four or five miles from a Russian advance guard operating north of Kostanzi on the Solenik Lom. Mehemet Ali sent forward a force to cover Eshreff's retirement, consisting of 4,000 infantry with two squadrons and six guns under Aziz Pasha. The force ran into the Russian advance guard, to the surprise of both parties, and there was a sharp skirmish at close quarters at the village of Essirdji, in which both sides lost heavily. Among the dead was Aziz, regarded as one of the most promising leaders of the Turkish army.

Prince Hassan, son of the Khedive of Egypt, and commander
of the detachment his father provided. (Ollier)

The setbacks at Plevna had effectively paralysed Russian operations on the Lom as elsewhere, and the Tsarevich's army remained virtually static throughout the early part of August. It occupied an extended line, in which there were large gaps, from Rustchuk almost as far south as Osman Bazar. The XII Corps covered Rustchuk by posting the 12th Division at Pirgos, on the Danube about ten miles from the fortress; the 33rd Division stood on the Lom, from Kadikoi south to Nisava. The XIII Corps had the 35th Division on the line of the Kara Lom from Kacalyevo to Opaka. The 1st Division was in a slightly more forward position, with its left resting on the Solenik Lom at Sadana, and its right at Yaslar on the Kara Lom. Units of the 1st Division maintained contact with the main body of the Russian army at Kozarevica, five miles east of Tirnova. Cossack patrols were thrown forward in advance of these positions, covering to a limited extent some of the gaps in the Russian line. The most serious of these was between the XII and XIII Corps, more or less opposite Rasgrad, where the largest body of Turkish troops was stationed.

Mehemet Ali had soon set about redeploying his army, bringing forward the units that had been concentrated around Shumla to a strong position from Rasgrad to Eski Dzuma. He at once set his infantry to the construction of earthworks along this line, devoting particular attention to those in front of Rasgrad. He had no confidence in Ahmed Eyoub, who commanded there, but the latter was an influential man among the more conservative pashas, and Mehemet Ali did not feel strong enough to bring about his removal. Ahmed Eyoub remained, therefore, in command of one of the two corps in which the army was organized. It was to consist of three divisions, each of sixteen battalions, six squadrons and four batteries, commanded respectively by Fuad, Assuf and

Baker Pasha, a former British officer who rendered good
service to the Turks during the War. (Ollier)

Nedjib Pashas. In addition there was an independent brigade led by Hassan Pasha, of
six battalions and one battery; a flying column commanded by Mehemet Bey, consisting
of three battalions, six squadrons and half a battery; and a cavalry brigade under Emin
Pasha of eighteen squadrons, a section of horse artillery and 2,000 Circassian cavalry.

Mehemet Ali had to put up with a lot of attention from the international press.
Wentworth Huyshe, the correspondent of the *New York Herald*, who accompanied the
Turkish army, described the effect on the Commander in Chief of the journalists who
besieged his headquarters:

> Poor Mehemet Ali, who had been frightened by the deluge of English officers, was
> now appalled by the avalanche of pressmen, but he made the best of it, and, instead
> of bullying and insulting us as his predecessor had done, he assumed an attitude of
> friendly reserve. 'Wait, *messieurs*, till I am ready, and then you shall see' – that was
> his stock phrase for his interviewers.[9]

Mehemet Ali was also not given the opportunity of making his own choice as
commander of his 2nd Corps. Aged twenty three, and with little military experience,
though a favourite of the Sultan, Prince Hassan was the eldest son of the Khedive of
Egypt and had arrived in command of the Egyptian contingent that had arrived at
Varna and which was now considered almost ready to take the field. A French journalist
offered an ironic opinion of its military capacity:

A Russian supply column. (*Russes et Turcs*)

A few months ago some fine men-of-war brought to Varna several thousands of nice little soldiers with chocolate faces and uniforms of dark blue cloth; they were so pretty, so prim, so well dressed, that one began to hope it would not rain for fear they should melt away. One could have sworn that they had all come out of boxes of toys from the Black Forest. It was natural to suppose that these elegant troops were not intended to take part in the hardships of warfare, for which they seemed no more fitted than a lady of fashion for work in the fields.[10]

On joining the army, the Egyptian soldiers, well equipped and well paid, were inclined to look down on their rougher Turkish comrades. They were more energetic and efficient in the matter of digging entrenchments, but were not, however, to prove as effective when it came to fighting. Political necessity compelled Mehemet Ali to accept Prince Hassan as commander of the 2nd Corps, which stood in front of Eski Dzuma. It was composed of three divisions. The 1st Division (Ismail Pasha) was of fourteen battalions (nine of which were Egyptian) and four batteries; the 2nd Division (Salih Pasha) had eighteen battalions, a cavalry regiment and four batteries; and the Reserve Division (Salim Pasha) had fifteen battalions and three batteries. There were three flying columns; the first of these, which would be assigned to Baker Pasha, consisted of three battalions, 1,000 Circassian cavalry and three guns, while Ibrahim Pasha and Mustapha Bey each had two battalions and eight squadrons of Circassians.

A Russian encampment in a cemetery, Karahassankoi. (Ollier)

Mehemet Ali had therefore 109 battalions, 56 squadrons and 153 guns at his disposal. Based on an average battalion strength of 500 men, and a squadron strength of 120 men, it has been calculated that the total of the army amounted to about 70,000 men. It was something to go to war with, and was certainly strong enough to justify Russian fears for the threat it posed to their entire operation.[11] Maurice observed that the Russian position 'was as remarkable as any to be found in the whole course of military history,' strung out as it was on a huge arc with a circumference of about 180 miles, which covered nothing except the bridges over the Danube:

> There were no general reserves: everywhere the Russian armies were reduced to acting on the defensive, and there was no immediate prospect of dealing the enemy a decisive blow. It was impossible to withdraw from the extended position taken up, for this would have meant abandoning the Christian populations of those districts which had enthusiastically welcomed the Russian flag, to the savage revenge of the Muslim soldiery. It would also have meant a loss of prestige and morale, which the Russian leaders dared not face in view of the careless confidence with which they had entered on the war.[12]

One of the steps taken by Mehemet Ali to strengthen the leadership of his army had been to send for Baker Pasha, at that time organising the new Turkish gendarmerie. Valentine Baker, who held the rank of *Mirliva* in the Ottoman Army, had been a highly promising cavalry colonel until he was cashiered from the British Army after an incident in a railway carriage that led to his conviction for indecent assault. His appointment to head the gendarmerie came as a result of an intervention by his friend the Prince of

The Battle of Karahassankoi. (*Illustrated London News*)

Wales who, like very many of those who knew Valentine Baker, was convinced of his innocence. Baker had kept in touch with the Prince of Wales, and in November 1876 had written to him to report on the positions that he had indentified which Britain could, if necessary, occupy to prevent a Russian occupation of Constantinople.[13] Baker, who arrived at Shumla on August 16, was appointed as a military adviser to Mehemet Ali, taking part in the discussions at headquarters as to the strategy immediately to be followed.

He had arrived to find Mehemet Ali pondering the rejection by the War Council of his plan to bring a large part of Suleiman's army over the Balkans. Discussing the alternatives of remaining on the defensive, or of launching an offensive towards Biela, Baker found neither option attractive. To stand fast meant inevitable defeat when the large scale Russian reinforcements, known to have been called up, actually arrived, while operating against the fortifications which were believed to have been thrown up to cover Biela with an army unused to manoeuvring in the open field was particularly hazardous. Baker strongly urged Mehemet Ali to strengthen Prince Hassan's corps, and then to move forward cautiously in such a way as to oblige the Russians to attack. If such operations were successful the army might then, he thought, go over to the offensive.[14]

Mehemet Ali agreed that Prince Hassan's corps should be strengthened, and was cautiously in favour of a limited forward movement. He then went off to Rasgrad, leaving Baker with Salih, who was in temporary command of the corps pending the arrival of Prince Hassan.

Baker had previously accompanied Mehemet Ali on a personal reconnaissance of the Russian positions near Popkoi, and had been impressed by the defensive potential of the position at Yenikoi, on the wooded heights in front of Eski Dzuma. It had been briefly occupied by the Russians in July, but in the general alarm after the second battle of Plevna had been abandoned, even though it commanded Eski Dzuma, and would have made it impossible for the Turks to hold that place. Hahn, whose headquarters were at Popkoi, realised when he observed the Turks busily fortifying Yenikoi what a serious mistake it had been to give it up, and decided to attempt to retake it. On August 21 he sent forward a force in two columns from Yaslar, which pushed back the Turkish outposts to Sarnasuflar and Rassimpachakoi.

Baker was soon heavily involved in the defence of the centre of the Turkish position near Yenikoi. In the course of fierce fighting the Russian assault was repulsed. The heat was brutal; on both sides the troops were exhausted. On August 22 the commander of the key sector of the Turkish defences, the Eshek Tepe, suddenly retreated, and the Russians, taking advantage of this, threatened the whole position. Fortunately for the Turks, two companies pushed forward by Baker surprised the attacking column, and the Tepe was reoccupied.[15]

It was clear to Salih that although this Russian assault had failed, the Yenikoi position would continue to be at risk while the Russians held Yaslar, and on August 22 he crossed the Lom with a strong column and drove out the two battalions which held the village. This, in turn, threatened the Russian position at Popkoi, and Hahn ordered an immediate counter-attack by Prokhorov's 1st Division. It was as late as 10.00 pm that the attack went in, and fighting continued all night before the Russians retook Yaslar. Salih was not done with, however, and concentrated the whole of his division, which put in three assaults during August 23, all of which were driven back. A fourth attack, however, succeeded, and Prokhorov fell back two miles to Sultankoi. Coming after Mehemet Ali's reinvigoration of the army, this victory, albeit a modest one, resulted in a disproportionate improvement in general morale.

Reinforcements continued to arrive. On August 26 the Egyptians came up to the front, and impressed Baker rather more than they had the French journalist previously quoted:

> They were fine, lithe, active-looking men, uncommonly well dressed and drilled; in fact, very far superior to the Turks in both respects, and they formed a strong contrast to the ragged battalions that had fought so well a few days before.[16]

On August 28 Prince Hassan arrived and took command of the corps. Mehemet Ali came to Eski Dzuma, and met with Prince Hassan, Salih and Baker to consider the situation. It was agreed that the time had now come to take the offensive. Popkoi was an obvious target; but the Russians had been heavily entrenching their position there since the engagement at Yaslar. The XIII Corps appeared to be concentrated in and around Popkoi, and on the left bank of the Kara Lom, but Karahassankoi, on the right bank, was not strongly held. After a lengthy debate, it was agreed that this should be the objective.[17] Prior to this, Mehemet Ali had carried out reconnaissances in force, both to determine the extent of the defences of Karahassankoi and, further north, towards Kairkoi to concentrate the attention of the XII Corps in that direction.

Apart from the fact that Karahassankoi was only lightly defended, another reason for selecting it as the point of attack was that it marked the junction between the two

The Battle of Karahassankoi. Key – 1) Sadina, 2) Karahassankoi, 3) Gagovo, destroyed by bombardment, 4) Popkoi, 5) Haidarkoi, (there is no 6), 7) River Lom, 8) Cossack squadron, 9) Bashi Bazouks, 10) Turkish troops coming from Rasgrad, 11, 12, 14,

15) Russian batteries, 13) Turkish battery near Rasgrad firing on 11 and 12, 16, 17, 18, 19) Turkish batteries, 20) Turkish infantry crossing the Lom. (Ollier)

Russian trenches at Karahassankoi. (*Illustrated London News*)

Russian corps. Hahn's position extended from Sultankoi, held by the 1st Division, to Gagova, held by Baranov's 35th Division. His line extended over the Kara Lom, through Karahassankoi and on to Sadina and Kisil-Moura. Major-General Leonov had held Karahassankoi for several weeks with a small force of cavalry; following the Turkish reconnaissances, he was reinforced with an infantry regiment and some field guns, bringing the total number of these to ten.

Mehemet Ali advanced on August 29. Nedjib's division of the 1st Corps was on the right. Preceded by a large number of Circassians his troops moved unnoticed under cover through the cornfields, before being launched in an assault on Sadina, which was immediately successful in driving the Russians from the village. On the left, the men of Sabit's brigade of Salih's division also advanced unobserved, moving forward behind a ridge before advancing in two columns, one on Haidarkoi and one on Karahassankoi. By noon they had deployed under cover of heavy artillery fire and were ready to attack; the overmatched Russian guns responded gamely, but by 2.00 pm had been reduced to silence. The Turkish columns advanced through the high standing maize stalks, being still scarcely visible to the attackers.

Leonov had in all some 3,000 infantry with 500 cavalry, and was heavily outnumbered as he struggled to hold his position. In the intense heat the Turkish infantry forced their way forward, the Russians retreating yard by yard in front of them. An eyewitness accompanying Leonov described the battle:

> All around and in front of us bullets were falling in showers. The dark foliage of the hillsides opposite, the whole crest of the flat ridge in fact, was dotted with puffs of blue smoke, and all about us sprung sudden clouds of dust and earth, showing

how well the Turks knew their mark. We anxiously looked towards Gagova for the expected help; for from the moment the ridge was taken our only hope of holding the village lay in the arrival of reinforcements.[18]

In fact the only reinforcement which Leonov received, at about 2.00 pm, was about 300 men. This was just enough to repel an attack by Nedjib, whose division had moved forward from Sadina on the right. For about two hours there was a lull in the fighting, which caused Baker, watching from the Sakar Tepe, the most intense frustration:

> It was perfectly maddening to remain a spectator on our point of observation, and to see a battle so completely thrown away. I could stand it no longer, and begged Mehemet Ali to let me go down and order a general advance on the village. It had originally been intended that the assault on Haidarkoi should be made directly Karahassanoi had fallen, but it was evidently no time to wait, and the chief ordered an immediate attack. Collecting my English staff – Colonel Allix, Colonel Briscoe, and Major Jenner, and accompanied by Major Sartorius, we pushed rapidly down the steep declivity and galloped off in the direction of Bachiler.[19]

Reaching Sabit's brigade, Baker found that its commander had gone off to look for Nedjib, to coordinate his assault. Baker sent Allix to find him, and tried unsuccessfully to get the Turkish skirmishers to move forward. At this moment the Russian artillery opened fire again, heralding a counter-attack; Baker's horse was killed, and that of Briscoe wounded. It was a dangerous moment; the Russian infantry advanced and at about half a mile short of the Turkish line halted and opened fire. At this juncture a Turkish battery, which Baker had ordered up from Bachiler, arrived and began firing. It was the turning point; as the Russian infantry wavered and then fell back the Turkish troops rose up and dashed forward. These Russian troops had been moving up to support the garrison of Karahassankoi but, checked by Baker's intervention, made no further progress. The village was now assailed by the troops of Nedjib's division and by Sabit's brigade, and by 7.00 pm it was in Turkish hands. At the same time two Egyptian battalions advanced and drove the Russians out of Haidarkoi.

As a result of this battle Hahn had been obliged to abandon the line of the Kara Lom. Had the success been immediately followed up, an even more comprehensive victory might have been won. Baker was extremely discontented with the performance of the Turkish staff in particular, which had confirmed the assessments he had received from foreign military *attachés* that the Turkish army was unable to manoeuvre effectively:

> The inefficiency of the Turkish staff had been singularly apparent. In the Turkish army the staff occupies a position towards its general very different from that of any other army in Europe. Young officers are trained at the Staff College. They attain a certain amount of theoretical proficiency which is not, as a rule, prevalent among the generals whom they serve, but they lack experience in practical maneuvring in the field. At the same time they are eaten up with the knowledge which they think they have acquired.[20]

On August 30 Mehemet Ali held a council of war before leaving Prince Hassan's Corps to go to Rasgrad, when it was agreed that Ahmed Eyoub's Corps should move forward to occupy to occupy the whole of the line of the Kara Lom. The Turks were gaining in confidence after the Battle of Karahassankoi; no very accurate figures of the losses sustained by either side were published, but Greene records a Turkish estimate of about 1,800 Russian casualties as against 1,000 Turkish.[21]

22

Cerkovna

Having pushed back the left wing of the XIII Corps, it was Mehemet Ali's intention to do the same to the right wing of the XII Corps, and thus separate them. The 33rd Division with the 1st Brigade of the 12th Cavalry Division constituted Vannovsky's right wing, which was at Kacalyevo and Ablava, the former a village on the right bank of the Kara Lom and the latter on the left bank. Lieutenant-General Baron Driesen was in command of this force, which consisted of 12 infantry battalions, 8 squadrons and 46 guns, amounting in all to about 10,000 men. Of these, Major-General Arnoldi commanded 5 battalions and 8 guns at Kacalyevo, while the remainder of the 33rd Division was posted along the plateau behind Ablava.

In order to conduct this operation with the maximum strength possible, Mehemet Ali restored Nedjib's division to the 1st Corps, and reinforced the corps with Reschid Pasha's brigade of Egyptian troops. In addition, in order to keep the left wing of the XII Corps occupied, which consisted of the 12th Division, he ordered Ahmed Kayserli, the commandant of the fortress of Rustchuk, to make a sortie in the direction of Kadikoi. Ahmed Eyoub was to direct Fuad's division on Kacalyevo and Sabit's brigade on Ablava. All being well, Reschid's brigade was to make a wide turning movement around Arnoldi's left with a view to seizing the bridge at Stroko and thus threatening the Russian line of retreat to Biela. Assaf's division remained in reserve at Rasgrad. The intention was that the 2nd Corps should advance against Popkoi to prevent the XIII Corps from assisting Driesen's force.

It would have been better had the Turkish army been ready to embark on these offensive movements immediately after the Battle of Karahassankoi; but it was four days before Ahmed Eyoub's corps moved forward. Fuad set out from Rasgrad on the morning of September 2, reaching Esserdji that night. Next day he marched to Solenik, having to go out of his way to get round an impassable wood, arriving that night. He was soon rejoined there by the rest of the corps. On September 4 the advance continued, and by the afternoon the Turkish divisions began to deploy in a half circle around the Kacalyevo-Ablava position. Seeing that an attack was imminent, Driesen sent for reinforcements; two infantry regiments were sent to him, although not all these troops arrived in time to take part in the fighting on the following day.

Fuad was ready to attack on the morning of September 5. Arnoldi's men were strongly entrenched, and the artillery was well sited. The ground over which the Turkish infantry must advance was broken up with ravines and watercourses, and the artillery could not at once be got forward. As a result, Fuad's first attacks, unsupported, broke down. By 7.00 am however, the Turkish artillery was in position and opened fire with great effect. The next infantry attack went in at 10.00 am and it was immediately apparent to Arnoldi that he was heavily outnumbered, and he began to withdraw in as good order as possible across the Kara Lom. To effect this he held the second line of his entrenchments for as long as he could. The Turkish cavalry at this point tried to work their way around Arnoldi's left, but this manoeuvre was prevented when the Cossacks and dragoons forming part of his force launched a successful charge which culminated in a bitter hand-to-hand fight.

Some of the reinforcements for which Driesen had applied having reached him, he sent forward at about noon the 130th Regiment and one battery from Ablava, which forded the Kara Lom and moved on Kacalyevo. By the time it neared the position the last of Arnoldi's troops had retreated across the river; but the regiment's arrival at least served the purpose of stopping any Turkish pursuit.

By 3.00 pm the Turks, in their turn, forded the Kara Lom and advanced on Ablava. This attack was led by Ibrahim Pasha, commanding part of Sabit's brigade, and was undertaken without orders. Ibrahim's battalions had not so far been engaged, but had been suffering all day from artillery fire from Driesen's batteries, and Ibrahim had had enough. Pushing on through the village of Ablava, Ibrahim led his men up to the heights beyond, convinced that reinforcements would be sent up to support him. Mehemet Ali, however, always the cautious commander, believed that Driesen had two divisions there, and Ibrahim, on his own, could not resist the Russian counter-attack, and fell back across the river. The total Russian losses were 1,339 killed and wounded; the Turkish losses were about the same, including about 150 casualties sustained by Ibrahim's force.[1]

Driesen's position above Ablava was, following Arnoldi's withdrawal, untenable, and next day he fell back through Orendzik and Sinankoi and across the Banicka Lom. The Turkish forces opposing him followed, albeit very slowly.

It had been intended that in support of the attack on Kacalyevo the 2nd Corps should operate against Popkoi, to force the XIII Corps away from the XII Corps. Salih, upon whom Mehemet Ali particularly relied to conduct the actual operations of Prince Hassan's corps, proposed on September 6 to attack Popkoi. His batteries dominated the village; when that morning after a heavy preparatory bombardment the Turkish infantry went forward they soon compelled the Russians to begin a retreat. At this point, believing that enough had been achieved, Prince Hassan halted the attack. Next morning it was clear that the Russians were pulling out of their positions altogether, and Baker and Salih went to Prince Hassan to urge an immediate pursuit, while they were in a state of confusion and encumbered by a mass of transport. Hassan at first was inclined to agree, but was then talked out of doing anything by his staff in the absence of instructions from Mehemet Ali. 'Utterly depressed,' as Baker wrote in his account of the war, he and Salih rode forward behind the cavalry they had sent on to follow the Russians. It was abundantly clear to them, as they watched their prey retreating out of their reach toward Biela, that if they had been allowed to press forward with two brigades, as they had advocated, 'nothing could have saved a large portion of the Russian XIII Corps.'[2]

Salih, outraged at the loss of this opportunity, reported what had happened to Mehemet Ali when he arrived next day. When the latter carried out operations himself he was successful, 'but his own lieutenants took it upon themselves to render his success useless.' He seemed powerless to procure obedience:

> When he arrived at Shumla in July he had reason to believe himself invested with the most extensive powers, an illusion which was now dispelled. Suleiman Pasha had his party at Constantinople, and he profited by it to disobey the orders of the Generalissimo, play his own game, and betray the interests of his country. As to

Prince Hassan, the Sultan had a particular friendship for him; and courageous indeed must have been the man who should have interfered with him. What could the foreigner, Mehemet Ali, do in the midst of these intrigues, with nothing but his talents to recommend him?[3]

When Baker and Salih returned to Hassan's headquarters to report what they had seen, they found the Prince in a remorseful frame of mind, 'aware, on reflection, that he had made a mistake, and had lost an opportunity.' This was certainly true, and it allowed the Russians to retreat to the safety of their position in front of the Jantra. There, their left flank rested on the Danube at Batin and their right at Koprivca on the Banicka Lom. The front of the Tsarevich's army had been shortened to about 25 miles. The Russian high command also hastened to cover the gap between the Tsarevich's right and the XI Corps on the Tirnova-Osman Bazar road, posting the newly arrived 26th Division (Dellingshausen) at Cerkovna and the 1st Brigade of the 32nd Division at Cairkoi.[4]

In spite of the ineptitude of both his corps commanders, Mehemet Ali's operations had been successful in driving back the Tsarevich from the line of the Solenik Lom to that of the Banicka Lom. He had fought and won two battles and had inflicted not inconsiderable losses on his opponent. Including the force from Rustchuk, he had about 60,000 men along the right bank of the Banicka Lom, covering a front of about 35 miles. 10,000 men were at Kadikoi; 30,000 at Kacalyevo; and 20,000 at Popkoi. Mehemet Ali located his headquarters for the moment at Sarnasuflar, and paused to consider his options.

Meanwhile his army moved forward, following the retreat of the Russian army. On September 14, pressed uncomfortably closely by Assaf's division, the Russians turned to

The Battle of Sinankoi, September 14 1877 (Strantz)

attack the advancing Turks in order to disentangle themselves. They ascended the heights on the left bank of the Banicka Lom, and began to move down towards Sinankoi, about two miles beyond the opposite bank. A successful Russian advance here, if followed up, would have compelled the Turks to retreat from the centre of their line, and would leave the 2nd Corps very exposed. Assaf, however, who had twelve battalions and five batteries, occupied a strong position on a plateau south of Sinankoi, and all the Russian assaults broke down. When Sabit arrived after an hour's fighting, bringing with him the twelve battalions of his division, it was the Russians whose situation became dangerous, as their retreat was menaced by a force of six battalions which moved on their flank at Goluburaar. They quickly fell back; although this amounted to another minor Turkish victory, the immediate Russian objective of getting back to their defensive position without further interference had been achieved.

In the discussions at Turkish headquarters as to what should next be done, it soon became apparent that before Mehemet Ali had left Ahmed Eyoub the latter had very strongly urged upon him the desirability of an advance from the direction of Rustchuk against the left of the Russian position. Baker, Salih and Hassan were strongly opposed to this. The Biela position was particularly strongly fortified on that side, and the more open country would give the Russian artillery and cavalry much greater opportunities to manoeuvre. And if the Turks were beaten, it would give the Russians the chance to move forward and threaten the line of retreat to Rasgrad. The alternative view was that there should be an offensive movement on the Turkish left. The fact that the headquarters of the 1st and 2nd Corps respectively each advocated an operation based on their own sector cannot have come as much of a surprise to Mehemet Ali. His own confidence had begun to evaporate. In his heart he did not believe that he could beat the Tsarevich, and would much have preferred to fall back to his former strong positions. But he was in no doubt that if he retreated, he would be severely reprimanded, and there was little chance that at this distance he could convince Constantinople of the unwisdom of attacking. His perplexities were, however, soon resolved; an imperative order arrived that an attack should be launched on Biela, prompted perhaps by the news of the capture of Lovtcha.

Mehemet Ali's diffidence about following up his victories at Karahassankoi and Kacalyevo has puzzled commentators. Greene put it down to his lack of confidence in his subordinates:

Russian cavalry at Biela. (*The Graphic*)

The only reason which has ever been assigned for the inaction which Mehemet Ali displayed was that his army, though composed of good fighting men, was so badly officered as to greatly diminish its efficiency for offensive purposes; and especially was this incompetence noticeable among the chiefs of regiments and brigades, who desired to conduct their men on their own responsibility, and without subordinating themselves to the general plan of campaign, or even to the orders of the Commander in Chief, who on account of his foreign birth never had the confidence of his generals.[5]

This was certainly an analysis which Baker would have endorsed. In the short time that he had been with the army he had seen plenty of examples of disobedience and ineptitude among senior officers, and the advice which he tendered to Mehemet Ali took this into account.

Arguing for an advance on the southern side of Biela, Baker pointed out that the Russian fortifications there were known to be far weaker than on the northern side:

Then, even if on our arrival the position appeared to have been too strongly fortified for us to incur the risk of a direct attack, we might either pass the Jantra at Kosna Kosowa, or a portion of our force might strongly entrench the positions east of the Banicka Lom, whilst a part might be detached to act with the force of Mehemet Salim to sever the Russian communications between Tirnova and Biela. In fact, we urged a concentration instead of a dispersion of force.[6]

Baker and Salih were both men who commanded Mehemet Ali's respect, unlike his two corps commanders, and their arguments carried the day. It was resolved to make an attack on the point of junction between the XIII Corps and the XI Corps, and to concentrate the attack on the latter's 32nd Division. Ahmed Eyoub, meanwhile, was to make a demonstration to occupy the attention of the Russian left and centre. As to this, Mehemet Ali gloomily observed that it was extremely doubtful if Ahmed Eyoub would thoroughly do his part.

The necessary movements of the Turkish army began on September 12. The weather had broken, and the troops advanced in heavy rain, delaying the progress of the operation considerably. There was little contact between the Russian and Turkish forces except that at Sinankoi on September 14; this did, however, add to Mehemet Ali's pessimism, and his movements thereafter were characterised by extreme caution. Instead of the concentration so strongly advocated by Baker and Salih, his forces remained strung out over a wide area. On his right Mustapha Zefi's brigade covered his flank at Kadikoi, while behind the northernmost end of his line Nedjib stood at Kacalyevo. Fuad held a position from Stroko through Cernica to Ostrica. Next came Assaf, from Sinankoi to Osikova, and behind him was Sabit, at Jenidzesi. Salih's division prolonged the line south from Osikova to Vodica, with Ismail's division from Vodica to Karatas. The left flank was protected by Salim's brigade, which was covering Osman Bazar. For Maurice, these dispositions told their own story as to Mehemet Ali's intentions:

Had he had any fixed idea of making a resolute advance he would most certainly have concentrated the greater part of his army and screened his concentration by

The Battle of Cerkovna. (Ollier)

a lightly held line of outposts. Circumstances had given him the advantage of the initiative, and he was in a position to throw superior force against some one part of the Tsarevich's necessarily extended line; but to do this successfully it was essential for him to be able to manoeuvre rapidly, and this was impossible with his troops scattered over such a wide front.[7]

Baker records that in order that the projected advance should be given as much support as possible, a message went to Suleiman urging him to bring at least part of his force over the Balkans in the direction of Elena. This produced no response at all, which is what Mehemet Ali no doubt expected; and this was in spite of the fact that the War Council in Constantinople had sent urgent orders to Suleiman as well as Mehemet Ali to move forward in an effort to relieve the pressure on Osman in Plevna.

The rain stopped on September 21 and next day the sun began to dry the rain-sodden roads, enabling the Turkish troops to move forward early to their positions from which the attack was to be launched, on the right bank of the Banicka Lom. Five batteries were concentrated at Cerkovna, and at 11.00 am these opened fire on the Russian positions. The Russians were by no means taken unawares by the attack; they had been alerted for several days by the Turkish activity behind Cerkovna. The Russians at this point were commanded by Lieutenant-General Tatischev, of the 11th Cavalry Division. He had posted his troops on either side of the road which, after crossing the Banicka Lom, ran through Cairkoi to Kesarova and on to Tirnova. To defend the position he had two regiments of the 32nd Division (the 125th and 126th), one regiment from the 1st Division (the 1st) and one of the 26th Division (the 101st). This gave him 12 battalions, about 10,000 men; the 102nd Regiment had also been sent to him, and was marching down from Biela. Tatischev also had the 11th Dragoons and 11th Lancers, five batteries of field artillery and one of horse artillery.

The Turkish plans for the ensuing battle had been the subject of further spirited debate while the army was slowly moving forward during the previous few days. Although

Baker, with Salih's support, had persuaded Mehemet Ali to attack at the southern rather than the northern end of his line, he lost the argument as to how the attack should be launched. Regarding Fuad's division as being with that of Salih the best in the Turkish army, Baker wished to bring that down to Cerkovna to join with Salih's division on the attack over the Banicka Lom. It was to be expected, however that Ahmed Eyoub would let out howls of protest, and Mehemet Ali's own staff persuaded him to agree to a turning movement around the Russian right. Baker was unable to get Fuad's division involved at all, but he did, however, get his own way as to the location of the Turkish gun line in the position described above.[8]

The principal opponent of Baker's plan had been Rifaat Pasha, and it was his brigade, of four battalions, that was given the task of attacking the Russian centre. On his right three more battalions, under Ali-Reza, were to attack the Russian left, which Baker in particular regarded as the weak point of the line. The Russian right wing was to be attacked by three battalions under Salim Pasha. In reserve there were ten battalions of Egyptian infantry under Hassan.

The Turkish attack began on the right at 1.00 pm when Salim's brigade began to debouch from the woods near Yurukler. Driving back the Russian cavalry in his front, Salim pressed on either side of the village. One company of infantry held him up; Tatischev realised that this movement of Salim's was an attempt to turn his right flank, and was the real attack, nothing more than a demonstration having so far been made against his centre, and he sent forward a battalion with several guns by way of reinforcement. Salim continued to feed fresh troops into the struggle and almost surrounded the Russian troops opposed to him. Had any part of the reserve been sent to him, he would have swamped Tatischev's left flank.

With, as he hoped, Russian attention focused on Salim's attack, Mehemet Ali at about 3.00 pm launched Ali-Reza's battalions against the Russian left. A squadron of lancers in front of Verbovka opposed them as they crossed the valley and began to climb up the vine-covered terraces. The lancers fell back slowly, using the terraces to hold up the attackers. It was clear, however, to Mehemet Ali that Ali-Reza had struck at the weakest point of the Russian defence, and he sent for Hassan's Egyptian battalions to come forward and support the attack. However, the roads were still very heavy, and these reserves simply could not get up to the front in time. The lancers continued to resist, although growing weaker, and did so long enough for Tatischev to bring up a battalion and a fresh battery to hold the position. The Turks fell back, before Ali-Reza committed his last battalion which he led up the hill in a desperate assault which reached the village of Verbovka. There, however, the 102nd Regiment arrived in the nick of time after its march from Biela. The exhausted Turkish infantry, with no support, could do no more, and fell back to their start line.

While all this was going on the contribution of Rifaat and his force was confined to a demonstration in front of the Russian centre. He went so far as to put his battalions in column to make a feint against the enemy, but made no attack. As night fell, the Turks remained in their positions all along the front. It was clearly a Turkish defeat, but Mehemet Ali's army was unbroken, and certainly in a position to launch a further attack if he had been so minded. However, Turkish casualties had been extremely high, given the nature of the battle; Hozier puts the number killed at about 800, with from 1,500 to 2,000 wounded. The total Russian loss was recorded as 501. The disproportion

Turkish infantry near Biela, showing the type of field defences frequently
used in the battles of 1877-78. (*Illustrated London News*)

was ascribed first to the fact that the Turks were attacking the Russians, who were in
prepared positions; and secondly to the fact that the 26th Division was equipped with
the Berdan rifle, which had a much greater range than the Krenk. Against the latter
weapon the Turks had always enjoyed a pronounced advantage of range with their
Peabody-Martinis, and the difference came as an unpleasant surprise to them.[9]

On the night after the battle yet another Council of War was held at the Turkish
headquarters. Baker and Salih bitterly opposed the suggestion of a retreat; if it was
necessary to pull back from the heights of Verbovka, then an effort should be made to
turn the Russian right, and move on Tirnova. A movement by about 2,000 cavalry in
this direction had been made on September 19, but came to nothing.

Against Baker and Salih were Sabit and those who supported Ahmed Eyoub,
and these in the end got their way. Mehemet Ali, thoroughly disenchanted with the
performance of many of his commanders, was very ready to return to a strong defensive
position. On September 24 Prince Hassan's corps retreated briskly to Sarnasuflar,
abandoning a good deal of materiel in its haste; and next day Ahmed Eyoub, whose corps
had not fought at all, began a retreat to Rasgrad. By October 1 the whole of the army
was behind the Kara Lom, and the Russian pickets were back in their former positions.[10]

On October 2, as he returned from an inspection of his positions, Mehemet Ali
found a letter waiting for him. Its contents were perhaps not unexpected to some of those
around him, but came as a complete surprise to him. He was relieved of his command
with immediate effect, and ordered to return to Constantinople. He was to be succeeded
by Suleiman. Baker went to say goodbye to him:

I found the Marshal, with a very small escort, sitting in the verandah of a house, and he welcomed me warmly. He was evidently much depressed and discouraged by the heavy blow which had fallen upon him, and he now began to see how thoroughly he had been playing into the hands of his enemies. The result which I had anticipated had been completely verified. The very men who had urged the Marshal to change his plan of operations at this critical period of the campaign were the first to urge against him the delay and want of decision which this change of plans had brought about.[11]

Baker said farewell to Mehemet Ali with the greatest regret, both on military and personal grounds: the Commander in Chief's 'kindness of heart and general good nature had much endeared him to all the officers by whom he was surrounded.' The choice of Suleiman as his successor was more surprising than Mehemet Ali's removal; it was widely understood that Suleiman's refusal to cooperate had been largely responsible for the failure of the offensive. In commenting that the latter's expensive failure at Shipka should have led to a court martial, Hozier observed: 'In a country of intrigue rewards are not obtained by merit, but by favour, and Suleiman Pasha was named Generalissimo.'[12]

23

Lovtcha

Osman's failure to follow up his defeats of the Russians in the first two battles of Plevna left his opponents the opportunity of putting into practice at least one lesson which they had learnt, and that was to embark on the construction of strong defensive positions around Plevna. The month of August passed with no significant move on the part of the Turks, and the Russian works were every day strengthened. For the moment it was the Grand Duke's policy to stand on the defensive while waiting for the reinforcements that had been sent for. The Turkish failure to carry into effect the coordinated offensive called for by the War Council at Constantinople at a time of the greatest Russian vulnerability let slip the best opportunity which the Turks were ever to have.

Osman, however, had not been idle. He too had energetically been constructing defensive works at both Plevna and Lovtcha, and had been bringing up reinforcements and stores of all kinds. By August 22 he had at Plevna forty-nine battalions, twelve squadrons and fifty-four guns, while Lovtcha was held by ten battalions with two squadrons and six guns.[1] He also organised a mobile column with which to conduct operations in the field, consisting of nineteen battalions, eighteen squadrons and three batteries, together with some irregular Circassian cavalry. This force, organised in two brigades under Tahir Pasha and Emin Pasha, was led by Hassan Sabri; Adil Pasha was

The quarters of the Tsar at Gorni Studen. (Ollier)

in command of the troops left to garrison Plevna. Rifaat Pasha was in command of the garrison of Lovtcha.

Once the negotiations for the participation of the Roumanian army had been completed, its four divisions were available for the immediate reinforcement of the Western Army. The 1st Roumanian Division remained posted on the north bank of the Danube opposite Widdin. The 2nd Division had crossed at Nicopolis at the end of July. The 3rd and 4th Divisions crossed the Danube some twenty-two miles up river from Nicopolis, apparently with the intention that they should operate against Plevna on the left bank of the Vid. However, after a few days they were brought over to the right bank. MacGahan believed that this was due to the cooperation between Russians and Roumanians being 'not very good', reporting that one Roumanian regimental commander had declined to receive an order from Zotov.[2]

Effective command of the Russian forces around Plevna had passed to Zotov immediately after the second battle. In addition to the Roumanian units and his own corps he had the IX Corps. He had detached one regiment and part of another from the IV Corps and sent them to Selvi to join Skobelev and his Caucasian Cossack Brigade. This brought Skobelev's force up to a total of five battalions, ten squadrons and two horse artillery batteries. His orders were to occupy Kakrina, just north of the Lovtcha-Selvi road, and to watch the Turks in Lovtcha.

With the troops he already had, the newly arrived reinforcements from Russia, and the Roumanians, the Grand Duke would have a total of almost 105,000 men with which to conduct operations against Plevna and on his right flank. There would be no more substantial reinforcements until at least the latter part of September. The question for the Russian high command was what to do about Plevna in the immediate future. On August 21, to the great surprise of the Russian command, Osman embarked on a sortie. Quite why he chose to do so then is unclear; it has been variously suggested that it was to mark the start of Ramadan or alternatively to celebrate the anniversary of Abdul Hamid's accession to the throne. During the night of August 30/31 Hassan Sabri's column was assembled close to the Ibrahim Redoubt, and at daybreak on August 31 moved out on the Pelisat road. At 6.30 am the Russian outposts reported the movement; Zotov took it to be merely a demonstration intended to occupy his attention while the real attack was made on the Roumanian army. About a mile west of Pelisat the Turkish batteries unlimbered and opened fire, while the infantry rapidly advanced. Their objective was a lunette built by the Russians on a long undulation formed by some hills in front of Pelisat and Sgalievitza. Shouting 'Allah il Allah!' the Turkish troops rushed up the plateau and drove the Russian defenders out of the lunette; the latter fell back but upon being reinforced the 62nd Regiment counter-attacked and retook the position, driving back the Turks for half a mile.

In their turn the Turks brought up further troops and drove forward again to retake the lunette. Maintaining a heavy artillery bombardment, from batteries posted along the crest of the ridge, they prepared to assault the main Russian positions around Pelisat, and in trenches to the south and west of Sgalievitza. The attack began at 1.00 pm; the Turkish column moving on Pelisat was held up by the Russian artillery, and after an hour broke off the fight and retreated. To the south of Sgalievitza the Turks had greater success, occupying a battery and some trenches. After about three hours, however, they

Lieutenant-General Imeretinsky. (*Illustrirte Geschichte des Orientalischen Krieges von 1876-1878*)

were driven back by the 120th Regiment, arriving from the reserve which Zotov had directed to Poradim. He had by now realised that he had to take this attack very seriously.

Momentarily successful in occupying some trenches north of Sgalievitza, the Turks appeared to be gaining the upper hand; but again fresh Russian troops appeared and drove them out. Undaunted, at about 3.00 pm the Turks mounted further attacks, but were beaten off with heavy loss, and they began steadily to withdraw to the ridge where their artillery was posted. Zotov, who was by now on the scene, personally directed the pursuit of the retreating Turks, following them for three miles. At this point, however, Hassan Sabri launched a counter-attack with his reserve, which threatened to take the pursuing Russians in the flank, who thereupon withdrew to Pelisat. When the sortie began, the general opinion at Russian headquarters that it was only a demonstration induced MacGahan not to go and see for himself. After a while, however, he became impatient and rode towards Pelisat, encountering large numbers of Bulgarian refugees escaping the Turkish advance. He soon realized that this was a serious assault, and stayed to record the battle as it swayed to and fro. He was impressed by the courage of the Turkish infantry as they sought to push forward:

> Encouraged by their success in taking the redoubt, and believing they could also take this line, they had no sooner withdrawn from the Russian fire than they formed and went at it again. They dived down into the Valley of Death to struggle there amid smoke and fire, a death struggle of giants; for there is nothing to choose between Russian and Turk on the score of bravery. Many bodies of Turks were

A view of the terrain over which Major-General Dobrovolski attacked at Lovtcha, with Hills 3 and 4 in the background. (Springer)

Russian troops in action at Lovtcha. (*Album della Guerra Russo-Turca del 1877-78*)

found within ten feet of the Russian trenches. The little slope, on the crest of which the trenches were situated, was literally covered with dead. I counted seven on a space of not more than ten feet square. The battle here was terrible, but the Turks were again repulsed, and again they retreated up the hill. It will hardly be believed that they went at it again; and yet they did so.[3]

The sortie had been expensive; the Turks lost about 2,000 men in killed and wounded, while the total Russian losses were 975.[4] The Turks had fought bravely, and had been well led in an assault which took the defenders entirely by surprise. It was, though, unwise:

> The whole enterprise, however, can only be regarded as a most useless and wasteful expenditure of blood. It was too extensive to be regarded as a mere reconnaissance, and far too feeble to break through the massive girdle now rapidly being drawn around Plevna.[5]

In his conduct of the operation Osman had made the same mistake as had the Russians in their first two assaults on Plevna; he had attacked in insufficient strength and had failed to support his assaulting columns.

With the defeat of this sortie the initiative now passed to the Russians. Their immediate objective was Lovtcha, which was in a key strategic position so far as any

Russian infantry taking a Turkish redoubt at Lovtcha. (Ollier)

assault on Plevna was concerned. Indeed, it has been suggested that if this town had been held in force instead of Plevna it might have proved an even greater nuisance to the Russian invasion of Bulgaria. It had speedily been taken by Osman in the course of his advance to Plevna, and remained in his hands as a valuable part of his defences. It prevented the total investment of Plevna, and threatened the rear of any Russian assault on the place. From the outset Skobelev in particular had been a fervent advocate of an assault on Lovtcha.

On August 6 Skobelev had conducted a reconnaissance in force against the town so boldly and skilfully that he obliged the garrison to develop its whole strength. His topographers were able to make a detailed map of the position, which he was able to examine personally before retreating to Kakrina. Lovtcha is some twenty miles southeast of Plevna by the high road, although the extremities of each set of defence works were only about twelve miles apart. It is located in what amounts to an amphitheatre, surrounded by a ring of hills with a diameter of about ten miles. The hills are about 600 feet high. Through the valley flows the River Osma; on its right bank the ridges form four peaks, which the Russians designated as Hills 1, 2, 3 and 4. Hill No 1 was also known as Mont Rouge. Behind this chain of heights, two further heights (called Mounts A and B) stand either side of the road to Selvi. Finally, at the bottom of the valley behind Lovtcha, close to the road to Plevna, the Turks had constructed a powerful redoubt on an isolated hill. A network of trenches linked the various fortifications.[6]

Skobelev issued an inspirational order of the day to his troops, setting out his instructions for both the infantry and the artillery. He concluded with a reminder of the importance of order and silence:

> You should not shout 'Hurrah!' except in cases when the enemy are near, and when you are preparing to charge with the bayonet. I direct the attention of all the soldiers to the fact that in a bold attack the losses are minimised, and that a retreat – especially a disordered retreat – results in considerable losses and disgrace.[7]

On August 31 Skobelev was ordered to advance up the road from Selvi and to seize Mounts A and B in order that batteries might be established there preparatory to an attack, an operation which he carried out with the minimum of fuss on September 1. During the night he worked hard at entrenching the position and preparing epaulments for the batteries; he installed the eight guns he had with him.

Overall command of the operation had been entrusted to Prince Imeretinsky. In addition to Skobelev's detachment, he had the 2nd Division, the 2nd Brigade of the 3rd Division, the 3rd Rifle Brigade and the 30th Don Cossacks. Skobelev's detachment was on the left; the remaining units, on the right, were under the command of Major-General Dobrovolsky. Having sent Skobelev forward on September 1 to secure the heights, Imeretinsky ordered Dobrovolsky to move up that night to be ready for an assault on the following day.

At 6.00 am on September 2 fifty-six Russians guns opened fire from Mounts A and B; it was half an hour before the Turkish artillery responded, but when it did it was once again apparent that its Krupp guns had a much greater range than those of the Russians. Alfred Krupp had an agent with Osman Pasha reporting on the performance of his guns, and had been very pleased with the information which he had received. In August

A panoramic view of the action at Lovtcha, as seen from the Russian batteries.
The widely-dispersed skirmish lines are particularly notable. (Budev)

he showed the Belgian Director General of Artillery, Colonel Nicaire, a telegram from his agent, about which the British Chargé d'Affaires at Brussels reported to the Foreign Secretary:

> The result of this great trial, the agent says was admirable, the guns not only carrying further than the Russian, but the precision of their fire was quite remarkable while the destructive power of the shells was double that of the ordinary shells. As to the Turkish artillerists, their mode of handling the guns was beyond all praise.[8]

However, although the Russian artillery was unable to master its immediate opponents, it inflicted heavy casualties on the Turkish infantry sheltering in their trenches on Mont Rouge and Hills 2, 3 and 4. The heavy artillery preparation for the assault entirely achieved its object; by the time the attack came in the Turkish soldiers were completely demoralised. In addition, considerable attention had been paid to the needs of the Russian troops who were to make the assault:

> Probably for no other engagement during the war were troops more thoroughly prepared in every respect, than for this attack on what was regarded as the chief outwork of Plevna. The men were well rested and refreshed, extra rations were provided, and a special detachment was set apart for conveying supplies of water into the ranks – a more important duty than may at first appear, the day of assault

being so insufferably hot that, in spite of every care, many of the men were rendered quite ill and had to leave the ranks[9].

The intention had been to defer the infantry assault until 2.00 pm; but so effective was the Turkish artillery fire that Dobrovolsky, seeing the effect on the morale of his men, felt obliged to go forward at once. By 10.00 am his troops had taken Hill 4, and driven the Turks over the Osma. Imeretinsky now ordered Skobelev's column forward, and in less than half an hour the other three hills were in Russian hands, thanks to the thoroughness of the artillery preparation. There remained only the powerful redoubt on the Plevna road, the capture of which was essential to the success of the operation, and which was a much tougher nut to crack. The redoubt was rectangular in layout, 160 yards long and 60 yards wide, with a heavy 24-foot parapet on which the Russian guns had made little impression. It stood on the Pordim hill, which was some 300 feet high.

At 5.30 pm Imeretinsky gave the order for the assault to commence. It was carried out by a force of eight battalions which moved on the right of the redoubt, while four more battalions crossed the river lower down and attacked the left of the position. There ensued a furious conflict. The redoubt was heavily shelled by the Russian artillery, while the Turkish infantry responded with a hail of rifle fire on the attacking columns, which took heavy losses as they climbed the hill, taking cover wherever they could. After twenty minutes the Russians collected together several hundred men in a patch of dead ground; then, as the defenders' attention was distracted elsewhere, they stormed up the slope, led

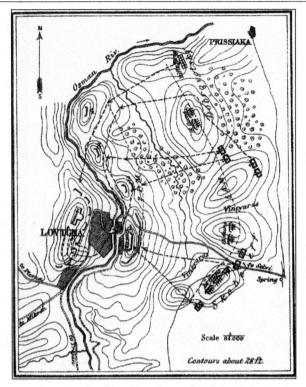

Battle of Lovtcha, September 3 1877

by the colonel of the 5th Regiment, with only a cane in his hand. As the Russian infantry poured over the parapet and into the redoubt, the Turkish infantry fell back, only to find that its only exit was blocked by an ammunition cart of which the horses had been killed. There followed a savage hand-to-hand fight, in which fearful casualties were suffered on both sides before the Turkish resistance was overcome; there were few survivors among the defenders of the redoubt.

The rest of the garrison of Lovtcha retreated into the hills to the west, pursued energetically by the Cossacks, who cut down many of the battered Turkish infantry, and took many more prisoners. In the rugged country, however, and as night fell, the Cossacks were unable to cut off Rifaat's retreat, and he succeeded in bringing all of his guns and what remained of his infantry into Plevna two days later, by way of side roads through the hills. Russian losses during the battle were reported as being 319 killed, with 1,145 wounded and 52 missing. Estimates of the Turkish casualties varied. The Russians claimed to have buried 2,200 Turks within the entrenchments; in addition many casualties were sustained during the subsequent pursuit. Throughout the war the losses claimed or admitted were wildly inaccurate, and this battle was no exception, as Thilo von Trotha pointed out:

> The statement of Prince Imeretinsky at the conclusion of his report, that 3,000 Turks (the number occurs more than once, and is therefore not a misprint) were cut down in their flight, bears too much the stamp of inordinate exaggeration to be

Prince Imeretinsky's corps following the Battle of Lovtcha. (*Russes et Turcs*)

of any value whatever, the more when it is considered that the pursuing Cossacks could barely have numbered more than 1,000 horses.[10]

Osman had first become aware of the threat to Lovtcha on September 1, when the guns of Skobelev's advance guard could be heard at Plevna. Soon after this the telegraph was cut, but for some time Osman attached no great importance to the situation, in spite of the reports which he received from Rifaat. Next day, however, news reached him of the strength of the force attacking Lovtcha, and he realised the danger. He assembled a force of twenty battalions, two squadrons of regular cavalry and a regiment of irregular cavalry, about 100 Circassian cavalry and three batteries of artillery. This column was not, however, ready to move off towards Lovtcha until noon on September 3. Osman took personal command of the force. It was not long before Cossack patrols spotted the Turkish columns as they marched southwards towards Bogot. Osman detached a flank guard to cover his left, and moved by a mountain track through Laskav to Zilkova, bivouacking for the night of September 3 just short of that place, about ten miles from Lovtcha.

That night Imeretinsky ordered Skobelev to take the units comprising his original detachment, and to occupy a position covering Lovtcha on the north, and early next morning Skobelev's men were dug in behind a brook flowing into the Osma near Pridunsec.

As dawn broke Osman resumed his march, his leading troops in touch with the screen of Cossacks that was monitoring his movement. At about midday his advanced patrols reported Skobelev's position. The fact that no firing could be heard suggested that the relief column was too late. Osman halted his march near Lisec and rode off by a side track to a point where he could see the town. It was clear that it was now strongly held by the Russians, and he saw little prospect of retaking it in the face of Imeretinsky's substantial force. He called a Council of War of his senior officers; it was reluctantly concluded that the relief column must return to Plevna. On September 5 he skilfully withdrew to the west through Miras and Peternica, going back all the way to Widdin, which he reached next day. This movement ensured that he was not cut off by the Russian forces around Plevna, and persuaded Imeretinsky that a movement to the south of Lovtcha was intended, as a result of which he dug in around the town rather than attempting any pursuit.[11]

24

The Third Battle of Plevna: The Assault

By the beginning of September, although the operations on the Lom were not going particularly well, the Russians were in an altogether stronger position than had been the case during August, and there were signs at headquarters of a mounting confidence that the worst was over, in Bulgaria at any rate. The Shipka Pass had been successfully defended; Osman's sortie from Plevna had been repulsed; and, on September 3, Lovtcha had been taken. Above all, there had been a steady stream of reinforcements, to such an extent that consideration must now be given to how to use them. One option, of course, was to wait until the arrival of the Guards and Grenadiers completed the reinforcement that had been arranged. This, however, would involve remaining on the defensive at least until mid-October, which would not look good in public relations terms. It would also give the Turks more time to concentrate their forces and, most significantly of all, would mean that a winter campaign was inevitable.

The offensive choices open to the Grand Duke were three. None of them were straightforward. To reinforce the Tsarevich, with a view to defeating Mehemet Ali and driving him back, might give the opportunity to cross into Eastern Roumelia and turn against Suleiman. It might also, though, result in Mehemet Ali retreating on Rustchuk, Shumla or Rasgrad and from a secure position menace the left and rear of the Russian advance just as Osman was doing on the right.

War artists and correspondents as sketched by a Russian Cossack officer. (Rogers)

The next option was to reinforce the troops holding the line of the Balkans, and to advance against Suleiman. Once he had been defeated in the field, the road to Adrianople would be clear. Or would it? The Turks were known to have substantial reserves of unused troops which could be sent up to reinforce Suleiman; and the Turks could also move troops rapidly by sea to Burgas, to threaten the left flank. It would also leave Mehemet Ali the option of moving part of his army southwards through Slivno against the Russian rear. This option was the boldest; but to Nicholas it also seemed the riskiest.

The third option was to launch a major assault on Osman in Plevna, driving him back so far that he no longer offered a threat to a Russian move south. It was a possibility which would enable Nicholas to employ the whole Roumanian army; the deal with Prince Charles had placed restrictions on where they might operate.[1] Furthermore, success here might inspire Serbia to enter the war. This, therefore, was the option chosen.

MacGahan, for one, considered that fighting in fortifications was a mistake. It would be better, he thought, writing on September 1, to take advantage of the Russian ability to manoeuvre more effectively, and to draw the Turks into open country:

> Their want of military science, good officers, and the impossibility of executing manoeuvres on the field of battle could have put them at a great disadvantage with the well-drilled Russian troops. The Russians have always been wanting the Turks to come out and fight in the open field, yet they entrench themselves in such a manner that the Turks have no temptation to come out, and find it impossible to do so when they try.[2]

The arrival of Prince Charles of Roumania to take command of the army before Plevna. (Ollier)

The reason for the choice of Plevna was, however, probably political rather than strategic. The Russian defeats there had caused considerable damage to the military reputation of the Russian army, as Maurice observed:

Plevna had seriously affected Russian prestige, and the Grand Duke Nicholas held it to be his immediate duty to remove the blot from the Russian arms by driving Osman from that place at the earliest possible moment... Still, however expedient it may have appeared to order another attack on Plevna, this decision is not one which would have been approved by a great commander.[3]

History does not record whether there was a great deal of consideration given to alternatives to an assault on Plevna, but it seems likely that there was not. One voice at any rate was raised in opposition; Nepokoitschitsky apparently argued against it at the Council of War when it was discussed. The army was not sufficiently prepared to be sure of success, he thought, the concentration of all the available troops was incomplete, and there was not yet a sufficient store of ammunition for a lengthy battle.[4] This at least was a rational military argument. The reason for the selection of September 11 as the date for the assault was not; it was the Tsar's name-day.

The headquarters of the Grand Duke, and of the Tsar, had throughout August been located at Gorni Studen; the Grand Duke moved to Poradim on September 3, where Prince Charles and Zotov were also based. Next day orders went out for the concentration of all the units that were to take part in the planned assault. On the night of September 6/7 they moved forward to the positions assigned to them in front of the Turkish redoubts.

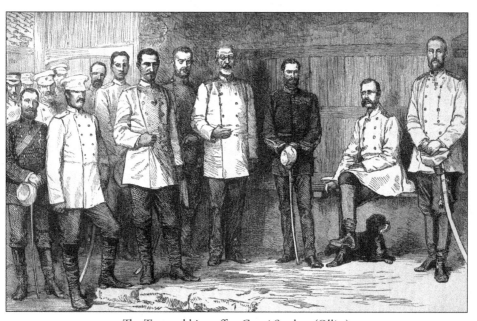

The Tsar and his staff at Gorni Studen. (Ollier)

Osman had almost 60,000 men in Plevna, although the Russians credited him with having between 70,000 and 80,000. They were now organised in three divisions. On the left the 1st Division (Adil Pasha) was responsible for the defence of the northern and eastern sectors; in the centre the 2nd Division (Hassan Sabri Pasha) covered the southern front. The reserve of ten battalions, under Rifaat Pasha, occupied the town of Plevna, the Vid river bridge, and the headquarters hill. Osman's total force consisted of 46 battalions, 19 squadrons and 80 guns, with about 500 Circassian cavalry.[5]

Given the strength of the position as it had been at the time of the two previous assaults, and the considerable and very visible improvements to it that had since been made, the Russians were embarking on a very dangerous venture. The total size of the attacking force was, in the view of many commentators, inadequate for the task. This was not merely hindsight; Sir Henry Havelock, who was at Plevna, estimated that at least 120,000 men would be required to have a good prospect of success. The increased range of modern weapons had materially shifted the balance:

> A defending force, well entrenched and strengthened by formidable redoubts, can now pour such a perfect stream of fire upon assaulting columns as to nearly annihilate them, without being seriously inconvenienced itself. The Germans, in their war with France in 1870, practically admitted the madness of such point blank assaults by the numerous important sieges they undertook; but after two unsuccessful assaults upon Plevna already, it would seem to have needed the sacrifice of an additional 20,000 lives to make this truth equally clear to Russian military leaders.[6]

The half-circle of Turkish redoubts began in the northern sector with two at Opanetz and one at Bukova. Along the Janik Bair were three more. At the eastern end of the ridge there were the two Grivitza redoubts above that village. These perhaps enjoyed a more fearsome reputation than was justified due to the Russian failures to capture them in July. They were not really the key to Osman's position, being lower than other redoubts and unlike them, not dominating a steep incline and not covered by efficient cross fires. Next, on the southern bank of the Grivitza brook, there was a cluster of six redoubts, connected with lines of trenches, covering the east of Plevna town, and running round to the Tultchenitza brook, and facing Radischevo. Finally, south-west of the town, there were six more redoubts to the west of the Green Hills; the southernmost of these, above the village of Krishin, was known as the Yunous Redoubt, after the name of Yunous Bey, who commanded here. These redoubts had been thrown up after the second battle, in which Skobelev's success in this sector had shown up a weakness in the defence.

The Russian forces facing this formidable position were located from the banks of the Vid in the north to the Tultchenitza brook in the south. In the north were the 3rd and 4th Roumanian Divisions, with the 2nd Division in close reserve, facing the line of redoubts from Opanetz to Grivitza No 2. Krüdener's IX Corps was to take up a position running from a point a mile and a half east of Grivitza on the main Rustchuk road to the Plevna-Pelisat road. Krylov's IV Corps, consisting of the 16th Division (less the 64th Regiment with Skobelev), the 30th Division (less one battalion of the 118th Regiment with Skobelev) and their two artillery brigades (less one battery with Skobelev), was to move to the high ground just south-east of Radischevo. Imeretinsky's detachment,

Troops from the Russian IV Corps take up their positions prior to the assault. (*Russes et Turcs*)

which consisted of sixteen battalions with ten batteries of 76 guns, was ordered to take post at the village of Tultchenitza. Lockarev's 9th Cavalry Division was assigned to cover the right flank of the IX Corps, keeping in touch with the left of the 4th Roumanian Division. Covering the left of the IV Corps was Leontiev's 1st Brigade of the 4th Cavalry Division, which maintained a connection with Imeretinsky's detachment. The extreme left of the Russian forces was protected by the Caucasian Cossack Brigade and the Don Cossack Brigade, together having 18 *sotnias* and 6 guns. The general reserve consisted of three infantry regiments (20th, 119th and 120th), two cavalry regiments (4th and 9th Hussars) and five batteries. It amounted in all to nine battalions, three squadrons and 38 guns, and was located at Pelisat.[7]

The proper employment of the Russian artillery during the attack was the subject of dispute among the principal artillery officers. Zotov, who assembled a meeting on September 2 to discuss the matter, was of the view that no assault should be launched until, following a continuous bombardment of the Turkish works, there were signs that the fortifications had been seriously damaged and heavy loss inflicted on the garrison. This view encountered serious opposition:

> It was objected that field guns could do but little injury to earthworks, and that neither the supply of ammunition nor the pieces themselves were equal to so heavy a call upon them. A counter proposition was then made that the redoubts should be swept by so heavy a fire as would destroy their armament, render them no longer a secure retreat for the reserves, and that by pouring a heavy fire on the approaches to them the advance of reinforcements should be rendered difficult. It was held by other members of this council that the destruction of the works should

not be attempted, nor their continuous bombardment persevered in, but that the approaches alone should be cannonaded.[8]

In the end no consensus was arrived at, and no consistent policy was adopted, with the unsurprising result that the Russian field artillery performed ineffectively during the battle.

Zotov's intention for the assault was to concentrate on the south-eastern and southern sectors. In accordance with the opinions he had expressed, it would be preceded by a lengthy bombardment of the Turkish position. The infantry would advance under cover of darkness in order to seize the positions required for the Russian batteries. Once installed, the artillery would commence the bombardment, to last several days. The field artillery was supplemented by two batteries of very large siege guns, originally intended for the siege of Rustchuk. They had been waiting in Roumania for a call to the front. It took no less than 1,500 oxen to drag these monsters and their platforms to the Sistova bridge, and from there to the Radischevo ridge, where they arrived at 10.00 pm on September 6. Working parties from the IX Corps and from the Roumanian divisions toiled through the night to prepare the batteries both for the siege guns and the field artillery for the bombardment that was intended to begin at 5.00 am next day.

In the morning, however, a thick mist shrouded the valley of the Grivitza and the Turkish positions, and it was not until 6.30 am that the bombardment commenced. Although the assault was known to be imminent – on September 6 Osman had published an order of the day warning that an attack was expected on the following day – the Turks were amazed to see, when the mist had cleared, the extent to which the Russians had been able to prepare their artillery positions during the night. It was not until 8.00 am that the Turkish guns began to respond. The Russian infantry, meanwhile, had moved up under cover into positions generally sheltered from the fire of the enemy. The bombardment continued all day. The Russians had 88 field guns and the 20 siege guns in action at ranges from 2,700 to 5,200 yards. Much of their fire was concentrated on the Grivitza No 1 redoubt, in which the Turks had 8 guns. Since the latter returned fire all day, it seemed that the Russian guns had not inflicted much damage. Nor had they sustained much, their losses being minimal.[9] Osman appears to have thought that the concentration on the south and south-east sectors of the defence was merely a feint, for about noon he transferred two battalions from Tahir to reinforce Adil.[10]

As night fell on September 7 it was clear to Prince Charles and Zotov that the bombardment must continue on the following day. During the night the Russian artillery continued to fire at intervals, the object being to prevent the Turks making good the damage sustained. The effort was in vain; at daylight next day it was apparent that not only had the damage been repaired, but in a number of places the works had been considerably improved. Meanwhile it had been decided that on September 8 Imeretinsky should advance on the Lovtcha-Plevna road and seize the ridge due east of Krishin, while Lockarev was to move to the extreme right of the Russian position, passing behind the Roumanian divisions to cross the Vid and operate in the rear of Osman's army, cutting the road to Sofia by making contact with the 1st Brigade of the 4th Cavalry Division on the extreme left of the army.

During the night the Russian batteries were advanced to within 1,600 yards of the Turkish works, and were reinforced by bringing forward five Russian and five

The Russian grand battery before Plevna. (Ollier)

Roumanian batteries. Next day their fire was concentrated largely on the Grivitza No 1 redoubt and the Ibrahim redoubt, the most easterly of the redoubts above Radischevo. The artillery duel continued until the Turkish response began to slacken at about 2.00 pm; by nightfall it had ceased altogether.[11]

Skobelev, with the advance guard of Imeretinsky's detachment, had the 5th and 8th Regiments, the 9th and 10th Rifle Battalions, four batteries, four siege guns and the 21st and 26th Don Cossacks. During the night of September 7/8 he had moved up to Brestovetz and to the Red Hill immediately to the east, and from here opened fire on the Yunous Redoubt at a range of 4,000 yards, and on the Turkish troops seen to be in occupation of the ridge to the east. Imeretinsky, with the rest of the detachment, was above a mile and a half behind in the direction of Bogot.

On the afternoon of September 8 Skobelev began a forward movement, advancing with the 5th Regiment, supported by two battalions of the 8th Regiment to take the 'first knoll,' as it was known, immediately north-east of Brestovetz. From here he pushed on to the second knoll, which was the ridge east of Krishin, which was held by several Turkish battalions. After a vigorous struggle the Turks retreated, and Skobelev moved forward to take the third knoll, which put him at 5.00 pm only about a mile south of the edge of Plevna. The Turkish artillery in the two redoubts close to the town and in the Krishin redoubt brought him under heavy fire; Osman brought up reserves from Plevna and Skobelev was driven back to the second knoll. During the night news came that the general assault which had been planned for September 9 had been postponed; believing that in his present position he was too exposed, Skobelev retreated to the first knoll, and there entrenched himself. It had been a bold stroke, but in the end had accomplished little; it had cost the Russians over 900 men killed and wounded.[12]

MacGahan, who had been watching the bombardment in the Radischevo area, was told by a Cossack that something more interesting was happening on the left. Making his way back over the ridge, he saw Skobelev's force moving forward. He watched as it took first one knoll, and the others, before falling back. As the battle raged, visibility deteriorated:

> At the time the Russians were advancing down the hill, the whole valley was filled with smoke. The town of Plevna, as well as the Turkish redoubts and even part of the wood where the Russians were, had become invisible. The sun was now just setting behind a mass of clouds, but it was seen for a few minutes like a fiery blood-shot eye, which tinged the smoke hanging over everything with the colour of blood. Then it suddenly disappeared behind the mountain, and darkness settled down over the scene. The fire continued for some minutes longer, and from the redoubt, as from the foot of the slope and the foot of the mountains, sprang forth thousands upon thousands of jets of flame like fireflies. Then the fire suddenly ceased. The fight for the night was over.[13]

Elsewhere Lockarev had succeeded with his large force of cavalry in occupying Dolni-Dubnik, brushing aside a force of Turkish cavalry. This, for the moment, did cut the road from Plevna to Sofia. The bombardment of September 8 was, however judged not to have been sufficiently effective, which was the reason for the postponement of the general assault. During the night the Russians again maintained a random fire, but were no more successful in preventing the Turkish infantry repairing the damage. On their

Camp followers watching the bombardment of Plevna. (*Illustrated London News*)

side the Russians constructed new batteries, so that at dawn on September 9 they had 220 guns ready to resume the bombardment.

It continued as before throughout the day, except that the siege guns were running low on ammunition. The Turkish response was in some cases more muted; in particular the Grivitza redoubts were silent. Sensing a possible opportunity here, the Roumanians pushed forward a reconnaissance to Grivitza No 2, but the Turkish infantry drove them off with murderous rifle fire. The barrage was now having a cumulative effect on the Turkish earthworks, and in spite of all the defenders could do the parapets were steadily falling in. Zotov reckoned that the field artillery could keep up the pressure on their own, and had eight of the siege guns moved to a new battery above Radischevo during the night of September 9/10. Meanwhile there had been considerable activity on Skobelev's front. At 5.00 am the Turks launched an infantry assault on his trenches on the first knoll, which was beaten back. A second assault three hours later got within 60 yards of his position before it too failed. Thereafter Skobelev was left undisturbed for the rest of the day; although Osman had sent three battalions under Emin Pasha to reinforce this sector, a planned assault was postponed. At the end of the day two more battalions joined Emin and during the night three more arrived. Emin kept his force concentrated in front of the redoubts, ready for an assault on the following day.

The bombardment continued unabated on September 10. The Grivitza redoubts were silent, the Turks having pulled most of their artillery out of these works, which had been severely damaged. The Russian artillery was also running low in ammunition in places, while a number of guns had suffered substantial wear and tear as a result of being fired at high elevation. During the afternoon the weather took a hand; heavy rain fell during a succession of violent thunderstorms. Everywhere the ground rapidly turned to a pasty black mud, which seriously hampered movement and in particular the bringing up of ammunition.[14]

Skobelev, who was no longer under the command of Imeretinsky, had been authorised to launch a preliminary assault on September 10. At the same time Emin had prepared to advance to drive back Skobelev and to seize the first knoll, but after a personal reconnaissance he reported back to Osman that it would be impracticable to hold it, even if it was possible to take it. He therefore moved forward to occupy only the second knoll with a skirmish line, with six battalions in support. When he launched his attack Skobelev was able without difficulty to drive back Emin's skirmish line and occupy the second knoll; but it was clear that any further advance would be vulnerable, and he contented himself with entrenching the position, which he held with two regiments and 16 guns, with two more regiments and two rifle battalions in reserve.

Zotov and Prince Charles had during the day decided that the artillery preparation had gone on long enough, and that the assault should be launched on September 11. The plan was for a heavy bombardment to begin at daybreak, which was to end abruptly at 9.00 am. It would be resumed again at 11.00 am but be halted at 1.00 pm, resuming at 2.30 pm. The infantry assault would go in at 3.00 pm.

The appalling weather afflicted both sides equally. In his redoubt on the Janik Bair, Herbert had suffered little from the bombardment, but was much affected by the heavy rain as he and his men awaited the assault:

The first day of the actual battle opened with a drizzling rain and in a white mist. The latter cleared towards noon; the rain continued all day, occasionally with a heavy downpour, mostly in a demoralising spray. The ground was a swamp; the wet penetrated our clothing; it invaded our sleeping-apartments and store-chambers and precautions had to be taken to keep the ammunition dry.[15]

A platform had been erected from which the Tsar and his staff could watch the assault. Descriptions of this by various correspondents as a 'grandstand' attracted a good deal of unfavourable comment in the Western press, as did the provision of lunch there. Wellesley described the arrangements that had been made:

There was no grand stand in the usual acceptation of the term, but a small wooden platform with a railing round it, and capable of holding about fifty persons, had certainly been erected for the Emperor's use. Many disagreeable remarks were also made with regard to the preparation of a great luncheon near the stand for the Emperor and his staff after witnessing the assault from this place of safety. It cannot be denied that the luncheon table was there, with its display of white tablecloths, knives, forks, champagne etc, close to the little stand, and I could not but think that the whole scene would have been more in keeping with a small provincial race meeting than with a field of military operations of so momentous a character.[16]

The general assault had been timed for 3.00 pm, but in the southern sector Skobelev had concluded that if his objective at that time was to be the two redoubts closest to Plevna, he must first advance and retake the third knoll. In front of him was Emin's force, which had been further reinforced to a total of 19 battalions and 11 guns. Skobelev had the 61st and 62nd Regiments of the 16th Division, the 9th, 10th, 11th, and 12th Rifle

Colonel Wellesley's quarters. (*The Graphic*)

Battalions and the 7th Regiment from the 2nd Division, a total of 13 battalions and 60 guns. Skobelev's artillery opened fire at daybreak against the Yunous redoubt and the two redoubts on the south-western edge of Plevna, while the infantry concentrated behind the second knoll. The countryside south of the town was covered with vineyards, which greatly reduced visibility; on the morning of September 11 the thick mist additionally made it hard to see more than a few yards.

Before commencing his assault Skobelev, with two officers and six Cossacks, rode forward to reconnoitre the Turkish positions. In his trademark white uniform, on a white horse, he was an obvious target. He and his party got so close in the fog to the Turkish infantry that, when they were spotted, they drew the fire of an entire company. Within moments, the two officers and four of the Cossacks were shot dead, and the other two Cossacks wounded; only Skobelev escaped unscathed.[17]

At 10.00 am the 61st Regiment and the 10th Rifle Battalions began their advance. Passing Emin's left in the fog, they fell upon his right wing and drove it back, quickly securing the third knoll. By 11.00 am the fog had begun to lift, and Emin launched a counter-attack. Skobelev reinforced his troops on the northern and western slopes of the third knoll; although according to the general order the bombardment should cease at 11.00 am, it was clearly impossible to break off the action. He brought up another battery to the second knoll, and ordered the 62nd Regiment to meet the counter-attack. The Turks were driven back into their works, and Skobelev took advantage of this to reform his troops which had become disordered during the fighting. Meanwhile, on his left, Leontiev's cavalry brigade had taken the village of Krishin and kept the Yunous Redoubt under fire. By 1.00 Skobelev had begun his preparations for his main assault on the two redoubts that were his principal objective.

It was remarkable that the vigour of the Turkish activity in this sector did not alert Zotov or the rest of the Russian high command to the importance that Osman evidently attached to its defence:

> It was the vital point; if the south-western heights had been taken, Osman Pasha would have been obliged to evacuate Plevna; while to close round them, and bar the Sofia road, would cut off all supplies. In spite of the excessive inquietude the Turks manifested each time they were threatened at this point, the fact was entirely overlooked by everyone on the Russian staff.[18]

Skobelev seems to have applied to Zotov for permission to bring forward the time for his assault, but only to have received this at 2.30 pm. It was not, therefore, until 3.00 pm that his troops advanced down the slope of the third knoll in two lines of company columns, with bands playing. They drove the Turkish skirmishers out of a line of rifle pits at the foot of the slope and began the climb up towards the two redoubts, reaching a point two hundred yards from the Turkish positions before being pinned down by heavy rifle fire. Seeing this, Skobelev sent the 7th Regiment forward, while the artillery kept up a heavy fire on the redoubts. The attack remained stalled, however, until Skobelev rode forward with two rifle battalions. His horse was killed in the charge, but he led forward his men on foot and stormed into the 'middle redoubt', this being the more westerly of the two.

MacGahan watched Skobelev's charge into the redoubt with the two rifle battalions:

Skobelev had now only two battalions of sharpshooters left, the best in his detachments. Putting himself at the head of these, he dashed forward on horseback. He picked up the stragglers; he reached the wavering, fluctuating mass, and gave it the inspiration of his own courage and instruction. He picked the whole mass up and carried it forward with a rush and a cheer. The whole redoubt was a mass of flame and smoke, from which screams, shouts and cries of agony and defiance arose, with the deep-mouthed bellowing of the cannon, and above all the steady awful crash of that deadly rifle fire. Skobelev's sword was cut in two in the middle. Then a moment later, when just on the point of leaping the ditch, horse and man rolled to the ground, the horse dead or wounded, the rider untouched. Skobelev sprang to his feet with a shout, then with a formidable, savage yell the whole mass of men streamed over the ditch, over the scarp and counter-scarp, over the parapet, and swept into the redoubt like a hurricane. Their bayonets made short work of the Turks still remaining.[19]

The Turks fell back about six hundred yards to a fortified camp, from which they kept up an incessant fire. Soon a counter-attack, in the course of which Emin was wounded, was launched from the next redoubt to the west, which seriously threatened the Russians in the middle redoubt; seeing this, Captain Kuropatkin, who was serving as Skobelev's Chief of Staff, collected about 300 men to meet the Turks head on in the open. A fierce hand-to-hand fight ensued in which, in spite of heavy casualties, the Russians succeeded in driving back the attackers.

Another group of Russian infantry made an assault on the eastern redoubt, but practically the whole force was shot down. Then Colonel Shestakov, from Imeretinsky's staff, came up the slope to the redoubts with three companies, collecting stragglers on the way to create a force of 1,200 men. With these, and a further group of infantry from the middle redoubt, he launched an attack on the eastern redoubt which, at 5.30 pm, was successful.

During these assaults, however, the Russians had suffered fearfully, their total casualties of 3,000 representing about a quarter of the force engaged. And, as night fell, Skobelev's position was now extremely precarious. Having occupied two redoubts he had created a wedge in the middle of the Turkish positions. In this vulnerable situation he sent off a message to Zotov by Colonel Orlov, an aide de camp to the Grand Duke, to explain that unless reinforced his position would become untenable, and that further forces should be sent against the Yunous Redoubt which threatened his rear. Meanwhile he would hold on as long as he could.[20]

While this success was being achieved on the Russian left, the other two assaults had been launched at the appointed time. In the centre the Russian batteries, located between the roads to Rustchuk and Bogot had opened fire at 7.00 am, and the infantry of Krylov's IV Corps had begun to get into position for their assault. By 11.30 am the 63rd and 64th Regiments, due to attack the Omar Redoubt and the works between it and the Tultchenitza, with the 117th and 118th Regiments in support, had been collected on the spur above Radischevo. Just before noon, as the mist cleared, some Turkish troops were seen moving near to the Russian outpost trenches. This, and the sound of Skobelev's battle, suggested that a Turkish attack was imminent. One battalion of the 63rd Regiment was ordered forward to cover the artillery; but due to confusion as to the object of the move the whole regiment, followed by the 117th Regiment, went on down the slope and launched an entirely premature assault against the Omar Redoubt. It failed completely, being stopped about 500 yards short of the Turkish trenches. Having lost more than 30 percent of their strength, the two regiments fell back to Radischevo. At 3.00 pm the 64th Regiment moved forward against the redoubt and the 118th Regiment against the trenches between it and the Tultchenitza. Neither made any greater impression than the previous assault, and by 4.00 pm they had been driven back with heavy loss. No reinforcements had been provided to replace the 63rd and 117th Regiments, and nor was the artillery moved forward.[21]

Two piecemeal attacks having failed, it might have been expected that some lessons had been learned. At 4.30 pm the 123rd and 124th Regiments, which had been covering the guns on the ridge south of Grivitza, were brought forward to attack the Omar Redoubt, a move which met the same fate as the preceding assaults. Finally, another abortive attack was made by the 20th Regiment, with the same result. The Turks had resisted these assaults with a force of six battalions and six guns, although reinforced later in the day with a further battalion, so the total strength of the defenders was much about the same as the attackers in each assault – a ratio which was certainly not one which should have given confidence to the Russian commanders. As it was, the assault on the Turkish centre had been a complete failure, and had cost the Russians 4,434 casualties.[22] The Tsar, who had previously been watching the fighting in the northern sector, arrived in the late afternoon to witness the defeat of the IV Corps:

> There were tears in his eyes when he saw his brave soldiers, decimated by the grapeshot, waver, stop, then fall back once again under the defenders' fire, and finally fly in disorder in every direction. His officers were scarcely able to induce him to leave the mournful spot, but they did at last succeed in getting him, in a greatly dejected state, to set off for the headquarters at Poradim.[23]

The Tsar's distress was apparent to all who saw him; Forbes later wrote of his profound anxiety as he watched the assaults on the Grivitza redoubts: 'As he stood there in solitary anguish, he was a spectacle of majestic misery that I can never forget.'[24]

In the northern sector the morning mist had been particularly thick and took even longer to clear. Here, the rigid timetable for the bombardment to begin and end appears not to have been followed, and there was little or no coordination between the Russian and Roumanian artillery. There was, however, a worse problem. From the north, in the front of the 3rd Roumanian Division there could be seen only the Grivitza No 2 Redoubt. From the east, in the front of the 4th Roumanian Division and from the south-east, in the front of the 1st Brigade of the 5th Russian Division, there could be seen only the Grivitza No 1. The objective of all three assaulting units was to be the Grivitza No 2, which they were to attack simultaneously. It did not apparently occur to the Russian staff to explain to them that there were in fact two redoubts.

At 3.00 pm the 4th Roumanian Division advanced from the east against Grivitza No 1, led by the 1st Brigade to two lines with the 2nd Brigade in reserve. The Turkish shelter trenches were soon taken when, to their amazement, the attackers found that the redoubt was still 600 yards away, the other side of a steep ravine. When the two brigades advanced across the ravine against the redoubt itself, they reached the ditch, but could

A panoramic view of the Battle of September 11. Key – 1) Russian batteries, 2) Grand siege battery, 3) Roumanian batteries, 4) Redoubt captured by the Roumanians on September 8; 5) Russian infantry reserve, 6) Russian infantry regiment moving forward, 7) General Zotov and staff officer, 8) Caissons of the reserve, 9) Grivitza village, 10) ridge behind which part of Plevna lay, 11) Attack by the Russian1st Brigade of the 5th Division, 12) Roumanian assault,

13) Turkish Grivitza redoubt, taken in the evening of September 11, 14) Further Turkish redoubt, 15) Turkish entrenched camp, 16) Turkish lines, 17) Redoubts in the Turkish centre, 18) Turkish redoubt attacked by Russian 30th Division, 19) Turkish redoubts, 20) Road from Plevna to Biela, 21) Road from Plevna to Pelisat, 22) Red Cross ambulance, 23) Location of the Tsar, Grand Duke Nicholas and Prince Charles of Roumania during the battle. (*Russes et Turcs*)

Roumanian chasseurs assault the Grivitza Redoubt at Plevna. (*Russes et Turcs*)

get no further. Support had been expected on both flanks, from the 3rd Roumanian Division and the 1st Brigade of the 5th Russian Division respectively, but this did not arrive, and the attackers fell back to the shelter trenches at 5.00 pm. Meanwhile the 3rd Roumanian Division had advanced to the assault at 3.00 pm as planned, one regiment advancing against the easternmost of the Janik Bair redoubts and the trenches running to Grivitza No 2, while the remaining regiment and a rifle battalion attacked the latter redoubt. The rest of the division, which constituted the reserve, got lost in the fog, and did not arrive in time to be of help, and the assault on Grivitza No 2 was beaten off with heavy loss.

The Russians assaulting Grivitza No 1 had advanced at 3.00 pm to take up a position just below the redoubt. Major-General Rodionov, commanding the 1st Brigade, believed that his orders required him to cover the left flank of the Roumanian 4th Division rather than to attack the redoubt. It was only after the Roumanian attack had failed that he decided to attack, sending the 17th Regiment forward against the southern face of the redoubt and two battalions of the 18th Regiment against the western face. On becoming aware of the Russian assault, the 4th Roumanian Division poured out of the shelter trenches on the eastern side of the redoubt. This attack coincided with the successful assault of the 17th Regiment, and the allies took possession of the redoubt. A Turkish counter-attack was briefly successful in driving them out again, but after a savage hand-to-hand fight the Turks were driven out in their turn. Throughout this time the allies had endured fierce fire from Grivitza No 2, which dominated the position. The total Roumanian losses, among which there were more killed than wounded, amounted to 2,566, while the Russians lost in all 1,327 men.[25] For this high price the reward was five guns and a flag, and the possession of the redoubt. The value of that, however, was made

Roumanian *Dorobantsi* fighting within the Grivitza Redoubt. (*Russes et Turcs*)

painfully clear on the following morning when it was realised that it was completely commanded by Grivitza No 2, which was as large, as strong, and as powerfully armed as the redoubt that had been taken.

25

Aftermath

No further assault had been planned for September 12, so that on both the northern and central sectors there was little activity. The day dawned bright and clear, after nearly two days of continuous rain and mist, but a cold wind swept the battlefield. It was with the southern sector that Osman was particularly concerned, since Skobelev still held the two redoubts, and he was in no doubt that this gravely threatened the entire defence of Plevna. It was a view which Skobelev shared, and he anxiously awaited Zotov's response to his appeal for reinforcements. It finally reached him at 7.00 am in the form of a copy of a laconic order from Zotov to Imeretinsky:

> By direction of the Commander-in-Chief, I order you and General Skobelev to entrench and maintain yourselves in the positions captured today. We cannot send reinforcements, because we have none. (signed) Zotov, Lieutenant-General.[1]

During the night of September 11/12 both sides had been extremely busy in the southern sectors, since it was obvious that fighting would be resumed next day. Yunous Bey had five battalions in and around the three southernmost of the redoubts. What remained of Emin's force, consisting of eight battalions, was now commanded by Riza

Burial of the dead near the Grivitza Redoubt on the evening of September 11. (*Russes et Turcs*)

Bey; Rifaat, who had taken over when Emin was hit, had now himself been wounded. It was sited at the Baghlarbashi Redoubt, to the west of the two redoubts occupied by Skobelev. It included the company led by Herbert, whose battalion had been one of those sent south from the Janik Bair during the afternoon of September 11. In the early morning an order from Osman was read out to the effect that an attack was to be made on the lost redoubts: 'With God's help we shall recover our positions and win the battle. At every point save this the Russians have been defeated, and have suffered heavily.'[2]

On the Russian side feverish efforts were made to repair the captured redoubts and to entrench the ridges facing the Turkish redoubts. On the third knoll Skobelev collected about 1,000 stragglers, from every battalion, and posted them to meet any assault from Baghlarbashi. Imeretinsky had sent up three battalions to Krishin and the ridge above the village – the second knoll – together with four batteries to cover Skobelev's rear.

While the northern and central sectors remained quiet, Skobelev had already been in action on September 12 by the time he received Zotov's response. At 6.00 am the Turkish artillery opened fire from all the western redoubts, while the infantry in the entrenched camp on the north delivered a heavy rifle fire. On the left of Skobelev's position an assaulting column from the Yunous Redoubt at 7.00 am got to within 300 yards of the Russian line before being driven back. During this attack the Turkish artillery had been able to give little support, having run short of ammunition, but at about 9.00 am fresh supplies reached the guns in the redoubts, which opened fire with renewed force.

Grivitza Redoubt (No 2) as seen from the Roumanian
positions at Grivitza Redoubt (No 1). (Strantz)

Russian troops in the trenches before Plevna. (*Illustrated London News*)

At about 10.30 a fresh Turkish assault came forward, reaching the trenches in front of the middle redoubt. The exhausted Russian infantry, worn out after 30 hours of continuous fighting, were beginning to drop out and make their way to the rear. Skobelev, who was on the third knoll, rode over 'and expostulated, threatened, ordered and encouraged the men, and got them back into the redoubt again.'[3] In spite of all he could do, however, the defence was on the point of collapse when Tahir Pasha, unexpectedly and for no apparent reason, ordered a withdrawal. It bewildered his men, among whom there was much discussion later of the possibility that he might be court martialled. Herbert learned later that Tahir's decision had been motivated by a fear that the Russian cavalry operating to the west of Plevna might fall upon his rear. Osman was understandably furious, relieving Tahir of command in this sector, and he ordered that a fresh attempt be made to retake the two redoubts, under the command of Tewfik Bey.

It was at about this time that Skobelev received a further order from Zotov, brought by Colonel Orlov:

> By order of the Commander in Chief, if you cannot hold the captured positions, you are to fall back – if possible not before evening – in the direction of Tultchenitza, covered by the cavalry of General Leontiev. Communicate this order, which is to be kept secret otherwise, to General Prince Imeretinsky. The Grivitza redoubt is in our hands, but the attack is not to be continued. 8.30 am (signed) Zotov, Lieutenant-General.[4]

Skobelev, always an optimist, did not give up hope even after receiving this order; he thought that the IV Corps would perhaps move forward against the central redoubts and in particular the Omar Redoubt, which would take some of the pressure off him. The Turkish artillery in the Omar Redoubt was causing him particular problems. In the middle redoubt two of the four guns were no longer operational and there were scarcely enough gunners to man the other two, so Skobelev ordered up three guns from the third knoll to replace them. Unfortunately the only ammunition wagon brought up to the middle redoubt was hit by a Turkish shell, and blew up, wounding Major-General Tebjanik, who commanded there, and Captain Kuropatkin.

At 2.00 pm the last available reserves sent up by Imeretinsky arrived, consisting of two battalions and about 200 riflemen. Four companies went to the redoubts, while the rest covered the left and right flanks of the position on the third knoll, and the riflemen were held behind the second knoll as a reserve. Their arrival was timely, for Tewfik was preparing the assault ordered by Osman. For this he had three battalions drawn from the central sector, three battalions under Mehmet Nasi which had previously been withdrawn into reserve, and the troops in the Baghlarbashi Redoubt who had carried out the abortive attack under Tahir. Tewfik split his force into two parts; one would advance against the two redoubts from the direction of the town, making as much noise and show of force as possible, while the other would be concealed among the vineyards on the Namasguiah hills to the west of Plevna.

All the time the Turkish artillery maintained a heavy fire. An abortive attack was made from the Yunous Redoubt soon after 2.00 pm. At about 2.30 pm the Turkish troops in the Baghlarbashi Redoubt began to form up for the assault. At 3.00 the column advancing from Plevna made its move; twenty minutes later the Baghlarbashi column left its trenches and marched on the middle redoubt, while the column hidden in the vineyards emerged and rushed forward. By 5.00 the leading troops had reached the redoubt. The Russian defenders, by now utterly exhausted, began to give way. Some 200 men under Major Gortalov remained to the end but were cut down to the last man in a vicious hand-to-hand fight. By the time the Baghlarbashi column arrived the Turks had taken the redoubt.

Mehmet Nasi's column from Plevna pressed on to the smaller redoubt, to which a number of companies that had entered the middle redoubt also advanced without orders. By now it was obvious to Skobelev that there was no hope of retaining it, and he gave orders for a withdrawal. Meanwhile elements of the 118th Regiment, sent by Krylov on his own initiative in response to the heavy firing in Skobelev's sector, had begun to arrive. It was too late for them to play any part in the struggle to hang on to the redoubts; all they could do was to cover the retreat of the defenders as they struggled back first to the third knoll and then to the second knoll. As night fell, Skobelev brought his whole force back to the first knoll, above Brestovetz, where he remained all night.

MacGahan saw Skobelev after he had been forced to retreat from the redoubts, and sent his readers his famous description of the young general:

> He was in a fearful state of excitement and fury. His uniform was covered with mud and filth; his sword broken; his cross of St George twisted round on his shoulder; his face black with powder and smoke; his eyes haggard and blood-shot, and his voice quite gone. I never before saw such a picture of battle as he presented.[5]

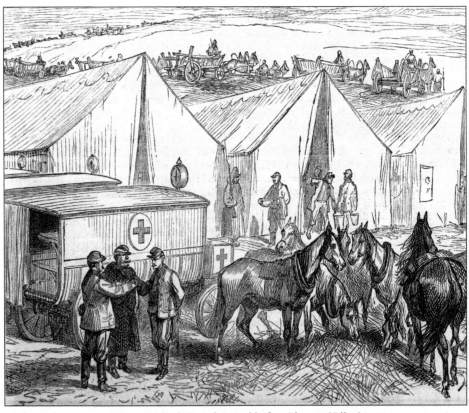

A Russian Red Cross hospital before Plevna. (Ollier)

Later that night MacGahan saw him again, and was struck by his composure as he discussed the events of the day. MacGahan asked him why he had been refused reinforcements; who was to blame? 'I blame nobody. It is the will of God,' was Skobelev's reply.

Skobelev remained in his position throughout September 13. Evidently the Turks had sustained quite enough casualties in restoring the position in this sector to think of following up their success by a further assault. And it had certainly been a success, due in Herbert's opinion not only to Tewfik but also to Yunous, who both deserved the praise heaped on them by Osman. He did not fail, however, to note the distinction between Skobelev and many of his colleagues, regarding the young general as possessing 'impetuosity, science, personal bravery, and astounding, almost uncanny, influence' over his men.[6] Skobelev's total losses in the battle were 160 officers and over 8,000 men, out of 18,100 engaged.[7] It was a fearful price for which the Russians had in the end nothing to show.

On September 13 and 14 the Russians gradually withdrew, although maintaining their occupation of the Grivitza No 1 Redoubt. During this time their batteries bombarded the town, to no great effect; and on the evening of September 14 the Turks launched an infantry assault on Grivitza No 1 which was, however, driven off.

The Third Battle of Plevna had therefore the same result as its predecessors. The Russians had 75,000 infantry present, of which some 60,000 came into action. Their total loss was computed at 18,581. The Turkish losses are unclear. Osman later observed that his losses in the southern sector exceeded those of Skobelev. The best estimate that was made of the total Turkish loss was that it was between 12,000 and 15,000 men.[8]

The decision not to send reinforcements to Skobelev has been ascribed to Levitsky, possibly on the basis that a decision to pull back had already been effectively made after the defeat of the IV Corps. The other explanation, that there were no reinforcements available, seems less plausible. By nightfall on September 11 the Russian had eleven regiments disposed in a half-circle from the village of Grivitza to the Tultchenitza river, and of these, as Greene pointed out, five had not been engaged at all. Since there was no plan to conduct offensive operations anywhere else on September 12, it is extremely surprising that no greater effort was made to take advantage of Skobelev's success. Osman could see its potential; his opponents could not.

The principal reason for the Russian failure was seen by observers as the lack of effective control in the conduct of operations. Prince Charles was nominally in command of the forces attacking Plevna but in practice it was Zotov who took the key decisions. Maurice found it astonishing that not only should the reserve have been so small, at less than ten per cent of the whole force, but that it should have been located behind the weakest of the three attacks to be launched, an attack that was directed at the strongest part of the Turkish line. There was no unity of command in the northern sector; the Russian and Roumanian units attacked independently of each other.[9]

The headquarters of Grand Duke Nicholas at Gorni Studen. (Budev)

Osman Pasha sketched on campaign. (*Illustrated London News*)

Tactically, the bombardment by the field artillery was misconceived in its purpose; to be fully effective it should gradually have increased in intensity up to the moment of assault. The pause in the bombardment of September 11 served no purpose, and the overall effectiveness of the Russian artillery preparation may be judged by the fact that as it proceeded the Turkish works were strengthened rather than weakened. Nor, with the exception of Skobelev's operations, were the infantry well used; as so often before, attacks went in piecemeal, one after another as each in turn failed.

During the bombardment on September 7-10 the volume of the Russian artillery fire had steadily declined. Skobelev's Chief of Staff, Kuropatkin, subsequently examined the expenditure of ammunition, calculating that during the four days a total of some 30,000 shells were fired; each gun averaged about 50 rounds on the first day, 40 on the second and only 30 on each of the third and fourth days.[10] This certainly contributed to the resilience of the Turks in making good the damage suffered. Even more worrying, however, was the reluctance of the field artillery (except that under Skobelev's direct control) to move forward to shorten the range in support of the attacking infantry. A conviction that the Turkish artillery was decidedly superior, and a pronounced fear of taking casualties from rifle fire, led many batteries to hang back and fire at a range where they were ineffective. Kuropatkin quoted Thilo von Trotha with approval:

Todleben. (*Histoire de la Guerre d'Orient 1877-1878*)

A battery which fires at the decisive point with destructive effect for five minutes – and is then lost, has done better service to the whole command than ten batteries which from well chosen rearward positions have maintained a well aimed, but in the end rather useless, fire.[11]

Zotov deserves, perhaps, some sympathy. He was obliged to conduct the operations under the gaze not only of Nepokoitschitsky and Levitsky, but also of the Grand Duke. Levitsky had come to Zotov several days before the battle to explain the Grand Duke's wishes. Perhaps even more importantly, the Tsar was present throughout the battle, and so was Miliutin. Although the Tsar was there merely to encourage his troops, and hopefully to witness their victory, it was not possible, as Greene pointed out, for him to be solely a spectator. For every Russian soldier, his will was law at all times.[12]

On September 13 and 14 lengthy councils of war were held, presided over by Alexander, at which Nicholas, Miliutin, Prince Charles, Nepokoitschitsky, Levitsky, and Zotov were present. These discussions, conducted with the spectacle of the fearful casualties sustained fresh in the minds of the participants, led to a firm conclusion. The right way now to deal with Plevna, it was concluded, was investment. There would be no more assaults, no more expensive attacks on a well-entrenched enemy. To conduct the investment the veteran General Todleben was recalled from retirement. The hero of the siege of Sebastopol, Eduard Todleben was born in Latvia in 1818. During the Crimean War he had risen from the rank of Lieutenant Colonel to Lieutenant-General, and he was the one Russian military leader who emerged from that war with credit. After the war he was appointed assistant to Grand Duke Nicholas, and became Chief of the Department of Engineers with the rank of General. Francis Greene described him thus:

> He has grown with advancing years, but he is still full of activity, both physical and mental. In personal appearance he bears a strong resemblance to Bismarck, and is a man who at once impresses you by his agreeable manners, polished address, and dignified bearing.[13]

Todleben was appointed to take the place of Zotov, who returned to the command of the IV Corps. Prince Charles continued in nominal command of the forces around Plevna. Krylov became commander of the cavalry forces operating on the left bank of the Vid. Imeretinsky became Chief of Staff of the Western Army, while Skobelev was appointed to the command of the 16th Division. Both of them were promoted to the rank of Lieutenant-General. Gourko, having come back from St Petersburg, was placed in overall command of all the cavalry. Two other casualties of the reshuffle were Hahn, who was held to blame for the defeats on the Lom, and who was replaced as commander of the XIII Corps by Korsakov, and Shakofskoi, who was succeeded in command of the XI Corps by Dellingshausen. As reinforcements poured into Bulgaria over the Sistova bridge, Todleben arrived on September 24 to take up his duties. An entirely new phase of the war had begun.

26

The Great Powers Watch:
May-September 1877

Once war had been declared it was evident that it could only be brought to an end by decisive military victory or by some extremely persuasive mediation. The latter seemed not, at least in the early stages of the war, at all likely to be necessary. The Russian expectation was that the war would be short, and that the forces available were sufficient to provide a quick victory. This confidence had been enough for the Russians to discourage Serbia from taking action and to refuse the offer of a Greek alliance; and although Roumania had proclaimed its independence as early as May 13, and declared war on Turkey, her offer to join Russia as an ally had been refused. Prince Charles was told on May 25 that the Russian army was strong enough and did not require Romanian assistance.[1]

The British government was particularly sensitive to the way in which the Russians set about winning the war, and how far they limited their objectives. In order to give a response to the British declaration of conditional neutrality of May 6, Shuvalov had gone to St Petersburg to persuade his government to seek a swift end to the war after the crossing of the Danube and the achievement of a military victory. Passing through Berlin, he told Bismarck of his intention. Reporting this to Lord Odo Russell, Bismarck told him that the only sensitive issues between Britain and Russia were Constantinople and the navigation of the Straits.[2] From St Petersburg, however, came a warning from Loftus that Gorchakov was playing Britain along until it was too late to stop the Russians occupying Constantinople. This, and the reports from his military *attaché* that the Turks faced a major defeat in the Caucasus, prompted Layard to suggest to Lord Derby on May 24 that a mediation proposal be put forward before the Russians crossed the Danube. Derby, almost certainly correctly, was extremely dubious about this:

> Personally I am not inclined to be hopeful of the success of an attempt to bring the combatants to terms at present. Even supposing the Sultan and his advisers to be favourably disposed, I doubt much whether the Russians would as yet consent to conditions such as could be accepted at Constantinople.[3]

Shuvalov, Loftus reported, would leave St Petersburg on June 4 with the Russian response to the British declaration. Meanwhile Andrassy had responded to the British enquiry with a statement of his position, which defined the essential interests of Austria on which he would insist, and for which if necessary he would stand up by force of arms. The British Cabinet liked the sound of this, which offered the prospect of joint action.

The official Russian answer was delivered by Shuvalov on June 8. This sought to offer reassurance as to Egypt and the Suez Canal, but was equivocal about the Straits and Constantinople, describing these as matters of common interest. This was

Romanian cavalry crossing the Danube. (*Album della Guerra Russo-Turca del 1877-78*)

obviously unsatisfactory. Shuvalov also set out the peace terms which Russian would accept, up to the point at which her forces crossed the Balkans. These included a 'small' autonomous Bulgaria, territorial gains for Serbia and Montenegro, Austria to have part of Bosnia-Herzegovina if necessary, Russia to regain Bessarabia (with Roumania being compensated by the Dobrudja) and to receive Batum. Although at first considering the terms reasonable, after a lengthy meeting of the Cabinet Disraeli changed his mind; committing Britain to remain neutral would prevent her mounting any expedition to Turkey, as he reported to the Queen:

> The probable result ... would be, that Russia would take care that Turkey would decline to make peace, and then Russia would march into Constantinople, having previously occupied the Dardanelles, and would dictate her terms to Europe. Lord Derby seems for peace at any price, and Lord Salisbury seems to think that the progress of Russia is the progress of religion and civilisation. Lord Beaconsfield does not believe that this is the feeling of the British people, and that if they woke one morning to hear that the Russians are in Constantinople, they will sweep the Ministers ... off the board of public life altogether.[4]

He went on to ask the Queen to write to the Foreign Secretary, which she did, advising him to be firm and energetic in the face of Russian perfidy; hesitation could be fatal. Derby's reply was to the effect that the Turks would not get better terms.

When the terms were put to Layard, he replied that they would not be considered by the Porte, and that if Britain tried to mediate on this basis it would lose all influence in the Ottoman Empire and among Muslims in India. Behind the Foreign Secretary's back, Disraeli had written to Layard secretly to see whether the Turks could be persuaded to request a British occupation of Gallipoli and for the fleet to go to Constantinople. He also tried to negotiate direct with Andrassy, fearing that Derby might sabotage the Anglo-Austrian talks; but von Montgelas, at the Austrian Embassy, whom he sought to use as an intermediary, refused to go behind the back of von Beust, his ambassador. Instead, Disraeli pressed Derby to put forward to Austria as energetically as possible an alliance based on the Austrian statement of their essential interests, telling him on the other hand not to believe anything that Shuvalov might say.

Political opinion in London was becoming extremely jittery at this time. Count Münster reported to Berlin some of the more absurd rumours that were circulating:

> In the papers and in conversation at times of vague excitement, such as these, wild notions are apt to come out. Amongst other rumours, it is now being noised abroad that Germany intends to undertake the role of mediator. She is agreeing to an increase of Russia's influence in the East, but is prepared to admit extension of the British sphere presumably in Egypt, only on condition of being assured of acquiring Holland on the German Ocean.[5]

Even the Queen, he wrote, had believed this nonsense until Odo Russell had convinced her to the contrary when visiting Balmoral. Münster also reported the warlike steps being taken by the British government: 'Preparations for an expedition are quietly going forward here in respect of transports and every sort of supplies.'

Bismarck's view was that it would suit German interests to promote a compromise between Russia and England, which might be followed by the rapprochement of both to Germany. This had been a feature of Bismarck's thinking for some time, and he had been emphatic in the comments which he made to Russell, telling him that 'he would give his last effort to bring about a cordial and intimate understanding between England and Russia to which Germany would become a party.' He was, however, looking beyond a settlement of any Anglo-Russian disputes. He asked Russell to convey to Derby 'his earnest, sincere and anxious desire to bring about an intimate and lasting alliance between England and Germany.'[6]

Bismarck was not well at the time, and was taking the cure at Kissingen, where he dictated a note on June 15 as to what he saw as the most desirable consequences of the Eastern Crisis:

> If my health permitted me to work, I could fill in and develop in greater detail the picture which floats before my mind. It is not one portraying any acquisition of territory, but rather one showing a combined political situation in which all the Powers, except France, have need of us, and are removed from the possibility of coalescing against us by the nature of their relations towards each other.[7]

In the constantly changing kaleidoscope of diplomatic discussions, this was perhaps a rather optimistic objective; but it was certainly at odds with the devious cunning of which Bismarck was suspected by just about every European statesman. So far as a war between Russia and England was concerned, if it could not be prevented the aim should be a peace satisfying to both, at Turkey's expense.

Meanwhile in London Disraeli was having trouble in keeping the Cabinet together. To Derby, to whom he wrote for support, he hinted that Salisbury's departure would not weaken the government; but he did not at this moment want to lose his Foreign Secretary: 'How grievous would be to me the blow that severed our long connection and faithful friendship.' Derby's response was to say that they would have no difficulty in agreeing 'at least in the present stage of the affair.' Evidently he saw armed intervention

A Roumanian *Dorobantsi* infantryman sketched on campaign by a Russian Cossack. (Rogers)

as some considerable way off. The immediate need was to get the vote of credit for which Disraeli had asked agreed to by Parliament; after that, if it came to sending troops to Gallipoli and the fleet to Constantinople, then both Derby and Salisbury would still refuse, if not resign, as the Queen recorded. Those steps were, she thought, essential, if Britain was not 'to kiss the feet of Russia.'[8] On June 30, however, after the Russians were over the Danube, Disraeli induced the Cabinet to accept three proposals. First, it was decided to seek Austrian agreement to a protocol to prevent the occupation of Constantinople. Secondly, the Mediterranean Fleet was to be strengthened; and finally it was to be sent to Besika Bay.

Decazes, the French Foreign Minister, told Lord Lyons on July 4 that he was pleased that the fleet was to go to Besika Bay. He hoped that this would be regarded by British public opinion as all that was needed. For her part, he said, France was 'comparatively indifferent to Russian progress in the East, and would view with quite as much jealousy an increase of English as an increase of Russian influence.' In Berlin, Bismarck confirmed to Russell that any peace terms acceptable to Britain, Russia and Austria would be agreeable to Germany. He thought, though, that the movement of the fleet was premature; it was a step that might be more effective later.

Disraeli's hope of an active alliance with Austria was to be disappointed. At the outset, soon after the outbreak of war, his approach through the Austrian embassy had been to ask: 'How much money do you want?' This was not, however, Andrassy's principal concern at that moment.[9] Negotiations continued until August, in the course of which Andrassy could not be tempted to make any explicit commitments. His deal with Russia had obliged him to remain neutral, but he did not want to end discussions with Britain in case Russia did not fulfill its side of the bargain. In the end all that was agreed was a 'moral understanding' of what each of the two Powers would object to. At the same time Franz Joseph was giving Alexander a much more specific assurance, in a letter brought by the Austrian military *attaché*, Baron von Bechtolsheim, to the Tsar's headquarters in August:

> Whatever happens and whatever turns the war may take – nothing can induce me to recede from my given word. England has been informed in a decisive manner that she cannot count, in any event, on an alliance with Austria.[10]

It was not the only manifestation of Andrassy's determination to stick to the Bucharest agreement; he told Prince Alexander of Hesse that it would be madness to think of adopting a hostile attitude to Russia, a comment which he knew would be reported back to St Petersburg.

Disraeli, finding that he was getting nowhere with Austria, the only Great Power to share British concerns about Constantinople, tried on July 14 to get the Cabinet to agree that Russian occupation of the city would be regarded as a *casus belli*. He was disappointed in this, and had to settle for an agreement that 'the occupation of Constantinople, or an attempt to occupy it, will be looked on as an incident which frees us from all previous engagements,' as he reported to the Queen. Derby recorded in his diary that the Cabinet meeting has been 'the best conducted and most orderly discussion that I remember for a long while'; however, the effect on Disraeli had not been good:

> I thought the Premier better in health, with more bodily energy than when we met last, but uncomfortable and not in his happiest mind. He has never before been exposed to the annoyance of having to waive or modify his ideas to meet those of his colleagues. In my father's time he settled all with him, and what the two agreed on, the Cabinet always accepted.[11]

The Queen was extremely annoyed at this further exhibition of pusillanimity on the part of her Cabinet in the face of the reports of Gourko's crossing of the Balkans and of alleged Russian atrocities. She asked Disraeli to tell the Cabinet meeting of July 17 of her 'shock and disappointment' that nothing had yet been done to send the fleet to Constantinople. Disraeli, who had perpetually encouraged the Queen in her anti-Russian views, was unable to give satisfaction; he had previously explained that although willing to lose both Derby and Salisbury if necessary, all but two of the members of the Cabinet refused to go as far as he wanted in giving the *casus belli* warning.

On July 17, however, Disraeli was able to get agreement to the reinforcement of British garrisons in the Mediterranean. It was at this time that the feasibility of occupying the Gallipoli peninsula was being explored, which was something that Admiral Hornby, the commander of the Mediterranean Fleet, wanted, in order to protect his ships if they had to pass through the Dardanelles route to Constantinople. On the other hand,

Admiral Sir Geoffrey Hornby, commander of Britain's Mediterranean fleet.

his second in command, Vice-Admiral Commerell, thought it unnecessary. Four days later the Cabinet went further, with Salisbury surprisingly in the lead, in approving the dispatch of 3,000 troops to Malta, and agreeing that if Russia took Constantinople and did not at once promise to withdraw quickly, then it would be war. This cost Disraeli one Cabinet Minister, Lord John Manners, the Postmaster General, because the latter demanded an immediate declaration of war if Russia entered the city.

Disraeli's mounting desire for a firm position to be taken had been driven by a fear of the Russian military successes. From Constantinople Layard sent an alarmist telegram on July 27, reporting Russian advances south of the Balkans which could soon put them at Adrianople, only 'a few short marches' from the Gallipoli peninsula. This prompted the Cabinet meeting on July 28 to take a much harder line (with the exception of the Foreign Secretary). It was resolved to send a telegram to express a readiness to send the fleet to Constantinople, and plans to ensure that Gallipoli was secured were also discussed. Derby reluctantly complied with a request that Shuvalov should be told that Britain was ready to help obtain an honourable peace, but that she might be obliged to send up the fleet. The Foreign Secretary, replying to a telegram from the Queen on the subject of the occupation of Gallipoli, told her that he was 'quite satisfied that the great bulk of the nation desires nothing so much ... as the maintenance of peace.'[12] Disraeli drafted the royal response to the effect that she was 'convinced to the contrary, and believes that there will soon be no controversy on the subject.'

The Queen was getting very much angrier with Derby, as she made clear to Disraeli on August 1:

It maddens the Queen to feel that all our efforts are being destroyed by the minister who ought to carry them out. The Queen must say that she can't stand it! For Russia <u>will</u> have her own way and <u>we</u> be humiliated if not ruined.[13]

Disraeli sought to soothe her, saying that there had been no change in the Cabinet's opinion.

On the battle front, however, there had been a significant change in the situation. Osman's seizure of Plevna, and his subsequent repulse of two attempts to dislodge him, materially altered the diplomatic situation. Krüdener's defeats, and that of Gourko south of the Balkans, together with a check to the Russian advance in the Caucasus, led European statesmen to review their policy. Andrassy toyed with the idea of taking advantage of the Russian setbacks to intervene; however, the Austrian military, who were on the whole pro-Russian, raised serious objections to what, in retrospect, seems a curiously unconsidered piece of opportunism.

In London, meanwhile, the arrival of Colonel Wellesley offered further reassurance. The Tsar had agreed to his going home to reassure the British Cabinet, and to say that Alexander was still willing to make peace on the terms that Shuvalov had brought on June 8, with the addition of extending Bulgaria south of the Balkans. Wellesley saw Disraeli and the Queen, Derby being out of town for the first meeting. Wellesley told them that Alexander was well meaning but weak and needed help to bring the war to an end. After further meetings in which the Foreign Secretary participated, Wellesley was given a formal response to take back, reiterating the government's desire for peace and its intention not to depart from its conditional neutrality. Disraeli and the Queen decided, however, also to entrust Wellesley with a secret message, unknown to Derby or the rest of the Cabinet, 'with a private but very clear warning to the Tsar against prolonging the conflict or planning a campaign for the following year.'[14]

Bismarck reacted calmly to the news of Russian military setbacks. If it reduced the temperature of Anglo-Russian relations, well and good. As it was, however, he was encountering afresh a problem that had plagued him earlier in his career, and that was the propensity of the Prussian and British royal families to communicate direct. After a dinner attended by Prince Henry of Reuss with the Duke of Edinburgh on which he reported to Bismarck on July 10, the Chancellor added a sharp note:

I expressed myself very fully in Berlin against the British ambassador and against interference by England. From unofficial meddling on the part of Royalty and from any personal appeal made by His Majesty to Queen Victoria over the heads of the British Ministers I expect only confusion in our relations with England and moreover, for the peace no practical success. Henceforward Prince Reuss should write 'confidentially,' and this letter must be placed among the secret documents.[15]

Disraeli, under the continuous stress of a situation which he sought unsuccessfully to master, vented his frustration in the form of a withering attack on his key ambassadors:

I wish we could get rid of the whole lot. They seem to me to be quite useless. It is difficult to control events, but none of them try to. I think Odo Russell the worst of all. He contents himself with reporting all Bismarck's cynical bravadoes, which he evidently listens to in an ecstasy of sycophantic wonder. Why does he not try to influence Bismarck as the Prince controls him? … Why does he not confidentially impress upon Bismarck that Turkey has shown such vigour and resource that she has established her place among the sovereign Powers of Europe, and that if they continue to play their dark game of partition they must come in collision with England, who will not permit the breaking up of the Ottoman Empire.[16]

During the first half of August the Cabinet was extremely busy, meeting on four occasions to consider a number of issues arising from the prospect of war with Russia, such as the British potential for an offensive from India, as well as the diplomatic steps to be taken to oppose a second campaign in Bulgaria if, as now appeared probable, the Russians remained held up before Plevna. During the Parliamentary recess both Disraeli and Derby were to remain in London, although the Cabinet was to be on call to meet in an emergency. Meanwhile Wellesley had returned to Bulgaria to deliver both the official British message and the secret message from the Queen and the Prime Minister. It has been suggested that the latter may have had the opposite effect to that intended in causing the Tsar not to suspend military operations during the winter in the hope of winning a victory without the need for a further campaign in 1878.[18] The secret message brought no reply, which 'perplexed and astonished' Disraeli.

Queen Victoria remained extremely concerned about all aspects of the situation, continuing to bombard the Foreign Secretary with demands for action. She insisted that he lodge a protest against Russian atrocities, and that he should appeal to the other Great Powers to urge Serbia not to join the war. This latter step had now become a real possibility. Whereas before the Russians had crossed the Danube they had discouraged

Roumanian chasseurs on the march. (*Russes et Turcs*)

The camp of the Roumanian 4th Division near Plevna. (*Illustrated London News*)

Serbia from taking part, the military setbacks they had encountered led them to seek some diversionary pressure on the Turks. The Tsar sent a personal appeal to Prince Milan to declare war, telling him that he would consider it to be a 'considerable personal service' for which he would pick up the bill. The Serbs were now not so keen to come in; their army was not ready and they were discouraged by the military situation.[18]

Nor did the Russians do better with Greece. A proposal from Gorchakov that Greece should receive Thessaly and Epirus if the Ottoman Empire disintegrated should, the Greeks felt, be embodied in a formal agreement. Gorchakov was reluctant to do this; and in any case the Greeks were under strong pressure from Austria and from Britain to do nothing. The proposal was tempting, but in the end nothing was what they did.

These diplomatic failures had obliged Russia to reconsider its position with regard to Roumanian support. This had been offered in the form of an alliance, which the Russians, mindful of their intention to take Bessarabia, and reluctant to accept commitments to the Balkan states, did not want. Roumania's position remained unchanged; she was not prepared to accept a secondary part in the proceedings, and the Russians had been obliged to accept this, as well as that Prince Charles should have overall command of the troops around Plevna, albeit with a Russian chief of staff.

The heavy Russian defeat in the third battle of Plevna was well received by the British press and by Disraeli and the Queen. The latter did not, however, relax her attitude to the development of British policy. She had proposed to the Prime Minister that the Great Powers should be asked to join Britain in bringing about an end to the war; if Russia refused reasonable peace terms, then Britain should become Turkey's ally. This, she explained, was put forward to prevent a second campaign; meanwhile the Cabinet Ministers who in rotation attended her at Balmoral were subjected to a continous expression of her frustration and anger.

Russian bivouac before Plevna. (*Illustrated London News*)

One of these, the Secretary of State for War, Gathorne Hardy, made at the end of September a proposal which delighted Disraeli. He suggested that Britain should come forward as a mediator, putting forward reasonable peace terms to Russia, including the acceptance by Turkey of the London Protocol, Bessarabia to Russia, Roumania to Austria and Montenegro to have what she could occupy by the end of the war. If refused, Britain would end its neutrality and intervene if Constantinople was threatened. Disraeli asked Derby to bring this plan before the Cabinet; the Foreign Secretary, mindful of the conclusion reached by Bismarck and Andrassy at a recent meeting that mediation was presently impossible, would have none of it:

> I am not prepared to support the proposal which you suggest, still less to put it forward; but a preliminary discussion will be of use as showing how far ... there is likely to be agreement among us as to the course which we ought to take.[19]

In retrospect the most extraordinary part of this proposal was the suggestion that Austria should have Roumania; but none of the ministers to whom Disraeli submitted the proposal seem to have found it remarkable enough to comment upon it. The Queen, still anxious to avoid a second campaign, was all for the plan. She did, however, have one continuing concern about Cabinet discussion, saying that the Prime Minister 'must insist on the decision of the Cabinet not being communicated to wives, above all, not to foreign ambassadors.' This was, of course, a reference to Lady Derby, and her propensity to relay to Shuvalov the most confidential matters discussed by the Cabinet. If her husband had been at first unaware of his wife's indiscretion, he certainly knew of it later, and appears to have done nothing to prevent it.[20]

Disraeli's desire for a forward policy was constantly being thwarted by the Foreign Secretary's reluctance to take any action. It was this that had led him to send the secret message to the Tsar via Wellesley; and with a similar desire to cut Derby out of the loop, he wrote privately to Layard in August to explain his position as to Turkey:

> The danger is, if the Russians rally, again successfully advance and reach Adrianople this autumn. What then is to be done? With her suspicions of England, Turkey would be ruined. That is why I should like to see our fleet in her immediate waters, and Gallipoli in our possession as a material guarantee, and with her full sanction. We should then be able to save Turkey.[21]

Disraeli had always had a very bullish view of the military capacity of Britain. When Derby pointed out to him that Britain had no allies, his response was that apart from Turkey none was needed. It was not for Britain to reconquer Bulgaria; but 'we were masters of the sea, and could send a British force to Batum, march without difficulty through Armenia, and menace the Asiatic possessions of Russia.'[22] It was perhaps just as well that Disraeli was not obliged to take charge of British grand strategy in a wartime context.

Catastrophe on God's Mountain

As a result of the Russian retreats following the Battle of Zevin and the relief of Bayazid, they found themselves at the beginning of August back where they had started, with the exception of Ardahan, which remained in their hands. The news of Zevin, when it reached the Imperial headquarters in Bulgaria, prompted the immediate mobilisation of the 1st Grenadier Division (Roop) and 40th Infantry Division (Lazarev) and their dispatch to Armenia. At the same time the 20th and 21st Infantry Divisions, based in Dagestan and along the River Terek, were also mobilised, but the fear of insurrections in this region led to their being retained there for the time being.

The new reinforcements had a long way to go; the 1st Grenadier Division had 1,400 miles of rail travel to Vladikavkaz and a 200 mile march to Alexandropol, while the 40th Division had a journey of 1,000 miles by boat and train from Saratov to Vladikavkaz. Units of the latter division began to arrive at Alexandropol in mid-August; the last of the Grenadier units did not reach there until on September 25.

Following the retreat from Zevin Loris-Melikov had taken up a strong position in front of the River Kars, facing south-west. His right was at Kuruk Dara, his centre at Kizil Tepe (the 'Red Hill') and his left at the ruined city of Ani on the River Arpa. It was about 15 miles in length. Holding the position were the Caucasus Grenadier Division, the 1st Brigade of the 39th Division, the 2nd Brigade of the 38th Division and the 2nd Brigade of the 19th Division. The total strength of the force was about 35,000 men and 5,000 Cossacks. Facing Loris-Melikov, Mukhtar had a field army of 20,000 infantry, 54 guns and 6,000 cavalry, as well as with the garrison of Kars, which amounted to 15,000 infantry, 30 field guns and 1,000 cavalry, together with the 300 siege guns of the fortress.[1]

Mukhtar's position, which if anything was even stronger than that of Loris-Melikov, was on the southern side of the lengthy ravine above which the Russians were entrenched, and ran parallel to the Russian position. His left was some ten miles in front of Kars, on two mountains, the Little Yagni and the Great Yagni. His centre was on the Aladja Dagh ('God's Mountain'), opposite Kizil Tepe, and his right ran to the River Arpa near Ani. The environment of this area was not pleasant:

> This corner of Armenia is of remarkable aridity; water is rare, and vegetation is scarcely anywhere to be seen; the mountains, washed by the rains of thousands of years, present to the view only monotonous lines of a geometrical regularity, nowhere broken by the rounded shapes of trees; the plains on which these heights rise, like an island out of the sea, frequently look as level as a sheet of water.[2]

Mukhtar's position was some eighteen miles long, which meant that it was only thinly held. A weakness of the position was on the left, which was separated both from

General Lazarev, commander of the Russian 40th Division. (*Russes et Turcs*)

Kars and from the centre; Mukhtar concentrated some of his best troops there. He also erected strong defensive works close to the village of Vizinkoi to baulk any Russian attempt to turn his left, and cut him off from Kars. One other drawback facing the Turks was the fact that, perched on the barren ridges of the Aladja Dagh, all their supplies, even including water, had to be brought up from Erzerum via Kars over very bad roads. The Russians, on the other hand, were close to their base at Alexandropol, with good communications; they were well supplied, with ample access to water.

In addition to the relative comfort enjoyed by the Russian troops, they had the encouraging signs of a steady flow of reinforcements. For the Turks, on the other hand, there was no prospect of additional support. On short rations, unpaid, and totally neglected, it is unsurprising that the rate of desertion began inexorably to rise. The Circassians in particular, never a particularly reliable part of the Turkish army, began to melt away, with the result that Mukhtar progressively lost nearly all of his cavalry. As things stood, he was perfectly aware that he would have little chance of beating the Russians in the open field, and in spite of having achieved a considerable run of success the most he could hope to do was for the most part to stand on the defensive.

For his part Loris-Melikov had no intention of engaging in any substantial offensive operations either, while he waited for sufficient reinforcements to come in. He was, however, concerned about the possibility of a Turkish advance against Tergukassov in the direction of Igdir. This town was the centre of the numerous Armenian communities that had settled there since 1828-1829; it has been suggested that both Loris-Melikov and Tergukassov, both themselves Armenian, were anxious for the safety of their countrymen.[3]

Igdir was Tergukassov's advance base, connected by poor roads to Erivan, forty miles to the north-east; partly surrounded by marshes, it was an unhealthy place for the troops. To the south and south-west of Igdir lay the forbidding tracks over the mountains, of which the best and most direct was the Cengel Pass, due south of Igdir; along this road Tergukassov located the bulk of his troops, in the belief that Ismail's main force was at Bayazid.[4] In this he was wrong; Ismail had selected Diyadin for his base and most of his troops were in the Balik valley.

On August 4, on the strength of local Kurdish advice that the Zov Pass, nine miles west of Cengel, was suitable, Ismail launched 4,000 Kurds, with six infantry battalions and six guns, in an attack on the Cossacks holding the position, and advanced to Alikocak four miles to the north. The infantry and artillery took up a position there; the Kurds pushed on to a point five miles from Igdir, before a counter-attack by the Pereyaslav Dragoons drove them back to Alikocak. It was not a very significant movement in military terms, but the Armenian population took fright and fled back over the River Aras. Tergukassov pulled back his troops at Cengel to Igdir, and sent for reinforcements. The great fear was that Ismail might push on and interpose between the forces of Loris-Melikov and Tergukassov. As the historians of the campaigns in the Caucasus have pointed out, however, Ismail had all the failings of a Kurdish chieftain, being lazy, incompetent and irresolute, and he made no further move.[5]

The threat he posed, however, was enough to prompt the sending of reinforcements to Tergukassov so that he might mount an operation against Ismail. In order to distract attention from this, a movement was undertaken against Mukhtar.

After two days of considerable activity behind their lines, the Russians on August 18 advanced against Mukhtar's positions. Following a demonstration against his centre an assault was launched on the Turkish positions on Great Yagni and Little Yagni. This was preceded by an advance of the Russian cavalry under Komarov, who engaged in a short but bloody encounter with all the Circassian cavalry which Mukhtar could muster, which ended by both sides falling back on their infantry. The Russian infantry now came

Turks making coffee in camp. (*The Graphic*)

on, but could make no progress against heavy rifle fire; when Hussein Pasha, the Turkish commander in this sector, launched his infantry in a counter-attack, the Russians were obliged to retire.

Mukhtar, who was possessed of an excellent intelligence system, had become aware of the planned attack on Ismail, and reckoned that the detachment of reinforcements to Tergukassov might give him an opportunity. He secretly brought up reinforcements from Kars, and prepared for an attack on the Kizil Tepe. Determined to surprise the Russians, he took steps to ensure that there was no general communication of the plan to the units concerned until the night of August 24/25, when he summoned a meeting of his senior commanders to tell them what was to occur.

Kizil Tepe, about 800 feet high, was one of the hills rising steeply from the plain to four irregular summits surrounding a crater. It was a key point in the Russian position, and was regularly held by a battalion and four guns. Mukhtar's plan was for a night attack by an overwhelming force; three battalions were to advance on each flank, while the columns to storm Kizil Tepe, consisting of two brigades led by his best commander, the German Mehmet Bey, were to move down the slopes of the Turkish positions and across the valley. These moved out about midnight, pausing for a rest in the valley before silently climbing towards the Russian positions. They got to within half a mile before being challenged by a sentry. The artillery, kept back previously because of the sound of the wheels, was now rushed forward and opened fire on the Russian positions. The Russian gunners were ineffective in their reply, being unable to depress their guns sufficiently to sweep the slopes. The Turkish infantry then ran out of ammunition and fell back, which prompted a counter-attack by the Russian infantry. They were met by

The Battle of Kizil Tepe. (Ollier)

a hail of artillery, however, and retreated again, whereupon the Turks charged with the bayonet and drove them off the hill.

Recovering from their surprise, the Russians regrouped. A grenadier brigade advanced against the Yagni hills. The flanks were protected by cavalry, while in the centre an infantry brigade from Devel's division and Komarov's five battalions prepared to retake Kizil Tepe. By 7.00 am the whole line was in action, and the infantry assault went in, supported by the fire of 72 guns which pounded the crater, raising clouds of red dust. The Turkish infantry sheltered under the rocks, but the gunners held their ground on the edges of the crater, replying vigorously to the Russian artillery. Finally the Russians abandoned their assault, and fell back to a fresh position.

Meanwhile Devel, who had been on the march to join Tergukassov, had heard the sound of firing from the Kizil Tepe, and at 6.00 am learned that it had fallen to the Turks. Irresolute, he was uncertain what to do, but was persuaded by his senior officers that he must march to the sound of the guns. Recrossing the Arpa at 11.00 am with six infantry battalions, some Cossacks and four mountain guns, he approached the scene of the fighting and sent a runner to Loris-Melikov's headquarters at Karayal to seek instructions. In reply, Dukhovsky, the chief of staff, told him that reinforcements were on the way, but that if the Russian position at Poldervan was abandoned he should retreat on Alexandropol. Seeing that the infantry on his right was retiring, he withdrew to the crossing over the Arpa at Kuyucuk; urged by his senior officers to launch an attack on the Turks on the Kizil Tepe, he refused, and ordered his troops back across the river, remarking bitterly that next day they would say he was to blame for all that had

Removing Turkish wounded during the Battle of Kizil Tepe. (Ollier)

happened.[6] In fact much of the blame was attached to Dukhovsky for communicating by runner rather than by field telegraph.

Kemball reported that the Turkish losses amounted to 430 killed and 1,401 wounded; he reckoned that the Russian casualties would have been much greater. Reflecting on the outcome of the battle, he wrote to Layard:

> It is probable that the Turks might have improved their victory or at least have completed the discomforture (sic.) of the Russians by advancing upon the villages of Kadikler, distant, the first about a mile and a half, the third as much further, from Kizil Tepe; but these villages appeared to be defended by earthworks and trenches, and are situated on ground rendered difficult of access by the precipitous banks of the Magrak, and the organisation of the Turks not being favourable to rapid or extended movements, Mukhtar Pasha did well, I think, to rest satisfied with the important success he had gained.[7]

Williams, who had accompanied Kemball throughout the battle, and found the latter's coolness under fire 'appalling,' reckoned that the Russian losses were about 3,000. He had been particularly struck by the behaviour of the Turkish irregular cavalry, as to which 'nothing could have been worse:'

> Wherever one looked within our front line there were to be found these fellows spending valuable hours in pretending to water their horses, or more flagrantly skulking and going to sleep in the shadow of corn ricks or even sponging upon the villagers in the rear, when they might at least have been picking up stragglers of the enemy.[8]

He thought that 'perhaps shooting a few of them for cowardice might have its effect.'

One immediate result of the battle was that a proposal to send troops from Alexandropol to join Tergukassov was abandoned. Another was the entrenchment of the new position between Bach-Kadikler and Poldervan; only outposts were left in the previous positions at Utch Tepe and Ani. The Grand Duke Michael now arrived at headquarters to take personal command, overtly at any rate. Quite how much this Imperial reinforcement added to the strength of the Russian high command must be doubtful; Williams, on another occasion, was dismissive of the Grand Duke as being 'ever ready to push himself into prominence elsewhere than in the field.'[9]

Following the battle Mukhtar advanced his lines down into the plain, and these were at once entrenched. The previous position was, however, retained, to provide a line to fall back on if necessary. In Constantinople the news of the victory at Kizil Tepe was received with delight. It seemed that Mukhtar's run of success was continuing, and the Sultan sent him a sword set in brilliants, two handsome Arab horses, and the Cross of the First Class of the Osmanli, and conferred on him the title of Ghazi, or Conqueror.[10]

During September there was little action, although in fact events behind the front lines were occurring that would decisively influence the future course of the war in Asia. On the Russian side, reinforcements continued to stream in, a fact that was well known to Mukhtar, as Kemball reported to Dickson, the military *attaché* at the embassy. He also conveyed news of the disastrous supply situation facing the Turkish army, which Dickson passed on to Layard:

> Sir A Kemball also reports in a letter of the 10th instant from the Turkish headquarters at Kerkhaned, that the army under Mukhtar Pasha has been mainly rationed and supported from the supplies of food, etc, at Kars, and this important fortress is spoken of as almost denuded of provisions. Every exertion ought to be made to revictual Kars, else it may be placed in great jeopardy for want of means, and it ought to be provisioned for at least twelve months.[11]

By the end of September the total Russian strength was over 60,000 men, with 200 guns; Mukhtar, on the other hand, was still growing steadily weaker as a result of both sickness and desertion, and in spite of calling up all the troops covering his line of communications and part of the garrison of Erzerum, his field army was no more than 35,000 strong, with 84 guns. His front was now some thirteen miles. His position was suitable as a jumping off point for an offensive, but he did not have nearly enough troops to contemplate this; on the other hand, his force was insufficient for the defence of such a long line. He had tried, and failed, to get reinforcements from Dervish at Batum and from Ismail.[12] He now set about the task of strengthening the field works that he occupied. Since Ismail had declined to provide him with additional troops, Mukhtar pressed him to take the offensive against Tergukassov. Rather reluctantly, this was what Ismail now did, advancing towards Igdir. An attack on Halfali on September 19-20 failed to shift the Russian defenders there, and another attack a week later on Corukca also failed, whereupon Ismail retreated into the mountains. Tergukassov left him alone there, feeling that any offensive operations were beyond his exhausted troops.

Bashi-Bazouks marching to headquarters. (*Illustrated London News*)

No further assistance for Mukhtar was to be expected from this quarter, although Ismail did grudgingly agree to release six battalions and two batteries to reinforce the position on the Aladja Dagh. There, the best that Mukhtar could hope for was to hang on to his present positions until winter came to put a stop to campaigning. The Russians, however, were determined to make use of their reinforcements to put paid to Mukhtar's army while it was still practicable to do so.

The Russian plan, drafted by Obruchev, was to seize the Yagni hills, to cut off Mukhtar from Kars, and to overwhelm him on the Aladja Dagh. For this purpose Loris-Melikov was assigned 20,000 men, in three columns; on his right, Roop was to attack Little Yagni, in the centre Sheremetiev was to attack Great Yagni, and on the left Schack was to prevent the Turks reinforcing the position. Heimann, with the 4th Caucasian Grenadier Division, was to launch a feint attack on Kizil Tepe while Shelkovnikov was to make a diversionary movement towards the Aladja Dagh. Mukhtar's spies picked up the news of an intended offensive, but also the disinformation which the Russians circulated to the effect that the principal target was to be Kizil Tepe, and he concentrated his troops in that direction. Mukhtar's decision to await an attack was criticised by a number of his officers; and on October 1, following a conference with Omer Pasha and Hussein Pasha, newly arrived from Constantinople, he sent a telegram seeking permission to withdraw to his spring positions in the Saghanly Dagh. He got no reply, but it was too late anyway; next morning the Russians attacked.

The Great Yagni, an immense truncated cone rising 650 feet above the plain, was regarded by the Russians as being almost impregnable, and Sheremetiev's main task was to distract attention from Roop's assault on Little Yagni. Great Yagni had three tiers of entrenchments, but on October 2 was held only by one battalion of about 500 men. Little Yagni, on the other hand, was occupied by about 4,000 men with twelve heavy guns, under the command of Mehmet Bey When Sheremetiev began his demonstration against Great Yagni, at about 6.00 am, it soon became evident that the Turkish entrenchments were weakly manned. As soon as he realised this, Loris-Melikov converted the demonstration into a general assault. Soon the slopes of the hill were covered with Russian grenadiers as they climbed towards the lines of entrenchments, undaunted by the rifle fire of the defenders. When they got into the trenches, the grenadiers easily overwhelmed the Turks and by 8.00 am the whole position had been taken. Only 140 of its defenders survived to be taken prisoner.

Roop's attack on Little Yagni fared less well. At first, however, the heavy bombardment from 50 guns forced the Turkish infantry to abandon their trenches, and the Russians moved forward; but the Turks returned, and opened a heavy rifle fire on the attackers, who fell back with a loss of nearly 400 men. Reinforcements sent up by Mukhtar, to whom the Russian intentions had by now become apparent, ensured that Little Yagni was held.

In the centre, Mukhtar had concentrated the strongest part of his army at the base of the Olya Tepe, a flat-topped mountain separated from the Aladja Dagh by a ravine. The position was well fortified, although the summit itself was unoccupied, a fact discovered by the Russian cavalry, which had found no Turkish troops at all across the only line by which they could retreat. Loris-Melikov had plenty of troops available; he and Heimann conferred, discussing what would be needed for an assault, and the latter declared that his own division could take the position while the rest of the units in hand were deployed against Little Yagni.

Heimann's optimism proved unwarranted; his assault on Olya Tepe failed, and the Turks were able to hold their position. On their right, however, Shelkovnikov had been unexpectedly successful. His move across the Arpa towards Ani and his recrossing of the river towards the spurs of the Aladja Dagh took the Turks by surprise, and he was able to take the line of entrenchments in his front. He did not, however, have sufficient troops to hold them, and when Mukhtar sent forward two brigades under Hussein Pasha and Chefket Pasha against him, Shelkovnikov's six battalions and two cavalry regiments were bundled out of the trenches and forced back to the Arpa. *En route* they were surrounded and only got back to their start line by forcing their way through, with the help of some reserves sent forward to support them.[13]

Next day Mukhtar went over to the attack, moving out towards noon and advancing towards Karayal. However, the Russians were ready for the Turks and prepared what was effectively an ambush, rows of soldiers lying down concealed in the rocky terrain. The Turks moved forward confidently, since it appeared that they had only two battalions to deal with. As they approached the Russian lines they realised the size of the force awaiting them, and opened a heavy fire. The Russians, rising up, returned the fire. After a short while, as the Russians began to advance, the Turks fell back, contesting each area of higher ground until after night fell, when they reached their previous positions. The Russian troops spent the night on the battlefields before withdrawing next day to their original lines.

The Russians soon found that although they were now in possession of the Great Yagni, it would be scarcely possible to hold it. It was exposed to artillery on three sides; there was no water; and the Turks, being still in occupation of the village of Subatan, could at any time attack it in the rear. Either more ground must be gained by a further battle, or the Great Yagni must be abandoned. As one of the few tangible proofs of success, it was hard to give up; but common sense prevailed, and on October 4 the Russians pulled back, retiring in good order. The Turks retook possession to find that the defences had been improved by the erection of redoubts for artillery. Nothing had therefore changed, but the fighting had cost both sides heavy casualties. The Russian losses were reported to be 960 men killed and 2,400 wounded. The Turkish losses were of the order of 1,000 killed and 3,200 wounded.[14]

The Turkish loss was, expressed as a proportion of their army, very much greater than the Russian. In addition, it seemed to Loris-Melikov and his senior commanders that the fighting around the Yagni hills had demonstrated that Mukhtar's forces were too stretched to hold a line that was thirteen miles long. They resolved, therefore, to launch a major offensive. Meanwhile, on the other side of the hill there were strong differences of opinion as to what should be done. Faizi and some others, facing the reality of their position, again urged a retreat to the Saghanly Dagh, reinforcing Kars by 20,000 men *en route*; the fortress, thus strengthened, should hold up a very large part of the Russian army for up to six months. The remainder of the Turkish army should, Faizi thought, take up a naturally strong position near Zevin, on the plateau of Horundozou, and there await reinforcements. Mukhtar took a different view. He believed that having failed in their attempt on the Yagni hills, the Russians would go into winter quarters and await the following spring, snow having already fallen. Mukhtar's view of the situation displayed a lack of understanding of his opponents, as Colonel Brackenbury pointed out:

> The Russians hold that the winter is of all seasons the most favourable for their military operations, because their army consists of men inured to all the rigours of frost and snow. Nothing was more unlikely than that they should give up the campaign at this point.[15]

Although minded to reject Faizi's advice, and remain in a forward position facing the Russians, Mukhtar was growing increasingly anxious about the increasing disparity of force, as the Russian reinforcements continued to arrive. He decided to concentrate his army, since it was strung out over too great a front, and on the night of October 8/9 he pulled his troops back from Great Yagni, Kizil Tepe and the villages of Hadji Vali and Subatan, retreating to the Aladja Dagh. He left a small outpost in front of Little Yagni. The movement escaped the attention of the Russians – it was conducted during a particularly dark and stormy night – until dawn on October 9. At first they suspected that this might some kind of trick on Mukhtar's part, but soon advanced to occupy the deserted position. So rapidly did they push forward that Mukhtar sent forward three battalions in skirmishing order to check the Russian advance. In the ensuing engagement, fought at long-range, the Turks lost about 500 men killed and wounded; the Russian loss is not recorded.[16]

If Grand Duke Michael's coming added little, the intellectual capacity of the Russian headquarters had been markedly improved by Obruchev's arrival, who had on the advice of Miliutin been posted to the Caucasus front by the Tsar in an effort to stem the tide of reverses. He had arrived in September in time to put forward the plans for the attack on the Yagni hills. Now, since Mukhtar had withdrawn from his position, Obruchev saw an opportunity to atone for the losses in that assault; but since the withdrawal might be a precursor to a retreat to the Saghanly Dagh, he believed that he must take action urgently.[17]

His new plan was aimed at the total destruction of Mukhtar's army, calling for a demonstration by Loris-Melikov with 32 battalions and 112 guns against the front of the Turkish positions while Lieutenant-General Lazarev, with 23½ battalions, 29 squadrons and 73 guns was to execute a wide turning movement around Mukhtar's right flank and thence into his rear. Coordination between the Russian forces was essential; Obruchev relied on the field telegraph to achieve this.

Lazarev set out on his long march during the night of 9/10 October, initially with 17 battalions of infantry, 22 squadrons and 70 guns. *En route* he was joined by two detachments from Tergukassov which brought his force up to its planned strength of about 20,000 infantry, and 3,000 cavalry. He crossed the Arpa into Russian territory and then some miles further south at Kizil-Kiliskly recrossed the river, reaching Digor on October 12. Lazarev ordered a rest day for the following day. Remarkably, he had so far encountered no hostile forces during his march. He had been paying out the telegraph line behind him, enabling him to keep in touch with headquarters throughout. Mukhtar's lack of cavalry meant that apart from accidents Lazarev might reasonably expect not to have his communications interrupted.

While Lazarev was engaged in his march the remainder of the Russian army was moving into position for the combined assault. On the right, Major-General Grabbe had 3 battalions, 8 guns and 15 squadrons between the Kars River and the high road north of Little Yagni. In the centre Heimann had 24 battalions (about 20,000 men), 8 squadrons and 104 guns; his force was posted from Great Yagni to Hadji Vali. On the left, under Major-General Kouzminsky, 8 battalions (6,000 men) with 24 squadrons and 24 guns were located in front of Kizil Tepe. The reserve, under Major-General Dehn, consisted of 6½ battalions (5,000 men) 8 squadrons and 24 guns; it was posted behind Kulveran. The right and left wings and the reserve were under the command of Roop. The intention was that once Lazarev was securely in the Turkish rear Heimann should assault the Turkish centre on the heights of Avliar, while Roop and Lazarev attacked and surrounded the Turkish right.

On the morning of October 13 Mukhtar, still sublimely unaware of the serious threat posed by Lazarev's movement around his right rear, came to the conclusion that he had been unwise in giving up Great Yagni, and determined to try and recapture it. He sent out a strong force before dawn in the hope of surprising the Russian defenders. The Turks reached the base of the hill before their advance was discovered; unluckily for them it was a moment when the Russian trenches were crowded with troops that had come up to relieve the overnight garrison, and they received the Turks with such a murderous rifle fire that after an hour the attackers retreated, leaving 123 dead on the slopes of Great Yagni.[18] Later in the day the Russian artillery, having located Mukhtar's position, began shelling the area; one shell burst only twenty yards from where the Turkish commander was standing. This cannonade was part of the Russian endeavours to keep Turkish attention on their immediate front.

Turkish infantry assault the Great Yagni, October 13. (*Russes et Turcs*)

At some point during the day Mukhtar became aware of Lazarev's turning movement, and he hurriedly cobbled together a force to resist it, sending a detachment about 6,000 strong under his brother in law Reshid Pasha, including three battalions that had arrived from Ismail to take up a position between Orlok and Bazardjik. Lazarev continued his march on October 14 after the rest day at Digor, and in the afternoon his advance guard ran into Reshid's force in a strong position south-east of Bazardjik. Reshid had had some opportunity to start preparing entrenchments; but Lazarev wasted no time in launching an immediate assault, his troops climbing the slopes of the position under heavy fire before driving the Turks back at the point of the bayonet. Mukhtar was himself quickly on the scene, bringing up reinforcements. These were, however, charged by Lazarev's cavalry, and fell back in the face of what could now be seen as a much superior force.

The Turks retreated to a second position, which commanded the whole country between Vizinkoi and Bazardjik; both sides could see that if that went, then there was nothing to stop the Russians falling upon the Turkish rear. Lazarev sent Shelkovnikov forward with a large force of infantry. Under cover of a heavy artillery bombardment the Russians swept forward, and by nightfall were firmly in occupation of the position. Mukhtar was now in serious trouble; there was only one road left to him, and to retreat by night towards Kars would involve a difficult and dangerous march. He was also reluctant to abandon the strong position on the Aladja Dagh. He ordered the baggage and supplies to start the journey back to Kars, while his troops remained in their earthworks, to await the morning. It was a fatally mistaken decision.

That night the field telegraph proved its value. Lazarev sent back at 2.30 am a full report of all that had occurred and the position he had occupied. The opportunity of a decisive victory was readily apparent, and orders were at once issued for an attack at dawn on October 15. Heimann, with the Caucasus Grenadier Division and 64 guns was to storm the Olya Tepe position. Lazarev was to advance against Vizinkoi, while Roop was to advance on Kerchane and, if Heimann's attack succeeded, was to assault the Aladja Dagh.

As dawn broke on October 15 Heimann's artillery moved forward to a line only 1,500 yards short of the Turkish works on the Olya Tepe. From here they opened a heavy fire on the Turkish position, using on this occasion shrapnel, which had not hitherto been employed to any great extent. The bombardment was, at this range, fearfully effective, causing heavy casualties. The position on the Olya Tepe was naturally very strong:

> All round the conical height of the Olya Tepe, formed of entirely bare rocks, the Turks had established a continuous entrenchment composed of a ditch for sharpshooters, five feet wide and three feet deep, provided with salient and re-entering angles.[19]

Heimann advanced with three regiments to the northern side of the Olya Tepe, remaining there until the artillery preparation had caused sufficient damage. Mukhtar observed that one of these regiments was too far advanced and reckoned that it might be vulnerable. At 10.00 am he sent seven battalions forward towards the right of the Russian column, but their assault failed in the face of heavy artillery fire from Great Yagni, and from the concentrated rifle fire of the infantry. By noon Heimann decided to launch his assault, and the Russian infantry began to climb the slopes of the Olya Tepe.

Turkish cavalry. (*Album della Guerra Russo-Turca del 1877-78*)

The garrison maintained a heavy fire for as long as they could, but as the Russian masses came on they abandoned first their outpost line of trenches, and then their position on the crest. The Russian infantry pursued them in a fierce bayonet charge, and the Turks fled in confusion. Heimann rode forward to the summit and ordered an immediate pursuit, while the artillery advanced between the Olya Tepe and Great Yagni, from where they could cover the only line of retreat from the Aladja Dagh.

Meanwhile Lazarev had advanced against the heights between Vizinkoi and Magaradjik. Eight battalions in two columns moved forward to drive the Turks out of the position. As they retreated they encountered the demoralised survivors retreating from the Olya Tepe, and the whole body fled in confusion in the direction of Kars. Mukhtar, who had been posted on a hill behind the Olya Tepe with Kemball and the members of his staff, watched as the left wing of his army dissolved. The *Daily News* correspondent described the scene:

> At this juncture the Marshal left the hill on which he had stood since morning … The line of retreat was all but impassable. Lingering convoys still struggled over the strong surface; and a couple of battalions, with a haste scarcely dignified, were making for Sari Tepe. I must here state that through all the confusion which followed, Mukhtar Pasha bore himself like a true soldier, retiring only when his soldiers left him no other choice.[20]

The successes of Heimann and Lazarev now opened the way for a decisive assault on the Turkish positions on the Aladja Dagh. At about 2.00 pm Heimann was ordered to cross the ravine and attack from the north-west, leaving sufficient troops to hold Vizinkoi and the Olya Tepe. Lazarev was to attack from the south-west, and at the same time to bar all the escape routes near Bazardjik which the Turks might attempt. Finally Roop was to assault the Aladja Dagh from the north. In fact, the latter had already made his move, seeing signs that Omer Pasha, commanding in this sector, was getting ready to withdraw his artillery. Ordering the charge to be sounded all along his line, Roop pushed forward his infantry. The Turks replied with a fierce rifle fire, but actually Omer's position was already impossible. Although it was already becoming dark, Roop resolved to make a final attack on the Turkish trenches. Just as the advance was beginning, the sound of cheers could be heard from the southern slopes of the Aladja Dagh, and from the direction of Bazardjik, where Omer had sent envoys under a white flag, the news spreading like wildfire. Grand Duke Michael, on the Vizinkoi heights, sent orders to Loris-Melikov to ratify the surrender, on terms that officers could retain their arms, personal goods and horses, but that the surrender of the army, its equipment and stores should otherwise be unconditional.

The surrender began at 2.00 am on October 16, the Turkish soldiers leaving their weapons in their trenches and marching down unarmed. A Russian officer described the scene to the *Moscow Gazette*:

> It was a fine picture and well calculated to rejoice our hearts. On both sides a living hedge – our soldiers – and in the middle a long motley line of disarmed Turks winding down the path; at the foot of the mountain, the silent masses of our troops waiting with sloped arms. The descent of the Turks lasted a long time – nearly two hours.[21]

It had been a crushing victory. Seven pashas, among whom were Reshid and Omer, had been taken, together with 36 guns and 2 battalions. During the two days following the battle the Russian cavalry picked up further prisoners, together with 9 guns. Altogether the Turks lost 5,600 men killed and wounded, and 12,000 prisoners. By comparison the Russian losses were modest, at 230 killed and 1,611 wounded. Of the 35,000 or so with which Mukhtar had started the battle almost half were lost, and his army, as an organised force, had been effectively destroyed.[22] Mukhtar himself declared that he was 'beaten by the Russian artillery,' which on this occasion at least was remarkably effective. Mukhtar was really beaten by the fact that the reinforcements which the Russians received were sufficient to make possible the turning movement prescribed by Obruchev; and perhaps also by the field telegraph, which enabled the various Russian forces to be coordinated.

Major May, after reviewing the evidence of observers at the battle, offered another explanation, concluding that the Russian success was largely due to the effectiveness of the field artillery, which in contrast to that at Plevna had engaged the enemy at close range. He quoted the Russian official account describing the performance of the artillery:

> It was worked on this day with a precision and activity which had not distinguished it on former occasions, and, as was remarked by an independent witness on the Russian side, instead of confining itself to a shell fire at impossible ranges – where neither accuracy nor effect could be expected, and where its fire was soon masked by the advance of its own troops – moved forward this time in support of the infantry, and materially cooperated towards the result of the day.[23]

The Camel's Neck

Mukhtar had made his way through the shattered remnants of his army to Kars, where by nightfall on October 16 a total of 16,000 troops had been assembled. He took the immediate decision to leave the larger part of these for the defence of the fortress, and to retreat with the rest to the Saghanly Dagh, where he hoped to effect a junction with the forces of Ismail. Hussein Hami Pasha was left in command at Kars. On the afternoon of October 17 Mukhtar left the fortress with about 2,800 men and a few guns, marching west in heavy rain over the mountains to the Olti valley, and then making his way to Zevin, which he reached on October 19. The entrenchments were still there, but although he was joined by some 8-10,000 men that he had ordered up from Erzerum, it was clear to him that his force was insufficient to hold the position. This left him no alternative but to fall back to Erzerum, which he finally reached during the night of October 29/30. Faizi had gone on ahead and selected a position to defend the city at Deve Boyun (the 'Camel's Neck') about seven miles to the north-east.

Kemball, who had accompanied Mukhtar throughout the campaign, wrote an account of the events of the retreat:

> We have passed in Armenia many 'mauvais quart d'heures' and critical moments since Mukhtar's defeat on the 15th. Nothing could be more admirable than his behaviour, both before and after the event of which you have heard the details, though worn out in body and depressed in mind. He very nearly broke down during our hazardous retreat from Kars. With a Russian force plainly visible at Begli Ahmed we were liable to be intercepted or attacked on the flank at any moment. Had the Cossacks shown themselves on the intervening range which covered our line of march, our dispirited troops would certainly have dispersed. The weather, in its very badness, though aggravating their sufferings, favoured their escape.[1]

Kemball went on to bemoan the lack of cavalry; Mukhtar told him that he had no more than 200 horsemen with which to harass the rapidly lengthening Russian lines of communication. It was this weakness that had so hindered the Turkish operations throughout the campaign in Armenia. It was again to have a significant effect on the defence of Deve Boyun.

Ismail, meanwhile, as soon as he learned of the defeat on the Aladja Dagh, had abandoned his sick and wounded (about 4,500 men) and retreated up the Araxes valley, pursued by Tergukassov, when the latter was belatedly informed of the Turkish defeat. The Kurds that formed a large part of Ismail's force now deserted in a body, and by the time that he joined Mukhtar he was not much more than 8,000 strong. In the course of Ismail's retreat, which he conducted with uncharacteristic speed, he was largely ignorant of the position and strength of his pursuers. However, he lost his rearguard when two battalions were surrounded and forced to capitulate at Hassan Kale. Mukhtar now had

Minarets at Erzerum. (Ollier)

about 18,000 men in all with 60 guns in the Deve Boyun position; although it was naturally strong, the force available to hold it was inadequate. The Camel's Neck Pass is a narrow valley opening on to the plain of Hassan Kale. Faizi had prepared three entrenchments covering the entrance to the pass; but these gave Mukhtar a front of many miles to defend with a force cobbled together from those he had brought from Kars, some convalescents and armed civilians from Erzerum, and Ismail's force.

Opposing the Deve Boyun position was Heimann, whose division had closely pressed Ismail during his retreat, and who had cut off the rearguard at Hassan Kale. As soon as Tergukassov joined him in front of Deve Boyun, Heimann resolved on an immediate attack, intending to bounce Mukhtar's defeated and demoralised troops out of the position while the impetus of his advance was still with him. He had available some 24,000 men with 120 guns, and 5 Cossack regiments. He divided his force in two, either side of the high road to Erzerum. The right was under Tergukassov and the left under Devel, with the cavalry in reserve, and Heimann planned for the assault to take place on November 4.[2]

Mukhtar assigned the defence of the crucial Ouzoun-Ahmet plateau, on the left of the position, to the reliable Mehmet, now promoted to the rank of Pasha; the right was commanded by Ismail, although no doubt having a pretty clear idea of the latter's limitations, Mukhtar sent Faizi to assist him. He himself remained in the centre, from where he intended to conduct the battle, and from where he could personally supervise the defence of the Deve Boyun itself.

The first shots in the battle were fired by the Turks at 9.45 am, while the Russians were still deploying, and soon the artillery was in action along the whole front. The Russian artillery, advancing to a range of less than two miles, replied with a tremendous fire, the guns on the right flank concentrating on Ouzoun-Ahmet. This was to be attacked by a column on the right of Tergukassov's force, under Colonel Prince Amirajibi, while the remaining column, under Bronevsky, deployed in front of the village of Pousi Dara. In touch with this column was Devel's right wing, under Avinov, while his other column, under Schack, formed the extreme left of Heimann's force.

Schack's advance was directed against the village of Gulli, which was soon taken. Ismail, however, collected a force of some eight battalions and launched these in a counter-attack against Schack's flank. During the confused fighting which ensued, in which the Russian infantry were reinforced by a regiment brought up in the nick of time, Faizi was wounded in the arm, but he continued to direct his troops. Mukhtar was alarmed by the success of Schack's advance, taking it to be the principal point of attack, and sent four battalions to reinforce Ismail, who employed them in a desperate attempt to retake the positions occupied by Schack's troops. Although failing to drive the Russians out of Gulli, this attack effectively stopped any further advance on this flank.

It was at the other end of the line, however, that the crucial action was being fought. Amirajibi had begun by launching a storming column in a direct assault on the plateau; this failed, but seeing that a fresh attack was being prepared Mehmet asked for and got three battalions and two batteries as reinforcements. These began to arrive as the second assault came in, and this too was repelled at the point of the bayonet. At 1.00 pm a third attack was made. This also failed, and Tergukassov decided to approach the problem from a different direction. Mehmet had posted one battalion and the artillery on a hill

A Russian assault at the Camel's Neck. (Ollier)

in front of the Tchoban Dagh, on his left flank, and from this position had been able to fire on the Russian attacks in flank. Bringing up two battalions, Tergukassov launched an assault on the hill and soon took it; the Russian artillery advanced to within a mile of Mehmet's position, and in a short time silenced the Turkish artillery at the top of the Deve Boyun defile.

At 4.00 pm the Russian artillery commenced a heavy bombardment with shrapnel of the Turkish trenches, following which Amirajibi's troops advanced and seized the small hills at the foot of the plateau. So accurate was the Russian artillery fire that one experienced Turkish officer observed to the correspondent of the *Daily News*: 'I don't believe that Russian officers direct those guns; they are English or they are Prussian.' Mukhtar, too, remarked on the considerably improved performance of the Russian guns.[3] The Turkish artillery responded, firing on the attackers from three sides, but in spite of this the Russians continued to press forward, taking the first line of trenches at the point of the bayonet. Establishing themselves in them, the Russians soon forced the Turks to retreat to the right of the plateau. After five hours fighting, the outcome remained in the balance, the Russians having taken some of the outlying positions but the Turks still holding the principal works. At this point a remarkable incident decided the course of the battle.

Heimann had, on seeing the initial success of Amirajibi's attack, wrongly thought that a complete breakthrough had been achieved, and ordered up the cavalry to advance through the pass and harry the Turkish retreat, supported by a grenadier regiment. Major-General Amilakhvari advanced at the head of 2,000 cavalry into the defile, but since Amirajibi had not been able to get any guns up to the plateau the horsemen were unprotected by artillery or rifle fire. Mukhtar, seeing Amilakhvari's advance, jumped to the conclusion that it was a reconnaissance that had been drawn on too far. Waiting until the Russian cavalry had come near enough, he ordered eight battalions forward out of their trenches to attack them:

> Very soon the Turks found themselves more than a thousand yards from their trenches. On the ridge where Mukhtar's staff was posted everyone held his breath. The Russian cavalry occupied ground much too irregular for free manoeuvring, and their annihilation seemed certain, more specially as two batteries of horse artillery were sent to assist in routing them.[4]

Amilakhvari halted beneath the slopes of Ouzoun-Ahmet, which Amirajibi's last attack had carried. As the Turks pressed forward, they found that it was they who had been trapped. From Ouzoun-Ahmet on their left, from the Erivan Grenadier Regiment in their front (which had been under cover and not observed), and from Bronevsky's troops on their right in front of the Tchoban Dagh, a storm of fire was poured on the advancing infantry. The suddenness of the attack, at short-range, in a confined space, panicked the Turkish troops, who turned and fled, several hundred being taken prisoner. Mukhtar, seeing what had happened, rushed forward with two battalions to try to check the Russian advance, but it was too late. Believing that all was lost, Ismail's division crumbled in spite of all that Faizi could do, falling back in confusion, throwing away weapons and munitions, and abandoning guns. The narrow road back from Deve Boyun was blocked by the dense crowd of fugitives.

British war correspondents with the Turks. (*The Graphic*)

Faizi and Mehmet rallied two brigades and succeeded in holding up the Russian advance long enough for the remnants of the army to reach Erzerum. Safety, however, was not at first to be found within the city, the governor having given orders for the gates to be shut. For a while there was the deeply unedifying spectacle of the defeated Turks engaging in a violent struggle to force their way into the city, finally prising open the gates. During the night which followed the battle stragglers continued to reach the city, while the Russians sought to make the most of their victory, their cavalry overrunning the plain of Erzerum. Heimann had the satisfaction of being able to spend the night sleeping in Mukhtar's tent.

The Turkish defeat had been comprehensive; they had lost 42 guns, including 8 heavy howitzers, 3,000 men killed and wounded and 1,000 taken prisoner, and another 3,000 deserters scattered over a wide area. The Russians, on the other hand, had lost no more than 1,200 men killed and wounded.[5] Heimann's reputation, which was based on his impulsive disposition always to attack, was greatly enhanced; it was burnished by the legend which grew up that the ambush of the Turkish infantry in the Camel's Neck Pass had been deliberately planned. It is clear, however, that it was entirely accidental, arising from Amilakhvari's rash advance and the unexpected appearance of the Erivan Grenadier Regiment.

The Russians did not, however, follow up their success by an immediate assault on the city. Had they done so, they might well have carried it, since the troops within were completely demoralised, and the civilian population was dead against putting up any resistance. On November 5 however, a reinforcement of 4,000 men, well equipped and organised in six battalions, reached the city and occupied the line of forts; the Russians, meanwhile, began to erect a redoubt on the crest of the Deve Boyun Pass. Next day the municipal authority petitioned Mukhtar, appealing to him to surrender the city to spare the inhabitants a siege and assault. Mukhtar's reaction was to say that this would be a matter for the Sultan, to whom he would telegraph for instructions. While waiting for these, he then received a summons from Heimann to surrender; he asked for three days' grace to reply, a period which the Russians used to erect an additional redoubt on the heights to the east of the city. The spectacle further alarmed the population, who again begged Mukhtar to surrender; but well within the three days he received orders to defend the city to the last man, and he sent to Heimann to tell him so.

Heimann's reaction was to repeat his demand for a capitulation, warning that in three days his bombardment of the city would commence. Mukhtar however, had not lost his nerve. Having toured the fortifications, and talked to their defenders, who had been joined by further reinforcements from Batum, he was convinced that the city could be held. At a meeting with all the civil and military authorities he carried them with him in his resolution to defend the place to the utmost.

Erzerum was surrounded by the old town walls, some four miles in circumference, which were high and wide and supported by numerous bastions. There was a moat, twenty-five feet deep in places. A number of additional works had been built; Medjid and Azizi on the Top Dagh, Surp Nisan to the north of these, and Keremetli at the south-west corner of the walls. South of the main road to Kars was Fort Ahali. Overall, the defences of Erzerum were formidable, but they did require a stronger force than Mukhtar possessed for them to be adequately garrisoned.[6]

Heimann, determined to avoid the rigours of a prolonged siege during the winter months, decided to try to take the city by a *coup de main*. He reckoned, almost certainly correctly, that the key to the defences of Erzerum was the Top Dagh, to the east of the city. If this could be taken it would be impossible for Mukhtar to continue to defend the place. Heimann planned a night attack on November 9/10, to be made by 10 battalions, with two batteries and a cavalry regiment. The force was split into two columns, with a view to a simultaneous attack on both sides of the Top Dagh. Unfortunately, the two columns lost contact with each other in the darkness, and only the advance guard of the right-hand column, of three battalions, arrived at the point of assault, Fort Medjid, about 1,300 yards in front of Fort Azizi, at the appointed time. Led by a spy familiar with the terrain, the Russians burst into the fort and captured its garrison. Meanwhile Mehmet, hearing the sound of battle, came out of Fort Azizi, and charged into Medjid at the head of half a battalion. A desperate hand-to-hand struggle ensued; after twenty minutes the Turks were again in possession of the fort.

At this point the rest of the assaulting force came up and launched a fierce attack on Fort Medjid. As dawn broke, the heavy guns of Fort Azizi were brought to bear on the attackers, and it became clear that the position was too strong to be taken. The Russians fell back, chased down the slopes by Mehmet's men, and by a mob of armed inhabitants that poured out of the city by the Kars gate.[7] The success greatly heartened the Turks,

Mukhtar Pasha sighting a Krupp gun at Erzerum. (Ollier)

and Mukhtar won the cooperation of the population in his resistance, for which he ordered up as much in the way of supplies and ammunition as it was possible to send. Fourteen more battalions arrived from Trebizond, their entry into the city not being opposed by the Russians, whose forces were quite insufficient to invest the place.

Heimann had lost some 700 troops killed and wounded and 130 taken prisoner in his assault on Fort Medjid, but he had not given up, and on November 12 made another assault on Fort Azizi; but again, after initially succeeding in entering the fortifications, the Russians were driven out by Mehmet. Soon after this, heavy snow began to fall, and within a few days further operations were effectively halted by the weather. Although by the beginning of December sufficient troops had become available to develop an investment of Erzerum, the weather continued to prevent any effective action against the city. The inhabitants, meanwhile, endured a winter of fearful privation; supplies of food began to run short, while a typhoid epidemic caused thousands of deaths. There was, however, no further fighting; the Russians were themselves suffering heavily from outbreaks of typhoid and cholera. As a result they merely maintained a blockade of the city until the general armistice brought hostilities to a close, having completed its investment when they were able to cut the Trebizond road on January 12 1878. Meanwhile, just before this occurred, Mukhtar was recalled to Constantinople.

29

The Storming of Kars

The forts that surrounded Kars were a very different kettle of fish from the modest earthworks that protected Plevna. They had almost all been built since the Crimean War, during which Kars had held out for five months until starved into surrender, and they had enormously strengthened the defensive potential of the fortress. Kars lies on the western side of the plain and on the river of that name. To the south-west, west and north of the city rise volcanic spurs jutting out from the Saghanly Dagh range. The river runs around the base of these spurs; to the north of the city it runs through a deep ravine in the mountains several hundred feet deep. On the north-east lies the Kara Dagh, or Black Mountain. The only weakness in a fortress so well protected by nature was on the south and south-east, where it was open to the rocky plain.

The citadel was built in masonry on a perpendicular rock overhanging the gorge just north of the city. Around the city were twelve detached forts. Two of these were on the north-east and east of the city (Fort Arab and Fort Karadagh). These were built on the bare rock; the earthworks were composed of earth brought to the site and there were no ditches or traverses. They commanded all the ground around, including the works on the Tchanak Dagh to the west and north-west. The forts were of a very considerable size. Fort Arab had an interior crest of 600 yards, with a curtain 300 yards long. Fort Karadagh, on the Black Mountain, consisted of a bastion with a curtain on either side enclosing a battery some 21 feet above the crest. The two forts were linked by a line of trenches.

On the Tchanak Dagh there were three smaller forts – Moukliss, Inglis and Veli Pasha, facing north and north-west. Next, to the west, the works on Shorak Dagh were as high as those on the Black Mountain. Here there were three forts, of which the most commanding one was Laze Tepessi, consisting of three batteries each with a front of 80 yards. Tik Tepessi was a square bastioned redoubt about 100 yards a side, with a ditch 9 feet by 7; a battery with a width of 60 yards was situated in front of it. Tekmass had two small square redoubts with an earthen parapet across the gorge.

The most powerful forts, understandably, were those covering the south-eastern sector. Fort Hafiz Pasha was a square redoubt, 400 yards a side, with bastions at the angles, traverses on the parapet and covered way, a ditch 12 feet by 6, and a three storied casemated barrack closing the gorge. Fort Kanly consisted of two small redoubts 150 yards square, behind which was a lunette with a two storied casemated barrack closing the gorge. Finally there were two small forts on the banks of the river, Forts Souvari and Tchim, (also called Vassif Pasha) which were simple lunettes without ditches or traverses.[1]

These fortifications had suffered little during the operations around Kars in May and June. Since then work had gone on to strengthen them, increasing the size of the ditches, and digging trenches to connect the forts on the south-eastern side. In resisting a siege Kars had a number of advantages; the forts were on commanding heights, were

A field hospital near Kars following the storming of the city. (*Russes et Turcs*)

close enough to lend each other support, and the fact that they were built on rocky ground meant that they could not be mined. On the other hand, the forts were not far enough from the city to prevent its bombardment; they lacked sufficient storehouses and access to water; and in a number of instances the forts lacked sufficient defensive features such as *caponnières* and traverses. Above all, the River Kars split the defence in two, preventing the swift movement of reserves.

Greene made a careful calculation of the garrison that would have been required properly to defend these works:

> The total armament of the place is about 200 guns (303 were captured at the assault, including a large proportion of field guns). The total development of the line of fire for infantry is about 6,000 yards, 4,000 in the works on the right bank and 2,000 in those on the left. Allowing 2 men to a yard, and 50 per cent in reserve, the proper garrison would be 18,000 infantry, and with 25 men to a gun, 5,000 artillery, or in all 23,000. This was almost exactly the strength of the garrison at the time of the assault.[2]

A different view of the adequacy of the garrison effectively to man the fortifications was taken by Hozier, who estimated that the city required at least 40,000 men:

> In order to have defended it properly there should have been sufficient reserves in each of the three lines of defence to man the entire length of the entrenchments; for owing to the nature of the ground, the rugged slopes and absence of roads, a rapid movement of reinforcements from one quarter to another was quite precluded.[3]

Nor, in Hozier's view, were the troops actually available sensibly distributed; the five strong forts on the west and north, which unlike those in the south covered each other, contained the bulk of the garrison, while the more vulnerable forts in the south and east were manned by Arab and Kurdish troops of doubtful quality, and were without reserves. Hozier judged that Hussein Hami, although a courageous divisional leader, had already shown that he was not up to the command of the fortress.

Even had the garrison not had twenty per cent of its number sick or wounded in the desperately overcrowded hospitals within the city, and the remainder been traumatized by the disaster on the Aladja Dagh, Kars would not have been impregnable. However, the size and strength of its redoubts undoubtedly made it a very tough nut to crack, and with the Russian experiences before Plevna very much in their minds, the Grand Duke and Loris-Melikov pondered hard on their options. A direct assault was plainly a very risky venture, but with the grim prospect of a lengthy winter siege as the alternative it seemed worth making the attempt. Besides, the Russian troops had their tails up after the victories of the Aladja Dagh and Deve Boyun, while the morale of the Turks was obviously correspondingly low. On the other hand, a siege would be a long affair; the garrison appeared well provisioned, and it was a type of warfare in which the Turks excelled. Supplying the besiegers would itself be a difficult undertaking, and the troops would be subjected to considerable and prolonged suffering.

All these considerations prompted the decision to launch an assault as soon as possible. Command of the Army of Kars was given to Lazarev, operating under the orders of the Grand Duke and Loris-Melikov. It consisted of the 1st Grenadier Division, the 40th Division, and parts of the 19th, 38th and 39th Divisions, comprising 41 battalions of 30,000 infantry, with 53 squadrons and 144 guns. Siege guns were sent up as quickly as possible, 48 of which arrived on November 4. They were established in twelve batteries around the east and south-east of the city, at a range of some 3,000 yards from the fortifications. The focus of the assault was to be Forts Hafiz, Kanly and Souvari, against which the siege batteries opened fire on November 11, keeping up the bombardment by day and night.[4]

Hussein Hami was not a robustly confident commander. The obvious intention of the Russians to press their advantage, whether by an energetically conducted siege or by a direct assault was all too evident, and he sent a gloomy report to Mukhtar soon after the bombardment commenced saying that his men were so demoralized that he was afraid that the fortress would fall at the first assault. Meanwhile the weather continued bitterly cold, although so far not a lot of snow had fallen.

The Turks made a spirited response to the Russian bombardment, on November 5 pushing forward to a position east of Fort Hafiz where they constructed a battery which caused a good deal of damage to Russian working parties. To deal with this a force under Alkhazov moved forward and compelled the battery to withdraw. At the same time two battalions of the Kutaisi Grenadiers, under Fadeyev, advanced from the direction of Vizinkoi, intending to cut off the battery's retreat. Fadeyev, realising that the guns had already been withdrawn, remained within a mile of Fort Hafiz in a depression, out of sight of the garrison. After nightfall, he moved forward to the fort, which had only a shallow ditch, and decided to launch a surprise attack. Shouting 'Come on, boys, here is glory for the Kutaisi Grenadiers,' Fadeyev led his men over the wall before the startled garrison could respond, and drove them out. He realised that he could not hope to hold the fort, and spiked the guns before withdrawing with eighty prisoners. His total casualties in this adventure were 42 killed and wounded; it raised great enthusiasm among the Russian troops.[5]

This success made a major contribution to the Russian decision-making process. It suggested that the garrison of Kars might not be as resolute as had been supposed, and that an immediate attack might be even more desirable. This view was reinforced by the large number of Russian soldiers reporting sick as they endured the bitter weather in their advanced positions around the city.[6]

The weather, indeed, was a major consideration. It had been planned to launch an assault on the night of November 13/14, in order to take advantage of a full moon; but the weather deteriorated to the point that the attack was called off until it improved. This was a matter of real concern to the Russians, who had taken extreme precautions to prevent the Turks becoming aware of the imminence of the assault. They went to the lengths of assuring even those newspaper correspondents with whom they had a good and trusting relationship that such a thing as an assault was not even being contemplated. This secrecy appears to have been effective, for there is no sign that the Turks anticipated the attack when it came, or the direction from which it would come.

On the afternoon of November 16 the weather began to moderate, and the assault was fixed for the night of the following day. In all, 35 battalions were assigned to carry out the attack and the supporting demonstrations and by nightfall on November 17 those attacking the south-eastern sector had been concentrated in and around two villages about two and a half miles from the forts. The attacking force was organised in seven columns. The first column, under Komarov, of 6 battalions and 16 guns, operating north of the river, was to launch a demonstration against Fort Tekmass but then, following the ravine, move against Fort Tchim. Parallel with this advance on the other side of the river, the second column, under Lieutenant Colonel Prince Melikov, of 3 battalions, was to attack Fort Souvari. Next came the third and fourth columns, commanded by Major-General Grabbe. He had 10 battalions and sixteen guns in all, and was to attack Fort Kanly. He personally led the left column while Colonel Vodjakin led the right. The fifth column, under Major-General Alkhazov, of 5 battalions and 8 guns, was to attack Fort Hafiz. A demonstration against Forts Laze Tepessi and Mouklis was to be made by the sixth column, commanded by Colonel Tchereminissov with 5 battalions and 24 guns; a similar demonstration against Forts Arab and Karadagh was to be made by Major-General Rydzevsky, with 6 battalions and 24 guns. These last were to convert their demonstrations into substantive attacks if the opportunity offered.[7]

Lazarev had given careful thought to the tactics to be adopted, applying lessons learned from previous assaults. He firmly believed in a night attack, but that it should be when sufficient moonlight enabled the assaulting columns to find their way. They should avoid a long march, but be concentrated gradually about three-quarters of a mile from the point of attack. Night patrols were sent out in the preceding days to accustom the Turks to skirmishing near the forts. Above all, the bombardment was to be stepped up in the three or four days before the assault, but not particularly so on the last day.[8]

Loris-Melikov joined the columns to assault Fort Kanly at about 6 pm November 17, and about two hours later they moved off:

There was a touch of frost in the air, and the full moon shone brightly. The plain and the lower hills and valleys seemed to slumber peacefully in the dark, but above them loomed the snow-wrapped mountain ridges glimmering in the beams of the moon. The greatest care had been taken to preserve silence and secrecy as long as possible, and the men were forbidden to smoke or speak. The skirmishers, in open order, marched in advance, followed by the assaulting troops, who at first marched in compact columns, deploying into columns of companies as they approached the line of attack[9].

At about 9 pm the Turks seem to have become aware that something was up, and there was some firing from their outposts. To concentrate their attention on the northern sector, the Russians opened fire with their artillery on the forts there. In the south no reply was made to the Turkish fire, which ceased for a while, before bursting out again at about 9.30 pm, when the Russian columns were about to reach their objectives.

The first to do so was Melikov's column, which stormed into Fort Souvari before its defenders realised that the Russians were so close. Attacking with the bayonet, they overwhelmed the defenders in a few minutes, spiked the guns, and then charged forward through a party of Turkish cavalry to reach, and ford, the icy water of the River Kars in order to attack Fort Tchim on its left and rear. To the right of Melikov's advance, however, the attack on Fort Kanly was encountering stiffer opposition.

Count Grabbe, leading his column on horseback, passed around the western redoubt in order to attack the rear of the main work. A few yards from the parapet he fell dead, shot twice in the chest. The command passed to Colonel Belinsky; as he cheered his men

The storming of Kars on the night of November 18 1877. (Strantz)

on, he too was shot dead. As the assaulting troops struggled to reach the parapet, it was found that the scaling ladders were too short, and the Russian troops had to scramble up the rugged sides of the wall. Entering the redoubt, there was a desperate hand-to-hand struggle before the outworks and batteries were taken. Next day some 500 Turkish bodies were found in this part of the fortification. The battle for Fort Kanly was not yet over, however. The two-storey barrack held out, and its defenders poured such a hail of fire on the Russians that they were forced for the moment to quit the fortifications they had taken and retreat to the edge of the parapet and the ditches. Hearing of the casualties among the senior officers, Loris-Melikov sent Colonel Bulmering of the engineers to take command of the troops at Fort Kanly. Two battalions and two companies from the reserve were sent forward and Loris-Melikov directed Prince Tchavtchavadze, who with 17 *sotnias* of Cossacks was at the bridge which carried the high road to Erzerum over the river, to advance into the area between Kanly and the city, and to support the troops in and around the fort. Meanwhile the Turks, encouraged by the lull in the fighting, had sortied from the barrack in an abortive attempt to force the Russians from the top of the parapet; at about midnight 250 dismounted Cossacks arrived in time to drive the Turks back into the barrack.

Bulmering now split his forces; he led one column which cleared the trenches leading to Fort Souvari, and advanced to the edge of the city, while the other, under Colonel Karassev, occupied the eastern part of the fort. Bulmering, returning to the fort, demanded the surrender of the barrack, threatening to knock it to bits with his artillery. The demand was refused, and firing continued until shortly before 4.00 am. Bulmering had had enough of this, and shouted that unless the barrack surrendered at once he would blow it, and its occupants, to pieces with dynamite. On being assured that the lives of his men would be spared Daoud Pasha, who was in command, surrendered with 300 men, who were all that remained of the garrison.

At Fort Hafiz Pasha, Alkhazov's troops had also been split into two columns. As they approached they were fired on not only by the fort but also from the trenches connecting it to the Black Mountain and the batteries constructed on its southern slope. To clear this threat, Colonel Fadeyev with 2,500 men succeeded in taking part of the trench system, driving the defenders towards the town and Fort Karadagh. Having cleared these trenches, Alkhazov turned his attention to the fort itself, which had been badly damaged by the Russian artillery, the casemated barrack building having been completely destroyed. Alkhazov led two battalions to the assault in the front and left of the fort, his troops pouring over the parapet. The Turks fell back behind the ruins of the barrack; but as they did so another battalion, sent around by the left, took them in rear, and after a bayonet charge the defenders were virtually wiped out.

Meanwhile Fadeyev's force had made considerable progress. Following up the Turks retreating towards Fort Karadagh, he pressed them closely, his troops chasing the enemy up the slopes of the mountain until reaching the fort itself. Climbing on each other's shoulders, some of them entered the fort from the rear. The defenders took refuge in the inner work, but before they could gather their wits the Russians were upon them. Soon, half the garrison had been bayoneted or knocked senseless, and the survivors fled along the trench system to Fort Arab. A party of Russians pursued them, but by now the Turks were beginning to recover, and practically annihilated their attackers before forming up for a counter-attack on Fort Karadagh. Fadeyev had, however, received reinforcements from Alkhazov in the form of the 158th Regiment, and resisted all the Turkish attacks.

By 2.00 am the Russians had taken all the works on the right bank of the river from Souvari to Karadagh, apart from the isolated barrack at Fort Kanly which was still holding out. Lazarev, riding along the lines, could see the extent of his success, and sent forward parties of troops taken from Alkhazov and Bulmering to take possession of the city. However, on the other side of the river things had not been going so well for the Russians.

Komarov had, in accordance with his orders, made a feint attack against Fort Tekmass with 2 battalions of the 3rd Grenadier Regiment, occupying Mount Moukha, some 3,500 yards from the fort. The remaining battalion and the artillery he held in reserve, sending Colonel Boutchkiev with the three battalions of the 151st Regiment along the ravine to attack Fort Tchim. At about 9.00 pm, as soon as firing was heard from the direction of Souvari, the regiment advanced from its position near the Kutchukkoi bridge. However, as it neared the ravine it ran into Turkish outposts in trenches at its entrance. The exchanges of fire that followed alerted the Turks in camp behind Fort Tekmass, who advanced to the edge of the ravine and poured a destructive fire on the Russians. Changing direction, Boutchkiev led his men up the slope and drove the Turks back towards Tekmass. Following them up closely, he went forward to the attack of the fort; as he charged forward he was killed instantly, and his disheartened troops fell back to the ravine, having suffered heavy casualties.[10]

Meanwhile Melikov's column, having crossed the river partly by a bridge of boats and partly by fording the icy waters, had launched an attack on the rear of Fort Tchim. In fierce fighting Melikov was mortally wounded, and many of his officers went down. The column retreated in some disorder to a cemetery on the south-west edge of the city. Komarov now sent forward the whole of his reserve along the road through the ravine in an attack on Fort Tchim, under heavy fire from that fort and from Fort Tekmass. The artillery unlimbered close to Fort Tchim and opened a heavy fire on it, while the infantry reached the cemetery and kept up a furious fusillade. This made little impression, though, and the Russians were by now taking heavy casualties from crossfire. Komarov had no choice but to pull back his troops and they, and the survivors of Melikov's column, fell back along the river bank to the Kutchukkoi bridge. The attack on this sector of the fortifications had thus failed with heavy loss. It had however, succeeded in keeping the attention of Hussein Hami, and limited the opportunity of reinforcements being sent to the south-eastern sector of the defences.

The remaining operations, along the northern flanks of the fortifications, were under the command of Roop. The column under Tchereminissov launched an attack on Fort Laze Tepessi at about 9.00 am. Initially successful, Tchereminissov's men stormed the trenches in front of the batteries and reached the ice-covered parapet. Here, however, they were held up, but hung on for several hours until the arrival of Turkish reinforcements drove them back into the trenches. Ryzdevsky's column, further east, maintained a heavy artillery fire on Forts Arab and Karadagh, which softened up the garrison of the latter before Fadeyev launched his assault. When Ryzdevsky heard of the capture of Karadagh fort he switched all his forces and launched an impromptu but vigorous assault on Fort Arab led by the 160th Regiment. This was entirely successful;

the survivors of the garrison fled back towards the city. There, the citadel had fallen, offering little resistance to the 152nd Regiment advancing from Fort Hafiz.

As the sun came up, Hussein Hami took stock of his position. For a long time the successful repulse of the attacks on Souvari, Tchim and Laze Tepessi, and the prolonged defence of Fort Kanly, had led him to believe that overall the Russian assault had failed. By 2.00 am, however, the true situation had become apparent.[11] All the forts on the right bank of the river were now in Russian hands, as was the citadel and the rest of the city. Although between 12,000 and 15,000 men still held out in the forts on the heights on the left bank of the river, it was entirely clear to him that there was no prospect of recapturing the lost positions. To remain where they were meant their inevitable surrender to the Russians, and he collected all the troops available to him, assembling them between Fort Tekmass and Fort Laze Tepessi. In thick columns these moved out in the direction of Olti, in an effort to break through the Russian cordon and then make their way through the mountains to Erzerum.

Roop alerted his cavalry, ordering an attack on the flank of the Turkish columns while his infantry, at the villages of Bozgala, Samovat and Aravartun, held them in front. At Bozgala, the largest Turkish column was surrounded, and quickly laid down its arms. At the other two villages the Turks broke through, and continued their march into the mountains. It was an opportunity for cavalry commanders to dream of. Pursued by Cossack cavalry, with horse artillery batteries, the columns were picked off one by one, surrendering by battalions after they had been ravaged by shrapnel fire. Gradually the whole Turkish force was overwhelmed in this way, until only about 150, on horseback, remained. During the pursuit of these, the Cossacks cut down about 100; the remainder,

The burial of Russian soldiers fallen during the storming of Kars. (Strantz)

Turkish officers captured at Kars. (*Album della Guerra Russo-Turca del 1877-78*)

thanks apparently to the quality of their horses, got away, reaching Erzerum, after a desperate ride, on November 27. Among this group was Hussein Hami, together with two or three of his senior officers.

The storming of Kars was a remarkable achievement. It was an extremely powerful fortress, well equipped and provisioned. Its garrison was equipped with modern breechloading rifles. There had been no preliminary siege operations, no painstaking approach by parallels, and Hozier called it 'an incident almost unequalled in modern warfare.'[12] 17,000 prisoners were taken, with 303 guns, 25,000 small arms and a huge quality of stores and ammunition. 2,500 Turkish bodies were found in all, while nearly 5,000 wounded were found, in the hospitals and on the field. The Russian losses were not inconsiderable, amounting to 488 killed and 1,785 wounded. The proportion of officers among the casualties was noticeably high, a tribute to the way in which they had led their men forward.[13]

Hozier described the grim aftermath of the battle:

The scene in the town after the assault was terrible. The Turkish dead lay in heaps in and behind the trenches, all frozen stiff in the attitude in which they had expired. The wounded Russians were removed and treated by their surgeons, who were thus fully occupied, while the unfortunate Turks, utterly neglected by their own surgeons, were left for days tortured by their wounds and exposed to the bitter cold without assistance … For more than a day the town was given up to anarchy and disorder ... The Turkish rule was broken, and that of the Russians was not established. The camp followers of the Russian army, and the rabble inside the city, made full use of the interval to gratify their love of plunder.[14]

Following the seizure of Kars, and the Russian check before Erzerum, the winter closed in, and brought virtually to an end all active military operations. Ultimately, the campaign in the Caucasus had ended in a decisive Russian victory. Initially, the Russian strategy had been markedly confused, and it then had to face a remarkable recovery led by the outstanding Ahmed Mukhtar. This was only overcome by the arrival of strong reinforcements and with the development of a clearer set of objectives. The higher leadership had not on the whole distinguished itself, although some notable victories had been won. Perhaps the outstanding Russian leader was Lazarev, who displayed a more consistent talent than the mercurial Heimann; like the competent Tergukassov, as well as Loris-Melikov, he was of Armenian origin. What they could all depend on was the patient, loyal and brave Russian soldiers, who endured great hardship without complaint.

On the Turkish side, the infantry also displayed great endurance and, especially in defence, fought well throughout the campaign. As on the Bulgarian front, they were mostly poorly served by their junior and middle ranking officers. Mukhtar did have a number of excellent subordinates, such as the Hungarian Faizi and the German Mehmet; but he also had some dreadful senior officers with which to deal, such as Faik and Ismail.

30

Gorni Dubnik

The Council of War held at Russian headquarters on September 13 after the crushing defeat at the third battle of Plevna had been an emotional affair. During the course of the discussion the Grand Duke Nicholas offered as his advice that the correct course of action would be to retreat to the Danube, establishing a fortified bridgehead there, and await reinforcements. Alexander then asked Miliutin for his view. He disagreed with the Grand Duke, reckoning that Osman was neither strong enough nor mobile enough to launch an attack, and that while reinforcements should be sent for they should be awaited in the army's present position. Nicholas was greatly offended: 'If that is your opinion, General Miliutin, you had better assume the command of the army yourself.' Alexander intervened to say that Nicholas should remain in command but that Miliutin's advice should be followed. Three months later, as Wellesley recorded, the Tsar had not forgotten the exchange; when the news of the surrender of Plevna reached him, he took Miliutin's hand and, with tears coursing down his cheeks, said that he should have the Grand Cross of the Order of St George. The Minister of War said that he had done nothing to deserve it, having been merely in attendance on the Tsar:

> Whereupon the Emperor, pointing across the valley to the hillock on which the Council of War was held on that fateful September day, said, 'I owe Plevna to you. Do you think I shall ever forget the advice you gave us on yonder hillock? And if he,' pointing to his brother in the valley, 'were here now, he should thank you in my presence for the counsel you then gave.'[1]

In truth, Nicholas had to some extent been a busted flush since the disastrous failure at Plevna. No clearer demonstration of this could be found than in the summoning of Todleben to headquarters. There had been considerable surprise at the outbreak of war that Russia's greatest military hero should have no command. These feelings were intensified when, after the first two battles of Plevna, Nicholas continued to resist pressure that Todleben should be sent for. His belated arrival was greeted with delight on all sides, coupled with an increasing public feeling against Nicholas:

> The resentment was the greater because the reason of the Grand Duke's antipathy to the great engineer was pretty well known. It appears that as chief of the engineer corps, of which the Grand Duke Nicholas was the Inspector-General, Todleben had put a stop to certain malpractices in the department, or, at any rate, had done all in his power to check them, and this action on his part had given umbrage to those who had derived profit from the old state of things.[2]

Although there was naturally a feeling of discouragement at the Russian headquarters, there was also a clear determination to carry the war through to the bitter end, although

The Russian Imperial Guard marching to Plevna. (Ollier)

this view might not have been shared in the Ministry of Finance, where concern about the cost of the war was mounting. MacGahan wrote from headquarters on September 19:

> I find the feeling here not so gloomy as I had expected. Military men acknowledge that they have been beaten, but as much by their own errors as by the bravery of the Turks, and there is not the slightest sign of hesitation, or weakening of the determination to fight it out. The idea of peace is not entertained. Everybody feels that it is a death struggle in which Turkey or Russia must go to the ground irretrievably, and the final issue is not doubted for a moment. Although the struggle must be hard, and may be long, Russia must ultimately crush her adversary, it is held, if only by mere brute force, in default of science, skill and generalship.[3]

The steps necessary to achieve a complete investment of Plevna were not taken immediately. During the third battle Lockarev's cavalry had operated very freely to the west of the city, and by September 11 had established contact with Leontiev's cavalry at Dolni-Dubnik, theoretically completing the ring. Patrols were sent to the west over the Isker and to the south-west towards Radomirtza, but no substantial contact was made. On September 18, however, Lockarev was ordered to the east of the Vid to a position on the left of the force in front of Plevna, on the Lovtcha road. All the rest of the cavalry, operating to the west of the Vid, was now placed under Krylov, following Zotov's resumption of command of the IV Corps. Krylov, with about 4,000 cavalry, was given a number of tasks; he was to clear the country as far as the Isker of Bashi-Bazouks, seize all the food and forage, break up Osman's lines of communication, reconnoitre towards Sofia and Widdin and prevent supplies or reinforcements reaching Osman.[4]

It was a formidable list, and Krylov soon encountered difficulties. On September 21 a reconnaissance found about 10,000 Turkish infantry dug in around Telis; next day Krylov's patrols reported a strong force moving out from there towards Dolni-Dubnik, and he ordered Lockarev to cross the Vid to take it in the rear. However, when he learned that another force (under Atouf) was advancing from Plevna to meet the column from Telis, he gave up the attempt to interfere, and retreated no less than fifteen miles to the north, fearful of being taken between two fires.

The Telis column, which was commanded by the able Ahmed Hifzi Pasha, who had recovered from the wound he sustained at Plevna in July, was escorting an immense convoy of some 1,500 wagons laden with supplies and ammunition. With Krylov out of the way it was able successfully to complete its journey to Plevna unscathed. It consisted of three brigades under Hakki Pasha, Edhem Pasha and Veli Bey, and had set out from Orkhanie on September 18. It was here that the Turks were assembling supplies for Plevna, under the direction of Chefket Pasha. He had become notorious as the officer principally responsible for the atrocities in Bulgaria in 1876 and had, indeed, been sentenced to death in response to insistent demands from the Western Powers. The Sultan commuted the sentence to banishment; all that this had amounted to, however, was a posting to a command at Batum.[5]

While Chefket was putting together the next convoy for Plevna, Krylov spent five days in reconnaissance along the Widdin road and towards Rahova. He encountered little except a few parties of Bashi-Bazouks, and by October had returned to his base at Trestenik, where he concentrated his force, sending patrols down the Sofia road. While he was thus engaged, Osman had sent Ahmed Hifzi's column on a successful foraging expedition around the villages to the south-west of Plevna. Aware that Chefket's next convoy was *en route*, he sent Ahmed Hifzi out to Dolni Dubnik to meet him. Chefket left Orkhanie on October 6 with an escort of 15 battalions, 4 cavalry regiments and two batteries, reached Telis next day and on October 8 entered Plevna with a convoy of 500 wagons. Apart from a brush with some of Krylov's cavalry at Radomirtza, the principal obstacles to this successful mission had been the appalling weather, which had swollen the streams to torrents, and the bridges destroyed by the Russians which had to be repaired. Krylov had, it is true, no infantry with which to bar the progress of these convoys; but he had a strong force of cavalry, and the long line of wagons presented a target which any vigorous cavalry commander would have longed for.

It had been apparent to Osman after the third battle of Plevna that the correct course would now be to withdraw from the city, falling back through Orkhanie to the line of the Balkans. There could be no doubt that to remain in Plevna was ultimately for his army to be lost. It was inevitable that, with overwhelming forces at their disposal the Russians would invest the city, and that now was the last opportunity for extricating the army. When Osman sought permission to do so, however, what Spenser Wilkinson described as the 'secret debating society' at Constantinople refused to entertain the

Cossacks foraging. (*Russes et Turcs*)

proposal; Plevna, he was told, was too important to be abandoned, and must be held at whatever cost. Maurice pointed out the military absurdity of the decision:

> It is difficult to conceive a more unjustifiable answer to the request of a gallant commander. The importance which Plevna had acquired was due to the menacing position of Osman's army, which from that place was a constant danger to the Russian right flank and to their communications. Once the Russians were able to accumulate sufficient force to make an offensive movement by Osman Pasha impossible the importance of Plevna was gone. To order Plevna to be held because it had proved to be a strategically important point under quite different conditions was to sacrifice uselessly a brave leader and a gallant army. The only possible defence of the policy of holding on to Plevna at any cost is that it was intended to take advantage of the fact that the Russians were concentrating the greater part of their strength against that place, and to throw every available Turkish soldier against one of the other Russian armies, and by overwhelming it compel the Russians to give up their operations against Plevna. But any such resolute action as this was far from the thoughts of the Sultan's advisers.[6]

The true reason for this foolish decision was political; the defence of Plevna had radically altered the international perception of Turkey. No longer appearing as a corrupt and brutal empire on the verge of a well-deserved final collapse, the Ottoman Empire was now displaying sufficient vitality for it to survive. As such its preservation might again be a reasonable policy objective for those Great Powers such as Britain and Austria that had previously regarded this as essential.

There is also one other aspect of the matter which the authorities at Constantinople might reasonably have taken into account. For Osman's army to get away from Plevna reasonably intact it would require speed and manoeuvrability, which were qualities it almost certainly did not possess. Although the troops had shown great courage during their defence of Plevna, they were not well trained. There was an inadequate force of cavalry to protect the marching columns; and the officers were of a decidedly variable quality. All this suggests that Osman's army was unlikely to prove a match for the Russian army in the open field. The Russians had a large force of cavalry, and their infantry heavily outnumbered the Turks. The route that Osman must take to extricate himself was towards Sofia. No doubt his troops would have put up a good fight when, as they would certainly have had to do, they turned to face their pursuers. But casualties would almost certainly have been high; it would have been difficult to prevent parts of the army being cut off in the course of the retreat. Of course, if the Turks had put together a strong enough force to move north to meet Osman, all these problems would have been materially reduced; but, as Maurice observed, this would have required a clear-sighted determination which was totally lacking.

Bashi Bazouks on vedette. (*Russes et Turcs*)

The need to pull out of Plevna while there was still time was also obvious to the foreign military *attachés*. On September 5, before the third battle began, Liegnitz was noting that the time had come for the Turks to withdraw, but believed that this would not happen because 'the Turkish soldier has no understanding of the strategic retreat.'[7]

Osman, therefore, must necessarily make plans to prolong the defence of Plevna for as long as he could. When Chefket arrived there with his second convoy the two men sat down to plan for the regular revictualling of the fortress. It was agreed that there should be a fortnightly supply convoy which would follow the excellent road from Sofia to Plevna. On either side of the road there would be a cordon of cavalry, and at regular intervals of five or six miles works would be constructed as halting places for the convoys, which would have up to 1,000 wagons. These places included Dolni Dubnik, with a garrison of 5 battalions and 2 guns; Gorni Dubnik, with 6 battalions, 4 squadrons and 4 guns; and Telis, with 7 battalions and 4 guns. These were all under Osman's command; the sector from Telis to Orkhanie was the responsibility of Chefket, who commanded a total of 23 battalions, 12 squadrons and 12 guns. The works constructed at the halting places might also serve another purpose; if Osman was ultimately to retreat from Plevna, they would provide him with positions at which to hold up any Russian pursuit.[8]

The weather, meanwhile, had steadily deteriorated, rendering bad roads almost impassable. By the beginning of October snow had fallen in the Balkans, and elsewhere prolonged heavy rain turned Bulgaria into a quagmire. These conditions particularly affected the bringing up of Russian reinforcements and supplies, since there were no metalled roads running from the bridges over the Danube. Broken wagons and wrecked carriages littered such roads as there were:

> It was a scene of hopeless wreck: fragments of shattered vehicles emerged from the black, semi-fluid mixture, and dead horses, which no one even tried to drag out, were lying half buried in the mud nearly everywhere. Everything that passed along the roads cut them up more and more, and all tended to create a scene of dirt and confusion beyond conception.[9]

Krylov's inept attempts to interdict the Turkish supply system came to an end with the formal announcement on October 4 of the new command structures in an order of the day. Todleben's position, officially, was to be 'Adjunct to the Commander of the West Army', with Imeretinsky as Chief of Staff; Krylov was to proceed to Russia as Inspector of Cavalry Remounts, leaving Gourko with the responsibility for operations against Osman's supply line. Meanwhile the Russian works around the east of Plevna had been strengthened, and new batteries established from which the siege guns could reach every point in the Turkish defences on the Janik Bair. On the Turkish side also the fortifications were repaired and strengthened, and a chain of redoubts and shelter trenches was constructed to cover the hitherto unfortified heights to the west of the city.

Todleben, now the effective commander of all the Russian troops around Plevna, was perfectly clear that no further assaults should be attempted, but that the investment should be completed as soon as possible. This he deferred until the further reinforcements arrived, since the intelligence available to him suggested that Osman had as many as 80,000 troops in the city; the true figure was actually about 50,000. It was not until the arrival of the Guards that Todleben felt he could take active measures to complete the

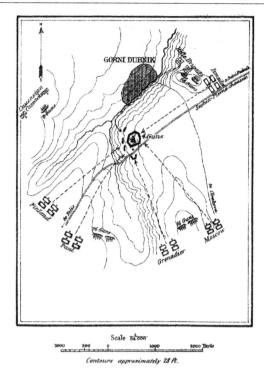

Battle of Gorni Dubnik October 24 1877

circle of investment. On October 21 Gourko was given command of a strong force to capture the Turkish posts on the Sofia road. For this task he was given the 2nd Guard Cavalry Division, Krylov's cavalry division, the 1st and 2nd Guard Infantry Divisions, the Guard Rifle Brigade, another regiment from the 3rd Guard Infantry Division, and an engineer battalion. The force comprised 40 battalions, 60 squadrons and 146 guns, and its first objective was to be Gorni Dubnik.[10]

At the same time Todleben intended to close the Plevna-Lovtcha road and complete the investment on the south of the city, an operation that would also cover Gourko's movement. This task was assigned to Zotov, with the 16th Division, now commanded by Skobelev, one brigade of the 30th Division, 3 regiments of the 3rd Guard Infantry Division, 3 battalions of the 3rd Rifle Brigade, an engineer battalion and 184 guns. These operations were to be carried out on October 24, and were to be accompanied by a bombardment of the Turkish positions by all the batteries around Plevna.

Gorni Dubnik had been selected as the point at which the Sofia road should be cut because of its proximity to the besieging forces and because it was considered that the ground in front of the village offered tactical advantages to the attacker. It was also, however, the strongest of the positions fortified by Chefket on the Sofia road. There was a large redoubt on the northern side of the road, surrounded by extensive advanced entrenchments and a lunette on the other side of the road. The position was commanded by Ahmed Hifzi, who had a total of between 7,000 and 8,000 men, with 4 guns, and who was, accordingly, heavily outnumbered. Of course, the position was not far from the whole of Osman's army, and Chefket's force, at Radomirtza, was not far away either.

Gourko, having reconnoitred the Turkish position on October 22, crossed the Vid in the early hours of October 24. He planned to attack on the north, east and south sides of the Turkish position, and to send a Cossack brigade and two regiments of Roumanian cavalry to the west to cut off the Turkish retreat. On the right of the attacking columns was Major-General Ellis, with the 4 battalions of the Rifle Brigade, 3 *sotnias* of Cossacks and 16 guns. In the centre Major-General Zeddeler had the 8 battalions of the Moscow and Grenadier Regiments, the sapper battalion, one *sotnia* and 16 guns. On the left, Major-General Rosenbach had the Paul and Finland Regiments (8 battalions) with 16 guns. The three columns reached their jumping off points at 8.30 am, about 1,800 yards from the Turkish positions, and all the artillery opened fire. The bombardment was supported by the Cossack horse artillery of 6 guns which had arrived on the north-west of Gorni Dubnik, so that by 9.00 am 56 guns were shelling the Turkish redoubt.

At about 10.00 am Colonel Lioubovitsky led the Grenadier Regiment forward, capturing the lunette and following the Turks up to the redoubt. There the advance halted; driven back by a murderous fire, the grenadiers took refuge behind the lunette and in the ditches beside the high road. Zeddeler now sent the Moscow Regiment forward with two batteries. The infantry joined the grenadiers in the ditches on the high road while the artillery pressed to within 900 yards of the Turkish position, only to be obliged to retreat owing to the accuracy with which the Turkish infantry picked off the gunners. By now Lioubovitsky was down, and so were Zeddeler and Colonel Scalon, his chief of staff; the infantry remained pinned down in the ditches, about 60 to 80 yards from the redoubt.[11]

Both Ellis and Rosenbach, seeing the whole of the centre column engaged, took it to mean a general attack, and each sent forward their columns to attack the redoubt.

The attack of the Russian Imperial Guard at Telis, October 24. (*Russes et Turcs*)

Ellis, with the Rifle Brigade, was held up by heavy fire from the trenches north-east of the redoubt, while Rosenbach's assault failed in the face of a terrible fusillade of rifle fire, the Paul Regiment falling back to a position behind the Grenadier Regiment and the Finland Regiment to a dead angle at the bottom of the ravine south-west of the redoubt. In this attack Rosenbach was wounded and Colonel Rounov, commanding the Paul Regiment, was killed.

By noon, therefore, Gourko was staring defeat in the face, and an intervention by either Osman or Chefket at this point would have been conclusive. However, Osman had his hands full, with the heavy bombardment of his positions and the movement by Zotov's force. Chefket, on the other hand, was disinclined to get too close to the Russians; it was widely believed that if caught, he would be hanged by the Russians for his part in the Bulgarian atrocities, and he refrained from advancing out of Radomirtza. Ahmed Hifzi, therefore, was obliged to fight his battle unaided. At 2.00 pm Gourko, reviewing the position of his forces, received very bad news. He had, in order to cover his attack on Gorni Dubnik, sent a column of 4 rifle battalions, with 17 squadrons and 20 guns, under Colonel Tchelistchev, towards Telis, with orders to capture the Turkish works there if possible, and to protect the left flank of the attack on Gorni Dubnik.

Arriving in front of the Telis redoubt, the riflemen launched their attack at about 10.00 am, and soon cleared the Turks out of a line of rifle pits in its front. These were, however, very shallow and offered no protection from the fire of the redoubt, so the riflemen must either retreat or go forward to the redoubt. They chose to attack, courageously rushing forward under heavy fire, but could not reach the redoubt. They took cover for a while in some broken ground until Tchelistchev, hearing that Turkish reinforcements were approaching, ordered the regiment to fall back, retiring about a mile and a half. A dreadful scene ensued:

> From 200 to 300 wounded Russians remained on the ground; and when the Turks came out immediately after the retreat of Tchelistchev's column, they were all killed, after being subjected to the torture of most horrible and disgraceful mutilations.[12]

This atrocity appears to have been perpetrated by Bashi-Bazouks. There was no doubt that it occurred; two English surgeons, serving with the Turkish garrison and later made prisoner, confirmed the incident. The riflemen had suffered terribly, losing a total of 973 men killed and wounded. Although the Turks made no attempt to follow them, their retreat left the road to Gorni Dubnik open, exposing Gourko's force to an attack from the rear, and it was clear to him that there was not a moment to lose. He ordered an attack from all sides at 3.00 pm, to be signalled by a succession of three volleys to be fired in turn by the batteries on the left, then in the centre and then on the right, after which all the infantry should assault the redoubt. Gourko went to the left column, giving the necessary orders to Lieutenant-General Count Shuvalov, the commander of the 1st Guard Division. However, at this point the artillery of the right column fired three volleys, and the infantry charged forward to the assault. Gourko, in his report of the battle, described what followed:

> It was with a sinking heart that I followed what was about to take place; there were going to be isolated assaults one after another, of which the success was more than

The Battle of Gorni Dubnik. (Fauré)

doubtful. To remedy matters as far as possible, and to sustain the column on the right, which had already begun the assault, I sent orderly officers in all directions to give the troops the order not to wait any longer for the signal, but to support the attack of the column on the right. As was to be expected, a series of attacks one after another took place. Received by an extremely murderous fire, no one body of troops could reach the great redoubt.[13]

Pinned down by the incessant fire, the attackers found what shelter they could, and held the ground that they had won, apart from the Finland Regiment, which was caught in open ground and forced to fall back to the dead space on the slope of the ravine, losing its commander Major-General Lavrov, killed at the head of the regiment. The assaults were over by 4.00 pm. The Russian artillery had ceased fire for fear of hitting their own men, while a withdrawal from the temporary shelter found by the troops would have caused enormous losses. Dusk began to fall, and with it a silence over the redoubt, until two battalions of the Ismailov Regiment, crawling forward, got within 50 yards of the redoubt. Simultaneously the rest of the infantry rushed forward, and stormed into the redoubt:

> The artillery also advanced to within 100 yards of the Turkish redoubt; and at this short distance poured in an effective and deadly shell fire, the effect of which was to create a scene of indescribable horror. The blockhouses within the redoubt were speedily in flames; the wounded and the horses were being burnt alive; the trappings of the artillery were on fire, and the explosion of cartridges which lay about mingled with the cries of the sufferers, the rattle of the infantry fire, and the thunder of the guns. The atmosphere of the camp was a thick yellow mist of dust and smoke, made lurid by the scarlet tints of the setting sun.[14]

At about 6.00 pm Ahmed Hifzi hoisted the white flag. The Russians took 2,289 prisoners and 4 guns. The Turks had lost about 1,500 men killed and wounded. About 5,000 of the garrison did, however, manage to escape, making their way into Plevna or back down the road to Telis. The Russian losses were heavy; 829 men had been killed and 2,980 wounded. Two regimental commanders and a battalion commander were among the dead, while two brigade commanders, a regimental commander and three other colonels were wounded, together with the divisional chief of staff and three of his officers.[15]

Greene, reflecting on the heavy casualties which had been sustained during the battle, observed:

> The blow was a heavy one, for the troops were all picked regiments of the Guards, and their officers nearly all belonged to the nobility; it brought the sufferings of war home to the higher classes in a way they had previously no idea of. The fault was not so much Gourko's, but rather that of the men themselves and their subordinate officers; yet it was a generous fault, for they had rushed forward impetuously in advance of their orders, filled with the pride of their birth and position.[16]

The Tsar was broken-hearted when he read the casualty lists, so many of the individuals being personally known to him; the extent of the butcher's bill almost led to Gourko being relieved of his command.

Gorni Dubnik had thus been cleared, but it was obviously necessary that Telis should be taken as well, since Gourko was for the moment uncomfortably situated between two enemy forces. Accordingly he assembled most of his force and on October 28 was in front of Telis. At 11.00 am he opened fire on the works with 70 guns, and by 2.00 pm the Turkish artillery had been silenced, preparing the way for an assault. At this point, however, showing a good deal less resolution than Ahmed Hifzi at Gorni Dubnik, the Turkish commander Ismail Hakki Pasha sent out a white flag. Upon being assured that his officers would be allowed to keep their personal property, he agreed to surrender. The Russians moved forward to occupy the Turkish positions. As they did so, however, they came upon the unmistakable evidence of the massacre of their wounded on October 24, and in spite of all their officers could do they violently attacked the Turkish troops, killing about 50 before order could be restored. Over 3,000 prisoners were taken, together with four guns and a large quantity of small arms ammunition intended for the garrison of Plevna.

Meanwhile Osman, still apprehensive that another general assault on the city was planned, recalled the garrison of Dolni Dubnik to Plevna. This made its way into the defences of the city during the night of October 31/ November 1, just as Gourko was massing his forces to storm the place. When the Russians occupied the fortifications of Dolni Dubnik next day, the investment of Plevna was complete.

31

Baba Konak

Gourko having shown that he was one of the few superior commanders to have discovered the secret of success, it was no surprise that it was he who was charged with the responsibility for conducting operations in the open field west and south-west of Plevna. At the beginning of November it had became known that the Turks were assembling an army to relieve Plevna in the area between Orkhanie and Sofia, and that it was apparently intended that Mehemet Ali should command this force. To deal with any attempt at relief a covering force was necessary, and this task was assigned to Gourko. Before, however, he commenced operations he was to await the final tranche of reinforcements, due to arrive on November 15.

Meanwhile, although there had been little general activity around the perimeter of Plevna since the investment had been completed, there had been two significant operations. The first of these was an assault by the Roumanians upon Grivitza No 2. By mid October the siege works around the fort had been advanced to within forty yards, and although the capture of the fort would have little effect on the investment, the Roumanians were keen to make an attempt to seize it. The plan was to take the fort by a sudden assault in immense force, trusting to the short distance to be crossed to limit casualties. On October 19 the assault took place, strong columns of infantry rushing forward, albeit in the face of fierce rifle fire from the Turkish defenders, who were well prepared. In spite of this the Roumanians succeeded in taking the fort and for twenty minutes held it under heavy fire. At the end of that time, the casualties steadily mounting and with no supporting activity on either flank, they fell back, having lost about 1,000 men killed and wounded. It had been a brave but ultimately pointless effort, and served only to demonstrate the futility of assaults upon the well-fortified Turkish positions.[1]

On the southern side of the city an operation was mounted with a more logical purpose. Since the third battle the Turks had held, and heavily fortified, the Green Hills that had been the scene of Skobelev's prolonged struggle in this sector. In particular the hill immediately above and to the north-east of Brestovetz (the first knoll) had been a considerable nuisance to the Russians, projecting the Turkish line into the lines of investment and obliging the Russians to undertake a journey of six or seven miles between Skobelev's position and that of Zotov. Todleben saw this as a weak point in the Russian lines, and ordered that the hill be taken. The task was assigned to Skobelev, now in command of the 16th Division. On November 4 he occupied Brestovetz, his troops digging in around the village. The attack was carefully prepared; Skobelev concentrated between 11,000 and 12,000 troops there for the assault, which went in during the early evening of November 9, his columns scrambling up the slopes on the east, south and west of the hill. The Turks were taken completely by surprise, and although putting up a brave resistance were driven off the hill by a bayonet charge. In the course of the fighting Skobelev was, for the first time, himself slightly wounded. The Russians now fell to the task of entrenching the position; by the morning of November 10 a great deal had been done to render the hill secure, and all that day the work continued, albeit under continuous fire from the Turkish positions. That night the Turks launched two powerful attacks in an effort to retake the heights, requiring Skobelev to throw in all his reserves before they were driven back. Over the next three days further attacks were made, all of which failed with considerable loss. After this the Turks contented themselves with the construction of fresh redoubts, one of which was no more than 150 yards from Skobelev's positions.[2]

Apart from these operations, the activity on both sides was confined to the strengthening of the existing defences and the construction of new works, particularly on the west side of Plevna, and opposite Bukova, where the Roumanians extended their right flank opposite the Turkish works on the heights of Opanetz. Todleben reckoned that Osman could not have provisions for more than two months, and he was in no doubt that investment was the correct course to follow, as he reported after the fall of the city:

> It only remained to follow strictly this line of action, without making any attempts at assault, which could lead to no definite result, and would have only increased the number of our losses: it was necessary simply to endeavour to make the circle of investment as close as possible, and to take all the necessary measures to prevent the enemy from being able to force it at any point.[3]

Meanwhile the War Council at Constantinople had indeed decided that Mehemet Ali, who had been intended for the command of the Turkish forces in Bosnia and

Russian medical services in action near the front. (Budev)

Herzegovina, should be appointed to the army to be assembled for the relief of Plevna. On his way to Sarajevo, therefore, he received a message to take up instead the command at Sofia. The troops being collected for this army came from various sources. Some units, earmarked to join Suleiman's army around Shumla and Rasgrad, were also diverted to Mehemet Ali. A number of Arab regiments, and some from Armenia, were identified as available, together with a considerable number of Circassians, while a somewhat battered Bosnian division was transferred from the Shipka sector. It was not an impressive force:

> Many who came would have been better away, had the commander in chief been able to select his men; but that was impossible, and the consequence was that the bulk of the army consisted of a rabble, hurried together with a view to numerical force alone, and without any regard to efficiency. Without unity or cohesion, ignorant of each other, composed to a great extent of conscripts, badly victualled and without any staff – such an army constituted the poorest and most imperfect instrument of offence.[4]

It was far too late to improvise such a force; the opportunity to do so was after Osman's victory in September. Nonetheless, Mehemet Ali did put together some 20,000 infantry, 2,000 cavalry and 36 guns, which he organised in two divisions under Chakir Pasha and Redjib Pasha, with a cavalry brigade and a reserve brigade under Valentine Baker who, disenchanted with Suleiman's leadership, had left him in the hope of being able to take part in operations to assist Osman in Plevna.

It was evident to Mehemet Ali that this force was incapable of confronting Gourko in the open field, and he concentrated the bulk of his troops at the Baba Konak Pass, with detachments at Orkhanie, Etropol and Slatitza. The crucial task as he saw it was to hold the line of the Balkans, and to cover Sofia; it was simply not realistic to undertake an offensive in the direction of Plevna, let alone to relieve the city. A different view was held in Constantinople, however, as Baker had found when arriving there from Shumla:

> A kind of spell seemed to hang over the military authorities at Constantinople at this time, which induced them to completely ignore common-sense views. They had scrambled together all the newly-raised *Mustafiz* battalions that could be collected, and they were rapidly assembling at Sofia. Mehemet Ali would command, I was assured, eighty-seven battalions; with those the relief of Plevna ought to be easy. It was in vain that I pointed out that good troops would be requisite, and that guns, cavalry, and an effective administrative department of supply would be necessary to feed an army that had to advance for so considerable a distance.[5]

Before leaving to take up the promised command of a force under Mehemet Ali, Baker paid a final visit to Edhem Pasha, the Grand Vizier, and made a last appeal that some of the good troops should be withdrawn from the Montenegrin and Serbian frontiers, 'but was met by the stereotyped answer that every part of the Empire must be watched and guarded.' Baker had one pleasant surprise on his journey to Sofia; on the station platform at Adrianople he caught sight of his friend, the dashing Captain Frederick Burnaby of the Blues. He had come to Turkey determined to make his way

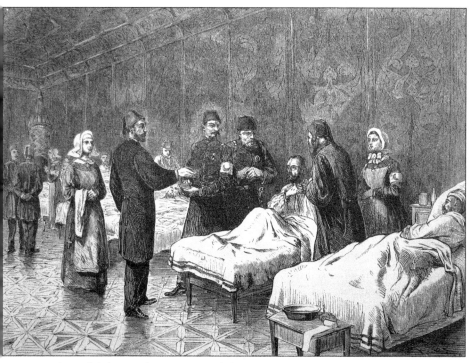

Sultan Abdul Hamid visiting wounded in a Constantinople hospital. (Strantz)

into Plevna, a project that horrified Baker. Burnaby agreed to accompany Baker to Sofia, and to discuss his plan with Mehemet Ali.

The force with which Gourko was to deal with any attempt to relieve Plevna consisted of the 1st and 2nd Guard Divisions, the Guard Rifle Brigade, the 2nd Guard Cavalry Brigade and the Caucasian Cossack Brigade, a total of 36 battalions, 36 squadrons and 120 guns, amounting in all to about 36,000 men. By this time the reinforcements arriving at Plevna had brought the total Russian forces there to a total of 191 battalions, 120 squadrons and 650 guns, or about 160,000 men, which meant that a detachment of the size of Gourko's force could easily be spared.[6] Even before he embarked on his march southwards the 3rd Infantry Division, based at Lovtcha, had marched south to Trojan and from there, on October 31, moved on Tetevan, which it captured after a brief combat. The division was not strong enough to advance any further for the moment, and was ordered to await Gourko's movement.

Gourko set off on November 15, the bulk of his force taking the high road to Sofia. Before this, to his right, 20 squadrons of cavalry entered the Isker valley and thence southwards to Vratza, a place which they captured on November 9. The Cossack brigade had previously taken Jablonitza; on November 18 Gourko's infantry marched into the town, where they were joined by the 2nd Brigade of the 3rd Division from Tetevan. Gourko's immediate concern was with the strong position at Orkhanie, which provided Mehemet Ali with a firm base of operation from which he could advance in the direction of Plevna. If it was possible by taking the offensive that the principal passes through the mountains could be seized, it would effectively shut the gate in Mehemet Ali's face.

Gourko's patrols found the Turks occupying a strong position at Pravetz, on the east side of the road to Orkhanie. It appeared to him to be too strong to fall to a direct attack, and he decided to combine such a forward movement with a flanking movement. For this he assigned Rauch, with one regiment of the Guard, two rifle battalions, one horse artillery battery and six squadrons. This force was to move up the valley of the Little Isker, to the left of the high road.[7] The high road itself was in good condition, although it followed a sharply twisting route through the mountains and often was as steep as 1:10. The other roads, such as those Rauch was to traverse, were primitive in the extreme.

Rauch's column would be one of three under the overall command of Lieutenant-General Shuvalov. Major-General Ellis, with five battalions, three *sotnias* and fourteen guns was to take the high road and attack the front of the Pravetz position, while five battalions, two squadrons and eight guns constituted the reserve. Another part of Gourko's force was under the command of Major-General Dandeville; the 12th Regiment, with eight guns and three *sotnias* was to take the road from Tetevan to Etropol; the Preobrazhensky Regiment, with four guns and three sotnais to follow the road through the Little Isker valley towards Etropol; four battalions, the 4th Dragoon Regiment and twenty four guns stood in reserve. Dandeville's mission was to make a strong demonstration against Etropol, although if he judged that the weakness of the enemy justified it he could launch a serious attack.[8] Gourko retained three regiments, with two squadrons and seventy-two guns, as a general reserve on the high road at the junction with the Etropol road, and dispatched two cavalry regiments in the direction of Lutikova, on the left of the Turkish position at Orkhanie.

Rauch's men had a fearful time of it. They set off from Jablonitza on November 21, with orders to march all night. The force was led by a party of men, working in two reliefs of sixty each, using the 120 picks and shovels which were the only tools available. The route was extremely difficult:

> The path led along a ravine where the Mali-Isker twisted and turned among the crags; and before they left the river to take the direction of the village of Kalugerovo, the next village on the route, they had crossed it ten times – each time with much trouble. The way led over great ledges of hard, flinty rock, full of seams and fissures, so difficult for the horses to pass that the feet of several were caught in the crevices and the hoofs torn from the bone.[9]

Due to reach the position assigned to him by noon on November 22, it was not until the following afternoon that Rauch arrived, after a march which Hozier thought was 'one of the finest achievements of the campaign.' On the morning of November 23 Rauch's troops encountered Turkish resistance for the first time, and were held up for two hours by a Turkish force on the heights above a ravine through which they were advancing.

Shuvalov had arrived in position on November 22 as arranged, to carry out the frontal assault in conjunction with Rauch; when the latter did not appear, he engaged in an artillery bombardment on that day and the following day. When Rauch's men arrived on November 23 on the flank of the Turkish position they were confronted by an enemy force posted to prevent a turning movement, but which had not had time to entrench itself. In spite of their exhaustion, Rauch's troops were at once launched in an assault, and drove back their opponents. Harried from one position to another, and under a heavy cannonade from Shuvalov's advance in their front, the Turks broke and fled, covered as they went by a thick mist, which hampered any pursuit. Thus the Russians took the strong Pravetz position at the remarkably low cost of 72 killed and wounded.

While this was going on, the cavalry force sent towards Lutikova had got into serious trouble, running into what amounted to a *cul de sac* in the mountains. Surrounded and cut off by Turkish infantry, a large part of the force had to fight their way out of the trap, abandoning two guns by throwing them over a precipice and losing a third to capture by the Turks. 79 men were killed or wounded. The setback had one positive aspect; the appearance of the cavalry on their left flank may have focused Turkish attention on this sector rather than on Pravetz, the key point of the Russian attack.[10]

Dandeville's advance on Etropol encountered much of the difficulty that Rauch had faced. He finally reached the Turkish positions around the town by November 23. The Turks here were commanded by Mustapha Pasha, and occupied a position of some considerable strength based on a series of redoubts on heights which were regarded as inaccessible. Mehemet Ali, who had arrived at Vrachesti, a few miles behind Orkhanie, on November 22 to inspect the positions held by his troops, had no expectation that a Russian assault was imminent, and his forces were disposed in anticipation of an advance to the north rather than in preparation to face an attack.

He was, therefore, dismayed to see on November 23, when he rode out with his staff to the position taken up in front of Orkhanie, the Russian advance guard coming down the high road from Plevna, evidently aiming to launch an attack on the first line of the position. Unfortunately for him, this line was held only by *Mustafiz* troops, and as soon as the Russians got near enough to attack, they panicked and ran back to the second line of defence. Mehemet Ali hoped to make a stand here; but the retreat had uncovered the entrance to the Orsikovo Pass, through which Gourko was able to advance to the village of Jasan. With the Russians almost on top of them again, the undisciplined Turkish infantry panicked again, and could not be made to stand and fight, and Mehemet Ali was obliged to fall back to the third line of fortifications directly in front of Orkhanie. Even here there was chaotic disorganisation and the *Mustafiz* troops began to fall back into the town before Chakir Pasha restored some sort of order with a regiment of regular troops.

This was bad enough; but at this point Mehemet Ali heard from Mustapha, at Etropol, that his situation there was critical, and seeking permission to evacuate and burn the town. Reluctantly, he gave his consent if it was absolutely necessary to retreat. Mustapha needed no more; at 8.00 am on November 24 he began his retreat from Etropol, pursued by Russian troops who threatened to cut off his artillery and baggage train. Ultimately he made it to the road over the Balkans, reaching Tashkessen in considerable disorder. Gourko occupied Etropol on November 25.

Mehemet Ali was utterly disheartened by the rapid collapse of his troops, observing to Valentine Baker, when the latter arrived at his headquarters, that as a result he expected to be recalled. He spoke to Burnaby about the latter's plan to make his way through the Russian lines to Plevna:

> You are an English officer, full of energy and courage, but there are plans which are so hazardous that it becomes folly to attempt them … and I feel so strongly that you

would be throwing away your life for no useful purpose that I must urgently advise
you to give up all thought of proceeding further with your enterprise.[11]

Burnaby reluctantly accepted this advice, but stayed on with Baker, serving on the
latter's staff.

At Orkhanie things went from bad to worse. The fall of Etropol gave the Russians
access to an old road from the town which joined the high road to the south of Orkhanie.
Down this road now advanced a column led by Prince Alexander of Oldenburg, and it
was immediately apparent to Chakir that to remain where he was in front of Orkhanie
was to court disaster. On November 25 he pulled out of the position there, abandoning
large quantities of stores, including three million rounds of small arms ammunition, and
retreating to Vrachesti. This position also proved untenable, with further troops from
Etropol threatening its rear, and on November 29 Chakir retired to the Baba Konak
Pass, where strong defensive works had been built. These took the form of six redoubts,
one behind the other, commanding each ridge in turn as the mountains rose and
culminating in the Yildiz redoubt, at 5,000 feet above sea level the key to the Turkish
position.

In eight days, at a cost of less than 500 men killed and wounded, Gourko had
dislodged the Turks from a series of strong positions in the foothills of the Balkans, and
had driven them back to their principal defensive position on the line of the mountains.
MacGahan had gone down from the lines around Plevna to pay a visit to Gourko's
headquarters, and on his return sent a dispatch reporting on the events there:

> I was much struck with the manner in which General Gourko handles his forces.
> He is more cautious than in the summer. There is much more order and foresight
> displayed, and also more precision in the movements, which begin to remind one

Fighting near the Baba Konak Pass. (*The Graphic*)

of the Prussians. I predict a great success for General Gourko, unless his plans are foiled by the weather.[12]

Gourko now prepared to attack the Turkish position at Baba Konak. He disposed his troops along the Greote ridge opposite the line of redoubts and about four thousand yards from it. The Turkish line was about seven thousand yards in length on both sides of the high road, and contained 15 guns, and was about fifteen hundred feet above the Greote ridge.

Facing the right of the Turkish position was Rauch, with the Preobrazhensky and Simeonov Regiments, with the 11th Regiment in reserve. Dandeville, with the Ismailov, Finland and 12th Regiments occupied the ridge from Mount Greote to the high road, while Ellis, with the Moscow Regiment and the Rifle Brigade, took up a position west of the high road. The Turks showed on December 1 that they were not yet completely done with; a fierce attack was launched on this day on Ellis's position inflicting 150 casualties before it was driven back.[13]

The Russians now made a determined attempt to storm the Yildiz redoubt. The position was, however, much too strong, and the assault was driven back with the loss of some 300 men killed and wounded. A *Daily News* correspondent with the Turks reported on the attack:

A tremendous fire met the assailants, whose weakened ranks were unsupported, and just as everything depended upon their having ample reserves to bring up, the Turks made a rush out of the redoubt, and drove the foremost back at the point of the bayonet. The descending tide carried dismay into the remainder of the advancing column, the retreat had to be sounded, and the day was lost. Six Russian battalions were engaged in the attack. Great was the relief of Mehemet Ali at the result of the day's fighting. Strong reinforcements had just arrived at the very moment when fortune looked its blackest for him. He openly declared that had the battle been lost he could not have answered for the consequences. Even as it is, his position is far from secure.[14]

Although the Russians, by dint of superhuman efforts, succeeded over a period of four days in hauling up sixty guns and placing them in position on the heights they occupied, their use was seriously hampered by dense fog which hung over the ravines between the ridges. In any case, the use of shrapnel against the earthworks was, as usual, ineffective, and it was reckoned that the position was too strong to be carried by a direct assault. For the moment, therefore, Gourko was content to observe the Turkish works, while maintaining a desultory artillery fire.

Frank Millet, another correspondent of the *Daily News*, made his way up to the Russian positions in the mountains:

When the snow covered the ground the picturesqueness of the mountain bivouacs was without parallel. The tree trunks came out sharply with their deep grey colour against the pure white, and every figure was in distinct silhouette. Now, the grey overcoats of the soldiers harmonise exactly with the colours of the carpet of dead leaves, and it is difficult to distinguish the men from the ground they lie on. In the snow, too, was written more plainly than with words, the history of the movements of each man in the skirmish line. One could follow every step of the advance of the Russians.[15]

On December 4 Mehemet Ali got the order that he had been gloomily expecting; he was recalled to Constantinople and Chakir appointed to the command of the troops at Baba Konak. Mehemet Ali's recall was not, however, a mark of disgrace; the reason that he was sent for was to prepare the defence of the capital.

32

The Fall of Plevna

O nce the circle of investment around Plevna had been completed, neither Osman nor Todleben nor any other well-informed observer could have been in any doubt as to the ultimate outcome. For Osman, his duty was to preserve his army as long as he could. For a while he may have entertained some hope that a relieving army might come to his aid, but it was not long before the faint prospect of this was extinguished. There was, however, a great deal of suffering to be endured, not only by the garrison of Plevna but by its unfortunate civilian population. Many years later Herbert described the situation:

The Plevna camp was one vast cemetery, with the town for its central charnel-house. An army of 40,000 men was slowly dying of exposure, privation, and illness. The weather grew worse and worse; the cold became intense. The mortality was appalling. There was hardly a man who was not suffering from something or other – exhaustion, fever, dysentery, rheumatism, ague, bronchitis, galloping consumption, open wounds, frostbites, broken limbs. There were cases of smallpox, typhoid fever, diphtheria, even leprosy and insanity; there were deaths from starvation and exposure; there were even cases of that, among Turks, extremely rare event: suicide.[1]

On November 13 Nicholas had sent in a *parlementaire* summoning Osman to surrender. After pointing out the successes at Gorni Dubnik and Telis, and the completion of the investment, he went on:

In the name of humanity and to prevent further bloodshed, for which your Excellency alone will carry the responsibility, I request you to cease all resistance, to name a place where we can negotiate the conditions of the capitulation.

Osman replied at once:

The imperial troops under my command have never ceased to show proof of courage, perseverance and energy. In all the battles up to now they have been victorious; because of this His Majesty the Tsar has been forced to bring as reinforcements the corps of the Imperial Guard and the Grenadiers ... My troops are in want of nothing and they have not yet done everything which they must to safeguard the Ottoman military honour. Up to today we have joyfully shed our blood for our country and our faith; we will continue to do so rather than surrender. As to the responsibility for the bloodshed, it falls in this world as in the next on those who provoked this war.[2]

The Russian camp before Plevna. (Ollier)

The contents of this exchange were circulated through the Turkish army; Herbert noted that 'the sentiments expressed in Osman's letter in such noble and dignified language were endorsed and applauded throughout the camp.'

However, the reality of the situation was becoming increasingly clear to everyone in Plevna. Unless the relieving army could arrive very soon, the game would be up. On December 1 Osman summoned a council of war attended by all his senior officers down to regimental level, instructing them to put to all their officers the question whether the army should remain in Plevna until all the food was exhausted, and then surrender, or should make an attempt to force the lines of investment. When the replies were taken back to the council of war it at first reached no decision; but on the following day it met again, when it was unanimously decided to attempt a sortie. Osman had made no secret of the desperate nature of the operation, saying:

> Let no man deceive himself as to the chances of success of such an attempt. They are infinitesimal. But I think that the honour of our country and the fair fame of our army render it incumbent upon us to make a last and supreme effort.[3]

The decision to launch a sortie, however small might be the prospect of success, was the product of a remorseless military logic. Having been condemned to ultimate defeat by Constantinople's insistence on defending Plevna to the last, Osman saw no alternative but to attempt to cut his way out. It was a decision that inevitably subjected both the soldiers and civilians trapped in Plevna to a final terrible tragedy; but in military terms it had to be done.

A line of Turkish outposts at Plevna. (*Russes et Turcs*)

One reason Osman gave to Todleben after the fall of Plevna for remaining in his positions there after the third battle was his conviction that the Russians would mount yet another attack, which he was in no doubt he could defeat. Unknown to him, as the investment proceeded, there were indeed voices at the Russian headquarters calling for just such an assault. Inspired by the news of the brilliant success of the storming of Kars, some of the bolder spirits on the Grand Duke's staff called for a similar assault on Plevna. These arguments, however, cut no ice with Todleben. While the date of Osman's capitulation could not be predicted, it was nonetheless a certainty; to choose on the other hand the uncertainty of an expensive assault was a most dangerous risk. Todleben's influence was now strong enough to put paid to adventurous suggestions of this sort, and his views prevailed.[4] MacGahan, on the other hand, thought that in not making an assault, the Russians were erring on the side of timidity.

In Todleben's view an assault was not only risky, but could lead to no definite result and could only add to the number of Russian casualties. As he wrote later in his official report:

> It was necessary simply to endeavour to make the circle of investment as close as possible, and to take all the necessary measures to prevent the enemy from being able to force it at any point. These measures consisted in strengthening the lines of investment by digging lines of rifle pits and trenches, in erecting batteries, and in

General Ganetsky, commander of the Russian Corps of Grenadiers. (*Russes et Turcs*)

establishing lunettes and redoubts upon the most important points. It was above all necessary to concentrate the fire of our artillery upon the enemy's fortifications, and to carry forward our trenches and ditches to a point near enough to those of the enemy to remove as far as possible from our batteries the fire of the enemy's musketry.[5]

Todleben's positions around Plevna extended for forty-six miles. He divided them into six sectors, each under a separate commander, each of whom was given a summary of the possible moves that Osman might make, and a plan to meet each of them. Todleben's six sectors were as follows:

- First Sector (Cernat): between Bivolar and the Grivitza Redoubt (Roumanian Corps).
- Second Sector (Krüdener): from the Grivitza Redoubt to the Galitz Redoubt near Radischevo (31st Division and 2nd Brigade 5th Division – eighteen battalions and ten batteries).
- Third Sector (Zotov) from the Galitz Redoubt to the Tulchenitza ravine (2nd Division and 12th Rifle Battalion – thirteen battalions and six batteries).
- Fourth Sector (Skobelev): from the Tultchenitza ravine to the Karputschaven ravine (16th Division, 30th Division, 9th, 10th and 11th Rifle Batttalions and 9th Regiment – twenty-seven battalions, twelve batteries and six *sotnias*).
- Fifth Sector (Kataley): from the Karputschaven ravine to the right bank of the Vid at Tyrnen (3rd Guard Division, two Guard squadrons and a Cossack battery – sixteen battalions, two squadrons and seven batteries).

- Sixth Sector (Ganetsky): along the left bank of the Vid to Bivolar (2nd and 3rd Grenadier Divisions, 1st Brigade of the 5th Division, 4th Roumanian Division, three cavalry regiments and a Cossack regiment – thirty battalions, eighteen squadrons and nineteen batteries).[6]

The substantial increase in responsibility given to Skobelev is apparent from the foregoing. He had by now been promoted to Lieutenant-General.

Todleben reckoned that if Osman did make an attempt to break out it would be in the fifth or sixth sectors, and, a few days before Osman made his attempt, he conducted some exercises in these sectors principally in order to get an idea of how long it would take to concentrate to defeat a determined sortie. Signs began to indicate that this might be imminent during the first week in December, when spies reported that three days' rations, 150 rounds of ammunition and a pair of sandals had been issued to each Turkish soldier. It was in any case always going to be difficult to conceal entirely the preparations for a break out, since there was no part of the Turkish position that was not visible from some point in the Russian lines. The information from deserters confirmed the observations from all around the besieging line that preparations for a sortie were in hand. The rate of fire of the Turkish artillery had begun to reduce on December 8 and on the following day the Turkish guns were almost silent. The movement of troops between the city and the river was noted, which confirmed Todleben in his view as to the sector likely to be attacked.[7]

He therefore took steps to reinforce the sixth sector, ordering Skobelev to cross the Vid at daybreak on December 10 with one brigade of the 3rd Guard Division, in order to be able to support Ganetsky when required. Four Roumanian battalions were to cross the river and stand behind Ganetsky's left. In moving Skobelev in this way Todleben was clearly determined to ensure that his most effective fighting general would be in the right place. Major-General Schnitnikov took Skobelev's place in command of the fourth sector.

On the night of December 9/10 the Russian observers peered through the sleet and snow to see what could be made of the Turkish preparations. Many lights were seen moving about the town, itself a most unusual occurrence. In Plevna, Herbert's battalion had been intended to form part of the Turkish rearguard, but was switched to reinforce the right wing of the assault. He recalled the tension among the troops during the night before the sortie:

The blackness of the night was lighted by sparse bivouac fires. Gaunt, lean figures of men and beasts illumined by the flickering flames threw monstrous shadows. The men, although excited and eager for the fray, were quiet and subdued in voice and manner, for silence had been enjoined. This vast bivouac of carts and beasts, extending over an area of two or three square miles in a desolate winter landscape, associated with the idea of the dread morrow that would decide betwixt life and death, victory and defeat, liberty and captivity, impressed one gloomily and unpleasantly.[8]

Osman's plan for the breakout was straightforward. His intention was to aim not for the Sofia road, for he thought there was little chance of making progress in that

Newspaper correspondents in the advanced trenches before Plevna. (Ollier)

direction, but to move due west towards the Isker which he would cross at Mahaletz, his ultimate objectives being first Kugasha and then Milkovatz. Thereafter, after a wide loop around to the west he would march south towards Sofia to join hands with Mehemet Ali's army. He divided his army into two roughly equal parts of 20,000 men. The first part, commanded by Tahir Pasha, preceded by thick lines of skirmishers, was to attack Ganetsky's positions across the Vid. Battalions in reserve were to move close on the heels of the attackers to exploit any success. The remainder of the army, led by Adil Pasha, was to stay on the banks of the Vid, with orders not to advance until two hours after the first assault; its mission was essentially to protect the flanks of the troops attacking the Russian positions.

Although the Russians had been on the alert for signs that Osman was on the move, his precautions had been sufficiently effective to prevent discovery until 3.30 am on December 10, when a deserter was brought in to Skobelev's headquarters with the information that the redoubts in the fourth sector had been abandoned. A reconnaissance went cautiously forward, returning with the news that the redoubts on the Green Hills were empty and that sounds could be heard from the Krishin redoubt indicating that that also was in course of being abandoned. Skobelev at once reported this to Todleben, and to the Grand Duke, and Ganetsky was warned to expect an imminent assault.

The Russian position on which the attack would fall consisted of a total of six redoubts, connected by trenches. On the right wing, including two redoubts, was posted the Kiev Grenadier Regiment with three batteries with the Tauris Grenadier Regiment in immediate reserve, and with the 2nd Brigade of the 2nd Grenadier Division further

Roumanian *Dorobantsi* in the forward trenches at Plevna. (Budev)

back at Dolni Dubnik. In the centre, the Siberia Grenadier Regiment was in the front line, with three batteries, supported by the Russia Minor Regiment. The second reserve consisted of the Fanagoria and Astrakhan Regiments at Gorni Netropolie. Finally, on the left stood the Archangel Regiment and two Roumanian divisions; in reserve came the Vologda Regiment and two batteries. Further back, at Demirkioi, came the 4th Roumanian Division.[9]

During the night cavalry patrols reported the concentration of Turkish forces on the banks of the Vid. At daybreak, under cover of a dense fog, the Turkish assaulting columns crossed the river by the main bridge, by a new bridge near Opanetz, and by several fords. They deployed in a large fold in the ground and the Turkish artillery behind them unlimbered on the higher ground and opened fire. The assault went in at about 7.30 am in the direction of Gorni Netropolie. Major-General Danilov, the commander of the 3rd Grenadier Division, moved the Russia Minor Regiment forward towards the first line, and the regiments at Gorni Netropolie were also ordered to move up. It was on the Siberia Regiment, defending Redoubts No 3 and 4, that the Turkish assault fell, and it suffered fearful casualties in an ultimately unsuccessful attempt to hold the redoubts. By 8.30 am the Turks were in possession of both of them, and had in the process captured 8 guns.

When the Russia Minor Regiment arrived, it advanced between the two redoubts, and succeeding in holding up the Turkish advance, although at the cost of heavy casualties, which included all three battalion commanders. Osman, who had led the attack in person, mounted on a magnificent chestnut stallion that had been presented to him by the Sultan, now had cause to regret his caution in ordering his second detachment

Osman Pasha's sortie from Plevna, December 10. Key – 1) bridges, 2) road out from
Plevna, 3) Russian grenadiers, 4) Russian batteries, 5) Turkish redoubts. (*Russes et Turcs*)

under Adil to wait for two hours before advancing. Had he had these troops with him in or near the front line, it is possible that he might have cut his way through what remained of the battered grenadier regiments that sought to bar his way. As it was, the attack began to lose momentum. When Major-General Stroukov arrived with the rest of the 2nd Grenadier Division, his troops charged the Turks with the bayonet, and a savage struggle ensued, in the course of which the Russians drove back their attackers and retook the guns which had been lost, pushing forward to recapture their most advanced trenches. For a while there was stalemate; the two lines, at a distance of between 200 and 300 yards, kept up a heavy fire upon each other, but with neither attempting to advance. Osman was waiting for Adil's troops to deploy and Ganetsky for the arrival of Skobelev.

While waiting for the deployment of Adil's troops, Osman's horse was killed under him, and he sustained a wound from a bullet that struck his calf. News of his fall, which exaggerated the severity of his wound, quickly spread through the Turkish army, and the infantry began to fall back in disorder towards the river. Meanwhile Ganetsky felt that he could wait no longer for the arrival of Skobelev's troops which, owing to a misunderstanding on the part of their commander, had been halted for two hours, and he launched a furious attack on the disintegrating Turkish lines. The Turkish retreat became a chaotic flight, sweeping through a convoy of 200 or 300 vehicles carrying Turkish civilians out of Plevna, that had closely followed the marching columns of the assault force. Many of the vehicles were overturned and there ensued a scene of utter confusion. Herbert had been sent by his commanding officer for instructions, and was caught up in the chaos:

> I was simply drawn along in a mad stream of men, horses and vehicles. Resistance to this torrent of panic-stricken humanity was as useless as opposition to the rush of the incoming tide. The officers of all degrees did their utmost to restore order and get their men to make a stand against the enemy, who did not by any means press hard … As far as my eyes could reach, all over the plain there were countless streams of soldiers making for the two bridges. The train got mixed with the infantry and the batteries, and the confusion baffles description.[10]

Meanwhile the Russian troops in the other sectors all began to advance, meeting little resistance, and soon occupied Plevna itself. The Tsar, arriving at Radischevo from his headquarters at Gorni Studen at about noon, was able to watch his troops entering the city, and taking possession of the redoubts and entrenchments that had resisted his army for so long. The only serious resistance encountered was at the Opanetz redoubts where, after a short struggle, the defenders gave up, and the Roumanians captured 2,000 men and three guns; and in the south, in Kataley's sector, where he was obliged to fight for possession of the three redoubts in his front. Capturing them, he took 3,854 prisoners and four guns.

Effectively, the Turkish break out had been defeated by 10.00 am, but along the Vid the battle continued for three hours more. At about 1.00 pm, however, the firing began to die away on both sides, and soon stopped completely. It was apparent to both sides that the Turkish situation was now hopeless; and an immense cheer went up from the Russian troops when it was seen that a white flag had been raised on the road leading beyond the bridge. The Turkish officer who arrived at the Russian front line was sent back by Ganetsky, by reason of his junior rank. When another arrived, he too went back, bearing a message for Osman to the effect that Ganetsky, who knew that the Turkish commander was wounded, could only deal with an officer able to represent him.[11]

Tewfik Pasha, Osman's chief of staff, rode out to say that the Turkish army surrendered, as did Osman himself, but that as the latter's wound prevented him coming out himself, he asked that Ganetsky come to him. In the first instance, Ganetsky sent Stroukov, who found Osman in a small house, with his surgeon tending his wound. Stroukov told him that Ganetsky could only accept an unconditional surrender. Osman remarked to his surgeon: 'One day follows another, but no two days are alike; one brings success, another misfortune,' and told Stroukov that he submitted to the wishes of the Russian commander in chief. Ganetsky arrived half an hour later; after some hesitation, Osman took off his sword and handed it to Ganetsky and gave the order for his troops to lay down their arms. It was an order which, in spite of their desperate situation, the Turks obeyed only reluctantly.[12]

Later that evening, as he was returning to Plevna, Osman's carriage was overtaken by Nicholas, who shook his hand, and congratulated him on his defence of Plevna, which he described as 'one of the most splendid military feats in history.' Next day the Tsar asked Osman to luncheon. Supported by his servant, and by a Cossack, Osman entered the Imperial headquarters. Wellesley watched as he entered the yard of the building in which the emperor was waiting:

> To the credit of the Russians be it said, that the moment it was realised that the wounded man they beheld was Osman Pasha, a spontaneous cry of 'Bravo, Osman!'

Turkish troops during the last sortie at Plevna. (Ollier)

arose from the entire staff, which must have consisted of between two and three hundred officers. All rose to their feet and saluted the wounded foe as he passed, and what impressed me was the fact that I did not see a single face among the Russian officers that was not moistened by a tear of pity and admiration.[13]

The fighting during December 10 before the final capitulation had been ferocious. It was estimated that the Turkish casualties during the break out were between 5,000 and 6,000 men, while the Russians lost nearly 2,000. The Russians took a total of 43,340 prisoners, while about 4,000 sick and wounded were found in the city.[14] The sufferings of the Turkish army were, however, far from over. Although the final capitulation was obviously close at hand, no provision had been made by the Russians to deal either with the prisoners or the wounded:

> The result was that the army which had fought so gloriously in defence of Plevna, and had spread the fame of Osman Pasha throughout the world, were subjected to heart rending sufferings and brutal treatment, such as have seldom disgraced a military triumph. The winter, which had hitherto been comparatively mild, suddenly became excessively rigorous. The severe cold which ensued was accompanied by heavy snow storms; and the unfortunate Turks, who were without cloaks or warm clothing, and frequently without shoes, perished miserably by scores every day.[15]

A *Daily News* correspondent encountered a column of Turkish prisoners marching north, led by an escort with fixed bayonets:

The Tsar, Grand Duke Nicholas and Prince Charles of Roumania are greeted on their entry into Plevna. (*Russes et Turcs*)

Following are a few Turkish officers, either on ponies or on foot. Behind them came the men who once kept the flower of the Russian army at bay round Plevna. How spiritless and broken they look as they trudge wearily along the road to their captivity. Half-starved, almost dead with fatigue and the severe cold, many with fever burning in their eyes – mere stalking bones and foul rags – come the brave troops who made the fame of Osman Pasha. We get well to the windward of these poor creatures, for typhus and smallpox linger round them on the frosty air. Many are even now falling out of the ranks to lie down and die.[16]

To war. (Konstantin Savitsky, 1888)

Men from the Russian 140th Infantry Regiment (35th Infantry Division) halt
during a march, summer 1877. (Pavel Kovalesvky, date unknown)

The Russian crossing of the Danube at Simnitza, June 27 1877. (Nikolai Dmitriev-Orenburg, 1883)

Tsar Alexander II crossing the Danube. (Ivan Aivazovsky, 1878)

The storming of the fortress of Ardahan, May 17 1877. (Alexander Kivshenko, date unknown)

A Turkish steamer attacked by the Russian cutter *Shutka* on
the Danube, 1877. (Alexey Bogolyubov, 1882)

Observing the actions around Ala Dagh, June 21 1877. (Simon Agopyan, 1910)

The defence of the citadel at Bayazid, June 1877. (Lev Lagar'o, 1891)

The entry of Grand Duke Nicholas into Tirnovo, July 1877.
(Nikolai Dmitriev-Orenburg, date unknown)

Before the attack – Plevna. (Vasily Vereshchagin, 1881)

After the attack – dressing station near Plevna. (Vasily Vereshchagin, 1881)

Site of the battle fought on July 18 1877 in front of the Krishin
Redoubt near Plevna. (Vasily Vereshchagin, 1880)

Action between the Russian *Vesta* (left) and Turkish *Vechta-Bulend*
in the Black Sea, July 1877. (Ivan Aivazovsky, 1877)

The assault on Shipka. (Cevat, 1911)

Defence of the Shipka Pass. (Alexander Kivshenko, date unknown)

Fighting around Shipka, August 1877. (Simon Agopyan, 1910)

The defence of the 'eagle's eyrie', Shipka Pass, August 23 1877. (Andrei Popov, 1893)

Major-General Michael Skobelev. (Nikolai Dmitriev-Orenburg, 1883)

The Russian grand battery at Plevna. (Nikolai Dmitriev-Orenburg, 1880)

Night attack at Plevna. (Simon Agopyan, 1910)

The capture of the Grivitza Redoubt, Plevna, September 11
1877. (Nikolai Dmitriev-Orenburg, 1885)

Defeated. Requiem. (Vasily Vereshchagin, 1878-79)

Episode from the Battle of Telis, October 24 1877. (V. Mazurovsky, 1888)

The Nizhny Novgorod Dragoons pursuing the Turks on the road to Kars during the fighting around the Yagni hills, October 3 1877. (Alexander Kivshenko, 1892)

The final battle at Plevna, December 10 1877. (Nikolai Dmitriev-Orenburg, 1889)

Attack on a Turkish convoy, winter 1877/78. (Pavel Kovalesvky, date unknown)

The capture of the Turkish steamship Messina by a Russian ship on
the Black Sea, December 13 1877. (Ivan Aivazovsky, 1877)

The Battle of Shenovo, January 8 1878. (Alexander Kivshenko, 1894)

Skobelev at Shenovo, January 8 1878. (Vasily Vereshchagin, 1878)

'Back from the front'. (Sami Yetik, 1920)

33

Elena

While the story of Plevna proceeded towards its ultimately tragic conclusion, there had been action on the other fronts in Europe. At the Shipka Pass, Suleiman had, after the repulse of his expensive assaults of August, limited his activity to desultory artillery and rifle fire for the next two weeks. His passivity suggested that he had given up his attempts to force the Shipka Pass, and that instead he would try to cross the Balkans elsewhere. Radetzky therefore sent back more than half of his troops to the north, for the protection of his communications in the event of an attack from Elena or through the Trojan Pass. Suleiman did still hold some of the positions captured during the August fighting, although the bulk of his army had been withdrawn behind Shipka village and to Kazanlik.

Suleiman had not, however, given up on the Shipka Pass, and his next plan was to use mortars and siege guns, the Russian positions on St Nicholas being almost out of range of field artillery. On September 11 the Russians were treated to the spectacle of the Turks returning in large numbers to their advanced positions, and with immense effort dragging up the mortars and siege guns. Clearly a fresh attack was in prospect, and next day the bombardment commenced, half of the guns targeting St Nicholas and the rest being aimed at the road along which must come any Russian reinforcements. The mortars had been very well sited behind the Turkish-held ridge, the shells falling with great accuracy, and compelling the Russian gunners to withdraw into shelter. Even so, it was supposed that this project of Suleiman was merely intended to distract attention from movements elsewhere.

This view was, however, incorrect. The Turkish victory in the third battle of Plevna had emboldened the high command at Constantinople, and as a result orders were issued to Mehemet Ali, at that time still in command on the Lom, and to Suleiman at Shipka, that steps must be taken to strike a decisive blow. Mehemet Ali's operations have already been described; Suleiman now put in hand his preparations for an assault on Radetzky's position, optimistic that the defences would have been considerably softened up by his bombardment.

The spearhead of the assault was formed by a task force of 3,500 volunteers, composed principally of regulars, with a few hundred Arabs. In three columns, they were to move during the night of September 16/17, each man wearing something white on his left arm for identification. Once in position, an attack was to be launched simultaneously, one column assaulting the south-east corner of St Nicholas, one the south-west corner, and the third, further south-west, was to aim for the summit through a break in the wall of rock. Once the height was taken, a general attack was to be launched, Redjib from the east and south-east, Salih from the south and south-west and Vessil from the west and north-west. Each of these had six battalions for the assault.[1]

The volunteers left the principal camp at about 11.00 pm, in two hours reaching the three groups of infantry which were already in position to follow up a successful attack.

At 3.30 am they set off again towards Mount St Nicholas. The first column, from Redjib's camp, was spotted by the Russians before it was half way to its objective, and came under heavy fire. The Turks replied with equal vigour, throwing themselves forward and up the steep rocks, hurling hand grenades as they ascended the bare slope of St Nicholas, before engaging the companies of the Podolsk Regiment in a murderous hand-to-hand fight. Colonel Doukhonine, in command on St Nicholas, reported back to Major-General Petrouschevsky, Dragomirov's successor in command of the 14th Division, and the latter sent forward two companies of the Zhitomir Regiment to reinforce him. As the desperate struggle continued, Radetzky arrived to take personal charge of the battle, and fed in one company after another as they reached the scene. The Russian fire was concentrated on the first Turkish column, which sustained huge losses, but in spite of this the Turks continued to climb the mountain, and began entrenching themselves. A counter-attack by three Russian companies was thrown back, suffering heavy losses in their turn.

Stalemate had been reached on this part of St Nicholas, defenders and attackers both suffering heavy casualties during a prolonged exchange of fire. The Russian battery on the eastern side of St Nicholas poured a continuous rain of shells on the Turkish attackers, while the mortars and siege guns on the Turkish side kept up a continuous bombardment of the Russian positions. At this point the second column, unnoticed by the Russians, suddenly debouched on the summit from the south-west. Taken by surprise, the Russians switched their fire to this new assailant, which permitted the first column to establish itself on the south-eastern crest of St Nicholas. The arrival of the second column was wholly unexpected, for it was believed that the summit was completely inaccessible from the south-west. A correspondent of the *Augsburger Zeitung* testified to what had been a remarkable achievement:

Turkish officers observe an assault in the Shipka Pass. (Ollier)

On the following day I saw the men of this column; their clothes were in shreds; the buttons were either torn out or rubbed off; they all had their pantaloons in holes at the knee, and the bleeding sores which appeared beneath showed what unheard of efforts they had been obliged to make.[2]

Soon after sunrise the third column arrived on the summit, having suffered heavy losses when its advance was discovered. However, once there, it was able to resist the three violent counter-attacks made by the Russians, although Hamdy Bey, the commander of the column, was one of those who fell during the fierce fighting. Half an hour after sunrise, therefore, a Turkish standard had been planted on top of St Nicholas, and this success was reported to Turkish headquarters. There, Suleiman had been watching in the distance the progress of the volunteers, marked by the flashes of the heavy exchanges of gunfire. He telegraphed the news that Shipka was taken to Constantinople, from where it was transmitted all over Europe.

The news was, however, premature. Although Vessil and Salih had, as arranged, attacked the Russian positions as soon as the assaulting columns had reached the summit of St Nicholas, their troops storming forward with immense courage, they failed to take any of the Russian positions in front of them, suffering heavy losses in the process. Everything therefore turned on the success of Redjib, who was due to attack from the east. Although the volunteers on St Nicholas shot down the gunners in the Russian batteries below them in an effort to facilitate Redjib's advance, it did not come. For whatever reason, his troops remained in their positions and, with the defeat of the columns of Salih and Vessil, the volunteers on St Nicholas were totally unsupported. Radetzky put together an attacking column, led first by Colonel Tiajelnikov and then, when he was wounded, by Colonel Prince Khilkov. After a desperate struggle the Turks were thrown back, in some cases literally, as they retreated down the mountainside, suffering further heavy losses.

A remarkable opportunity had been wasted; the *Augsburger Zeitung's* correspondent was scathing in his assessment of the reason for the failure:

> A brilliant début degenerated into a total defeat. Why? Because the Pashas are always men who would allow themselves to be slain by the side of their cup of coffee before quitting it, and because the subordinate officers are worthless. With Turkish soldiers one would be able to conquer the world, on condition that their officers should be dismissed. Among the 800 wounded treated here today, only one officer was found.[3]

Casualties on both sides had been heavy; the Russians had lost over 1,000 officers and men killed and wounded, while the Turkish loss was much greater. In his official report of the battle, Radetzky estimated that the total of the enemy casualties was of the order of 3,000 men.[4] After the failure of the attack there was a lull in the fighting, while Suleiman pondered his next step. On September 20, having established some fresh mortar batteries, he renewed the bombardment, concentrating his fire on St Nicholas. This continued for ten days, in the course of which the Russians learned how to protect themselves against this form of cannonade. When this became apparent to the Turks, they changed target, now aiming at the road up which all the Russian supplies and ammunition came. After some early Turkish success in this process, Radetzky ordered that such movements must take place only at night, which effectively put paid to Suleiman's efforts to disrupt his communications.

At the beginning of October Suleiman's insidious campaign in Constantinople finally bore fruit, when Mehemet Ali was dismissed as commander in chief, and replaced by Suleiman. His position as commander of the forces in front of the Shipka Pass was taken by Raouf Pasha, until then holding office as Minister of Marine, as well as a subordinate position under Suleiman. He appears to have disapproved of Suleiman's elevation, at first resigning his post before retracting this and taking up his command.

If the members of the council in Constantinople expected an immediate increase of activity on the part of the army in the Quadrilateral as soon as Suleiman arrived, they were to be disappointed. He soon decided that the Tsarevich's army occupied a position far too strong to be attacked, while the position of his own army at Kadikoi was unsatisfactory due to the difficulty of obtaining sufficient supplies. On October 19 he withdrew the divisions of Nedjib and Fuad to Rasgrad, leaving only Assaf's division and Mustapha's column to cover the railway. Suleiman's passivity surprised the Russian high command; in anticipation that he would pursue the aggressive policy he had adopted at the Shipka Pass, the 2nd Grenadier Division had been earmarked to reinforce the Tsarevich. This order was now revoked, and the division was sent to Plevna. Thereafter on both sides preparations were made for a winter campaign. The Turks were issued with warm cloaks, and a programme of building winter huts was put in hand. On the Russian side supplies of sheepskin coats began to arrive, and there too the soldiers were set to work building their winter quarters.[5]

By mid November the desperate situation of Plevna had concentrated the mind of the War Council on the possible steps that might be taken. The assembly of Mehemet Ali's relief army had begun, but it would clearly take time to put it sufficiently in order to be able to advance. Considerable dissatisfaction was felt at Suleiman's inaction, and he was ordered to take immediate steps to assist Osman. Suleiman accordingly embarked on a series of reconnaissances in force at various points on his line, the most significant being at Pirgos on the Danube on November 19. Here his troops gained a temporary advantage, driving the two Russian companies holding Pirgos back to Metchka, before reinforcements arrived to restore the position. Suleiman had, however, learned enough from this action to conclude that the Russians had few troops immediately south of the Danube, and that another thrust in this area might succeed in reaching the recently completed bridge at Batin, over which passed the Tsarevich's line of communications.

On November 26 Suleiman launched an attack over the Lom with a force of some forty battalions, with fifty-four guns, some regular cavalry and 500-600 Circassians. Commanded by Assaf, the force was divided into three columns. On the right Salim Pasha was to attack Pirgos; in the centre Ibrahim Pasha was to attack Metchka and support the third column, led by Osman Bey, whose objective was Trestenik. The Russian position to be attacked was commanded by Lieutenant-General Firks. On the left at Metchka Major-General Tsitliadzev had a brigade of the 12th Division, with sixteen guns, while at Trestenik Major-General Fofanov had the other brigade of the 12th Division, the Bessarabian Regiment from the 33rd Division, and forty-four guns. The rest of the 33rd Division was in reserve.[6]

The Turkish assault at Metchka. Key – A, B) Russian batteries, C, D) Second and third lines of Russian entrenchments, E) Russian advance posts abandoned at the start of the

action, F) Turkish skirmishers advancing against Pirgos, G) Pirgos road, H) Pirgos village, I) Monitor *Nicopol*, J) Turkish reserves, K) Russian batteries at Parapan. (*Russes et Turcs*)

Suleiman Pasha dictating orders. (Ollier)

The Turkish assault went in at 8.00 am, and quickly overran the Russian outpost line, except at Gol-Tchesme, where two battalions held out. Salim took Pirgos, and advanced along the bank of the Danube between the river and Metchka, occupying the village but failing in two assaults on the Russian entrenchments behind it. In these he was joined by Ibrahim. Meanwhile Osman, after a lengthy struggle, drove out the garrison of Gol-Tchesme, which fell back on Trestenik with heavy loss. Firks, fearing that the considerable numerical superiority of the Turks would lead to the loss of Trestenik, ordered Tsitliadzev to launch a counter-attack on Salim, which he did with immediate success. His advance drove Salim first out of Metchka, then back to Pirgos and finally, at about noon, down the road to Rustchuk. He was unable to exploit his advantage, however, as Ibrahim, who had fallen back in the direction of Trestenik, advanced again towards Metchka, threatening to outflank Tsitliadzev, who was obliged to break off his pursuit of Salim to meet this danger. Meanwhile Osman Bey continued his movement on Trestenik. The battle was fought in appalling weather. In bitter cold, and high winds, icy rain beat down on the combatants. By 3.30pm Tsitliadzev was making progress against Ibrahim, and Firks, who had been able to reinforce Trestenik, reckoned that the time had come for a general counter-offensive. The Russians advanced all along the line, and Assaf retreated across the Lom. He had sustained total casualties of about 1,200; the Russian loss in killed and wounded was 766.[7]

Thwarted in this endeavour, Suleiman now prepared to assault the opposite end of the Tsarevich's line, calculating that this would have been weakened as the Russians withdrew forces to meet the threat from Assaf. His earlier reconnaissances had indicated

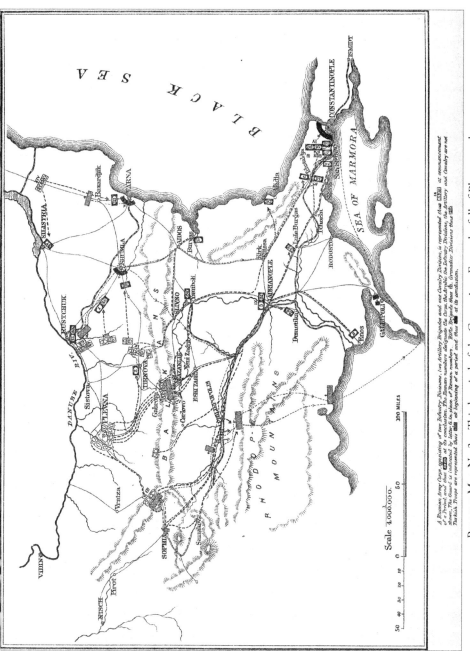

Progress Map No 3 – Third period of the Campaign. From the fall of Plevna to the conclusion of peace at San Stefano, December 10 1877 to March 3 1878

that Tirnova might not be strongly defended on its eastern side, and he resolved to launch a major attack on Elena. From there he would move on Tirnova, obliging Radetzky to retreat from the Shipka Pass, through which Raouf could then advance to join hands with him. Suleiman also sent an order to Mehemet Ali to support him by making an advance in the west towards Lovtcha. His intention was extremely ambitious, since he hoped in this way to oblige the Russians to concentrate against him, and for this to provide Osman with an opportunity to break out of Plevna.

Russian patrols soon picked up the fact that a Turkish force was concentrating around Osman Bazar, and steps were taken to reinforce the garrison of Elena, which at the beginning of December consisted of a brigade of the 9th Division, commanded by Major-General Dombrovsky, with a dragoon regiment and three batteries. An advanced position in front of Elena, based on the Mareni ravine, covered the roads. On the night of December 3/4 the Russian outposts reported the fires of an enemy camp, and gave the alarm. There was no suspicion of the fact that Suleiman had skillfully assembled a force of 20,000 infantry, 8,000 Circassians and Bashi-Bazouks, and twenty guns. At 6.30 am on December 4 the Turks advanced on Mareni, which was held by two battalions, with four guns and three squadrons. Demonstrating against the Russian centre, Suleiman sent an attacking column around the left, and once this was engaged sent a further column against the Russian right. A battalion of the Orel Regiment now came up, and led by the regimental commander, Colonel Kleveshahl, delivered a bayonet charge. This momentarily drove the Turks back; but the heavy preponderance of numbers meant that the battalion was soon surrounded, and Kleveshahl wounded. An eyewitness described the outcome:

> A revolver in each hand, the heroic leader performed prodigies of valour, but, receiving a second wound, fell from his horse, and, placed on an ambulance stretcher, was being carried off the field, followed by several other wounded officer, when the Turks threw themselves upon the group, killed the bearers, finished several of the wounded, and were about to do the same by the colonel. But struck with his brilliant uniform, for he still wore that of the Guard from which he had just been transferred, they thought they had taken an officer of very high rank, and lavished attention upon him.[8]

Only one officer and a few soldiers managed to cut their way out, the whole of the rest of the battalion being killed or captured.

Dombrovsky sent up all reserves to assist what remained of the detachment at Mareni. A counter-attack could make no headway against vastly superior numbers and the Russians slowly fell back into Elena, where Dombrovsky had a well fortified position. He put the battered troops from Mareni in the second line; his first line was held by seven companies, with a battery of nine guns on a height on his left and another of fifteen guns on the right. Suleiman sent a column at 10.00 am around Dombrovsky's left, in the mountains between Slatavitza and Elena, and another to the south of the town. In spite of brilliant charges by the Russian cavalry, the turning movements penetrated into the rear of the defenders, and Dombrovsky had no choice but to order a retreat, abandoning nine of his guns as he did so. He fell back to a position at Jakovitza, having lost about 1,800 men killed or wounded; in addition, the Turks had taken some 500 prisoners, a sufficiently unusual circumstance for Greene to remark on it, adding that they were sent to Constantinople and well cared for.[9] The Turkish losses were of the order of 2,000 men killed and wounded, having achieved a considerable victory, described by Hozier as, after the victories at Plevna, 'the most brilliant success gained by the Turks in Europe during the whole war.'[10]

So far so good; but Suleiman's advance had been based on a plan whereby the Turkish force at the Shipka Pass would cooperate. No help, however, had been forthcoming from that quarter, nor was likely to do so. This force had been drastically weakened by the detachment of a large part of the force to join the army assembling under Mehemet Ali at Sofia. With only about 12,000 effective troops available, and with deep snow lying on the mountains around the pass, it was in no state to make any headway in this sector. Nor was the command of the force in the slightest way encouraging. Raouf had now been appointed military governor of Adrianople, and his place at Shipka had been taken by Ahmed Eyoub Pasha. Layard, writing to Lord Derby on November 27, was trenchant in his observations on the appointment:

> Ahmed Eyoub Pasha was recalled, it is generally believed, from his command in the Army of the Danube on account of his having left Mehemet Ali Pasha without support, notwithstanding the instructions which he had received, in the attack on the Russian positions at Bejir Verbovka, thus causing its failure. He has the reputation of being slow, incompetent, and obstinate. I have not yet been able to ascertain how he has obtained his new command – probably through some intrigue. It is to be feared that his former jealousy of Mehemet Ali Pasha will not have diminished, and that he will not be disposed to afford much help either to that general or to Osman Pasha.[11]

On the same day Layard had reported that the War Council at Constantinople had been dissolved, 'Namyk Pasha admitting that it was the cause of more mischief than good, and that the Sultan had done right to put an end to it.'[12]

The lack of any support from the Shipka Pass seems to have paralysed Suleiman, and although in holding Elena and Slatavitza he had what Hozier described as 'the two keys of Tirnova,' he did nothing to exploit his victory. To do so he must act fast, for although for the moment Suleiman had the odds very much in his favour, the Russians had immediately set about bringing up reinforcements to restore the position. During the night of December 4/5 Prince Mirsky, the commander of the 9th Division, who had arrived at Jakovitza with a battalion from his 2nd Brigade, was reinforced by the 4th Rifle Brigade from Tirnova, and next day the 2nd Brigade of the 11th Division arrived.

Mirsky was sensitive to the criticism at the Imperial headquarters as to the extent of the casualties which his division had sustained in the fighting around Elena and Jakovitza. Describing the events later rather defensively to Captain Richard von Pfeil-Burghausz, a Prussian officer who had been granted a commission in the Russian army, he explained the critical situation that could have led to the fall of Tirnova:

> Now, I ask you whether our losses, which were certainly great, were not counterbalanced by the preservation of our chief place in Bulgaria, the fall of which just before the surrender of Plevna would have made the much desired junction

of Osman and Suleiman Pasha practicable. The consequences of this could not possibly be stated. Now, what followed? This defeat was grist to the mill of my enemies in the Grand Duke's headquarters. Only my most gracious Emperor saw what had really been done, and he at once sent a hundred crosses of St George for the men.[13]

On December 5 Suleiman, who had been trying to contact the Turks at Shipka, made a half-hearted advance, sending a column to occupy Minde on his right and launching an assault on Jakovitza. The attack lasted no more than an hour before it was broken off. His determination appears to have deserted him completely, and the opportunity was lost. The Russians continued to bring up reinforcements, so that by December 8 they had the equivalent of three and a half divisions in position to bar any further advance on Tirnova.

Having evidently concluded that he was going to make no further progress here, Suleiman returned to his earlier project of an attack on the extreme left of the Tsarevich's army. In doing so, he reckoned that the Russian positions on the northern end of the line would have been weakened by the dispatch of reinforcements to the southern end. He was able to put together a large force for the operation, assembling over sixty-eight battalions, or 40,000 men, which he placed under the command of Fazli Pasha, in place of Assaf, who had been sacked after his failure on November 26. On December 10 Suleiman personally accompanied a reconnaissance in force to test the strength of the Russian positions. On the following day the Turkish forces began to concentrate for an assault, thirty-eight battalions crossing the Lom and a further thirty battalions emerging from Rustchuk.

Suleiman's hope that the position between Metchka and Trestenik might be less strongly held was disappointed; the whole of the XII Corps was now in line there, supported by the 2nd Brigade of the 35th Division. At about 10.00 am on December 12 the Turkish artillery on the heights between Pirgos and Metchka, consisting of twenty guns, opened fire and the infantry advanced down into the ravine. Here they were met by a furious artillery fire from the Russian batteries behind Metchka, and were forced to retreat. Fazli brought up reinforcements, and launched another attack, supported by a heavy artillery bombardment on the Russian left; this too failed, as did three other assaults on the Russian right. Grand Duke Vladimir, watching the battle from Trestenik, was waiting his moment for a counter-attack. At about 1.00 pm he judged that the time was ripe, and launched the 2nd Brigade of the 35th Division against the Turkish left. The attack was supported by the 2nd Brigade of the 12th Cavalry Division, which in fact came into action first, and got into some difficulty on the plateau of Gol-Tchesme before the infantry stormed the Turkish shelter trenches. With these troops practically in Fazli's rear, Vladimir sent forward the 2nd Brigade of the 33rd Division against the Turkish troops in front of Metchka. Sweeping down on the Turkish infantry sheltering in the ravine, the Russian troops drove them up the opposite slope with the bayonet; as they retreated, the Turkish infantry were raked by the Russian artillery, and suffered heavily. Their retreat across the Lom continued under heavy fire not only from the guns of Vladimir's Corps, but also from the Russian batteries over the river at Parapan, and from the captured Turkish monitor now renamed *Nikopol*.

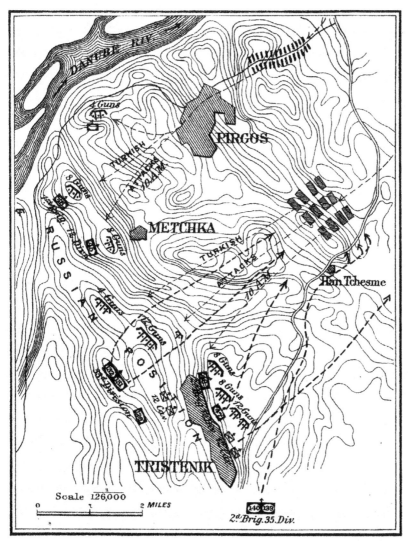

Battle of Metchka-Tristenik, December 12 1877

Suleiman's assault had proved a total failure, and an expensive one. His losses amounted to nearly 3,000 men, of whom some 800 were killed. The total Russian casualties amounted to 799 men. The bulk of the Turkish casualties had been caused by the shrapnel of the Russian artillery.[14] This was effectively the end of the campaigning on the Lom; apart from the garrisons of the fortresses, the troops that Suleiman had so unsuccessfully employed in an effort to relieve the pressure on Plevna were withdrawn to Roumelia. Overshadowed by the battles around Plevna, and the more spectacular fighting in the Balkan mountains, by its operations the Tsarevich's army had successfully carried out its task of protecting the left flank of the Russian invasion of Bulgaria, and of masking the Turkish fortresses of the Quadrilateral.

34

Tashkessen

The fall of Plevna was of course of crucial importance for the future conduct of the war, but it did not mean that all was over bar the shouting. Certainly the Russians could now proceed in the knowledge that the total forces available to them in Bulgaria were double those of the Turks, and that the latter might well be demoralized by the turn that events had taken. The practical problems of taking the next steps towards ultimate victory which the Russians faced were nonetheless considerable. From their own territory on the Pruth to the Balkans, their line of communications was 500 miles in length, and had been interrupted on the Danube where drifting ice had carried away all the bridges. The Balkans offered a significant obstacle, and the weather was beginning to deteriorate substantially. Until the fall of Plevna it had been tolerably mild, but on December 15 it began to snow heavily, and continued to do so for a week, at the end of which movement became extremely difficult. There were, in any case, only two good roads available to the Russians, those between Plevna and Sofia and between Sistova and the Shipka Pass. The rest were a sea of mud.[1]

In addition to this severe weather, which came as no surprise to the Russians, and with the problems of which they were not unfamiliar in their own country, there was one aspect of it peculiar to the Lower Danube with which they were not acquainted. This was the *Krivitza*, as it was known to Roumanians and Bulgarians, a hurricane of snow that lasted two or three days raging with such colossal violence that no one dared to leave their houses:

> It uproots the strongest trees, and even carries off the roofs of houses; while everyone outside runs the risk of being buried under the snow. The trains are compelled to cease running while the tempest lasts; and warned of its approach, the people make preparations as if for a week's siege; for although the *Krivitza* only lasts three days, at least three more are needed to reopen communications with the outside world.[2]

The unexpected ferocity of these storms caused a number of Russian disasters. A convoy of wounded, trapped by such a storm, was unable to move, and the snow built up until it was entirely overwhelmed. There were few survivors. In another place an entire camp was buried, and several thousand soldiers had to dig out the men there, some of whom were found dead under the snow. A supply convoy *en route* from Sistova to Biela was overtaken by the *Krivitza*, and only escaped, with the loss of part of its train, when its commanding officer ordered an immediate retreat. During these storms the Russians lost thousands of horses and cattle. In the Shipka Pass both sides had to withdraw their outposts in so heavy a snowstorm that visibility was less than fifteen yards.

It had not needed an awareness of what the weather was to lead Todleben to the conclusion that a winter campaign should be avoided. He calculated that the Turkish strategy would be to fall back to Adrianople, and that the Russians would therefore arrive

Russian troops on the march during a snowstorm. (*Illustrated London News*)

there in the depths of winter, with a supply line that could not be maintained across the chain of mountains behind them. His firm view was that the proper course would be to put the army into winter quarters along the main roads north of the Balkans, and to assemble a large force around Rustchuk to invest that fortress. During the winter a regular siege would lead to its capture, and in the following spring the army would be in good shape to cross the Balkans and advance on Constantinople. This did not commend itself to Nicholas, who even before the fall of Plevna had reached the conclusion that the army should conduct a winter campaign in spite of all the practical difficulties. His main concern was to keep the pressure up; ceasing active operations in the field would give the Turks a chance to recover and, worse still, would give time for international diplomacy to interfere. In particular, the longer the war continued the greater was the risk of British intervention. Apart from Skobelev and Gourko, the Russian generals preferred Todleben's policy; but on this occasion Nicholas prevailed and as soon as Plevna fell he had therefore taken steps to ensure that Gourko was given the resources necessary to push southwards.[3]

As has been seen, Gourko had paused in front of the Turkish position in the mountains early in December, to await the reinforcements that would be released by the fall of Plevna. The first units moved out on December 14, but were soon held up by the deterioration in the weather, and it was not until December 23 that Gourko received at

Orkhanie the last of the additional troops promised to him. By that date the Russian forces in Bulgaria were organised in three separate armies, together with the troops in the Dobrudja, which were not under one command. Gourko had the Guard Corps, of three divisions, and the IX Corps of two divisions; one rifle brigade, and two cavalry divisions. In all, he had 84½ battalions, 54 squadrons, 256 field guns and 24 of horse artillery, a total of 80,000 men. His mission was to beat Mehemet Ali, to capture Sofia, and then to march eastwards past Philippopolis to Adrianople.

Radetzky, whose objective was to defeat the Turkish army at Shipka and then to advance to Adrianople, had the VIII and IV Corps, with the Bulgarian Legion, two rifle brigades and a cavalry division. This gave him 74 battalions, 18 squadrons, 240 field guns and 12 of horse artillery, amounting in all to 66,000 men. The Tsarevich, whose task continued to be the protection of the lines of communication running south from the Danube, as well as the siege of Rustchuk, had the XII and XIII Corps, a cavalry division and eight Cossack Regiments. His strength was 72 battalions, with 60 battalions, 288 field guns and 36 of horse artillery, a total of 71,500 men. Finally, in the Dobrudja there were a further 76½ battalions, with 92 squadrons, 320 field guns and 60 of horse artillery, a further 80,000 men. Tying up so much of the army in the Dobrudja does suggest an excess of caution on the part of the Russians, at odds with the bolder policy now to be adopted elsewhere in Bulgaria.

Gourko, who had what might reasonably be described as the cream of the Russian army at his disposal, outnumbered his immediate opponent by more than two to one. The Turks had some 25,000 men in their defensive line where the high road crossed the Balkans, with 15 guns; about 5,000 men and 4 guns at Lutikova and the same at Slatitza; and a reserve of about 10,000 men at Sofia. Gourko had used the lull in active operations to familiarise himself with the territory into which he must now advance and which, indeed, might offer a more effective obstacle to his progress than the Turkish army. The strength of the defensive positions which confronted him was such that he resolved if possible to turn them.

It was clear to Millet, though, who arrived at Gourko's headquarters on Christmas Eve, that Gourko must do something soon:

> It has been evident for some time that General Gourko would either have to retire from the positions he had taken on the mountains near the Baba Konak Pass, or else cross the range at any cost, for the severity of the weather made it almost impossible to bring up the supplies and ammunition, and life in the bivouacs on the mountain became daily more and more difficult. Scarcely a night passed but frozen hands and feet were counted by hundreds. Thirty soldiers were frozen to death during four days of the storm, and the number of sick from exposure amounted to more than 2,000.[4]

The deep mud, which was all that the roads consisted of, had frozen solid, and, on any incline, steps had to be cut with axes; they were otherwise impassable. Gourko's investigation of the possibility of finding a way over the mountains to outflank the Turkish position bore fruit when a Bulgarian shepherd was found who identified not one but two paths which might give Gourko what he wanted. Lieutenant Colonel Stavrosky, of the General Staff, was sent to check this out, and reported that the shepherd was right,

Russian troops advancing from Etropol towards Sofia. (Strantz)

and that each of the routes could be used. Gourko made his plans accordingly, intending to move in three columns. Two of these would take the paths that had been discovered, which would outflank the Turkish position to the west, while the third, moving from Etropol, would pass to the east side of it and, having concentrated the enemy's mind on this threat, ultimately descend into the Slatitza valley at Bunova or Mirkovo and cut the Petricevo road. The rest of Gourko's army he placed under the command of Krüdener, whose orders were to remain where he was in front of the Turkish position, bombarding it, and holding himself ready to follow up any retreat. Once the routes had been identified Gourko set his engineers to work to create a passable road, an operation that was carried out under Stavrosky's direction.[5]

On the Turkish side no significant reinforcements had reached Chakir. There had, however, been a change in the command structure, Suleiman having been recalled to Constantinople with a view to his taking personal charge of the defence of the whole Turkish line along the Balkans. He arrived in the capital on December 19, and at once set off to visit the units bracing themselves for the Russian advance. He reached Sofia a few days later, and made his headquarters there; his intention was that a large part of the troops withdrawn from the Lom should move via Tatar Bazardjik and Ichtiman to Sofia. He had, as Baker later wrote, 'the wild idea of maintaining the whole of the Balkan line, and at the same time resisting the certain attack of the Serbian army upon the position to the west of Sofia.'[6] Baker had already realised that in the changed circumstances the line of the Balkans would be impossible to defend successfully, advocating the immediate retreat of all the Turkish forces in the west all the way back to Adrianople; any that could not retire by this route should be evacuated through Salonika to the capital. Chakir, who forwarded Baker's paper outlining this plan to Suleiman, emphatically endorsed it, but it cut no ice with the commander in chief, who merely responded to say that his troops from the Lom were beginning to arrive at Sofia.[7]

Suleiman's capacity for doing the wrong thing had already been demonstrated on many occasions, and his determination to try to hold the entire line of the Balkans was yet another instance of this. Greene's observations on the policy that should have been adopted to defend a long river or mountain line were an endorsement of the plan put forward by Baker:

> All military writers are agreed that the proper means of defence of such a line is to post small bodies in observation at the various points of passage, and keep the main body of the defenders at some central point in rear, from which, as soon as the enemy's real attack is made clear, a force can bear down upon him and strike him before his troops have all crossed the mountains or river. Such a point in this case was Adrianople, in itself a naturally strong position, and now defended by numerous half-finished earthworks, and from which high roads lead to Sofia, Shipka, Slivno and Aidos, and railroads to within three days' march of Sofia, two days' of Shipka, and one day's of Slivno.[8]

Instead of this, Suleiman began to increase the force around Sofia to 40,000 men, the Shipka garrison to the same figure, and left only 10,000 at Adrianople. Of the western army, 15,000 men were at Sofia itself, and the remainder in the mountains.

Gourko may have supposed that his preparations for his outflanking movement had been concealed, and various accounts suggest that the Turks were unaware of the threat. This was, not, however, the case. Baker was very much alive to the danger:

> Before the departure of Mehemet Ali, and frequently since, I had expressed my anxious fears relative to the pathway over the mountain leading by Tchuriak to Potop. It was impossible to trust to the Circassians, who were supposed to guard the mountains on the Sofia plains; but these men had long ago reported that a party of Russian cavalry occupied the village of Tchuriak. I had begged Mehemet Ali to allow me to start some day with three battalions, and to clear the whole of this pass from Russian occupation.[9]

Mehemet Ali, however, had felt unable to spare the troops necessary for such an operation, as did Chakir when he assumed the command. On December 24 Baker made a reconnaissance in the direction of Tchuriak. He could see that the village was occupied but not in great strength. After testing the defences briefly, he concluded that Tchuriak was held by an infantry battalion and a Cossack regiment. Since guns had been seen on the mountain crest, it was obvious that the Russians had constructed a road from the mouth of the pass to the summit. Next day he took Chakir to see for himself and they agreed that this would be the direction from which a Russian advance would come, but Chakir, conscious that his force had dwindled to a strength of 12,500 men, still felt unable to detach any part of it to allow Baker to conduct a spoiling operation at Tchuriak.[10]

Baker's staff was temporarily augmented at about this time by the arrival of Lieutenant H H Kitchener R E. Baker took him on one of his visits to the Turkish positions, some 6,200 feet above sea level. Kitchener evidently enjoyed the experience, writing in an article on his return to England:

> The sun threw a rosy tinge over all, making the most perfect scene imaginable. There were the Russians, just below us in their trenches. We could see them relieving guard, and they could easily have been picked off with a rifle ... The whole positions both of the Turks and the Russians were laid out below us as on a map.[11]

Gourko had begun his movement on Christmas Day. The advance guard, under Rauch, consisted of 13 battalions, with 16 field guns and 11 *sotnias* with 4 horse artillery guns, left at 5.00 am, the intention being to reach Tchuriak 24 hours later. Climbing the steep road, covered with a thick layer of ice, the troops struggled to bring up the artillery. By noon on December 26 only four four-pounders had reached the summit. As night fell, a fresh snowstorm further hampered the advance, but before they bivouacked for the night the leading infantry had reached the head of the valley and were over the Balkans. The problems of movement were, however, so acute that it was not until December 30 that the whole of the column had finally concentrated at Tchuriak. Meanwhile on December 27 Gourko, aiming to take advantage of having got at least the leading units of his force over the mountains, ordered the occupation of the hills that separate the Tchuriak valley from the Sofia plain, a task which the Preobrazhensky Regiment accomplished without difficulty. The advance guard had been followed by two further echelons which made up the 3rd Guards Division under Kataley.

The flanking columns to the right and left experienced even greater difficulties than Rauch's advance guard. On the right Veliaminov, with six battalions, sixteen squadrons and sixteen guns started, like Rauch, from Vrachesti, and was to cross the Oumourgatch Mountain before descending to Jeliava; but this force encountered such deep snow drifts on this route that it was compelled to abandon its advance and fall back to the route taken by Rauch's column. The column finally reached Tchuriak very much the worse for wear after five days' march on December 28. On the left, Dandeville had fared even worse. He had nine battalions, six squadrons and sixteen guns, and set off from Etropol on December 25. In spite of deep snow, its advance guard succeeded in reaching the highest point of the mountains before it bivouacked that night. Next day it was joined by the rest of the column, together with four guns, and on December 27 an infantry battalion got as far as the southern slope, with two guns, causing great alarm to the Turks in their fortified position. On December 28, under cover of gunfire from the four guns which had now been brought up, the 11th Regiment moved towards Shandarnik and a battalion of the 124th Regiment in the direction of Mirkovo. This represented the limit of their progress. During the night a fierce snowstorm cut off communication between the various units, and Dandeville could not get orders through until late on December 29. It was clearly impossible to proceed, and he directed the whole column to retreat to Etropol, where it reassembled on December 30. 823 men reported sick with frostbite and 53 had died from the extreme cold.[12]

On the afternoon of December 27, when Baker reached Chakir's headquarters, he found that news had arrived that the Russians were over the mountains in force at

Tchuriak, and that the telegraph wire to Sofia had been cut, presumably by Cossacks operating on the high road. Clearly, if the Russians could take the Tashkessen Pass, the whole of Chakir's army would be lost. Chakir asked Baker to take six battalions to hold the position; on enquiring which battalions had been selected, Baker found that the worst *Mustafiz* battalions had been chosen. This would not do, and he told Chakir so; instead, he took the three Albanian and Bosnian battalions which he had been leading; the Edirné battalion of *Mustafiz* had by mistake joined the others, but in view of its poor reputation, Baker left it behind, and marched during the night with his three battalions to Tashkesssen which he found, to his relief, had not yet been occupied. At the head of the pass he came upon a large khan, a strongly built stone building, with many windows, which would serve as a key defensive point.[13]

The Sofia road runs through the Tashkessen Pass, the name of which in Turkish means 'the cut rock', the pass resembling an incision in the rocky heights. Coming over the crest, Baker had seen the camp fires of the Russians extending for several miles northwards on the high road, and he estimated that their strength was about 20,000. With only three battalions to deal with, it would be all too easy for the Russians to turn the position. Baker had no expectation that any appeal to Suleiman could produce any assistance, even if it got through; and he resolved to ride back to Chakir to stress how dangerous was the situation. Chakir, in the absence of orders from Suleiman, was reluctant to retreat; but Baker overcame his doubts, and Chakir agreed to do so if no orders came through during the day, and promised him reinforcements in the morning. Baker had another hair-raising ride along the icy tracks to return to Tashkessen, where he found that the Edirné battalion had turned up after all; though 'a useless body of men,' it did have an excellent commander. It was clear to Baker that if he could delay the Russians at Tashkessen, Chakir would have a chance of escape, and he made his plans for what would obviously be a desperate defence.

Fortunately, the Russians were slow to move, and Baker had time to get his infantry and guns into position. About an hour after dawn, on December 29 the Russians could be seen to be preparing to advance. Baker described what he saw:

> It was impossible to imagine a more beautiful scene of war. From the stony crest we looked down on a most extensive panorama. The whole country was covered with a white sheet of snow. On the distant hills the black masses of the enemy were gathering fast. Below us, on the little ridge, our cavalry vedettes stood quietly at their posts. In rear, and hidden from the enemy, the supporting squadrons were mounted and ready. Amongst the rocks on the crest the brave Albanian and Bosnian battalions lay calmly waiting.[14]

Baker, watching the Russians deploy, estimated that a Russian division of 16 battalions lay in his right front; he could tell from the uniforms that it was a Guards division. Aiming to convince the Russians that his position was strongly occupied, he ordered his artillery to open fire as soon as they came within range. His hope was that the enemy would pause to bring up further troops, and to his delight he saw the advancing column move to the right to occupy a low range of hills and begin to entrench. That evening he received two more battalions; the El Bassan battalion of regular troops, and the Eski Cheir, 'a miserable little *Mustafiz* battalion that could not be trusted' which was only about 220 strong.[15] Baker's small force was not to be tested on the following day, when heavy snowstorms made movement difficult until late in the afternoon. As a result the Russians deferred their assault. Chakir sent Baker another battalion, the Tchengueri; he regarded this one as 'indifferent.'

The Russian advance finally began on December 31. By now some 25,000 men had been concentrated in front of the Tashkessen position. With their huge preponderance in numbers, the Russians began to envelop both the right and left of the Turkish position, and it was evident to Baker that he must pull back. At this moment he noticed a gap on the Russian right, as it moved around his flank, and he sent forward his tiny force of cavalry. This cheeky move gave him time to concentrate his centre on the road and around the khan, where he concentrated all his seven guns. It was not a moment too soon; wave after wave of Russian infantry stormed forward against the position, but all were repulsed. As the Russians came forward a great roar rose up from their lines; Baker was determined that this should be answered, and ordered his bugler to sound the Turkish cry of 'Allah':

> Springing to their feet, the gallant Prizrend shouted their appeal to the God of battles. Battalion after battalion took it up, and it echoed back from the distant mountain peaks. It was a glorious sight to see the confidence of the scanty little band of Turkish troops, as the great Muscovite wave rolled up against our position.[16]

During the afternoon Baker received word from his aide de camp, Colonel Allix, that Chakir had deserted him, and was in full retreat. If true, this would have meant that Baker's little force must necessarily be cut off. Baker, however, doubted the accuracy of this report and another to the same effect, and held his ground. His instinct was correct; what Allix had seen was Chakir's baggage and guns, escorted by an infantry brigade, retreating towards Tatar Bazardjik, in accordance with the agreement that Chakir and Baker had made that this train would be sent away first while Chakir held his position

Turkish prisoners, winter 1877/78. (*The Graphic*)

on the mountains; the plan was that once this long convoy was safely on its way Chakir would commence his retreat while Baker held off the Russians.[17]

The fighting around the khan had been particularly fierce. As the Russian assault began, Baker intended to put the Edirné battalion, of dubious merit, in the building itself. In the face of Russian rifle fire, the men of the battalion refused to enter the building:

> It was in vain that Islan Bey and my friend Captain Burnaby used their sticks on the backs of the skulkers. The wretched battalion hesitated, while only about a dozen more adventurous spirits crept forward to the corner of the building, but would not enter.[18]

In the end the battalion broke completely, bolting down the road and threatening to disrupt the deployment of the Uskub battalion which was forming up. Fortunately this stood firm, and Baker was able to get four companies into the khan, which proved crucial to the defence of his line.

As night fell, the Russians launched a final assault, pressing up the slope to the final crest of the Turkish position, under heavy fire from the defenders, whose numbers had been heavily depleted. As they neared the summit, the Bosnian battalion launched a bayonet charge, which drove the Russians back. Within a few minutes the firing died down, and Baker could assemble his little force, and start on the retreat to Tatar Bazardjik. With not much more than 3,000 men he had held off at least 17,000 men of the Russian Imperial Guard; and the delay which he had imposed on Gourko's advance enabled Chakir to escape unscathed from a position in which he would otherwise have been utterly destroyed.

The violence of the engagement may to some extent be judged by the expenditure of ammunition. Accurate records of the amount used during the various battles are usually hard to come by, and could only be compiled from unit war diaries if they ever existed and had survived. And, of course, the mere quantity of the expenditure of rifle ammunition does not carry with it any indication that it was well used. On the Turkish side in particular the infantry were very apt to fire constantly and at random, a practice that did however on occasion inflict a considerable number of casualties. At Tashkessen, though, so great was the total expenditure of rifle ammunition that it does demoustrate how heavily the Turkish troops were engaged. During a battle that lasted eight hours, the Prizrend battalion fired 292 rounds per man, and the other two battalions not much less – or over 30 rounds per man per hour.[19]

Philippopolis

Millet, the *Daily News* correspondent, had been with Gourko throughout the passage of the Balkans and the Battle of Tashkessen. Reporting on the events of January 1 he described the moment that the Russian forces that had crossed the mountains through Tchuriak joined hands with those following up Chakir's army through the Baba Konak position:

> At this moment General Gourko turned around and said earnestly, 'Now we can say, in all conscience, that we have crossed the Balkans, in every phase of the undertaking,' and he shook hands warmly with every one, congratulating those who counted this as their second passage.[1]

Meanwhile there had been action on the high road to Sofia, where Veliaminov had moved to Gorni Bugarovo on December 31, taking up and entrenching a position along the crest of a low bluff twelve miles from the city. Next day the Governor of Sofia, Osman Pasha, advanced from the city with 5,000 men. Deploying in front of Gorni Bugarovo, Osman began to envelop Veliaminov's right flank, while keeping up a heavy rifle fire. To this, the Russian infantry did not respond, and encouraged by their silence Osman launched his troops in an assault. When the column got within 50 yards of the Russian position, its defenders sprang up and delivered several volleys, which at that range caused heavy casualties. This was followed by a bayonet charge which caused the Turkish column to break and flee. The Turkish casualties were fearful; 800 dead were left on the field, while 1,600 wounded were taken back to Sofia. The total Russian loss was 243.[2] Osman, who had talked of emulating his namesake and making Sofia a second Plevna, now lost heart completely.

On the evening of January 1 Gourko completed his preparations for the pursuit of the Turkish force under Chakir, and for the capture of Sofia. The latter task was assigned to Rauch, with 16 battalions and 26 guns, who was to leave Tashkessen at 2.00 am the following morning and march down the high road to Sofia. The pursuit of Chakir was to be undertaken by Kataley with the 3rd Guard Division consisting of 16 battalions and 16 guns; *en route* he was to pick up Dandeville's force, which had by now finally made it across the mountains to Bunova. The remainder of the force, being the detachments of Shuvalov and Schilder-Schuldner, were to go into bivouac near Malinne, after bringing down the guns from the mountains.

Rauch reached the River Isker at Vrajdebna, about eight miles from Sofia, on the evening of January 2. He found that the covered bridge there was defended by three battalions of infantry and a cavalry regiment. He advanced with the 2nd, 3rd and 4th Rifle Battalions on the Turkish entrenchments, sending the Preobrazhensky Regiment and the 1st Rifle Battalion to the left, to look for a ford or, if possible, to cross on the ice. The frontal attack encountered stout opposition, in spite of the fire of the two batteries which Rauch brought up in support. However, the turning movement proved decisive; although the ice was scarcely thick enough, the Russians succeeded in crossing the river, and as soon as it was clear that they were in considerable strength, the defenders retreated, setting fire to the bridge as they went. The riflemen dashed forward, and began to throw water and snow on the blazing timbers with their cooking pots. Gourko, who had accompanied Rauch's column, was the first to cross the bridge through the flame and smoke, followed, somewhat apprehensively, by his staff. The seizure of the bridge was an important success; if it had been destroyed the delay in getting over the Isker would have been considerable.[3]

Next day Gourko made a personal reconnaissance of the defences of Sofia. Sofia was a well built city of between 40,000 and 50,000 inhabitants; for the Ottoman Empire it had always been of great strategic importance. Osman's hope of making a lengthy stand there was not without some reasonable foundation. Six large redoubts covered the various roads into the city, and several lines of trenches and batteries had been constructed. There were at least twelve field guns to support a garrison of about 12,000 men. Osman was reported as saying that he would defend the place foot by foot, 'burn all the houses, blow up all the powder magazines and not even leave a whole blade of straw for the Russians.' This kind of bombast may have been intended to reassure the Turkish population or to cow the Bulgarian; but the shocking defeat at Gorni Bugarovo, and the rapid advance that followed, caused panic among the 20,000 Muslims among the population, and all kinds of transport were requisitioned to take them to safety. Many of them, and particularly the large number of wounded in hospital at Sofia, never reached it, perishing in large numbers on the dreadful roads in the appalling weather.[4]

Gourko concluded that the weakness in the city's defences lay on the northern side, where no redoubts existed, and he selected this point for the assault. The experience on both sides during the war suggested that it might be an operation that was not without risk, at least of heavy casualties; but Gourko was convinced that if it had to be done, it should be done at once. He ordered Veliaminov to move to the north of the city with 8 battalions and 12 guns, while Rauch, with 20 battalions and 42 guns, was to move down the high road from Plevna. A cavalry brigade of the Guard was moved to cut the road to Philippopolis. This left only the road to Radomir, running south-west from the city, as a line of retreat. From there, a road ran to Dubnitza, giving a chance of retreating to Tatar Bazardjik, if that was what Osman decided to do. It did not take him long to make up his mind. During the night of January 3/4 he evacuated the city. When at noon on the following day a Cossack rode in to Gourko's headquarters to report this, it was not at first believed. In fact, Rauch's advance guard had been in the city since 10.00 am, and during the afternoon his main body arrived. Millet watched them as they marched in:

> They were not quite as trim as when they crossed the Sistova bridge, their caps were warped out of shape, their overcoats occasionally tattered and burned, and their faces and hands brown and roughened with the constant exposure, but they were as tidy as could be expected, and marched with a swing and regularity that was refreshing to see after the forced disorder of the mountain marches. A total stranger could not have failed to notice how perfectly General Gourko had his troops in hand, for the tone in which they answered his customary salutation, the expression

Russian troops in the Balkans. (*Album della Guerra Russo-Turca del 1877-78*)

of the individual faces as he passed, and the way in which they received the caution not to pillage in the city, were proof of this.[5]

While all this was going on, Baker was conducting a fighting retreat down the road through Petricevo in the direction of Otlukoi. For the first two days after he had retreated from Tashkessen he had seen little of the enemy, but by the afternoon of January 2 contact had been made with his pursuers. In one of the many skirmishes Lieutenant-General Kataley and one of his brigade commanders, unwisely riding ahead of his column, were killed by snipers. Chakir, meanwhile, had got well ahead in his retreat towards Otlukoi, which he reached unhindered, to learn that Suleiman had gone off to Adrianople leaving instructions that Chakir was to remain at Otlukoi for the present. What the point of this was Suleiman had not made clear. Baker, when he got to Otlukoi, proposed to Chakir that they should turn upon their pursuers who could not yet be in great strength, and deliver an assault which would not only check the pursuit, but would raise the morale of the troops. Chakir rejected the proposal, but agreed to a reconnaissance in force towards Matchka, where the head of the Russian column was taken to be.[6] Baker conducted the operation with his customary belligerence, and succeeded in driving back the Russians for long enough to put Matchka to the torch before retiring. His achievements at Tashkessen had been conveyed to Constantinople, and he received a personal telegram of thanks from the Sultan, which informed him of his promotion to the rank of *Ferik*, the equivalent of Lieutenant-General.

Baker and his colleagues at Otlukoi were surprised to learn that they might expect a visit from Suleiman, and the commander in chief turned up there on January 5, making a perfunctory examination of part of the Turkish position. Baker noted that he was 'in a most undecided and unsettled state of mind,' possibly due to rumours of his imminent supersession. Unfortunately for the troops under his command these rumours were not well founded. The Turkish forces had for the moment found a breathing space at Otlukoi, where there were no untoward incidents between the troops and the Bulgarian inhabitants, who were able to do a thriving trade in supplying goods to their temporary visitors. Suleiman's orders suggested to Chakir that the stay of his force there might be for some time, but on January 10 news arrived of the capture of Vessil Pasha's army at Shipka, and Suleiman hurriedly departed to Bazardjik. From there he sent orders for an immediate retreat, which was not going to be easy, since Chakir was encumbered with a large quantity of military stores which considerably delayed the movement.

In order to enable him to turn the flank of any position taken up by the retreating Turkish forces, Gourko divided his army into four parts. On the right Veliaminov was to advance to Samakov, and endeavour to cut off Osman's force, and to move on to Banja. He had 8 battalions of the IX Corps, 12 *sotnias* of Cossacks and 8 guns. In the centre Shuvalov, with 30 battalions, 12 squadrons and 76 guns, all of the Guard, was to move down the high road to Ichtiman. There it was to deploy and operate against any position occupied by the Turks at Trajan's Gate, a deep gorge through which the high road ran. On the left Krüdener, with the rest of the Guard units, and the remainder of his own IX Corps, amounting to 24 battalions, 16 squadrons and 58 guns, was to advance through Petricevo to Otlukoi. Behind the left and centre groups a force of 6 battalions and 8 guns under Schilder-Schuldner was to keep up communication between them. Gourko also sent a small force detached from the 3rd Division to work its way along the base of the Balkans as far as Karlovo, while a reserve of 8 battalions, 8 squadrons and 14 guns covered the rear at Sofia.

On January 9, as much to the surprise of the Turkish commanders as to their opponents, an order came from Constantinople to cease hostilities as an armistice was being sought. Parlementaires were sent forward to the effect that an armistice had been agreed; in the face of this, the local Russian commanders felt obliged to cease firing and to apply for instructions. On the Turkish side Baker and his immediate colleagues, having for the moment escaped their pursuers, reckoned it would be best to retrace their steps and take up a position covering the pass in front of Otlukoi. Baker's chief of staff, Shakir Bey, was sent forward under a flag of truce, and it was agreed that neither side would attack until the position had been clarified. When he got back, Shakir reported that the Russian Guards officers to whom he spoke were utterly sick of the war, and blamed England for its outbreak.[8]

Nothing therefore happened on January 10; but next day the Russian headquarters made clear that no armistice had been agreed and operations were to be resumed. As usual, the Turkish staff work of getting a march under way proved inadequate to the task, and it was not until the afternoon that the retreating columns began to move, in response to an order from Suleiman, in the direction of Bazardjik.

To the west, the question was whether Osman's force, which had been at Samakov until forced to retreat by Veliaminov, could get to the Maritza valley before Shuvalov, coming down through Ichtiman, could cut them off. As it turned out, the dreadful weather conditions, which left the roads thick with ice, delayed the Russians, since their artillery had to be manhandled up and down each slope. The Turks got a lead of a few miles into the valley, which they maintained to Bazardjik, albeit with the loss of some 300 ox carts carrying their baggage, which were captured by Shuvalov's leading unit. At Bazardjik a defensive position had been taken up some days earlier by Fuad, with about 8,000 men, along the Topolnica River. It was strong enough for the leading Russian units to have to wait for further forces to come up before it could be attacked, and it enabled the Turks from Samakov to come in.

Chakir and Baker, with Redjib, made their way to Suleiman's headquarters, where they met Fuad. It was clear to all what should be done:

> We found at once that all the generals of division were in perfect accord, that golden moments had been lost, and that the safety of the army depended on an immediate retreat upon Adrianople; but great doubts were expressed as to whether this movement could now be accomplished.[9]

Baker was still convinced that such a retreat was no longer possible, and devoted further study to the routes open to the army to the southward through the Rhodope Mountains. He found Suleiman's staff to be ignorant of what roads were open, whether to the south or to the east through Philippopolis, but it was clear that the whole of their forces would shortly be concentrated along the line of the Maritza. Suleiman, when he met his generals, was in a state of 'wild confusion,' which cannot have inspired much confidence in them. Fuad, indeed, was utterly dismayed, as he made clear in a conversation with Baker:

> He was in distress at the general state of mismanagement that was apparent everywhere, and evidently thought that Suleiman was a traitor, and endeavouring to lose army after army by arrangement with the Russians.[10]

It seemed pretty clear to Gourko, after he personally reconnoitred the position held by Fuad, that the Turks did not intend to make a serious stand at Bazardjik even though Fuad now had about 20,000 men under his command. Nevertheless, in planning his attack on the town for January 14, Gourko had some reason to hope that he might, by enveloping it from both north and south, be able to cut off and surround its defenders, and he made his plans accordingly. Krüdener was to get as far to the east as he could, coming down on the high road at Tchernogol to cut off a retreat to Philippopolis, while Shuvalov and Veliaminov were to envelop Bazardjik from the north and south respectively. During the night of January 13/14, however, the Turks got away, marching eastwards, their retreat being skillfully covered by Fuad.

When Shuvalov's leading troops entered Bazardjik, they found a scene of utter desolation, as Millet described:

A British ambulance with the Turkish army. (Ollier)

The streets were barricaded with broken cases, shutters, and the confused débris of the shops. Every house was opened and gutted. Bedding, groceries, furniture, small wares of all kinds, fairly paved the streets leading towards the railway station. The bright sun shining through clouds of smoke from a hundred burning houses lighted the scene of destruction and devastation with a reddish glare, and here and there a dead body with pools of blood still fresh about it completed a perfect picture of war in its most dramatic aspect.[11]

Shrewdly, Fuad did not retreat directly along the main road to Philippopolis, where he might have been caught in the open by Gourko's cavalry, but instead fell back over the Maritza, and followed the line of the railway which ran eastwards to the south of the river. Baker had been extremely exercised about the need to destroy the bridge over the Maritza at Bazardjik, and was not at all impressed with the airy assurances of the headquarters staff that it was made of wood and could easily be burnt or blown up. Although it was built of wood it was on stone buttresses and covered with two feet of concrete.[12] The problem was that the concrete could not be removed until Fuad's troops had been able to cross; the best that Baker could do, in the absence of any gunpowder, was to select the two spans adjoining either bank and pile up wood underneath them. As it was, it was only after houses adjoining the bridge had caught fire that Fuad's cavalry arrived to cross the bridge, which they hesitated to do because of the smoke and flame that enveloped the buildings on both sides of the street. In the end, however, they got across, and the piles of wood, with tar and petrol, were ignited on both sides of the river, and the last of the rearguard retreated.

Philippopolis is some twenty-four miles from Bazardjik by the route taken by the army, but the troops were marching well, and it was Baker's hope that they would reach it by nightfall on January 14. Once there, three good roads were available for the continued retreat to Adrianople if, but only if, the army could outdistance its pursuers. The generals of division met during the afternoon, and agreed that the men should be given a short rest until evening and then push on to Philippopolis. Reporting this to Suleiman, they were astounded to learn that instead of this he proposed to turn back to deal with a small Russian force which had crossed the Maritza near Adakeni. All the generals argued fiercely with this decision, Baker saying that it would lead to the loss of the whole army or at least its guns and matériel. Suleiman would have none of it:

> He replied that there was great reason in my argument, but that he had determined to halt the next day, and to move back upon Adakeni. This decision destroyed any remaining confidence that was felt by the generals of division in the Commander in Chief. The whole course of events, since the appearance of Suleiman with the Western Armies, had excited the greatest distrust amongst the senior officers.[13]

The disrepute in which Suleiman was held by Baker and his senior colleagues was shared by the military *attachés* and correspondents on the Turkish side. Hozier, in his history of the war, reviewed his performance and suggested that Suleiman would have now understood its consequences:

> Suleiman surely must have felt at last how much evil he had done his country. It was he who had been to a great extent instrumental in causing the fall of Osman

Turkish sentinels in the Balkans. (*Russes et Turcs*)

Pasha by his disobedience to Mehemet Ali; it was he who had disorganised all the commands; it was he who had persisted in retaining at Shipka, at Arab-Konak, and at Sofia armies which the Russians had beaten and annihilated in detail; it was he who had left Adrianople without any defenders; and finally, it was he who had brought Turkey's last army into the desperate situation in which it now found itself. His influence was traceable in all the misfortunes of his country, and the consciousness of the fatal part he had played must have caused him bitter regret at this moment – when he was himself all but lost.[14]

Whether he really did realise how far he was to blame, rather than supposing himself simply to have been unlucky, is doubtful. The stupid indifference he had shown in ordering attacks that resulted in appalling and unnecessary casualties does not suggest that he was capable of much reflection on his own inadequacy.

By now the only hope for the army was to retreat as quickly as it could to Hasskoi. It might then be possible to move south of the River Arda, and from there march to Demetoka and then north to Adrianople. But it would require a celerity of movement of which the army probably was not capable, and in any case Suleiman appeared not to have grasped the need for haste, summoning a council of war for January 15. This proved pointless; the generals of division repeated their views, but Suleiman obstinately rejected them. It broke up without any fresh orders being given, and the generals were left to cope with the developing situation. Gourko had sent Krüdener along the Philippopolis road, Schilder-Schuldner toward Hadji-Ali-Dermen, Veliaminov along the right bank of the Maritza and the cavalry in a wide sweep to the north of Philippopolis to cross the river to the east of that place. On the Turkish side it was again Fuad who had the task of screening the efforts of the rest of the army to retreat into Philippopolis. Baker's fear was that the Russians might get round to the south of the city and cut off the escape route through the mountains, and he took two brigades to ensure that this was kept open. Fortunately for the Turks, the Russian advance was not pressed very vigorously, and during the night Fuad was able to retreat through Philippopolis and reestablish contact with the main body.[15]

During January 16 Fuad continued to act as the rearguard as the rest of the army headed south from Philippopolis towards Stanimaka. Fuad took up a position near Dermendere, and at about 3.00 pm launched an energetic assault on the most advanced units of Shuvalov's column. These were from the 31st Division, and they repeated their tactics of Gorni Bugarovo, holding their fire until their attackers were within fifty or sixty yards, and then delivering a furious fusillade. Three times the Turks attacked, each time suffering heavy casualties, leaving some 600 dead in front of the Russian positions; Russian casualties were only about 60.[16]

Meanwhile the rear of Suleiman's main body got into difficulties; a mixed brigade of dragoons, followed by an infantry brigade mounted on cavalry horses under Major-General Krasnov, had been sent by Gourko to ford the Maritza two or three miles west of Philippopolis. They caught the retreating Turkish columns near Karagatch, and carried the village with a loss of some 260 men, capturing 18 guns. The Turks then launched a counter-attack in a vain effort to recapture the guns, before retreating into the mountains. The Russians, expecting further attacks, retreated with the guns to

Ahlan overnight. Suleiman, however, made no attempt to follow, continuing his retreat through the mountains, leaving Fuad to extricate himself as best he could.

Throughout January 17, fighting with his back to the mountains, Fuad endeavoured to clear a route for his force towards Stanimaka; but his attack failed and he was forced back, abandoning more of his guns. Baker had realised that the artillery would be a fatal impediment to the retreat, and had previously urged its abandonment. Now, in disorder, Fuad's troops retreated through the mountains in small parties, struggling in the deep snowdrifts which barred their way. One part of Fuad's force was trapped in the Beleschnitza gorge, and suffered fearful casualties as they were assailed by artillery and rifle fire on three sides. An eyewitness who visited the scene in the evening described what he found:

> At the entrance of the gorge there is a frightful jumble of cannon, caissons, wagons, bodies of men and horses, forming a barricade several feet high. As far as the eye can reach, the interior of the gorge is covered with the bodies of dead and wounded, standing out against the snow clad ground; and I may say without exaggeration, that the little stream at the bottom of the pass has become quite red with blood.[17]

It was estimated that there were 2,000 dead alone lying there.

Baker, meanwhile, had reached Stanimaka where he again found his commander in chief in a state of confusion, having lost touch both with Fuad and with Chakir. It was clear that the last chance of getting away to the east towards Adrianople through Hasskoi and Hermanli had now been lost, and that the only course was to fall back through the Rhodope mountains to the Aegean. There seemed to be one possible route through Tahtali, and steps were taken to cover this. Heavy gunfire could be heard from the direction of Markova and Beleschnitza, and Baker sent a message to urge Suleiman to order an advance in that direction to support Fuad. Suleiman sent a reply that he agreed, but appears to have done nothing; describing this, Baker remarked derisively that 'Suleiman, as usual, when any stirring events were taking place, was occupying his house in the town.'[18]

During the night the battered columns of Suleiman's army began their retreat through the mountains. Baker observed that 'the gross negligence which characterised the Russian outposts throughout the campaign again stood us in good stead.'[19] Once again the Turks were able to make a night retreat unhindered. Their officers, however, had lost heart completely, incapable, as Baker remarked, of fighting out a beaten game, and resigned to the loss of the army. As the retreat continued, Baker prevailed on Suleiman to order the abandonment of the guns, and this the senior officers agreed to do. Still encountering deep snow, and in bitter cold, the remnants of Suleiman's army trudged on through the mountains. The enemy now was not the Russians, but starvation, as the last supplies of biscuit were exhausted. Finally, though, the last of the mountains was crossed, and Baker and his men could see in the distance the blue waters of the Aegean. By January 28 some 40,000 men, in a state of complete disorganisation, had been assembled, near to Enos, where a fleet of transports under Manthorpe Bey, an English officer, had been collected to transport them to Gallipoli and Constantinople.[20]

Although at times the pursuit by Gourko of the retreating Turks might have been pressed even more relentlessly, he had achieved a remarkable success. In the fighting between Sofia and Philippopolis he had suffered a total of 1,250 killed and wounded, a modest casualty list compared to the scale of his accomplishment. The Turkish army opposed to him had been completely broken up; he had taken 2,000 prisoners, 114 guns and a huge quantity of rifles, ammunition and stores. The Turks had lost some 5,000 men in the fighting around Philippopolis alone.[21]

The remorseless tragedy that had overtaken the Turkish army under Suleiman's command might have been avoided, if instead of his dilatory and wrongheaded orders he had grasped the reality of his situation. So serious, however, was the mistrust felt by his commanders that many of them believed that his conduct could only be explained by treachery. There was no evidence to confirm this, but he was arrested on his return to Constantinople and in December 1878 was tried by court martial; he was sentenced to complete degradation and confinement in a fortress for fifteen years. He died in 1892.[22]

36

Shenovo

While Gourko was setting off from Sofia in his pursuit of Suleiman's army, an even greater drama was being enacted in the high passes of the Balkans at Shipka. The Russian high command's strategy for conducting a winter campaign called not only for the offensive by Gourko across the Balkans in the direction of Sofia, but a major operation by Radetzky's army, and early in January Skobelev arrived at Gabrova with substantial reinforcements, consisting of the 16th and 30th Divisions and the 3rd and 4th Rifle Brigades. These brought the total number of infantry at Radetzky's disposal to 56,000 men in 74 battalions in addition to artillery and cavalry. Out of these, however, Radetzky had effectively lost the use of the 24th Division; sent to the Shipka front in late November as a relief for the 14th Division, it had lost several hundred men through freezing during the severe December storms, and by Christmas Day had no less than 6,013 men unfit for duty due to frost bite and sickness caused by the extreme exposure.[1]

With the additional troops made available to him, Radetzky planned to take out the Turkish force at Shipka. Vessil Pasha, in command there, had some 40,000 men with 93 guns. The Turkish position had been greatly strengthened, particularly during the long period of inactivity caused by the bad weather. The village of Shipka was now the nucleus of a large fortified camp, and the pass was blocked by a series of redoubts and entrenchments. Eight redoubts lay on the west and four on the east of the road, linked by trenches, and forming a semi circle from Shenovo through Dolni Gouzovo, Gorni Gouzovo and Yanina. It could prove a very tough nut to crack.

Radetzky planned to envelop the Turkish position, and for this purpose he divided his army into three groups. On the right Skobelev, with the 16th Division, the 3rd Rifle Brigade, 7 Bulgarian battalions, and the 9th Don Cossack Regiment, with 6 guns and 6 mountain guns, was to take a mountain trail leading from Zelenodrevo to the summit of the mountains only two and a half miles to the west of the Turkish position on Bald Mountain. From there he was to descend to the village of Imetli in the Tundja valley and then swing to his left to attack the western side of the Turkish position. Meanwhile, on the left, Prince Mirsky was to advance from Triavna following a trail over the Seltsis hill, crossing into the Tundja valley at Gusevo, where he would turn to his right to attack the Turks' eastern flank. His column consisted of the 3rd, 34th and 36th Regiments of the 9th Division, the 30th Division, the 4th Rifle Brigade, a Bulgarian battalion, the 23rd Don Cossack Regiment, 16 guns and 6 mountain guns. The operation was to commence on the morning of January 5 and it was hoped that both columns would be in a position to attack on the morning of January 8. Meanwhile the rest of Radetzky's army, under his direct command, would remain in the Russian position in the Shipka Pass. He had there the 14th Infantry Division, and the 35th Regiment of the 9th Division. In addition to the principal operation, a small force under Major-General Kartsov, consisting of two regiments of the 3rd Division, a battalion from the 3rd Rifle Brigade and the 24th and

Russian troops resting high in the Balkans. (Ollier)

30th Don Cossack Regiments, was to endeavour to cross the Trojan Pass to the west and make contact with Gourko's army.[2]

All three movements faced dreadful difficulties in their passage over the Balkans in the appalling weather conditions that prevailed, but it was Kartsov's column that encountered the most considerable obstacles:

> In the region the Balkans attain their greatest general elevation, and here its loftiest summits are found; the most conspicuous being the Maré-Haidouk, whose top is lost in clouds, fogs and snow; the few footpaths which exist are only practicable for foot-passengers or solitary horsemen, not for bodies of troops. It was not, therefore, without cause that the best military writers had considered the Trojan Balkans impassable.[3]

It was these conditions that presented the greatest threat to Kartsov's mission, since the Turkish defences were modest; about 2,000 men occupied four redoubts. Kartsov split his force into three, each part setting off at intervals of one day from Koliba, his starting point, commencing on January 4. He took with him eight guns, mounted on sledges, each of which required 24 buffaloes, a company of infantry and a *sotnia* of

Cossacks to drag it up the mountains. They reached the summit on January 5, through quagmires and snowdrifts, the sappers painfully clearing the way. Lieutenant Colonel Sosnovsky, the commander of the rifle battalion which led the advance, attempted a surprise attack on the principal Turkish redoubt, but his men were spotted within two hundred yards, and were driven back by heavy rifle fire.

The main redoubt was linked to the other three by a system of trenches, and it was evident that a frontal attack was out of the question. Two days were spent in reconnoitring a route to turn the position, and in hauling up the artillery. On January 7 Kartsov's guns opened fire on the redoubt, while a column moved around it to the east. Once it had got to a position from which it could descend on the Turkish right, another column attacked in front. The defenders broke, and fled down the mountains, and Kartsov was able to make his way to Karlovo, where he was joined by other units of the 3rd Division which had moved along the south side of the Balkans through Slatitza.[4]

Even before the fall of Plevna Skobelev had turned his mind to the crossing of the Balkans, and the prolonged delay which followed was a source of intense frustration to him. Eventually he had set out for Gabrova on December 22, marching over appallingly bad roads in bitter weather. Part of his artillery was left at Plevna, as each gun required eight horses rather than six. A Russian observer described Skobelev's troops *en route*:

> When the detachment began the march, it defiled before its beloved chief singing gaily as it marched by. He was accustomed to greet them with great geniality, recalling the battles in which they had taken part, and talking sometimes of the soldier's position, and sometimes of subjects far removed from the scenes of the campaign. The privates, instead of being, as usually is the case, awkward in the presence of their chief, were put perfectly at their ease, and showed themselves at their best whenever they had the kind and hearty greeting of Skobelev.[5]

Arriving at Shipka, Skobelev conferred with Radetzky and Mirsky. The planned operation was clearly going to be difficult, not least because it would be a serious problem to coordinate the attacks on the Turkish position once the Russians were through the mountains. Writing to Kuropatkin, his Chief of Staff, Skobelev disclosed his uneasiness in the minute instructions which he gave for the preparations to be made. Confidence generally, however, was high, as Pfeil, who was to accompany Mirsky, observed:

> The Russian headquarters, which, owing to the ignominious defeats at Plevna, the failure at the Lom, and the conspicuous success of the Turks at Elena, had lost all power of decision, had now pulled itself together and determined to proceed with vigour. With the changeableness peculiar to the Russian character, which is despondent today and exultant tomorrow, after the events of Plevna they looked down with contempt on the adversary of whom they stood in mortal fear only a few days previously. The plan for crossing the Balkans was worked out in a corresponding spirit.[6]

Mirsky had further to travel than Skobelev, and his force began its march at dawn on January 5. He had twenty-eight miles to cover to reach Gusevo, from where he was to attack, whereas Skobelev, who started out on the evening of the same day, had to march

Russian troops bivouacking in the Balkans. (Ollier)

only twelve miles to his objective at Imetli. The assumption was, therefore, that Mirsky would have to make forced marches to reach his destination, while Skobelev should pace himself to arrive at the same time. As it turned out, however, the physical obstacles encountered by the latter meant that it was his force that was behind schedule.

Mirsky's advance was preceded by some 1,500 Bulgarians who worked to clear the snow, and for a while good progress was made. Once the force caught up with the road sweeping operation, however, the march was slowed by the need to take particular care to negotiate the steep precipices. At about noon the column halted; Mirsky came to the conclusion that it was not practicable for the field artillery to complete the march without causing enormous delay, and he decided to proceed with the mountain guns alone. Darkness had fallen at 6.30 pm, but the column trudged on, aiming to bivouac for the night on the southern slope of the mountains, while the staff were to go to Seltsis, a village marked on the map. In the pitch dark, in biting cold and a savage wind, the men had to wade knee deep through the snow. Pfeil was struck by the fortitude of the soldiers:

There was of course no possibility of lighting fires or making any kind of shelters, and cooking was out of the question; but, often as I went through the ranks of the brave fellows, I never heard a single word of discontent; only the officers abused everybody roundly and did not trouble themselves in the least about their men.[7]

As they struggled forward news came that Seltis consisted only of three half burnt out huts, and that in any case it appeared that the road was impracticable at night, so Mirsky was deprived of accommodation. Nearly all his staff had vanished, evidently having found bivouacs with the Bulgarians; Mirsky's composure deserted him entirely and 'he complained loudly that the troops had to suffer so much, and declared that he would just throw himself upon the snow and let everything take its chance.' Pfeil, however, revived his spirits, and with the aid of three Cossacks got his commander to Seltsis where, after all, accommodation was found and where the Prince's baggage shortly arrived with his valet; they dined on cold meat and 'some excellent Madeira.' Mirsky's column rested for the whole of January 6, to allow the 30th Division, marching as the reserve, to arrive. On January 7, in much easier conditions, the force resumed its march to Gusevo, which was taken after a brief action. Mirsky sent one brigade of the 30th Division under Schnitnikov to occupy Magilish, six miles to the east of Kazanlik, to cover his left flank and rear, and settled down to prepare for the beginning of his assault on the following day, although he was, however, still in ignorance of Skobelev's progress.

This had been by no means as rapid as had been hoped. Although making good time on January 6, marching seven miles before bivouacking for the night, next day it was possible to move only slowly. As had been the case with Mirsky's column, movement of the field artillery created tremendous problems, and all save six guns had to be left behind; even the mountain guns demanded tremendous efforts in being dragged through the snow. The column, much of the time marching in single file, stretched for miles. The men had provisions for six days, part of which was carried in their packs, and the rest by packhorses. Cattle were driven along the track to provide sufficient meat. Each man had ninety-six cartridges, and a similar quantity was carried by the train. There were even a number of camels, brought from Central Asia; these hardy animals were of great assistance in pulling the guns.[8]

Although by January 7 the descent to Imetli had begun, and that village was occupied before nightfall, Skobelev's troops were still strung out for miles, and by dawn on January 8 he had not yet succeeded in concentrating his force, having encountered resistance from a body of Turks entrenched in his front. Mindful of instructions that he had received from Radetzky that he was not to attack until he had his force well in hand, he sent a messenger to report that he would not have all his force up until the evening of January 8. While waiting for a response, he had to endure the frustration of hearing the sound of battle to the east, where Mirsky had began his attack. Radetzky responded to Skobelev's report with an order to concentrate his force and attack on the morning of January 9, establishing contact with Mirsky if this was possible. He added that the 1st Cavalry Division was being sent forward to reinforce him.[9]

Radetzky had taken his stand on the morning of January 8 on the crest of St Nicholas, from where he would be able to see the advance of the columns of both Mirsky and Skobelev. He was soon able to see Mirsky's troops moving forward to the assault. Deploying about noon, they advanced to the attack of the Turkish positions. Mirsky, like Radetzky, had heard the sound of gunfire from the west, where Skobelev was clearing away the opposition which he had encountered, but as the day wore on this died away, and there was no sign of an attack from this direction. Mirsky's orders were, however, to attack on January 8, and this he proceeded to do. In his front line came the 4th Rifle Brigade, deployed as skirmishers, supported by the mountain guns and the 33rd Regiment. In his second line were the 34th, 36th and 117th Regiments. The 20th Regiment remained at Gusevo, and Schnitnikov's two regiments (118th and 119th) were ordered to advance from Magilish towards Kazanlik.

The advance guard, led by Colonel Krock, took the villages of Yanina and Haskioi after a short but sharp struggle, but beyond these were held up by a small range of hills covered with several tiers of rifle pits. Under heavy shellfire from the Turkish artillery, to which only the small mountain guns were able to reply, the Russian troops advanced to the assault, sustaining heavy casualties as they did so. The colonel of the 33rd Regiment was wounded, and the line began to waver before Mirsky sent forward the 36th Regiment in support. A lucky shot from a mountain gun exploded a Turkish caisson; the Russian line moved forward and captured the Turkish trenches with three guns and 100 prisoners. These Turkish guns had been in a battery on the right flank of the Russian lines which had picked out the party of Mirsky's headquarters staff and had caused it several casualties.[10]

As dusk fell the Russians approached the last line of Turkish defences, which was a series of redoubts to the south of Shipka village. The exhausted troops were running out of ammunition, and at this point the Turks launched a violent counter-attack. It failed, however, in the face of volley firing by the Russian infantry. Nonetheless, Mirsky was very exposed. Although Kazanlik had been found to be unoccupied, his left flank was in the air; his troops were pinned down only 200 yards from strong enemy positions; and his back was to a high range of mountains into which retreat would be difficult if not impossible.[11]

Skobelev's failure to launch an attack, for whatever reason, had caused intense bitterness among Mirsky's staff, and it seemed to Pfeil that their commander was beginning to lose his nerve:

> Prince Mirsky now began to doubt of success; his mind reverted to the defeat he had suffered at Elena, and he remarked to me that this day would bring new shame on his head. A sort of council of war was called, in which we three and the commander of artillery took part, and the Prince put his views before us. As he said, he had done his duty, and attacked at the time ordered, but had been shamefully left in the lurch, and there was nothing left for him but to save his army, and with this view to withdraw it to the Balkans. The artillery general, a fat, helpless personage, who the whole day had kept out of harm's way, gave his unconditional support to this course.[12]

The Chief of Staff, Colonel von Raben, and Colonel Sobelev, attached to Mirsky from the General Staff, were for holding on; Pfeil agreed, suggesting that the pioneers be sent to Kazanlik to fortify the place. This last suggestion was acted upon; Mirsky accepted his subordinates' advice, although sending off a pessimistic report to Radetzky that unless reinforced he must retreat. He had lost more than 1,500 men. Radetzky responded that he must hold on for another twenty-four hours; he would launch a frontal attack next day, when Skobelev would also attack from the west.[13]

Radetzky planned to launch his frontal attack on January 9 at noon, reckoning that if Skobelev began his advance at 8.00 am he would reach Shipka at about that time. As dawn broke, St Nicholas was enveloped in a thick mist, and nothing could be seen, but heavy firing from the east suggested that Mirsky was under attack. This was indeed the case; after a heavy artillery preparation the Turks launched an attack all along the line. The situation was critical; without support any retreat might degenerate into a rout, and Pfeil found Mirsky in a desperate state of mind:

> From the Prince's face I saw what a struggle was going on in his mind. For some moments we rode silently alongside one another, our eyes fixed on the battlefield, and then suddenly he looked round at me with an angry look, such as I never before or since saw on his face, and said, 'I was a fool to take your advice and not insist upon following out my own plan and withdrawing my troops. You see, I shall lose my army! As I had fulfilled my orders, and attacked Shipka, and as Skobelev did not arrive, I could have withdrawn with all honour.' He stared at me, and was silent. These were the only words we exchanged on our ride up to the scene of action.[14]

The Turkish attacks continued, and appeared to be making headway, to the point when it appeared that the Russians might have to retreat. At this point a message arrived from Colonel Krock on a scrap of paper: 'Hurrah! Skobelev is advancing with bands playing. Krock.' Pfeil thought it a moment one would have to have lived through to understand, and compared their feelings to Wellington's when at Waterloo he heard the news of Blücher's arrival. Prince Mirsky gave Pfeil a look which, he wrote, he would never forget.[15]

Early on January 8 Skobelev's leading regiments, the 63rd and 64th, had moved on a hill to the south-east; this was soon taken by the 64th Regiment. However, although he probed towards Shenovo, Skobelev felt bound by his orders from Radetzky not to attack until all his force was in hand, and he held back from launching an attack. During the night all his force was assembled at Imetli, with the exception of the 62nd Regiment. On the morning of January 9 this unit could be seen descending the mountain, and Skobelev felt he might now reasonably launch an attack. This began with the capture, not without heavy loss, of a hill on his right flank, west of Shenovo. He also sent a force of cavalry in a wide swing to his right, and it was they who had established contact with Krock and Mirsky's advanced guard.

Immediately in his front, Skobelev faced four Celtic tumuli, where Gourko had camped during the previous July. These the Turks had fortified, linking them by épaulements. In front of Shipka there was a semi-circular redoubt, with four guns, prolonged with a redan and three lines of trenches, while in its turn behind this lay a huge earthwork surrounding the entrenched camp, with another circular redoubt. All these works had been constructed among the woods and bushes around Shenovo, making it difficult to assess their strength.[16]

At 7.00 am Skobelev deployed his force. In the first line were the 63rd Regiment and the Bulgarian Legion; behind these were the 61st and 64th Regiments and the Rifle Brigade. Skobelev located his mountain guns in the centre and took up his position there. With bands playing, the assault force moved towards the redoubts, received by a very heavy fire. Response to this was difficult, for the defenders were largely concealed among the trees and bushes. As the line moved forward Major-General Count Tolstoy fell, seriously wounded, and the heavy casualties which the infantry were taking caused the attack momentarily to falter. Colonel Panioutine, of the 63rd Regiment, on seeing this formed a column of attack on a front of two companies and personally led it forward into the storm of rifle fire. Every fifty yards or so the attacking column lay down for a brief rest before springing up and rushing forward again. Finally, the base of the principal redoubt was reached, and Panioutine led his men into the earthwork, where a savage hand-to-hand fight ensued with the bayonet. Eventually, the Turks fell back to their second position, pursued by the Russian infantry. Giving them no time to regroup, Panioutine, the regimental flag in his hand, was the first over the top.

Meanwhile Skobelev had personally led forward his centre while on the left the Bulgarian Legion stormed the tumuli. In the chaotic fighting which followed the Turkish units broke, and retreated, some towards Shipka and the rest in the direction of Kazanlik. Vessil, his nerve now completely gone, sent forward an officer with a white flag, surrendering his entire force to Skobelev without attempting to negotiate any conditions.

It was an utterly spineless decision. In the east, his forces were still holding their own against Mirsky, while in the centre Radetzky's attack had quickly run into difficulty. Advancing down the narrow road from the Shipka Pass, the attackers could only move five or six abreast. Preparations for the attack had been concealed by the thick mist, and the leading troops almost at once carried the first line of entrenchments. The attackers, however, were exposed to the cross fire of 22 battalions, 10 mortars and two batteries of howitzers, and the defenders threw hand grenades into the tightly packed masses of Russian infantry with deadly effect. Making a supreme effort, Radetzky's men stormed the second line of trenches, but could make no impression on the third, suffering fearful casualties. Pinned down in the position which they had reached, the Russians had lost more than 1,700 men in the space of three hours.

However, although immediately unsuccessful, Radetzky's attack had had the effect of concentrating Vessil's attention on his centre, which he at first took to be the main focus of the assault. Half his army and almost all his artillery was engaged in the defence of this part of his position, and it was only when his left flank began to disintegrate under Skobelev's attack that he realised his peril, upon which he panicked. Had he pulled back his troops facing Radetzky, he could probably have forced a way through to the southward, saving at least part of his army.

As it was, 12,000 men immediately in Skobelev's front surrendered at Shenovo. Steps were immediately taken to disarm them, while Skobelev sent Stoletov to report to Radetzky. He also insisted that Vessil send an immediate order to the rest of his army to lay down their arms, an order that was only grudgingly obeyed. When the Turks in Mirsky's front began to show white flags, Mirsky sent Pfeil off to Skobelev; as the senior officer, he wished to take control of the process of disarming the prisoners. When Pfeil reached Skobelev, he found him on the point of making a triumphal ride on his white horse to thank his troops; Skobelev invited him to accompany him, as his men crowded round their general with deafening shouts. Once this spectacular ride was completed, Skobelev rode with Pfeil to meet with Mirsky.

Prince Nicolai Ivanovich Sviatopolk-Mirsky, of an impeccably aristocratic background, was contemptuous of Russia's great military hero and thought him an arriviste and a glory hunter, as he told Pfeil:

Turkish prisoners on the plains of Shipka. (*Russes et Turcs*)

Prince Mirsky had always the lowest opinion of Skobelev's character, and said that he was an officer with whom, in time of peace, no one would shake hands. His grandfather was a drummer, and under Catherine II, I know not for what reason, became an officer; and his father, who like himself, was a lieutenant general and aide de camp to the Emperor, had gathered together the whole of his great fortune in Asia and in various high posts which he had held.[17]

Regrettably, Mirsky's staff reached the unwarranted conclusion that Skobelev had delayed his advance deliberately in the hope that Mirsky would be defeated and Skobelev could then arrive to save the day.

Vessil's army, when surrendered, consisted of 41 battalions totalling 36,000 men, of whom some 6,000 were sick and wounded. 98 guns, including twelve mortars, were captured. The Russian casualties had, however, been considerable, 1,122 being killed and 4,362 wounded. 1,755 casualties were suffered by Radetzky, while Mirsky's losses were 2,201 and Skobelev's 1,528.[18]

It had been a spectacular victory, and it has been justly described as inflicting a blow on the Ottoman Empire even more terrible than the fall of Plevna. At a stroke, its last army had been eliminated, and although many thousands of men might still be collected in front of Constantinople, there was no longer any realistic chance that the Russian advance could be halted.

The Great Powers after Plevna

The undeniable prospect of an imminent Russian victory gave the Great Powers a good deal to think about. The prospect of the fall of Plevna alarmed Queen Victoria extremely, and Disraeli was obliged to calm her down, writing to her on November 16:

> Unquestionably the fall of Plevna ... would be a calamity to this country, but it would not be a disgrace ... Now, we have adopted and announced a different policy [from the one of 1854]: one of neutrality, conditional on no British interest being menaced or attacked. We have defined those British interests. The occupation by Russia of Constantinople, or the Dardanelles, would assail one of those interests.[1]

The Cabinet having approved the proposal that a request be made to the Russian government for a promise not to take such a step, Disraeli had to press his reluctant Foreign Secretary to prepare a draft. Derby thought it 'a very awkward paper' but finally produced a draft. It included a paragraph promising continued neutrality if the Russians did not occupy Constantinople, and Disraeli struck this out, to Derby's fury. Ultimately, after a Cabinet meeting, Disraeli prevailed, although Derby made an attempt during the discussion to distinguish between a threatened and an actual occupation of the city; the Prime Minister insisted that either must be a *casus belli*.

The capitulation of Plevna, expected though it was, caused an enormous reaction in Britain. Although the bulk of the press called for mediation, the *Pall Mall Gazette* called for a demonstration, and the *Morning Post* for a declaration of war if hostilities did not end immediately. In all this it was the threat to Constantinople that occupied everyone's attention, as expressed in the bellicose music hall song that gave the word 'jingo' its special meaning. Written by G W Hunt, and performed by 'The Great MacDermott,' it was an immediate success; the Prince of Wales even asked for it to be sung to him at a private audience. There is no evidence to suggest that its sentiments were the product of official encouragement, but they must have reassured Disraeli in his belief that his policy was soundly based on popular feeling. The verses of the song outlined the misdeeds of the 'Russian Bear,' but it was the chorus that caught the public's mood:

> We don't want to fight, but by jingo if we do ...
> We've got the ships, we've got the men, and got the money too!
> We've fought the Bear before, and while we're Britons true,
> The Russian shall not have Constantinople.

When it came to it, Britain certainly had the ships, and no doubt the money; but its ability to put a substantial number of men into the field was much more doubtful. The only force immediately available was in Malta, and was 4,000 strong. The Queen was,

The entrance to the Dardanelles. (Ollier)

A view of Constantinople. (Ollier)

predictably, profoundly affected by the news from Plevna, writing to her daughter, the Crown Princess of Germany, on December 17:

> The fall of Plevna was a bitter pill, a true grief to me who feels too strongly to speak of it! I cannot express in words my indignation. But please God we shall assert our feeling and position[2].

The Queen certainly did manage to express her own feelings, bombarding Disraeli with letters calling for firmness on the part of the Cabinet. He was not to hesitate, she said, about calling for Derby's resignation. Her fear was that doing nothing would reduce Britain to a 'subservient, second rate, cotton spinning power.'

On December 14 Disraeli put to his Cabinet proposals to summon Parliament, to seek a large increase in military spending, and to insist on mediation. Derby strongly objected; his position now was that he did not regard even the occupation of Constantinople as a *casus belli*, an approach which led Northcote, the Chancellor of the Exchequer, to express his concern to Salisbury that there would be 'the most serious consequences if Derby cannot rouse himself to take a lead and give us a line of his own.'[3] Salisbury thought Disraeli's proposals would put Britain on 'the steep slope which leads to war,' and that Constantinople was in fact in no real danger. Another heated Cabinet meeting followed on December 17, and yet another on the following day, when Derby's proposal to call Parliament and ask for money, but not to attempt mediation was rejected in favour of Disraeli's plan; the Prime Minister got his way partly by a threat of his own resignation.

Derby had seen no prospect of mediation being successful, and his attitude was shared elsewhere. Bismarck preferred direct talks between Russia and Turkey, and so did Andrassy. Wellesley reported from St Petersburg that Alexander was in favour of peace, but was not interested in mediation. In fact, the British proposal for this was never delivered, as the Porte formally confirmed its desire that Britain should ask Russia if it would consider overtures for peace. When this was communicated to St Petersburg Gorchakov's reply, on December 29, was that 'Russia desired nothing better than to arrive at peace,' but that the Porte must apply to the Russian commanders in chief in Europe and Asia, who would state the terms required for an armistice.[4]

The British Cabinet continued to meet very frequently although, due to the serious divisions that characterised its discussions, very ineffectually. Not unreasonably, it was anxious to persuade the Russians that armistice negotiations should be between governments rather than generals in the field. Gorchakov was adamant, however, and the Porte was advised to send representatives to the Russian headquarters. At this stage, ironically, both sides were deliberately dragging their feet; the Russians were anxious to press on with their advance to Constantinople while keeping an eye on British intentions as they were clarified after the recall of Parliament on January 17, while the Turks still clung to the hope of active British assistance. It was Layard who was responsible for this, repeatedly displaying such sympathy and encouragement that it is not surprising that the Turks deceived themselves into believing that British intervention was possible. Prince Reuss, the German ambassador, was blunt in his criticism of Layard:

He has never ceased to dissuade the Porte from following the correct path, i.e., that of direct negotiations with Russia, and on the other side, he is urging his own Government, as I learned from speeches made by him, to pursue an active Turkophil policy. I am not alone here in conjecturing that his action will tend considerably to postpone the end of the War, and that this policy will, therefore, have been full of consequences for Turkey.[5]

In his opinion, it was Layard's daily comments to Server Pasha as to the attitude of Britain that led to the postponement of the dispatch of plenipotentiaries to Grand Duke Nicholas.

Queen Victoria's passionate desire to see Britain taking affirmative action was expressed regularly in her correspondence with her Prime Minister; she wrote excitably for instance on January 10:

> She feels she cannot remain sovereign of a country that is letting itself down to kiss the feet of the great barbarians, the retarders of all liberty and civilisation that exists ... Oh, if the Queen were a man, she would like to go and give those Russians, whose word one cannot believe, such a beating. We shall never be friends again till we have it out. This the Queen feels sure of.[6]

On the same day Layard urged that the fleet should be brought nearer to Constantinople, and next day suggested that the Turks be advised to garrison the Bulair lines to defend Gallipoli. Disraeli thought this a good idea, and told the Queen of his intention to propose to the Cabinet on January 12 that the Dardanelles be occupied. He was also at pains to reassure her of the steps being taken to massage the Press, something that the Queen took very seriously. She had been particularly enraged by *The Times*, writing to her daughter:

> Surely you must have known long ago, that *The Times* is a mere tool in the hands of Russia, takes its inspiration from Count Shuvalov, is, I believe, even bribed – and its reports from the seat of war are utterly unreliable, as Colonel Mansfield writes, having been written with only one object, viz for Russia.[7]

Demonstrating that spin doctoring was an art already being practised in the 19th century, Disraeli told her that his secretary, Montague Corry, 'sees the editors of *Telegraph, M.[orning] Post* and *Pall Mall* every day, and guides, instructs and inspires them. And the *Standard* also, though the writers of that print are very dull.'[8]

Layard's violent denunciations of Russia and his explanations and excuses for Turkey in his correspondence with Derby, were repeated to a wide audience. To the Foreign Secretary, he suggested that in relation to the allegations of atrocities by the Circassians, 'the tendency to exaggerate among the Christians and Europeans in this country is the source of infinite mischief: it is impossible to get at the real truth.' In a letter to Lord Lytton, the Viceroy of India, he suggested without any evidence whatever that it was Russia's aim to remove the entire Muslim population from a new Bulgaria.[9] As well as misleading the Turks with his sympathy and advice, Layard also continued to wind up Disraeli. Not that the Prime Minister needed much encouragement; when Parliament

'The Attack on the Redoubt' -- knowledge of the Siege of Plevna penetrated even children's games of the time. (*Illustrated London News*)

met on January 17 he was insulting and threatening by turns when he spoke of Britain's resolve to fight for 'precious interests.'

Meanwhile, the Russian advance towards Adrianople continued. On January 10 the Turks made telegraphic contact with Grand Duke Nicholas, whose reply confirmed that negotiations for an armistice could only take place with him, and that first the bases of peace must be agreed. On January 13 Nicholas sent a telegram to the effect that the bases of peace would be communicated to a person sent with powers to accept them. A meeting should be held for the purpose at Kazanlik. This brought the Ottoman Council of Ministers at last to believe that they must do something, and after a lengthy meeting that day it was agreed to send Server Pasha and Namyk Pasha to Kazanlik on the following day. In fact, they did not leave until January 15, and it was January 19 before they reached their destination, having been delayed by the Russian advance. Two meetings were held with the Grand Duke next day, but matters were only discussed very generally, no specific terms being put forward. Both sides still seemed content to temporise, and it was only the imminence of the Russian occupation of Adrianople that led to a meaningful discussion on January 21, when Nicholas finally spelled out the only terms on which an armistice could be agreed.

HMS *Alexandria*, Hornby's flagship. (*Illustrated London News*)

The Russian terms were stark and it was made clear that they were not negotiable. Bulgaria was to be an autonomous state, including Roumelia. Montenegro was to be independent, with increased territory. Roumania and Serbia were to be independent, the former to have 'an adequate territorial indemnity' and the latter a frontier rectification. Bosnia and Herzegovina were to be autonomous. Turkey was to indemnify Russia for the expenses of the war; the nature of the indemnity, whether territorial or pecuniary, was to be settled later. The question of the Straits was to be settled between the two countries later.

Meanwhile Disraeli was beginning to get his own way with his Cabinet, which met on the afternoon of January 23 and, in the face of bitter objections from Derby, and from Lord Carnarvon, the Colonial Secretary, agreed to send the fleet to Constantinople. Orders went that evening to Admiral Hornby to that effect:

Sail immediately for Dardanelles and proceed with the fleet now with you to Constantinople. Abstain from taking any part in contest between Russia and Turkey, but waterway of straits is to be kept open, and in the event of tumult at Constantinople, protect life and property of British subjects.[10]

Hornby had been at anchor in Besika Bay since the end of June, and he and his officers had settled down to enjoy themselves. There was much shooting to be had, and a pack of beagles was brought out from England on November 10, and before long a number of horses were brought down, enabling the Admiral to go hunting. At the end of December the fleet had been moved to Vourla, the southerly winter gales making the Besika anchorage very dangerous. Hornby (after making fresh arrangements at Vourla for kennels and stables) had gone to Malta, but a week later the deteriorating situation had necessitated his return to the fleet. He was gloomy about the orders to sail, writing to complain to his wife that the vacillation they had revealed showed 'that we are not well commanded, and I do not anticipate much credit will accrue to the country.'[11]

His pessimism was well founded; on the evening of January 24 he was ordered to return to Besika Bay. The reversal was due to information received in London from Layard, setting out the Russian peace terms which the ambassador understood would be accepted. Since the government had just announced that it would seek a vote of monies if the Russians did not put forward peace terms, it was felt that the even graver step of sending the fleet to Constantinople should not now be proceeded with.

In the meantime, however, both Derby and Carnarvon had resigned. Disraeli was perfectly ready to accept both resignations, and the Queen was particularly happy that he should do so; but Dyke, the government chief whip, and Northcote, the Chancellor of the Exchequer, feared the electoral consequences, while Salisbury considered that Derby's departure would be taken to mean that the government meant to go to war. Carnarvon went, but Derby was persuaded to stay; Disraeli would have liked to move him to another post, but the Foreign Secretary was only prepared to continue in that office.

The Queen had expressed her 'immense satisfaction and relief' when told of Derby's resignation, so Disraeli had a considerable task on his hands to assuage her disappointment at the retention of the Foreign Secretary. He wrote to her to tell her that practically every member of the Cabinet wished him to remain, and that his retirement was 'producing disastrous results on the Conservative party, both in Parliament and out of doors; a general disintegration is taking place.'[12] The Queen had to put up with the situation, but she did not hide her regret.

In Parliament, the debate on the motion to add £6m to the Army and Navy estimates began on January 28 and went on for five nights, providing all shades of opinion with an opportunity for an airing, often in most extravagant language. George Trevelyan remarked of the Prime Minister that he had 'never disguised his desire to plunge the nation into war,' while Gladstone, speaking at Oxford on January 30, described the Cabinet as a bag in which 'all the warning winds of heaven are shut up.' Disraeli, hearing of this, described Gladstone as a 'vindictive fiend' rather than a pious Christian. In the end the Government's motion was carried by a comfortable majority.

Meanwhile Disraeli had been hoping for some sort of accord with Austria. Andrassy had made no secret of his belief that he had been deceived by the Russians, but his discontent with the situation did not lead him to accept that a Russian entry into Constantinople was one of the points on which Austria and Britain had agreed to support each other. On the other hand, Andrassy was determined that the Russian terms for peace should be submitted to the Great Powers, and suggested the convening of a conference. To this Gorchakov sent a conciliatory reply, stating that the preliminary

HMS *Sultan* saluting the Turkish flag at Chanak. (*Illustrated London News*)

terms were provisional as far as they concerned Europe. Thereafter, discussions began about the possibility of a conference, and especially about the venue; Gorchakov was not prepared to consider Vienna, suggesting a small German resort such as Baden-Baden.[13]

Although even Derby admitted that there might be circumstances to justify sending the fleet to Constantinople, and there was widespread concern about a possible Russian occupation of the city, the reality was that Britain alone did not possess the military resources to prevent it. The fear of such a step was increased by the news, which reached London on February 1, that the Turks had agreed to an armistice. The deepening crisis would put the divided Cabinet under even greater strain in the days to come. The news that the bases of the armistice had been agreed, but without confirmation of their signature, enhanced fears as to what the Russians were up to, as Derby observed in his diary on that day:

> The unexplained delay causes great suspicion and irritation here, it being thought that the Russians are playing their usual tricks, and that time is being wasted in order to allow of an occupation of Constantinople. Schou. explains it by the difficulty of communication, there being only a field telegraph across the Balkans, which is easily put out of order. But that would not account for our hearing nothing from the Porte.[14]

38

Armistice

The delays during January in getting any armistice talks started had enabled the Russians to achieve what the army in particular wanted – to press on with their advance in order to underline the completeness of their victory. The defeat of Suleiman's army at Philippopolis and Vessil's ignominious surrender at Shipka left only disordered Turkish forces in the path of a Russian advance to Adrianople, and Nicholas wanted to waste no time in capturing the city. On January 22 Gourko's infantry marched off in three echelons, totaling 52 battalions with 128 guns. The first echelon reached Adrianople on January 26; the rest of the force was delayed by the rising of the river. Gourko, in his official report, gave credit to his troops for their remarkable achievement. Between January 6 and 27 they had marched 230 miles in fearful weather, crossing the Maritza at the worst time of the year, and fought a three-day battle:

> My soldiers have marched without a murmur, and almost without repose, tens and hundreds of *versts*; they have carried on their backs provisions for eight days as well as hundreds of cartridges, so that I have not had any trouble about transport; they dragged the artillery across the mountains, and I was thus enabled to descend into the plain with my guns, and finally overtake the enemy.[1]

Russian troops enter Adrianople – note the camels! (*Album della Guerra Russo-Turca del 1877-78*)

Gourko had however, been preceded at Adrianople. The cavalry of Skobelev's advance guard under Major-General Stroukov had set off from Eski Zagra on January 14. This force, which comprised the 1st Brigade of the 1st Cavalry Division, consisted of the 1st Moscow Dragoons, the 1st St Petersburg Lancers, and a *sotnia* of Cossacks. With nine squadrons, Stroukov rode away into the heart of European Turkey. His first objective was the seizure of the two railway lines from Philippopolis and Ternova. The roads he took were covered in ice; on either side lay deep and soft snow. During the first day Stroukov covered 36 miles, reaching Alagda, where he first made contact with the enemy. He discovered that the railway bridge over the Maritza at Semenli was held by a battalion of Turkish infantry, and that reinforcements were expected from Hermanli. Stroukov determined to strike while the iron was hot, and sent forward a squadron of dragoons to reconnoitre and if possible seize the bridge. Driving back the Turks to the middle of the 400 yard long bridge, the dragoons pushed on under heavy fire. They could not, however, reach the far end, and in the end retreated to rejoin their regiment.

Next morning, reckoning that there would be great confusion on the enemy's side, Stroukov pushed forward with his whole force. Seeing them come, the Turks tried to set the woodwork of the bridge on the far side on fire; Stroukov dismounted his leading squadron, and led them over the bridge; the Turks fell back and the dragoons put out the fire. Stroukov reported these events to Skobelev, who sent forward an infantry battalion by a forced march to Ternova in order to secure this key position, which deprived the Turks of the use of the railway in their retreat.

Although he was still thirty miles ahead of the main body of Skobelev's force, Stroukov pushed on. The speed of his advance outran a Turkish force of some 25,000 men from Slivno, under Kerim Pasha, which was struggling to reach Adrianople. As Stroukov neared the city on January 20 he heard the sound of explosions, and was then amazed to receive a deputation from the inhabitants made up of representatives of all the different ethnic communities in Adrianople, begging him to occupy the city to save it from the Bashi-Bazouks. There were, Stroukov was told, a large number of these poised to pillage the city.

Next morning he moved on Adrianople, hardly believing that it would be possible to take the second city of the Ottoman Empire without a blow being struck. But there was no response to his advance from the 32 forts which encircled Adrianople; the garrison, commanded by the ineffable Ahmed Eyoub Pasha, had pulled out, heading for the Chataldja lines in front of Constantinople. On the following day Stroukov received the consuls of Britain, France, Austria and Greece, who congratulated him on having saved the city from the depredations of the Bashi-Bazouks. In return, Stroukov was able to tell them that Skobelev, with his whole force, would reach the city within a few hours.[2]

Since by now the Turkish plenipotentiaries were already at Russian headquarters, it was crucially important to push on, occupying as much territory as possible before any armistice was agreed. On January 22 Stroukov moved out again, heading southwards to Lule-Bourgas, which was taken on January 25. On January 28 he went on towards Constantinople. Behind him, the 2nd Guard Cavalry Division moved towards Gallipoli, occupying unopposed Demetoka and Ouzoun-Keupri. Skobelev, with his advance guard, pressed on down the line of the railway toward the capital.

Turks working on trenches near Gallipoli. (*Illustrated London News*)

Millet, who was still with Gourko, wrote from Adrianople on January 27 a lengthy account of the dreadful sufferings of the long column of civilian fugitives flooding southwards in the direction of Constantinople:

> Seventy miles of utter desolation, seventy long miles strewn with the household effects of many thousand families, seventy weary miles of a continuous, ghastly, sickening panorama of death in every form, and in its most terrible aspect – such is the road from Philippopolis to Hermanli. This route has been for many weeks the theatre of scenes, and here has been enacted a tragedy of such colossal proportions and horrible character, that it is quite impossible for any one who has not witnessed part of it to conceive in the most moderate degree the nature of the diabolical drama.[3]

Millet noted that 'the peculiar nature of the war has made it impossible to avert the partial ruin of the people where the armies have passed,' but he was clear that this catastrophic exodus of the population might have been prevented; the refugees might have been stopped as far back as Sofia if Suleiman had not ordered them on in advance of his retreating army.

When Valentine Baker had reached Gumurdjina he had found Suleiman there, from whom he learned that the Russians, having taken Adrianople, were marching on Constantinople and Gallipoli. This news led him to assume that Britain must now intervene, making the defence of the Bulair lines and Gallipoli of prime importance. Eighteen months earlier Baker had previously paid attention to the defences of the capital, urging the then Minister of War, Redif Pasha, to construct a line of fortifications from Lake Derkos on the Black Sea to Buyuk-Tchekmedji, on the Sea of Marmora. His advice was dismissed, *Redif* pointing out that the Turks would never let the Russians cross the Danube, but even if that occurred, they could never pass the Balkans. 'Why then, should we waste time in throwing up fortifications only thirty miles in front of Constantinople?' he asked.[4]

Baker was not put off by this, and had spent two months studying the very strong position he had identified. Later, the British government had sent a team of engineers to survey the position, but it was not until after war had broken out, and Gourko had demonstrated that the Balkans were passable, that work had hurriedly been put in hand. Even now, it would not have been too late to give the capital a respectable line of defence:

> The great advantage of the Buyuk-Tchekmedji-Derkos position lies in the fact that a long hilly chain extending from sea to sea slopes down by a succession of spurs to the broad valley of the Kara-Sou, and these spurs which cover more than two-thirds of the extent of the whole position, completely command the broad plain which lies in front of them.[5]

The position was thus one of remarkable natural strength. Greene observed that the length of the position was no more than twenty miles, of which twelve miles was occupied by broad lakes extending inland from either shore, while of the remaining eight miles at least half consisted of impassable or difficult swamps, and the rest of almost impenetrable thickets. Behind this line of lakes, swamps and thickets ran the continuous ridge described by Baker, on which had been begun the construction of thirty redoubts:

Russian soldiers in a bazaar at Adrianople. (Ollier)

These redoubts were only half finished, but they still afforded complete protection for infantry; they would have mounted about 150 siege guns and as many more field guns, and their proper garrison would have been 60,000 to 75,000 men. With such a garrison – since the flanks of the line rested on the sea, and could not be turned or invested – these lines might fairly be called impregnable.[6]

However, instead of fortifying the line, work had begun on two entrenched camps behind it; then, once Gourko had retreated, work stopped. When he passed through Constantinople in November, Baker again pointed out the importance of completing the city's defences, but nothing was done.

Baker, convinced that Britain would now be acting 'promptly and energetically,' expected that the Malta garrison would be sent to Bulair and that the fleet would be ordered through the Dardanelles. The 4,000 men from Malta would not, however, be enough to stop the Russians at Bulair, so he asked leave to go there to see what could be done to strengthen the position. After a rather hazardous journey, he arrived at Gallipoli, only to learn of Hornby's arrival and almost immediate departure. Some 3,000 Turkish troops were in the Bulair lines, and Baker immediately disembarked the 5,000 men he had brought with him, while 3,500 more under Redjib Pasha were expected. Having designated the positions to be occupied, Baker set off for Constantinople, where he found that 30,000 men had been collected under Mukhtar, who had taken command of the capital's defences. With the rest of Suleiman's army, amounting to some 25,000 men, due to arrive shortly, Baker advised that the defences could be held for several weeks.

The Council of Ministers had expected that with armistice talks under way, the Russians would halt their advance, but were dismayed to discover that this was not the case. Russian cavalry was reported in Chataldja, only four miles in front of the defensive line. The detailed terms of the armistice were not, at that stage, known; and it was only on the evening of January 31 that news arrived that the Turkish negotiators had agreed that the Buyuk-Tchekmedji-Derkos position should be given up, to form a neutral barrier between the two armies. Next morning Baker saw Raouf Pasha, who confirmed the news. For Baker, after all he had suffered for the Ottoman Empire, it was the last straw:

> Utterly disgusted, and determined not to be a witness of the unnecessary retreat of the Turkish army, I requested immediate permission to return to England on leave of absence, and started for London via Brindisi on the following afternoon.[7]

The Russians had been advancing on all fronts. In the Dobrudja, where Zimmerman had been standing on the defensive immediately after crossing the Danube, it was now considered safe for him to move south. After having had no previous opportunity to distinguish themselves while victories were being won elsewhere, his troops won a victory at Bazardjik on January 27, capturing the town after a brief but bloody encounter. In front of the army of the Tsarevich, however, there was no resistance, the Turkish forces in the Quadrilateral retreating into the fortresses of Rustchuk and Shumla. Pushing forward, the Russians occupied Osman Bazar on January 27, Rasgrad on January 28 and Eski Djuma on the following day. Todleben, with the XII Corps and the 32nd Division, invested Rustchuk and prepared to besiege the place when news came of the armistice

The signing of the armistice at Adrianople. Left to right – General Nepokoitschitsky,
Server Pasha, Nelidof, Grand Duke Nicholas, Namyl Pasha. (*Russes et Turcs*)

that had been signed on January 31. Rustchuk was surrendered, in accordance with the
agreed terms, on February 20.[8]

Meanwhile, away to the west, the Turks had had a new enemy to face. On December
12, after the news of the fall of Plevna, Serbia declared war. Ever since hostilities had
begun in April 1877, the Serbian army had been preparing to enter the war. When
Prince Milan sent the formal declaration of war, the reasons given were the ill treatment
of refugees and the alleged Turkish intrigues against Serbia; but the real reason was the
chance that Serbia now had to gain independence and perhaps territory.

The Serbian Army consisted of about 70,000 infantry and 3,000 cavalry, with 250
guns, organized in five corps. It effectively covered the Russian right, and rear, after the
taking of Sofia. In the forty-eight days during which it moved forward, the Serbian army
claimed the capture of thirty-nine fortified positions The taking of the fortress of Nish
was its greatest achievement, the garrison of 7,000 surrendering after six days of heavy
fighting, in which the Serbs sustained total casualties of some 1,500 men. The Serbs also
could claim the capture of seven other towns, with 250 guns, several thousand rifles and
3,000 prisoners.[9]

Advancing from Nish, the Serbs encountered a force that had been sent to relieve the fortress, which had fallen back subsequently to Pristina. Splitting into two columns, the Serbs completely surrounded the Turkish force, and were preparing to attack when news came of the armistice, and hostilities were suspended.

Meanwhile the Roumanians were trying to strengthen their position. After the fall of Plevna, while the Russian forces were moving southward, it was agreed that the Roumanian army should take Widdin as its objective. Prince Charles had applied for this, partly because it meant only short lines of communication but principally because he wanted to have some territorial asset in hand when it came to bargaining at the end of the war. Under the command of General Haralambie, a force of 15,000 infantry, 2,000 cavalry and 84 guns advanced towards Widdin, attacking the advanced Turkish positions around the city on January 24. After bitter house to house fighting in the villages of Tatardjik and Rupca, the Turks were driven back into the city. Time was running out; an armistice was clearly imminent, and there was no time to embark on a siege. An attempt was made to reduce the city by a bombardment from both sides of the Danube, but before it could take effect news came of the signing of the armistice on January 31.

In Asia, as the war drew to its close, the Russians made a final attempt to capture Batum. Oklobju, thwarted in his attempts to seize the place, had remained on the defensive, and posed so little threat that the Turks withdrew a large number of regular troops to strengthen their forces in Bulgaria. Oklobju was succeeded by Denibekov, who was ordered in January 1878 to prepare an attack. The forces available were reinforced, and the aggressive Komarov was put in command. On January 30 he launched a vigorous assault on the Turkish positions, having made the most extensive preparation including the construction of roads through the forest to enable artillery to be brought up. It was all to no avail:

> The valley of the Kintrish became a veritable valley of death; for once in the open the guns of the Turkish men of war could play upon their flank, whilst before them were the trenches, rising tier upon tier to the redoubts crowning the heights.[10]

Throughout the war, the Turks had dominated the Black Sea by means of their powerful fleet. Although the Russians had fitted out four unarmed vessels, equipping them with two Krupp 9 cm and five 6 inch mortars, and adapting their boats for use as torpedo launches, they could not challenge the Turkish command of the sea. Two were based in Sebastopol and two in Odessa, and they did succeed in capturing a number of colliers used for resupplying the Turkish fleet. The Turks could, however, safely use the sea for the movement of men, munitions and stores to Bulgaria or Asia Minor by the transports and ironclads of the fleet. Although no especially brilliant feats were achieved, the Turks had been able to land, and subsequently withdraw, their troops at Soukhom Kaleh; while, as has been seen, the fleet played a significant part in the defence of Batum. Hobart, with perhaps understandable exaggeration, claimed that 'if the Russians could have disposed of the Turkish fleet they would have easily taken Batum.'[11]

Namyk and Server, negotiating the armistice at Adrianople, felt in the end that they had no option but to accept the terms laid down by the Russians. In addition to accepting all the bases for a peace treaty prescribed by the Grand Duke, they agreed to surrender the fortresses of Widdin, Rustchuk and Silistria (with the curious option of withdrawing their matériel or selling it to the Russians). The Russians were to occupy Bourgas and Midia on the Black Sea coast, and could use these ports to resupply their army. The Turkish blockade of the Russian Black Sea ports was to be lifted. Finally, the Buyuk-Tchekmedji position was to be abandoned.[12] These terms effectively precluded any resumption of hostilities should the negotiations for the peace treaty be stalled, leaving the Turks with virtually no cards in their hand to play.

39

San Stefano

The severity of the terms imposed by the Russians reflected the loss of influence of Gorchakov who, once the war had begun, was sidelined in Bucharest; in the position in which he found himself he felt, he said, like 'a station master.' Real authority was now to be found at the Tsar's military headquarters; Gorchakov was not even invited to a meeting held there at the end of November to discuss the peace terms to be demanded.[1] The military leaders played their cards very close to their chest; the Roumanians were not invited to participate in the armistice negotiations, and Prince Charles was refused a copy of the armistice agreement. When, after Plevna, the Tsar returned to St Petersburg, the Foreign Ministry representative at army headquarters complained of being left uninformed and uninstructed.

The full details of the armistice terms did not reach London until February 8. The debate in Parliament had meanwhile taken place, and the Cabinet, now in a state of the greatest alarm, was meeting almost daily. Public opinion grew daily more excitable, as did Queen Victoria, insisting that Disraeli make good his promise to prevent by force the occupation of Constantinople:

> She cannot speak strongly enough, for Great Britain's safety and honour are at stake … She cannot rest day or night till she hears that strong measures are taken to carry out these principles.[2]

On February 8, compelled by the pressure of events to do something, the Cabinet grasped the nettle and sent orders to Hornby to proceed to Constantinople 'to protect life and property of British subjects,' an earlier attempt to induce Austria and Italy to join a combined naval entry into the Sea of Marmora having proved abortive. Hornby, who told his wife that he 'had just ended a nice little run with the beagles,' did not get the order until the following day, when he was told that the ambassador had been directed to ensure that the necessary orders had gone to the Dardanelles forts to allow his passage. Hornby set off at once, sending *Salamis* on ahead to get Layard's instructions; but to his dismay, she returned, to say that there were no orders, and that the local commander had protested against the fleet's entry. Hornby ruefully reflected that he 'had been rather too quick, and made a mess of it.'

> Well, luckily it was dark, and there was no one to see our movements except the lookout men on the lower forts, six miles below us. So we turned round and anchored at the mouth of the Straits.[3]

Without permission, and in the face of the reminder that to proceed was a breach of international law, Hornby felt obliged to retreat once more:

The British fleet at Volo. (Ollier)

As it was not yet daylight, and as it was clear the Government telegram could not have reached the Ambassador, I thought it was no use stopping there, looking as if we wanted to go up and couldn't, so we weighed, and at daylight were to be seen returning majestically to our own quarters.[4]

While this further humiliating débacle was taking place, Gorchakov had learned of the dispatch of the fleet, and of the previous suggestion of a joint naval demonstration. He instructed Shuvalov that as this step was being taken to protect the subjects of the nations concerned, the Russian government would send part of its army into the capital for the similar purpose of protecting Christian life and property. Salisbury, for much of the time a relatively pacific influence in the Cabinet, was concerned about Britain appearing ridiculous, urging Disraeli to order the fleet to force its way in. On February 11 the Admiralty order to do so went to Hornby, instructing him to enter the Straits on the morning of February 15:

If fired upon by Forts and ships struck, return fire – but do not wait to silence Forts, unless absolutely necessary to insure passage into Sea of Marmora. Take what force you consider necessary, and take up position near Constantinople – safe from surprise and attack.[5]

This time, after a courtly exchange of letters with Hussein Pasha, the Governor General of the Dardanelles, Hornby and his fleet entered the Narrows without incident,

Count Andrassy, Austria's Foreign Minister. (Ollier)

albeit in thick and snowy weather. There was a brief delay when the ironclad *Alexandra* briefly went aground; but she was soon got off, and during February 14 Hornby went on with *Alexandra, Achilles, Sultan* and *Temeraire*:

> Early next morning they found themselves off Constantinople, that most beautiful of all cities as seen from the sea in the early morning, the dark cypresses rising about the uneven red tiled roofs, and, still higher, the white minarets standing out against the sky.[6]

Andrassy, meanwhile, was struggling to maintain some initiative in the complex diplomatic manoeuvres that followed the end of the fighting, and on February 4 he formally invited the Great Powers to a conference at Vienna. France, Italy and Britain were quick to accept. Bismarck, who had no great interest in the precise terms of settlement, was concerned only that they should be agreeable to both Austria and Russia. In particular, he wanted to secure Andrassy's position, as Herbert Bismarck explained to Bülow on February 2:

> We cannot be certain that Andrassy's successor will not belong to one of the anti-German parties in Austria. We therefore wish to maintain Count Andrassy in office.[7]

Bismarck certainly did not want to oppose Russia either, for fear of driving her into the arms of a revanchist France. This even handed approach to his two allies led him to reject Andrassy's suggestion of an Austro-German defensive alliance. It would certainly be seen in Russia as a hostile act, while William's affection for his nephew Alexander in any case precluded such a deal. It was to push the peacemaking forward, therefore, that Bismarck made his speech to the Reichstag on February 19, publicly setting out his own position and famously likening himself to 'the honest broker' who gets the business done.

Next day, after hearing from his ambassador in London that an early meeting of the proposed conference was the last chance of avoiding war, Bismarck thought he had better give Gorchakov a nudge, writing to Schweinitz in St Petersburg:

> The postponement of the conference, which according to your telegram, No. 45, is imminent, may produce far reaching consequences. Prince Gorchakov is quite aware what he is about and does not need our advice; but I beg that you will give the foregoing facts to him.[8]

Discussions about the date and venue of a conference continued. The second week of March was seen as too soon by Gorchakov, who also said that he would only attend if Bismarck and Derby did so as well.

While these Great Power contacts continued, the situation between Russia and Britain remained on a knife edge. In response to continued threats of a Russian occupation of Constantinople unless the fleet withdrew, Layard and Hornby decided that it would be less provocative to move the fleet from the Princes' Islands, where it lay at anchor, to Mondania Bay, about ten miles further off. Meanwhile the Sultan declined a secret British offer to buy the four most powerful Turkish ironclads, suggesting as an

The headquarters of Grand Duke Nicholas at San Stefano. (Strantz)

alternative an alliance, which Layard passed on. Layard, Hornby and Dickson were all in favour of military cooperation with the Turks; their concern was the defence of Bulair. However, on February 18 Gorchakov undertook not to occupy Gallipoli or the lines of Bulair, adding that he expected that in return no British troops would be landed. In a sense, both sides were bluffing; the Russians could really not afford to provoke a war, while the British military threat was negligible.

Although this understanding appeared to have averted war for the moment, the danger was by no means past. The Russians now threatened the Turks with an occupation of Constantinople unless the Turkish fleet was surrendered; the British response was to threaten the withdrawal of their ambassador and a refusal to attend the conference if the Russians moved in without the Sultan's consent. At the same time Disraeli maintained his contact with Andrassy; the Austrian concern was to know how much might be a British subsidy, in the event of war with Russia, and Disraeli made optimistic noises about this. However, the most he could get from his Cabinet was agreement to guarantee an Austrian loan rather than a subsidy.[9] Seeking some idea of Bismarck's attitude in case of war, all Disraeli got was an assurance of German neutrality. When Russell, the British ambassador in Berlin, suggested that such neutrality benefited Russia more than Austria, Bismarck denied it:

> The object of the strictly neutral position he wished to observe was to be able to give his support to a peaceful issue at the first favourable moment. At Gastein he had promised Count Andrassy that he would 'befriend' him and that promise was sacred. Besides which the sympathies of the people of Germany were for Austria and in opposition to the Russian sympathies of the reigning families in Germany.[10]

On February 18 he again reassured Russell, and repeated his earlier suggestions that Britain should occupy Egypt, which he saw, together with an Austrian occupation of Bosnia and Herzegovina, as a way of solving the Eastern Question.

As February drew to a close it became evident that the only generally acceptable location for the conference would be Berlin, and at the beginning of March this was agreed by Britain, and by Germany, although Bismarck expressed his reluctance. Russia, on the other hand, agreed more readily, which suggested to both London and Vienna that it was an attempt to buy time while imposing harsh terms on the Turks. The negotiations between the two belligerents were being conducted at San Stefano, about six miles from the outer walls of Constantinople; in an effort to defuse the crisis over the Turkish fleet the Sultan had agreed in response to a demand by the Grand Duke to the occupation of San Stefano on February 23 by 10,000 Russian troops.[11]

It was altogether a most peculiar situation and an extremely dangerous one, in which a trifling incident could have the most far reaching consequences. The Russians, now camped close to the capital, were while engaged in negotiations with the Ottoman Empire to end the war, at the same time evidently on the brink of another. There is no doubt that Queen Victoria, whose ironclads lay at anchor within easy reach of the city, wanted to go to war with Russia, and her Prime Minister's warlike ambitions had never been concealed. Disraeli may have been rather more circumspect than the Queen, due principally to the opposition he encountered in his Cabinet; but he had readily taken on board the inflammatory content of the advice he received from Layard. As long ago

The house at San Stefano at which the treaty was signed. (Ollier)

The Russian Imperial Guard entering San Stefano. (Ollier)

The saloon of Grand Duke Nicholas at San Stefano. (Ollier)

as August 6 of the previous year he had speculated to his ambassador as to what might develop:

> If there is 'a second campaign,' I have the greatest hopes this country will interfere and pronounce its veto against a war of extermination, and the dark designs of a secret partition, from which the spirit of the 19th century recoils. As we have command of the sea, why should not a British *corps d'armée* (via Batum) march into Armenia and even occupy Tiflis? We might send another to Varna and act on the Russian flank.[12]

But that had been written at a time when all was not going well for the Russians; now, with the war duly won, everything turned on the negotiations at San Stefano and their outcome, and the way in which this outcome was received by the Great Powers.

The Russian delegation at the peace talks was led by Ignatiev, itself a circumstance to cause uneasiness on the part of the British government. The question for the Russians was how high to pitch their demands of an enemy so comprehensively defeated that it must accept virtually whatever terms it could. The Russian government was perfectly aware that the negotiations at San Stefano were not being conducted in a vacuum. However much it may have resented the fact that the terms of peace would be reviewed one way or another by the Great Powers, this was the reality of the situation. To settle on very harsh terms, which were then modified in the face of pressure from the other Powers, was to expose Russia to the risk of a humiliating climbdown. Gorchakov was aware of this; in the discussions in St Petersburg before Ignatiev set off to negotiate, he

Illuminations arch over Nevsky Prospect, St Petersburg, to celebrate peace. (Ollier)

Signing the treaty of peace at San Stefano. (Ollier)

Grand Duke Nicholas is greeted by the Sultan at the Dolmabahce palace. (Strantz)

had recommended that a more general protocol should be agreed with the Turks, leaving him with greater flexibility to deal with a final settlement with the other interested Great Powers.

On the other hand, it was not altogether surprising that Ignatiev, like many in Russia and particularly the military leadership, took the view that it would be best to strike as hard a bargain as possible in the light of its victory, and then see what must be conceded from that position of advantage. It was, however, unwise; as Professor Medlicott wrote in his account of the Congress of Berlin, 'it is difficult today to regard the treaty [of San Stefano] as anything but a blunder of the first magnitude.'[13] What the terms might be had already caused profound uneasiness in London; Derby told Shuvalov that it was essential' that the British government be told of them with as little delay as possible. Disraeli severely criticised the Foreign Secretary for the civility of the enquiry, to which Derby huffily replied that he 'did not understand that it was the desire of the Cabinet to shape their enquiry so as to bring about a refusal to answer it.'[14]

The Treaty of San Stefano was signed on March 3. Ignatiev then went to Constantinople to obtain its ratification from Abdul Hamid, before returning to St Petersburg on March 17. Gorchakov caused a good deal of alarm in London by continuing to refuse a reply to Derby's request on the grounds that it would be dangerous to give an incomplete version of the terms, and it was not until March 23 that these were officially received by the British government. This ensured that in any event their reception would be extremely hostile; before that time a lot had happened in London and elsewhere.

The final terms of the treaty were indeed extremely harsh. The first articles brought substantial increases of territory to both Serbia and Montenegro, whose independence was recognised, as was that of Roumania. Six articles dealt with Bulgaria, creating an autonomous principality with a Christian government. It was to be a 'Big Bulgaria,' so much objected to by Britain and Austria, encompassing most of Macedonia together with the provinces of Bulgaria and Eastern Roumelia; the territory stretched west to include Monastir and Lake Ochridon, south to the Aegean and east to the Black Sea. Territorially it was a great deal larger than had been proposed in 1876. It was to be garrisoned by 50,000 Russian troops for two years. Its size meant that the Russians were certainly in breach of their agreement with the Austrians. The Russians could argue, with some convincing evidence, that ethnically the boundaries were justifiable; but this was not of much concern to those such as Andrassy and Disraeli who saw the whole thing in terms of European power politics.[15] Russia's war indemnity was to be 1,410m roubles, but since Turkey did not have the money, in lieu of 1,100m roubles the Dobrudja was to be assigned to Russia, (with the right to exchange it for that part of Bessarabia transferred in 1856) together with a wide swathe of territory in Asia, including Ardahan, Kars, Batum and Bayazid.[16]

40

The Congress of Berlin

Although Gorchakov had stoutly declined to release the terms of San Stefano until they had been officially ratified, they were known unofficially, and the governments of the other Great Powers reacted strongly. The conclusion of the treaty concentrated their minds, and Austria brought forward a revised proposal for the congress to be held in Berlin. This followed a suggestion from Gorchakov, to which Bismarck had no objection. France and Italy agreed as well and so, provisionally, did Britain. Derby told Parliament that British acceptance was subject to the submission of the whole of the treaty to the congress. He told Münster on March 6 of another concern, as the ambassador reported to Berlin:

> Lord Derby also fears that public opinion might imagine (rightly or wrongly he would not say), that the congress, if held in Berlin, would assume a more Russian complexion. If it were certain that Prince Bismarck was to be its President, much of the distrust concerning it would disappear; but there was a fear that out of courtesy and under pressure of his other engagements Prince Bismarck would concede the office of President to Prince Gorchakov, and this was not desired.[1]

What was evident to everyone concerned was that a great deal of negotiating would have to be done to get all parties to Berlin with a respectable chance of getting a generally acceptable settlement. Bismarck, for his part, made it clear that he would insist that no questions should be discussed that did not arise immediately out of the terms of the treaty. He would himself have preferred that a congress be held at Baden-Baden rather than Berlin, since he disliked the idea that he would be saddled with a certain amount of responsibility. He also made it clear that there could be no congress without British participation.[2]

The potential sticking point was Britain's insistence that the whole of the treaty must be before the congress, to which Gorchakov replied with an evasive answer on March 19. In the meantime the risk of war between Russia and Britain appeared during March to be increasing, both sides actively making preparations. Among these was an attempt by Disraeli to create a league to protect common Mediterranean interests, consisting of Britain, France, Austria, Italy and Greece, which his Cabinet received with scepticism. He also raised the desirability of obtaining a naval station in the Eastern Mediterranean to protect British maritime interests, with which the Cabinet (but not Derby) did agree. On March 27 Disraeli went further, proposing to the Cabinet that the reserves should be called out, troops brought from India, and suitable naval stations be occupied (apparently Alexandretta and Cyprus). The Cabinet approved the calling out of the reserves, and also in principle the other proposals. Disraeli, like Gorchakov, was playing with fire; he cannot have been surprised that at the end of the Cabinet meeting Derby asked Northcote to give Disraeli his resignation. He was replaced by Salisbury, whose position at the India Office was taken by Hardy, the Secretary of State for War. The latter was succeeded by Frederick Stanley, Derby's younger brother.[3] Derby, whose health had been affected by the long struggle to avoid war, went with a good deal of relief.

At Constantinople, Layard and Hornby were getting ready for war. The ambassador was told by Abdul Hamid that if given advance notice Turkey would fight alongside Britain. The admiral was preparing plans to carry the war into the Black Sea, as he explained to the Admiralty:

> If I went, I should try to go up by night, taking as many colliers as I could. My object would be to prevent the Russians communicating with Sulina, Kunstedje, Varna, Bourgas and Midia … If two or three fast corvettes, say honest 12-knot ships, could be sent up by night, they would be very useful. I have nothing of the sort here at present.[4]

He was also concerned with the safety of Gallipoli; his second in command, Sir Edmund Commerell, was planning, with part of the fleet, to operate in cooperation with the Turkish army if the Russians made a move there, and this was expressly approved by the Admiralty.

Meanwhile Salisbury communicated to all the Great Powers a circular setting out the British position on San Stefano, which argued that signatories to the treaties of 1856 and 1871 could not lawfully withdraw from their obligations unilaterally; that the effect of the treaty was the suppression of Turkish independence; and that it was not compatible with British interests. The firm note which it struck ensured a favourable reception in Britain; Gorchakov and Shuvalov were not at all happy about it, the former complaining that the circular stated what Britain did not want, but not what it did want. This was a view shared by Andrassy.[5]

Throughout April Disraeli pursued his discussions with the Austrians, but Andrassy was reluctant to commit himself to anything like the extent that Disraeli required, even after a direct question was put on April 20 as to Austrian willingness to insist on limiting the new Bulgaria to the region north of the Balkans. By the end of the month the discussions petered out. Meanwhile another effort was made to defuse the situation that existed at Constantinople when Bismarck was asked to mediate the withdrawal of the Russian army and the British fleet from their proximity to the capital. Both sides were keen on such a deal, although neither could be seen to suggest it, the British because Hornby's fleet was not of much use where it was, and the Russians because their troops were in a decidedly exposed position. The suggestion was that the fleet should return to Besika Bay, and the Russian army should retire to Adrianople. Bismarck agreed to help, adopting the proposal as his own, but the negotiations beame bogged down in detail, and in the end neither force was withdrawn until after the Congress of Berlin.[6]

Shuvalov, who with Derby had worked tirelessly to avoid a warlike situation from developing, was now deprived of the steady flow of Cabinet information which arose from his equivocal relationship with Lady Derby. Salisbury was polite but cold, at first declining for the moment even to state how Britain wished to revise the San Stefano treaty. The new Foreign Secretary was, however, sympathetic to Shuvalov's plan to go back to St Petersburg to discuss the situation at first hand, not least because he felt that if Gorchakov retired, as seemed likely, he would much prefer Shuvalov to succeed him

The British fleet passing through the Dardanelles. (Ollier)

rather than Ignatiev. Accordingly, he relented, and gave the ambassador a note of the British conditions; the removal of Bulgaria from the Aegean, support for Greece, and the preservation of Turkish independence. Bulgaria was to be limited to the north of the Balkans; Russian territorial claims in Armenia were to be reduced; and the position as to the war indemnity clarified. Shuvalov was to be away for two weeks; he pleaded that nothing controversial should be done in that time.

The reference to Greece was significant. The Greeks, unlike the Serbs, had taken no part in the war, and were beginning to regret the fact, as it appeared that they might not make the kind of territorial gains that they desired, particularly in Thessaly. In February the Greek government announced that it had 'resolved to occupy provisionally with its army the Greek provinces of Turkey'.[7] This particular scavenger had, however, left it too late; there would be no support forthcoming for an attack on Turkey at this time, and the government climbed down on an assurance that 'an Hellenic question be discussed at the Congress.' Notwithstanding this, there were insurrectionary movements in Thessaly which continued until May. The territorial arrangements of the Treaty of San Stefano were, of course, extremely disagreeable to Greece.

Shuvalov's trip to St Petersburg was of crucial importance; it has been said that 'the question of peace or war rested temporarily in the hands of a skilful, ambitious, and mildly unscrupulous ambassador,' and this was certainly the case. Having seen Bismarck *en route* he arrived at St Petersburg on May 12. He found the Russian capital in a considerable state of excitement, but in spite of this he achieved a good deal. Through Loftus, he obtained a British assurance that the provisions as to Serbia and Montenegro would not be interfered with if Britain got her way on other matters; and he overcame Ignatiev's influence with Alexander to get agreement to a limited Bulgaria. On his way back through Berlin, therefore, Shuvalov asked Bülow now to move to establish a formula for the Congress; Bismarck agreed to this, the basis being a 'free discussion of the entire Treaty of San Stefano.'[8]

The proposals which Shuvalov brought back formed the basis of an Anglo-Russian accord, the terms of which were quickly agreed. Russia agreed effectively with the British position as to a divided Bulgaria, the boundary of which was to be the line of the Balkans. The northern part was to be politically autonomous, while the southern part administratively so. In Asia, Bayazid was to be restored to Turkey; the San Stefano provisions for Montenegro and Bessarabia were to remain. Britain accepted the terms of Bismarck's invitation to the Congress. The agreement, in spite of the reservations of Disraeli and the Queen, was signed on May 30.[9]

Events now moved swiftly. On June 4 an Anglo-Turkish Convention was concluded, by which if Russia retained at the Congress her conquests in Asia, Britain would defend the Ottoman Empire against further attack, and would be allowed to occupy Cyprus.

This was to remain a secret until the Congress had completed its deliberations, although it appears that in fact its terms were not as much of a surprise as had been thought; hints had been dropped earlier, especially to the French, the power that was most likely to be concerned with Britain's acquisition of a key point in the Middle East. Finally, on June 6 an Anglo-Austrian agreement was signed. This secured Austrian support for the British position as to the boundaries of Bulgaria, British support for Austria's position as to Bosnia and Herzegovina (whatever that turned out finally to be) and an agreement to cooperate in negotiations over the withdrawal of the Russian army.[10]

With these agreements behind the curtain having been concluded, the way was clear for the opening of the Congress. The British delegation was led by Disraeli, supported by Salisbury and Lord Odo Russell. Disraeli was handicapped by his imperfect command of French, and was persuaded by his colleagues that he should therefore address the Congress in English. Count Münster offered Bismarck an insight into the personalities involved, and in particular the Prime Minister:

> Your Highness will find it very difficult to keep up a serious conversation with this very vain man, who is already showing the weakness of age. At the same time he frequently expresses witty and illuminating ideas, but fails in the higher conception – moral grip. His Private Secretary, Mr Montagu Corry, is devoted to his Chief. He is a very pleasant man, but is vain, and spoilt by Society. He has great influence with Lord Beaconsfield. He uses every bit of gossip to retain his influence with his aged Chief, and is therefore to be handled with great caution ... Lord Salisbury is known to Your Highness. His experience at Constantinople and during late years has been of the greatest use to him. Before long he will be Prime Minister, and a leading figure in England.[11]

Keeping the road clear for the guests to the banquet at the Royal Palace, Berlin. (Ollier)

The Congress which opened on June 13 has been described as 'one of the most brilliant political assemblies of modern times, not unworthy of comparison with the congresses of Vienna and Paris,' and those participating included most of Europe's leading statesmen.[12] Bismarck led the German delegation, with Bülow and Prince Hohenlohe, then serving as ambassador in Paris. Gorchakov, in spite of his infirmity, was the first member of the Russian delegation, although frequently Shuvalov, the second Russian member, was effectively its leader. Salisbury unkindly observed of Gorchakov that 'if some kindly fit of gout would take him off we would move much faster.' The third of the Russians was Oubril, their ambassador in Berlin. The flamboyant Andrassy led the Austrian delegation, supported by Count Karolyi, the ambassador at Berlin, and Baron Haymerlé. The French delegates were Waddington, the Foreign Minister, and Count Saint Vallier, the ambassador to Berlin. From Italy came Count Corti, the Foreign Minister, and Count de Launay, the ambassador to Berlin. The composition of the Turkish delegation had caused some difficulty at Constantinople, where it was decided that the responsibility for what could not be other than an unfortunate outcome should not be taken by a pure Turk. Accordingly, the chief of the delegation was a Phanariot Greek, Caratheodory Pasha. The second delegate was Sadullah Bey, the ambassador at Berlin, and the third was the unfortunate Mehemet Ali – unfortunate because Bismarck appeared greatly to resent a German-born individual representing Turkey. Indeed, Bismarck throughout treated the Turkish delegation disrespectfully, making it clear that the function of the congress was not to save territory for the Turks but to ensure international peace.[13]

Although much had been done to hammer out agreements between the Great Powers before the Congress assembled, there were still a number of key issues that remained to be

The sitting of the Congress of Berlin. (Ollier)

Crowd outside the Radziwill Palace, waiting to see the
plenipotentiaries to the Congress of Berlin. (Ollier)

settled. Of these, perhaps the most important was the evolution of an agreement between
Austria and Russia. In addition there were the questions of the Russian occupation of
Bulgaria, the Straits issue, the future status of Batum, Armenian reform and of course
the Cyprus Convention. Even where understandings had been reached beforehand, the
Russians and Turks were prepared to argue every point. Nor had other key relationships
been clearly defined, such as that between Austria and Turkey.[14]

There were also a number of peripheral issues, such as the Roumanian treatment
of the Jews. Since 1866 Austria, England, France and Germany had been pressing the
Roumanian government to improve the condition of the Jews, and latterly Germany
had been particularly active. As to Serbia, deserted by the Russians, there was no option
but to seek Austrian support; this, Andrassy was prepared to give, but only on his terms.
Then there were the ambitions of Greece, which were supported by the French, not least
because it gave them something to do beyond listening, and agreeing with what was
decided by others.

All this meant that Bismarck had, as president of the Congress, a lot of work to do.
When the delegates arrived, they were greeted by a Chancellor unfamiliar in appearance,
Bismarck having unexpectedly grown a beard. He was hopeful that a week or ten days
would suffice to produce a general agreement but it took all his considerable skill to
achieve the compromises necessary to keep the Congress moving. The most difficult
question was of course the future of Bulgaria, and Bismarck put that first on the
agenda. Discussion of the issue effectively began on June 17; the British attitude was
uncompromising, due to the publication in the London *Globe* of the terms of the Anglo-
Russian agreement, which had caused public fury at home to which Disraeli felt obliged

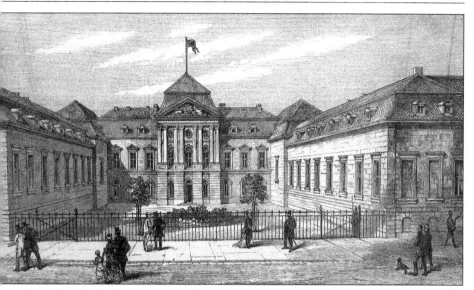

The Radziwill Palace, meeting place of the Congress of Berlin. (*Illustrated London News*)

to respond. Over the next nine days, the issue was hotly discussed. Disraeli told Corti that he took 'the gloomiest view of affairs' and that if the British view did not prevail, he would wreck the Congress. He chose Corti, because the latter was well regarded by Bismarck, for whom the message was intended. Famously, Disraeli put it about that he had ordered a special train to enable him to stage a theatrical departure. Bismarck took this calmly, and visited Disraeli to broker an agreement as to the frontiers of the new Bulgaria, whereby the Sanjak of Sofia and the port of Varna would be included.

After the Bulgarian question had been settled, Bismarck, who had now shaved off his beard, proposed that the boundary changes affecting Bosnia, Montenegro, Serbia and Roumania should be next on the agenda. Andrassy was concerned to achieve the right to occupy Bosnia and Herzegovina but only if this was proposed by another of the Powers; he did not want it to be Germany's suggestion, however, because he did not want to appear to be publicly beholden to Germany or, if it came to that, to Russia. In part his problem was domestic, because in Austria and Hungary there was a strong body of opinion that was opposed to the inclusion of more Slavs within the Empire. Bismarck sardonically observed:

> I have heard of people refusing to eat their pigeon unless it was shot and roasted for them, but I have never heard of any one refusing to eat it unless his jaws were forced open and it was pushed down his throat.[15]

Andrassy got his way; in return for his support to Britain during the discussions on Bulgaria, Salisbury proposed the occupation of Bosnia and Herzegovina, seconded by Bismarck and it was generally agreed.

The question of Russia's Asiatic acquisitions had been largely covered by the agreement with Britain, except for the status of Batum. Salisbury now threatened to propose a change in the regulations affecting the Straits if Russia did not give up the

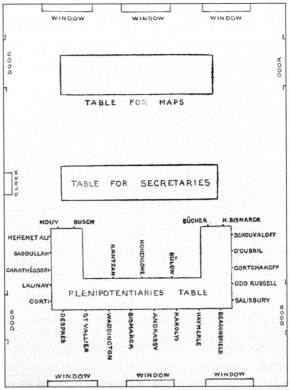

Plan of the hall of the Congress of Berlin, showing the seats
of the plenipotentiaries. (*Illustrated London News*)

port; ultimately, after the intervention of both Gorchakov, who spoke to Disraeli, and Bismarck, it was agreed that Batum should become a free port. Meanwhile the existence of the Cyprus Convention, with which Batum's future was connected, began to be generally known. The Turkish government refused at first to issue a *firman* permitting the immediate occupation of the island by Britain, but was finally persuaded to do so on July 6. Time was pressing and Salisbury now had to hasten to Waddington to calm French reactions to the occupation of Cyprus; at Bismarck's suggestion, Salisbury assured Waddington that Britain would leave France a free hand in Tunis, and this was enough to pacify the French Foreign Minister.

Meanwhile the other territorial questions had been settled. Russia got back Bessarabia, and Roumania got the Dobrudja as compensation. Serbia gained territory to the south-east, and Montenegro got Antivari. For the Greeks, however, there was no immediate satisfaction; all that the Congress did was to invite Turkey to reach an agreement with Greece as to any frontier adjustments.

The Congress concluded on July 13. Disraeli and Salisbury, claiming that they had achieved peace with honour, were welcomed back to London as the heroes of the hour. In spite of his almost criminal recklessness in bringing Britain to the edge of war with Russia, Disraeli had got away with it, and was rewarded with the Order of the Garter from a grateful monarch. And perhaps he deserved it; as Bismarck observed: 'der alte

Jude, das ist der Mann.' In spite of Münster's warning, the two men had got on well together, and could reasonably claim to have been responsible between them for winding up the Russo-Turkish War.

Professor Medlicott has pointed out that the 'real clue to the proceedings and decisions' of the Congress of Berlin was to be found in the agitated state of public opinion in various countries, and especially in Austria, Russia and Britain:

> The determining factor in the various compromises arrived at was the desire of all the governments to appease this public excitement without recourse to war. The concentration of prestige and ability tended, on the whole, to have a steadying effect on the deliberations ... only Bismarck, and perhaps Beaconsfield during the first fortnight, succeeded in establishing over the other delegates something of the personal ascendancy they enjoyed in their own cabinets. Bismarck's vast reputation and achievements would have made him, in any circumstances, the outstanding personality, but the position of president gave him additional prestige which he exploited to the full. The other delegates were soon to find that his sweet voice and careful enunciation could not long disguise his determination to speak with the most outrageous bluntness wherever the acceleration of business made it necessary.[16]

The Roumanians had good reason to feel particularly discontented with the final settlement. After the Treaty of San Stefano they had protested about the provision by which Russia reserved the right to cede the Dobrudja to Roumania in exchange for Bessarabia. The Russian response was to occupy Bessarabia with far more troops than were required to protect the lines of communication, and to threaten that if Roumania refused to agree to the proposed exchange, the whole country would be occupied and the army disarmed. Prince Ghica, the Roumanian envoy in St Petersburg, took the matter up with Gorchakov, complaining that this was a breach of the convention that Russia would protect Roumania's integrity. Prince Charles, in his memoirs, recorded the strikingly discreditable and disingenuous response:

> Prince Gorchakov gave Prince Ghica the following curious explanation: when Russia signed the convention in view of a war against Turkey, she undertook by that article to defend the integrity of the Roumanian territory only against the Turks. The prescriptions of this article have no reference to Russia and her relations with Roumania.[17]

In Berlin, Roumania was allowed only to make a formal protest before the Treaty ratified the exchange.

For Turkey, the overall outcome, if less catastrophic than the Treaty of San Stefano, was of course seriously prejudicial. As Count Corti observed of the negotiations in Berlin: 'Everybody was telling everybody else to take something which belonged to somebody else,' and it was nearly always Turkish property which was concerned. Russia, on the other hand, had had to accept that part of the fruits of her victory had been taken from her. It could not, of course, have been otherwise. Russia had been militarily exhausted by the war, and reality compelled her to give up some of the gains which Ignatiev had wrested from the Turks at San Stefano. In the end, the two empires, having fought a bitter war at a fearful cost in human suffering, ended it by sharing in this way a feeling of humiliation.

41

Conclusion

The war of 1877-1878 was the last major European war of the 19th century. It was much the most comprehensively covered by war correspondents, who had access to modern technology that enabled their editors to satisfy the demands of their readers for immediacy of information in a way never before possible. The war was studied carefully by military men for the next three decades, searching for the key lessons that might be learned from it, until another equally avoidable war fought by the Russian Empire replaced it as a subject for detailed military analysis. It did not, however, provide as much enlightenment as the Franco-Prussian War of 1870-1871, nor did it influence military thinking to anything like the same extent.

It had seemed, before the war began, that it was a war which Russia would certainly win; and in the end the outcome was as expected. Along the way, however, there were a considerable number of alarms, sufficient to demonstrate that the margin between victory and defeat was much narrower than anyone expected. With rather more effective leadership on the part of some of the Turkish commanders, and a bit of luck, the result could have been different. Although it was always highly improbable that the Russians could have been totally defeated or their armies destroyed, it was possible that they might have been fought to a standstill, and obliged to bring the war to an end without having defeated the Turkish armies. As it was, although by the end Turkish military capability had been almost completely destroyed, the Russians themselves were not in good shape to have gone on fighting very much longer, not least because financial difficulties were becoming acute.

No nation's leaders, embarking on hostilities, can be unaware of the death, destruction and misery that must ensue. In 1877 Russia's generals hoped for and anticipated a quick victory. It was a state of mind in which military men have frequently set off down the road to Armageddon, but as has so frequently been the case in the course of human history the hopes of winning without paying a high price were to be disappointed.

Both sides began the war by making fundamental mistakes, but those made by the Turks were the more serious and less easily made good. As Moltke had pointed out, initial errors have lasting consequences:

Even the first deployment of the army – assembling the fighting means in readiness – cannot be planned without a previous plan of operations, at least in a very general sketch. One must consider in advance what one intends in the defence, just as for the attack … Even a single error in the original assembly of the armies can hardly ever be made good again during the entire course of the campaign.[1]

The Turkish mobilisation and initial deployment demonstrated this in full measure. Although the likelihood of war with Russia was evident throughout 1876 and still more so early in 1877, the mobilisation was conducted at a languid pace. This, according to

The Tsar returns from Kishinev to St Petersburg. (Strantz)

Valentine Baker, was the fault of Redif Pasha, the Minister of War, whom he described as 'a man of a low order of intellect, but bold and unscrupulous,' and whose measures to prepare for the coming war were 'stamped with incapacity.' For the mobilisation to be successfully conducted, the military system must be efficient. Baker noted the extent of the War Minister's responsibility:

> During the Serbian War, Redif Pasha had so completely broken up the system of army organisation which had been established by Abdul Aziz that all the military departments were in confusion.[2]

Redif's incompetence also extended to the part he played in the selection of field commanders, a process in which the Sultan insisted in taking a hand. In Europe, the key appointment was of course the overall command of the forces to defend the Danube and the Balkans, and the choice of the seventy-year old Abdul Kerim proved, as has been seen, to be a particularly serious error. Mukhtar's appointment to the command in the Caucasus, on the other hand, proved an inspired choice. Less happy was the decision by Abdul Hamid to set up a war council in Constantinople as the supreme decision making body, composed effectively of the most elderly and incompetent generals that were not engaged in the field. He also established a separate private military advisory council, composed of members with close connections to the palace but lacking in military ability. Thus the War Ministry had to compete for the Sultan's attention with two other bodies without any definition of their proper responsibilities.[3]

Abdul Kerim's decision to concentrate the bulk of his army in the Quadrilateral was, as has already been noted, based on his intention to offer a purely static defence. As Maurice observed, 'except as one more example to prove that a passive defence is no defence there is nothing to be learned from Abdul Kerim's strategy.'[4] It was a decision that effectively gave up any defence of the line of the Danube and discarded one of the Ottoman Empire's principal advantages in a war with Russia, namely the command of the sea. Not only would this have enabled a Turkish seizure of Reni, Galatz and Braila, thus taking up a position on the flank of any Russian advance; it also provided a strong river flotilla with which an active defence of the Danube could have been conducted.[5]

The Turkish General Staff was, as has been previously observed, grossly incompetent, and this was noted frequently by the military *attachés* and war correspondents. Not only was it utterly inefficient when it came to organising the movement of troop units; it could not even arrange to keep commanders well informed. Early in the war, Kemball commented to Layard on the

utter helplessness of the Turkish commanders not only in the matter of interchanging information between their several corps and positions, but of learning with any degree of certainty what is passing within even twenty miles of their respective centres.[6]

On the Russian side there had been partial mobilisations on November 1 1876 and April 3 1877, but these failed to provide sufficient resources to conduct the campaigns against the Ottoman Empire. Both in the European campaign and that in the Caucasus the Russians began with what had appeared to be strong enough forces but which it was soon evident were not. The lack of sufficient manpower meant that the bold plan of Obruchev to cross the Danube and plunge straight forward to the Balkans with defensive screens on either side became a victim of those at Russian headquarters arguing for a more cautious strategy. In the Caucasus, the troops immediately available achieved some initial success before becoming bogged down; it took a further mobilisation in July to bring Grand Duke Michael's forces to a level sufficient to take on Mukhtar's army.

With a few exceptions, Russian generalship was not a great deal better than the Turkish. The Grand Duke Nicholas was of limited ability, although to his credit he did grasp the importance of keeping up the pressure after Plevna even though it meant a winter campaign. Todleben's arrival brought much needed stability to the Russian headquarters. Skobelev was outstanding, and Gourko and Radetzky were effective: in Asia, much the best of the Russian leaders was Lazarev.

Reference has already been made to the superior weaponry with which the Turkish army went to war. The adoption of the Peabody-Martini rifle gave the Turkish infantry a significant advantage, while the performance of the new Krupp steel cannon entirely lived up to expectations. By comparison the Russian artillery struggled to make sufficient impact; the flat trajectory of their field guns generally meant that they were unable to inflict high casualties when the Turks were in secure fortifications. Todleben gloomily estimated that it required one day's battery firing to kill a single Turk.

The Russian infantry stoically endured the most fearful conditions without complaint, and almost invariably displayed outstanding courage in battle. Their officers provided inspiring leadership, especially at regimental level, and paid a high price in the casualties which they sustained. Medical services had improved dramatically since the Crimean War, the mortality rate for sick and wounded having fallen to about one-third of the previous level.[7] Supply services, on the other hand, were completely inadequate; as the army's line of communication lengthened, the situation steadily deteriorated. This applied not only to the provision of sufficient food, but also to boots and winter clothing, a problem that caused severe suffering in the dreadful weather conditions which the troops endured.[8] Greene paid a particular tribute to the Russian soldiers to whom he ascribed the principal cause of the Russian success in the winter campaign:

> From the time the movement was well under way the men never saw their knapsacks, which remained north of the Balkans till some time after the armistice. They marched and fought and slept in snow and ice, and forded rivers with the thermometer at zero. They had no blankets and the frozen ground precluded all idea of tents ... their clothing at night was the same as in the day, and it differed from that of the summer only in the addition of an overcoat, woollen jacket, and a 'bashlik' or woollen muffler for the head ... there was more than one instance where the men fought, and fought well, not only without breakfast, but without having tasted food in twenty four hours. Yet, in face of these unusual privations and hardships, there was not a single case of insubordination.[9]

Greene was, however, well aware of the downside of the characteristics of the Russian soldier:

> He instinctively looks for orders, and obeys them with a blind instinct, without stopping to question their merit; left to his own resources, he is almost helpless, and will often get killed from sheer stupidity in standing still and waiting for an order when everyone is dead who has the right to give one ... Deprived of their officers, a body of Russian soldiers may degenerate into a helpless, inert mass, and be slaughtered by means of their very cohesiveness, but will never take a panic.[10]

Compared to the Turkish artillery, the Russian gunners, much less well equipped and with horses that were often worn out, were frequently ineffectual, although their courage in bringing their guns into action usually matched that of the infantry which they supported. The Russian cavalry, frequently poorly commanded, achieved less than might have been expected of them; on the whole the Cossack units seem to have done better than the regular cavalry. Menning suggests that cavalry commanders failed to employ their troops in conjunction with infantry as a result of the changing role of cavalry on a battlefield in which the killing power of weapons had so markedly increased.[11]

The Turkish regular infantry of the *Nizam* and *Redif* generally displayed just as much courage and endurance as their Russian adversaries, coming forward to attack enemy positions with great determination. They were, however, badly led; the quality of Turkish officers at all levels was poor. This in particular was the cause of the collapse of morale that on occasion led Turkish infantry to break and flee. The *Mustafiz*, frequently largely composed of troops with little training, were much less reliable. Overall, the quality of individual units was, as Baker for instance speedily learned, extremely uneven. The Turkish infantry did of course have the Peabody-Martini and it was also much better clothed than previously in the history of the Ottoman army – better, too, in the matter of winter clothing, than the Russian infantry.[12] It, too, endured the dreadful conditions of the winter campaign with immense fortitude.

It was generally agreed by observers, military *attachés* and war correspondents alike, that the infantry on both sides were basically of high quality. Wellesley reported:

> As far as the individual soldier is concerned, without in any way detracting from the stubborn courage and powers of endurance which characterize the Russian, it has been proved that the Turk is quite his equal.[13]

And another British observer suggested that 'man for man the Turkish soldier seems the better, but is very badly officered, which must tell in operations on a large scale in the open,' a view that was repeatedly borne out in the course of the war.

The Turkish artillerymen generally made effective use of the superiority of their guns, especially when employed in the defence of prepared positions. In the open field they were handicapped by the poor quality of their horses. Their performance would have been improved had more attention been paid to their technical instruction. The regular cavalry were badly mounted and poorly trained, and there were not nearly enough of them; Mukhtar in particular was gravely handicapped by the lack of sufficient horsemen to provide a screen and to gather intelligence. The irregular cavalry were, generally, worse than useless, more concerned with looting than in making any effective contribution in battle. Hirschfeld, the German military *attaché* at Constantinople, thought that the Turks 'received not the slightest bit of support from this material,' while Colonel Lennox considered that their discipline was 'infinitesimal':

The Sultan decorating wounded Turkish soldiers. (*The Graphic*)

They march when and as they please, there is no roll-call; their actions are almost independent of all authority and after pillaging they quietly drive off cattle to their homes which may be literally hundreds of miles away.[14]

Although the Ottoman army was thus better clothed and equipped than it had ever been, the rear services remained disastrously bad. Medical services were lamentably inadequate, although the devoted service of a considerable number of foreign doctors somewhat assuaged this problem. Ammunition was generally well supplied, but other stores and provisions were often lacking. Transport, or the lack of it, remained a serious handicap throughout the war in both theatres.

The many foreign observers, military *attachés*, war correspondents and volunteers that accompanied the armies brought back accounts of a number of aspects of the fighting to illustrate the military lessons to be derived from the war. Of these, much the most important feature was the use of field fortifications in the context of the development of firearms. Temporary fortifications were a response to the range, precision and rapidity of fire of modern rifles, so much so that it could be said that during the war 'the combination of trench and breechloader attained such a perfection, that the whole campaign may be said to have consisted – tactically – of the attack and defence of more or less hastily fortified positions.'[15]

Greene illustrated the stopping power of the latest rifles by a calculation that four hundred men occupying a redoubt with a front of one hundred yards could deliver 24 shots to a range of a mile and a quarter in twelve minutes, the time to be taken by an attacking force to cover that distance. If only five per cent of the bullets found a target the defenders could have put out of action three times their own number. Greene put it thus:

> The above illustration is sufficient to call attention to the great fact of modern tactics, viz., that in the last few years the defence, behind fortifications, has enormously gained upon the attack, owing to the improvement in small-arms; or in other words, that any attacking force is now at a very much greater disadvantage than it was fifteen years ago.[16]

The necessity of being able to construct field fortifications quickly applied to the attackers as well as the defenders. Three decades after the war, reviewing the lessons to be learned from it, General Langlois noted that Skobelev 'never advanced a foot without making sure of his position by field fortifications,' and that he constantly complained of the entrenching tools available:

> If we consider in how short a time the Russians ultimately were able to construct very efficient cover, although they were poorly supplied with the necessary tools, we shall come to the conclusion that the rapid construction of field works, which are of such high value nowadays, is quite as much a factor at the disposal of the attack as it is of the defence. It allows the attack to firmly establish itself at each stage of its progress. Skobelev understood this and made use of all the advantages that the offensive could gain from this new feature in war.[17]

Not all Skobelev's colleagues grasped the point as clearly as he did, and throughout the war the Turks were much more proficient in strengthening their positions rapidly in this way, as a result of which the Russian infantry frequently sustained heavy casualties when coming forward to attack while unable to make an effective reply.

Greene was irritated by the talk of Russian officers who spoke of the Turkish use of earthworks as 'a new method of making war,' reporting to Washington that 'the lessons of our civil war have unfortunately not been studied by the Russians.'[18] Kemball, however, had noted, as had other observers, the extent to which some at any rate of the Russians had learned from their adversaries, reporting to Layard:

> In illustration of the caution with which their reverses in this campaign have inspired the Russians I may mention that the battlefield is ploughed up on every side with rifle-pits and shells-trenches dug by them on their first advance upon the Turkish lines or in the successive steps of their retreat as well as to secure the flank and rear of the main column.[19]

However, an instance of one Russian commander, at any rate, who had not learned the lesson properly occurred as late as the final crossing of the Balkans, when Prince Mirsky rejected a suggestion put forward by Pfeil:

> I was not always able to carry my own views through. For example, I proposed that various field fortification works should be executed during the night, so as at all events to secure our line of retreat. Neither the Prince nor the two colonels would, however, hear of them.[20]

The reliance placed by the Turks on their effective field fortifications was partly responsible for the mindset of commanders who were reluctant to conduct a war of manoeuvre; this hesitation was also, quite justifiably, prompted by an awareness of the inability of the staff to organise movement in the face of the enemy with any degree of efficiency. Werder, writing after the Second Battle of Plevna, mourned the opportunity that he felt had been lost, due to the Turkish lack of energy and initiative when on the offensive compared to that which they displayed when standing on the defensive; another army, he thought, would at once have taken steps to threaten the position of the Tsarevich's army.[21]

In her comprehensive assessment of the reports of the foreign military *attachés* who accompanied the armies, Maureen O'Connor observed that in considering the lessons that might be learned from the war, they had to take account of the fact that 'these were not European armies officered by European men playing by European rules.'[22] This view was particularly strengthened by their experience of the atrocities which they encountered. The evidence of the *attachés* as to these may be more to be relied on than that of the war correspondents, who were writing for a popular audience and able to give free rein to their portrayal of what they saw. On the whole, however, the accounts given by the war correspondents were remarkably consistent with the reports of the *attachés*.

The war had begun against the background of the painfully explicit accounts of the most revolting barbarity with which the Turks had suppressed the Bulgarian insurgency. Even now the stately Victorian prose in which these events were reported still has the power to shock the modern reader. If MacGahan's letters from Bulgaria were written in the most emotional terms, the horrors that he described were amply confirmed by others, such as Eugene Schuyler, who as a US consular official reported them from a different standpoint. MacGahan was clear in what he wanted to achieve:

> The crimes that were committed here are beyond the reach of exaggeration. There were stories related to us that are maddening in their atrocity, that cause the heart to swell in a burst of impotent rage that can only find vent in pitying, useless tears … If I tell what I have seen and heard it is because I want the people of England to understand what these Turks are.[23]

After publication of the reports of the appalling barbarities that had occurred in 1876, it was accordingly to be expected that once the fighting had begun there would be allegations and counter-allegations made of atrocities committed by both sides. Many battles ended with a detailed report of such acts, perpetrated both on opposing troops and upon the civilian population. It is necessary to consider whether the conduct of the troops on either side went substantially beyond the casual and murderous brutality that has been the characteristic of soldiers in battle down the ages. This had been a war between two ancient enemies, one of which was culturally not really on a par with the countries of Western Europe, and the other in which mediaeval barbarity was still a feature of everyday life; it was always going to be fought with an extreme ferocity that was shocking to the Western observers.

The existence of the perceived cultural and social difference between Russia and Turkey on the one hand and the remaining Great Powers on the other was something of which observers were obliged to take account, in their assessment both of the fighting qualities of the troops involved and of their behaviour as a whole. Attitudes in Russia sometimes came as a considerable surprise; Wellesley, for instance, was shaken by what he found at Russian headquarters:

> No words can describe its filthy condition. It was absolutely innocent of all sanitary arrangements, and although, as I have elsewhere pointed out, Russia is the strangest mixture of luxury and barbarism, it always appeared to me inconceivable that the Emperor, who was continually moving about the camp, should have tolerated such a disgusting state of things.[24]

This kind of thing confirmed the foreign military observers in their belief that this was not, fundamentally, a European war.

It was not long before they began to experience personally some of the appalling aspects of warfare between these two nations. The incident witnessed by Liegnitz in July 1877 during Gourko's defence of the Shipka Pass, when the Turks fired on a flag of truce, was an early indication that not only the Turkish irregular cavalry were capable of the most appalling atrocities but that at times the regular infantry, usually very disciplined, could behave very badly, and could do so on the orders of their officers. MacGahan, who was present, and reported the mutilation of the Russian dead and wounded, considered the reason for the incident:

Evidently a pure outburst of savage ferocity; the rage of the savage who finds himself beaten on all hands by a civilised enemy, and flings a deliberate defiance at civilised modes of warfare and revenges himself in the only way his barbarous nature can find satisfaction by violating the most sacred law of civilised warfare.[25]

The massacre at Eski Zagra also appears to have taken place with the connivance of Turkish officers as well, it was suggested, of Suleiman himself; it was alleged that he had 'reduced the entire town to ashes on account of the "treason" of the inhabitants in asking the Russians to come there.'[26] In this case the victims were the Bulgarian population, but the ferocity of the attack upon them may have been exacerbated by the fact that it was troops of the Bulgarian Legion that had opposed the Turks there.

The evidence of Turkish atrocities, in both the European and Caucasus theatres, was convincing, although it was from time to time exaggerated in the reports of pro-Russian observers. On the other hand Layard, of course, was always prepared to put the best face he could on the Turkish position. He pointed out that the atrocities that had been committed against Christian populations were 'assigned by all trustworthy authorities' to the Circassians and the Bashi-Bazouks. While, he wrote, the Turkish government had to accept responsibility for their actions, he implausibly offered excuses:

> But it must not be forgotten, at the same time, that Turkey has been forced into this struggle for existence, and that she has been compelled to have recourse to every available means to defend all that is dear to men – honour, country, religion, and life.[27]

The Turkish authorities endeavoured to suggest that the Russian troops were also guilty of grave crimes on a regular basis; although there were certainly atrocities committed against the Turkish civilian population, these seem to have been the work of Bulgarian civilians. A large number of observers reported on what they had found in relation to the Turkish allegations; perhaps the most magisterial of the published accounts came from Archibald Forbes, in an article for the *19th century* for November 1877, in which he set out in detail his conclusions:

> Of the multitudinous atrocities on Turkish refugees charged against the Russian soldiery with so great persistent circumstantiality by Turkish authorities and their abettors, I have never found the smallest tittle of evidence, and on soul and conscience believe the allegations thereof to be utterly false.[28]

In a lengthy article, he refuted the suggestions that the Russian soldier was a 'brutal ignorant boor' and reported that, to the contrary, he had found them 'delightful comrades, of inexhaustible good humour, light hearted under hardship, humane, of a genuine, if unobtrusive humanity.'[29] Forbes's account was emphatically confirmed by Colonel Brackenbury, in a lengthy article published a month later in *The Times*. None of this was, of course, to the taste of those engaged in whipping up anti-Russian feeling in England. These views of the Russian soldier were matched on the other side; Herbert, serving with Turkish regulars inside Plevna, found much the same qualities in his comrades there.

One Turkish commander at any rate made plain to his troops the behaviour he expected of them. In a proclamation which he published to his troops early in October 1877 when he was contemplating an advance across the Russian frontier, Ahmed Mukhtar made an emphatic statement of his position:

> By the grace of the All Powerful the enemy has been obliged to retreat from our country, beaten and humiliated. Since then, our most ardent wish is about to be fulfilled; we are going to take the offensive and cross the frontier. Although we have had in our country to endure iniquitous, illegal and barbarous acts at the hands of the Russians, I expect each one of you to conduct himself sympathetically towards the oppressed people of Erivan. In accordance with your inmost feelings and your traditional generosity you will avoid any actions to satisfy base passions; you will not break our holy Law which is above civil law and no man among you will shame himself by committing acts of pillage and oppression as the Russians have done. It is a horrible crime, against our law, to kill a human being, the most wonderful creation of God. Therefore you will forebear from unjust killing or acts of pillage … As thinking men, take these precepts to heart, obey your leaders and respect your holy Law.[30]

But if the Russians may be acquitted of actively perpetrating outrages of the kind suggested, they must nevertheless be found guilty of the most appalling treatment by default of the prisoners that fell into their hands after Plevna. No provision had been made for the huge numbers with which they had to deal, even though it had been obvious for a long time that sooner or later Plevna would fall and the problem of caring for them would immediately arise. Their fate, illustrated by the war artist Frederick Villiers in his drawing of the 'Death March of the Turkish Prisoners,' was dreadful beyond words. As they were marched off into captivity, scantily clad and barefoot, in fearsome weather, it was estimated that 5,000 died before they reached Bucharest; of the 43,000 that were sent northwards, only 15,000 reached Russia.[31]

Every war is a profound tragedy for the people of the country in which it is fought. Humanity, decency, kindness and mercy may be largely suspended, even by the civilian population. For the people of Bulgaria, Christians and Moslems alike, the experience of 1877-1878 was peculiarly dreadful, coming as it did after the well-documented atrocities of the repression of the Bulgarian uprising. The war left a ruined country. True, Bulgaria had taken a long stride towards freedom and independence, but the price paid was fearful, in the loss of life, the devastation of towns and villages and the destruction of the framework of society. Consul Fawcett wrote to Layard after visiting the districts south of the Balkans that the war 'had probably caused more human misery than even the invasion of the Visigoths, who fourteen centuries before desolated these same fertile countries.'

Understandably, most of those involved in the war looked back on it as an outstanding event in world history. For Francis Greene, the heroes were the Russian soldiers:

> Their self abnegation and cheerfulness under great physical suffering, to which their brilliant success was pre-eminently due, are excelled by nothing of which we have any record in history, and they entitle every man of those trans-Balkan columns

to the lasting gratitude of their own countrymen and the friends of Christian government everywhere, no less than to the admiration of the entire world, which still appreciates the value of military heroism.[32]

On the other side of the hill, William von Herbert reflected not only on the horrors of the battle for Plevna:

It is also rich in features which lay bare all that is most beautiful and most noble in human nature. Even if no moral, whether strategical or tactical, historical or political could be drawn from it, even if it could not form the basis for a whole superstructure of conjectures for the future, it shows the sublime grandeur to which men can rise who fight (or imagine they fight) for a righteous cause.[33]

Appendix I

Strengths of Russian Infantry and Cavalry Regiments 1877

Strength of an Infantry Regiment

	Combatants		Non-combatants		Train	
	Officers	Men	Officers	Men	Horses	Waggons
4-battalion Regiment – War footing	80	4,057	7	226	186	44
4-battalion Regiment – Peacetime	64	1,897	7	185	52	17
3-battalion Regiment – War footing	76	3,081	6	136	174	41
3-battalion Regiment – Increased Peacetime footing	60	2,363	6	135	135	41
3-battalion Regiment – Peacetime	60	1,793	6	105	49	16

Strength of a Cavalry Regiment

	Combatants			Non-combatants		Train	
	Officers	Men	Horses	Officers	Men	Horses	Waggons
4-squadron Regiment	33	728	593	6	141	64	16

The above establishment was maintained in peace and war save for the train, which, in peacetime, contained 15 horses and 9 waggons.

Order of Battle
Russian Army of the South
March 3 1877

Commander in Chief: Grand Duke Nicholas
Chief of Staff: Adjutant General Nepokoitschitsky
Assistant Chief of Staff: Major-General Levitsky
Artillery Commander: Prince Massalsky

IV Corps

Lieutenant General Zotov
    16th Infantry Division: Major-General Pomerantsev
        1st Brigade:
            61st (Vladimir) Infantry Regiment
            62nd (Suzdal) Infantry Regiment
        2nd Brigade:
            63rd (Oglitz) Infantry Regiment
            64th (Kazan) Infantry Regiment
    30th Infantry Division: Major-General Schnitnikov
        1st Brigade:
            117th (Jaroslavl) Infantry Regiment
            118th (Shuisk) Infantry Regiment
        2nd Brigade:
            119th (Koloma) Infantry Regiment
            120th (Serpukov) Infantry Regiment
    4th Cavalry Division: Lieutenant General Krylov
        1st Brigade:
            4th (Ekaterinoslav) Dragoon Regiment
            4th (Kharkov) Lancer Regiment
        2nd Brigade:
            4th (Mariopol) Hussar Regiment
            4th Don Cossack Regiment
    Corps Artillery:
            16th and 30th Artillery Brigades
            7th and 8th Horse Batteries

XIII Corps

Lieutenant General Hahn

1st Infantry Division: Lieutenant General Prokhorov
    1st Brigade:
        1st (Neva) Infantry Regiment
        2nd (Sophia) Infantry Regiment
    2nd Brigade:
        3rd (Narva) Infantry Regiment
        4th (Kopor) Infantry Regiment
35th Infantry Division: Major-General Baranov
    1st Brigade:
        137th (Nieshin) Infantry Regiment
        138th (Volkhov) Infantry Regiment
    2nd Brigade:
        139th (Morshansk) Infantry Regiment
        140th (Saray) Infantry Regiment
13th Cavalry Division: Major-General de Raden
    1st Brigade:
        13th Dragoon Regiment
        13th (Vladimir) Lancer Regiment
    2nd Brigade:
        13th (Narva) Hussar Regiment
        13th Don Cossack Regiment
Corps Cavalry: 31st Don Cossack Regiment
Corps Artillery:
        1st and 35th Artillery Brigades
        20th Horse and 6th Don Cossack Horse Batteries

XIV Corps

Lieutenant General Zimmerman
    17th Infantry Division: Major-General Prochovnikov
        1st Brigade:
            65th (Moscow) Infantry Regiment
            66th (Butyr) Infantry Regiment
        2nd Brigade:
            67th (Tarutino) Infantry Regiment
            68th (Borodino) Infantry Regiment
    18th Infantry Division: Major-General Narbut
        1st Brigade:
            69th (Ryazan) Infantry Regiment
            70th (Riajsk) Infantry Regiment
        2nd Brigade:
            71st (Bielev) Infantry Regiment
            72nd (Tula) Infantry Regiment
    Don Cossack Division: Lieutenant General Shamshev
        1st Brigade:
            15th Don Cossack Regiment
            16th Don Cossack Regiment

2nd Brigade:
    17th Don Cossack Regiment
    18th Don Cossack Regiment
Corps Artillery:
    17th and 18th Artillery Brigades
    16th and 17th Don Cossack Horse Batteries

VII Corps

Lieutenant General Ganetsky
  15th Infantry Division: Lieutenant General Shostak
    1st Brigade:
      57th (Modlin) Infantry Regiment
      58th (Prague) Infantry Regiment
    2nd Brigade:
      59th (Lublin) Infantry Regiment
      60th (Zamosc) Infantry Regiment
  36th Infantry Division: Lieutenant General Vierevkin
    1st Brigade:
      111th (Mojaisk) Infantry Regiment
      112th (Zvenigorod) Infantry Regiment
    2nd Brigade:
      143rd (Dorogobouje) Infantry Regiment
      144th (Kaschira Infantry) Regiment
  Corps Cavalry:
    2 Cossack Regiments
  Corps Artillery:
    15th and 36th Artillery Brigades

VIII Corps

Lieutenant General Radetzky
  9th Infantry Division: Lieutenant General Prince Sviatopolk-Mirsky II)
    1st Brigade:
      33rd (Jeletz) Infantry Regiment
      34th (Sievsk) Infantry Regiment
    2nd Brigade:
      35th (Briansk) Infantry Regiment
      36th (Orel) Infantry Regiment
  14th Infantry Division: Lieutenant General Dragomirov
    1st Brigade:
      53rd (Volhynia) Infantry Regiment
      54th (Minsk) Infantry Regiment
    2nd Brigade
      55th (Podolia) Infantry Regiment
      56th (Zhitomir) Infantry Regiment
  Corps Cavalry:
    23rd Don Cossack Regiment

Corps Artillery:
9th and 14th Artillery Brigades

IX Corps
Lieutenant General Krüdener
5th Infantry Division: Lieutenant General Schilder-Schuldner
1st Brigade:
17th (Archangel) Infantry Regiment
18th (Vologda) Infantry Regiment
2nd Brigade:
19th (Kostroma) Infantry Regiment
20th (Galicia) Infantry Regiment
31st Infantry Division: Lieutenant General Veliaminov
1st Brigade:
121st (Penza) Infantry Regiment
122nd (Tambov) Infantry Regiment
2nd Brigade:
123rd (Koslov) Infantry Regiment
124th (Voronezh) Infantry Regiment
Corps Cavalry:
34th Don Cossack Regiment
Corps Artillery: 5th and 31st Artillery Brigades

X Corps
Lieutenant General Prince Voronzov
13th Infantry Division: Lieutenant General Richter
1st Brigade:
49th (Brest) Infantry Regiment
50th (Bialystok) Infantry Regiment
2nd Brigade:
51st (Lithuania) Infantry Regiment
52nd (Vilna) Infantry Regiment
34th Infantry Division: Lieutenant General Baron Korf
1st Brigade:
133rd (Simferopol) Infantry Regiment
134th (Theodosie) Infantry Regiment
2nd Brigade:
135th (Kerich-Yenikale) Infantry Regiment
136th (Taganrog) Infantry Regiment
Corps Cavalry:
2 Cossack Regiments
Corps Artillery: 13th and 34th Artillery Brigades

XI Corps
Lieutenant General Prince Schakofskoi
11th Infantry Division: Lieutenant General Khrapovitzky

1st Brigade:
    41st (Seleguinsk) Infantry Regiment
    42nd (Yakut) Infantry Regiment
2nd Brigade:
    43rd (Okhotsk) Infantry Regiment
    44th (Kamchatka) Infantry Regiment
32nd Infantry Division: Major-General Aller
    1st Brigade:
        125th (Kursk) Infantry Regiment
        126th (Rylsk) Infantry Regiment
    2nd Brigade:
        127th (Poutivl) Infantry Regiment
        128th (Starioskol) Infantry Regiment
Corps Cavalry:
    2 Cossack Regiments
Corps Artillery: 11th and 32nd Artillery Brigades

XII Corps

Lieutenant General Vannovsky
    12th Infantry Division: Lieutenant General Baron de Firks
    1st Brigade:
        45th (Azov) Infantry Regiment
        46th (Dnieper) Infantry Regiment
    2nd Brigade:
        47th (Ukraine) Infantry Regiment
        48th (Odessa) Infantry Regiment
Corps Cavalry:
    2 Cossack Regiments
33rd Infantry Division: Lieutenant General Timofeiev
    1st Brigade:
        129th (Bessarabia) Infantry Regiment
        130th (Kherson) Infantry Regiment
    2nd Brigade:
        131st (Tiraspol) Infantry Regiment
        132nd (Bender) Infantry Regiment
Corps Cavalry:
    2 Cossack Regiments
Corps Artillery: 12th and 33rd Artillery Brigades

7th Cavalry Division

Lieutenant General Manzei
    1st Brigade:
        7th (Kinburn) Dragoon Regiment
        7th (Olivopol) Lancer Regiment
    2nd Brigade:
        7th (White Russia) Hussar Regiment

7th Cossack Regiment
Artillery:
13th and 14th Horse Batteries

8th Cavalry Division

Major-General Prince Manvelov
1st Brigade:
8th (Astrakhan) Dragoon Regiment
8th (Voznesensk) Lancer Regiment
2nd Brigade:
8th (Loubny) Hussar Regiment
8th Cossack Regiment
Artillery:
15th Horse Battery
1 Cossack Horse Battery

9th Cavalry Division

Lieutenant General Lockarev
1st Brigade:
9th (Kazan) Dragoon Regiment
9th (Bug) Lancer Regiment
2nd Brigade:
9th (Kiev) Hussar Regiment
9th Cossack Regiment
Artillery:
16th Horse Battery
2nd Cossack Horse Battery

10th Cavalry Division

Major-General Dediouline
1st Brigade:
10th (Novgorod) Dragoon Regiment
10th (Odessa) Lancer Regiment
2nd Brigade:
10th (Ingremanland) Hussar Regiment
10th Cossack Regiment
Artillery:
17th Horse Battery
3rd Cossack Horse Battery

11th Cavalry Division

Major-General Tatischev
1st Brigade:
11th (Riga) Dragoon Regiment
11th (Tchougouiev) Uhlan Regiment
2nd Brigade:

11th (Isoum) Hussar Regiment
11th Cossack Regiment
Artillery:
18th Horse Battery
4th Cossack Horse Battery

12th Cavalry Division

Major-General Baron Driesen
1st Brigade:
12th (Starodoub) Dragoon Regiment
12th (Bielgorod) Uhlan Regiment
2nd Brigade:
12th (Akhtyrka) Hussar Regiment
12th (Cossack) Regiment
Artillery:
19th Horse Battery
5th Cossack Horse Battery

Also assigned to army:

1 Brigade of 4 Battalions of Rifles, each with 4 companies
12 Regiments of Don Cossacks, each with 6 sotnias
1 Scout Corps, with 4 Cossack Regiments, each of 6 sotnias
2 Don Cossack Horse Batteries, each with 6 guns
10 Mountain Batteries, each with 6 guns
1 Siege Park with 100 guns
3 Sapper Battalions

Order of Battle of the Roumanian Army, March 1877

Commanding Officer: Prince Charles of Roumania
Chief of Staff: Colonel Slaniciano

1st Corps

General Lupu
    1st Division: Colonel Cherchey
        1st Brigade:
            4th Chasseur Battalion
            1st *Dorobantsi* Regiment[1]
        2nd Brigade:
            4th Infantry Regiment
            2nd *Dorobantsi* Regiment
        Cavalry Brigade:
            1st Light Cavalry Regiment
            2nd Light Cavalry Regiment
        Artillery:
            2nd Battery, 2nd Artillery Regiment
            Engineering Detachment
    2nd Division:Colonel Logadi
        1st Brigade:
            1st Chasseur Battalion
            1st Infantry Regiment
        2nd Brigade:
            2nd Chasseur Battalion
            3rd Infantry Regiment
            4th *Dorobantsi* Regiment
        Cavalry Brigade:
            3rd Light Cavalry Regiment
            4th Light Cavalry Regiment
        Artillery:
            5 Batteries of the 2nd Artillery Regiment
            Engineering Detachment

---

1   The *Dorobantsi* were the Roumanian territorial army infantry, a conscript force.

2nd Corps

General Radovici

    3rd Division: Colonel Angelesco

        1st Brigade:

            3rd Chasseur Battalion

            2nd Infantry Regiment

            1st Battalion 6th *Dorobantsi* Regiment

        2nd Brigade:

            8th Infantry Regiment

            3rd *Dorobantsi* Regiment

        Cavalry Brigade:

            2nd Squadron 5th Light Cavalry Regiment (1)

            6th Light Cavalry Regiment (4)

        Artillery:

            4 Batteries of the 2nd Artillery Regiment

            Engineering Detachment

    4th Division: Colonel Mano

        1st Brigade:

            5th Infantry Regiment

            7th *Dorobantsi* Regiment

            8th *Dorobantsi* Regiment

        Cavalry Brigade:

            7th Light Cavalry Regiment

            8th Light Cavalry Regiment

        Artillery:

            3 Batteries of the 1st Artillery Regiment

            Engineering Detachment

         Artillery Reserve & Park

            6 Artillery Batteries

            Munitions Column

        Cavalry Reserve:

            1st Hussar Regiment

            2nd Hussar Regiment

Appendix IV

Order of Battle, Russian Army of the Caucasus, March 1877

Commander in Chief: Grand Duke Michael
Second in Command: Lieutenant General Loris-Melikov
Chief of Staff: Major-General Donkhovskoi
Artillery Commander: Major-General Gubski

Caucasus Grenadier Division: (Lieutenant General Tarkhan-Mouravov)
  1st Brigade: (In Tiflis)
    13th Erivan Leib Grenadier Regiment
    14th Georgia Grenadier Regiment
  2nd Brigade: (In Tiflis)
    15th Tiflis Grenadier Regiment
    16th Mingrelia Grenadier Regiment
  Caucasus Grenadier Artillery Brigade

19th Division: (Major-General Komarov II)
  1st Brigade: (In Stavropol)
    73rd Crimea Infantry Regiment
    74th Stavropol Infantry Regiment
  2nd Brigade:
    75th Sebastopol Infantry Regiment
    76th Kuban Infantry Regiment
  19th Artillery Brigade

39th Division: (Lieutenant General Devel)
  1st Brigade: (In Tiflis)
    153rd Baku Infantry Regiment
    154th Derbent Infantry Regiment
  2nd Brigade: (In Akhaltsyk)
    155th Kouba Infantry Regiment
    156th Elisavetpol Infantry Regiment
  39th Artillery Brigade

41st Division: (Leiutenant General Oklobju)
  1st Brigade: (in Kutais)
    161st Alexandropol Infantry Regiment
    162nd Akhaltsyk Infantry Regiment
  2nd Brigade: (in Khan-Kendy Camp)

163rd Lenkoran Infantry Regiment
164th Zakatala Infantry Regiment
41st Artillery Brigade

Caucasus Cavalry Division: (Lieutenant General Count de Toulouse-Lautrec)
   1st Brigade: (In Tiflis)
      15th Tver Dragoon Regiment
      15th Nijni-Novgorod Dragoon Regiment
   2nd Brigade: (In Piatigorsk)
      17th Sieversk Dragoon Regiment
      18th Pereiaslaw Dragoon Regiment

Local & Sedentary Troops
   Alexandropol Fortress Infantry (3 battalions)
   Local detachments (2 battalions and 12 detachments)
   Cadres (1 battalion & 12 detachments)

Irregular Troops
Combined Caucasus Cossack Division: (Major-General Sheremetiev)
      Kuban Cossack Regiment
      Caucasus Cossack Regiment
      1st Yeisk Cossack Regiment
      1st Gorsko-Mozdok Cossack Regiment

Other Irregular Troops without divisional assignments
Kuban Cossack Regiments
      1st & 2nd Tamane Cossack Regiments
      Poltava Cossack Regiment
      1st & 2nd Ekaterinodar Cossack Regiments
      1st & 2nd Oumane Cossack Regiments
      Ouroupa Cossack Regiment
      1st & 2nd Laba Cossack Regiments
      1st & 2nd Khoper Cossack Regiments
      2nd Yeisk Cossack Regiment
      5 Cossack Horse Batteries
      2 Cossack Scout Battalions

Terek Cossack Regiments
      1st & 2nd Volga Cossack Regiments
      1st & 2nd Kislar-Grebenski Cossack Regiments
      2nd Vladivkavkaz Cossack Regiment
      1st & 2nd Sounja Cossack Regiments
      2nd Gorsko-Mozdok Cossack Regiment
      2 Cossack Horse Batteries

Units in Reserve
20th Division: (Lieutenant General Heimann)
    1st Brigade: (In Grozny)
        77th Tenguinsk Infantry Regiment
        78th Navaguinsk Infantry Regiment
    2nd Brigade: (In Grozny)
        79th Kourin Infantry Regiment
        80th Kabarda Infantry Regiment
    80th Artillery Brigade

21st Division: (Lieutenant General Petrov)
    1st Brigade:
        81st Apcheron Infantry Regiment
        82nd Daghestan Infantry Regiment
    2nd Brigade:
        83rd Samoura Infantry Regiment
        84th Shirvan Infantry Regiment
    21st Artillery Brigade

38th Division: (Lieutenant General Tergukassov)
    1st Brigade:
        149th Black Sea Infantry Regiment
        150th Taman Infantry Regiment
    2nd Brigade:
        151st Piatigorsk Infantry Regiment
        152nd Vladikavkaz Infantry Regiment
    38th Artillery Brigade

Other units
    1st, 2nd, 3rd, 4th, 5th, 6th and 7th Caucasus Frontier Battalions
    Instructional and indigenous troops

Bulgarian Legion, May 1877

Commanding Officer: General Stoletov
Chief of Staff: Lieutenant Colonel Rinkevich

1st Brigade (Colonel Korsakov)
    1st Battalion (Lt. Col. Kesiakov)
    2nd Battalion (Maj. Kurtianov)

2nd Brigade (Colonel Viazemsky)
    3rd Battalion (Lt.Col. Kalitin)
    4th Battalion (Maj. Redkin)

3rd Brigade (Colonel Tolstoy)
    5th Battalion (Lt. Col. Nischenko)
    6th Battalion (Maj. Beliaev)

Appendix VI

Strength of the Turkish Army of the Danube, June 1877

At this time the forces under the direct control of Abdul Kerim were loosely organised in six corps, with a total strength of 220 infantry battalions, 46 squadrons and 64 field batteries. This total included the garrisons of the Quadrilateral fortresses and other places.

1st Corps – Widdin: *Mushir* Osman Pasha
   9 *Nizam* Battalions
   3 Light Battalions
   43 *Redif* Battalions
   6 Cavalry Squadrons
   15 Field Batteries

Of these forces, 14 battalions constituted the garrison of Widdin. 26 battalions, the cavalry and most of the artillery were based in Rupfa, Bellarada and along the Danube. Of the rest, there were two battalions in each of Artchew-Palanka and Kossovo, four battalions and a battery in Lom-Palanka; there were five battalions and two batteries in Rahova.

2nd Corps – Rustchuk: *Mushir* Eshref Pasha
   6 *Nizam* Battalions
   3 Egyptian Battalions
   2 Light Battalions
   34 *Redif* Battalions
   6 Squadrons
   12 Field Batteries

The garrison of Rustchuk comprised 29 battalions, 2 squadrons and 7 batteries. There were 9 battalions, 4 squadrons and 3 batteries at Nicopolis, 4 battalions and 2 batteries in the Sistova area, 2 battalions at Plevna and 1 battalion at Biela.

3rd Corps – Silistria: *Ferik* Selami Pasha
   5 *Nizam* Battalions
   2 Light Battalions
   27 *Redif* Battalions
   6 Squadrons
   9 Field Batteries

The garrison of Silistria comprised 2 battalions, 2 squadrons and 5 batteries; that of Turtukai 6 battalions, 2 squadrons and 5 batteries. There were two battalions at Rossova.

4th Corps – Dobrudja: *Ferik* Ali Pasha

    5 *Nizam* Battalions

    2 Light Battalions

    17 *Redif* Battalions

    12 Squadrons

    7 Field Batteries

This force was widely scattered. The largest part was at Matchin, where there were 5 battalions, with 4 squadrons and 3 batteries. Other locations included Toltcha, where there were 3 battalions and 2 batteries) Isaktcha, (5 battalions and 1 battery), Babadagh, (2 battalions and 2 squadrons), Hirsova (3 battalions, 2 squadrons and 1 battery), Tchernavoda and Medjidie (1 battalion and 2 squadrons), and Kustendje (1 battalion).

5th Corps – *Ferik* Raschid Pasha

    9 Egyptian Battalions

    12 *Redif* Battalions

    4 Squadrons

    9 Field Batteries

The whole of this force was concentrated at Varna, apart from 3 battalions, 4 squadrons and 1 battery in Bazardjik, and 2 battalions with 1 battery in Pravadi.

6th Corps – Shumla: *Mushir* Ahmed Eyoub Pasha

    10 *Nizam* Battalions

    3 Light Battalions

    28 *Redif* Battalions

    12 Squadrons

    12 Field Batteries

The bulk of this force, consisting of 29 battalions, 6 squadrons and 9 field batteries, was located in and around Shumla. The remainder was as follows: In Rasgrad, 3 battalions, 2 squadrons and 1 battery; along the railway from Rasgrad to Pravadi, 3 battalions, 2 squadrons and 2 batteries; in Kazan, 1 battalion and 2 batteries; in Eski Djuma, 2 battalions; in Eski Stambul, 3 battalions; and in Yenikoi, 1 battalion

Order of Battle, Turkish Army of Plevna, July 29 1877

Commanding officer: *Mushir* Osman Pasha
Chief of Staff: *Mirliva* Tahir Pasha
Staff: *Kaim-makam* Hairi Bey; *Kaim-makam* Talahat Bey
Commander of cavalry: *Miralai* Osman Bey
Commander of artillery: *Miralai* Ahmed Bey
Surgeon-in-Chief: *Miralai* Hassib Bey

1st Division
Commander: *Ferik* Adil Pasha
  1st Brigade: *Miralai* Emin Bey
    1st Regiment: *Kaim-makam* Mehemd Nazif Bey
      1 light battalion (*Nizam*)
      2 infantry battalions (*Nizam*)
    2nd Regiment: *Miralai* Omer Bey
      1 infantry battalion (*Nizam*)
      2 infantry battalions (*Redif*)
      1 field artillery battery (6-pounders)
      1 horse artillery battery (4-pounders)
  2nd Brigade: *Mirliva* Kara Ali Pasha
    3rd Regiment: *Kaim-makam* Mehemed Bey
      3 infantry battalions (*Redif*)
    4th Regiment: *Kaim-makam* Suleiman Bey
      1 infantry battalion (*Nizam*)
      2 infantry battalions (*Redif*)
      1 field artillery battery (6-pounders)
2 cavalry squadrons (*Nizam*)
100 irregular cavalry

2nd Division
  Commander: *Mirliva* Hassan Sabri Pasha
  3rd Brigade: *Mirliva* Tahir Pasha
    5th Regiment: *Miralai* Yunous Bey
    6th Regiment: *Miralai* Said Bey
      1 infantry battalion (*Nizam*)
      2 infantry battalions (*Redif*)
      1 field artillery battery (6-pounders)
      1 mountain artillery battery (3-pounders)

4th Brigade: *Mirliva* Atouf Pasha
    7th Regiment: *Kaim-makam* Ibrahim Bey
        2 infantry battalions (*Nizam*)
        1 infantry battalion (*Redif*)
    8th Regiment: *Miralai* Hamdi Bey
        1 infantry battalion (*Nizam*)
        2 infantry battalions (*Redif*)
    1 field artillery battery (6-pounders)
2 cavalry squadrons (*Nizam*)
100 irregular cavalry

Reserve

Commander: *Mirliva* Sadik Pasha
Adjutant: *Kaim-makam* Abdullah Bey
Infantry: *Kaim-makam* Hairi Bey
    2 infantry battalions (*Nizam*)
    7 infantry battalions (*Redif*)
Cavalry: *Miralai* Osman Bey
    2 cavalry squadrons (*Nizam*)
    2 Ottoman Cossack squadrons
    200 irregulars
Artillery: *Miralai* Ahmed Bey
    2 batteries (6-pounders)
    2 sections (4 guns) (6-pounders)
    1 horse artillery battery (4-pounders)
Engineers: 1 company

Total in Plevna: 33 battalions, 9½ batteries, 8 squadrons, 400 irregular cavalry, 1 company engineers; or, 20,000 men with 57 guns.

Garrison of Lovtcha

Commander: *Mirliva* Rifa'at Pasha
Adjutant: *Miralai* Tewfik Bey
    1 light battalion (*Nizam*)
    1 infantry battalion (*Nizam*)
    4 infantry battalions (*Redif*)
    1 battery (6-pounders)
    100 irregular cavalry

Total of Plevna army, including Lovtcha garrison: 39 battalions, 10½ batteries, 8 squadrons, 500 irregular cavalry, 1 company engineers; or, 24,000 men with 63 guns.

Order of Battle, Russian Army at Plevna, July 30 1877

IX Corps
Lieutenant-General Baron Krudener
    5th Infantry Division: Major-General Schilder-Schuldner
        1st Brigade: Major-General Knorring
            17th (Archangel) Infantry Regiment
            18th (Vologda) Infantry Regiment
        2nd Brigade:
            19th (Kostroma) Infantry Regiment
            20th (Galitz) Infantry Regiment
        5th Brigade Field Artillery
            6 field batteries (48 guns)
    31st Infantry Division: Lieutenant-General Veliaminov
        1st Brigade: Major-General Belokopilov
            121st (Penza) Infantry Regiment
            122nd (Tamboff) Infantry Regiment
        2nd Brigade:
            123rd (Kozloff) Infantry Regiment
            124th (Voronetz) Infantry Regiment
        31st Brigade Field Artillery
            6 field batteries (48 guns)
    9th Cavalry Division: Major-General Loschkarev
        1st Brigade:
            9th Dragoons
            9th Lancers
            1 horse artillery battery
        2nd Brigade:
            9th Hussars
            9th Don Cossacks
            1 horse artillery battery

Not present on July 30: 19th Infantry Regiment, 9th Dragoons, 9th Hussars, 2 field and 1 horse artillery batteries. The 124th Infantry Regiment arrived near the end of the battle.

XI Corps
Lieutenant-General Prince Shakofskoi
    32nd Infantry Division

1st Brigade: Major-General Tchekov
     125th Infantry Regiment
     126th Infantry Regiment
32nd Field Artillery Brigade:
     6 field batteries (48 guns)
11th Cavalry Division
     1st Brigade
         11th Dragoons
         11th Lancers
         1 horse artillery battery

Not present on July 30: 3 field batteries.

IV Corps

30th Infantry Division: Major-General Powzanov
     1st Infantry Brigade:
         117th Infantry Regiment
         118th Infantry Regiment
     2nd Infantry Brigade:
         119th Infantry Regiment
         120th Infantry Regiment
     30th Field Artillery Brigade:
         6 field batteries (48 guns)

United Cossack Division

Caucasian Cossack Brigade: Colonel Tutolmin
     2 regiments, 1 mountain battery, with 1 horse artillery battery attached.

Ammunition Expenditure of the Russian Army at the Second Battle of Plevna, July 30 1877

| Unit | Number of weapons in action | | | Ammunition expenditure | | | | | Rounds used per weapon | | |
| | | | | Artillery rounds | | | Small arms rounds | | | | |
	Guns	Rifles	Revolvers	Shells	Shrapnel	Canister	Rifle	Revolver	Gun	Rifle	Revolver
117th Infantry Regiment (Jaroslavl)	-	2,393	-	-	-	-	55,144	-	-	23.0	-
118th Infantry Regiment (Shuisk)	-	2,775	-	-	-	-	91,000[1]	-	-	32.8	-
119th Infantry Regiment (Koloma)	-	2,836	-	-	-	-	54,644[2]	-	-	19.3	-
120th Infantry Regiment (Serpukov)	-	2,820	-	-	-	-	42,010	-	-	14.9	-
17th Infantry Regiment (Archangel)	-	1,839	-	-	-	-	66,832	-	-	36.3	-
18th Infantry Regiment (Vologda)	-	1,391	-	-	-	-	73,185	-	-	52.6	-
20th Infantry Regiment (Galicia)	-	2,371	-	-	-	-	5,196	-	-	2.2	-
121st Infantry Regiment (Penza)	-	2,051	-	-	-	-	69,580	-	-	33.9	-
122nd Infantry Regiment (Tambov)	-	1,440	-	-	-	-	4,032	-	-	2.8	-
123rd Infantry Regiment (Koslov)	-	2,421	-	-	-	-	56,448	-	-	23.3	-
125th Infantry Regiment (Kursk)	-	2,873	-	-	-	-	175,251	-	-	61.0	-

Unit	Number of weapons in action			Ammunition expenditure					Rounds used per weapon		
				Artillery rounds			Small arms rounds				
	Guns	Rifles	Revolvers	Shells	Shrapnel	Canister	Rifle	Revolver	Gun	Rifle	Revolver
126th Infantry Regiment (Rylsk)	-	2,226	-	-	-	-	84,600	-	-	38.0	-
11th Dragoon Regiment (Riga)	-	644	96	-	-	-	3,868	480	-	6.0	5.0
11th Uhlan Regiment (Tchougouiev)	-	127	134	-	-	-	156	72	-	1.2	1.3
2nd Kuban Cossack Regiment	-	740	36	-	-	-	11,100	180	-	15.0	5.0
Vladikavkaz Cavalry Regiment	-	500	-	-	-	-	18,500	-	-	37.0	-
1st Battery, 30th Artillery Brigade	8	-	-	153	-	-	-	-	19.1	-	-
2nd Battery, 30th Artillery Brigade	8	-	-	7	37	-	-	-	5.5	-	-
3rd Battery, 30th Artillery Brigade	8	-	-	80	-	-	-	-	12.0	-	-
5th Battery, 30th Artillery Brigade	8	-	-	227	46	-	-	-	34.1	-	-
6th Battery, 30th Artillery Brigade	8	-	-	61	1	-	-	-	7.8	-	-
1st Battery, 5th Artillery Brigade	7	-	-	229	174	-	-	-	57.6	-	-
2nd Battery, 5th Artillery Brigade	7	-	-	77	183	-	-	-	37.1	-	-
5th Battery, 5th Artillery Brigade	8	-	-	147	224	4	-	-	46.9	-	-
6th Battery, 5th Artillery Brigade	8	-	-	3	-	-	-	-	0.4	-	-

Unit	Number of weapons in action			Ammunition expenditure					Rounds used per weapon		
				Artillery rounds			Small arms rounds				
	Guns	Rifles	Revolvers	Shells	Shrapnel	Canister	Rifle	Revolver	Gun	Rifle	Revolver
1st Battery, 31st Artillery Brigade	8	-	-	203	105	-	-	-	38.5	-	-
2nd Battery, 31st Artillery Brigade	8	-	-	172	100	-	-	-	34.0	-	-
3rd Battery, 31st Artillery Brigade	8	-	-	272	-	-	-	-	34.0	-	-
4th Battery, 31st Artillery Brigade	8	-	-	56	30	-	-	-	10.8	-	-
6th Battery, 31st Artillery Brigade	8	-	-	8	76	-	-	-	10.5	-	-
1st Battery, 32nd Artillery Brigade	8	-	-	258	90	-	-	-	43.5	-	-
3rd Battery, 32nd Artillery Brigade	8	-	-	385	180	-	-	-	70.6	-	-
4th Battery, 32nd Artillery Brigade	8	-	-	70	217	-	-	-	35.9	-	-
6th Battery, 32nd Artillery Brigade	8	-	-	115	115	-	-	-	28.8	-	-
8th Don Cossack Battery	6	-	-	80	3	-	-	-	13.8	-	-
18th Horse Artillery Battery	6	-	-	8	1	-	-	-	1.5	-	-
Totals	154	29,447	266	2,611	1,582	4	811,546	732	27.3	27.6	2.8

Notes
1   The Regiment also lost 1,008 small arms rounds.
2   The Regiment also lost 54,644 small arms rounds.

Appendix X

Russian Reinforcements to Bulgaria, August 15 1877

Guard Corps

His Imperial Highness the Crown Prince
  1st Guard Division: Grand Duke Vladimir
    1st Brigade:
      Preobrazhensky Guard Regiment
      Simeonov Guard Regiment
    2nd Brigade:
      Ismailov Guard Regiment
      Guard Jäger Regiment
    1st Guard Artillery Brigade
  2nd Guard Division: Lieutenant General Tchertkov I
    1st Brigade:
      Moscow Guard Regiment
      Guard Grenadier Regiment
    2nd Brigade:
      Pavlov Guard Regiment
      Finland Guard Regiment
  3rd Guard Division: Lieutenant General Shuvalov
    1st Brigade:
      Lithuania Guard Regiment
      Kexholm Guard Regiment
    2nd Brigade:
      St. Petersburg Grenadier Guard Regiment
      Volhynia Guard Regiment
  Guard Jäger Brigade:
      1st Emperor Guard Jäger Battalion
      2nd Guard Jäger Battalion
      3rd Finland Guard Jäger Battalion
      4th Guard Jäger Battalion
  1st Guard Cavalry Division: Lieutenant General Pouchkin
    1st Brigade:
      Chevalier Guard Regiment
      Guard Lancer Regiment
    2nd Brigade:
      Guard Dragoon Regiment
      Guard Hussar Regiment
      Combined Guard Cossack Regiment - formed by:

        Emperor Guard Cossack Regiment (2 sqns)
        Ataman Crown Prince Cossack Regiment (2 sqns)
        Ural Guard Cossack Squadron
    3rd Brigade:
        Emperor Guard Lancer Regiment
        Grodno Guard Hussar Regiment
  Corps Artillery:
        1st 2nd and 3rd Guard Artillery Brigades
        Guard Horse Artillery Brigade:

V Corps
Lieutenant General Rall
    7th Infantry Division:
        1st Brigade:
            25th (Smolensk) Infantry Regiment
            26th (Mohilev) Infantry Regiment
        2nd Brigade:
            27th (Vitebsk) Infantry
            28th (Polotsk) Infantry
    8th Infantry Division:
        1st Brigade:
            29th (Tchernigov) Infantry Regiment
            30th (Poltava) Infantry Regiment
        2nd Brigade:
            31st (Alexopol) Infantry Regiment
            32nd (Krementsoug) Infantry Regiment
  Corps Artillery:
        4th and 8th Artillery Brigades

XV Corps
Lieutenant General Kostanda
    2nd Infantry Division:
        1st Brigade:
            5th Infantry Regiment
            6th Infantry Regiment
        2nd Brigade:
            7th (Revel) Infantry Regiment
            8th Infantry Regiment
    3rd Infantry Division:
        1st Brigade:
            9th Infantry Regiment
            10th Infantry Regiment
        2nd Brigade:
            11th Infantry Regiment
            12th Infantry Regiment

15th Cavalry Division:
    4 Don Cossack Regiments
Corps Artillery:
  2nd and 3rd Artillery Brigades
  15th Horse Artillery Brigade

XVI Corps
Lieutenant General Rievousky
  27th Division:
    1st Brigade:
      105th (Orenburg) Infantry Regiment
      106th (Oufa) Infantry Regiment
    2nd Brigade:
      107th (Troitsa) Infantry Regiment
      108th (Saratov) Infantry Regiment
  37th Division: Lieutenant General Tchengey
    1st Brigade:
      145th (Novocherkassk) Infantry Regiment
      146th (Tsaritsyn) Infantry Regiment
    2nd Brigade:
      147th (Samara) Infantry Regiment
      148th (Caspian Sea) Infantry Regiment
  16th Cavalry Division:
    4 Don Cossack Regiments (2nd tour)
Corps Artillery
    27th and 37th Artillery Brigades
    16th Horse Artillery Brigade

Appendix XI

Order of Battle, Turkish Army of the Danube, August 1877

Commanding Officer: Mehemet Ali Pasha

1st Corps (Rasgrad)
Ahmed Eyoub Pasha
> Division: Fuad Pasha
>> Brigade: Hussein Pasha
>> Brigade: Mustafa Pasha
>>> 16 Battalions, 6 squadrons & 4 batteries
> Division: Assaf Pasha
>> Brigade: Osman Pasha
>> Brigade: Mehmet Pasha
>>> 16 Battalions, 6 squadrons & 4 batteries
> Division: Nejib Pasha
>> Brigade: Ali Pasha
>> Brigade: Hamid Pasha
>>> 16 Battalions, 6 squadrons & 4 batteries

2nd Corps (Eski Dzuma)
Prince Hassan
> Division: Ismail Pasha (Egyptian forces)
>> Brigade: Savfet Pasha
>> Brigade: Reschid Pasha
>>> 3 Egyptian Regiments, 1 *Nizam* Regiment
>>> 2 Light Battalions
>>> 14 battalions and 4 batteries
> Division: Salih Pasha
>> Brigade: Sabit Pasha
>> Brigade: Assim Pasha
>> Brigade: Mehmet Pasha
>>> 18 Battalions, 1 cavalry regiment & 4 batteries

Reserve Division
Salim Pasha
> Brigade: Tahir Pasha
> Brigade: Mehmet Pasha
>> 15 Battalions & 3 batteries

Appendix XII

Order of Battle of the Roumanian 3rd and 4th Infantry Divisions, August 30 1877

Column of Attack of the 3rd Infantry Division
Commander: Colonel Grigore Ipătescu

First attack echelon:
Skirmish line: 1st and 3rd Companies, 1st Battalion/10th *Dorobantsi* Regiment
Main body: 2nd, 4th and 5th Companies, 1st Battalion/10th *Dorobantsi* Regiment
                1st-4th Companies, 1st Battalion/8th Infantry Regiment

Second attack echelon:
                2nd Battalion/10th *Dorobantsi* Regiment
                2nd Battalion/8th Infantry Regiment

Column of Attack of the 4th Infantry Division
Commander: Colonel Grigore Borănescu

First attack echelon:
Skirmish line: 1st and 2nd Companies, 2nd Chasseur Battalion
First line: 3rd and 4th Companies, 2nd Chasseur Battalion
Second line: 1st Battalion, 16th *Dorobantsi* Regiment
Third line: 1st Battalion, 14th *Dorobantsi* Regiment
                2nd Battalion, 5th Infantry Regiment

Second attack echelon:
                1st Battalion, 5th Infantry Regiment
                1st and 2nd Battalions, 6th Infantry Regiment

Appendix XIII

Order of Battle, Turkish Army of Plevna, September 6 1877

Commanding Officer: *Mushir* Osman Pasha
Chief of Staff: *Mirliva* Tahir Pasha
Staff: *Mirliva* Sadik Pasha; *Miralai*s Hamdi Bey, Hairi Bey; *Kaim-makam*s Raif Bey, Abdullah Bey
Principal Aide-de-Campe: *Kaim-makam* Talahat Bey
Commander of cavalry: *Miralai* Osman Bey
Commander of artillery: *Mirliva* Ahmed Pasha
Surgeon-in-chief: *Miralai* Hassib Bey

Each regiment contained 3 battalions.

1st Division
Commander: *Ferik* Adil Pasha
    1st Brigade: *Mirliva* Edhem Pasha
        1st Regiment: *Kaim-makam* Mehemed Nazif Bey
        2nd Regiment: *Kaim-makam* Mehemed Bey
    2nd Brigade: *Mirliva* Kara Ali Pasha
        3rd Regiment: *Miralai* Hafouz Bey
        4th Regiment: *Miralai* Suleiman Bey
    2 squadrons *Nizam* Cavalry
    Detachment of Circassians
    4 batteries (each 6 guns)

2nd Division
Commander: *Ferik* Hassan Sabri Pasha
    3rd Brigade: *Miralai* Tewfik Bey
        5th Regiment:
        6th Regiment: *Miralai* Said Bey
    4th Brigade: *Mirliva* Atouf Pasha
        7th Regiment: *Kaim-makam* Ibrahim Bey
        8th Regiment: *Miralai* Omer Bey
    2 squadrons *Nizam* Cavalry
    Detachment of Circassians
    3 batteries (each 6 guns)

3rd Division
Commander: *Mirliva* Tahir Pasha

5th Brigade: *Kaim-makam* Riza Bey
   9th Regiment:
   10th Regiment: *Bimbashi* Issa
6th Brigade: *Miralai* Yunous Bey
   11th Regiment: *Kaim-makam* Ali Riza Bey
   12th Regiment: *Kaim-makam* Talahat Bey
2 squadron *Nizam* Cavalry
Detachment of Circassians
2 batteries (each 6 guns)

Reserves

Commander: *Mirliva* Rifa'at Pasha
   Infantry: *Mirliva* Emin Pasha
      10 battalions
   Cavalry: *Miralai* Osman Bey
      1 *Nizam* squadron (escort to headquarters)
      2 Ottoman Cossack squadrons
      10 squadrons Salonika auxiliaries
      Detachment of Circassians
   Artillery: *Mirliva* Ahmed Pasha
      3 batteries (each of 6 guns)
      1 company of engineers

Total: 46 infantry battalions, 19 cavalry squadrons, 500 Circassians, 12 batteries, 1 company engineers; or, 30,000 men with 72 guns.

Appendix XIV

List of the Turkish Fortifications and Positions at Plevna, with their Commanders and Garrisons, September 6 1877

		Btns	Guns
Left wing			
Opanetz redoubts	Suleiman Bey	2	6
Bukova redoubts	Mehemed Nazif Bey	4	3
Janik Bair redoubt (west)	Adil Pasha	3	6
Janik Bair redoubt (east)	Edhem Pasha	2	3
Bash Tabiya	Hafouz Bey	2	4
Kanli Tabiya	Kara Ali Pasha	1	2
Totals		14	24
Centre			
Atouf Tabiya	Atouf Pasha	2	4
Araba Tabiya	Tewfik Bey	3	4
Omer Tabiya	Omer Bey	3	2
Ibrahim Tabiya	Ibrahim Bey	2	4
Chorum Tabiya	Ibrahim Bey	2	4
Totals		12	18
Right wing			
Tahir Tabiya	Tahir Pasha	3	4
Issa Tabiya	Bimbashi Issa	1	-
Kavanlik Tabiya	Riza Bey	1	2
Yunuz Tabiya	Yunous Bey	2	3
Talahat Tabiya	Talahat Bey	1	3
Milas Tabiya	Ali Riza Bey	1	-
Baghlarbashi Tabiya	*Bimbashi* Rassim	1	-
Totals		10	12
Reserve			
Ikhtihat Tabiya	Rifa'at Pasha	3	6
Headquarters Hill	Ahmed Pasha	4	6
In Plevna	Ahmed Pasha	2	-

Vid bridge	*Bimbashi* Kazim	1	6
Totals		10	18

Summary

		Btns	Guns	Sqdns
Left wing, or First Division	Adil Pasha	14	24	2
Centre, or Second Division	Hassan Sabri Pasha	12	18	2
Right wing, or Third Division	Tahir Pasha	10	12	2
Reserve	Rifa'at Pasha	10	18	13
Totals		46	72	19

Appendix XV

Order of Battle, Turkish Army of the Danube, October 1877

Commanding Officer: *Mushir* Suleiman Pasha
Second in Command: *Ferik* Fazli Pasha
Chief of Staff: *Mirliva* Husni Pasha
General Staff: *Miralai* Mustafa Isset Bey
    Kaim-makam Bessim Bey
    Bimbashi Bedri Bey
    Bimbashi Zekki Bey
    Yuzbashi Mehmed-Ali Effendi
    Yuzbashi Adni Effendi

1st Division
Ferik Fuad Pasha
    1st Brigade: *Mirliva* Hadji Raschid Pasha
        1st Regiment
            1st 2nd and 3rd Battalions, 3rd *Nizam* Regiment
        2nd Regiment (*Kaim-makam* Nouri Bey)
            Rize *Redif* Battalion
            Gazze *Redif* Battalion (2nd *Ban*)
            Philippopolis *Redif* Battalion
            Aidin Auxiliary Battalion
    2nd Brigade: *Mirliva* Azmi Pasha
        3rd Regiment (*Miralai* Rustem Bey)
            Brousse *Redif* Battalion
            Kirmasti *Redif* Battalion
            Koutahia *Redif* Battalion
        4th Regiment (*Kaim-makam* Said Bey)
            Boli *Redif* Battalion
            Kotch-Hissar *Redif* Battalion
            Constantinople Auxiliary Battalion
    Reserve Regiment: (*Miralai* Mustafa Remzi Bey
        2nd *Nizam* Light Battalion
        Sofia *Redif* Battalion (1st *Ban*)
        Philippopolis *Redif* Battalion (1st *Ban*)
        Lovtcha *Redif* Battalion (1st *Ban*)
    Cavalry:
        1 squadron 3rd *Nizam* Cavalry Regiment
    Artillery: Lt. Colonel Ahmed Bey

1st, 2nd and 3rd Batteries, 4th Reserve Regiment
2nd Battery, 1st Reserve Regiment

2nd Division
Ferik Assaf Pasha
  1st Brigade: *Mirliva* Ibrahim Pasha
    1st Regiment (Kaim-makam Ismail Firkri Bey)
      Sofia *Redif* Battalion (2nd *Ban*)
      Philippopolis *Redif* Battalion (2nd *Ban*)
      Lovtcha *Redif* Battalion (2nd *Ban*)
    2nd Regiment (*Miralai* Osman Bey)
      1st, 2nd and 3rd Battalions, 1st *Nizam* Regiment
      Altouni-Zade Auxiliary Battalion
  2nd Brigade: *Mirliva* Osman Bey
    3rd Regiment (Kaim-makam Zihni Bey)
      1st and 2nd Battalions, 2nd *Nizam* Regiment
      Rasgrad *Redif* Battalion,
    4th Regiment (Kaim-makam Nusret Bey)
      Damascus *Redif* Battalion
      Beirut *Redif* Battalion (1st *Ban*)
      Jerusalem *Redif* Battalion (1st *Ban*)
      Cheich Auxiliary Battalion
  Reserve Regiment: (Kaim-makam Osman Bey)
      Antalya *Redif* Battalion
      Gazze *Redif* Battalion (3rd *Ban*)
      Homs *Redif* Battalion
      Nablus *Redif* Battalion
  Cavalry:
      2 squadrons Adrianople Gendarme Regiment
  Artillery: Lt. Colonel Ali Bey
      1st, 2nd and 3rd Batteries, 2nd Artillery Regiment
      3rd Battery, 5th Artillery Regiment
      Half Mountain Battery

3rd Division
Ferik Nedjib Pasha
  1st Brigade: *Mirliva* Osman Pasha
    1st Regiment (Kaim-makam Ismail Bey)
      Balikesser *Redif* Battalion
      Nigde *Redif* Battalion
      Ineboli *Redif* Battalion
      Ada-Bazar *Redif* Battalion
    2nd Regiment (Kaim-makam Nouri Bey)
      Sofia *Redif* Battalion (3rd *Ban*)
      Eregli *Redif* Battalion
      1st and 2nd Sultanie Auxiliary Battalions

2nd Brigade: *Mirliva* Reschid Pasha
    3rd Regiment (Kaim-makam Ahmed Fehmi Bey)
        5th *Nizam* Light Battalion
        Brousse *Redif* Battalion
        Kirmasti *Redif* Battalion
        Shumla *Redif* Battalion
    4th Regiment (Kaim-makam Atta Bey)
        Eski-Chehir *Redif* Battalion (3rd *Ban*)
        Demotika *Redif* Battalion
        Hasskeui *Redif* Battalion
        Aidin Auxiliary Battalion
Cavalry:
    2 squadrons Adrianople Gendarme Regiment
Artillery: *Miralai* Mustafa Bey
    1st 2nd and 3rd Batteries, 2nd Artillery Regiment
    1st Battery, 1st Artillery Regiment

4th Division
Ferik Sabit Pasha
    1st Brigade: *Mirliva* Assim Pasha
        1st Regiment
            2nd Battalion, 6th *Nizam* Regiment
            Eski-Chehir *Redif* Battalion (2nd *Ban*)
            Kaissarie *Redif* Battalion
        2nd Regiment (Kaim-makam Mustafa Bey)
            Tachkeupru *Redif* Battalion
            Tchoroum *Redif* Battalion
            Kirchehir *Redif* Battalion
            Yozgad *Redif* Battalion
    2nd Brigade: *Mirliva* Hassan Pasha
        3rd Regiment (Kaim-makam Husni Bey)
            1st, 2nd and 3rd Battalions, 1st *Nizam* Regiment
        4th Regiment
            1st, 2nd and 3rd Tirnova *Redif* Battalions
Cavalry:
    2 squadrons Adrianople Gendarme Regiment
    2nd Cavalry Regiment
Artillery:
    1st, 2nd and 3rd Batteries, 1st Artillery Regiment

Army Cavalry
Mirliva Kerim Pasha
    1st, 2nd, 3rd and 4th *Nizam* Regiments
    Military School Regiment
    Polish Auxiliaries
    Circassian Auxiliaries

Aidin Auxiliaries
Shumla Auxiliaries

Army Artillery
Miralai Mehmed Bey
    3 Horse Artillery Batteries, Reserve Regiment

Appendix XVI

Disposition and Strength of the Turkish Army of the Quadrilateral, October 1877

Station	Infantry		Cavalry	Artillery	
	Battalions	Men		Field Guns	Men
Varna	9	7,446	269	36	2,243*
Hadji Oglar Bazardjik	13½	8,637	1,591	22	522
Silistria	18½	10,776	389	12	2,022*
Rustchuk	20	12,630	60	12	1,767*
Kadikoi	18	10,730	}	26	}
Rasgrad Camp	25	13,552	}	65	}
Rasgrad Town	1	463		-	
Solenik	13	7,429	} 1,585	18	} 2,347
Near Djelin Jenikeui	3	1,973	}	-	}
Djumaa and Karahassankoi	20	11,196	1,369	30	628
Jaila	13	7,757	208	22	539
Slimnia and Kasan	10	7,832	-	-	-
Shumla	8	4,817	284	18	1,411*
Totals	172	105,238	5,755	261	11,479

* Including garrison artillery.

Appendix XVII

Bulgarian Legion, October 1877

Commanding Officer: General Stoletov
Chief of Staff: Lieutenant Colonel Keller

1st Brigade (Colonel Depreradovich)
    1st Battalion (Col. Kesiakov)
    2nd Battalion (Maj. Kurtianov)
    7th Battalion (Lt. Col Tizenhausen)
    8th Battalion (Capt. Ilin)

2nd Brigade (Colonel Viazemsky)
    3rd Battalion (Maj. Chiliaev)
    4th Battalion (Maj. Redkin)
    9th Battalion (Lt.Col.Lvov)
    10th Battalion (Lt. Col. Tselitsa)

3rd Brigade (Colonel Tolstoy)
    5th Battalion (Maj Popov)
    6th Battalion (Maj. Beliaev)
    11th Battalion (not known)
    12th Battalion (Maj. Kornilovich)

Order of Battle, Turkish Army of the West, November 1877

Commanding Oficer: *Mushir* Mehemet Ali Pasha
   Staff: *Miralai* Zia Bey
      Miralai Omer Bey
      Bimbashi Nazim Bey
      Bimbashi Chaukir Bey
      Bimbashi Izzet Bey

1st Division

Ferik Chakir Pasha
   1st Brigade: *Mirliva* Ibrahim Pasha
      1st Regiment (*Kaim-makam* Moustafa Bey)
         1st, 2nd and 3rd Battalions, Bosnia *Nizam* Regiment
         Kiangueri *Redif* Battalion,
      2nd Regiment (*Kaim-makam* Kiamu Bey)
         Eregli *Redif* Battalion
         Uskub *Redif* Battalion
         Tire *Redif* Battalion
   2nd Brigade: *Mirliva* Mehmed Zekki Pasha
      3rd Regiment (*Kaim-makam* Ahmed Chukri Bey)
         3rd Battalion 4th *Nizam* Regiment
         Salonika *Redif* Battalion
         Pergama *Redif* Battalion
         Ourfa *Redif* Battalion (3rd *Ban*)
      4th Regiment (*Kaim-makam* Kiamil Bey)
         Ourfa *Redif* Battalion (1st *Ban*)
         Jerusalem *Redif* Battalion (3rd *Ban*)
         Kaissarie *Mustafiz* Battalion
   Reserve Regiment (*Kaim-makam* Bey)
      2nd Battalion 3rd *Nizam* Regiment
      Drama *Redif* Battalion
      Adrianople *Redif* Battalion
   Artillery:
      2 Field Batteries

2nd Division

Ferik Redjib Pasha
   3rd Brigade: *Mirliva* Chukri Pasha

1st Regiment (*Kaim-makam* Chefki Bey)
   1st *Nizam* Light Battalion
   Tchoroum *Redif* Battalion
   Boli *Mustafiz* Battalion
   Tarsis *Redif* Battalion
2nd Regiment (*Kaim-makam* Ali Bey)
   3rd Battalion 3rd *Nizam* Regiment
   Tiran *Redif* Battalion
   Sandoukli *Mustafiz* Battalion,
4th Brigade: *Miralai* Nazif Bey
   3rd Regiment (*Kaim-makam* Izzet Bey)
   2nd Bosnia *Nizam* Battalion
   Karahissar *Mustafiz* Battalion
   Elbassan *Redif* Battalion
   Tchoroum *Mustafiz* Battalion
   4th Regiment (*Kaim-makam* Ali Bey)
   Beyrouth *Redif* Battalion
   Kiangueri *Mustafiz* Battalion
   Nigde *Mustafiz* Battalion
Reserve Regiment (Ahmed Bey)
   Ischtib *Redif* Battalion
   Eregli Moustahfiz Battalion
   Pristina *Mustafiz* Battalion
Artillery:
   2 Field Batteries

Reserve

5th Brigade: *Mirliva* Baker Pasha
   1st Regiment: (*Kaim-makam* Islam Bey)
      Uskub *Redif* Battalion
      Eski-Chehir *Mustafiz* Battalion
      Tripoli *Redif* Battalion
      Nish *Mustafiz* Battalion (1st and 2nd *Ban*)
   2nd Regiment: (*Kaim-makam* Emin Bey)
      Nish *Mustafiz* Battalion (3rd *Ban*)
      Tuzla (Bosnia) *Redif* Battalion
      Prizrend *Mustafiz* Battalion
      Jerusalem *Redif* Battalion (1st *Ban*)
      Prizrend *Redif* Battalion
Artillery:
   2 Field Batteries
Cavalry:
   Four *Nizam* Regiments
   Ottoman Cossack Regiment
   Fethie Circassian Auxiliaries
   Nusretiye Circassian Auxiliaries

Selimiye Circassian Auxiliaries
Balikesser Volunteer Cavalry
Aleppe Volunteer Cavalry
Smyrna Volunteer Cavalry
Eski-Chehir Volunteer Cavalry
Aidin Volunteer Cavalry

Other Units

Garrison of Sophia: *Ferik* Mehmed Pasha
    5 Infantry Battalions
    3 Squadrons
    1 Battery (6 guns)
Loutikovo: *Mirliva* Ali Pasha
    5 Infantry Battalions
    1 Battery (6 guns)
Pirot: *Mirliva* Yahia Pasha
    5 Infantry Battalions
    1 Battery (6 guns)
Dorouk Pass: Lieutenant *Miralai* Refik Bey
    3 Infantry Battalions
    1 Battery (6 guns)
Slatitza: *Miralai* Omer Bey
    11 Infantry Battalions
    Auxiliary Cavalry
    1 Mountain Battery (8 guns)

Appendix XIX

Order of Battle, Turkish Army of Plevna, December 10 1877

Commanding Officer: *Mushir* Ghazi Osman Pasha
Chief of Staff: *Mirliva* Tahir Pasha
Staff: *Miralai* Veli Bey, Hairi Bey; *Kaim-makam* Tahir Bey
Principal Aide-de-Camp: *Kaim-makam* Talahat Bey
Commander of artillery: *Mirliva* Ahmed Pasha
Commander of cavalry: *Miralai* Bekir Bey
Commander of train and convoy: *Miralai* Said Bey
Surgeon-in-Chief: *Miralai* Hassib Bey

1st Division
Mirliva Tahir Pasha
    1st Brigade: *Mirliva* Atouf Pasha
        1st Regiment: *Kaim-makam* Raif Bey
            1st, 2nd and 3rd Battalions, 2nd *Nizam* Regiment
            Ischtib *Redif* Battalion
        2nd Regiment: *Kaim-makam* Eyoub Bey
            Ineboli *Redif* Battalion
            Gumuldjina *Redif* Battalion
            Yozgad Battalion
            Drama *Redif* Battalion
        Artillery:
            2 Field Batteries (12 guns)
    2nd Brigade: *Miralai* Yunous Bey
        3rd Regiment: *Kaim-makam* Zini Bey
            1st, 2nd and 3rd Battalions, 4th *Nizam* Regiment
            Silistria *Redif* Battalion
        4th Regiment: *Kaim-makam* Abdullah Bey
            Nish *Redif* Battalion (1st *Ban*)
            Nish *Redif* Battalion (2nd *Ban*)
            Kiangueri *Redif* Battalion
            Prizrend *Redif* Battalion
        Artillery:
            2 Field Batteries (12 guns)
    3rd Brigade: *Mirliva* Tewfik Pasha
        5th Regiment: *Kaim-makam* Mehemed Nazif Bey
            5th *Nizam* Light Battalion

Monastir *Redif* Battalion
Tchoroum *Redif* Battalion
Pristina *Redif* Battalion
6th Regiment: *Kaim-makam* Rassim Bey
Ankara *Redif* Battalion
Gumuschhane *Redif* Battalion
Bey-Bazar *Redif* Battalion
Eregli *Redif* Battalion
Artillery:
2 Field Batteries (12 guns)
Cavalry: *Kaim-makam* Chefki Bey
1 cavalry regiment (*Nizam*) (5 squadrons)

2nd Division

Ferik Adil Pasha
4th Brigade: *Mirliva* Hussein Wasfi Pasha
7th Regiment: *Kaim-makam* Natou Bey
1st *Nizam* Light Battalion
1st Battalion 7th *Nizam* Regiment
Ada-Bazar *Mustafiz* Battalion
Simaw *Redif* Battalion
Nigde *Redif* Battalion
8th Regiment: *Kaim-makam* Hourshid Bey
3rd Battalion 6th *Nizam* Regiment
Kiangueri *Redif* Battalion
Sparta *Mustafiz* Battalion
Aintab *Redif* Battalion
Kilis *Redif* Battalion
Artillery:
2 Field Batteries (12 guns)
5th Brigade: *Mirliva* Sadik Pasha
9th Regiment: *Miralai* Hafouz Bey
1st, 2nd and 3rd Battalions, 3rd *Nizam* Regiment
Nizam with Magnesie *Mustafiz* Battalion
Simaw *Redif* Battalion
Mustafiz-Seres *Redif* Battalion
10th Regiment: *Kaim-makam* Latif Bey
Slivno *Redif* Battalion
Assi-Yosgad *Redif* Battalion
Choumia *Redif* Battalion
Kirchehir *Redif* Battalion
Artillery:
2 Field Batteries (12 guns)
6th Brigade: *Mirliva* Edhem Pasha
11th Regiment: *Kaim-makam* Kazim Bey
2nd *Nizam* Regiment

2nd *Nizam* Light Battalion
2nd *Nizam* Battaliion, *Nizam* Regiment
Zafranboli *Redif* Battalion
12th Regiment: *Miralai* Suleiman Bey
3rd Battalion, 5th *Nizam* Regiment
3rd Battalion, 2nd *Nizam* Regiment
Nablus *Redif* Battalion
Djeunis *Redif* Battalion
Koula *Redif* Battalion
Artillery:
2 Field Batteries (12 guns)
Cavalry: *Kaim-makam* Haki Bey
1 cavalry regiment (*Nizam*) (4 squadrons)
½ cavalry regiment (Salonika auxiliaries) (5 squadrons)

Convoy Brigade

7th Brigade: *Miralai* Said Bey
13th Regiment: *Kaim-makam* Pertev Bey
1st, 2nd and 3rd Battaliions, 5th *Nizam* Regiment,
Assi-Yozgad *Redif* Battalion
Bey-Bazar *Redif* Battalion
14th Regiment: *Kaim-makam* Ali Mehemed Bey
3rd *Nizam* Light Battalion
Milas *Redif* Battalion
Tireboli *Redif* Battalion
Serres *Redif* Battalion
Auxiliary Battalion
2 Ottoman Cossack squadrons
1 squadron mounted volunteers of Vodena

Corps cavalry

Commander: *Miralai* Bekir Bey
½ cavalry regiment (Salonika auxiliaries) (5 squadrons)
2 squadrons Circassians

Reserve artillery

1 battery (4 guns) (6-pounders)

Engineers

Commander: *Kaim-makam* Tiflik Bey
3 companies

Escort to Headquarters

1 battalion volunteers of the Ottoman Union

Totals

Infantry	58 battalions	22,000 men
Cavalry	9 squadrons regulars	}
	2 squadrons Ottoman Cossacks	}
	10 squadrons Salonika auxiliaries	} 1,500 men
	2 squadrons Circassians (200)	}
	1 squadron mounted volunteers of Vodena	}
Artillery	14 batteries @ 6 guns each	} 88 guns
	1 battery @ 4 guns	} 1,500 men
Engineers	3 companies	}
Escort to Headquarters: 1 battalion		} 9,000 men
Non-combatants, convalescents and wounded		}
Grand total	34,000 men	

Distribution of the Russian Army in Bulgaria, December 25 1877

Commanders	Gourko		Radetzky		Tsarevich		{Zimmerman, Fanetzky, Kartzov} {Dellinghausen, Kartzov}			Semeka[1]	
Army Corps	Guard	IX	VIII	IV	XII	XIII	XIV	Grenadier	XI	VII	X
Infantry Divisions	1, 2, 3	5, 31; 3[2]	9, 14	16, 30; 21	12, 33	1, 35; 32, 2	17, 18	2, 3	11, 26; 3[3]	15, 36	13, 34
Rifle Brigades	1		Bulgarian Legion	3, 4							
Cavalry Divisions	2	4 Caucasian Cossack Don Cossack		1	12	8 Don Cossack[4]	1 Cossack 7[5]	11, 13	9 Don Cossack[6]	7[7]	10
Total	84½ battalions = 65,000; 54 squadrons = 6,000; 256 field guns = 9,000; 24 horse artillery guns = 1,000; Total = 80,000 men		74 battalions = 56,000; 18 squadrons = 2,000; 240 field guns = 7,500; 12 horse artillery guns = 500; Total = 66,000 men		72 battalions = 54,500; 60 squadrons = 6,500; 288 field guns = 9,000; 36 horse artillery guns = 1,500; Total = 71,500 men		76½ battalions = 58,000; 92 squadrons = 10,000; 320 field guns = 10,000; 60 horse artillery guns = 2,500; Total = 80,000 men			48 battalions = 40,000; 28 squadrons = 8,000; 192 field guns = 6,000; 18 horse artillery guns = 1,900; Total = 50,900 men	

Notes

1 This command constituted the Coast Army, mostly stationed at Odessa, with detachments in the Crimea and the Lower Danube.

2 11th and 12th Infantry Regiments, 1½ battalions 10th Infantry Regiment.

3 9th Infantry Regiment, 1½ battalions 10th Infantry Regiment.

4 Consisted of 31st, 36th, 37th and 39th Don Cossack Regiments. In the middle of January sent over the Balkans via the Shipka Pass, under Lieutenant-General Skobelev I, and joined General Gourko's command at Philippopolis.

5 One brigade only.

6 One brigade only (24th and 30th Don Cossack Regiments).

7 One brigade only.

Glossary

The question of the proper treatment of names in a history of the Russo-Turkish War of 1877-1878 is peculiarly difficult to resolve. For an English language history most of the sources come from the 19th century; commentators such as journalists, military attachés and historians used transliterations of Russian, Bulgarian and Turkish names with a cheerful inconsistency, and it is by no means easy to follow a straight path. Much of the difficulty stems from the fact that names, especially place names, were recorded phonetically, and their transfer to the written page descended on what the listener thought he heard, and the language which he himself spoke.

Since this is a history in English, I have followed the sources that are historically most familiar, and have not attempted to use the modern day equivalents – a decision which I realise will offend the purists. I have, however, had great assistance from Robert Williams with regard to Russian names. He has pointed out that in the 19th century English writers did a particularly bad job of transliterating these. Thanks to his help I am able to set out below the spelling of various names as they appear in the text, with their proper transliteration as well as the Russian version. Where possible, two transliterations are given for foreign names, the first being the spelling in the original language and the second being the exact transliteration from the Russian.

Bulgarian place names present even more difficulty. Both the Bulgarian and Turkish versions of such place names were used interchangeably by 19th century writers, with all their phonetic misspelling; and in any case they often bear little relation to their modern equivalents. I have therefore used the formulation most frequently used by contemporary writers.

Finally, there are the names of Turkish places and individuals. Modern Turkish produces very considerable variations in the spelling of both; again, I have followed the 19th century version.

The senior Turkish ranks are given in Turkish; their approximate Western equivalents are as follows:

Mushir	Marshal
Ferik	Lieutenant General
Mirliva	Brigadier General
Miralai	Colonel
Kaim-makam	Lieutenant-Colonel
Bimbashi	Major
Yuzbashi	Captain

Russian Names

Name in Text	Correct transliteration	Original Russian
Alkhazov	Alkhazov	Алхазов
Amilakhvari	Amilakhvari	Амилахвари
Arnoldi	Arnoldi or Arnol'di	Арнольди

Name in Text	Correct transliteration	Original Russian
Astafeev	Astafeyev	Астафеев
Avinov	Avinov	Авинов
Baranov	Baranov	Баранов
Bariatinsky	Baryatinsky	Барятинский
Belinsky	Belinsky	Белинский
Biskoupsky	Biskupsky	Бискупский
Boreisha	Boreysha	Борейша
Boutchkiev	Buchkiyev	Бучкиев
Bronevsky	Bronevsky	Броневский
Brunnow	Brunnov	Бруннов
Bulmering	Bulmering or Bul'mering	Бульмеринг
Cherniaev	Chernyayev	Черняев
Chernozubov	Chernozubov	Чернозубов
Chernyshev	Chernyshyov	Чернышёв
Danilov	Danilov	Данилов
De Firks	Firks	Фиркс
Dehn	Dehn or Den	Ден
Dellinghausen	Dellinghausen or Delensgausen	Деленсгаузен
Denibekov	Denibekov	Денибеков
Derozhinsky	Derozhinsky	Дерожинский
Devel	Devel or Devel	Девель
Dobrovolsky	Dobrovolsky	Добровольский
Dolgorukov	Dolgorukov	Долгоруков
Dombrovsky	Dombrovsky	Домбровский
Doukhonine	Dukhonin	Духонин
Dragomirov	Dragomirov	Драгомиров
Driesen	Driesen or Drizen	Дризен
Dubassov	Dubasov	Дубасов
Ellis	Ellis	Эллис
Fadeyev	Fadeyev	Фадеев
Fofanov	Fofanov	Фофанов
Ganetsky	Ganetsky	Ганецкий
Gorchakov	Gorchakov	Горчаков
Goremykin	Goremekin	Горемыкин
Gortalov	Gortalov	Горталов
Gourko	Gurko	Гурко
Grabbe	Grabbe	Граббе

Name in Text	Correct transliteration	Original Russian
Hahn	Hahn or Gan	Ган
Heimann	Heimann or Geyman	Гейман
Ignatiev	Ignat'yev	Игнатьев
Imeretinsky	Imeretinsky	Имеретинский
Karassev	Karasev	Карасев
Kartsov	Kartsov	Карцов
Khilkov	Khilkov	Хилков
Khomenko	Khomenko	Хоменко
Kiselev	Kiselyov	Киселёв
Kleinhaus	Kleinhaus or Kleyngaus	Клейнгаус
Klenveshahl	Kleveshahl or Klevezal'	Клевезаль
Knorring	Knorring	Кнорринг
Komarov	Komarov	Комаров
Korf	Korf	Корф
Korsakov	Korsakov	Корсаков
Kouzminsky	Kuzminsky	Кузминский
Kovalevsky	Kovalevsky	Ковалевский
Kravchenko	Kravchenko	Кравченко
Krock	Krock or Krok	Крок
Krüdener	Krüdener or Kridener	Криденер
Kuropatkin	Kuropatkin	Куропаткин
Lavrov	Lavrov	Лавров
Lazarev	Lazarev	Лазарев
Leonov	Leonov	Леонов
Leontiev	Leont'yev	Леонтьев
Levitsky	Levitsky	Левицкий
Lioubovitsky	Lyubovitsky	Любовицкий
Lipinsky	Lipinsky	Липинский
Lockarev	Lashkaryov	Лашкарёв
Loris-Melikov	Loris-Melikov	Лорис-Меликов
Martinov	Martynov	Мартынов
Maximilianovich	Maksimilianovich	Максимилианович
Miliutin	Milyutin	Милютин
Muraviev	Murav'yev	Муравьев
Nepokoitschitsky	Nepokoychitsky	Непокойчицкий
Novikov	Novikov	Новиков
Obruchev	Obruchev	Обручев
Oklobju	Oklobzhio	Оклобжио

Name in Text	Correct transliteration	Original Russian
Orlov	Orlov	Орлов
Pamoutine	Panyutin	Панютин
Panin	Panin	Панин
Petrouschevsky	Petrushevsky	Петрушевский
Philippov	Filipov	Филипов
Popov	Popov	Попов
Prokhorov	Prokhorov	Прохоров
Radetzky	Radetzky or Radetsky	Радецкий
Rauch	Rauch or Raukh	Раух
Rodionov	Rodionov	Родионов
Rodzevich	Rozdevich	Роздевич
Roop	Roop	Рооп
Rosenbach	Rosenbach or Rozenbakh	Розенбах
Rosenbaum	Rosenbaum or Rozenbaum	Розенбаум
Rostovsev	Rostovtsev	Ростовцев
Rounov	Runov	Рунов
Rydzevsky	Rydzevsky	Рыдзевский
Scalon	Scalon or Skalon	Скалон
Schack	Schack or Shak	Шак
Schildner-Schuldner	Schilder-Schuldner	Шильдер-Шульднер
Schnitnikov	Shnitnikov	Шнитников
Schwabe	Schwabe or Shvabe	Швабе
Shakofskoy	Shakhovskoy	Шаховской
Shelemetiev	Shelemet'yev	Шелеметьев
Shelkovnikov	Shelkovnikov	Шелковников
Shestakov	Shestakov	Шестаков
Shuvalov	Shuvalov	Шувалов
Skobelev	Skobelev	Скобелев
Sobelev	Sobolev	Соболев
Stroukov	Strukov	Струков
Sukhozanet	Sukhozanet	Сухозанет
Sviatopolk-Mirsky	Svyatopolk-Mirsky	Святополк-Мирский
Tatischev	Tatishchev	Татищев
Tchelistchev	Chelishchev	Челищев
Tchereminissov	Cheremisinov	Черемисинов
Tebjanik	Tebyakin	Тебякин
Tergukassov	Tergukasov	Тергукасов
Tiajelnikov	Tyazhel'nikov	Тяжельников

Name in Text	Correct transliteration	Original Russian
Todleben	Todleben or Totleben	Тотлебен
Tolstoy	Tolstoy	Толстой
Tsertelev	Tsertelev	Цертелев
Tsiliadzev	Tsitlyadzev	Цитлядзев
Tsvietsinsky	Tsvetsinsky	Цвецинский
Tutolmin	Tutolmin	Тутолмин
Vannovsky	Vannovsky	Ванновский
Veliaminov	Vel'yaminov	Вельяминов
Vodjakin	Vodyakin	Водякин
Vorontsov	Vorontsov	Воронцов
Wielopolski	Wielopolski or Velyopol'sky	Велёпольский
Yolchine	Yolchin	Елчин
Zamoyski	Zamoysky	Замойский
Zeddeler	Seddeler or Zeddeler	Зедделер
Zimmermann	Zimmermann or Tsimmerman	Циммерман
Zotov	Zotov	Зотов

Notes

Chapter 1: The Congress of Paris

1. Norman Rich, *Why the Crimean War?* (Hanover NH 1985) p167
2. ibid, p178
3. AJP Taylor, *The Struggle for Mastery in Europe* (Oxford 1954) p81
4. ibid
5. Alan Palmer, *The Decline and Fall of the Ottoman Empire* (London 1992) p122
6. Quoted George Villiers, *A Vanished Victorian* (London 1938) p271
7. Quoted Rich, p183
8. Taylor, p83
9. Quoted Rich, pp195-196
10. Taylor, p85
11. William E Echard, *Napoleon III and the Concert of Europe* (Baton Rouge LA 1983) p70
12. Hugh Seton-Watson, *The Russian Empire 1801-1917* (Oxford 1967) p331

Chapter 2: Political and Social Reform in Russia

1. Quoted W Bruce Lincoln, *Nicholas I* (London 1978) p350
2. Hugh Seton-Watson, *The Russian Empire 1801-1917* (Oxford 1967) p332
3. Edward Crankshaw, *The Shadow of the Winter Palace* (London 1976) p152
4. H Seton-Watson, p333
5. ibid, p335
6. ibid, pp347-348
7. ibid, p404-407
8. William C Fuller, *Strategy & Power in Russia 1600-1914* (New York 1992) pp276-277
9. H Seton-Watson pp290-292
10. ibid, pp442-443
11. ibid, pp416-417
12. ibid, p377
13. ibid, p445
14. Taylor, pp160-161

Chapter 3: The Ottoman Empire

1. Quoted Palmer, p137
2. ibid, p128
3. Quoted Jason Goodwin, *Lords of the Horizons* (London 1998) p313
4. William Miller, *The Ottoman Empire 1801-1913* (Cambridge 1913) p333
5. ibid, pp259-260
6. Echard, p133
7. ibid, p139
8. Quoted Echard, p144

9. Palmer, pp134-135
10. ibid, p136
11. ibid, p139
12. Quoted Palmer, p142
13. Miller, p369
14. Palmer, p145

Chapter 4: The Eastern Question

1. Taylor, p215
2. Taylor, p216; William L Langer, *European Alliances and Alignments* 1871-1890 (New York 1950) p11
3. Misha Glenny, *The Balkans. Nationalism, War and the Great Powers 1804-1999* (London 1999) p124
4. Quoted Glenny, p130
5. Quoted Langer, p71
6. Langer, p74
7. ibid, p81
8. Taylor, p236
9. Mihailo D Stojanovic, *The Great Powers and the Balkans* (Cambridge 1939) pp86-87
10. I S Kartsov, quoted David Mackenzie, *The Lion of Tashkent* (Athens GA 1974) p127
11. Gale Stokes, *Politics as Development: The Emergence of Political Parties in 19th century Serbia* (Durham NC 1990) p111
12. Mackenzie, p165
13. Stojanovic, p24

Chapter 5: The Approach to War

1. Quoted RT Millman, *Britain and the Eastern Question 1875-1878* (Oxford 1979) p525n
2. Quoted Millman, p165
3. Elliot to Derby, September 4 1876, quoted R W Seton-Watson, *Disraeli, Gladstone and the Eastern Question* (New York 1972) p63
4. Quoted Millman, p144
5. ibid, p154
6. Quoted Stojanovic, p96
7. R W Seton Watson, p57
8. Glenny, p110
9. Stojanovic, p103
10. Gordon Craig, *The Politics of the Prussian Army* (Oxford 1964) p264
11. Prince Otto von Bismarck, *Reflections and Reminiscences* (London 1899) II p334
12. Quoted Langer, p100
13. Langer p103; Stojanovic p122
14. Quoted Langer, p104
15. Stojanovic, p128
16. Millman, p215
17. Langer, p105; J R Vincent (ed), *A Selection from the Diaries of the 15th Earl of Derby between September 1869 and March 1878* (London 1994) p356

18. Quoted Millman, p234
19. Werther to Bülow, E T S Dugdale (trans) *German Diplomatic Documents 1871-1914* (London 1928) I p46
20. Quoted Millman, p247
21. Palmer, pp148-149

Chapter 6: Recourse to Arms

1. Millman, pp248-249
2. Quoted Millman, pp250-251
3. ibid, p251
4. Quoted Millman, p255
5. Otto Pflanze, *Bismarck and the Development of Germany* (Princeton NJ 1990) II p426
6. Quoted Millman, p261
7. Langer, p115; Vincent, p386
8. R W Seton-Watson, p167
9. Captain H M Hozier, *The Russo Turkish War* (London nd) I pp274-275
10. R W Seton-Watson, p196
11. ibid, p197
12. ibid, pp192-194
13. ibid, p195; Millman, pp295-296
14. Millman, p297
15. ibid, p274
16. R W Seton-Watson, p173; Millman, p281
17. Langer, pp116-117

Chapter 7: The Russian Army

1. Quoted Bruce W Menning, *Bayonets before Bullets* (Indianapolis IND 1992) p8
2. Forrestt A Miller, *Dimitri Miliutin and the Reform Era* (Vanderbilt TN 1962) pp9-13
3. ibid, p19
4. ibid, p31
5. Quoted Menning, p11
6. Menning, p14
7. ibid, p17
8. Robert F Baumann, 'The Russian Army 1853-1881' in *The Military History of Tsarist Russia* (New York 2002) p138
9. Menning, pp21-22
10. Francis V Greene, *Report on the Russian Army and its Campaigns in Turkey in 1877-1878* (New York 1879) p19-20 (cited hereafter as Greene; all page references are to the text volume)
11. Fuller, pp279-280
12. Menning, p29
13. Major F Maurice, *The Russo Turkish War* 1877 (London 1905) p12
14. Greene, p149

15. 'Daily News', *The War Correspondence of the* Daily News *1877-8* (London 1878) I p59
16. Francis V Greene, *Sketches of Army Life in Russia* (New York 1880) p150
17. 'Daily News', *Correspondence*, I p82
18. ibid, p136
19. Rupert Furneaux, *The Siege of Plevna* (London 1958) p25; Olga Novikova, *Skobeleff and the Slavonic Cause* (London 1883) p32
20. W E D Allen and Paul Muratoff, *Caucasian Battlefields* (Cambridge 1953) pp111 and 216

Chapter 8: The Ottoman Army
1. Field Marshal Helmuth von Moltke, *The Russians in Bulgaria and Rumelia in 1828 and 1829 during the campaign of the Danube, the sieges of Brailow, Varna, Silistria, Shumia and the passage of the Balkans* (London 1854) p13 (cited hereafter as Moltke)
2. ibid, p456
3. Field Marshal Helmuth von Moltke, *Briefe aus der Türkei* (Berlin 1873) pp377-400
4. Maurice, pp14-16
5. Mesut Uyar and Edward J Erickson, *A Military History of the Ottomans* (Santa Barbara CA 2009) p177
6. F W von Herbert, *The Defence of Plevna* (London 1911) p8
7. Maurice, pp16-17
8. Herbert, p10
9. 'Daily News', *Correspondence*, I p18
10. Herbert, p50
11. Maurice, pp38-38; Greene, p380

Chapter 9: Command of the Sea
1. B Langensiepen and A Güleryük, *The Ottoman Steam Navy 1828-1923* (London 1995) pp134-136
2. ibid, pp133-134
3. 'Daily News', *Correspondence*, I pp24-25
4. Admiral Hobart Pasha, *Sketches from My Life* (London 1887) pp107-108
5. Langensiepen, p3
6. Roger Fulford (ed), *Your Dear Letter* (London 1971) p145
7. Langensiepen, p3
8. ibid
9. Donald W Mitchell, *A History of Russian and Soviet Sea Power* (London 1974) p185
10. Fred T Jane, *The Imperial Russian Navy* (London 1899) pp180-181
11. ibid, p181
12. ibid, p175
13. Hobart, 117

Chapter 10: Plans of Campaign
1. Quoted Fuller, p296
2. ibid, p313
3. Fuller, pp314-316

4. R Rosetti, 'Roumania's Share in the War of 1877' in *Slavonic and East European Review* (March 1930) p552
5. Maurice, pp32-33
6. ibid, p34
7. Menning, p53
8. Maurice, p39
9. Greene, p161
10. Maurice, p40
11. Hobart, p117
12. ibid, pp119-120
13. Colonel FA Wellesley, *With the Russians in Peace and War* (London 1905) p169
14. ibid, p180
15. ibid, pp190-193
16. Vincent, p28
17. ibid, p420

Chapter 11: The Barboshi Bridge

1. Hozier, I p380
2. 'Daily News', *Correspondence*, I p39
3. ibid, p41
4. Greene p152
5. ibid, pp152-153
6. 'Daily News', *Correspondence*, I p65
7. Maurice, pp51-52
8. Greene, p151
9. ibid, pp153-154

Chapter 12: The Crossing of the Danube

1. Menning, pp39-40
2. ibid, pp40-41
3. Quoted Menning, p44
4. Greene, p157
5. Maurice, p56
6. 'Daily News', *Correspondence*, I pp170-171
7. Maurice, pp57-58
8. Menning, p56
9. Anon, *Historical Narrative of the Turko-Russian War* (London nd) I p150
10. Hozier, I p468
11. *Turko-Russian War*, I p153
12. Menning, p56
13. Maurice, p63
14. Greene, p159
15. 'Daily News', *Correspondence*, I p297
16. ibid, p160
17. Quoted Greene, p444
18. Maurice, p69

Chapter 13: Gourko

1. 'Daily News', *Correspondence* I p246
2. Greene, *Army Life in Russia* p144
3. Greene, pp164-165; Maurice, p71
4. Moltke, p46
5. ibid
6. Field Marshal Helmuth von Moltke, *Lettres Sur l'Orient* (Paris 1872) p139
7. Hozier, I p476;Greene p166
8. Hozier, I p477
9. ibid, I pp477-478
10. Col. Nikolai Epauchin, trans Col. Henry Havelock, *Operations of General Gurko's Advance Guard in 1877* (London 1900) p35
11. Moltke, p46
12. Epauchin, pp41-42; Greene, p167
13. Epauchin, p48
14. Greene, p168
15. Hozier II, p458
16. 'Daily News', *Correspondence* I pp262-263
17. Greene, p169
18. Epauchin, pp71-72
19. Greene, p169
20. 'Daily News', *Correspondence* I pp269-270
21. Hozier, II p489; Greene p169
22. Epauchin, p81
23. Greene, p170
24. 'Daily News', I p272
25. Greene, pp171-172; Epauchin pp98-105
26. 'Daily News', *Correspondence*, I p273
27. Greene, pp173-174

Chapter 14: Krüdener

1. Greene, p185
2. Maurice, p94
3. Herbert, p81
4. Greene, p187
5. ibid, p188
6. 'Daily News', *Correspondence*, I p251
7. Herbert, p91
8. ibid, p95
9. Maurice, p108
10. Greene, p189
11. ibid, p190
12. Maurice, p109
13. Hozier, II p568
14. Herbert, p113
15. Greene, p192

6. Maurice, p115

Chapter 15: Osman

1. Reginald Hargreaves, *The Enemy at the Gate* (London c 1944) p219
2. Herbert, p132
3. Sir George Sydenham Clarke, *Fortification* (London 1907) p70
4. Colonel C B Brackenbury, *Field Works* (London 1888) p276
5. Herbert, p129
6. Maurice, p117
7. ibid, p119
8. ibid, p121
9. Greene, p196
10. ibid, p198
11. ibid
12. Greene, p200; Maurice, pp126-127
13. Greene, pp200-201
14. Maurice, p130
15. Herbert. p164
16. Thilo von Trotha, *Tactical Studies on the Battles Around Plevna* (Kansas City KS 1896) pp67-74
17. 'Daily News', *Correspondence,* I p323
18. Rosetti, p556
19. King Charles of Roumania, *Aus dem Leben*, quoted Rosetti p570n

Chapter 16: Mukhtar

1. Hozier, II pp818-819
2. Greene, p378
3. Hozier, II p820
4. Greene, p380
5. Hozier, II p821
6. Allen and Muratoff, pp114-115
7. Hozier, II pp825-826
8. Greene, pp380-381; Charles Williams, *The Armenian Campaign* (London 1878) p4; 'Daily News', *Correspondence,* I p102; Hozier, II p821
9. Hozier, II p822
10. ibid, pp828-829
11. ibid, p834
12. ibid, p835
13. ibid, p839
14. Greene, p383
15. Allen and Muratoff, p119
16. Hozier, II p832
17. ibid, p841
18. Allen and Muratoff, p121
19. ibid, p135
20. Williams, p33

21. Hozier, II p356
22. F deMartens, *La Paix et la Guerre* (Paris 1901) p505
23. Allen and Muratoff p136
24. Greene, p384
25. Allen and Muratoff, p140; Williams, p42

Chapter 17: Batum
1. Hobart, p125
2. Hozier, II p842
3. Allen and Muratoff, p125
4. Hozier, p843
5. ibid, p846
6. Hobart, pp131-132
7. Quoted Hozier, II p848
8. Allen and Muratoff, p127
9. Hozier, II p849
10. Hobart, p133
11. Allen and Muratoff, p157
12. ibid, p130
13. ibid, p152
14. ibid, 153-154
15. ibid, pp215; Hozier, II p902

Chapter 18: Zevin
1. Hozier, II p858
2. ibid
3. Allen and Muratoff p142
4. Williams, p47
5. Allen and Muratoff, p143; Hozier, II p859
6. Hozier, II p860
7. Allen and Muratoff, p146
8. Hozier, II p861
9. Williams, p47
10. Hozier, II p862
11. Allen and Muratoff, pp150-151
12. William, p78
13. Hozier, II pp864-865
14. Allen and Muratoff, p146
15. Hozier, II p866

Chapter 19: Eski Zagra
1. Epauchin, pp138-139
2. ibid, pp146-147
3. Maurice, pp133-134
4. ibid, p135
5. Epauchin, p170

6. Greene, p181
7. ibid, p181
8. Hozier, II p510
9. ibid, p511
10. ibid, p512
11. Greene, p182
12. 'Daily News', *Correspondence,* I p275
13. Epauchin, p299
14. ibid
15. Hozier, II p515
16. Greene, p204

Chapter 20: Suleiman at Shipka

1. 'Daily News', *Correspondence,* I p276
2. ibid, p278
3. Greene, pp205-206
4. Hozier, II p632
5. Maurice, p149
6. Hozier, II p637
7. Greene, p209
8. Hozier, II p637
9. ibid, p638
10. Greene, p209
11. Hozier, II p640
12. 'Daily News', *Correspondence,* I p414
13. Greene, p211; Hozier, II p643
14. Hozier, II p643
15. 'Daily News', *Correspondence,* I p417
16. Hozier, II p645
17. Greene, p212
18. Hozier, II p647
19. ibid, pp648-649; Greene, p213

Chapter 21: Karahassankoi

1. Maurice, p298
2. ibid, p95
3. Hozier, II p502
4. ibid, p730
5. Moltke, p122
6. Maurice, pp96-97
7. ibid, p97
8. Hozier, II p738
9. Wentworth Huyshe, *The Liberation of Bulgaria* (London 1894) p198
10. Hozier, II p739
11. ibid, p740
12. Maurice, p143

13. Anne Baker, *A Question of Honour*, (London 1896) pp101-102
14. Lieut. Gen. Valentine Baker, *War in Bulgaria* (London 1879) I pp17-18
15. ibid, pp31-37
16. ibid, p46
17. ibid, pp48-49
18. Hozier, II p745
19. Baker, I pp61-62
20. ibid, p73
21. Greene, p219

Chapter 22: Cerkovna
1. Greene, p220; Hozier, II p748
2. Baker, I p105
3. Hozier, II p749
4. Greene, p220
5. ibid, p221
6. Baker, I p114
7. Maurice, pp239-240
8. Baker, I pp163-166
9. Hozier, II p754
10. Greene, p223
11. Baker, I p245
12. Hozier, II p745

Chapter 23: Lovtcha
1. Maurice, p160
2. 'Daily News', *Correspondence*, I p436
3. ibid, p439
4. Greene, p227; Hozier, II p661
5. Hozier, II p661
6. ibid, p662
7. ibid
8. FO 65/985 Mr Lumley to Lord Derby, August 11 1877
9. Hozier, II p663
10. Trotha, p88
11. Maurice, pp182-184; Furneaux, p98

Chapter 24: The Third Battle of Plevna: The Assault
1. Maurice, p193
2. 'Daily News', *Correspondence*, I p440
3. Maurice, p194
4. Hozier, II p666
5. Herbert, pp355-356; Greene, p235
6. Hozier, II p669
7. Maurice, pp205-206
8. Major E S May, *Achievements of Field Artillery* (London 1893) pp125-126

9. Greene, p238
10. Herbert, p183
11. Trotha, p97
12. Greene, p241
13. 'Daily News', *Correspondence,* I pp462-463
14. Greene, p240
15. Herbert, p193
16. Wellesley, pp242-243
17. Hozier, II p675
18. ibid
19. 'Daily News', *Correspondence,* II p480
20. Greene, p251
21. Maurice, p223
22. ibid, p228
23. Hozier, II p680
24. Archibald Forbes, *Czar and Sultan* (London 1894) p158
25. Greene, p245

Chapter 25: Aftermath

1. Trotha, p121; Greene, p252
2. Herbert, p211
3. Greene, p252
4. Trotha, p122; Greene, p253
5. 'Daily News', *Correspondence,* I pp482-483
6. Herbert, p222
7. Greene, p255
8. ibid, p256
9. Maurice, p233
10. May, p129
11. Trotha, p225
12. Greene, p258
13. Greene, *Army Life,* pp147-148

Chapter 26: The Great Powers Watch: May to September 1877

1. Stojanovic, p152
2. Millman, p557n
3. ibid, p293
4. Quoted Millman, p296
5. Dugdale, I p53
6. Langer, p123
7. Dugdale, I p55
8. Millman, p300
9. Taylor, p244
10. Quoted G H Rupp, *A Wavering Friendship: Russia and Austria 1876-1878* (Philadelphia PA 1976) p405
11. Millman, pp308-309; Vincent, p419

12. Quoted Millman, p315
13. ibid, p316
14. Langer, p128
15. Dugdale, I p58
16. Quoted W Taffs, *Ambassador to Bismarck* (London 1938) p203
17. Millman, p322
18. Stojanovic, p153
19. Quoted Millman, p324
20. Millman, p10
21. Stojanovic, p176
22. ibid, p177

Chapter 27: Catastrophe on God's Mountain
1. Greene, pp387-388
2. Hozier, II pp869
3. Allen and Muratoff, p161
4. ibid, p162
5. ibid, p163
6. ibid, p167
7. FO881/3320 Kemball to Layard, August 27 1877.
8. Williams, p124
9. ibid, p177
10. Hozier, II p873
11. FO881/3337 Dickson to Layard, September 26 1877.
12. Allen and Muratoff, p168
13. Hozier, II p876
14. Greene, p391; Hozier, II p877
15. Brackenbury, p318
16. Hozier, II p879
17. Menning, pp79-80
18. Hozier, II p879
19. ibid, p881
20. 'Daily News', *Correspondence,* I p581
21. Hozier, II p884
22. Greene, p396; Hozier, II p885
23. Quoted May p138

Chapter 28: The Camel's Neck
1. FO335/140/1 Kemball to Dickson, November 4 1877.
2. Hozier, II p888
3. 'Daily News', *Correspondence,* I p614
4. Hozier, II p890
5. Allen and Muratoff, p196
6. ibid, p197
7. ibid, p199

Chapter 29: The Storming of Kars

1. Greene, pp399-400; Clarke, pp71-72
2. Greene, p402
3. Hozier, II p896
4. Greene, p403
5. Allen and Muratoff, p204
6. Hozier, II p895
7. Greene, pp405-406
8. Allen and Muratoff, p205
9. Hozier, II p896
10. Greene, pp412-413; Hozier, II p898
11. Allen and Muratoff, p210
12. Hozier, II p900
13. Greene, p415-416
14. Hozier, II p900

Chapter 30: Gorni Dubnik

1. Wellesley, pp283-284
2. ibid, pp220-221
3. 'Daily News', *Correspondence,* I p490
4. Greene, p264
5. Hozier, II p687
6. Maurice, pp253-254
7. Quoted, Maureen O'Connor, 'The Vision of Soldiers' in *War in History* (London 1997) p272
8. Hozier, II p689
9. ibid, II p690
10. Maurice, p257
11. Greene, p274
12. Hozier, II p698
13. Greene, p276
14. Hozier, II p699
15. Greene, p277
16. Greene, *Army Life in Russia*, p145

Chapter 31: Baba Konak

1. Hozier, II p706
2. ibid, p707
3. Quoted Greene, p302
4. Hozier, II p707
5. Baker, I p334
6. Greene, pp290-291
7. Hozier, II p709
8. Greene, pp292-293
9. Hozier, II p79
10. Greene, p295

11. Baker, II pp65-66
12. 'Daily News', *Correspondence,* II p55
13. Greene, p297
14. 'Daily News', *Correspondence,* II p98
15. ibid, p85

Chapter 32: The Fall of Plevna
1. Herbert, p288
2. ibid, pp269-270
3. Herbert, p290
4. Greene, p300
5. Greene, p302
6. Trotha, pp181-182; Greene, p303
7. Trotha, p183
8. Herbert, p310
9. Trotha, pp185-186
10. Herbert, p328
11. Hozier, II pp719-720
12. ibid, pp721-722
13. Wellesley, pp277-278
14. Hozier, II p723
15. ibid, p724
16. 'Daily News', *Correspondence,* II p214

Chapter 33: Elena
1. Hozier, II p651
2. Quoted Hozier, II p652
3. ibid, p654
4. Greene, p282
5. Hozier, II pp757-758
6. ibid, pp758-759
7. Greene, p284
8. Quoted Hozier, II p761
9. Greene, p285
10. Hozier, II p763
11. WO106/2, Layard to Lord Derby, November 27 1877
12. ibid
13. Richard von Pfeil-Burghausz, *Experiences of a Prussian Officer in the Russian Service During the Turkish War of 1877-78* (London 1893) p145
14. Greene, pp287-288; Hozier, II p765

Chapter 34: Tashkessen
1. Greene, p321
2. Hozier, II p770
3. Greene, pp323-324
4. 'Daily News', *Correspondence,* II p285

5. Hozier, II p772
6. Baker, II pp71-72
7. ibid, p72
8. Greene, p322
9. Baker, II p64
10. ibid, pp85-87
11. Quoted Magnus, Sir Philip, *Kitchener: Portrait of an Imperialist* (London 1958) p34
12. Greene, p330
13. Baker, II pp91-96
14. ibid, p109
15. ibid, p115
16. ibid, p138
17. Hozier, II p777
18. Baker, II p143
19. ibid, p160

Chapter 35: Philippopolis

1. 'Daily News', *Correspondence,* II p302
2. Greene, p333
3. Hozier, II p780; 'Daily News', *Correspondence,* II p324
4. Hozier, II pp780-781
5. 'Daily News', *Correspondence,* II p317
6. Baker, II pp180-181
7. Greene, pp339-340
8. Baker, II pp199-201
9. ibid, p206
10. ibid, p210
11. 'Daily News', *Correspondence,* II p355
12. Baker, II p216
13. ibid, p241
14. Hozier, II p787
15. Baker, II p247; Hozier, II p791
16. Greene, p345
17. Quoted Hozier, II p793
18. Baker, II p260
19. ibid, p265
20. Greene, p347
21. ibid
22. ibid

Chapter 36: Shenovo

1. Greene, p349
2. ibid, pp348-350
3. Hozier, II p797
4. Greene, pp348-349
5. Quoted Novikova, p152

6. Pfeil, p162
7. ibid, p172
8. Hozier, II p799
9. Greene, p351
10. Pfeil, p188
11. Greene, p352
12. Pfeil, p194
13. Greene, p352
14. Pfeil, pp201-202
15. ibid, p203
16. Hozier, II p802
17. Pfeil, pp209-210
18. Greene, p356

Chapter 37: The Great Powers after Plevna

1. Quoted Millman, p330
2. R Fulford, ed, *Darling Child* (London, 1976) pp270-271
3. Quoted Millman, p339
4. Millman, p346
5. Dugdale, p59
6. Quoted Langer, p132
7. Fulford, *Darling Child*, p274
8. Quoted Millman, p574
9. R W Seton-Watson, pp286-287
10. Mrs Fred Egerton, *Admiral of the Fleet Sir Geoffrey Phipps Hornby* (London 1896) p229
11. ibid, p230
12. Quoted R W Seton-Watson, p301
13. Langer, p134
14. Vincent, p497

Chapter 38: Armistice

1. Quoted Hozier, II pp810-811
2. Hozier, II pp810-811
3. 'Daily News', *Correspondence*, II pp383-384
4. Baker, II p297
5. ibid, p299
6. Greene, p363
7. Baker, II p323
8. Hozier, II p812
9. ibid, II p795
10. ibid, II p902
11. Hobart, p128
12. Greene, p363

Chapter 39: San Stefano

1. M S Anderson, *The Eastern Question* (London 1966) p199
2. Quoted Stojanovic, p210
3. Egerton, pp237-238
4. ibid
5. Quoted Millman, pp388-389
6. Egerton, pp245-246
7. Quoted Nicholas Der Bagdasarian, *The Austro-German Rapprochement, 1870-1879* (Cranbury, New Jersey 1976) p219
8. Dugdale, p65
9. Stojanovic, p218
10. Quoted Stojanovic, p221
11. Anderson, p201
12. Quoted RW Seton-Watson, p218
13. W N Medlicott, *The Congress of Berlin and After* (London 1938) p12
14. Quoted Millman, p401
15. Langer, pp139-140
16. Michael Hurst ed, *Key Treaties for the Great Powers 1814-1914* (Newton Abbot 1972) pp528-546

Chapter 40: The Congress of Berlin

1. Dugdale, p70
2. ibid, p76
3. Millman, p415
4. Egerton, p257
5. Langer, p144
6. ibid, p145
7. Miller, p380
8. Millman, p435
9. Langer, pp147-148
10. ibid, p149
11. Dugdale, p99
12. Langer, p150
13. ibid, p152
14. Medlicott p30
15. Langer, p152
16. Medlicott p36
17. Quoted Rosetti, p577

Chapter 41: Conclusion

1. Daniel J Hughes, ed, *Moltke on the Art of War* (Novato CA 1993) p91
2. Baker, I pxvii
3. Uyar and Erickson, p184
4. Maurice, p39
5. Uyar and Erickson, p185
6. May 20, 1877, quoted O'Connor, p269

7. Menning, p82
8. ibid, p83
9. Greene, p369
10. Greene, *Army Life in Russia*, pp25-26
11. Menning, p85
12. Uyar and Erickson, p201
13. Lennox to Layard, July 29 1877, quoted O'Connor p270
14. Wellesley to Lord Derby, September 21 1877, quoted O'Connor p275
15. Greene, pp421-422
16. ibid, p422
17. General H Langlois *Lessons from Two Recent Wars* (London 1909) p36
18. Quoted O'Connor, p278
19. October 2 1877, quoted O'Connor, p277
20. Pfeil, p183
21. O'Connor, p287
22. ibid
23. Quoted Dale L Walker, *Januarius MacGahan* (Athens OH 1988) p181
24. Wellesley, p194
25. 'Daily News', *Correspondence*, I pp273-274
26. Greene, p182
27. Quoted Hozier, II p548
28. Quoted Hozier, II p523
29. ibid
30. Quoted A Le Faure, *Histoire de la Guerre d'Orient* (Paris 1878) p4
31. Furneaux, p216
32. Greene, *Army Life in Russia*, p125
33. Herbert, p345

Bibliography

ALBRECHT-CARRIÉ, René, *A Diplomatic History of Europe Since the Congress of Vienna* (London 1958)

ALLEN, W E D and MURATOFF, Paul, *Caucasian Battlefields. A History of the Wars on the Turco-Caucasian Border 1828-1921* (Cambridge 1953)

ANDERSON, M S, *The Eastern Question 1774-1923* (London 1966)

ANON, *Album della Guerra Russo-Turca del 1877-78* (Milan, 1878)

ANON, *Histoire de la Guerre d'Orient 1877-1878* (Brussels, 1878)

ANON, *Historical Narrative of the Turko-Russian War* (London nd [1886], 2 volumes)

ANON, *Russes et Turcs. Guerre d'Orient* (Paris 1878, 2 volumes)

BAKER, Anne, *A Question of Honour: The Life of Lieutenant General Valentine Baker Pasha* (Barnsley 1996)

BAKER, Lieutenant General Valentine, *War in Bulgaria: A Narrative of Personal Experiences* (London 1879, 2 volumes)

BAUMANN, Robert F, 'The Russian Army 1853-1881' in *The Military History of Tsarist Russia* (New York 2002)

BERNHARDI, General F von, *On War of Today* (London 1912)

BISMARCK, Prince Otto von, *Bismarck: The Man and the Statesman, Being the Reflections and Reminiscences of Otto, Prince von Bismarck, Written and Dictated by Himself after His Retirement from Office* (London 1899, 3 volumes)

BLANCH, Lesley, *The Sabres of Paradise* (London 1960)

BRACKENBURY, Colonel C B, *Field Works: Their Technical Construction and Tactical Application* (London 1888)

BROWNING, Oscar, *Wars of the Century and the Development of Military Science* (London 1903)

BRUNKER, Lieutenant Colonel H M E, *Story of the Russo-Turkish War (in Europe) 1877-78* (London 1911)

BUDEV, A., *Grabados Españoles de la Guerra Ruso-Turco de 1877-1878* (Sofia, 1977)

BULLARD, F.L., *Famous War Correspondents* (Boston, 1914)

CECIL, Lady G, *Life of Robert Marquis of Salisbury* (London 1921, 2 volumes)

CERNAT, General A, *Memorii: Campania 1877-1878* (Bucharest 1976)

CLARKE, Sir George S, *Fortification. Its Past Achievements, Recent Development and Future Progress* (London 1907)

CLAYTON, G D, *Britain and the Eastern Question: Missolonghi to Gallipoli* (London 1971)

COMAN, General I, (ed) *România în războiul de independență 1877-1878* (Bucharest 1977)

CRAIG, Gordon, *The Politics of the Prussian Army 1640-1945* (Oxford 1964)

CRANKSHAW, Edward, *The Shadow of the Winter Palace: The Drift to Revolution 1825-1917* (London 1976)

DAILY NEWS' *The War Correspondence of the "Daily News" 1877-78* (London 1878, 2 volumes)

JALE, E T S, (trans) *German Diplomatic Documents 1871-1914* (London 1928, 4 volumes)

HARD, William E, *Napoleon III and the Concert of Europe* (Baton Rouge LA 1983)

GERTON Mrs F, *Admiral of the Fleet Sir Geoffrey Phipps Hornby, a biography* (London 1896)

EPAUCHIN, Colonel N, trans Colonel H Havelock, *Operations of General Gurko's Advance Guard in 1877* (London 1900)

FAURÉ, A, *Histoire de la Guerre d'Orient (1877-1878)* (Paris, 1878, 2 vols)

FINKEL, Caroline, *Osman's Dream: The Story of the Ottoman Empire 1300-1923* (London 2005)

Focşeneanu, Colonel I, and CIACHIR N, *Acţiuni militare ruso-romîno-bulgare in războiul din 1877-1878* (Bucharest 1957)

FORBES, Archibald, *Memories and Studies of War and Peace* (London 1895)

FORBES, Archibald, and others, *Battles of the Nineteenth Century* (London nd, 7 volumes)

FULFORD, Roger, (ed) *Your dear letter: private correspondence of Queen Victoria and the Crown Princess of Prussia, 1865-1871* (London 1971)

FULFORD, Roger, (ed) *Darling Child: private correspondence of Queen Victoria and the Crown Princess of Prussia, 1871-1878* (London 1976)

FULLER, William C, *Strategy and Power in Russia 1600-1914* (New York 1992)

FURNEAUX, Rupert, *The Siege of Plevna* (London 1958)

GALL, Lothar, *Bismarck: The White Revolutionary* (London 1986, 2 volumes)

GEROLYMATOS, André, *The Balkan Wars. Conquest, Revolution and Retribution from the Ottoman Era to the Twentieth Century and Beyond* (Staplehurst 2004)

GLENNY, Misha, *The Balkans. Nationalism, War and the Great Powers 1804-1999* (London 1999)

GOODWIN, Jason, *Lords of the Horizons. A History of the Ottoman Empire* (London 1998)

GREENE, Francis V, *Report on the Russian Army and its Campaigns in Turkey in 1878-1878* (New York 1879, 2 volumes)

GREENE, Francis V, *Sketches of Army Life in Russia* (New York 1880)

HARGREAVES, Reginald, *The Enemy at the Gate. A book of famous sieges, their cause, their progress and their consequences* (London nd)

HERBERT, F W von, *The Defence of Plevna* (London 1911)

HOBART, Admiral A C, *Sketches from My Life* (London 1887)

HOLT, L H and CHILTON, A W, *The History of Europe from 1862 to 1914* (New York 1918)

HORSETZKY, General A von, *The Chief Campaigns in Europe since 1792* (London 1909)

HOZIER, Capt H M, *The Russo-Turkish War. Including an Account of the Rise and Decline of the Ottoman Power, and the History of the Eastern Question* (London, nd, 5 volumes)

HUGHES, Daniel J, (ed) *Moltke on the Art of War. Selected Writings* (Novato CA 1993)

HURST, Michael, (ed) *Key Treaties for the Great Powers* (Newton Abbot 1972, 2 volumes)

HUYSHE, Wentworth, *The Liberation of Bulgaria. War Notes in 1877* (London 1894)

JANE, Fred T, *The Imperial Russian Navy: Its Past, Present and Future* (London 1899)

LANGENSIEPEN, B, and GÜLERYÜK, A, *The Ottoman Steam Navy 1828-19* (London 1995)

LANGER, William L, *European Alliances and Alignments 1871-1890* (New York 1950)

LANGLOIS, General H, *Lessons from Two Recent Wars. The Russo-Turkish and South African Wars* (London 1909)

LE FAURE, Amédée, *Histoire de la Guerre d'Orient 1877-1878* (Paris 1878, 2 volumes)

LINCOLN, W Bruce, *Nicholas I: Emperor and Autocraft of all the Russias* (London 1978)

LOFTUS, Lord Augustus, *The Diplomatic Reminiscences of Lord Augustus Loftus, P.C., G.C.B.* (London 1894, 4 volumes)

MACKENZIE, David, *The Lion of Tashkent: The Career of General M.G. Cherniaev* (Athens GA 1974)

MAURICE, Major F, *The Russo-Turkish War 1877: A Strategical Sketch* (London 1905)

MAY, Major E S, *Achievements of Field Artillery* (London 1893)

MAY, Major E S, *Field Artillery with the Other Arms* (London 1898)

McELWEE, William, *The Art of War: Waterloo to Mons* (London 1974)

MEDLICOTT, W N, *The Congress of Berlin and After. A Diplomatic History of the Near-Eastern Settlement 1878-1880* (London 1938)

MENNING, Bruce W, *Bayonets before Bullets: The Imperial Russian Army 1861-1914* (Indianapolis IND 1992)

MILLER, Forrestt A, *Dimitri Miliutin and the Reform Era in Russia* (Vanderbilt TN 1962)

MILLER, William, *The Ottoman Empire 1801-1913* (Cambridge 1913)

MILLMAN, R T, *Britain and the Eastern Question 1875-1878* (Oxford 1979)

MITCHELL, Donald W, *A History of Russian and Soviet Sea Power* (London 1974)

MOLTKE, Field Marshal Helmuth von, *The Russians in Bulgaria and Rumelia in 1828 and 1829 during the campaign of the Danube, the sieges of Brailow, Varna, Silistria, Shumia and the passage of the Balkans* (London 1854)

MOLTKE, Field Marshal Helmuth von, *Briefe aus dem Türkei* (Berlin 1873)

NATIONAL ARCHIVES, Foreign Office and War Office Records

NOVIKOVA, Olga A, *Skobeleff and the Slavonic Cause* (London 1883)

O'CONNOR, Maureen P, 'The Vision of Soldiers in War in History' in *War in History Vol 4* (London 1997)

OLLIER, Edmund, *Cassell's Illustrated History of the Russo-Turkish War* (London nd, 2 volumes)

PALMER, Alan, *The Decline and Fall of the Ottoman Empire* (London 1992)

PFEIL-BURGHAUSZ, Richard von, *Experiences of a Prussian Officer in the Russian Service during the Turkish War of 1877-78* (London 1893)

PFLANZE, Otto, *Bismarck and the Development of Germany* (Princeton NJ 1990, 3 volumes)

RICH, Norman, *Why the Crimean War? A cautionary tale* (Hanover NH 1985)

RIKER, T W, *The Making of Roumania* (Oxford 1931)

ROBINSON, Major General C W, and others, *Wars of the Nineteenth Century reproduced from the 11th edition of the Encyclopaedia Britannica* (London 1914)

ΓI, R, 'Roumania's share in the war of 1877' in *Slavonic and East European _view* (March 1930)

P, G H, *A Wavering Friendship: Russia and Austria 1876-1878* (Philadelphia PA 1976)

ARAUW, Captain C von, *Der Russisch-Türkische Krieg 1877-1878 auf Grundlage der veröffentlichen officiellen russischen Rapporte dargestellt* (Leipzig 1878)

SCAFES, C I et al, *Armata română în războiul de independenţă 1877-1878* (Bucharest 2002)

SETON-WATSON, Hugh, *The Russian Empire 1801-1917* (Oxford 1967)

SETON-WATSON, R W, *Disraeli, Gladstone and the Eastern Question* (New York 1972)

SHANNON, R T, *Gladstone and the Bulgarian Agitation 1876* (London 1963)

SPRINGER, Anton, *Der Russisch-türkische Krieg 1877-1878 in Europa* (Vienna 1891-93, 7 volumes)

STANLEY, Francis, *St Petersburg to Plevna, containing interviews with leading Russian statesmen and generals* (London 1878)

STOJANOVIC, Mihailo D, *The Great Powers and the Balkans 1875-1878* (Cambridge 1939)

STOKES, Gale, *Politics as Development: The Emergence of Political Parties in Nineteenth Century Serbia* (Durham NC 1990)

STRANTZ, V von, *Illustrirte Kriegs-Chronik. Gedenkbuch an den Russisch-Türkischen Feldzug von 1876-1878* (Leipzig, 1878)

SÜER, H, *1877-1878 Osmanli-Rus Harbi Rumeli Cephesi* (Ankara 1993)

TALAT, Colonel A., *Plevne Savunmasi* (Ankara 1997)

TAYLOR, A J P, *The Struggle for Mastery in Europe* (Oxford 1954)

TROTHA, Thilo von, *Tactical Studies on the Battles Around Plevna* (Kansas City KS 1896)

UYAR, Mesut, and ERICKSON, Edward J, *A Military History of the Ottomans: From Osman to Atatürk* (Santa Barbara CA 2009)

VILLIERS, George, *A Vanished Victorian: Being the Life of George Villiers Fourth Earl oj Clarendon 1800-1870* (London 1938)

VINCENT, Professor J R (ed), *The Derby Diaries, 1869-1878: A Selection from the Diaries of Edward Henry Stanley, the 15th Earl of Derby, between September 1869 and March 1878* (London 1994)

WALKER, Dale L, *Januarius MacGahan: The Life and Campaigns of an American War Correspondent* (Athens OH 1988)

WELLESLEY, Colonel F A, *With the Russians in Peace and War: Recollections of a Military Attaché* (London 1905)

WILKINSON, Spencer, *War and Policy: Essays* (London 1900)

WILLIAMS, Charles, *The Armenian Campaign. A Diary of the Campaign of 1877 in Armenia and Koordistan* (London 1878)

ZIMMERMANN, M B, *Illustrirte Geschichte des Orientalischen Krieges von 1876-1878* (Vienna 1878)

Index

ning Source UK Ltd.
Keynes UK
06f0605211016

1UK00004B/6/P